Shrinking Cities

Volume 2 ▸ Interventions

COLOPHON

Shrinking Cities, Volume 2 ▸ Interventions
Volume 1 ▸ International Research (ISBN-10 3-7757-1682-3, ISBN-13 978-3-7757-1682-6)

The German edition of this book was published in conjunction with the exhibition "Shrinking Cities—Interventions," Galerie für Zeitgenössische Kunst Leipzig, November 26, 2005–January 29, 2006. This English edition is published in conjunction with the exhibition "Shrinking Cities," planned for the following venues: 10th International Architecture Exhibition, Venice, September 10–November 19, 2006; University of Tokyo, with AkiDeCo Museum, Tokyo, Fall 2006; Pratt Manhattan Gallery and Van Alen Institute, New York, November 2006–January 2007; Cranbrook Art Museum, Bloomfield Hills, Mich., and Museum of Contemporary Art Detroit (MOCAD), February–March 2007; Afoundation, Liverpool, Summer 2007; E-Werk, Saarbrücken, Germany, Fall 2007; Deutsches Architekturmuseum in Frankfurt (DAM), Frankfurt am Main, November 2007–January 2008; Pro Arte Institute, with State Museum of History, St. Petersburg, Spring 2008 (exhibition schedule as of May 2006).

Editor and concept: Philipp Oswalt; *Editorial team:* Philipp Oswalt, Elke Beyer ("Reorganizing" and "Imagining" chapters), Anke Hagemann ("Reevaluating" and "Reorganizing" chapters), and Anita Kaspar ("Deconstructing" chapter), with Füsun Türetken, Kristina Herresthal, Alexandra Hoorn, and Lena Feldhahn; *Translations:* Brian Currid ("Deconstructing" chapter), Jill Denton ("Deconstructing" and "Imagining" chapters), Nancy Joyce ("Survival Handbook"), Steven Lindberg (Introductory texts and "Reevaluating" chapter), Christina M. White ("Reorganizing" chapter); *Copyediting (German edition):* Miriam Wiesel, with Stefanie Oswalt; *Copyediting (English edition):* Ginger A. Diekmann and Niamh Warde; *Proofreading:* Niamh Warde, Greg Bond, and Rebecca van Dyck; *Production management (English edition):* Elke Beyer and Anita Kaspar; *Managing director:* Florian Bolenius (until February 2006), Karin Johnson (starting February 2006); *Graphic design:* Stephan Müller and Tanja Wesse; *Illustrations:* Tina Berning ("Deconstructing" chapter), Felice Bruno ("Imagining" chapter), Tom(as) Frey ("Reorganizing" chapter), and Maria Tackmann ("Reevaluating" chapter); *Reproductions:* Dr. Cantz'sche Druckerei, Ostfildern, and Licht & Tiefe, Berlin; *Binding:* Nething Buchbinderei GmbH & Co. KG, Weilheim/Teck; *Production and printing:* Dr. Cantz'sche Druckerei, Ostfildern; *Cover illustration:* Jacques Magiera

© 2006 Philipp Oswalt; authors, photographers, artists, and their heirs
© 2006 for the reproduced works by John Heartfield, Lucien Kroll, Les Levine, Gordon Matta-Clark, Robert Smithson, and Frank Lloyd Wright: VG Bild-Kunst, Bonn

Published by Hatje Cantz Verlag, Zeppelinstrasse 32, 73760 Ostfildern, Germany, Phone: +49 711 4405-0, Fax: +49 711 4405-220, www.hatjecantz.com

Hatje Cantz books are available internationally at selected bookstores and from the following distribution partners: USA/North America - D.A.P., Distributed Art Publishers, New York, www.artbook.com; UK - Art Books International, London, www.art-bks.com; Australia - Tower Books, Frenchs Forest (Sydney), www.towerbooks.com.au; France - Interart, Paris, www.interart.fr; Belgium - Exhibitions International, Leuven, www.exhibitionsinternational.be; Switzerland - Scheidegger, Affoltern am Albis, www.ava.ch. For Asia, Japan, South America, and Africa, as well as for general questions, please contact Hatje Cantz directly at sales@hatjecantz.de, or visit our homepage at www.hatjecantz.com for further information.

ISBN-10 3-7757-1711-0
ISBN-13 978-3-7757-1711-3
Printed in Germany

Volume 2 ▸ Interventions

Edited by Philipp Oswalt for the Kulturstiftung des Bundes
with the editorial assistance of Elke Beyer, Anke Hagemann, and Anita Kaspar,
with Füsun Türetken, Kristina Herresthal, Alexandra Hoorn, and Lena Feldhahn

Shrinking Cities is a project of the Kulturstiftung des Bundes (German Federal Cultural Foundation) in cooperation with the Project Office Philipp Oswalt, the Museum of Contemporary Art Leipzig, the Bauhaus Dessau Foundation, and the magazine *archplus*.

Table of Contents

Project Participants, Acknowledgments — 10
Foreword | *Hortensia Völckers and Alexander Farenholtz* — 11
Introduction | *Philipp Oswalt* — 13
Governmentalizing Planning | *Nikolaus Kuhnert and Anh-Linh Ngo* — 19
Without a Model: Experimental Urbanism | *Friedrich von Borries and Walter Prigge* — 25
Truth Discourses | *Barbara Steiner* — 31
Commissioned Contributions to the Exhibition — 36
Project Publications — 40
Notes on Contributors — 42
Illustration Credits — 45

DECONSTRUCTING — 48

Demolition City — 50
Planned Destruction | *Anthony Fontenot* — 52
Demolition and Urban Development: A Historical Sketch | *Gerd Albers* — 62
La Défense | *OMA* — 68
Leinefelde: Orderly Retreat | *Ulrike Steglich* — 70
Dismantling Infrastructure | *Matthias Koziol* — 76
Decamping Detroit | *Charles Waldheim and Marilí Santos-Munné* — 80
Gordon Matta-Clark | *Dan Graham* — 86
Demolitions: Opening Interior Gardens | *Lara Almárcegui* — 98
The Background Muzak of an Epochal Change | *Tina Veihelmann* — 99
Palast der Republik: Re-deconstruction | *Eric Tschaikner* — 106
The Solution: Vibach in 2042 | *Johannes Touché* — 108
Cretto | *Alberto Burri* — 110

Evolutionary City — 112
Robert Smithson and the Architecture of Absence | *Kai Vöckler* — 114
Continuous Conveyor Belt City | *Superstudio* — 131
Structures of Possibility | *Pierre Huyghe* — 132
Specific Indeterminacy: Witznitz Briquette Factory | *Florian Beigel Architects* — 136

Feral City — 142
Naturally Determined Urban Development? | *Jörg Dettmar* — 144
Duisburg-Nord Landscape Park | *Latz + Partner* — 151
Urban Agriculture | *Holger Lauinger* — 156
Tilbury Park | *muf architecture/art* — 165
Apple Tree Court: An Urban Oasis | *Anthony Milroy et al.* — 168
COW—the udder way | *Ulrike Steven et al.* — 169
Grow! | *anschlaege.de* — 174

Contraction City — 178
The Compact City: A Model for Eastern German Cities? | *Markus Hesse* — 180

Remaking Barnsley | *Alsop Architects* — 184
Bradford City Centre Masterplan | *Alsop Architects* — 185
Oswald Mathias Ungers's Urban Archipelago for Shrinking Berlin | *Jasper Cepl* — 187
Russian Disurbanism | *Christiane Post and Philipp Oswalt* — 196
Fiber City, Tokyo | *Ohno Laboratory* — 204

Depleted City — 212
The Shrinking and Perforated City | *Marta Doehler-Behzadi* — 214
Chemnitz-Brühl | *Matthias Grünzig* — 218
Core & Plasma | *L21* — 220
Wall It Up. And Take a Breath. | *Peter Arlt and letzelfreivogel architekten* — 222
The Suburbanization of Inner Cities | *Walter Prigge* — 225
Gas Station Urbanism, or What's Left of the City | *Orange Edge* — 232
On-Demand Infrastructure for Shrinking Regions | *Florian Böhm* — 235
Tourism in a Luxury of Void | *Michael Zinganel* — 244
[Inverse] Seasonal City | *Hans-H. Albers, Michael Hieslmair, Maruša Sagadin, and Michael Zinganel* — 250
Cities in an Aging Society | *Matthias Grünzig* — 257
Us Old Folk | *L21* — 260

Polarized Regional City — 268
MetroSachs | *Friedrich von Borries and Walter Prigge* — 270
The Last Bastion | *Bart Lootsma* — 276
Territorial Retreat | *Hans-Joachim Bürkner* — 282
Emscher Park International Building Exhibition | *Arnold Voß* — 293
Schkreutz City Map: 1st Edition | *SMAQ* — 301
Bitterfeld: A Translocal Region | *Urbanista* — 306
Hollocore | *AMO* — 308
The City Turned into a Region | *Robert Kaltenbrunner* — 310
The Upper Calder Valley | *John Thompson & Partners et al.* — 322
However Unspectacular: The New Suburbanism | *Interboro and CUP* — 324
Strategic Planning | *Manfred Kühn* — 330

REEVALUATING — 336

Temporary City — 338
Vacant Lots as Incubators? | *Klaus Overmeyer* — 340
Building Guards | *HausHalten e.V.* — 344
Community Gardens on Josephstraße | *Lindenauer Stadtteilverein e.V.* — 344
Dietzenbach: Definitively Unfinished | *Projektgruppe Stadt 2030* — 348
Sportification | *complizen Planungsbüro* — 350
Utilization of Vacant Space in Dessau-West | *Anonymous users* — 354
What Is Art Up To in Disused Buildings? | *Elske Rosenfeld* — 355
FURTHER Up in the Air | *Leo Fitzmaurice and Neville Gabie* — 362
Theater as Urban Intervention | *Andreas Hillger* — 366

Pioneer City 372
Space Pioneers | *Bastian Lange and Ulf Matthiesen* 374
These Start-Up Times: How Dessau Organizes Vacant Spaces of the Future | *Ulrike Steglich* 384
Alternative Investment in Shrinking Cities | *Birgit Schmidt* 386
Alternative Investment: International Models 392
Leipzig-Plagwitz: The Dark Land Behind the Marsh | *Kathleen Liebold and Heidi Stecker* 394
Struggling with the Creative Class | *Jamie Peck* 401
Werkleitz Gesellschaft e.V. 407
Chinati Foundation | *Donald Judd* 408
Los Topos | *Club Real and Peanutz-Architekten* 412
The Settlers ... In the Boondocks | *Claus Strigel* 417
Go East: On the Wild-West Rhetoric of Shrinking City Projects | *Anke Hagemann* 421

Reinterpreted City 426
Forty Years of Heterodoxy | *Juan Herreros* 428
Potteries Thinkbelt | *Cedric Price* 431
Against Necrophilia | *Stephen Mullin* 436
Bat Hat: Redesign of Battersea Power Station | *Cedric Price* 438
"Urban Renewal": Not Just Demolition | *Wolfgang Kil* 439
WiMBY! (Welcome into My Backyard!) IBE Rotterdam-Hoogvliet | *Crimson* 445
Battle of Matériel with No Winners | *Claudia Wahjudi* 454
Door Recycling | *Raumlabor et al.* 456
Automatenbar | *Automaten e.V.* 460
Recycling Projects | *Dan Peterman* 462

REORGANIZING 464

Do-It-Yourself City 466
Urban Self-Organization | *A Conversation with Marjetica Potrč* 468
Adamah | *Kyong Park/iCUE et al.* 474
Catherine Ferguson Academy | *G. Asenath Andrews et al.* 476
The Activating State | *Thomas Knorr-Siedow* 479
Can Social Capital Save Shrinking Cities? | *Christine Hannemann* 484
Contemporary Activist Art | *Stella Rollig* 489
Social Change, Self-Empowerment, and Imagination | *A Conversation with Irene Bude, XPONA, Anke Haarmann, Kristina Leko, Tadej Pogacar, and Isa Rosenberger* 499
The World Economic Crisis, Subsistence Economics, and Modern Urban Planning | *Markus Kilian* 503
The Buffalo Is Dead | *A Conversation with Frithjof Bergmann* 513
Out of Work, Into Reality! | *bankleer* 515
workstation | *WochenKlausur and ideenwerkstatt berlin e.V.* 518
Opera of the Unemployed | *Robert Linke and Hans-Joachim Schulze* 521

Strong City 524
In Times of Crisis – Back to the Cities | *A Conversation between Marta Doehler-Behzadi, Dieter Hoffmann-Axthelm, Stephan Lanz, Engelbert Lütke Daldrup, and Philipp Oswalt* 526
Wolfen: The Cost of Silence | *Tina Veihelmann* 534
The Experiment of Red Vienna, 1919–1934 | *Rudolf Kohoutek* 540
From Managerialism to Entrepreneurialism | *David Harvey* 547
The Urban Task Force and Its Urban Renaissance | *Anna Minton* 555
Rethinking Local Specificity and Community | *Ash Amin* 559

Commodified City 568
Communalization of Property? | *Holger Lauinger* 570
Reality Properties: Fake Estates | *Gordon Matta-Clark* 572
Acquisition of the Property at the Corner of Tibusstraße and Breul | *Maria Eichhorn* 576
Opening Empty Lots to the Public | *Lara Almárcegui* 580
Claiming Land | *Stefanie Bremer et al.* 581
Loans for Shrinking Regions | *Rolf Novy-Huy* 587
Fictitious Values, Imaginary Markets | *Matthias Bernt* 592
Collateral in Hand, Treuhand, and the Invisible Hand | *Andreas Siekmann* 597

Emerging City 600
Hoang's Bistro | *Christoph Schäfer* 602
Urban Transformation as Unintended Side Effect | *Robert Fishman* 608
Shrinkage and Immigration | *Franz-Josef Kemper and Olaf Schnur* 615
To Play with Shrinking – and Shrink Playfully? | *Friedrich von Borries* 622

Exceptional City 628
Exterritories | *fiedler.tornquist* 630
Recruitment of Settlers in the History of Prussia | *Carsten Benke* 638
Non-plan | *Reyner Banham, Paul Barker, Peter Hall, and Cedric Price* 644
Enterprise Zones in the United Kingdom | *Klaus Zehner* 649
Special Economic Zones in Poland | *Uwe Rada* 655
Special Tax Zones as a Fatal Strategy | *Corell Wex* 658
Special Social Welfare Zone Forst | *Jesko Fezer, Stephan Lanz, and Uwe Rada* 661
Temporary Autonomous Zone | *Hakim Bey* 669
Dresden's Colorful Republic of Neustadt | *Residents and other stakeholders* 670

IMAGINING 672

Communicating City 674
On the Crisis of Urban Public Life | *Jörg Dürrschmidt* 676
Le Week-End | *D. Gregor Mirwa et al.* 683
A Monument for the Women's Center | *Isa Rosenberger* 686
Conflict as Productive Potential | *Nina Möntmann* 689

[murmur] | *Gabe Sawhney, James Roussel, and Shawn Micallef* — 695
Immaginare Corviale | *Osservatorio Nomade/Stalker* — 696
Tenantspin (Superchannel) | *Superflex* — 698
Karlskrona2 (Supercity) | *Superflex* — 701
Blinkenlights | *Chaos Computer Club* — 704
Walk the City, Flex Your Mind | *Gregor Harbusch* — 706
Love at Leisure. Help Me Stranger. Roundabout. | *e-Xplo* — 708
Rainwater Retention Tanks on Land Awaiting Development – A City Walk | *Boris Sieverts* — 714
Communication with the Ones Who Left | *Mirjam Struppek* — 717

Marketing City — 722
City Marketing: Origin and Critique | *Stephen V. Ward* — 724
Promoting Detroit | *William J. V. Neill* — 730
De-TRO-it | *Ursula Faix, Anders Melsom, and Kathrine Nyhus* — 736
The Pott's Boiling | *Springer & Jacoby* — 738
Leipzig Freedom | *Orange Cross* — 742
The Guggenheim Effect | *Lorenzo Vicario and Pedro Manuel Martínez Monje* — 744
Architecture as Branding | *A Conversation with Will Alsop* — 753
Twenty-First-Century Homesteading: New Attempts to Resettle the American Frontier | *Kate Stohr* — 759
Flagship Developments | *Various Architects* — 766

Profiled City — 770
The Urban Self | *Anke Haarmann* — 772
The Secret of L.E. | *Anke Haarmann with Irene Bude* — 776
The National Museum of Statistics | *Eva Grubbauer, Martin Luce, Joost Meuwissen, and Johannes Weisser* — 778
International Building Exhibition "Urban Redevelopment Saxony-Anhalt 2010" — 784
Urban Identities | *Ulf Matthiesen* — 787
The City Must Be Invented | *Regina Bittner* — 793
Urban Blindness | *Ruedi Baur* — 797
The Railway Underpass at Tourcoing | *Intégral Ruedi Baur et associés* — 801
A Regional Image for Südraum Leipzig | *Unverzagt und Albrecht* — 802

Imaginary City — 804
To the Sisters of Carl Möglin | *Wiebke Loeper* — 806
The Battle of Orgreave | *Jeremy Deller* — 812
Making Museums of Industrial Heritage Sites | *Susanne Hauser* — 816
The Power of Desire | *Stephan Lanz* — 823
The Square of Permanent Reorganization | *Andreas Siekmann* — 826

```
S U R V I V A L   H A N D B O O K
with Perspectives on "Human Capital"
Authors collective, led by Wolfgang Engler
```

PROJECT PARTICIPANTS

Shrinking Cities is a project initiated by the Kulturstiftung des Bundes (German Federal Cultural Foundation) in cooperation with the Project Office Philipp Oswalt, the Galerie für Zeitgenössische Kunst Leipzig (Museum of Contemporary Art Leipzig), the Bauhaus Dessau Foundation, and *archplus* magazine.
Chief curator: Philipp Oswalt (architect/writer, Berlin)
Curatorial team: Nikolaus Kuhnert (*archplus* magazine, Berlin), Walter Prigge (Bauhaus Dessau Foundation), Barbara Steiner (Galerie für Zeitgenössische Kunst Leipzig)
Collaborators of project participants for the second project phase: Project Office Philipp Oswalt, Berlin—*managing director:* Florian Bolenius (until February 2006), Karin Johnson (starting February 2006); *research associates:* Elke Beyer, Anke Hagemann, Anita Kaspar, Kristina Herresthal, Alexandra Hoorn, and Füsun Türetken; *interns:* Lena Feldhahn and Sebastian Juhnke; *sponsoring:* Nicole Minten; *public relations:* Astrid Herbold (until mid-2005), Achim Klapp (starting mid-2005); *volume copyeditors:* Ginger A. Diekmann and Niamh Warde (English edition), Miriam Wiesel with Stefanie Oswalt (German edition); *Web site:* e27, Berlin; *EDP system administration:* united-data.net/Johann Dinges; *tax consultancy and accounting:* Eckhard Stranghöner with Regina Marks; Galerie für Zeitgenössische Kunst Leipzig—*exhibition and project coordination:* Kathleen Liebold; *press and publicity:* Heidi Stecker; *accounting:* Gisela Pataki; *interns:* Stefan Höhne and Stefan Pedersen; Bauhaus Dessau Foundation—*research associate/project coordination:* Friedrich von Borries; *intern:* Tobias Kurtz; *finances:* Manuela Falkenberg; *archplus* magazine—*research associates/project coordination:* Gregor Harbusch, Kristina Herresthal, Anh-Linh Ngo, and Susanne Schindler; *jury for the competition:* Azra Aksamija, Ruedi Baur, Regina Bittner, Anne Lacaton, Georg Schöllhammer; *preliminary selection for the competition:* Mitch Cope, Anke Hagemann, Sabine Kraft, Philipp Misselwitz, Sergei Sitar, Schirin Taraz-Breinholt, Jan Wenzel; *management:* Sabine Kraft
Expert advisors: Christine Hannemann (sociologist, Humboldt-Universität, Berlin), Wolfgang Kil (architecture critic, Berlin), Ulf Matthiesen (city and regional researcher, Institut für Regionalentwicklung und Strukturplanung, Erkner)
Exhibition design: Rasmus Koch and Jakob Trägårdh, Copenhagen
Graphic design (corporate design, publications): Stephan Müller and Tanja Wesse, Berlin
Collaborating institutions (as of January 2006) for entire project: Bildungswerk Weiterdenken in der Heinrich-Böll-Stiftung e.V., Dresden; Goethe-Institut, London; Kulturamt Leipzig; Sächsische Aufbaubank – Förderbank, Dresden; Internationales Leipziger Festival für Dokumentar- und Animationsfilm; Cineding Leipzig, Cinemathèque Leipzig, Kinobar Prager Frühling Leipzig, Passage Kinos Leipzig, Schaubühne Lindenfels, UT Connewitz e.V.; *for individual works:* Agentur für Arbeit Halle/Saale; Aus- und Weiterbildungsstätte "Arbeit und Leben" Schkopau; AWO Stadtverband Leuna e.V.; Soziales Dienstleistungszentrum Merseburg; Berliner Journalisten-Schule; Bunter Laden Leipzig; Frauenkommunikationszentrum Wolfen; Internationale Sommerschule Halle; Metal Culture, Liverpool; RAUM—Zeitgenössische Kunst und Philosophie, Wismar; St. Gabriel's Church Liverpool; Stadtplanungsamt Halle/Saale; Stadtplanungsamt Magdeburg; Stiftung Trias, Bochum; Verein der Freunde der Staßfurter Rundfunk- und Fernsehtechnik e.V.; Westcott Farm, Devon, Great Britain

ACKNOWLEDGMENTS

We would like to thank the Kulturstiftung des Bundes, above all Hortensia Völckers and Alexander Farenholtz, Uta Schnell, Fokke Peters, and Friederike Tappe-Hornbostel, who were always there with advice, ideas, and specific assistance. Important advice and support were provided by, among others, Omar Akbar, Harald Bodenschatz, the Inura Network, Stefanie Oswalt, Kyong Park, Andreas Ruby, and the Galerie Barbara Weiss. We also would like to thank Francesco Careri, Robert Jessop, Kieran Long, Gregor Mirwa, Toni Moceri, and Axel Sowa.
We are grateful to Hatje Cantz Publishers and its staff, especially Annette Kulenkampff and Christine Müller, for their helpful collaboration.
We are indebted to all those who actively participated, without whom this project never could have been realized.
We are grateful to the exhibition installation, education, and visitor services teams of the Galerie für Zeitgenössische Kunst Leipzig for providing the first exhibition venue in autumn 2005.
In addition to the funding received from the Kulturstiftung des Bundes, individual authors participating in the project were supported by the Royal Netherlands Embassy in Berlin; the Embassy of the Republic of Slovenia in Berlin; the British Council, Berlin; the Office of the Federal Chancellor of Austria, Department of Culture, in Vienna; the Danish Arts Council – Committee for International Visual Art, Copenhagen; the Austrian Embassy in Berlin – Kulturforum, Berlin; Eternit AG, Berlin; Mitteldeutscher Rundfunk, Magdeburg; Norddeutsche Landesbank NORD/LB, Magdeburg; Stadtplanungsamt Magdeburg; TechniSat Digital GmbH, Staßfurt; Wohnungsbaugesellschaft Magdeburg.
The exhibition was also supported by the IKEA Stiftung, MDR FIGARO – Das Kulturradio des Mitteldeutschen Rundfunks, and Ströer Deutsche Städte Medien GmbH, Dresden.

FOREWORD

The shrinking of cities is found in all areas of urban life. The consequences reach far beyond economic fault lines, fundamentally transforming the cultural and social structure of a city. On the basis of four urban regions in the United States, Russia, Great Britain, and Germany, the first exhibition and the accompanying book offered an informed and lucid survey of the international dimension of this development. The scope of what has been transformed for residents in their cities—reductions in schools and kindergartens, cutbacks in public transportation systems, new unutilized spaces and empty factories in neighborhoods, changes to the tempo of the city, and the attitude to life of those "left behind," to name just a few—were demonstrated impressively.

The first part of this project met with great public interest and a broad resonance in the national and international press, and that was because the situation it treated was neither minimized nor smoothed over. The exhibition and book heightened public awareness of the cultural dimension of shrinking cities and drew attention to the fact that shrinking cities are not a special case of urban development in, say, the former East Germany.

When taking stock in this way, it is all the more urgent to ask what opportunities for cultural innovation and what possibilities for creativity are opened up when we abandon the hope that the process of shrinkage is a short-term problem to be addressed through economic growth.

In dealing with shrinking cities, the disciplines of urban development, urban planning, and architecture, which traditionally have been guided by ideas for managing growth, reach their limits. For that reason, the second part of the project—the exhibition and this book— is rigorously focused on ideas, productive and debatable approaches, and even visions of how to approach shrinking cities. In addition to traditional urban development measures, we must test and explore possibilities for social, cultural, and communicative interventions. The restructuring of cities should be understood as an opportunity.

It would be unrealistic to expect that the concepts and ideas that you will read about here can provide simple recipes that can be employed directly to immediate effect. We see their significance rather as a way of playing through options and models, sometimes even with a utopian gesture, so that new aspects and images can be introduced to our notion of urban life. The point is to show that there is, and must be, a whole spectrum of possibilities for action.

The spectrum of views represented in this project is especially broad. It extends, for example, from portraits of specific people who have discovered individual ways to come to terms with shrinking opportunities to work and consume in their city, as a way of social survival that preserves self-respect and the practice of being responsible for oneself (the "Survival Handbook" by Wolfgang Engler et al.), all the way to a scenario—which sounds bizarre only at first—for a Chinese special economic zone for the region of Halle/Leipzig ("Exterritories" by Johannes Fiedler and Jördis Tornquist). This notion aims at a fundamentally new understanding of design and planning: rather than establishing and planning results, it aims to design and explore other sets of rules in which the outcomes are not determined in advance.

What we thus have before us is a kaleidoscope of ideas presenting possibilities for approaching shrinkage that range from individual, everyday strategies in shrinking cities to top-down political and social conditions and critiques thereof. Taken together, they transform our traditional idea of urbanism and can lead to a long-term rethinking that will affect both individual and social action. Cities will not be reconstructed until there is a reconstruction in our heads.

With the project Shrinking Cities the Kulturstiftung des Bundes (German Federal Cultural Foundation) entered terrain where the question of the scope of cultural production and intervention is a self-critical element of the project. We see the continual resurveying of this terrain as an important task and challenge for the future.

We would like to thank the chief curator, Philipp Oswalt, and his team as well as co-curators Nikolaus Kuhnert (*archplus* magazine, Berlin), Walter Prigge (Bauhaus Dessau Foundation), and Barbara Steiner (Museum of Contemporary Art Leipzig) for their outstanding work. Christine Hannemann (sociologist, Humboldt-Universität, Berlin), Wolfgang Kil (architecture critic, Berlin), and Ulf Matthiesen (city and regional researcher, Institute for Regional Development and Structural Planning, Erkner) have supported the project as advisors and offered productive guidance. We would like to thank them and all the participants for their valuable contributions.

We hope you find these readings inspiring and informative.

———
———

Hortensia Völckers, Artistic Director/Executive Board, Kulturstiftung des Bundes
Alexander Farenholtz, Administrative Director/Executive Board, Kulturstiftung des Bundes

INTRODUCTION
Philipp Oswalt

—

—

As the theme "shrinking" has moved to the foreground of public consciousness in Germany in recent years and is emerging in places like Japan and eastern Europe, the question of how to respond creatively to this unwanted urban change is raised all the more urgently. It is clear that the strategies pursued thus far have proved unable to formulate a satisfactory response, even if one accepts that in many places it simply will not be possible to reverse the shrinkage—an insight that has led to the prevalence of the term "shrinking cities."

The widespread call for artists is symptomatic of the enduring helplessness. Where community politicians, urban planners, architects, and property owners no longer know what to do, they invite artists to fill the vacuum. There is hardly an urban development proposal today that gets by without artists, hardly a neighborhood without artistic interventions in vacant spaces. From the building ministry to the district manager, from the investor to the neighborhood group: with the increasing skepticism about their own roles and disciplines, they are hoping for a quasi-religious redemption from the arts. Usually, of course, this just papers over more fundamental problems.

If we agree with the French sociologist Pierre Bourdieu that social space translates into physical space,[1] it must be said that social problems are reflected in the crisis of physical space in shrinking cities, and that without addressing this crisis, little of substance can be said about the transformation of cities. But that is not all. Not only are social constellations expressed in urban space, which can be read as a kind of mapping of them, but social questions are also reflected in the conception of the models for action themselves (and their crises).

Social Ideas

The classical model of urban planning took for granted control over the entire territory, the state as a central building developer, and the existence of welfare state models to achieve good living conditions for all residents. After this model underwent a crisis, for a number of reasons, in the 1970s, it was increasingly replaced by the postmodern model of island urbanism—though its effects continue to be felt in many areas even today, and occasionally it still dominates. This new model dispenses with any attempt to shape the whole, limiting itself to small, island-like areas for development, planned with increasing perfection and, often enough, later controlled, while the other areas of the city disappear from the sphere of interest and fail to attract attention. The goal of such planning is to acquire private investment to realize projects. And so this concept is also called the "entrepreneurial city."

Both models of urban development—that based on the classical welfare state and the entrepreneurial model—are, for the most part, ill suited for dealing with shrinking cities. Shrinking areas are characterized by both state and private disinvestment. Shrinkage goes hand in hand with radical cuts in financing, especially at the community level, as a result of increasing expenditures and reduced incomes. At the same time, in the context of a drop in demand, an excess of supply, and devaluation of the real-estate market, private investments fail to materialize. The process is exacerbated by the fact that banks are not prepared to lend money to those who are willing to invest, as shrinking areas are viewed as high risks.

The reaction to this dilemma in Germany—a society marked by neoliberal rhetoric, increasing privatization, and a large state share of gross national product—is characteristic. Whereas state direct investments are largely taboo, despite a state share of gross national product of nearly 50%, a simulated market economy is blossoming—a planned economy without a plan, so to speak. The state invests enormous resources as matching funds for inadequate private investment or even to create the illusion of private investment. It subsidizes jobs in large industry with six-figure euro sums per capita and builds enormous infrastructures to pave the way for private investments that often enough fail to materialize anyway. From an urbanistic point of view, of course, such policies do not result in consistent models. The funds spent according to various rules for subsidies are manifested in a fragmented patchwork rug of disconnected, often unfinished parts.

Neoliberal?
Criticizing such policies as neoliberal is pointless, as this is not a genuine rollback of the state but merely a different kind of state, employing its funds based on other criteria. The question is for what and to what ends they are used. Urban development demonstrates this exemplarily. For the so-called Stadtumbau Ost program (an urban renewal program for eastern Germany), a total of €2.6 billion of communal, state, and federal funds will be made available over a period of eight years—seemingly quite a large sum. For the same period, however, the federal government used to pay out about €80 billion in subsidies for private home ownership.[2] The subsidy for home ownership is by no means a form of welfare policy, for one has to have equity capital to qualify for such funding. It serves the lobby of the construction trades and provides for middle-class homeowners.

This is even more obvious using the example of the shrinking city New Orleans after the catastrophe of Hurricane Katrina in 2005. Certainly the negligent disregard of flood protection, the insufficient mobility of poorer residents, and the lack of catastrophe protection can be characterized as typical neoliberal practices. Yet the primary beneficiaries of reconstruction funds amounting to several billion dollars are several American firms that have direct personal connections to the White House. The direct distribution of the funds to those affected was never seriously considered. The journalist Naomi Klein observed, "'Reconstruction,' whether in Baghdad or New Orleans, has become shorthand for a massive uninterrupted transfer of wealth from public to private hands." The headline on the cover of *The Nation* in which Klein's article appeared sums it up: "Now the real looting begins."[3]

The production of ideology is not without consequences, even if it veils the facts: the consequence of neoliberal rhetoric and the invoking of supposed economic efficiency liberate state funds from the criterion of socially just distribution and clear the path to the shifting of social resources and influence.

In other respects, too, so-called neoliberalism is distinguished not so much by reductions in state power than by different forms of state power. In their essay "Neoliberalizing Space,"[4] the Anglo-Saxon urban geographers Jamie Peck and Adam Tickell demonstrate that, following a first phase of deregulation and the rollback of the Keynesian welfare state in the United States and Great Britain during the 1990s ("rollback neoliberalism"), a "neoliberal" rollout has long since returned in the form of an expansion of state controls, measures, and institutions under new premises.[5]

The Ambivalence of Modernity
Nevertheless, however ill-suited the neoliberal model may prove to be in dealing with shrinking cities, the conservation or restoration of the classical welfare state has also failed to provide a convincing perspective, not least because of a sad alliance with a rationalistic determinism. The fundamental ambivalence of this approach, which characterized the modern era into the 1970s, no longer can be ignored. The question of whether additional state welfare or more self-organization of civil society is desirable admits of no clear answer, and any decision has its disadvantages.

In the days of the High Modernism of architecture and urban planning, people still dreamed—building on the political ideas of socialism and a general faith in progress—of overcoming contradictions, of achieving harmony in an ideal society, of eliminating the contradiction between city and countryside. The positions of Ludwig Hilberseimer and the Russian disurbanists are examples of this. Essential to this model is the idea of overcoming disparities of social space and producing living conditions based on equal value. The presumption was that economic aid to lesser-developed regions was desirable not only for reasons of social policy but also for reasons of economic policy, for the funds invested there would have the greatest spin-off effects on growth.[6] Economic and social goals supported each other in a win-win situation—or so the assumption went. Today, the opposite view is prevalent: only in the existing growth areas of large agglomerations can economic development be pursued effectively with the maximum spin-off effect on growth. This view results in a dilemma: Should the existing funds be invested for the greatest effect on growth, thus maximizing the wealth of the society as a whole while simply putting up with increasing polarization of the social geography? Or should we renounce growth and concentrate on balancing differences in living conditions?

The most productive approach may be to try to break out of this dilemma by seeking other scenarios for development that do not futilely employ all available means to bring shrinking regions to the standards of growth areas but rather offer unique qualities that turn the differences into positives, without contributing to a polarization of society. The prerequisite is to abandon the idea of uniformity and consciously emphasize qualitative differences.

Shrinking cities question existing social practices, values, and models and thus call for a fundamental cultural reflection and reevaluation: Is urbanism conceivable without density? Can slowness itself represent quality? What role does property play in the use of space? Can unused spaces and materials be used in different ways? Are there informal practices that can be read as positive models for action? How do mentalities and identity crises influence urban space?

In such a process of searching for a new cultural orientation, the perspectives of different fields matter: architecture, art, media, sociology, ethnography, economics, and so on. In such a context, scholarly work and other approaches can be joined by artistic production—freed of the compulsion to formulate solutions and contribute directly to improving the situation—to provide essential stimuli and communicate knowledge.

Insoluble Problems

For the planning theorist Lucius Burckhardt, decision-making dilemmas are fundamental to urban development: "Urban planning is a doling out of comforts and sorrows; everything that urban planning plans brings some people advantages and others disadvantages.... Problems are insoluble, precisely because they are permeated with the doling out of sorrows. There is no best and definitive solution to problems. There are only possibilities for a society to muddle through reasonably well for a while. But insolubility does not mean that one shouldn't do anything at all..., on the contrary. Problems have to be 'dealt with.'"[7]

Every model for action is structurally incomplete: it may be successful in certain areas, but in others it will have little effect or even worsen the problems. The ideas behind the "entrepreneurial city" that have been practiced in shrinking cities like Manchester, Birmingham, and Baltimore exemplify this. On the one hand, they have achieved remarkable success at revitalizing city centers; on the other, they have tended to have negative effects on outlying districts because less public funding is available for them, and they continue to suffer from economic decline and population loss.

Any urban development plan is biased. Rather than offering an allegedly objective or neutral promise of salvation through planning, this bias has to be exposed and negotiated. There needs to be a discussion about what social ideas, what interests, and what goals manifest themselves in a given project. There needs to be a repoliticization of urban development without it being completely absorbed by politics, as happened in the 1970s.

Political Deficit

The architect Rem Koolhaas recently pointed to the political deficit as one of the fundamental weaknesses of contemporary architecture: "We have broken the connection with politics and have not been able to find a different domain of legitimacy apart from good and intelligent architecture. But that would be tremendously important. Architecture is only legitimate when it formulates a utopia. Since 1945, however, this idea of a social task has continually declined. The loss was compensated by a lot of attractive new inventions by architects. Only in the past ten years, however, as the number of projects for the public domain has increasingly diminished, and we architects find ourselves serving private interests, has it become very clear that the decline of our theoretical content is also a decline of architectural content."[8]

More concretely, in the context of shrinkage, there has to be a new debate over the instruments of planning—analogous to the beginnings of High Modernism: the development of new tools of action was essential to the formation of the architecture and urban development of High Modernism. On the basis of a new sociopolitical model, new clients and sponsors were created, as were new forms of financing, new models for taxation, new concepts for community politics, new institutions, and so on. Today we urgently need such topics to be addressed again. For years, countless urban development plans have been produced in reports and urban development proposals, in competitions and direct commissions, but they have not had any noticeable effect. The reason is that all the projects are based on growth-oriented models for action that do not take hold in shrinking situations: the plans are obsolete from the outset.

Reinforcing the Local
One essential point of departure for the new models for action that are required is empowerment of the local, a reinforcement of autonomous opportunities for action. Abandoning the enforcement of ideas of the unity of an entire country does not have to take the form of a tribute to the neoliberal policy of "locational competition." For the development of cities, the emancipation of the local means regaining the power to shape a situation that had increasingly evaporated in the face of the dominance of centralized state regulation, the fragmentation of jurisdictions, and the rise in power of external influences. These days, communes are degraded into administrative apparatuses that merely implement the directives of others, having lost any opportunities to shape policy because they lack freely available financial resources and are hampered by detailed regulations. Their empowerment through decision-making authority and financial means is a precondition for developing productive qualities within regional inequalities, which can serve as a basis for models for living that take into account local differences.

From this perspective, the disempowerment of the local that has been seen in many ways in eastern Germany since reunification has proven to be one of the central political problems. Along with the drying up of community finances, the impositions of the institutional apparatus of western Germany, the importation of elites from western Germany, and the properties that are largely held in western German hands have hindered any autonomous development. It is therefore hardly surprising that participation in social processes—by any measure of civil engagement, such as elections, parties, unions, or churches—is clearly lower in eastern Germany than in western Germany. Acquiescence was purchased in eastern Germany through transfer payments, but hardly any opportunities for autonomous development were created. Compared with Great Britain in the 1980s, the profound social transformation took place amid an almost ghostly silence; but the silence thus purchased cannot produce forward-looking perspectives.

Just how far this disempowerment has gone is demonstrated by the circumstance that the model of the participative budget practiced in Brazilian cities like Porto Alegre cannot be applied in many German communities because they no longer have any funds for investment. As a result of the centralized overregulation of their structures, much wealthier former industrial countries are sometimes less flexible politically than are significantly poorer countries.

Paradoxical Planning
Formulating approaches to shrinking cities necessitates regaining a form of planning that overcomes the neoliberal reduction of urban development to insular projects, that thinks of space as a whole, and that takes into account larger temporal horizons. At the same time, such an approach has to take the contradictions inherent in planning as the starting point for discussions: How can one take action without being able to solve problems? How can large areas and stretches of time be given shape when they can neither be surveyed nor predicted, much less determined? How can the incompleteness of planning be made productive?

In addition, urban development is influenced by many different forces that are based on a wide range of structures for decision-making, developmental processes, and power structures. Most of them lie outside the level on which urban planning and local action occur. Indeed, they extend across all conceivable scales: from the neighborhood to the globe. For this reason, giving shape to urban space cannot be limited to the local but calls for action on a broad range of levels that are only loosely connected. The urban sociologist Klaus Ronneberger speaks of a "policy of jumping scales" in this context: "Because places are not restricted locally, and power relationships are produced and reproduced in a variety of geographical units, the perspective should be constructed in such a way that the individual territorial levels are leapt over and thus the boundaries of neighborhood and city are also transgressed. A policy of jumping scales could open up a path to new forms of an urban practice that counteracts the neoliberal territorial strategies."[9]

Multiplicity

This book presents and discusses a number of models for action that address the various scale levels of the urban. It is divided into four fields of action. The field "Deconstructing" examines the questions of how urban rollback—that is, the process of de-urbanization—can be shaped and what qualities can be gained by that which remains. The field "Reevaluating" explores how the traditional, the abandoned, can be reappropriated and used differently. The field "Reorganizing" is concerned with the question of social organization: How can processes, structures, and programs be conceived differently in order to create new opportunities for development? Finally, the field "Imagining" addresses mental processes of communication, memory, the search for identity, and the production of desire, considering urban action from the perspective of the imagination.

The themes of the subchapters clarify the perspectives on the city on which the envisioned approaches to action are based. The eighteen urban ideas presented are in themselves incomplete and cover only part of the complex urban reality. At the same time, however, they represent the necessary conceptual model on which any form of urban action is based. They therefore give an initial sense of the ideological premises of the various practices, making them negotiable.

Philipp Oswalt, chief curator of "Shrinking Cities"

Translated from the German by Steven Lindberg

Notes
1   Pierre Bourdieu, "Site Effects," in *The Weight of the World: Social Suffering in Contemporary Societies* (Palo Alto, CA: Stanford University Press, 1999), 124.
2   The program Stadtumbau Ost will run from 2002 to 2009. The costs for the state subsidy for home ownership amounted to €11.4 billion in 2004 alone. Over the eight-year period, the sum would be eight times that. The planned elimination of the subsidy in the fiscal year 2007/08 will gradually reduce the annual costs in the future.
3   Naomi Klein, "Purging the Poor," *The Nation*, October 10, 2005.
4   Jamie Peck and Adam Tickell, "Neoliberalizing Space," *Antipode* 34 (2002): 380-404.
5   See also Loïc Wacquant, "How Penal Common Sense Comes to Europeans: Notes on the Transatlantic Diffusion of the Neoliberal Doxa," *European Societies* 1 (1999): 319-352.
6   On this, see Robert Kaltenbrunner, "The End of Homogeneous Space," trans. David Skogley, in *Shrinking Cities, Vol. 1, International Research*, ed. Philipp Oswalt (Ostfildern-Ruit, Germany: Hatje Cantz, 2005), 704-710.
7   Lucius Burckhardt, "Das Ende der polytechnischen Lösbarkeit," reprinted in idem, *Wer plant die Planung: Architektur, Umwelt und Mensch* (Berlin: Martin Schmitz Verlag, 2004), 119-128.
8   Rem Koolhaas, "Die Berliner Schlossdebatte und die Krise der modernen Architektur," in *Fun Palace 200X: Der Berliner Schlossplatz; Abriss, Neubau oder grüne Wiese?*, ed. Philipp Misselwitz, Hans Ulrich Obrist, and Philipp Oswalt (Berlin: Martin Schmitz Verlag, 2005), 45-46.
9   Klaus Ronneberger, "Von der Regulation zur Moderation," *dérive* 14 (2003), 18. See also David Harvey, *Spaces of Hope* (Berkeley: University of California Press, 2000), 234ff.

GOVERNMENTALIZING PLANNING
Nikolaus Kuhnert and Anh-Linh Ngo

If there is anything certain at all in the current debate on planning, it is the correlation between the emphasis placed on the diagnosis of a crisis in the discipline of planning and the level of significance attributed to so-called players. The player, as an active social subject conscious of problems, functions in a certain sense as a task force that must always jump in whenever there is a fire on the planning front. What significance does this have for a discipline that traditionally has derived its image of itself from its mandate to help turn the big wheels of society and that was able, to an extent equaled by few disciplines other than politics, to convey the impression that social processes could be controlled formally? What inferences can we draw from the fact that planning no longer is focused on instruments but rather players?

Obviously this development indicates the dissolution or rather extension of a hierarchical conception of (state) power. It also involves models for control that express this trend toward decentralization in society and in the theory of power. We give two discourses as examples here which help to describe these trends toward flat hierarchies and an extension of planning by means of "subplanning" instruments: the evolution from a government approach to a governance approach and Foucault's concept of "governmentality," which is well suited as a tool of critical analysis for penetrating these shifts in power conceptually. Ultimately the point is to discuss the player-based approach to the planning debate against the backdrop of a theory of power and to question the subjectification of planning instruments—emphasizing individual interventions and empowerment strategies.

Governmentality

With the rise of neoliberalism, the enthusiasm for planning—or, more correctly, for the possibility of controlling social processes—was sobered. Planning and controlling mechanisms survived this process of transformation as mere "phantom pains," as Rem Koolhaas sarcastically commented in "Whatever Happened to Urbanism?" At the moment, these pains are being felt especially intensely.

Planning is presently experiencing an unanticipated renaissance. This renaissance, however, is no longer based on cybernetic models but rather on the debate on the assessment of the state in relation to mechanisms for self-control by society. This debate was kicked off by Michel Foucault in the 1970s, in a famous series of lectures at the Collège de France in which he attempted to reconstruct the history of governmentality. The concept of "governmentality" derives from the French adjective *gouvernemental*. Using this approach, Foucault developed a genealogy of the modern state whose traces he followed from ancient Greece to its contemporary neoliberal forms.[1]

The concept of governmentality offers a way of considering power and subjectivity together. By exploring the "microphysics of power," Foucault conceptualizes the state or society as the result of many micro- and macro-political practices and relationships of social power. This specific understanding of government covers "not only ... the legitimately constituted forms of political or economic subjection but also modes of action, more or less considered and calculated, which were destined to act upon the possibilities of action of other people. To govern, in this sense, is to structure the possible field of action of others."2

In this context Foucault used the metaphor of a ship, comparing the art of government to the steering of a ship. Notably, however, Foucault used in this context not the concept of steering but the ambiguous concept of conducting, as the French verb *(se) conduire* can mean both "guide" or "steer" and "conduct (oneself)": "Perhaps the equivocal nature of the term 'conduct' is one of the best aids for coming to terms with the specificity of power relations. For to 'conduct' is at the same time to 'lead' others (according to mechanisms of coercion which are, to varying degrees, strict) and a way of behaving within a more or less open field of possibilities. The exercise of power consists in guiding the possibility of conduct."3

In this sense, governmentality can be understood as either the art of conduct or the art of government. But *government* is used in a comprehensive sense that includes not only its present meaning as governing the state by means of politics but also the many techniques of conducting oneself and others—the so-called technologies of the self. This connection to the older meaning of the word, which until well into the eighteenth century described a general field of problems relating to how one conducts one's life, pointed "beyond the management by the state or the administration [to] problems of self-control, guidance for the family and for children, management of the household, directing the soul, and so on."4 Social action takes place in this "field of possibilities" between technologies of domination and technologies of the self. The players are thus no longer determined in a one-sided way but are always guided by themselves and by others.

Governmentalizing the Players

This is precisely where the discourse of governmentality becomes productive for the current debate on planning, which is marked by, among other things, an emphasis on increasing commitment from members of society. In this discourse, the approach based on such players is, to a certain extent, a further development of an understanding of participation in which the importance is shifted from participation to "problem ownership"—that is to say, to the active assumption of the responsibility for addressing the problem.

As part of the neoliberal program of the "lean state," which calls for "rolling back the state," civic initiatives take on quasi-sovereign functions. They are enlisted for tasks that were previously the responsibility of state bodies. But they do not take over these tasks as a way of relieving the burden on the state but rather as a way of realizing new social goals. This approach abandons the traditional classifications not only of state and society but also of society and the individual. Hence the "self-esteem" movement in the United States sees the source of various social problems as based not in society and its structures but rather in the individual and the subjective—that is to say, in a lack of self-esteem among those affected.

How can such obvious strategies of exoneration be declared by the very movements that seek social change, particularly when such strategies tempt them to go along with "slimming the state" without playing a part? The analysis of governmentality is enlightening in two respects. First, it enables one to apply the concept of government even to such initiatives and to penetrate them with a conceptual analysis of power, for in the broad sense that Foucault gives to the concept of government, there is a clear continuum between the government of the state, the *oikos,* or "household," and the individual "conducting oneself." By "conducting oneself" he means the way in which "the technologies of domination of individuals over one another have recourse to processes by which the individual acts upon himself."[5] Individuals are "governments of themselves," balancing out control by oneself and by others.

For the above-mentioned strategy of "going along with, without playing a part," this means that an analysis critical of ideology is precluded from the outset, because it would proceed according to the old model of the dichotomy of state and society and hence would fundamentally fail to appreciate the subpolitical character of such strategies. It makes sense rather to penetrate such strategies through an analysis of power in order to grasp the new character of politics and the new role of the players. Understood in this way, the self-esteem or empowerment movements can be seen as an attempt to improve the ability of players to govern, because they understand themselves as factors in the power play as a result of this "self-empowerment." Consequently, they expand the field of possibilities for their action rather than see themselves as the playthings of power or as objects of planning.

The analysis of governmentality is also interesting for another reason. Through an analysis of the individual as part of technologies of conducting oneself and others, it re-enters the scholarly debate as a "social relationship." This approach, which is advocated by political anarchism and by the antiauthoritarian movements of the beginning and the end of the last century, becomes relevant again today in the debate on governmentality. Both definitions—the individual as "social relationship" and as "government of oneself"—lead to a concept of the player that provides enough ammunition for a debate with neoliberal strategies of deregulation, privatization, and liberalization that postulate the *homo oeconomicus* as the sole model for the future.

From Government to Governance
Since the early 1980s a concept has become established in organization theory and political science which tries to grasp these processes of deregulation, privatization, and liberalization in theoretical terms: governance. The concept itself can be traced back to the Greek verb *kubernán,* to "steer" or "guide," as a wagon or a ship; this is also the root of the word "cybernetics." Governance in general refers to the system of steering or regulating a political, social, or corporate unit. Originally introduced as an alternative to "government," its semantic context has since expanded to such an extent that it has become a fashionable term used in almost every context, from "corporate governance" to "good governance" and "urban governance": "Whereas 'government' stands for the hierarchical, centralist, and dirigiste character of traditional forms of running a state, 'governance' refers to decentralized, network-like forms of 'context guidance.'"[6] This distinction acknowledges that guidance and regulation are availed of not solely by the state (the "first sector") but also by the private economy (the "second sector") and the "third sector" (i.e., associations, societies, representative bodies).

Governance has in common with governmentality the skeptical view that politics can less and less be limited to governmental politics. Understood in this non-normative sense, governance suggests that the role of the state has to be redefined. In practice, however, the discourse of governance responds affirmatively, as a rule, to deregulation, privatization, and liberalization. Governance nonetheless fundamentally signals "a 'rollback to the political' in a phase in which the neoliberal transformation of society is increasingly proving to be subject to crises and is losing its legitimacy. Even confirmed liberals have begun to assume meanwhile that market fundamentalism has to be supplemented by an 'efficient state'.... In that sense, the governance discourse has at least in part revitalized the faith, dominant in the postwar period, in planning and optimization"[7]—Koolhaas's above-mentioned "phantom pains."

By contrast, governmentality both attempts to describe these trends toward the dissolution or expansion of hierarchical conceptions and enables "the development of a dynamic analysis that is not limited to observing a 'decline of the political' but decodes the 'rollback of the state' or the 'dominance of the market' itself as a *political* program. In that respect, neoliberal governmentality implies not so much a tendency for the political to end but rather its transformation that systematically restructures the relationships of social power. What we are observing is not a decline in the sovereignty of the state or in capacities for planning but rather a shift from formal to informal types of government. This includes a transfer of patterns of action defined in terms of nation-states to a level beyond the state as well as the establishment of new forms of 'subpolitics' that operate 'underneath,' as it were, what was traditionally the political."[8]

Unlike the planning models of the decades after the Second World War, however, the current model no longer embraces the classical *dichotomy* of state and society, which sees the state as an intervening player in the sense of the traditional "comprehensive planning" of the 1960s. Rather, it takes into account a new relationship of state and society in which the latter has divided into a number of subsocieties with tendencies to become "parallel societies." In this patchwork society, the state can intervene only in a limited way—namely, by guiding the context. Michael Haus and Hubert Heinelt speak of this circumstance as a "trichotomy" of state, market society, and civil society.[9] The contemporary governance debate is distinguished both by its decentering of politics and economics and by the greater value it places on civil society. This simultaneous mobilization of politics, market economies, and civil society is, according to Anthony Giddens, the paradigmatic quality of the above-mentioned "trichotomy." Constructing this triangle of forces implicitly calls for a balance in the relationships of power. And the achievement of this balance necessitates the mobilization and strengthening of the fundamentally weak forces of civil society by means of empowerment strategies.

Consequently, most of the proposals submitted for the competition "Shrinking Cities: Reinventing Urbanism," which the magazine *archplus* organized as part of the "Shrinking Cities" project, depend on a new understanding of players and of how to mobilize them.[10] The new forms of this "context guidance" are decentralized and network-like—no longer hierarchical, centralized, and dirigiste.[11] They are intended to develop the traditional connections between state and society in both directions and to create new mechanisms for cooperative action and communicative planning. In this sense, planning is strategic, cooperative, and dialogical: it is strategic because it has to react to different social contexts; it is cooperative because it can only create the contexts for various social players; and it is dialogical because the patchwork society can only be mobilized through dialogue.

The Planner as Player
The fact that a large majority of the competition entries focuses on constituting new players suggests that the model of society derived from the governance debate outlined above has been accepted as a general point of reference and that, correspondingly, interest is

now focused on the processes and problems of constituting players in civil society. The resulting demands to increase individual responsibility, self-provision, and self-government become problematic when they are intended to justify and implement neoliberal political goals.[12]

This is precisely where the aforementioned governmentalizing of players can offer another approach that preserves the critical potential of the idea of governmentality and escapes the precarious differentiation into state and society. In a way analogous to the governmentality discourse, the proposed works question in a cultural sense the limits and mechanisms of power, of interpretative authority, and of the production of the environment. Applying the above-cited remarks to the debate on planning, what we observe is not a decrease in the capacity for planning but rather a shift from formal to informal types of planning. This extension of the understanding of planning comprises new forms of "subplanning" that operate "underneath" what was traditionally considered planning. Rather than creating "plans," "planners" increasingly cooperate with other players to produce results, thus becoming players alongside other players. Planning in this sense becomes cooperative or—to borrow a phrase from Foucault again and thereby formulate it in terms of the question of power—an "acting upon an acting."

We are grateful to Thomas Lemke and Christine Hannemann for valuable suggestions.

Nikolaus Kuhnert, managing editor of the magazine *archplus* and member of the curatorial team of "Shrinking Cities"
Anh-Linh Ngo, editor of the magazine *archplus*

Translated from the German by Steven Lindberg

Notes
1   The transcripts of this extensive lecture series have been published in German translation in Michel Foucault, *Geschichte der Gouvernementalität I und II*, ed. Michel Sennelart (Frankfurt am Main: Suhrkamp, 2004). For an English translation based on this series, see Michel Foucault, "Governmentality," trans. Rosi Braidotti and revised by Colin Gordon, in *The Foucault Effect: Studies in Governmentality*, ed. Graham Burchell, Colin Gordon, and Peter Miller (Chicago: University of Chicago Press, 1991), 87–104.
2   Michel Foucault, "The Subject and Power," trans. Leslie Sawyer, in *Michel Foucault: Beyond Structuralism and Hermeneutics*, 2d ed., ed. Hubert L. Dreyfus and Paul Rabinow (Chicago: University of Chicago Press, 1983), 221.

3   Ibid., 220.
4   Thomas Lemke, "Neoliberalismus, Staat und Selbsttechnologien: Ein kritischer Überblick über die 'governmentality studies,'" *Politische Vierteljahresschrift* 41, no. 1 (2000): 31–47.
5   Michel Foucault, "About the Beginning of the Hermeneutics of the Self," *Political Theory* 21, no. 2 (1993): 198–227, esp. 203–204.
6   Ulrich Brand, "Governance," in *Glossar der Gegenwart,* ed. Ulrich Bröckling, Susanne Krasmann, and Thomas Lemke (Frankfurt am Main: Suhrkamp, 2004), 111.
7   Ibid., 114.
8   Thomas Lemke, Susanne Krasmann, and Ulrich Bröckling, "Gouvernementalität, Neoliberalismus und Selbsttechnologien," in *Gouvernementalität der Gegenwart,* ed. Ulrich Bröckling, Susanne Krasmann, and Thomas Lemke (Frankfurt am Main: Suhrkamp, 2000), 26.
9   See Michael Haus and Hubert Heinelt, "Politikwissenschaftliche Perspektiven auf den Stand der Planungstheorie," in *Perspektiven der Planungstheorie,* ed. Uwe Altrock, Simon Günter, Sandra Huning, and Deike Peters (Berlin: Leue Verlag, 2004), 167ff.
10 This volume documents the competition entries *COW—the udder way, Bau an!, However Unspectacular, Los Topos, Claiming Land, Exterritories, De-TRO-it,* and *The National Museum of Statistics.* Other works are published in *archplus* 173 (2005). Complete documentation of all the works is found in digital form in Philipp Oswalt, ed., *Shrinking Cities: Complete Works, Vol. 2, Interventionen/Interventions* (Aachen, Germany: ARCH+ Verlag, 2006).
11 See the concept of "decentralized context control" *(dezentrale Kontextsteuerung)* proposed by Helmut Willke and Gunther Teubner, in *Perspektiven der Planungstheorie,* ed. Altrock et al., 173.
12 See Barbara Steiner, "Komplizenschaft?" *archplus* 173 (2005), 78.

WITHOUT A MODEL: EXPERIMENTAL URBANISM
Friedrich von Borries and Walter Prigge

Shrinkage Radicalizes the Simultaneity of the Nonsimultaneous

The social spheres of "rich" and "poor," of "open to the future" and "hopeless," no longer divide according to "first world" and "third world"; in all worlds, shrinking is a way of adapting to global processes of transformation. What has been called growth in China—the emergence of islands of wealth in China within a generally low societal level—is identical in meaning with what has been called shrinkage in Europe, that is, the emergence of areas of poverty within a generally high societal level. This simultaneity of the nonsimultaneous is found on every street corner in the world today.

The space of experience of shrinking implies a limited horizon of expectation: the future shrinks down to the expected end—of a house, a neighborhood, or a city. Freed from these apocalyptic undertones, such knowledge can become productive if the future is no longer automatically predetermined by the pasts of an eternally expanding modernity. Modern progress is at an end, and the philosophy of the history of modernity will go into reverse: the demolition of modernization rather than its construction, modernization by means of demolition. The dismantler emerges as the hero of today.

This divergence between the historical space of experience and the present horizon of expectation is seen as positive in current conceptions of deceleration. The stasis manifested in shrinkage is seized upon as an occasion to invert as if in a mirror the ideology of progress. Nevertheless, shrinking lacks any idyllic potential; it is the result of the harsh modernization processes of economics and politics. Stasis means the future will happen elsewhere. "Shrinking" radicalizes this experience of nonsimultaneity between the third and the first worlds, between East and West, between prospering regions and structurally weak ones, between the stable and the unstable districts of a city. What seems right here becomes wrong there: growth and shrinkage always go hand in hand in this global zero-sum game.

Shrinkage Is the Result of Neoliberal Locational Politics

Shrinkage marks the turn not just from the modernist faith in scientific progress but also from the modern concept of uniform spaces and regions. If modernization already signifies urbanization, then the modern city was the guarantee for uniform socialization. Shrinkage is thus the farewell to the city as the location of societal modernization, the farewell to urbanism as a space of egalitarian socialization.

Modernization today, in many regions, means de-urbanization. In the logic of the global market economy, neither politics nor planning shapes these relationships. Nevertheless, shrinkage is not an anonymous, undirected strategy, as is particularly clear from the special case of former East Germany. Reunification was a deliberate transformation of the socialist system, conscious deindustrialization with intentional purging of the market of industrial sectors, and state-financed suburbanization to form middle-class social strata. These three sources of shrinkage fed West Germany's strategy for reunification, the results of which were predictable: shrinking is a strategy for modernization that pushes the East to the periphery, making it Germany's Mezzogiorno. The building of *Standort Ost* (eastern Germany as a location of economic investment) failed because it was nothing more than a traditional reproduction of the West. Despite continuing transfer payments, increased mobility, and growing flexibility, the locational politics of western Germany cannot establish a self-sufficient economy everywhere, neither in the East nor in the West (e.g., East Friesland, the Saarland, and the Ruhr region). The fragmentation and heterogeneity of social space in both the East and the West are the result of a locational politics that shrinks in favor of the seemingly omnipotent economy itself. The acceleration of the global economy has no uniform or continuous direction of growth; it produces a "polar inertia" (Paul Virilio) that can neither be controlled by politics nor be shaped by planning. And certainly not by a form of politics that reduces the relationship of space and location, global and local, to a simplistic economics based on the logic of location. How can the power to shape things be introduced into these relationships of space and location?

Shrinkage Reorganizes Space and Location

Shrinking cities indicate structural fissures in urban development—profound breaches in the materiality of city, space, and region. In order to understand these transformed relationships of space and location and distill from them the new typology of shrinking cities, the Bauhaus Dessau Foundation commissioned experimental urbanistic scenarios. These extensive study models operate between analysis and conception and are examples of a new linking of research and design: they offer new ways of reading the existing city and its fissures, analyzing the present developmental parameters of de-urbanization and shifting the parameters of the scenario in order to reveal implicit alternatives.

The Loose City: Geographic dispersion and suburban reorganization. When residents and jobs migrate to surrounding regions, spaces of post-Fordist logistics develop in between core cities. Along the linear traffic infrastructure, nonurban architectural forms like shopping malls, warehouses, and gas stations mix with old village structures and new developments of single-family homes, without any kind of urban planning relationship between these elements. Such posturban spaces are developing, for example, between Halle and Leipzig or Weimar and Erfurt, whose historical city centers are becoming part of a linear structure of strip cities. This nonurban form of growing agglomeration has no midpoint; the periphery becomes the center.

Growing City: De-urbanization and geographic concentration. The shrinking of one city means growth in another. What happens with the shrinking cities that lie outside areas of regional growth? Is there still a "growth corridor" within the extended shrinking of eastern Germany? In this scenario, the development of the network of cities Dresden/Leipzig/Halle/Erfurt is being forced ahead by means of the urban euthanasia for dying cities outside this corridor. These dying cities are being brought together into a growing metropolis in order to reconstitute the region of eastern Germany as a whole, thereby updating Koolhaas's bigness models for the European reality, in which the development of metropolises always means de-urbanization as well.

Translocal City: Fragmentation along a global geographical axis. Neighborhoods are defined not by geographical proximity but by networks of urban economies. "From Bitterfeld to the whole world" could be the marketing slogan for the translocal city Bitterfeld: Bitterfeld's neighboring cities include not just Wolfen, three miles away, but also Leverkusen, which is the site of the headquarters of Bayer AG, one of the most important economic players in Bitterfeld. Within this translocal neighborhood the city develops relationships of community whose economic parameters are experienced on a daily basis and have to be addressed both politically and culturally.

Seasonal City: Fragmentation along a temporal axis. The seasonal workers and weekend commuters of eastern Germany give their native cities a new, slower rhythm and thus reduce the urban structure to seasonal needs. Only gas stations continue to offer 24-hour service. Below a certain critical mass, the infrastructure disintegrates, similar to the situation in villages that have no grocery stores, schools, or children. The lack of support facilities has to be replaced by mobile infrastructure and temporary offerings. The seasonal city—familiar from agglomerations that are filled on a temporary basis, like those produced by mass tourism in the Alps or on the Mediterranean—becomes an urban model for shrinkage under quite different economic conditions.

Special Welfare City: Political dispersion and social reorganization. Special economic zones are thought to be driving forces behind economic growth: they stand for the neoliberal promise that growth can be generated through deregulation. The special welfare city is a radicalized form of the special economic zone for generating sociality. It shares with it the qualities of deregulation and self-government, but does this by encouraging the participation and involvement of society. The community is converted into an association or civic group run by the citizens themselves; they define their own criteria for distributing the state transfer monies that continue to flow in (e.g., those that guarantee a minimum income). This creates urban community and true self-government.

City of the Elderly: Integration of the unintegrated. The special welfare city reflects the large social problems in shrinking cities. It ensures the survival of the superfluous and the unemployed, and it does not matter whether someone is old, poor, or both—every citizen receives a guaranteed minimum income, and hence has the same status. That is also the prerequisite for a different kind of policy for elderly persons. An urban model for a social form of socialization of old people integrates the different cultures and themes of elderly persons: wellness and cultural education from middle-class paradises like Sun City or Majorca, farewells and asceticism from the spiritual cultures of church and religion, poverty and solidarity from the favelas and prefab concrete buildings.

These scenarios and models react to the transformed circumstances of space and location under post-Fordism. In the modern era, locations were subsumed under standardized geographical structures. The chain of growth from job offerings, population growth, use of space, infrastructure expansion, and the shaping of development produced the modern city, in which growth tended to be equal everywhere. Shrinkage interrupts or puts an end to these growth processes. The unequal development of space under discontinuous modernization reduces cities to locations within the global space of the economy and compels them to become individual through the employment of postmodern cultures of placemaking (e.g., reurbanization, marketing, identity politics, a role as cultural beacon). These kinds of locational strategies fail, however, because all of the communities are competing for the jobs and residents: this zero-sum game does not reflect the challenges of globalization but merely executes them on a local level. With the reflexive linking of space and location, the global and the local, shrinking cities and growing regions, the scenarios and models of an experimental urbanism offer ways of responding as an alternative to this submission to a simplistic locational logic of global urban development.

Shrinking without a Model

Shrinking cities spread and radicalize the universal experience of global city structures: increasing heterogeneity of social cultures (from the favela to the gated community) as well as fragmentation and insularity of urban spaces can be found in every growing city in the world, whether in Europe, Asia, or America. Following the same patterns of citadel and ghetto, the global geography of the city sets homogeneous design tasks for architecture and urban planning. Their market-oriented models are, however, unsuited to a reflective urbanism. What is needed, rather, are experiments that intervene in the practices of politics and design in order to change them. Starting out from the central urbanistic problems of the structures of work, space, and society, the Bauhaus Dessau Foundation commissioned experimental, prototypical interventions in concrete locations and situations in shrinking cities. As a complement to artistic and architectural projects, these projects generate and test urbanistic tools and concrete concepts for an experimental urban design.

Learning to Survive: Residents of shrinking cities develop social strategies to survive. Especially for the poor, the old, the unemployed, and immigrants, everyday life in shrinking cities is a constant struggle for survival, because their social connections have lost their normality and their living conditions have become precarious. What strategies ensure social survival?

Projecting Activity: A "We Inc." creates associations and secures livelihoods. The yardstick for possible jobs is not the existing job market but the ideas and potential of individuals who come together with their particular talents and interests to form self-organized activities: collective projects as counterparts to the neoliberal "Me Inc."

Putting the Useless to Use: Collective property activates unutilized areas. Formal plans for the use of and building on vacant areas are superfluous. Useless lots and buildings are reappropriated and used successfully by creative pioneers of space in informal ways. There is a need to develop political and legal procedures for the recognition of the informal and collective use of useless property.

Encouraging Individual Initiative: Local market economies make growth possible. Self-organized centers for independent entrepreneurs bring local companies and informal networks of sociocultural milieus together in order to strengthen and develop their opportunities and potential in the formal marketplace. Such autonomous initiatives for economic stimulation from below require subsidies from above as state assistance for self-help.

Broadcasting the Center: The fringe is the center. The function of city centers is communicated nowadays through decentralized communications media such as television. Do such "media transmissions" replace the experience of a social center and centrality? The "media-ization" of the world can be made evident when proximity and familiarity are transferred to images from afar and "televised."

Shaping Spaces: The forms of shrinkage require formal qualities. Beyond the master plans, situation-specific urban development tactics liberate urban entities, connect islands of buildings, generate improvised building types, and intervene with conceptions for municipal marketing: minimalist design defines new formal qualities in the discontinuity of the built world.

Producing Ruins: Unutilized areas determine the form of a city. The walling up of vacant buildings and neighborhoods changes the perception of a city. Consciously produced ruins that stand for transformation and change replace the perforation of a city by suburbanizing green spaces: a mysterious typology of useless and forgotten space from the past.

Phasing Cities Out: Shrinking ends with dying. Dying cities are the radical form of shrinkage. A mummifying approach to urban development, with partially renovated facades in front of empty and dilapidated buildings, is not a solution. Phasing out entire cities calls for a different plan: a "social plan" for abandoning the city, for giving up property, for remembering the lost legacy.

Planning Proactively: Acting in a way that is open to the outcome anticipates shrinkage. Planning means anticipating in one's thinking a desired state and reacting with practical methods and instruments in order to achieve that goal. Proactive methods and instruments that are open to outcomes replace reactive processes when the goal is to prepare locations for processes of shrinkage that might lie ahead.

Such approaches to action and urbanistic themes intervene in the design disciplines and politics of urban development and set themselves apart from urban planning design based on classical frameworks. Politics is dominated by the model of the "European city," which provides an "urban development" reduced to housing policy with no workable sociopolitical idea on which it can be based. However, the design disciplines currently have no "realistic" strategies either for implementing "radical" concepts that get to the roots of urban reality. This is all the more dramatic because the shrinking of cities does not appear to be a temporary phenomenon but rather part of global processes of modernization whose long-term consequences of social space must be shaped locally. And no one appears to be equipped to do this. If the deconstruction of buildings and neighborhoods is still a task for architects and planners, there is no overarching authority for the process of phasing out cities. In the form of urbanistic testing by means of experimental projects, such authority can be defined and conceived reflexively.

Shrinkage Politicizes Design
In an age dominated by economic constraints, the question of how the power to design can be reclaimed leads to a search for a new politics of urban design. This search for design as a form of action in which politics and design are meant to come together again can only happen without models. Models are elements of political orientation and authoritarian control within a hierarchical culture of planning that is concerned with goal-directed design in a planned order of foreseeable events. That was the criterion of the planning culture of the modern age; its hero was the architect and urban developer who designed modernism's normative promise of a better world and made its vision of the future evident.

The marketable images of the investors and the conservative postulates of urban development have also lost their persuasiveness in the face of the reality of shrinkage. Today they are being replaced by an open search for political design alternatives: the goal of exploring within an experimental arrangement in a way that is open to outcomes and unpredictable events is not to create culture on the basis of art but to politicize design practice. Such action in the form of experimental projects becomes reflective when it considers the boundaries and intersections between the elements of research (knowledge about space), design (social relationships), and presentation (visual politics) and links them anew in urbanism. Design then becomes political as a field of action for realpolitik beyond the limits within which the disciplines of politics, planning, social work and art, architecture, and urban planning demarcate and define the field of urbanistic design. This kind of politicizing is achieved by an urbanism that links the formation of structures of space and society to each other.

Walter Prigge, research associate of the Bauhaus Dessau Foundation and member of the curatorial team of "Shrinking Cities"
Friedrich von Borries, research associate of the Bauhaus Dessau Foundation during the "Shrinking Cities" project

---
Translated from the German by Steven Lindberg

TRUTH DISCOURSES
Barbara Steiner

―

―

After nearly three years of interdisciplinary collaboration on a joint project like "Shrinking Cities," the premises under which you joined transform almost by necessity. Not because you have become more pragmatic or more willing to compromise, but because such a collaboration, if you take it seriously, inevitably alters your own perspectives. The various disciplines from which we started out—architecture, urban planning, sociology, and the visual arts—and their respective approaches and methods collided frequently over those three years, created friction, and to some degree questioned one another.[1] Interestingly, however, it was precisely the interdisciplinary conflicts that helped in focusing on one's own discipline and its role in the thematic complex that was to be addressed as a group.

That artists were invited to a project like Shrinking Cities seems natural if one thinks of the many vacant buildings, usually former industrial complexes, that are now used for culture. For that reason, in the first volume I devoted my essay to that topic, basing it on developments in Manchester, Berlin, and Leipzig.[2] At the time, at least as far as Berlin and Leipzig were concerned, it still looked as if investments themselves would remain uncontrollable to a certain extent and not always bear fruit. Those involved in the project repeatedly discussed the role of culture/art and its potential co-optation by investors; the assessments, pro and con, differed. In the meanwhile, the former spinning mill in Leipzig has turned out to be a profitable business for its investors: commercial galleries from the city are setting up on the site; apartments are being finished at a rapid pace; stores of all kinds are moving in. At first glance, it would seem to be a very happy development: a vacant industrial monument was saved from decline; Leipzig galleries are attracting collectors from around the world; artists are selling their works; and the city is becoming more attractive. The role of culture and art is clearly stated in its connection with the enhanced status of vacant buildings and sites: when intellectuals and artists focus attention on certain ensembles and fill them with life, they produce welcome added value. But the resulting financial profit rarely remains in the hands of the artists; it usually is absorbed by the investors. The reflux is marginal. In other words, the symbolic revaluation is followed by an economic revaluation. There seems to be no alternative to this development; other forms of participation—say, with the contribution of "pioneers"—are not even open for discussion, at least when the area to be managed is relatively large and lucrative. Art, however, is not only welcome in connection with vacancy: since the 1980s urban planners have shown increasing interest in artistic works when it comes to implementing them as a so-called soft locational component and as a contributor to an image. The idea is to make urban space attractive as a location for consumption and experiences, distinguishing it from other cities so that it can hold its own in global competition. It goes without saying that not every manifestation of art is welcome. Critical positions, in the sense of a questioning of existing relationships, are not desired.

It is at least as obvious that art should pop up in the context of debates on shrinkage in which the issue is how to "activate" residents of such regions and cities, putting them in a position to generate new, positive perspectives on their own (desolate) situation and to take their lives into their own hands. The magic word is "self-empowerment." Cultural and artistic practices are employed to inspire people to appropriate existing spaces, structures, and situations; in short, to offer help for self-help. In this context, two points were discussed repeatedly by the curatorial team:[3]

1. To what extent do artistic practices themselves provide a perfect backdrop for the outsourcing of state tasks, and to what extent do artists involuntarily become the enforcers of dubious economic trends? In light of current developments, the instrumentalization of strategies of participation and self-empowerment is clearer than ever when the goal is to delegate social responsibility to those affected.[4]

2. To what extent is "empowerment" merely "cosmetic action" that leaves the social framework untouched? It is true that cultural or artistic strategies begin with the subject and his or her opportunities, whereas the basic political and economic parameters of action are only indirectly an object of intervention. This very point—the relationship between the subject and social developments—was again and again fiercely debated in the curatorial team over the past three years. "Empowerment" is probably the word that led to the most controversies within the group. The question that came up repeatedly is whether one should start with the subject or work directly with political and economic structures in order to achieve social change. The controversy encountered at first in (traditional) polarizations: on the one hand, the planners, who worked from a metaperspective; on the other, the artists, who dedicated themselves to the (oppressed) subjects. The call for committed local action and the acceptance of contradictions encountered a practice that tried to grasp the various developments equally and work out structural commonalities within the differences. Interestingly, the various arguments quickly turned out to be a question of disciplinary background in each case: whereas over the past three decades in the visual arts there has been a growing mistrust of metastructures and authoritarian postulates, in planning—apart from a few exceptions[5]—solutions are sought independently of such considerations of subjective states. There is still the question of the social relevance of artistic positions: In what way are they relevant if they do not intend to offer "solutions"? Or, conversely, is it perhaps the case that this distance is necessary if one wants to be socially relevant and establish a critical relationship to a given reality? After extensive discussions among ourselves and also with the artists involved, it became clear that that there is no simple either-or, that functional and nonfunctional are certainly found side by side and cannot always be separated. Artistic works that reject being functionalized from the outside can certainly pursue a self-imposed functional ambition. The artists whom we invited adopted various "concepts of functionalism," which could be warped, parodied, or mimetically appropriated.

According to Homi K. Bhabha, both culture and politics can be understood as being part of a collective that is defined by common features, values, and interests.[6] This community-based concept of culture essentially provides the "reason" for seeing oneself as part of a community that is capable of political action. In times of uncertain identities, however, as is the case during processes of shrinkage, culture itself becomes precarious. Several quite contradictory identities meet, and the process of identification that is crucial to developing cultural identities becomes more open, more variable, but also more contested. It results in "cultural uncertainty," a "significatory or representational undecidability" (Bhabha, following Frantz Fanon).[7] For Bhabha, this represents a fundamental opportunity to achieve a (new) understanding of identity. Although Bhabha developed these ideas in the course of debates on postcolonialism, it seems to me that this aspect can be transferred to our context. More than that, I believe that "cultural uncertainty" or "significatory or representational undecidability" are especially pronounced in shrinking cities. They do not permit of clarity because their political, economic, social, and cultural foundations have been shaken. "Significatory or representational undecidability" is, however, found in the Shrinking Cities project itself: it does not provide the desired cultural answer to pressing social problems. The answer fails to materialize; indeed, it *must* fail to materialize, when viewed against this backdrop. The absence of "decisive" urban planning projects in the *archplus* competition was striking: nearly all of the projects submitted were "indefinite/ambiguous" when it came to questions of design—one could even say they were "not exemplary" enough. And yet precisely that quality, as an "unexpected dimension of an ambiguous city," is particularly interesting because it makes it possible to turn the "in-between position of the urban subject ... into something liberating,"[8] and to make it a constructive point of departure for a debate on the politics of identity and image.

That is, however, just one perspective. In a way analogous to debates on functionalism, we immediately encounter "the flip side of the coin": precisely in times of uncertainty, the risk of co-optation of processes of cultural identification emerges when strong (old and new) representations are supposed to bridge or even unify contradictions and discrepancies. Hegemonically employed images—along the lines of "Gehry = Bilbao"—certainly adopt the function of producing (collective) amnesia if *one* dominant image for giving a city identity replaces a number of others and is intended to smooth over the inevitable conflicts. In shrinking cities especially, the search for models testifies to the effort to produce a (superior) cultural identification and avoid disturbing deviations by means of "beacon politics." Counteracting strong representations and instead making the case for "floating" or contingent identities, difference, and hybridity do not automatically lead to the emancipation of subjects. On the contrary, difference and hybridity, if efficiently organized, can certainly be co-opted and fit in well with a capitalist logic of exploitation. Some differences—for example, when having to do with preserving regional customs and other unique qualities—are definitely welcome as long as they do not disturb hegemonic politics.

Again and again, we on the curatorial team discussed (with great controversy) the social relevance of art. Artistic contributions may indeed seem marginal, even naive, in the face of political and economic power relationships. This is also reflected in the negligible value that society attributes to art, which scarcely plays a role at all in critical public debates. But how can that be changed? Art is not the only discipline wrestling with such questions. That every social change is difficult, even when the crises are great, is an observation for which we are indebted to Antonio Gramsci. In his analysis of the Italian state and Italian society after the defeat of the First World War, he noted that fundamental crises do not automatically lead to fundamental social change. External "ruptures" alone are not sufficient to change a social consensus. In order to prepare for a new consensus, Gramsci thus felt it was necessary to start with the civil society *(società civile)*, the place in society where debates over values and imaginations take place.[9] When Gramsci spoke of a struggle for a new culture, for a new way of living ("lotta per una nuova cultura, per un nuovo modo di vivere"), and at the same time a struggle for a new society ("lotta per una nuova civiltà"), he was alluding to the fact that the cultural system of a society is the point of departure for change.[10] Even if the basic parameters of society have changed in many respects since his analysis, his observations about the role of culture seem more relevant than ever. Political, economic, and social debates about the future will increasingly play out in the domain of culture when the point is to gain an understanding of controversial measures, acceptance, or trust in the face of massive ruptures; to generate social perspectives; or to support or even criticize existing power structures. In these processes of working out and negotiating values and identifications, I see a place for critical and politically committed art, even if its role might seem almost quixotic at first. As mentioned above, the structure of (symbolic) value has been set in motion by the change in the political system in the East and by economic pressure, and this has led to uncertainty. The artists we invited did not see it as their task to conceal, bridge, or resolve these crises; they knew that they cannot "serve as a substitute for education systems, urban planning, or other social disciplines."[11] Their art is, however, very much in a position to produce changes in the perceptions and attitudes of those affected. Seen from that perspective, artworks go beyond purely symbolic gestures, because the issue is suddenly about the *real* consequences of this production of visual symbols—that is to say, about the structure of society, immediate living conditions, and everyday actions.

If we review the debates that took place in the context of the Shrinking Cities project, it is clear that there is no simple answer to the question of the role of art in society or, in our case, of its contribution to the theme of shrinkage. It is important but not per se critical. It can certainly be affirmative and complicit in a capitalist logic of exploitation in the context of strategies for improving value, "branding," or "events culture." At the same time, art is in a position to encourage alternative identifications and (dissident) spaces in which various forms of thinking and acting are discussed but also developed, explored, and negotiated. Even after three years, we never achieved a consensus about the Shrinking Cities project, neither on the curatorial team nor among the various participants. Nevertheless, I see this as an opportunity to continue the debate. After all, the point is precisely this working out and negotiating of what society could be today.

Barbara Steiner, director and curator of the Museum of Contemporary Art Leipzig and member of the curatorial team of "Shrinking Cities"

Translated from the German by Steven Lindberg

Notes
1 Without "Shrinking Cities," we never would have had these discussions; in Walter Prigge's words, we had "truth discourses"—that is to say, discourses that are neither true nor false, that have to compete with one another and remain contradictory, but that nevertheless involve wrestling with an attitude.
2 See Barbara Steiner, "Protest, Resistance, Usurpation," trans. Christina M. White, in *Shrinking Cities, Vol. 1, International Research,* ed. Philipp Oswalt (Ostfildern-Ruit, Germany: Hatje Cantz, 2005), 438-441.
3 See also "Social Change, Self-Empowerment, and Imagination," an interview with the artists Irene Bude, XPONA, Anke Haarmann, Kristina Leko, Tadej Pogacar, and Isa Rosenberger, in this volume, 499-502.
4 I examined this ambivalent role of art and artists in my article for *archplus* dedicated to the winners of the international competition "Shrinking Cities: Reinventing Urbanism."
5 A recent example is found in *Hier entsteht: Strategien partizipativer Architektur und räumlicher Aneignung,* ed. Jesko Fezer and Matthias Heyden (Berlin: b-books, 2004), 13-14, 19.
6 The lecture was held on September 4, 1999, in the Haus der Kulturen der Welt in Berlin. It has not been published and is available only as a typescript, which cannot be quoted without permission.
7 Homi K. Bhabha developed his ideas by coming to grips with the work of Frantz Fanon. He made the case for the rupture that breaks up cultural assessments and interpretations, for an earthquake on the level of representation, which would bring us to define ourselves individually and collectively, to question the foundation on which (national, colonial) identities are constructed. See Homi K. Bhabha, *The Location of Culture* (New York: Routledge, 1994), 152-154.
8 See the essay by Anke Haarmann, "The Urban Self," in this volume, 772-775.
9 By "civil society" Gramsci meant the sum of values and imaginations as well as the sum of nonstate and noneconomic institutions in a given society (from the family to churches, unions, and political parties). See Antonio Gramsci, *Prison Notebooks,* trans. Joseph A. Buttigieg and Antonio Callari, 2 vols. (New York: Columbia University Press, 1991-1996). On the situation after the First World War and the preparation of a "potential for consensus" for times of social crisis, see Gramsci, "Number and Quality in Representative Systems of Government," in *Prison Notebooks,* 192-195.
10 See Wolfgang Fritz Haug, "Gramsci und die Politik des Kulturellen," *Das Argument* 167 (1988): 32-48, esp. 37.
11 Kristina Leko, in "Social Change, Self-Empowerment, and Imagination," in this volume, 499-502.

COMMISSIONED CONTRIBUTIONS TO THE EXHIBITION "SHRINKING CITIES—INTERVENTIONS"

PRIZEWINNERS IN THE *ARCHPLUS* COMPETITION "SHRINKING CITIES: REINVENTING URBANISM," 2004

anschlaege.de, designers, Berlin; with *Marcus Bassler*, entrepreneur, Berlin; *Krista Burger*, artist, Berlin; *Ronald Schulz*, mushroom grower, Berlin; *Nina Thibo*, artist and writer, Berlin; and *Johannes Touché*, architect and journalist, Berlin
Grow! (Bau an!)
Mushroom cultivation project and installation, 2004/05
"Grow!" studied the economic viability and tested the feasibility of creating a garden for growing edible mushrooms in the bathrooms and kitchens of an abandoned prefab concrete building in Gera.

Members of *bad-architects.network*, architects (*Ursula Faix*, Innsbruck; *Anders Melsom*, Oslo; and *Kathrine Nyhus*, Oslo); with *Ethan Zuckerman*, philosopher, Cambridge, Mass., and *Peter Dematté*, programmer and musician, Innsbruck
De-TRO-it di-PTY-ch
Media installation on two screens, 2004/05
A continually updated screen shows the media presence of various cities on the Internet. A second screen juxtaposes the intros of selected films that take place in Detroit, local news, and short films made about Detroit's residents.

Stefanie Bremer, urban planner, Dortmund; *Dirk E. Haas*, geographer and urban planner, Essen; *Päivi Kataikko*, architect, Essen; *Henrik Sander*, urban planner, Dortmund; *Andreas Schulze Bäing*, developmental planner, Liverpool; and *Boris Sieverts*, artist and tour guide, Cologne; with *Bas Princen*, photographer, Rotterdam and Los Angeles
Claiming Land
Photography/Wall chart, 2004/05
Discussions of the economic, social, cultural, and political implications of giving away unutilized land, using the example of a fictive action in Liverpool.

Center for Urban Pedagogy, New York (*Damon Rich*, designer, and *Rosten Woo*, political scientist) and *Interboro*, architects and urban planners, New York (*Tobias Armborst*, *Daniel D'Oca*, *Georgeen Theodore*, and *Christine Williams*)
However Unspectacular: The New Suburbanism/ Detroit Do Your Thing!
Photographs, planning materials, teaching materials, and video, 2004/05

On the one hand, the authors studied how residents of Detroit suburbanize the inner city through individual appropriations. On the other, they developed teaching materials to create an awareness of Detroit's specific problems and thus open up long-term possibilities for influence.

Michael Engel, architect, Sibiu, Romania; *Peter Ille*, architect, Dresden; *Uta Oettel*, designer and photographer, Potsdam; *Ulrich Trappe*, architect, Dresden; and *Brigitta Ziegenbein*, architect, Dresden and Weimar
i am in (ich bin drin)
Installation, 2004/05
Material on migration in Germany illustrates the thesis that the shrinking population in Germany should be countered with immigration. It results in an image of a future Germany as an ethnic archipelago.

fiedler.tornquist, architects, Graz; with *complizen Planungsbüro*, Halle
Exterritories
Discussion forum, installation, text, video, 2004/05
"Exterritories" discusses a fictive exterritorial special economic zone in the region of Halle an der Saale. A public discussion round with experts examined the opportunities and risks of a Chinese zone in eastern Germany.

Eva Grubbauer, architect, Graz; *Martin Luce*, architect, Berlin and Hamburg; *Joost Meuwissen*, urban planner, Amsterdam and Vienna; and *Johannes Weisser*, designer, Hamburg and Rotterdam; with *Jan Hoffmann*, carpenter, Hamburg, and *Stephan Kipke*, carpenter, Hamburg
The National Museum of Statistics (National Museum für Statistik)
Outdoor installation, 2004/05
The National Museum of Statistics in the park of the Galerie für Zeitgenössische Kunst Leipzig combined architectural references with a critique of the statistical method and contributed to the representation of local initiatives and residual identities in museums.

Cathy Hawley, architect, London, and *Annalie Riches*, architect, London; with *Patricia Hawley*, microbiologist, Norfolk
Migrations
Video and mural, 2004/05
Observations of migratory birds in the Manchester region exemplify a more sensitive perception of everyday life and help create a new image of the city.

Ulrike Steven, architect, London; *Paul Cotter,* filmmaker, London; *Gareth Morris,* architect, London; *Heidi Rustgaard,* choreographer, London; *Eike Sindlinger,* architect, London; and *Susanne Thomas,* choreographer, London
COW—the udder way
Performance in Liverpool and installation (indoors and open air), video, 2004/05
A one-week performance with cows in an inner-city residential district of Liverpool encouraged discussion of the possibilities of unconventional use concepts and individual action in unutilized areas.

PROJECTS COMMISSIONED BY THE BAUHAUS DESSAU FOUNDATION

Peter Arlt, sociologist, Linz, and *letzelfreivogel architekten,* Halle (*Gábor Freivogel* and *Nadja Letzel*)
Wall It Up. And Take a Breath. (Einmauern. Und Luftholen)
Installation, 2004/05
Walling up empty residential buildings is a possible alternative to tearing them down, as both serve the important goal of taking superfluous living space off the market. The strategy of walling up is discussed, using a concrete example.

Behles & Jochimsen, architects, Berlin; *Tobias Engelschall – Oda Pälmke,* architects, Berlin; *Jessen + Vollenweider,* architects, Basel; and *Kühn Malvezzi,* architects, Berlin/Milan/Vienna
Text: Laurent Stalder; coordination: Stefan Rethfeld
Shrink to Fit
Video installation, 2004/05
"Shrink to Fit" uses short film to present new possibilities of intervention that give new meaning to the existing spaces in shrinking cities through spatial, architectural, and symbolic interventions.

Friedrich von Borries, architect, Berlin, and *Walter Prigge,* sociologist, Dessau; with *Nicolas Bourquin,* graphic artist, Berlin; *Hannes Gieseler,* filmmaker, Dorfhain; *Nina Gribat,* architect, Berlin; *Johanna Leuner,* graphic designer, Berlin
MetroSachs
Planning material and videos, 2005
In the southern region of eastern Germany a new metropolitan area is evolving which integrates the entire population of these regions into a prospering agglomeration. The problem of shrinking cities is solved by phasing out the cities.

Thomas Busch, architect, Dessau; with *Team 40a,* graphic artists, Dessau, and *Stefanie Rumpler,* photographer, Dessau

A Financing Concept for the Malt House Center for Innovation (Finanzierungskonzept Innovationszentrum Mälzereigebäude)
Planning material, 2005
The Brauhaus Verein Dessau presents its experiences in developing an entrepreneurial center "from the bottom up" and its financing and implementation concept for converting two old malt houses into a center for innovation.

Institut für Städtebau der ETH Zürich (*Kees Christiaanse, Mark Michaeli, Tim Rieniets,* and students)
Deplanning
Planning material, 2005
This study project of the Eidgenössische Technische Hochschule Zürich (Swiss Federal Institute of Technology Zurich) is intended as a laboratory for developing and testing new urban planning methods and instruments that enable proactive planning for cities that are not yet shrinking.

Authors collective directed by *Wolfgang Engler,* sociologist, Berlin; with *Barbara Metselaar-Berthold,* photographer and filmmaker, Berlin
Survival Handbook (Handbuch des Überlebens)
Photography and text, 2005
Literary portraits and a series of photographs shed light on the perils and successes of reorientation in the lives of people who have fallen out of the normality of a society based on working for a living or never even found their way into it.

Jesko Fezer, architect, Berlin; *Stephan Lanz,* urbanist, Berlin; and *Uwe Rada,* journalist, Berlin
Special Social Welfare Zone Forst (Sonderwohlfahrtszone Forst)
Installation, interviews, and posters, 2005
As a synthesis of welfare project and special economic zone, the Special Social Welfare Zone Forst responds to the end of a society of labor and to urban shrinkage with a political experiment that radically rethinks the social and economic structure of a community.

L21, architects, Leipzig (*Lilly Bozzo-Costa, Tom Hobusch, Stefan Rettich,* and *Dirk Stenzel*); with *Franziska Buschbeck,* writer, Halle, and *Gitte Kießling,* writer, Halle
Us Old Folk (Wir Alten)
Installation with audio drama, 2004/05
L21 addresses the accelerating problem of the aging of eastern German society. On the basis of interviews with experts and young people, as the elderly people of the future, scenarios of a society of the elderly are outlined.

Holger Schmidt, urban planner, Dessau; with *Hannes Gieseler,* filmmaker, Dorfhain, and *Julia Schmidt,* cultural journalist, Berlin
**Dessau: City of Possibilities
(Dessau—Stadt der Möglichkeiten)**
Video, 2005
Three selected projects in the city of Dessau demonstrate the opportunities and risks of interim use and reactivation of buildings and lots. It results in proposals for new sponsors and integration of the parties involved.

SMAQ—architecture urbanism research, architects, Berlin and Rotterdam *(Sabine Müller* and *Andreas Quednau)*
**Schkreutz City Map: 1st Edition
(Schkreutz. Stadtplan. 1. Auflage)**
Cartographic intervention, 2004/05
Between the cities of Halle and Leipzig, around the Schkeuditz freeway interchange, a new peripheral city has emerged that is locally independent and that follows the mechanisms of the globalized economic context. The map displays this apparent periphery as the center of the contemporary city.

Urbanista, Hamburg *(Matthias Baxmann,* urban planner; *Rüdiger Kinast,* landscape architect; and *Julian Petrin,* urban planner)
**Bitterfeld: A Translocal Region
(Translokale Region Bitterfeld)**
Installation, 2004/05
Within its borders Bitterfeld may have shrunk, but as a place with new functional and perceptive links it has become a "translocal region" beyond territorial restrictions. A bundle of measures is proposed to support this development.

visomat.inc, Berlin *(Agata Kurecki,* landscape planner; *Torsten Oetken,* media and video artist; and *Michael Weinholzner,* media and video artist), and *Matthias Böttger,* architect, Berlin; with the *Verein Freunde der Staßfurter Fernseh- und Rundfunktechnik e.V.*
TV STASSFURT
Video installation, 2005
Dispersed and incomplete beginnings of an urban life in Staßfurt are broadcast by television and thus brought together. Peripheral places begin to interact with one another and simulate urban life.

WochenKlausur, artists' group, Vienna
We Inc. (Wir AG)
Workshop, 2005
During the course of the exhibition the artists' group WochenKlausur worked with the unemployed and jobseekers to found "We Inc.'s" as alternatives to the "Me Inc." supported by employment offices.

Michael Zinganel, architect, Graz; with *Hans-H. Albers,* architect and urban planner, Graz; *Michael Hieslmair,* architect and artist, Vienna; and *Maruša Sagadin,* artist, Vienna
**[Inverse] Seasonal City
([Inverse] Saisonstadt)**
Installation, 2005
What kind of transfer of know-how and capital is taking place from Tyrol to eastern Germany when eastern Germans perform seasonal work in Austrian hotels? Is the seasonal city, which fills and empties in turn, the urbanist model for eastern Germany's future?

PROJECTS WITH GRANTS FROM THE MUSEUM OF CONTEMPORARY ART LEIPZIG

Anke Haarmann, artist and philosopher, Hamburg, and *Irene Bude,* filmmaker, Dresden and Hamburg
The Secret of L.E. (Das Geheimnis von LE)
Film poster, 3-5-min. film trailer, 60-min. video, 2004/05
Under the label [AHA], Anke Haarmann has been making portraits and self-portraits of various social groups since 1997. In collaboration with Irene Bude and the parties involved in each case, she has made a film about four characteristic approaches to urban space in Leipzig.

Kristina Leko, artist, Cologne and Zagreb
No Subject (A Conversation with Working People)
Multimedia installation, 2004/05
Kristina Leko's installation assembles various materials (biographies, stories, etc.) from the artist's participation-based collaboration with unemployed people along the number 5 streetcar line between Halle and Bad Dürrenberg.

Wiebke Loeper, artist, Berlin
**To the Sisters of Carl Möglin
(An die Schwestern des Carl Möglin)**
Installation, photography, 2004/05
In autumn 2004, Wiebke Loeper organized a project with young people in Wismar in which they photographed the important things and places in the city with regard to the decision to "leave or stay." Alongside these photographs Loeper, whose grandparents live in Wismar, exhibits her own photographs of the town.

Commissioned Contributions to the Exhibition "Shrinking Cities—Interventions"

Tadej Pogacar, artist, Ljubljana, and *P.A.R.A.S.I.T.E. Museum of Contemporary Art,* Ljubljana
Treuhand Puzzle
Installation, 2005
An interactive puzzle illustrates the history and activities of the Treuhand (the German privatization agency) by showing the most important figures and institutions and their relationships to one another. An accompanying audio archive supplements the puzzle with interviews with those affected.

Isa Rosenberger, artist, Vienna
A Monument for the Women's Center (Ein Denkmal für das Frauenzentrum)
Installation (flag monument in Wolfen) and 20-min. video, 2004/05
Together with former working women, Isa Rosenberger designed and created a flag monument for the Wolfen women's center. A video documents the path from the research to the implementation of the monument and the reactions of local decision-makers.

Christoph Schäfer, artist, Hamburg; with *Deborah Schamoni,* camera operator, Berlin
Hoang's Bistro
Installation and video, 2005
A dance video shows dancers performing a fertility dance intended to attract people to Leipzig. It also documents the parallel economies created along the periphery of the city by migrants living in Leipzig.

Andreas Siekmann, artist, Berlin
Collateral in Hand, Treuhand, and the Invisible Hand: Theatrum Mundi Oeconomicus / Stages of a Market Mechanism (Faustpfand, Treuhand und die unsichtbare Hand. Theatrum Mundi Oeconomicus / Stationen eines Marktmechanismus)
Installation, 2005
A series of diagrams and an ensemble of mechanical figures illustrate the process of deindustrialization and capitalization of the economic structures of eastern Germany. Alongside the activities of the Treuhand after the fall of Communism, it sheds light on the current neoliberal approach to industry in eastern Germany.

Superflex, artists, Copenhagen (*Björnstjerne Christiansen, Jakob Fenger,* and *Rasmus Nielsen*)
Superflex Outsourcing Shrinking Cities
Installation, 2005
Superflex outsourced its task to an architecture and planning office in China. This office developed for Superflex strategies and possible interventions for shrinking cities.

XPONA group (*Dmytri Kleiner,* political economist and software artist, Berlin; *Tanja Ostojic,* artist and cultural activist, Belgrade and Berlin; and *David Rych,* artist and cultural activist, Berlin)
XPONA, exchange in post-nation
Interactive Internet project and media installation, 2005
XPONA is an Internet portal written in the open-source Internet language Wiki; it is designed to serve the nonmonetary exchange of skills and knowledge. www.xpona.net

Heimo Zobernig, artist, Vienna; with *Norbert Steiner,* architect, Vienna
A House without Qualities (Haus ohne Eigenschaften)
Collated material, 2005
Originally the artists wanted to work with a vacant building. Over the course of their work, however, fundamental doubts about their own intervention emerged, and they decided to abandon it. That decision is documented by reference materials.

———
———
———
———
———
———
———
———
———
———
———
———

The following research tasks regarding existing concepts for action were commissioned for project development:

Architecture: Katrin Hass and Helmut Thöle
Art: Emmanuel Post, Elske Rosenfeld (Argentina)
Landscape architecture: Susanne Hainer and Holger Lauinger
Media: Mirjam Struppek
Theater: Claudia Plöchinger
Entry illustration for the exhibition: Flag (Bastien Aubry and Dimitri Broquard), Zurich

PROJECT PUBLICATIONS

Shrinking Cities, Volume 1: International Research
Edited by Philipp Oswalt for the Kulturstiftung des Bundes. With editorial assistance from Elke Beyer et al., 736 pages, 503 illustrations, 389 in color, 17 x 22.5 cm, softcover
Hatje Cantz, 2005
€39.80, $55.00
ISBN-10 3-7757-1682-3
ISBN-13 978-3-7757-1682-6

German edition:
Schrumpfende Städte, Band 1: Internationale Untersuchung
Hatje Cantz, 2004
€39.80
ISBN-10 3-7757-1481-2
ISBN-13 978-3-7757-1481-5

This book examines the causes and dynamics of the process of shrinkage for the first time on an international level. Citing concrete examples from Manchester and Liverpool in Great Britain, Detroit in the United States, Ivanovo in Russia, and Halle and Leipzig in Germany, it compares living conditions and cultural change in shrinking urban regions. Artistic intercessions help sensitize the public to a global phenomenon that poses a completely new social challenge.

Contains: Global Processes of Shrinkage, Dying Cities—Redundant Spaces, Moving Cities Unstable Places, Panic City—The Psychogeography of Fear, Imagining the City—Cultural Representations, Space Pioneers—The Avant-Garde of Shrinking, Everyday Survival—Do It Yourself, Growth : Shrinkage—Dynamics of the Periphery, The Myth of Planning—Automatic Urbanism, Deconstructed Values—Mentalities in Flux. With portraits of the individual locations and a Japan insert.

Shrinking Cities, Volume 2: Interventions
Edited by Philipp Oswalt for the Kulturstiftung des Bundes. With editorial assistance from Elke Beyer, Anke Hagemann, Kristina Herresthal, Anita Kaspar, Füsun Türetken et al., 864 pages, 478 illustrations, 369 in color, 17 x 22.5 cm, softcover
Hatje Cantz, 2006
€39.80, $55.00
ISBN-10 3-7757-1711-0
ISBN-13 978-3-7757-1711-3

German edition:
Schrumpfende Städte, Band 2: Handlungskonzepte
Hatje Cantz, 2005
€39.80
ISBN-10 3-7757-1558-4
ISBN-13 978-3-7757-1558-4

archplus, 173, "Shrinking Cities"
Journal for Architecture and Urban Planning, volume 38, May 2005, 82 pages, 75 color illustrations, German
ARCH+ Verlag, 2005
€14.00
ISSN 0587-3452

In 2004, as part of the "Shrinking Cities" project, *archplus* held the international and interdisciplinary competition "Shrinking Cities: Reinventing Urbanism." This issue of the journal documents all nine prize-winning projects and five additional works from the competition, discussing them in the context of current discourses on planning and government.

Atlas der schrumpfenden Städte / Atlas of Shrinking Cities
Edited by Philipp Oswalt and Tim Rieniets. With editorial assistance from Elke Beyer, Anke Hagemann, Kristina Herresthal, and Henning Schirmel. 160 pages, 37.5 x 26.7 cm, with numerous color illustrations, German/English
Hatje Cantz, spring 2006
Circa €39.80
ISBN-10 3-7757-1714-5
ISBN-13 978-3-7757-1714-4

Which cities shrink? Where are these cities? What processes lie behind shrinkage? *Atlas of Shrinking Cities* has approximately thirty world maps, fifty diagrams, forty city portraits, fifteen lexical essays, and an index of cities to document this global phenomenon and make it comprehensible visually by means of an innovative graphic presentation. In four chapters, illustrations, charts, and statistics reveal the reasons behind urban shrinkage, which range from demographic developments and migration patterns to shortages of resources, the destruction of nature, and transformations in types of settlement. Case studies of shrinking cities from a variety of continents illustrate the concrete effects of global processes of transformation. The index shows population changes over the past fifty years for every shrinking city with more than one hundred thousand inhabitants.

Shrinking Cities: Complete Works 1 + 2
This publication is a digital documentation of the "Shrinking Cities" project. It includes video works, research material, and the presentation of contributions to the exhibitions, and complements the printed publications of the project.

Shrinking Cities:
Complete Works 1, Analyse / Analysis
Edited by Philipp Oswalt. With assistance from Andrea Andersen and Kristina Herresthal, A4-sized foldout broschure with a CD and a DVD, German/ English/Russian
ARCH+ Verlag, 2006
€15.00
ISBN-10 3-931435-02-4
ISBN-13 978-3-931435-02-8

CD with 2,000 pages of studies in German, English, and Russian by two hundred authors on the research locations Detroit, Manchester/Liverpool, Ivanovo, and Halle/Leipzig, including studies on cultural issues such as music, vandalism, film, and literature, and with music by Richard Kirk (live at the Volkspalast, Berlin, 2004) and Stefan Weihrauch, and a song collage. DVD with twelve film contributions (approx. 2.5 hours, German/English) by Robert Andersen, Benjamin Miguel Hernandez/Chris Turner, Laura Horelli/Kathrin Wildner, Jody Huellmantel/DCDC, Kyong Park, Kelly Parker, Antje Ehmann, Projektbüro Oswalt/1kilo, and extracts of films by Albrecht Schäfer and Clemens von Wedemeyer.

Shrinking Cities:
Complete Works 2, Interventionen / Interventions
Edited by Philipp Oswalt. With assistance from Anita Kaspar, Kristina Herresthal, and Füsun Türetken, A4-sized foldout brochure with a CD and a DVD, German/English
ARCH+ Verlag, 2006
Circa €15.00
ISBN-10 3-931435-03-2
ISBN-13 978-3-931435-03-5

CD with circa 1,200 pages of studies, mainly in German, on approaches to shrinking cities from the fields of architecture, urban planning, media, theater, and art, with a documentation of all the works produced as part of the "Shrinking Cities" project (including works from the competition "Shrinking Cities: Reinventing Urbanism").
DVD with circa two hours of videos by bad-architects. network, fiedler.tornquist, Anke Haarmann, Interboro/ Center for Urban Pedagogy (CUP), Isa Rosenberger, Christoph Schäfer, Holger Schmidt, and more.

NOTES ON CONTRIBUTORS

Gerd Albers (b. 1919 in Hamburg), urban planner, lives in Germering.
William Alsop (b. 1947 in Northampton, Great Britain), architect and professor of architecture at the Technische Universität Wien, lives in London.
Ash Amin (b. 1955 in Kampala, Uganda), geographer and professor of geography at the University of Durham, lives in Durham.
anschlaege.de—Christian Lagé, Steffen Schuhmann, and Axel Watzke, communication designers, Berlin.
Peter Arlt (b. 1960 in Linz, Austria), sociologist, lives in Linz.
Ruedi Baur (b. 1956 in Paris), designer and director of the Institut für Design Forschung Design2context Hgk Zürich, lives in Paris.
Claudia Becker (b. 1969 in Hagen, Germany), architect and city planner, lives in Darmstadt.
Florian Beigel (b. 1941 in Constance, Germany), architect and professor at the Architecture Research Unit of London Metropolitan University, lives in London.
Carsten Benke (b. 1970 in Berlin), city and regional planner, research associate at the Leibniz-Institut für Regionalentwicklung und Strukturplanung, Erkner, lives in Berlin.
Frithjof Bergmann (b. 1944 in Heiligabend, Germany), philosopher and anthropologist, lives in Michigan.
Matthias Bernt (b. 1970 in Bad Salzungen, Germany), political scientist and research associate at the Umweltforschungszentrum Leipzig-Halle and the Universität Leipzig, lives in Berlin and Leipzig.
Elke Beyer (b. 1974 in Rheydt, Germany), historian and research associate for the "Shrinking Cities" project, lives in Berlin and Zurich.
Regina Bittner (b. 1962 in Freiberg, Germany), cultural studies scholar and project coordinator of the Bauhaus-Kolleg at the Bauhaus Dessau Foundation, lives in Dessau.
Florian Böhm (b. 1970 in Frankfurt am Main), air and space engineer and assistant professor at the Institute for Aviation and Space Travel at the Technische Universität Berlin, lives in Berlin.
Friedrich von Borries (b. 1974 in Berlin), architect and research associate at the Bauhaus Dessau Foundation, lives in Berlin.
Stefanie Bremer (b. 1969 in Flensburg, Germany), urban planner and assistant professor at the Institute for Urban Development and Planning at the Universität Duisburg-Essen, lives in Dortmund.
Irene Bude (b. 1965 in Meißen, Germany), filmmaker and social pedagogue, lives in Hamburg.
Hans-Joachim Bürkner (b. 1954 in Hildesheim, Germany), geographer, professor of economic and social geography at the Universität Potsdam, and department head at the Leibniz-Institut für Regionalentwicklung und Strukturplanung, Erkner, lives in Berlin.
Jasper Cepl (b. 1973 in Düsseldorf, Germany), architect and assistant professor in the department of architectural theory at the Technische Universität Berlin, lives in Berlin.

Philip Christou (b. 1956 in Lethbridge, Canada), architect and senior research fellow at London Metropolitan University, lives in London.
complizen Planungsbüro—Andreas Haase and Tore Dobberstein, architect and MBA, Halle.
CUP (Center for Urban Pedagogy)—Damon Rich and Rosten Woo, designer and political scientist, New York.
Jörg Dettmar (b. 1958 in Kamen, Germany), city and landscape planner, professor of design and space planning at the Technische Universität Darmstadt, lives in Darmstadt.
Marta Doehler-Behzadi (b. 1957 in Berlin), architect and urban planner, lives in Leipzig.
Jörg Dürrschmidt (b. 1964 in Ludwigslust, Germany), sociologist and assistant professor in the department of macrosociology at the Universität Kassel, lives in Kassel.
Wolfgang Engler (b. 1952 in Dresden, Germany), sociologist and dean of the Hochschule für Schauspielkunst "Ernst Busch" in Berlin, lives in Berlin.
Alexander Farenholtz (b. 1954 in Helmstedt, Germany), specialist in business administration and administrative director of the Kulturstiftung des Bundes, lives in Halle an der Saale.
Jesko Fezer (b. 1970 in Stuttgart, Germany), architect, artist, and assistant professor at the Universität der Künste Berlin, lives in Berlin.
fiedler.tornquist—Johannes Fiedler and Jördis Tornquist, architects, Graz.
Robert Fishman (b. 1946 in Newark, N.J., USA), architect and professor of architecture and city planning at Taubman College of the University of Michigan, lives in Ann Arbor.
Leo Fitzmaurice (b. 1963 in Shropshire, Great Britain), artist, lives in Liverpool.
Anthony Fontenot (b. 1963 in Ville Platte, La., USA), architect and professor of architecture at Tulane University, New Orleans, lives in New Orleans.
Neville Gabie (b. 1959 in Johannesburg, South Africa), artist, lives in Stroud.
Dan Graham (b. 1942 in Urbana, Ill., USA), artist, lives in New York.
Annett Gröschner (b. 1964 in Berlin), writer, lives in Berlin.
Matthias Grünzig (b. 1969 in Berlin), freelance journalist, lives in Berlin.
Anke Haarmann (b. 1968 in Munich), artist and philosopher, lives in Hamburg.
Anke Hagemann (b. 1974 in Göttingen, Germany), architect and research associate for the "Shrinking Cities" project, lives in Berlin.
Christine Hannemann (b. 1960 in Berlin), sociologist and lecturer at Humboldt-Universität Berlin, lives in Berlin.
Gregor Harbusch (b. 1978 in Munich), student of art history, cultural history, and modern history. Freelance contributor to archplus magazine, lives in Berlin.
David Harvey (b. 1935 in Gillingham, Great Britain), geographer and professor of anthropology at City University New York, lives in New York.

Susanne Hauser (b. 1957 in Mönchengladbach, Germany), cultural studies scholar and professor of art history and cultural studies at the Technische Universität Graz and Humboldt-Universität Berlin, lives in Berlin and Graz.

Katja Heinecke (b. 1969 in Bergisch Gladbach, Germany), artist and architect, lives in Leipzig.

Juan Herreros (b. 1958 in San Lorenzo de El Escorial, Spain), architect and professor at the Escuela Técnica Superior de Arquitectura de Madrid and at Princeton University, lives in Madrid.

Markus Hesse (b. 1960 in Arnsberg, Germany), geographer and assistant professor in the department of geographical studies at the Freie Universität Berlin, lives in Berlin.

Andreas Hillger (b. 1967 in Dessau, Germany), cultural journalist and editor of the *Mitteldeutsche Zeitung*, lives in Dessau.

Dieter Hoffmann-Axthelm (b. 1940 in Berlin), urban planner and journalist, lives in Berlin.

Pierre Huyghe (b. 1962 in Antony, France), artist, lives in Paris and New York.

Interboro—Tobias Armborst, Daniel D'Oca, Georgeen Theodore, and *Christine Williams,* architects and urban planners, New York.

Project team [Inverse] Seasonal City—Michael Zinganel, Hans-H. Albers, Maruša Sagadin, and *Michael Hieslmair,* architects, artists, urbanists, Vienna and Graz.

Eva Jankowski (b. 1968 in Gotha, Germany), stage director, lives in Berlin.

Robert Kaltenbrunner (b. 1960 in Vilseck, Germany), architect and head of the Department of Construction, Dwelling, and Architecture at the Bundesamt für Bauwesen und Raumordnung, lives in Bonn and Berlin.

Franz-Josef Kemper (b. 1944 in Bonn), geographer and professor of population and social geography at Humboldt-Universität Berlin, lives in Berlin.

Wolfgang Kil (b. 1948 in Berlin), writer and freelance critic, lives in Berlin.

Markus Kilian (b. 1970 in Fulda, Germany), architect and assistant professor in the department of architectural history and theory at the Universität Wuppertal, lives in Cologne.

Thomas Knorr-Siedow (b. 1946 in Berlin), urbanist at the Leibniz-Institut für Regionalentwicklung und Strukturplanung, Erkner, lives in Berlin.

Rudolf Kohoutek (b. 1941 in Vienna), urbanist, lives in Vienna.

Matthias Koziol (b. 1954 in Pritzwalk, Germany), civil engineer and professor of urban technology at the Brandenburgische Technische Universität Cottbus, lives in Cottbus.

Martin Krems (b. 1963 in Kamen, Germany), historian and press spokesman for the IBA "Stadtumbau 2010," lives in Walbeck.

Manfred Kühn (b. 1960 in Gießen, Germany), planning scholar and research associate at the Leibniz-Institut für Regionalentwicklung und Strukturplanung, Erkner, lives in Kleinmachnow.

Nikolaus Kuhnert (b. 1939 in Potsdam, Germany), architect and managing editor of *archplus* magazine, lives in Berlin.

Bastian Lange (b. 1970 in Ostfildern-Ruit, Germany), geographer and research associate at the Leibniz-Institut für Regionalentwicklung und Strukturplanung, Erkner, and at the Bauhaus Dessau Foundation, lives in Berlin.

Stephan Lanz (b. 1963 in Kaufbeuren, Germany), urban planner and assistant professor in the department of economic and social geography at the Europa-Universität Viadrina in Frankfurt an der Oder, lives in Berlin.

Holger Lauinger (b. 1971 in Karlsruhe, Germany), freelance journalist, lives in Berlin.

Kristina Leko (b. 1966 in Zagreb, Croatia), artist, lives in Zagreb and Cologne.

letzelfreivogel architekten—Gabor Freivogel and *Nadja Letzel,* architects, Halle.

Kathleen Liebold (b. 1976 in Merseburg, Germany), cultural studies scholar and project coordinator at the Galerie für Zeitgenössische Kunst Leipzig, lives in Leipzig.

Wiebke Loeper (b. 1972 in Berlin), artist, lives in Berlin.

Bart Lootsma (b. 1957 in Amsterdam), historian, curator, and guest professor at the ETH Zürich/ Studio Basel, lives in Vienna.

Engelbert Lütke Daldrup (b. 1956 in Kranenburg, Germany), developmental planner and councilor for urban development and building for the city of Leipzig, lives in Leipzig.

Pedro Manuel Martínez Monje (b. 1963 in Santurtzi, Spain), sociologist and associate professor of sociology at the Universidad del Pais Vasco, lives in Bilbao.

Ulf Matthiesen (b. 1943 in Hamburg), sociologist and urban and regional scholar, professor of European ethnology at Humboldt-Universität Berlin, department head at the Leibniz-Institut für Regionalentwicklung und Strukturplanung, Erkner, lives in Berlin.

Anna Minton (b. 1970 in Newcastle, Great Britain), writer and freelance journalist, lives in London.

Nina Möntmann (b. 1969 in Hamburg), curator and critic, lives in Hamburg.

Stephen Mullin (b. 1940 in London), architect, lives in London.

Project team The National Museum of Statistics— Eva Grubbauer, Martin Luce, Joost Meuwissen, and *Johannes Weisser,* architects and designers, Graz, Amsterdam, Hamburg.

William J. V. Neill (b. 1953 in Belfast, Northern Ireland), urban planner and lecturer in environmental planning at the Queens University in Belfast, lives in Comber, Northern Ireland.

Anh-Linh Ngo (b. 1974 in Kontum, South Vietnam), architect and editor of *archplus* magazine, lives in Berlin.

Rolf Novy-Huy (b. 1957 in Castrop-Rauxel, Germany), bank employee and loan agent at the GLS Gemeinschaftsbank, Bochum, lives in Hattingen.

Hans Ulrich Obrist (b. 1968 in Zurich), curator, lives in Paris and Milan.
Hidetoshi Ohno (b. 1949 in Gifu, Japan), architect and professor of environmental technology at the University of Tokyo, lives in Tokyo.
Orange Edge—Stefanie Bremer and *Henrik Sander,* urban planners, Dortmund.
Philipp Oswalt (b. 1964 in Frankfurt am Main), architect and journalist, lives in Berlin.
Klaus Overmeyer (b. 1968 in Rhede, Germany), landscape architect, lives in Berlin.
Jamie Peck (b. 1962 in Nottingham, Great Britain), professor of geography and sociology at the University of Wisconsin-Madison, lives in Madison.
Tadej Pogacar (b. 1960 in Ljubljana, Slovenia), artist and director of the Galerie/Centre P74, lives in Ljubljana.
Christiane Post (b. 1961 in Ahlen, Germany), artist and art historian, lives in Berlin.
Marjetica Potrč (b. 1953 in Ljubljana, Slovenia), architect and artist, lives in Ljubljana.
Walter Prigge (b. 1946 in Bremen, Germany), urban and cultural sociologist at the Bauhaus Dessau Foundation, lives in Dessau.
Michelle Provoost (b. 1964 in Arnhem, The Netherlands), architectural historian, lives in Rotterdam.
Uwe Rada (b. 1963 in Göppingen, Germany), journalist and urban development editor for *tageszeitung,* lives in Berlin.
Stella Rollig (b. 1960 in Vienna), curator, journalist and director of the Kunstmuseum Lentos in Linz, lives in Vienna and Linz.
Isa Rosenberger (b. 1969 in Salzburg), artist, lives in Vienna.
Elske Rosenfeld (b. 1974 in Halle an der Saale, Germany), freelance translator, journalist, and artist, lives in Berlin.
Marilí Santos-Munné (b. 1965 in Santo Domingo, Dominican Republic), architect, lives in Basel.
Christoph Schäfer (b. 1964 in Essen, Germany), artist, lives in Hamburg.
Birgit Schmidt (b. 1963 in Dessau, Germany), urban planner, project developer and consultant, lives in Dessau.
Olaf Schnur (b. 1966 in Aschaffenburg, Germany), geographer and assistant professor in the geography department, division of population and social geography, at Humboldt-Universität Berlin, lives in Berlin.
Anne-Kathrin Schuhmann (b. 1982 in Gera, Germany), photographer, lives in Berlin.
Steffen Schuhmann (b. 1978 in Frankfurt an der Oder, Germany), designer and photographer, lives in Berlin.
Andreas Siekmann (b. 1961 in Hamm, Germany), artist, lives in Berlin.
SMAQ—Sabine Müller and *Andreas Quednau,* architects, Berlin and Rotterdam.
Heidi Stecker (b. 1964 in Leipzig, Germany), art historian at the Galerie für Zeitgenössische Kunst Leipzig, lives in Leipzig.
Silke Steets (b. 1973 in Gelnhausen, Germany), sociologist, lives in Leipzig.
Ulrike Steglich (b. 1967 in Berlin), freelance journalist and author, lives in Berlin.
Barbara Steiner (b. 1964 in Doerfles, Austria), art historian and director of the Galerie für Zeitgenössische Kunst Leipzig, lives in Leipzig.
Kate Stohr (b. 1973 in Chicago), freelance journalist, lives in Bozeman, Montana.
Mirjam Struppek (b. 1973 in Gelsenkirchen, Germany), urban planner and scholar, lives in Berlin.
Kathrin Swoboda (b. 1970 in Weißenfels, Germany), psychologist, lives in Berlin.
Johannes Touché (b. 1972 in Lübeck, Germany), journalist and architect, lives in Berlin and Valencia.
Urbanista—Matthias Baxmann, Rüdiger Kinast, and *Julian Petrin,* urban planners and landscape architect, Hamburg.
Anna Vandenhertz (b. 1953 in Potsdam, Germany), writer, lives in Berlin.
Tina Veihelmann (b. 1970 in Werneck, Germany), freelance journalist, lives in Berlin.
Lorenzo Vicario (b. 1963 in Bilbao, Spain), sociologist and associate professor of urban sociology at the Universidad del Pais Vasco, lives in Bilbao.
Kai Vöckler (b. 1961 in Hanover, Germany), artist and freelance journalist, lives in Berlin.
Hortensia Völckers (b. 1957 in Buenos Aires), art historian and artistic director of the Kulturstiftung des Bundes, lives in Berlin.
Arnold Voß (b. 1949 in Herne, Germany), developmental planner and research associate at the Technische Universität Berlin, the Technische Hochschule Aachen, and Columbia University in New York, lives in Herne.
Claudia Wahjudi (b. 1965 in Radebeul, Germany), cultural journalist and editor for the Berlin city magazine *zitty,* lives in Berlin.
Charles Waldheim (b. 1963 in Orlando, Fla., USA), architect and professor of landscape architecture at the University of Toronto, lives in Toronto.
Stephen Ward (b. 1948 in Wakefield, Great Britain), city and regional planner and professor of planning history at Oxford Brookes University, lives in Oxford.
Corell Wex (b. 1968 in Nuremberg, Germany), freelance journalist, lives in Nuremberg.
Martin Wilhelm (b. 1961 in Munich), freelance architect and adjunct lecturer of the Fachgruppe Stadt at the Technische Universität Darmstadt, lives in Frankfurt am Main.
Andreas Willisch (b. 1962 in Karl-Marx-Stadt, Germany), sociologist, lives in Schlemmin.
XPONA group—Dmytri Kleiner, Tanja Ostojic, and *David Rych,* artists and cultural activists, Berlin and Belgrade.
Klaus Zehner (b. 1957 in Cologne), geographer and lecturer in the department of geography at the Universität Köln, lives in Cologne.
Michael Zinganel (b. 1960 in Radkersburg, Austria), artist, architectural theorist, and assistant professor at the Technische Universität Graz, lives in Vienna.

ILLUSTRATION CREDITS

Willi Ahlmer, Rheine: 148/149
Hans-Hermann Albers, Graz: 247
Lara Almárcegui, Rotterdam: 98, 580
Alsop Architects, London: 184–186, 768 bottom right, 769 top
AMO, Rotterdam: 309
anschlaege.de, Berlin: 175, 176/177
Aral, Bochum: 233 bottom
Architectural Design (October 1966): 432–435
Archiv Peanutz-Architekten, Berlin: 456
Arid Lands and Sustainable Communities Trust, Salford: 168
Artangel and Channel 4, London; Martin Jenkinson (photographer), Sturminster Newton: 813–815
Leander Auer, Weimar: 356 bottom
Author unidentified: 349 top, 699 top
Claus Bach, Weimar: 398, 399
bankleer, Berlin: 515
Sven Barske, Hamburg: 824 top
Roland Beer, Leipzig: 345
Florian Beigel, London: 139 bottom, 141
Leonardo Benevolo, *Die Geschichte der Stadt* (Frankfurt am Main and New York: Campus-Verlag, 1990): 66 bottom, 182
Tina Berning, Berlin: 48/49
Rüdiger Böhme, Brandenburg an der Havel: 818 bottom
Michael Braun, Gefrath; Projektbüro Oswalt, Berlin; party responsible, Füsun Türetken: 739
Don Brockmeier, Eustis: 762/763
Pieter Bruegel the Elder, Antwerp, 1563: 115
Thomas Bruhns, Berlin: 407
Felice Bruno, Lucerne: 672/673
Tina Brüser, Berlin: 716 third row left
Bundesminister für Wohnungsbau, Berlin, 1957: 64 bottom
Janet Cardiff, Ontario/courtesy of Galerie Barbara Weiss, Berlin: 710–711
Center for Urban Pedagogy and Interboro, New York: 326–327, 329
Chinati Foundation, Marfa: 409 top
Philip Christou, London: 139 top
Oliver Claridge, Tilbury: 166
Marcus Coates, Berwick on Tweed: 363 bottom right
Contemporary Arts Center, Cincinnati: 766 bottom right
Mitch Cope, Detroit: 477–478
Copenhagen X, Copenhagen, and Zentropa Interaction ApS, Hvidovre: 624 bottom
Giorgio D'Ambrosio (camera), Matteo Fraterno, Cesare Pietroiusti, Francesca Recchia, Rome: 697 top right, second row
Cynthia Davidson, *Anywhere* (New York: Rizzoli, 1992): 610
Pia di Tardo (video graphics), Rome: 697 top left
Werner Durth, *Träume in Trümmern* (Munich: dtv, 1993): 66 top
Todd Eberle, New York: 409 bottom
Esto, Mamaroneck, photograph by Peter Aaron: 128/129
Ursula Faix, Kathrine Nyhus (graphic art), Innsbruck, Oslo: 624 top, 736–737

FAT Architects, London/courtesy of WiMBY!: 447
Jesko Fezer, Berlin: 664, 830/831
fiedler.tornquist, Rudi Gräf, Graz: 630–637
Leo Fitzmaurice, Liverpool: 363 bottom left
Benjamin Foerster-Baldenius, Berlin: 368 top, center, bottom left
Frank Lloyd Wright Foundation, Arizona: VG Bild-Kunst, Bonn, 2005: 159, 233 top
Tom(as) Frey, Lucerne: 464/465
Fritz-Schumacher-Kolloquium, *Stadterhaltung, Stadtumbau, Stadterneuerung* (Hamburg: Sautter + Lackmann, 1998): 66 center
Neville Gabie, Liverpool: 363 top, 364–365
Geheimes Staatsarchiv, Berlin: 640 bottom
Moisei I. Ginzburg, *Stroitel'stvo Moskvy*, 1930, no. 3: 198 top
Moisei I. Ginzburg, M. Barshch, *Sovremennaia arkhitektura*, 1930, nos. 1-2: 198 bottom, center, 200, 202 top
Gran Fury, New York: 491 right
Peter Granser, Stuttgart/courtesy of Galerie Kamel Mennour, Paris; Galerie 14-1, Stuttgart, and Galeria la fabrica, Madrid: 266–267
Matthias Grünzig, Berlin: 219
Anke Haarmann with Irene Bude, Hamburg: 773, 777
Dirk E. Haas, Essen: 582 bottom, 583 top
Bruce Harkness, Dearborn: 264–265
The Heartfield Community of Heirs: VG Bild-Kunst, Bonn, 2005: 491 left
Penny Herscovitch, Los Angeles: 163
Ludwig Hilberseimer, *The New City: Principles of Planning* (Chicago: Paul Theobald, 1944): 506
Ludwig Hilberseimer, *The New Regional Pattern* (Chicago: Paul Theobald, 1949): 507
Thomas Hillig, Berlin: 442 bottom
Hubert Hoffmann, Stiftung Archiv der Akademie der Künste, Berlin: 510
Franz Höfner, Berlin: 357 top
Martin Holtappels, Münster: 820
Florian Holzherr, Munich/courtesy of Chinati Foundation, Marfa: 410/411
Laura Horelli, Berlin: 535
Frank Hülsbömer, Berlin: 460–461
Timothy Hursley, Little Rock: 470
Pierre Huyghe, Paris: 134–135
IBA-Büro Dessau, Doreen Ritzau (graphic art), Dessau: 785
Imperial War Museum, London: 157
Indymedia, Hamburg: 671
Intégral Ruedi Baur et associés, Paris: 801
Interboro and Center for Urban Pedagogy, New York: 626
Annett Jummrich, Halle: 370 center left
Gert Kähler, ed., *Geschichte des Wohnens* (Stuttgart: Deutsche Verlags-Anstalt, 1996): 504
Werner Kaligofsky, Vienna: 471
KARO Architekten, Leipzig: 221
Heinz Kathe, *Preußens Adoptivkinder* (Berlin: Arani, 1985): 640 top
S. O. Khan-Magomedov, *Arkhitektura sovetskogo avangarda*, 2001, no. 2: 202 bottom
Lorenz Kienzle (photograph), Berlin; Joachim Steuerer (poster graphics), Dresden: 684 bottom, 685 bottom

Gert Kiermeyer, Halle: 367
Connie Klar, Halle: 351
Lucien Kroll, Brussels: VG Bild-Kunst, Bonn, 2005: 440
Klemens Kühn, Halle: 368 bottom right
Jörg Kutschke, Halle: 357 bottom
Heimo Lattner, Berlin: 708
Michael Latz, Stuttgart: 152/153, 154 bottom, 155
Maarten Laupman, Rotterdam/courtesy of WiMBY!: 451
letzelfreivogel architekten, Halle: 223-224
Les Levine, New York/courtesy of Museum of Mott Art, New York, and Galerie Brigitte March, Stuttgart: VG Bild-Kunst, Bonn, 2005: 495
Robert Linke and Hans-Joachim Schulze, Berlin: 522-523
Holger Lippmann, Berlin: 705
Wiebke Loeper, Berlin: 807, 808/809, 810/811
Jason Lowe, Tilbury: 167 top
Jan Mammey, Leipzig: 716 third row right
Grotest Maru, Berlin: 370 top, center right
Gordon Matta-Clark/courtesy of Centre Pompidou, Paris: VG Bild-Kunst, Bonn, 2005: 88-90
Gordon Matta-Clark/courtesy of David Zwirner Gallery, New York: VG Bild-Kunst, Bonn, 2005: 94-95
Gordon Matta-Clark/courtesy of the estate of Gordon Matta-Clark and David Zwirner Gallery, New York: VG Bild-Kunst, Bonn, 2005: 573
Thomas Mayer, Neuss: 768 top right
Birgit Meixner, Berlin: 684 top, 685 top
Roman Mensing, Münster/courtesy of Galerie Barbara Weiss, Berlin: 577
Henry Mertens, Dessau: 380/381
Metrotimes, Detroit, Tanja Wesse (photograph), Berlin: 475
Barbara Metselaar, Berlin: Survival Handbook insert 7, 11, 15, 19, 25
Reneé Meyer, Wolfen: 352/353
Shawn Micallef, James Roussel, Gabe Sawhney (concept), with Marlena Zuber (illustration), Toronto: 695
muf architecture/art, London: 167 bottom
Musée Carnavalet, Paris: 64 top
Museum of Contemporary Art, Chicago: 463 top
Museum of Contemporary Art, Chicago/courtesy of Galerie Klosterfelde, Berlin: 463 bottom
NASA Earth Observatory, Washington: 205 top
Peter Neumann, Berlin: 286/287
New Society Magazine, 1969: 645, 647
Rune Nielsen and Superflex, Copenhagen: 702-703
Matthias Noell, Diathek der Professur für Geschichte des Städtebaus, ETH Zürich: 110
Ohno Laboratory, University of Tokyo: 205 bottom, 209
OMA, Rotterdam: 68-69, 192, 277, 279
Onlab, Nicolas Bourquin and Johanna Leuner (graphic art), with Nina Gribat, Berlin: 272-273
Romolo Ottaviani, Michele Citoni, and Davide Ferraris, Rome: 697 third and fourth rows
Peanutz-Architekten and Club Real, Berlin: 412-416
Muck Petzet, Munich: 443 top
Picture-Alliance/dpa, Frankfurt am Main, photograph by Achim Scheidemann: 102/103
Marjetica Potrč, Ljubljana: 472
Presse- und Informationsdienst Stadt Wien, "Ausstellung Kommunaler Wohnbau in Wien," 1977: 542/543

Cedric Price, London: 240
Michael Price, North Palm Beach: 473
Bas Princen, Rotterdam: 583 bottom
Project Office Philipp Oswalt, Berlin; party responsible, Gabi Eisenreich (graphics), Berlin: 285
Project Office Philipp Oswalt, Berlin; party responsible, Lena Feldhahn (content and graphics), Berlin: 650, 656
Project team COW—the udder way, London: 171-173
Project team Dietzenbach 2030: 349 center, bottom
Project team National Museum for Statistics, Vienna, Amsterdam, Hamburg, Rotterdam: 779, 780/781
Kai Reichelt, Berlin: 442 top
Matthias Rick, Berlin: 370 bottom left, 457 bottom, center
Isa Rosenberger, Ruth Kaaserer (camera), Vienna: 687-688
Stefanie Rumpler, Dessau: 382-383
Christoph Schäfer, Deborah Schamoni (camera), Hamburg: 603-607
Christoph Schäfer, Hamburg: 824 bottom
Thomas Schulze, Leipzig: 161
Andreas Schulze Bäing, Liverpool: 582 top
Steffen Schumann, Berlin: 356 top
Dietmar Seidel, Lichterfeld-Schacksdorf: 818 top
Andreas Siekmann, Berlin/courtesy of Galerie Barbara Weiss, Berlin: 598-599, 827
Boris Sieverts, Cologne: 715, 716 top, second row, bottom
SITE, New York: 126-127, 130
SMAQ, Berlin, Rotterdam: 302/303, 304/305
Robert Smithson, Estate of Robert Smithson, James Cohan Gallery, New York: VG Bild-Kunst, Bonn, 2005: 117
Robert Smithson, Solomon R. Guggenheim Museum, New York: VG Bild-Kunst, Bonn, 2005: 118-119
Robert Smithson, Collection des Musées Marseille: VG Bild-Kunst, Bonn, 2005: 122-123
Der Spiegel 21 (1998), Tanja Wesse (photograph), Berlin: 749
Der Spiegel 48 (2002), Tanja Wesse (photograph), Berlin: 743
Tony Spina, Detroit: 731 bottom
Springer & Jacoby, Hamburg: 740-741
Stadtbauamt Leinefelde-Worbis (photograph): 72/73
Stadtbauwelt 36 (1972): 131
Claus Strigel, Munich, 2004; Waldemar Hauschild (camera): 418-419
John Struthers, *Glasgow's Miles Better* (Glasgow: Struthers Advertising & Marketing Ltd., 1986): 726
Superflex, Copenhagen: 699 bottom
Superflex, Copenhagen, and Tenantspin/FACT, Liverpool: 700
Syntosil, Zurich: 457 top
Maria Tackmann, Berlin: 336/337
Max Taut, *Berlin im Aufbau* (Berlin: Aufbau-Verlag, 1946): 505
Time + Timing, 1986: 438
Peter Trummer, Amsterdam: 236/237
Eric Tschaikner, Linz: 106-107
Oswald Mathias Ungers, *Die Stadt in der Stadt* (Cologne: Studioverlag für Architektur L. Ungers, 1977): 190-191
Unverzagt und Albrecht Kommunikation, Leipzig: 802-803
Upper Calder Valley Renaissance Group, Yorkshire: 323

Illustration Credits

Urbanista, Hamburg: 307
Jean-Luc Valentin, Frankfurt am Main: 443 bottom
Verfürth & Kraska, Essen: 294
Camilo José Vergara, New York: 230–231
Lorenzo Vicario, Bilbao, and Pedro Manuel Martinez-Monje, Santurtzi: 746/747
Charles Waldheim, Toronto, and Marilí Santos-Munné, Basel: 81–83
Walter P. Reuther Library, Wayne State University, Detroit: 731 top
Tanja Wesse, Berlin, after Patsy Healey: 183
Tanja Wesse, Berlin: 716 fourth row right
WFA, The Hague, photograph by Peter van Rijswijk: 56/57
WochenKlausur, Vienna: 519
Timo Wulf, Berlin: 370 bottom right
Wolfgang Zeyen, Leipzig: 226/227
Harf Zimmermann, Berlin: 154 top
Michael Zinganel, Hans-Hermann Albers, Michael Hieslmair, and Maruša Sagadin, Graz: 252–253, 254/255
Felix Zwoch, *Idee, Prozess, Ergebnis* (Berlin: Frölich & Kaufmann, 1984): 53

DEMOLITION CITY

Demolition is a means of adjusting shrinking cities to a drop in local demand. Tearing down the old to make way for the new has always been part of the history of urban development. Demolition today has gained a hitherto unknown quality: it is an end in itself. It hence becomes an issue in itself. The question of dying cities follows as a consequence: What does it mean when cities completely disappear?

PLANNED DESTRUCTION
MODERN PLANNING, WAR, AND PUBLIC HOUSING
Anthony Fontenot

If the twentieth century stands as an icon to an era of progress and development with its monuments in the form of skyscrapers and massive urban territories reconfigured by modern planning, the beginning of the twenty-first century seems to represent its inverse, a negative icon—a void, with its monuments being the immaterial sites of destruction, urban disinvestment, bombed cities, decay, and demolition, which collectively constitute some of the most powerful, yet repressed, aspects of urban restructuring over the past few decades. Whether executed by war or the bulldozer, planned destruction—the intentional effort to destroy the urban fabric—has been an intrinsic part of urban development and restructuring throughout the twentieth century and seems to be acquiring a greater intensity in recent years. From Haussmann's reconstruction of Paris, to the military's strategic destruction of cities from the Second World War to the present, to U.S. public housing policies that institutionalized the demolition of existing housing as a condition for funding, to the destruction of the World Trade Center, a new urban paradigm is emerging. The planned destruction of the built environment characterizes some of the most dynamic and active processes occurring in the transformation of cities today, yet remains obscure in the discourse of architecture and urbanism and is largely repressed from public discourse.

The world of late capitalism is plagued by rotting territories, shrinking cities, and obsolete postindustrial landscapes, offering a full spectrum of destruction from outright attack to slow disinvestment and decay that demands a rethinking of the ways in which modornization has been realized. Whereas con-struction and de-struction have always been inextricably linked in the discourse of modernism, the complex implications of the underside of modern planning are becoming evident in the early twenty-first century. As Paul Virilio states, "alongside progress—that is to say, the qualitative achievements of science, there is a quantitative logic. The more intense the progress, the more catastrophic and painful the accidents, the tragedies."[1] It is a strange irony that both the beginning and the end of postmodernism is marked by the infamous destruction of buildings designed by Minoru Yamasaki: the Pruitt-Igoe public housing project, constructed in 1955 and demolished in 1972, and the World Trade Center, constructed in 1972 and destroyed in 2001.

Trapped in cycles of disinvestment, many U.S. cities today allocate millions of dollars in funding for the demolition of thousands of buildings. For example, the Demolition Division of the City of Detroit is one of the most active organizations in the nation, demolishing between fifty and one hundred buildings every month. "The economically, politically and socially driven processes of creative destruction through abandonment and redevelopment are often every bit as destructive as arbitrary acts of war. Much of contemporary Baltimore (or Detroit, New Orleans, Cleveland, etc.), with its 40,000 abandoned houses, looks like a war zone to rival Sarajevo."[2] From urban disinvestment, to demolition, to the employment of military strategies of urban devastation, it is increasingly difficult to distinguish the results of the various methods of urban restructuring. In an effort to bring back life to the failing inner cities of the United States, the federal government has embraced

Demolition of the Pruitt-Igoe public housing project in 1972, Saint Louis, United States.

the "Hope VI" grant program as its new panacea for urban ills and since 1993 has allocated 218 million dollars for the demolition of 70,000 housing units.[3] Undoubtedly, the United States currently leads the world in new ways of developing that cyclically produce devastated urban landscapes with little recognition or reflection on the process. If the budgets for U.S. military practices and urban demolition continue to increase, it may be necessary to consider that "the art of destruction should be seen as an aesthetic as well as ethical discipline and should be taken up in the curriculum of schools of architecture and urban design."[4]

Public Housing

In the 1930s most American cities were occupied with overcrowded and dilapidated substandard housing. Robert Wagner, a senator from New York who had grown up in a tenement, pushed for housing reform. Wagner saw positive governmental action as a solution and used his legislative powers to promote public housing. In the sympathetic climate of the New Deal he won the passage of the Housing Act. On September 1, President Roosevelt signed into law the U.S. Housing Act of 1937, also known as the Robert F. Wagner Housing Act.

To prepare the designs for these new projects, cities (such as New Orleans, which became the first recipient of funds) employed modern architects who followed the latest planning scheme of independent slabs in an open greenfield. Le Corbusier's "Ville Radieuse" (Radiant City, 1931) was not only a manifesto for the creation of a new city consisting of the holy trio of sun, air, and green, but was also a proposal for the simultaneous demolition of the historic city, typified by density, poverty, and unhygienic conditions. Like so many European theoretical proposals, the new rational planning strategies employing separation, sorting, and classification were to find practical expression and application in America. The first American public housing projects directly absorbed the logic of the early European theories and planning schemes. As a result, the urban poor became even more circumscribed and isolated within spaces that were radically severed from the context of the city. Although different architectural styles were experimented with, it was the tower or slab typology in the green field that came to distinguish the "projects" throughout the United States.

The intention of the 1937 U.S. Housing Act was to provide cities with the means to clear their slums and provide decent housing for the poor. The "equivalent elimination" clause of the housing act stipulated that for the removal of each unit deemed a "slum" the government would finance construction of a new unit.[5] This also meant that federal money was not available simply to provide new public housing. It clearly stipulated that a "slum" unit must be demolished in order for federal monies to be disbursed to erect new housing in its place. Urban renewal was thus inconceivable without equivalent demolition.

This clause now put city officials in a position of not only having the power to deem certain parts of the city as slums, but the necessity to do so in order to be eligible for the program funding. In the competition to receive federal money, a kind of witch hunt for slums ensued across American cities. What areas were to be deemed slums? What were the criteria? These were far from being neutral questions. On the contrary, officials were now in a position to restructure entire urban regions both for the good of needy citizens as well as for the benefit of major federal contracts for the construction of the new city projects. Massive areas of cities were deemed slums and neighborhoods destroyed. Modernist ideals of decent housing for the poor and working classes frequently posited the traditional city itself as the enemy. It is, however, an easy transition from a critique of "substandard" housing—lacking running water, heat, and so forth—to an argument for massive demolition. The progression from single houses to a block to areas of twenty urban blocks—as occurred in New Orleans—produced incredible scenes of destruction and demolition stretching across the city. What had once been a bustling and thriving city was now a series of massive voids—on a scale of urban destruction that sometimes paralleled the destruction of European cities in the Second World War. The result was a self-induced war against the city, not from aerial bombing but by the ground forces of government policies and bulldozers. What might have started as a small-scale genuine desire to provide decent housing to the working poor ended as large-scale manipulation of land use (urban renewal) that allowed powerful developers to control and justify massive restructuring of the city. Major parts of the city were radically reorganized as the public housing projects eventually came not to belong to the neighborhood but to define it.

Housing Act of 1949

The U.S. Federal Urban Renewal Program was enacted by Congress in the Housing Act of 1949. The primary objectives of this program were to eliminate substandard and other inadequate housing through clearance of slums and blighted areas; to stimulate sufficient housing production and community development to remedy the housing shortage; and to realize the goal of a decent home and a suitable living environment for every American family. The act, however, pressed upon the authorities the new role of leading the battle against urban blight. "Blight" meant any unprofitable urban area and included commercial or residential districts that cost the city more in services than they generated in profits.[6] Such early signs of "creative destruction"—a term coined by Joseph Schumpeter in 1942—could be detected in the early years of public housing and urban renewal policy, whereby cities attempted to follow an economic-urban logic of self-regulation, destroying what was perceived as useless or unprofitable. The intention of the new act was to offer the opportunity to expand the public housing program. Therefore, a main objective of the act was to authorize new public projects on a massive scale. The development of the Magnolia Housing Project in New Orleans, for example, revealed the dangerously flexible uses of the concept of blight. The massive area claimed for the project was declared blighted and was destroyed. While this area did include some decaying houses, it also included the well-maintained homes of black doctors, ministers, and other professionals who made up the heterogeneous mix of residents in the neighborhood. The act was designed to increase public housing, making it available to a greater population; however, most cities across America employed this new program to fulfill a variety of agendas, such as redesigning their downtown districts, destroying more housing than they built. While Europe was still struggling with the urban devastation of its cities by war and massive population displacement, in neighborhoods across the United States a far more subtle, but none the less powerful, process of displacement and destruction was under way. Hundreds of thousands of families in cities across America received notices similar to the following: "The building in which you now live is located in an area which has been taken by the Boston Redevelopment Authority according to law as part of the Government Center Project. The buildings will be demolished after the families have been relocated and the land will be sold to developers for public and commercial uses, according to the Land Assembly and Redevelopment Plan presently being prepared."[7]

As Martin Anderson points out, the message is clear: this property is being taken by the government and destroyed; the government will then sell the cleared land to another party for private development; please move now. This extraordinary action was just one of many evolving from a federal program, the scope of which had rapidly increased following its enactment, and is largely responsible for establishing the legacy of modernization as an insensitive, brutal, and destructive process. This program was responsible for some of the largest urban reconstruction projects in the postwar era spanning over 750 cities across the United States.

Hope VI: Planned Destruction of Mass Public Housing
Since the 1970s, public housing in America has experienced a continuous setback and decline in resources. During the 1980s, at the height of the Reagan era, the budget of the U.S. Department of Housing and Urban Development (HUD) was slashed more aggressively than any other level of the domestic branch of the government, and during the 1990s the most active source of public housing funding came in the form of grants to facilitate the demolition and privatization of housing stock.[8] These initiatives were largely the response to a harsh critique of modernism and public housing following the demolition of the Pruitt-Igoe development in 1972. Decline in support for public housing increased as the image of public housing turned into ghettos of drug-infested high-rise towers occupying cancerous zones in the heart of the inner city. In order to broaden housing policy's overall impact on the economic health of urban neighborhoods and their residents,

Between 2000 and 2010, 200,000 apartments will be demolished in the Netherlands; as here in Voorburg, 2003.

Planned Destruction_Anthony Fontenot

HUD has now taken a new tack when it comes to inner-city investing. Through its Hope VI program, the department is using public housing money to leverage private investment in New Urbanist-style, lower-density development that includes market-rate housing and even commercial projects.

Many cities, rather than choose retention of their housing stock or new mixed income development, are using federal grants to divest themselves of their public housing regardless of its status of occupation. In a process of action as critique, the city now unleashes on the very products of its own process the demolition of thousands of public housing units across the United States. If the rational city of modernism saw the destruction of the historical city as a necessary means of moving forward, the irrational city of the early twenty-first century has inadvertently arrived at demolition as a new form of strategic planning. The grand-scale urban restructuring of the inner city has returned, not as the production but as the destruction of massive housing projects. This urban restructuring, while offering new opportunities for the redefinition of the inner city, is also forcing low-income families, many of which have been living in public housing for generations, into desperate predicaments concerning housing. Such issues beg new questions concerning the urban restructuring occurring in America, France, the Netherlands, Germany, and the United Kingdom, as massive "urban mistakes" are being demolished by the day. The neoliberal solution of relieving government of obligations concerning social issues does not work.

In producing a new kind of space within the context of early twenty-first-century development, there seems to be an ideological acceptance of little need for an invention of the new. Variations on the "traditional" model of housing have become the definitive model, resulting in a kind of no-design aesthetic that forms a composite of a phantom historic city now emerging in the inner cities. It is within this space of the demolition of the existing and the *reproduction of the known* that New Urbanism has flourished and has become the manifesto for a new kind of city.

The United States is not the only country with an urge to destroy. The governments of Great Britain, the Netherlands, France, and Germany have likewise implemented large-scale public schemes aimed at demolishing postwar urban developments. A new national regeneration program for *zones urbaines sensibles* (sensitive urban zones) has been in operation in France since 2003; by 2008, 200,000 apartments are to be torn down under this program. Great Britain's Pathfinder scheme foresees the demolition of almost half a million apartments over a fifteen-year period. The German program Stadtumbau Ost (Urban Reconstruction in Eastern Germany) will allocate around 2.5 billion euros between 2002 and 2009 primarily for the demolition of approximately 360,000 apartments.

Creative Destruction for the Twenty-First Century

The twenty-first century will be an era simultaneously concerned with the creative and destructive processes of capitalism as the confluence of economics, urban development, military operations, and disinvestment in "obsolete" urban territories increases. Collectively, these processes will be responsible for producing unimaginable urban devastation. A new kind of urbanism will be required for conceptualizing ways of incorporating grand-scale urban mistakes, accidents, and by-products of an advanced capitalist system. In short, this new century will be asked to make sense of a political-economic space that produces destruction as a systematic by-product of its development. This new kind of urbanism will become the medium through which we not only conceive of the renovation of the postindustrial city, but begin to reconcile the ongoing destructive processes of late capitalism.

According to the economic theories of Joseph Schumpeter, two basic aspects to be expected of the development of capitalism are its highly creative outcome as well as its destruction and devastation. In 1942, he coined the term "creative destruction" to denote a "process of industrial mutation that incessantly revolutionizes the economic structure from within, incessantly destroying the old one, incessantly creating a new one."[9] Schumpeter goes so far as to state that this process of creative destruction is the essential fact about capitalism. He explains that capitalism is not only equally as creative as it is destructive, but that in fact destruction is a basic prerequisite for development and progress. His theories help to explain modernity as a creative and energetic force that generates a destructive process of radical un-doing—from business to science, literature, art, architecture, and cinema, to politics and the law. This helps to explain a process that seems to be growing in intensity as it rids itself of the old and replaces it with new models.

In order to fully appreciate the implications of Schumpeter's theory in considering the relationship between economic investment and urban development, one would have to conceive of cities as commodities. In a recent article entitled "The Father of Creative Destruction: Why Joseph Schumpeter is Suddenly all the Rage in Washington," Frank Rose attempts to contextualize certain economic thinking currently dominant in Washington.[10] He cites former U.S. House Majority Leader Dick Armey as maintaining that "the market must clean itself out by taking resources away from the losers, so it creatively destroys the losing companies and reallocates resources to the winning companies. That's really what's going on."[11] If, as the former treasury secretary, Lawrence Summers, suggests, the economic future follows the patterns that Schumpeter has outlined, with creative destruction being the norm and innovation the main driver of wealth, then what does this mean for the future of cities and urbanism?[12] Schumpeter's theories suggest that both old and new urban models must be capable of responding to new economic conditions or run the risk of becoming obsolete. By extension, they also suggest that cities must be prepared to come into existence as well as fall out of existence according to the whims of the economy. But does this also mean that to resist this process would be to go against the very nature of development and progress of the current economic system? What exactly would this imply for the future of urban development? When Rem Koolhaas states that "the great originality of the Generic City is simply to abandon what doesn't work—what has outlived its use—to break up the blacktop of idealism with the jackhammers of realism and to accept whatever grows in its place,"[13] he is highlighting the fact that permanence is a thing of the past and that cities have now become the medium through which capital is invested and disinvested—cycles that move at an astounding speed. From commodities, to companies, to cities, just as war acts as an intensified extension of the economy—limiting, controlling, maintaining, and redirecting economic flows through strategies of defense and attack—the artillery of capitalism is investment and disinvestment.

What has long been ignored in the discourse of urbanism is that economic-urban development and destruction are inextricably linked, yet have remained segregated as separate studies. The relationship between urban planning and war exposes the fact that urban planning, development, modernization, and restructuring often involve devastation and ruination of cities, demolition, and forced resettlement similar to that which occurs in all-out war. This association is important because cities are unmade and annihilated, discursively as well as through bombs, planes, missiles, bulldozers, plans, and terrorist acts.[14] The inability to separate war and contemporary urban restructuring centers on the way in which this new economy manifests itself in various conditions around the globe. "The capacity for contemporary cities to overcome all manner of tribulations must in part be attributed to the fact that cities, in their capitalistic form, are hyperactive sites of 'creative destruction.' They dance to the capitalist imperative to dismantle the old and give birth to the new as expanding capital accumulation accompanied by new technologies, new forms of organization and rapid influxes of population (now drawn from all corners of the earth) impose new spatial forms and stresses upon the physical and social landscape. If, in making way for and creating the new, some of the old must first be destroyed, then why does it matter if this destruction is carried out by the wrecker's ball or inflicted by some contingent act of violence?"[15] Harvey's comments on the open-ended processes of "creative destruction" expose the precarious nature of cities as commodities under a dominant order that thrives equally on production as well as destruction, yet is a widely accepted economic philosophy. As Senator Armey implies, there will be winners and losers in this new economy—some will make it and others won't.

Is it important to distinguish between the abandonment of commodities, corporations, or cities as they become obsolete? If there is no distinction, and if what we are experiencing is an economic-urban paradigm where cities are made or destroyed interchangeably, then what is the role of urban planning in such a context? If this is the future of urbanism, then why have architecture and urban theory persisted exclusively with theories of design and construction, while excluding destruction? Furthermore, what does it mean for urbanism to absorb the spatial implications of a political-economic system that makes it increasingly difficult to draw a line between war, place annihilation, modern progress, and development? As economic destiny, this thinking allows the justification of the decimation of cities—whether through urban military operations or disinvestment—to be normalized, as in the case of Detroit. While creative destruction helps to explain certain patterns of urban invigoration and reinvention, as well as disinvestment, abandonment, decay, and rot, it also helps to explain federal and state attitudes towards such patterns.

If the economic future does in fact follow the patterns that Schumpeter has outlined, then it may require a global shift in thinking in order to account for a history of planned destruction as well as its new emerging manifestations as a natural by-product of the economic order. This long interdependent history of modernization and destruction is now becoming increasingly evident in all aspects of urban development. As new urban paradigms of destruction emerge from the dark side of modernization, driven by the highly creative and destructive impulses of the economics of late capitalism, the future of planned destruction promises to be all the more creative in the twenty-first century.

Notes
1   Paul Virilio, *Unknown Quantity* (New York: Thames and Hudson, 2003).
2   David Harvey, "The City as Body Politic," in *Wounded Cities: Destruction and Reconstruction in a Globalized World,* ed. Jane Schneider and Ida Susser (New York: Berg Publishers, 2003), 26.
3   Jason Hackworth, "Public Housing and the Re-scaling of Regulation in the US," *Environment and Planning,* A 35 (3), 537.
4   Thomas A. P. Van Leeuwen, "Architects, Demolish! The Dual Nature of Creation and Destruction," in *Shrinking Cities, Vol. 1, International Research,* ed. Philipp Oswalt (Ostfildern-Ruit, Germany: Hatje Cantz, 2005), 712.
5   M. R. Mahoney, "The Changing Nature of Public Housing in New Orleans, 1930-1974," (master's thesis, Department of History of the Graduate School of Tulane University, 1985), 21.
6   Ibid., 53.
7   Martin Anderson, *The Federal Bulldozer: A Critical Analysis of Urban Renewal, 1949-1962* (Cambridge, MA: MIT Press, 1964), 1.
8   Jason Hackworth, "The Neoliberal Turn and the Restructuring of Public Housing Policy in the United States," *Critical Planning* (Summer 2004), 11.
9   Joseph Schumpeter, *Capitalism, Socialism and Democracy,* 3rd enlarged ed. (New York: Harper, 1950), 83.
10 Frank Rose, "The Father of Creative Destruction: Why Joseph Schumpeter Is Suddenly All the Rage in Washington," *Wired* 10.03 (March 2002), 1-2.
11 Ibid., 1.
12 Ibid., 2.
13 Rem Koolhaas and Bruce Mau, *S,M,L,XL* (New York: The Monacelli Press, 1995), 1254.
14 Stephen Graham, "Cities as Strategic Sites: Place Annihilation and Urban Geopolitics," in *Cities, War and Terrorism: Towards an Urban Geopolitics,* ed. Stephen Graham (Oxford, UK: Blackwell, 2004), 31-53.
15 Harvey, "Body Politic," 25.

DEMOLITION AND URBAN DEVELOPMENT: A HISTORICAL SKETCH
Gerd Albers

"Building, breaking, rebuilding": the American poet Carl Sandburg used these words almost a century ago to characterize the dynamism of Chicago.[1] This sequence of building, breaking, and rebuilding has marked urban development for millennia. Often, fire or wartime destruction has led to reconstruction, but I will leave this aside in the discussion below. Instead, what is at issue here is the role that intentional demolition has played in the framework of urban development, a role that today is taking on a new dimension. In the past, two situations typically led to such targeted demolition programs: first of all, the implementation of new planning that had been hindered by existing buildings until the value of conservation was considered secondary to that of the new plans, and, second, the judgment that existing structures are longer adequate to meet current technical, functional, or social needs. This can, but must not necessarily, be expressed in a lack of demand.

Of course, such motivations can also overlap: for example, when an area is chosen for new planning where the structures seem worthy of demolition in other respects as well.

History offers many examples of the first category of demolition—examples that go back to long before the industrial age (to which this overview will limit its attention). The early industrial period is marked by one particularly spectacular measure: Eugène Haussmann's redesign of Paris, where the aim was not only to create serviceable streets for traffic between the various railway terminals on the outskirts of the city center, but also to provide maneuvering room for troops, with the help of which the "belly of the revolution" was to be cut open. The generous network of broad boulevards with a uniform architecture lining the streets led to the sacrifice of many older buildings, usually acquired on the basis of a law on renovation passed in 1850 (but seldom used elsewhere in France). These new boulevards, bustling with traffic, and their impressive architectural setting, would form the image of Paris around the world.

In other countries as well, it was primarily the building of new thoroughfares that led to comprehensive demolition programs, from Barcelona's Las Ramblas to Kingsway in London to Hamburg's Mönckebergstraße. Also worthy of mention is a traffic thoroughfare built in 1910 through the old center of Strasbourg—then part of Germany—as part of comprehensive demolition measures on the basis of the aforementioned French renovation law, which was still valid in Alsace, although it had already been repealed in the rest of France.[2]

In addition, some demolition measures developed solely out of the insight that existing buildings were no longer acceptable for technical and/or social reasons. These cases included the destruction of unsuitable working-class housing in Great Britain. Here, an individual legal basis had to be created for each particular case, beginning in 1866 in Glasgow. This approach was followed in 1875 by the Artizans' and Labourers' Dwellings Improvement Act, which was a generally applicable law.

At around the same time, a comprehensive demolition program was taking place in Hamburg, but for a completely different reason: the city-state's integration into the German customs area (though Hamburg maintained a customs-free zone around its port), which was agreed upon as part of the founding of the German Empire in 1871. The area that was to be used for the duty-free port had to be abandoned as a residential location, leading to the demolition of housing for around 24,000 inhabitants and their resettlement to other parts of the city. A little later, a cholera epidemic led to a similarly drastic measure in the same city: the rehabilitation of the Gängeviertel quarter around the turn of the last century. Here, after large-scale demolition, the neighborhood was completely rebuilt, in part with office buildings, including Fritz Höger's Chilehaus as well as Hans and Oscar Gerson's Ballinhaus. This was accompanied by a corresponding reordering of the street system.

If this redesigning of Hamburg's old city center in part attracted special attention because of the scope of the measures undertaken, the underlying problems could be found in many other cities as well. Joseph Stübben remarked on this in 1907 in the second edition of his standard work, *Der Städtebau:* "But there are also numerous old structures, alleyways, and neighborhoods that are an offense to health and traffic, that not only do not deserve any protection, but should be immediately torn down to provide air, light, and traffic on the basis of new street and building plans."[3]

Nonetheless, critical voices also made themselves heard around the same time: Hans-Christian Nußbaum, for example, warned in his *Hygiene des Städtebaues* against the "destruction of numerous small apartments of the cheapest kind," because "doing away with this one evil can lead to even graver problems."[4] And when Cornelius Gurlitt asked whether it "might not be better to leave the old parts of the city and to cure them from within, rather than destroy them," this was an early instance of the notion of "historical conservation."[5]

During the interwar years, the discussion of architectural renovation and renewal continued, but soon a certain shift in emphasis became evident. The diminishing stock of preindustrial buildings disappearing at the time was increasingly seen as worthy of preservation and renovation, while housing from the Wilhelminian period, with its severe problems of overcrowding, poor floor plans, and insufficient light and sun, moved to the center of critical discussion. These debates remained largely theoretical in nature, however, and little large-scale demolition was carried out. In contrast to these more or less pragmatic considerations were the ideas of radical proponents of modernism, like Bruno Taut and Le Corbusier, who advocated a complete rejection of the now outmoded city. For example, Le Corbusier's "Plan Voisin" called for the demolition of almost all of Paris's city center, with the exception of the significant architectural monuments. The megalomaniacal plans for the "Führer cities" of the Third Reich also foresaw the demolition of existing urban structures.

After the Second World War, in light of the extent of the destruction, the demolition of usable buildings was only considered in exceptional cases. In addition, the substantial reorganization aspired to in devastated areas was often hindered by economic limitations or restrictions related to proprietary rights, which led to necessary compromise. It took until the 1960s, when reconstruction had been by and large completed, for the critical voices to dominate. Too little had been torn down, it was argued, too much damaged substance had been maintained, and the chance for reordering urban structures on a large scale had thus been missed. This was a period of euphoria with respect to the magnitude of human capabilities, when the future seemed to be under control. It was the era of large-scale projects like Berlin's Märkisches Viertel and similar undertakings in other countries. Such plans were accompanied by the extensive demolition of older housing in Great Britain, in particular, and it is also there that many of the buildings

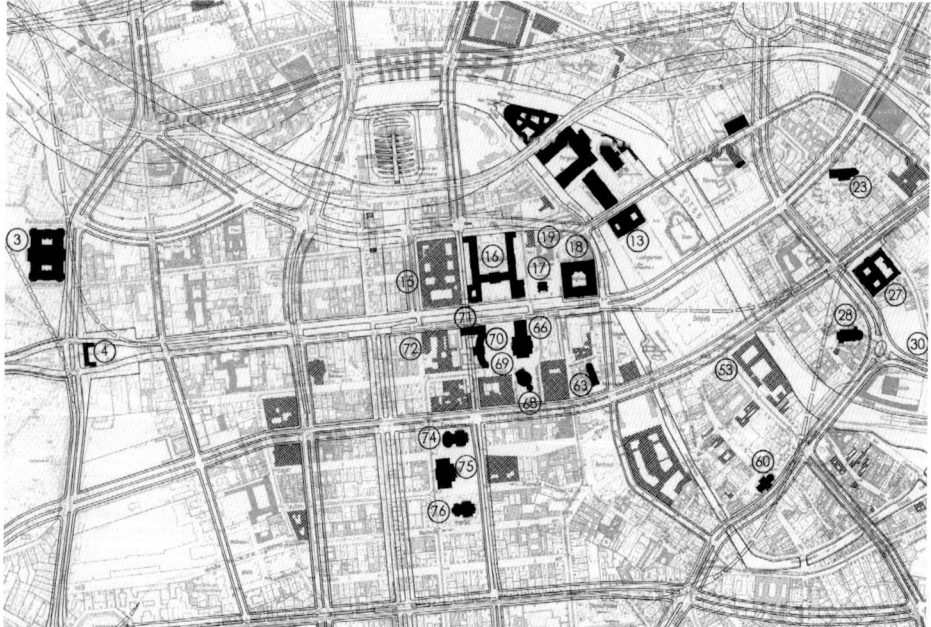

▲ History has repeatedly witnessed buildings being torn down for symbolic reasons, such as the Bastille in Paris in 1790. ▼ In classical modern urban architecture, however, the dominant trend was to destroy large areas yet preserve historical monuments, as shown here in the call for entries to the "Hauptstadt Berlin" (Capital City Berlin) competition in 1957.

erected in its place have in turn themselves been torn down, less for constructional than for sociopolitical reasons. A spectacular example of this kind is offered by St. Louis in the United States, with the destruction in 1972 of the Pruitt-Igoe housing development, an event which the critic Charles Jencks, oversimplifying somewhat, stylized as the death of modern architecture.[6] At an international planning congress held in 1993 in Glasgow, the "Gorbals" were presented—a central area of town where nineteenth-century residential dwellings had been completely replaced in the 1950s and 1960s with new buildings. But in the meantime these later buildings had themselves also been by and large cleared away—with the exception of two impressive, twenty-story apartment blocks, which, as a local colleague reported, had received an architectural prize in their day; "and they will come down next week."

But following this brief jump forward to the 1990s, let us now return to the mid-1970s, which marked a turning point in the overall climate of urban planning.

Visions of new technological possibilities, like the space structures envisioned high above the old cities that were to accommodate the most various uses, now lost their fascination; what was instead at issue was "a future for our past," as the slogan for European Architectural Heritage Year in 1975 put it. And the earlier criticism that postwar planners had been too timid, and that the remains of the past had not been done away with rigorously enough, thus leaving not enough room for the new, was now replaced with the accusation that too much that had been worth keeping, or too much that could have been repaired, had been torn down in the postwar years.[7]

Accordingly, demolition was now approached with more reluctance. A telling example here is Berlin's "Internationale Bauausstellung" (International Building Exhibition), which focused on the renovation of late nineteenth-century neighborhoods, where the aim was no longer building on vacant, emptied plots, but tearing down side wings or rear wings—and even this was not carried out unreservedly. In Charlottenburg, for example, rear wings of buildings were maintained and integrated into the new concept; this was usually true, however, of buildings that originally housed the more affluent, and were thus more generously proportioned. Similar measures were undertaken in Scandinavia, with the opening up of courtyard garden spaces by tearing down rear building wings, as well as the partial dismantling of buildings from the 1960s. In Göteborg, for example, the upper floors of a multistory prefab house were taken down and the two remaining stories were remodeled into terraced houses.

But the new fascination with the past also led to new demolition: for example, the postwar buildings on the eastern side of Frankfurt's Römer quarter were torn down to make room for copies of the lost half-timbered houses, and for the reconstruction of the Knochenhaueramtshaus in Hildesheim a building was sacrificed that had been highly regarded at the time of its construction in the 1950s. This "staging" makes clear how much a shift in the basis of evaluation can mold the spirit of the time.[8]

The question of value judgments plays an even more important role in the approach to historical buildings that bear witness to a controversial past. At the latest since the storming of the Bastille we have been familiar with the tearing down of buildings that symbolize an unloved past. Examples of this would include the demolition in Munich of the "Temples of Honor" for the Nazis killed in the 1923 Beer Hall Putsch, the tearing down of Berlin's Stadtschloss (City Palace) by the regime of the German Democratic Republic (GDR), and, in a repeat performance, the current decision to dismantle the Palast der

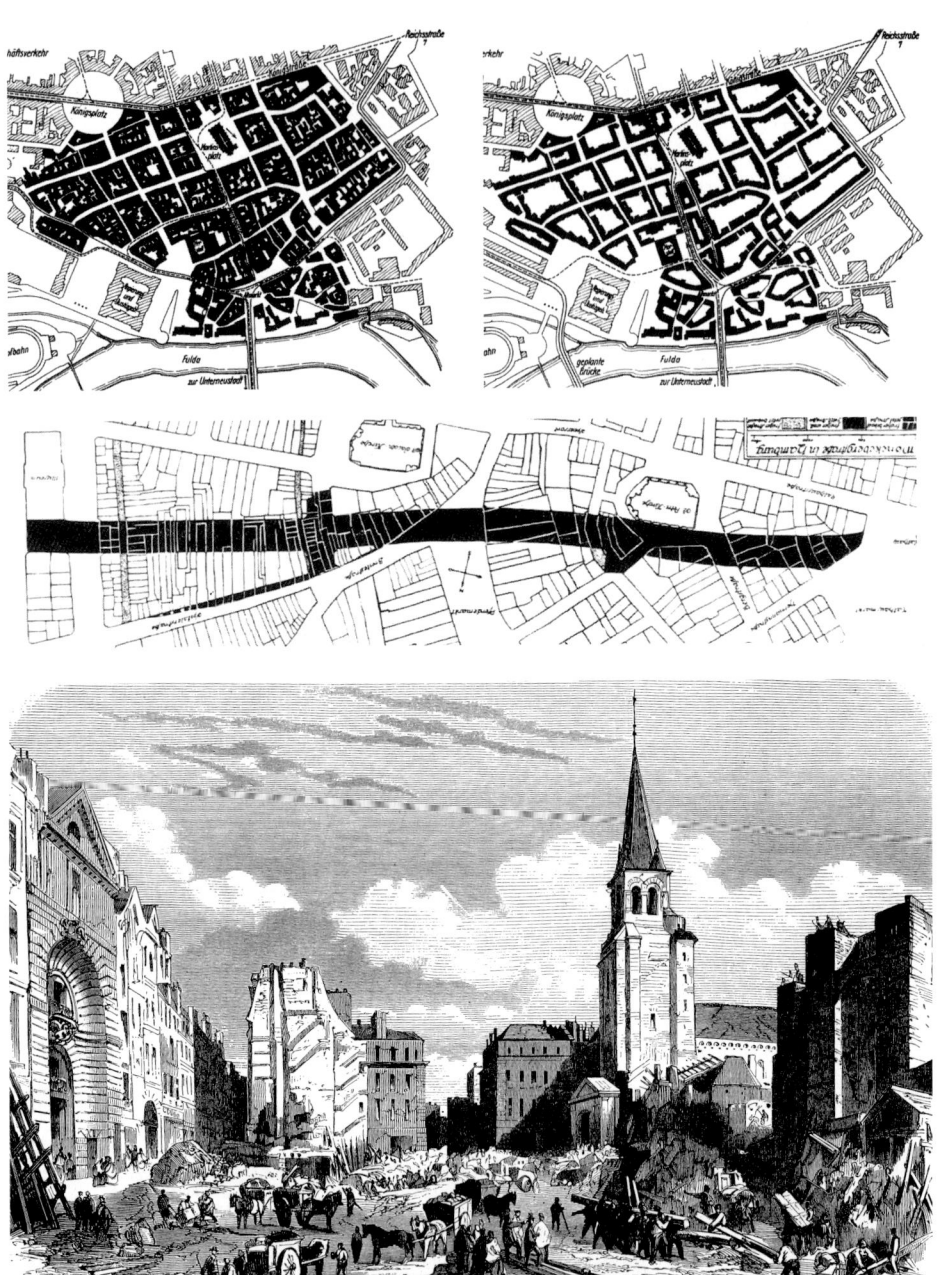

▲ Demolishing or even gutting historical districts became common practice in cautious urban regeneration programs: Kassel, 1926–1933. ▶ From the mid-nineteenth century onward, adapting densely built cities to new traffic requirements led increasingly to thoroughfares being forged through city-center areas: Mönckebergstraße ploughs through Hamburg, 1904–1912. ▼ Haussmann's rue de Rennes thoroughfare in Paris, 1868.

Republik, which had replaced the latter. This latest demolition has not yet been carried out, and it should be seriously reconsidered in the interest of realistic historical awareness.

A further aspect of demolition is illustrated by GDR housing policy and its fixation on the precast concrete apartment blocks known as *Plattenbauten*. This led in many places to the abandonment and subsequent decay of older buildings that were certainly worthy of "conservatory renewal." It was possible to save some of these buildings after 1989, but 1990s housing policy has encouraged demolition in a different way: suburban development and shopping malls cropping up on city green belts have caused the emptying of city centers, which now—in light of the demographic trend—has become an essential problem of the cities of eastern Germany and elsewhere.

The decline in population necessarily leads to vacancy and a lack of demand in the housing sector as well as in other areas of urban life. Suggestions for remedying this problem focus on removing "excess housing from the market." This stretches from the "mothballing" of unused housing stock to its targeted demolition.

These challenges can also be seen as chances for urban development—opportunities for improving urban living in terms of both structure and design. But new forms of collaboration will be required if this is to be done in a way that benefits all residents.

Translated from the German by Brian Currid

Notes
1 Carl Sandburg, "Chicago," in *The Oxford Anthology of American Literature,* ed. W. R. Benét and N. H. Pearson (Oxford, UK: Oxford University Press, 1941), 1171–1172.
2 Otto Schilling, *Innere Stadterweiterung* (Berlin: Der Zirkel, 1921).
3 Joseph Stübben, *Der Städtebau* (Stuttgart: Alfred Kröner, 1907), 237
4 Hans-Christian Nußbaum, *Hygiene des Städtebaues* (Leipzig: Göschen, 1907), 99ff.
5 Cornelius Gurlitt, "Besserung der Wohnungsverhältnisse in alten Städten," in *Verhandlungen des ersten Kongresses für Städtewesen Düsseldorf 1912,* ed. Stadtverwaltung Düsseldorf (Düsseldorf: Stadtverwaltung Düsseldorf, 1913).
6 Charles Jencks, *The New Paradigm in Architecture: The Language of Postmodernism* (New Haven, CT: Yale University Press, 2002), 9.
7 See Erwin Schleich, *Die zweite Zerstörung Münchens* (Stuttgart: JF Steinkopf Verlag, 1978); Wolf Jobst Siedler, *Die gemordete Stadt* (Munich: Herbig Verlag, 1964).
8 See Werner Durth, *Die Inszenierung der Alltagswelt* (Wiesbaden: Vieweg, 1977).

LA DÉFENSE
Paris, 1991
OMA (Rotterdam) with D.B.W. (Paris)

———

———

As a proposal submitted to an invited architectural bidding for extending the main axis of the Champs-Elysées beyond the commercial center at La Défense, OMA developed an urban renewal strategy for the already built-up area. The concept was based on the principle of a continuous tabula rasa, something inherent to the utilization logic of current architecture based on the economic reality of the rapid amortization of real estate investments and the low durability of construction materials.

Assuming that the buildings have a life span of thirty years, in five-year stages the district will be successively freed of its present construction—with the exception of several enduring, historical elements like the university, the prefecture, and a park—making room for new developments. This freeing of space will allow a process of re-organization to begin: a neutral grid isolates the timeless elements and at the same time transforms the rest of the area into a stage for unforeseeable progress. Since the pattern is neutral vis-à-vis different construction densities or building typologies, it does not imply any kind of homogenous space. Instead, the system regulates the co-existence between mass and empty space, and provides a guideline for the distribution of new programs and the urban future of this area. (Ed.)

———

———

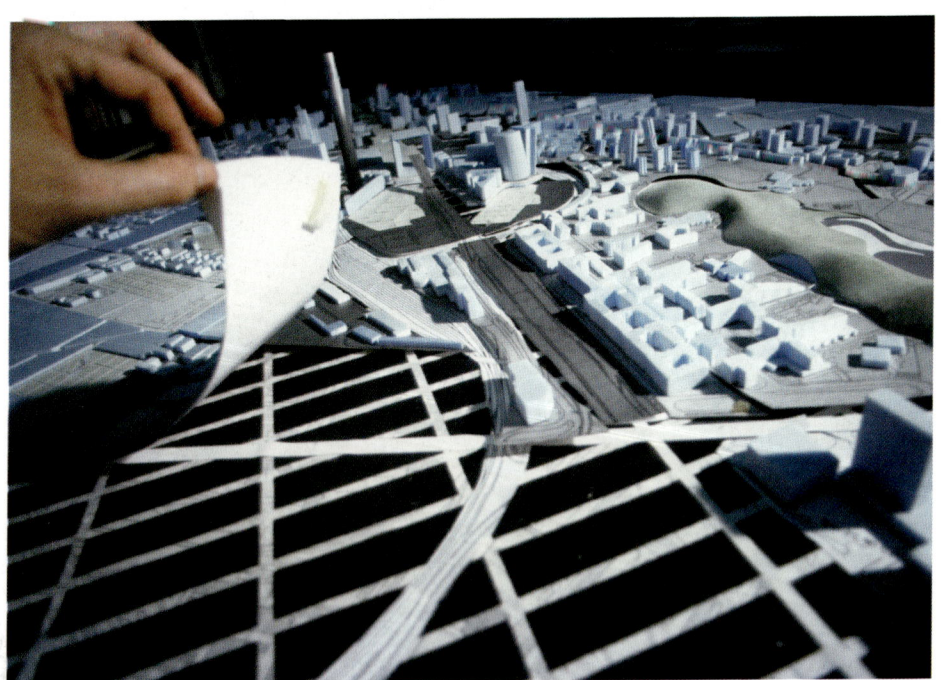

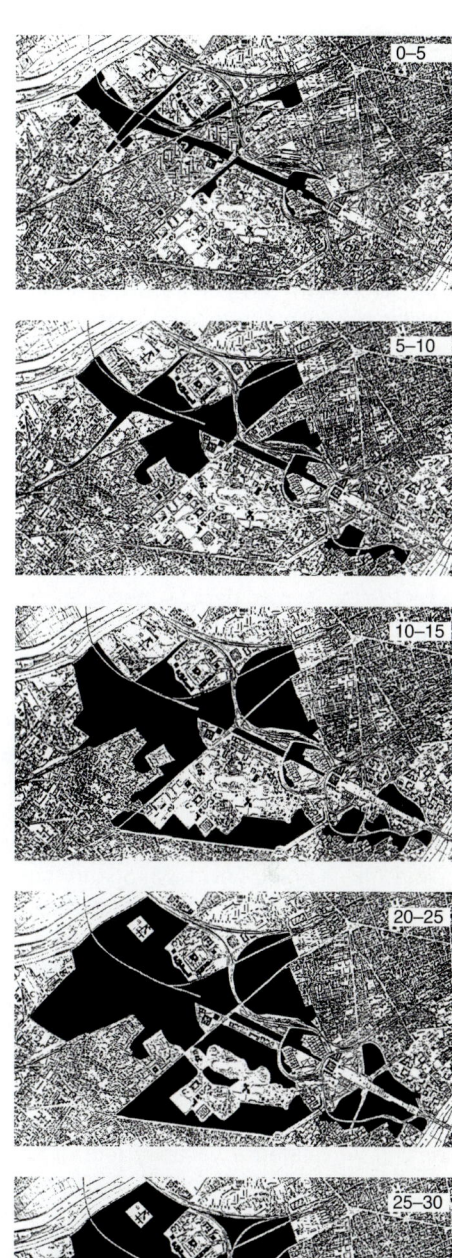

With the exception of isolated historical elements, the area around La Défense is being demolished in five-year phases to make room for new urban developments.

LEINEFELDE: ORDERLY RETREAT
Ulrike Steglich

Directly across from Leinefelde's train station, the supermarket chain Kaufland has opened a store. The huge red and white box doesn't exactly seem deserving of any kind of architectural prize. But for the town's mayor, Gerd Reinhardt, who indeed has already accepted several prizes for architecture and urban planning on behalf of his town, it is still a good sign. Not just because of the sixty jobs that the discount chain has created, but also because Kaufland has not chosen a location in the middle of nowhere, but rather one in the center of town.

Concentration on the center, demolition on the margins; this is how this town in the Eichsfeld region of Thuringia has strategically planned its shrinkage. Leinefelde has now come to be seen as an exemplary model in matters of city replanning and the structuring of the shrinking process, and has been awarded several prizes, including the 2004 European Urban Planning Prize. Whoever returns to the city after two, three, or four years not only notices the visible progress in replanning, but also a different feel: while Leinefelde is still a shrinking city with economic problems and too few jobs, it does not seem abandoned, left to its own devices, bleak, and hopeless like some other eastern German towns.

A crucial factor for Leinefelde was that its local government recognized the problem early on and reacted quickly, at a time when the promise elsewhere was still of "blooming landscapes" and the "eastern boom." The problem in question was what was to become of a large monoindustrial housing development that had lost its industry almost overnight.

Until the 1950s, Leinefelde was just a village. Industry was brought to the region following the implementation of the German Democratic Republic's Eichsfeld Plan in 1959,[1] and a huge textile factory was built in Leinefelde offering employment to many. The village's 2,500 inhabitants were joined by 13,000 new residents, who were housed in Südstadt Leinefelde—a brand-new town quarter comprised of four- to six-story *Plattenbauten* containing 5,600 units and constituting 90% of the entire residential housing of Leinefelde.[2]

But with the unification of the two German states in 1990, the situation in Leinefelde again changed dramatically. In the spinnery alone, only 250 of what were once 4,000 jobs remained; in the early 1990s the town lost a total of three-quarters of its jobs. "The most critical time was 1994," says Roland Senft, head of Leinefelde's building authority. Unemployment had soared to 25%, people were moving away, either in search of work or—if they could—into a single-family home, and the birthrate was falling. The municipal WVL Wohnungsbaugesellschaft (housing company), which owned two thirds of the town's housing, registered a vacancy rate of around 30%. The prognosis was a decrease in population, from 16,000 in the 1980s to only around 10,000 in 2010. Over the long term, only half of the apartments in the Südstadt development would be needed. Such problems could not be solved with conventional renewal measures.

There were several motives that led the town government to take leave of all illusions of growth so early on and to decide instead pragmatically in favor of "controlled shrinkage." On the one hand, migration away from Leinefelde was quickly driven to extreme levels by the collapse of what was once the town's largest employer, by a lack of alternative employment, and by the location of the town in the area where the state of Thuringia meets the western German states of both Bavaria and Hesse. Together, these factors meant that outward migration had already reached massive proportions in the initial years after 1989. On the other hand, the vacancies were not dispersed among a large number of individual property holders, but concentrated on two housing companies, with around 90% belonging to WVL and the cooperative LWG, the housing companies that owned the *Plattenbauten*. Within a short time, these found themselves financially with their backs to the wall, which in turn put the town under pressure. With no significant number of private investors in sight, Leinefelde was economically at first hardly able to compete.

On the other hand, this property structure also offered decisive advantages: the town government enjoyed immense possibilities of control, and the modest number of actors involved in this relatively small town made it easier to convince all parties to join efforts in a shared strategy. This allowed for intensive, ongoing communication, and consensus formation, quick agreement, and coordination.

Already in 1993, Leinefelde commissioned the urban planning firm GRAS to develop a framework with the goal of, on the one hand, better connecting the old town core and Südstadt and, on the other, reducing the stock of residential housing. To be able to flexibly react to still uncertain developments, infrastructure as well as modernization, reconstruction, and partial demolition were to be concentrated on the town core, while the complete demolition of apartment blocks was primarily left to the outlying areas, apart from some necessary "de-densification measures" in the core, to provide green areas and open spaces. Emphasis was also placed on reorganizing the town's infrastructure as well as developing a "green corridor" leading from the old town through Südstadt to the open landscape outside the town.

Then, little Leinefelde went all the way, holding an international architectural bidding contest together with the two housing companies to mark the launch of a reconstruction program that was to guarantee as much diversity as possible. Behind the catchy slogan, "Only the best will do for Leinefelde and its people," was the conviction that the usual paint-job renovations were quickly seen through, and that only high-quality, diverse housing could stand up to the competition over the long term. As a result of the bidding, the Munich firm Meier-Scupin und Petzet was commissioned with renovating Leinefelde's "Physiker" quarter and to this end developed a modular system of model ground plans, emphasizing the qualities of the existing structures, and proposed spatially sensible as well as affordable solutions; the slope on the square in front of the new residents' center, for example, was evened out with ground-down concrete slabs. Most impressive, however, is the residents' center itself: of the three parallel blocks that made up the quarter, two were torn down and the third was partially dismantled, leaving a one-story building that is used as an office, services, and citizens' center.

But this eagerness also led to some strange results, as can be seen by the area next to the residents' center in the midst of the development, which due to the lack of funds had initially been only provisionally restored. Then a group of Japanese planners that came to visit Leinefelde established contact between Leinefelde and the company that had organized the Osaka EXPO world exhibition; with their help the city created a Japanese garden. Now the settlement's leisure area is so exquisitely and expensively designed that a steel fence has been erected around it in order to protect it and teach the residents to treat it with care. Entrance to the garden costs twenty cents.

Demolition City

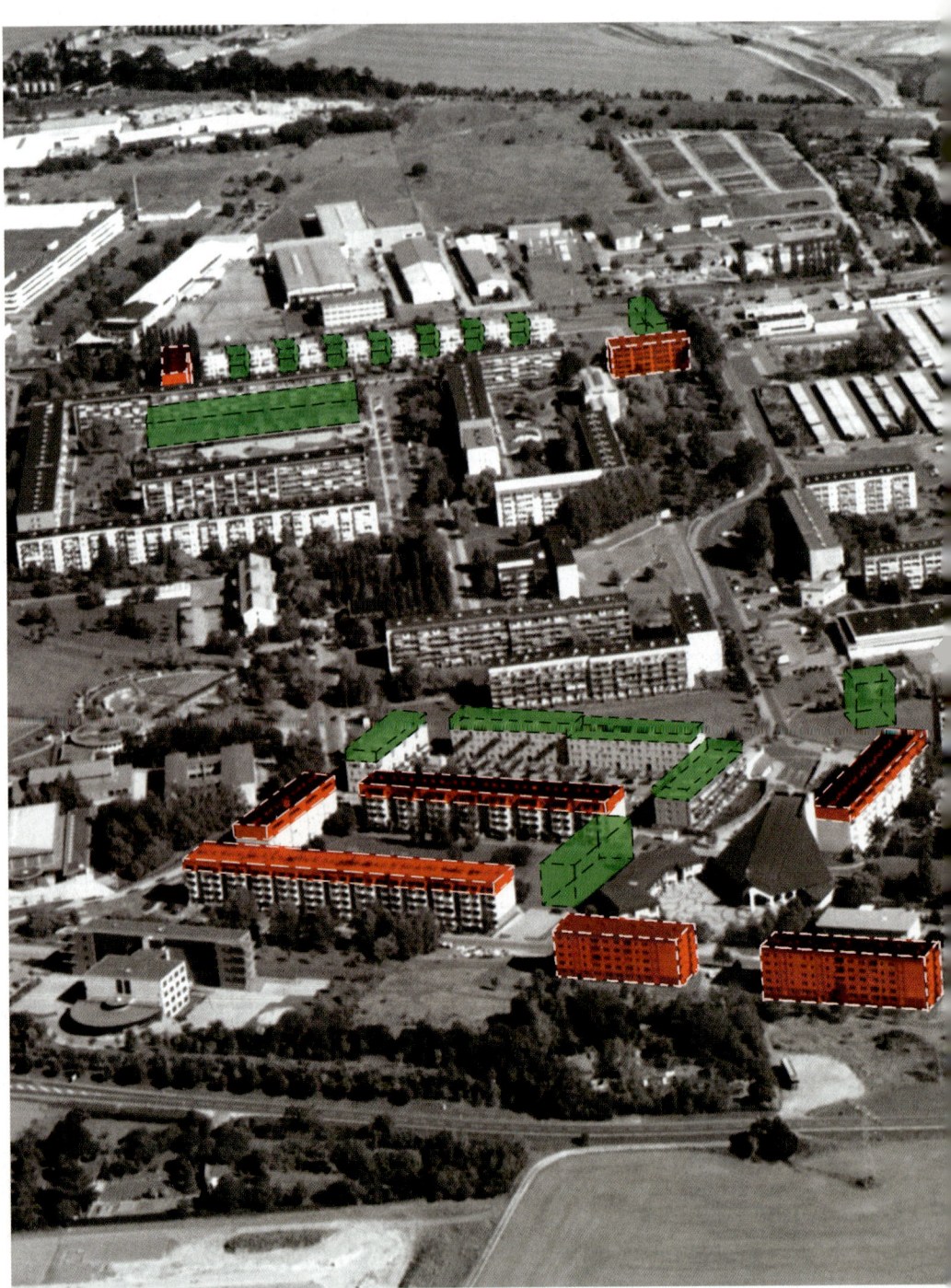

The demolition of Leinefelde's Südstadt district began in 1993 and will continue over the coming years.

Leinefelde: Orderly Retreat_*Ulrike Steglich*

Demolition complete
Demolition planned

The architect Stefan Forster, another winner in the bidding contest, experimented with the *Plattenbauten,* using their constituent parts to build summerhouses and widely admired townhouses for families. The concrete slabs proved to be astonishingly flexible, and there were also numerous uses for the remaining parts, for example in the construction of the new youth center.

Reconstruction, modernization, and demolition took place all at the same time, presenting a tremendous financial and logistic challenge to the two housing companies. The town's ambitious goal was to reduce vacancy to the usual rate of fluctuation and to break the negative cycle in which many cities and towns find themselves, where dismantling or demolition is in a permanent race against time with growing vacancy rates. "It was a huge effort," says Barbara Hahn, the managing director of WVL. But she adds that it worked because everyone cooperated and the projects were well coordinated. In order to shoulder the costs and to divide them fairly, the city and the two housing companies established a "financial pool": the German government is currently funding the dismantling at a rate of €60 per square meter. While €40 per square meter was enough to cover the cost of full demolition, partial demolition was more expensive at €90 per square meter, so the pool was redistributed in yearly blocks. By taking advantage of various funding programs, including a low-interest capital loan program, it was possible to keep the rents relatively affordable, even after modernization.

Particular tactfulness was required in interacting with the residents, since the attempt to break the cycle meant they often had to put up with living in construction sites. It was all the more important to get certain areas fully completed as soon as possible.

In the meantime, according to WVL, the vacancy rate in the modernized segments has reached the goal of 3%. Of the original 3,600 apartments, WVL still owns 2,600—of which half were fully modernized and 650 were partially modernized, 650 apartments were torn down, and the rest were privatized. Another 570 units on the outskirts of town now face demolition—the candidates have already been vacated in anticipation.

Leinefelde can be viewed as a huge jigsaw puzzle. A variety of measures are being undertaken, supervised, and coordinated at the same time by the ten-member "town development crew." No modernization takes place before the question of a sensible further use or conversion has been considered, especially in the case of infrastructure. In addition to the modernization and reduction of the residential housing, the nurseries were placed in the hands of private institutions and, due to the declining number of children, were in part converted—into a clothing collection center, a workshop for the handicapped, a vocational school, and a solar-power center. One former nursery was transformed into the town's social center and now houses various associations and initiatives; a school that was no longer needed became a vocational educational center. Substantial funds flowed into the infrastructure: the multipurpose Obereichsfeldhalle event center, a new youth center, a family swimming-pool complex, the redesign of the amusement park as a "green lung" with leisure and sport activities, the green corridor through Südstadt, new walkways and roads, to mention just a few parts of the puzzle. Commercial enterprises compatible with residential housing are consciously located toward the town center, while those less compatible are placed on former industrial sites on the outskirts of the town. At the east end of Südstadt, an area is also reserved for possible residential expansion, single-family houses, or the like.

There is hardly anything that Leinefelde would not have taken advantage of: the EXPO world exhibition, the Stadtumbau Ost (Urban Restructuring in Eastern Germany) program, the Soziale Stadt (Socially Integrative City) program,[3] architectural bids, student projects, model recycling experiments, combinations of various aid schemes, networking, and the establishment of a local administration for Südstadt in order to involve the residents by way of workshops, working groups, a neighborhood newspaper, senior citizen care, and other activities.

Leinefelde is contracting into a smaller dimension, becoming more compact. But it still seeks to remain a good-sized town. Mayor Reinhardt hopes that the population will stabilize somewhere between 9,000 and 12,000 residents. He relies on well-conceived solutions and high quality, instead of provisional answers. At the moment, the vacancy rate lies at around 19%, and it is due to fall to under 10% following the demolition planned for 2005 and 2006. Reinhardt wants to see the first phase of the "rigorous town reconstruction" completed by 2010. First successes are already evident: the migration flowing away from town has almost come to a complete halt, and Reinhardt reports a trend toward moving from the periphery back to the town center: "There's an increase again—albeit modest—in demand for housing in the center," he says. The wide variety of living units in modernized, green housing developments also attracts interest from the surrounding area. And the residents are clearly responding positively to the changes; Leinefelde has few problems with litter or vandalism, for example.

In the meantime, due to the fusion with eight other local governments, Leinefelde has become the town of Leinefelde-Worbis. This change is intended to strengthen the area economically and to secure Leinefelde's infrastructure over the long term, allowing it to remain a regional center, for this places the town in a better financial position. Since the arrival of the highway exit, the commercial areas are also more in demand.

Although Leinefelde has done everything right, the economy remains a sore point. "Companies are not quite queuing up to locate here," Reinhardt puts it cautiously. All the same, Leinefelde is able to profit from its status as a commuter center (Kassel and Göttingen are not far away). Unemployment is currently at 19%. A random resident—in this case an older taxi driver—asked about the current mood in Leinefelde complains about the lack of jobs. "The young people are moving away. My own son now works in Baden-Württemberg." "But," he adds, "it's great how the town has changed. Have you seen the new town houses?"

Translated from the German by Brian Currid

Notes
1 The Eichsfeld Plan was a program for the "socialist redevelopment" of the economically depressed region.—Ed.
2 The prefabricated concrete apartment blocks typical of the GDR are known as *Plattenbauten* (literally "slab structures").—Ed.
3 Die Soziale Stadt is a joint federal and state program for urban development introduced with the aim of counteracting the widening sociospatial divide in Germany's cities.—Ed.

DISMANTLING INFRASTRUCTURE
Matthias Koziol

Shrinkage: New Conditions for Local Infrastructure
Shrinkage, demographic shifts, and migration: these phenomena constitute a multilayered problem not just for residential housing companies, urban planners, and politicians. The operators of town and city infrastructural systems also find themselves confronted with a situation that is entirely new in both objective and subjective terms. Rapidly diminishing utilization due to changes in consumer behavior, modernization, and the decline in the number of customers or residents creates entirely new conditions for the economics, operation, and planning of capital-intensive utilities.

The demographic trend alone has predetermined these developments for the long term in many cities and towns across Germany. Only a massive policy of targeted immigration or a significant shift in consumer behavior could change things now.

German cities are not alone in this regard. Similar processes can be found in the shrinking cities of North America, like Detroit and Saint Louis, and also in Manchester and Liverpool in the United Kingdom.

The Impact of Shrinkage and Replanning on Systems and Networks: Critical Utilization Thresholds
In some eastern German towns and cities, underutilization has reached dimensions that are having a noticeable impact. The costs for odor prevention at Frankfurt/Oder's city waterworks have increased from around €10,000 to €60,000 per year over the last ten years. At the same time, the amount of wastewater needed to maintain the functioning of the wastewater network multiplied by a factor of six between 1999 and 2001, rising from 1,920 to 11,852 cubic meters. In 2003, the first attempt was made to raise the price for district heating by 10% so as to cover the costs of "urban replanning."

The level of utilization of networks is closely tied to both their efficiency and their economic viability. The economic consequences are basically identical for all supply media: fewer consumers overall mean a cost increase for each individual consumer. The principle of cost coverage means the existing fixed costs are distributed among all the consumers.

But in technical terms, we are faced with a quite differentiated range of problems:
- In the *drinking water network,* lower utilization leads to increased standing times for the water, and thus to a significantly increased risk of renewed contamination. This danger exists particularly in buildings with temporarily lower utilization over the summer months (schools and the like), in centralized warm water units, and in parts of the network where the firefighting water supply is fed by public drinking water. Here, flow speed is especially low due to the required large diameter of pipes. There is a significant danger particularly in new, still unused networks (in newly opened, unused industrial parks, for example) and in locations with high ambient temperatures (cellar pipes, for example). The main causes in eastern German towns and cities are the reduction of the average population density from three to under two persons per living unit and the decrease in daily

water consumption from 200–220 liters per resident to around 80–100 liters per resident. These two factors alone have caused around a 70% reduction in water-supply utilization and wastewater production. This is compounded by significantly reduced occupancy rates and decreased commercial and industrial usage. As a result, consumption of drinking water has fallen to well below 30% of the scheduled capacity in many affected areas.

For example, between 1990 and 2002, drinking water utilization levels in Schwedt, including areas in the Uckermark district, fell from around nine million to around three million cubic meters, despite an increase in the number of households and the significant expansion of the network.

Because of the failure to maintain the required minimum flow velocity in wastewater pipes, deposits can develop in the (now) oversized pipes, especially in those placed on low-grade inclines. Given flow durations of more than ten hours and lower oxygen content, sulfuric oxide can form, as—in the presence of condensed steam—can biogenic sulfuric acid. The consequences include odor problems and corrosion, for example of the concrete constituents of collecting basins and pipes, necessitating frequent scouring. Decreasing amounts of wastewater also lessen the efficiency of existing, increasingly oversized sewage treatment plants.

To simplify, considering the above-mentioned effects of low housing population density and changed consumer use, dispersed vacancies or demolition of more than 50% can as a rule be seen as critical.

- During the same period, the decline in the use of *district heating* in the larger eastern German cities was of a similar dimension. Causes include improved insulation, better technology, and changes in consumer behavior due to dramatic increases in prices and charges after 1990.

But in contrast to the drinking water and wastewater systems, the technical efficiency of the *district heating system* can as a rule still be maintained in the existing hot water networks despite the dramatically falling demand. Nonetheless, the declining demand is leading to a (relative) increase in heat loss, a decrease in efficiency and controllability, and surplus capacities in the power plants, and thus to an overall decline in system efficiency and cost effectiveness.

Urban Replanning Concepts Have a Decisive Influence on the Consequences for Technical Infrastructure

Urban replanning strategies have a decisive influence on the effects of shrinking processes for the technical infrastructure. Three important replanning strategies should be briefly discussed in this regard:

- The simplest method of dismantling technical infrastructure, the dispersed, *story-by-story method,* means that the network initially remains unchanged in structure and overall length. If underutilization of the supply networks does not reach any critical operational thresholds, the "only" result is an increase in expense due to the distribution of existing fixed costs among a declining number of consumers. Nonetheless, this does present a problem over the mid-term or long-term perspective. If critical operational thresholds still fail to be reached over the long term due to continued dispersed demolition, this will result in significantly higher operational costs due to the required regular scouring of pipes and/or investments in adjusting plant size and pipe systems.

- *Selective or segmentary demolition,* that is, the removal of individual buildings, is in many ways comparable in its effect on the network with story-by-story dismantling. (An exception here are cellar pipes for multiple buildings.) In this case, partial demolition can already lead in the replanning phase to additional investment for necessary "stopgaps" or the re-laying of pipes or relocation of plants.

Over the long term, both strategies lead to an increase in investments in network renewal per consumer since there is no decrease in the supply area and the whole network has to be renewed for significantly fewer consumers.

- The *large-scale, systematic demolition of buildings,* preferably from the ends of the supply networks inward, as a rule helps to avoid the need for network extension, the re-laying of supply lines, and the relocation of plants. It causes the least problems in terms of the network because the network is simply dismantled in the reverse direction of its original construction. Even closing down parts of networks is as a rule unproblematic. Over the long term, this strategy of demolition leads to a decrease in the area served and thus to shorter network lengths and lower replacement costs in the case of network renewal.

Assuming that the shrinking processes will continue as a result of the demographic transformation, large-scale area demolition, at best beginning at the ends of the network, is the only way to keep individual cost burdens for the technical infrastructure within reasonable limits over the long term.

Future Perspectives

As the vacancy rate rises and the occupancy rate declines, the amount of pipeline per resident increases. Thus, as a result of the posterior de-densification of residential areas, the demographic transformation is leading to a significant increase in committed loan capital and in the fixed costs per resident (around 50%–80% of the overall costs). Fees and prices for the technical infrastructure will thus increase under the principle of cost-covering distribution. In eastern German cities and towns, these account for a significant part of ancillary living costs, which in the case of unmodernized *Plattenbauten* are often just lower than the rent.[1] Full distribution of the direct and indirect costs of infrastructural adjustment among consumers is not possible for political and legal reasons. This allows us to draw several essential conclusions about urban replanning:

Urban replanning must be carried out in a cost-effective manner, that is, stop-gap solutions should be avoided in favor of intelligently planned dismantlement. Large-scale demolition, if possible from the ends of the networks inward, is basically preferable to scattered demolition. Partial dismantling or demolition should not decrease settlement density by more than 30%. Decentralized solutions should also be enabled where they promise long-term benefits.

The implementation of these proposals will not always be easy to reconcile with short-term housing and urban planning needs. For this reason, a comprehensive examination of strategies and measures as well as the overall coordination and management of city replanning processes is essential.

Translated from the German by Brian Currid

Note
1   The prefabricated concrete apartment blocks typical of eastern Germany are known as *Plattenbauten* (literally "slab structures").—Ed.

Literature

Freudenberg, Dieter, and Matthias Koziol. *Arbeitshilfe zur Anpassung der technischen Infrastruktur im Stadtumbauprozess: Fachbeiträge zu Stadtentwicklung und Wohnen im Land Brandenburg.* Frankfurt/Oder: Institut für Stadtentwicklung und Wohnen, 2003.

Koziol, Matthias. "Auswirkungen des Stadtumbaus auf die kommunale Infrastruktur." In *Stadtumbau: Bericht zum Fachkolloquium "Stadtumbau: Wohnen und Leben mit Rückbau, Risiken und Chancen schrumpfender Städte," 28. September 2001.* Frankfurt/Oder: Institut für Stadtentwicklung und Wohnen, 2002.

———. "Stadtumbau und Stadttechnik—was passiert unterirdisch und ebenerdig?" In *Fachbeiträge zu Stadtentwicklung und Wohnen im Land Brandenburg, Stadtumbau und Stadttechnik, Expertenanhörung und Erfahrungsaustausch am 11. April 2002 in Frankfurt/Oder (ISW-Schriftenreihe,* 2). Frankfurt/Oder: Institut für Stadtentwicklung und Wohnen, 2002.

Stadtplanungsamt Cottbus. *Stadtumbaukonzept Cottbus, Teil: Stadttechnische Netze.* Cottbus: Stadtplanungsamt Cottbus, 2002.

DECAMPING DETROIT
Detroit, 1995/96
Charles Waldheim and Marilí Santos-Munné

> One last question must now be asked: during a crisis period, will the demolition of cities replace the major public works of traditional politics? If so, it would no longer be possible to distinguish between the nature of recessions (economic, industrial) and the nature of war.
>   Paul Virilio, *The Overexposed City*[1]

In August 1990, Detroit's City Planning Commission authored a remarkable and virtually unprecedented report.[2] This immodest document proposed the decommissioning and abandonment of the most vacant areas of what had once been the fourth-largest city in the United States. With this publication, uninspiringly titled the *Detroit Vacant Land Survey*, the city planners documented a process of depopulation and disinvestment that had been under way in Detroit since the 1950s.[3] With an incendiary 1993 press release based on the City Planning Commission's recommendations of three years prior, the City Ombudsman, Marie Farrell-Donaldson, publicly called for the discontinuation of services to, and the relocation of vestigial populations from, the most vacant portions of the city: "The city's ombudsman ... is essentially suggesting that the most blighted bits of the city should be closed down. Residents would be relocated from dying areas to those that still had life in them. The empty houses would be demolished and empty areas fenced off; they would either be landscaped, or allowed to return to 'nature.'"[4]

In the second half of the twentieth century the city of Detroit lost half its population. Prior to this politically volatile plan for the city's decolonization, the planning professionals responsible could offer no solution to the ongoing demise of what had been the finest example of modern industrial urbanism.

While European proponents of modernist planning had originally imported Fordism and Taylorism from American industry and applied them to city planning, it was the American city (and Detroit in particular) that offered the fullest embodiment of those principles in spatial terms. While flexibility, mobility, and speed made Detroit an international model for industrial urbanism, those very qualities rendered the city disposable. Traditional models of dense urban arrangement were quite literally abandoned in favor of escalating profits, accelerating accumulation, and a culture of consumption. This of course was the genius of Ford's conception: a culture that consumes the products of its own labor while consistently creating a surplus of demand ensuring a nomadic, operational, and ceaselessly reiterated model of exurban arrangement. That ongoing provisional work of rearrangement is the very model of American urbanism that Detroit offers.

Detroit was the only city that dared to publicly articulate a plan for its own abandonment and conceive of organizing the process of decommissioning itself as a legitimate problem requiring the attention of design professionals. In a graphically spare document featuring maps blacked out with marker to indicate areas of vacant land,

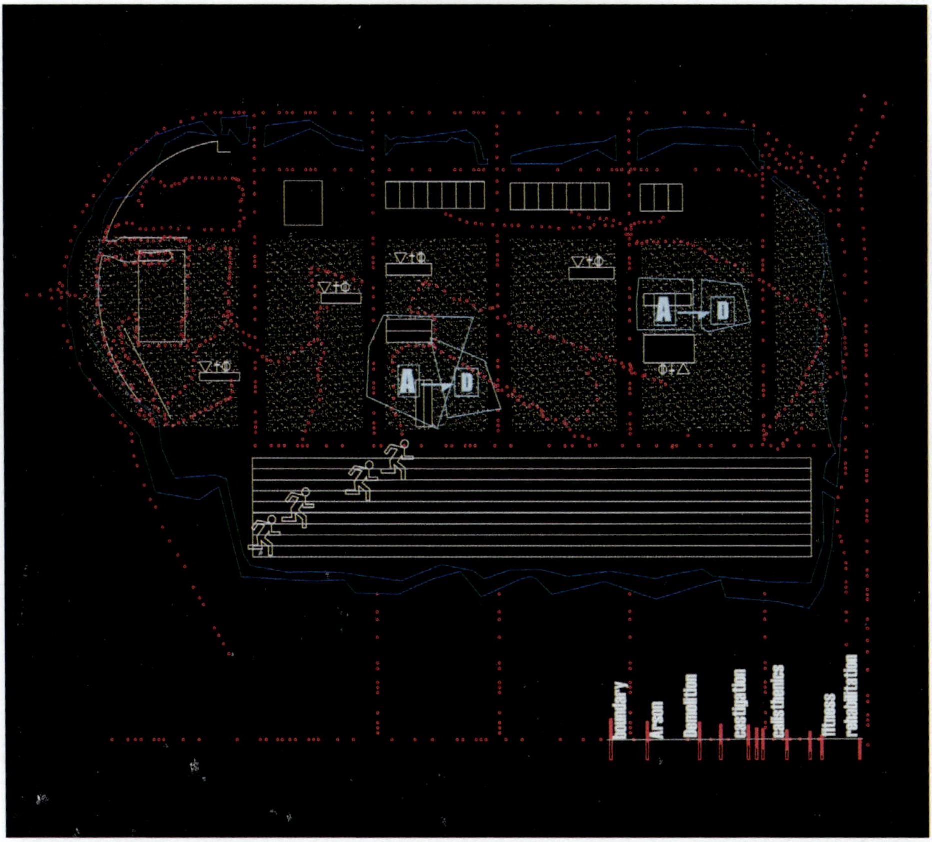

Exurban Survival Training Course/Boot Camp.

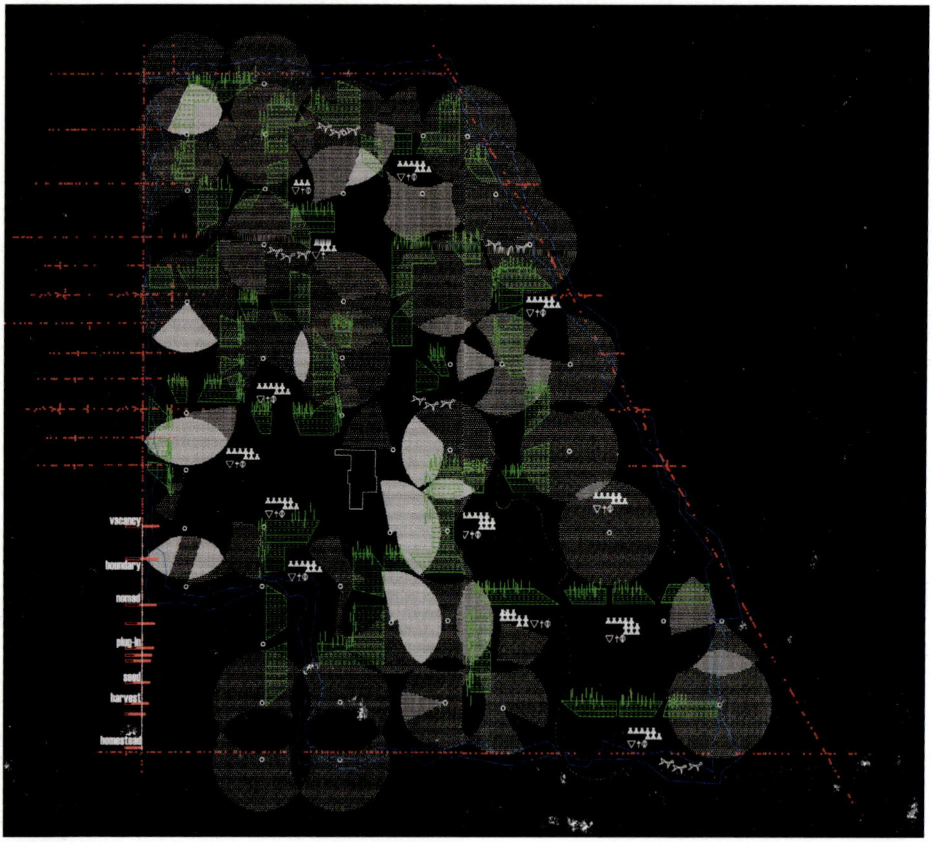

Demolition City

Migrant Worker Mobile Homesteads.

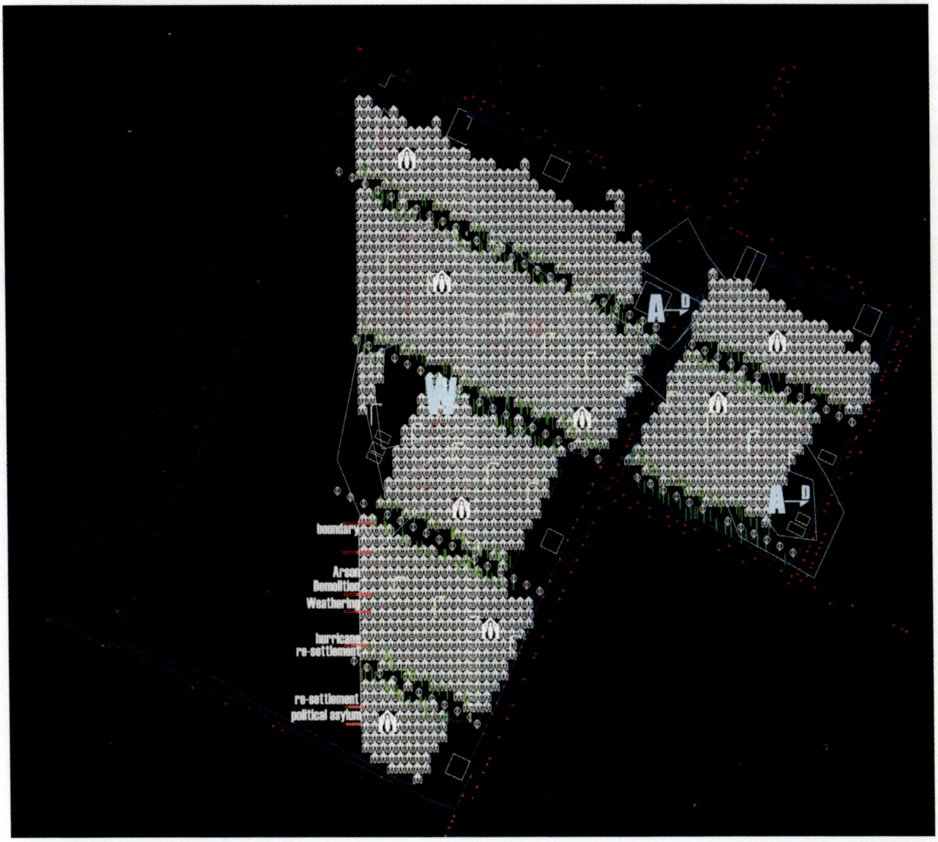

Decamping Detroit_*Charles Waldheim, Marilí Santos-Munné* 83

Federal Emergency Management Agency (FEMA) and Immigration and Naturalization Service (INS) Refugee Center.

Detroit's planners rendered an image of a previously unimaginable urbanism of erasure that was already a material fact.

Taking the city's proposal for the abandonment of the least viable lands at face value, "Decamping Detroit" describes a series of scenarios by which Detroit would be decamped. Based on the *Detroit Vacant Land Survey,* the project identifies seven bounded territories within the city surveyed as over 70% vacant land and proposes scenarios by which they might be reconstituted. Additional territories currently over 50% vacant are identified for future annexation. These urban abscesses are appropriated as sites for the staging of exurban landscapes of indeterminate status. The project proposes four stages in the eventual abandonment of these landscape territories: dislocation, erasure, absorption, and infiltration.

As Detroit decamps, it constructs immense empty spaces, tracts of land that are essentially void spaces. These areas are not being "returned to nature," but are curious landscapes of undefined status. In this context, landscape is the only medium capable of dealing with simultaneously decreasing densities and uncertain futures. The conditions recommending an urbanism of landscape can be found in both the abandoned central city and on the periphery of the still spreading suburbs. Ironically, the ongoing process of greenfield development at the perimeter of Detroit's metropolitan region brings up similar questions posed by the incursion of opportunistic natural environmental systems into areas of post-urban abandonment. For these sites, both brownfield and greenfield, what is demanded is a strategy of landscape as urbanism, a landscape urbanism for Detroit's postindustrial territories.

These reserves of open space necessitate infrastructural strategies for social and ecological arrangement. Also needed are collective conceptions of these spaces that are capable of rendering Detroit's postindustrial territories legible to various populations and constituencies. Rather than allowing these spaces to be legislated by naming activities, their future viability as true void spaces depends upon the imaginary and mythic conditions of their founding. Toward this end, the decommissioning of these territories requires the same kind of public participation and rites that attended to their original annexation and incorporation.

1. Dislocation: The first revision of the territories involves the voluntary relocation of those remaining residents wishing to be relocated, the discontinuation of city services, the capping of utilities, and the spatial demarcation or bounding of the newly constituted zones.

2. Erasure: The second phase of the project concerns the erasure and scrubbing of the newly evacuated Zones. The proposal authorizes and accelerates the ongoing arson of abandoned houses in the city by sanctioning regularly scheduled large-scale burns as a continuation of Detroit's Devil's Night festivities. These burns are complemented with the aggressive demolition of selective portions of the Zone, the release of captured wildlife species, and the insertion of plant species to hasten the natural deterioration.

3. Absorption: The third phase of the project proposes the ecological reconstitution of portions of the Zones through tree farming and the inundation of the ground through selective flooding.

4. Infiltration: The final stage in the project speculates on the future reappropriation of the decommissioned Zones and their annexation from agents and constituencies

outside the city by opportunistically occupying the physical residue of Detroit's exurban landscapes. Rather than master planning or scripting a particular material and spatial future for these Zones, "Decamping Detroit" speculates on the process of their decommissioning and the staging of their vacancy.

Zone 1 — Suburban Campground/Garden Annex
Zone 2 — Migrant Worker Mobile Homesteads
Zone 3 — Pigeon and Falconry Range/Rifle Range
Zone 4 — FEMA and INS Refugee Center
Zone 5 — Exurban Survival Training Course/Boot Camp
Zone 6 — Experimental Agriculture Cooperative Homestead
Zone 7 — Firefighters Academy/Arson Investigation Center

This contribution is an abridged version of Charles Waldheim and Marilí Santos-Munné, "Decamping Detroit," in *Stalking Detroit*, ed. Georgia Daskalakis, Charles Waldheim, Jason Young (Barcelona: ACTAR, 2001), 104–121. The original text is reprinted here in abridged form by kind permission of the authors.

Notes
1   Paul Virilio, "The Overexposed City," in *Zone 1/2: The Contemporary City,* ed. Michel Feher and Sanford Kwinter (New York: Zone Books, 1987), 18–39. In 1998, Detroit's mayor, Dennis Archer, secured $60 million in loan guarantees from the U.S. Department of Housing and Urban Development to finance the demolition of every abandoned residential building in the city. See "Dismantling the Motor City," *Metropolis,* June 1998, 33.
2   City Planning Commission of the City of Detroit, "Detroit Vacant Land Survey," unpublished report dated August 24, 1990. Also see M. S. Bruhn and J. F. Brahn, "Survey and Recommendations Regarding Vacant Land in the City" (unpublished report submitted to the City Council of Detroit, 1990).
3   Ibid., 3–5.
4   "Day of the Bulldozer," *The Economist,* May 8, 1993, 33–34.

GORDON MATTA-CLARK
Dan Graham

—

—

I

In the 1970s, artists attempted to leave the politically coercive bonds of the art gallery. They deserted the city to make neoprimitive earthworks, relocations, or simply maps of their walks in the landscape. But in the display (documentation) of this work to the public, ironically, the art gallery returned as a support. As Robert Smithson said in 1970, "Landscape [is] co-extensive with the gallery. I don't think we're dealing with matter in terms of a back to nature movement. For me the world is a museum."[1] Smithson wanted to deny any reading of his work in terms of the then currently fashionable ecology movement as well as any political reading; rather it was to be read as formalist art or as an ambiguously romantic stance.

Not only couldn't the earth artists escape the need for the gallery to document their work, but they were in danger of taking part of nature and exhibiting it as a found object. This was a great dilemma for Gordon Matta-Clark, a young artist and friend of Smithson's. He described his first work saying, "I made a series of visits to the ghetto area of the Lower East Side and the Bronx ... moving into spaces with a hand saw and cutting away rectangular sections of the floor or walls to create a view from one space into another. The sections were carefully removed from their original positions [and taken] to an art gallery."[2]

Matta-Clark came to the position that work must function directly in the actual urban environment. "Nature" was an escape, political and cultural contradictions were not to be denied. By making his removals public (similar to the chance spectacle of a demolition for casual pedestrians), the work could function as a kind of urban agitprop, like the actions of the Paris Situationists during May 1968—public intrusions or "cuts" in the seamless urban fabric. The Situationists' idea was to have their gestures interrupt the induced habits of the urban masses; this might then unrepress certain concealed realities. Similarly, Matta-Clark saw his "cuts" as probes, opening up socially hidden information beneath the surface to "create repercussions in terms of what else is imposed upon by a cut.... It was kind of the thin edge of what was being seen that interested me as much, if not more than, the views that were being created.... The layering, the strata, the different things that are being severed [provided] the simplest way to create complexity ... without having to make or build anything."[3]

II

Matta-Clark's work starts by setting up a dialogue between art and architecture on architecture's own territory. It doesn't generalize the art gallery as the site of a repressive architecture identified with the Establishment, but now links itself to the urban environment on an experienced political/architectural/historical basis that includes its relation to itself as a memory of archetypal architectural form. These ideas about architecture and the city have been espoused by the Italian architectural critic Manfredo Tafuri, who has criticized modern architecture for its destruction of the city as context.[4]

Tafuri starts with the assumption that the idea of regarding each new building as a self-sufficient, utopian vision began with the French revolutionary architects Etienne-Louis Boullée and Claude-Nicolas Ledoux. In each particular architectural proposal, individual works of architecture were unique symbols projecting a broad social vision that, however, was contained solely within the work's formal properties. During the nineteenth century new building forms proliferated on the urban landscape, as the Industrial Age produced both novel materials for construction and a taste for historical eclecticism. These new structures were seen as innovative formal utopias, while old buildings were seen as "reactionary" failures and torn down to make way for the more progressive forms. In fact, this process was connected to the capitalist organization of architectural practice; architectural practice was structured in terms of competitions in which the criterion by which each new building was judged was whether it superseded all previous buildings. Economically, the effect was to continually stimulate the consumption-production cycle as new buildings constantly replaced old ones. All of this development came at the expense of the cohesion of the city structure and tended to displace urban districts, which were redeveloped to generate money for an expanding economy.

Tafuri's position is Marxist in its commitment to a revolution of the oppressed underclass, but it opposes Karl Marx's ideological rejection of appeals to the memory of past events, which he felt obscured the implications of the potential future nascent in technological progress. Marx wanted to shed the ideological in favor of an empirical approach to history: "The social revolution of the nineteenth century can only create its poetry from the future, not from the past. It cannot begin its own work until it has sloughed off all superstitious regard for the past. Previous revolutions required recollections of world history in order to dull themselves to their own content. In order to arrive at its content, the revolution of the nineteenth century must let the dead bury the dead."[5]

On the other hand, Walter Benjamin argued that in this century, bourgeois ideology is *maintained* by the notion of progress supported by an empirical, "scientific" ideology of "objective" historical evolution. In opposition to the twentieth-century ideology of "progress," Benjamin proposed a recuperation of historical memory. Benjamin believed that without the concept of historical memory and the redemption of *past* oppression, Marxism could only fall into the trap of reducing itself to the dominant terms of rationalism. As he observed in his "Theses on the Philosophy of History,"

> The past carries with it a temporal index by which it is referred to redemption. There is a secret agreement between past generations and the present one.... Like every generation that preceded us, we have been endowed with a *weak* Messianic power, a power to which the past has a claim.... nothing that has ever happened should be regarded as lost for history.... [The oppressed have a] retroactive force and will constantly call in question every Victory, past and present, of the rulers.... The true picture of the past ... can be seized only as an image which flashes up at the instant when it can be recognized and is never seen again.... To articulate the past historically does not mean to recognize it 'the way it really was' (Ranke). It means to seize hold of a memory as it flashes up at a moment of danger.... Only that historian will have the gift of fanning the spark of hope in the past who is firmly convinced that even the dead will not be safe from the enemy if he wins.[6]

All of us are "living in a city [whose] whole fabric is architectural ... [where] property is so all-pervasive," noted Matta-Clark.[7] He wanted his work to expose this "containerization of the environment in the interests of capitalism." To achieve this, instead of building, restoring, or adding new elements to existing architecture to call attention to the "innovative" or "progressive" elements of each new "idea" manifested in a new work of architecture,

Conical Intersect, Gordon Matta-Clark, Paris, 1975.

Gordon Matta-Clark_*Dan Graham*

Demolition City

Matta-Clark proposed to attack the cycle of production and consumption at the expense of the remembered history of the city. More recently, these ideas have also been espoused by Tafuri, as well as the architects Aldo Rossi and Léon Krier.

But Matta-Clark's approach differs from, say, Krier's by a refusal to construct; Matta-Clark's practice, instead, was to subtract from architectural structures (and overlays of hidden architectural structures archaeologically below these) already in existence. No new buildings are added to the world; what is gained is a newly available historical time/popular memory of the city. Matta-Clark usually focused on a unique local syntax (e.g., terraced or twin houses). By means of his deconstruction he then accentuated the external relations of his chosen buildings (and by implication of other nearby or similar buildings), which were characterized by property boundaries and private codes of behavior.

III

"By undoing a building," Matta-Clark said, "[I] open a state of enclosure which had been preconditioned not only by physical necessity but by the industry that [proliferates] sub-urban and urban boxes as a context for insuring a passive isolated consumer."[8] These deconstructions can, paradoxically, still be a form of architecture; for the effect of stripping or cutting into buildings functions to enhance or preserve the site. Matta-Clark noted that in his work *Splitting,* "what the cutting's done is to make the space more articulated, but the identity of the building as a place, as an object, is strongly preserved, enhanced."[9]

To strip, to eviscerate, to deconstruct a building—these are statements against professional architectural practice. To destroy and not to construct (or reconstruct) a building amounts to an inversion of functionalist doctrine. While Mies, for instance, constructed in terms of materials such as glass and steel to reveal both the material structure and the previously unrevealed interior, Matta-Clark looked for already existing "gaps, void places that were not developed." These only exist as negation in modern architecture. In fact, the sheer glass-and-steel openwork, like the modern bureaucratic thinking it reflects, is often a measure taken by modern architecture to cover over these contradictions (particularly contradictions in the definition of public versus private property). A Matta-Clark work reveals contradictions as they have been developed in time as stratified, archaeological layers of otherwise normal building situations. Matta-Clark's exposures, unlike Minimal, Pop, or Conceptual Art, allow a historical time to enter: "There is a kind of complexity which comes from taking an otherwise completely normal, conventional, albeit anonymous situation and redefining it, retranslating it into overlapping and multiple readings of conditions past and present."[10]

IV

Since Matta-Clark grew up in both Paris and New York, his work must be viewed both in terms of twentieth-century French art history and in terms of contemporary American art, especially Minimal Art, reductivism, and progress art.

Many of Matta-Clark's American works deal with vernacular apartments or two-family house structures. The cuts reveal private integration of compartmentalized living spaces, showing how each individual family has coped with the imposed structure of his container. The constructional imposition, along with the private person's adaption to its concealed order, is revealed to the outside public in the form of "Sculpture."

Normally, it is only the specialized professional architects in society who can penetrate the facade and read general schematic structures to building units. This professional world is itself institutionalized and containerized in its own place of work: the engineer's or architect's office suite. "The Datum Cuts, for example, took place in an engineers' drafting rooms and offices. I couldn't deal with the outside because there wasn't enough exterior enclosure to really penetrate anything. What fascinated me was the interior central plan. The engineers took a small square, primitive hut shape and divided it in half to make one big drafting room. They divided the other half into a quarter which became the office, and divided the remaining quarter in half again for the coatroom and bathroom. And then divided that again to make a shower or something. Everything was progressively divided so that the remaining last piece was 1/32 of the whole. I used the idea of division around the center. Therefore, I removed a square section out of the roof apex, then projected that cut from the roof down into the building and spread it out laterally through the walls and doors."[11]

V

Matta-Clark fragments or splinters architecture, turning it into a kind of reverse cubism or "anti-monument," but one whose task is to reconstitute memory—not conventional memory as in the traditional monument, but that subversive memory that has been hidden by social and architectural facades and their false sense of "wholeness." "[There is] a type of space we all, all of us, have stored in memory: spaces that are detailed and precise, fragments generally, at all levels of reminiscence. And of course, once you get into reminiscence, an infinite number of associations emerge. Memory seems to create a unique kind of space setting up an about-to-disintegrate level."[12]

Unlike the conventional monument designed to smoothly link past to present to implied future, Matta-Clark's "monument" is profoundly pessimistic. It will be quickly demolished; as a work it is something of a useless gesture. It defies permanent symbolic form. It accepts its fate—to be remembered only as a photo/text representation as "conceptual art" *and* to disappear into the anonymous rubble. It is close to instant ruins—a photo of what was once a spark of hope and is now erased by more dominant forms. These are negative "monuments" or remembrances of works desired to "open up" history and historical memory, which could lead to a critical view of present oppression.

VI

In effect, Matta-Clark's work, although negative as to architectural practice, still hopefully opts, from the view of historical materialism, for a communication value. This is the ideal of Conceptual Art: "The determining factor is the degree to which my intervention can transform the structure into an act of communication."[13] Matta-Clark identified his deconstructions in terms of linguistic acts: "It's like juggling with syntax, or disintegrating some kind of established sequence of parts.... The piece is a way of imposing a presence, an idea, it's a way to disorientation by using a clear and given system."[14]

VII

His most (propagandistically) effective work was *Conical Intersect,* made in 1975 in the Les Halles district of Paris, which was then being demolished for the erection of the Centre Pompidou and luxury housing. The artist was well aware of the area's symbolic meaning for Parisians and of the visual alignment of the new Centre Pompidou with the Tour Eiffel—one a monument of nineteenth-century French progress, the other a symbol of contemporary French national ideology.

Matta-Clark used two seventeenth-century "twin" town houses from which he cut out a massive conical base four meters on the diameter. "The central axis made an approximately forty-five-degree angle with the street below. As the cone diminished in circumference, it twisted up through the walls, floors, and out the attic roof of the adjoining house."[15] The conical removals penetrated the buildings, the holes optically functioning like periscopes, directing the attention of people on the street to, specifically, the alignment of the buildings to both the Eiffel Tower and the new Centre Pompidou (as well as these two landmarks' relation to each other). With the aid of this "periscope," viewers could look not only into the interior of the Matta-Clark sculpture/building, but *through* the conical borings to these other buildings that embody past and present eras of Paris. The building—as Barthes said of the Eiffel Tower—"an object when we look at it, it becomes a lookout in its turn when we visit it, and now constitutes as an object, simultaneously extended and collected beneath it, that Paris which just now was looking at it."[16]

The Centre Pompidou's modernist infrastructure, with its throwback to a 1960s Archigram, science-fiction look, features dramatically exposed service ducts, which make it look like a circuitry diagram. Both interior and exterior pipes are color-coded, delineating for the public information concerning the technical functioning of the building. Its technological optimism seemed, at the time, a sharp contrast to the rubble of the rest of the neighborhood, one of the oldest sections of Paris. The new Centre, then, was a talisman, linking contemporary French technology/culture to the Paris of the Eiffel Tower. Appositely, Matta-Clark's "anti-monument" drew attention to both the destruction of the old historical *quartier* and the shattering of any real historical continuity between old and new Paris for those who live there. Its literally negative structure mimicked both the symbolic Eiffel Tower and the new Centre Pompidou. It took a gamble: that by deconstructing an existing architectural object, designed to be destroyed anyway (a kind of double negation being involved here), the work had *more* (not less) articulation or symbolic meaning than the two other competing monuments. In art terms, Matta-Clark's work in Paris evokes a succession of Parisian forms: it suggests cubism, but reversed—for while cubist collage consists of fragments of the real world brought into (gallery) art, Matta-Clark's works cut into/eliminate from the real world to make a sculpture; in this sense the sinuous forms of the conical borings also suggest Hector Guimard's Art Nouveau Métro entrances.

The stripping or cutting away in Matta-Clark's work reveals the usually hidden constructional and historical layering. This inverts the display of compositional or functional workings in the Centre Pompidou's architecture and challenges its implicit ideology of "progress." Matta-Clark's aim can be viewed as a form of urban ecology; his approach is not to build with expensive materials, but to make architectural statements by removing in order to reveal existing, historical aspects of vernacular, ordinary buildings. Thus, the capitalist exhaustion of marketable material in the name of progress is reversed.

VIII

In a certain sense, Matta-Clark's ideas have been reappropriated in the world of architecture. Frank Gehry's house, for example, has the fashionable "ecological" look; he has partially cut into the original house, exposing hidden beams and creating a complex

Bingo, Gordon Matta-Clark, Niagara Falls, New York, 1974.

Gordon Matta-Clark_*Dan Graham*

modern work of architecture in the "style" of Matta-Clark's work. But Gehry recontextualizes Matta-Clark's anti-architectural gesture, employing the notion of cutting buildings to play with formal or compositional ideas.

While Gordon Matta-Clark opposed such professional architectural styles, he was influenced by theories and existing examples of architecture. His restoration of the archetypalness of a typical house might be compared to Michael Graves's 1969/70 Benacerraf House in New Jersey. Graves's "add-ons" leave the former, old house intact but build onto it a schematic Corbusier-like or Léger-like front extension that places the house in dialectical juxtaposition with its "Heroic Modernist Revival," architect-built extension. Both, in a sense, are archetypalized. What holds the composition together is that the addition is actually derived from the elevation diagrams (hidden behind the facade of the house ... only known to Graves, the architect). Or compare Matta-Clark's deconstruction of a house to a new house by Robert Venturi. One of Venturi's most radical ideas is that architectural facades may be composed through inflection toward (mimicking) other publicly visible buildings in the surrounding, immediate environment. This is a way of looking at or reflecting the work as it actually is, and eliminating the authoritarian imposition of the architect's self-contained utopian building.

What Matta-Clark's projects attempted, but which is avoided by the many compositional stratagems of modern architects, is to expose to public view the property lines and general containerization of the space to which the urban space is subjected. This is usually hidden within the composition of the modern building by the architect's composition. To construct ... or to deconstruct? This question, which Matta-Clark's work raised, is still unanswered, unresolved. The architect builds; the artist destroys.

First published in an incomplete French version as "Gordon Matta-Clark," special issue, *Art Press* (Paris), no. 2 (Summer 1982). This version is a reprint from Dan Graham, *Rock My Religion: Writings and Projects 1965-1990*, ed. Brian Wallis (Cambridge, MA: MIT Press, 1993). With kind permission by the author.

Notes
1   Robert Smithson, interview by Liza Bear and Willoughby Sharp, "Discussions with Heizer, Oppenheim, Smithson," *Avalanche*, no. 1 (Fall 1970), 62.
2   Gordon Matta-Clark, "Interview with Gordon Matta-Clark, Antwerp, September 1977," in *Gordon Matta-Clark*, exhibition catalog (Antwerp: Internationaal Cultureel Centrum, 1977), 8.
3   Liza Bear, "Gordon Matta-Clark: Splitting (The Humphrey Street Building)," *Avalanche*, no. 10 (December 1974), 34.
4   Manfredo Tafuri, *Architecture and Utopia: Design and Capitalist Development*, trans. Barbara Luigia La Penta (Cambridge, MA: MIT Press, 1976).

5   Karl Marx, "The Eighteenth Brumaire of Louis Napoleon," in *Surveys from Exile* (Harmondsworth, UK: Penguin, 1973), 148.
6   Walter Benjamin, "Theses on the Philosophy of History," in *Illuminations,* ed. Hannah Arendt, trans. Harry Zohn (New York: Schocken Books, 1969), 254–255.
7   Bear, "Splitting," 34.
8   "By undoing a building there are many aspects of the social conditions against which I am gesturing: first, to open a state of enclosure which had been preconditioned not only by physical necessity but by the industry that [proliferates] suburban and urban boxes as a context for insuring a passive, isolated consumer—a virtually captive audience.... The question is a reaction to an ever less viable state of privacy, private property, and isolation." Gordon Matta-Clark, interview by Donald Wall, "Gordon Matta-Clark's Building Dissections," *Arts Magazine* 50, no. 9 (May 1976), 76.
9   Bear, "Splitting," 37.
10 Matta-Clark, "Building Dissections," 77.
11 Ibid., 77–78.
12 Ibid., 78–79.
13 Ibid., 77.
14 Bear, "Splitting," 36.
15 Matta-Clark, "Interview (Antwerp)," 12.
16 Roland Barthes, "The Eiffel Tower," in *The Eiffel Tower and Other Mythologies,* trans. Richard Howard (New York: Hill and Wang, 1979), 4.

DEMOLITIONS: OPENING INTERIOR GARDENS
Rotterdam, The Netherlands, 1999
Lara Almárcegui

Every demolition creates a new empty lot. But in Rotterdam, each time part of a block of houses disappears, the houses' interior gardens become visible. These interior gardens are one of the most significant green areas in the center of town and, although secret, they are carefully protected. For my project, I publicized where demolitions would take place and invited the public to visit the opening of a new green area.

THE BACKGROUND MUZAK OF AN EPOCHAL CHANGE
Tina Veihelmann

No creation without destruction. It is said that reconstruction in Germany after the Second World War was constantly accompanied by the detonation of wartime ruins and old symbols, as if the sound of explosions was the background music for postwar reconstruction. As can be read in the official reports of the time, hardly a week would go by in which bombs were not being defused and at the same time explosives being discharged in order to demolish a bunker, a smokestack, or a gas tank. The press eagerly followed the trail of one Berlin explosives expert, the perky Herta Bahr, famous for her meticulousness in the art of explosives. She enjoyed great popular acclaim. With the precision work of the perky Herta in mind, Gottfried Knapp sees a link between the attention demanded by the erection of the constructed world and the attention given to its destruction. Demolition explosions, he suggests in his essay "Am Anfang war der große Knall" (In the Beginning Was the Big Bang), also had a purifying effect on the "psychic and peristaltic household of the political system."[1] Demolition, he argues, became a ritual, celebrated a moment of departure, and opened the field for a new beginning.

Now, for the first time since the postwar years, demolition is again taking place in grand style. Only this time it is not bunkers and ruins that are falling, rather intact apartment houses and factories. The relics of Germany's industrial age are being done away with. These wastelands are now expanding: the word "periphery" is increasingly losing its power of description, for this condition of the world has ceased being a marginal phenomenon. The Western world is changing just as fundamentally and quickly as it did in the time of Knapp's big bang. But, this time, the big bang is missing. The background music to this epochal change is strangely muted.

Perky Herta stays at home, and there is no public acclaim, no celebration. Explosives are still used, but only when 100-meter-high smokestacks are felled. Now building demolition is approached like construction. For there is no other way to do it: the fall of the smokestack must be precisely calculated to ensure that the giant ends up exactly in its own bed and that no accidents happen, as did at the Schwarz Pumpe strip mine when one of the eight smokestacks being demolished turned on its axis and fell onto a supply pipe belonging to the district heating system. If things go well, the audience applauds. They've brought along folding chairs and thermoses, and some film the event on video. Some are former employees of the plant, whose trademark they are now tearing down. Clearing up is also work, and demands expertise, too. The onlookers appreciate the expertise required. The journalist from the radio station *Kulturradio* looks for sentimental sound bites, but cannot find any, for nobody is really choked up about it. Too many workplaces have already been done away with. "There's another smokestack" and "When will that one be demolished?" are often said in one and the same sentence.

Even less mourned is the disappearance of the housing that went along with the industry. The demolition equipment munches assiduously away like locusts at the structures, with no noise, no sparks, and usually without an audience. "Nibbling away," the housing companies call this process, the same housing companies that once had the buildings erected.[2] The mouth of a digger bites into the walls of former kitchens and children's rooms, ripping chunks out and throwing them onto a pile. Then the piles are taken away. But the event is no louder than the people next door closing a window. They'll be next.

Indeed, one or two cities have already been cleared in this way: 100,000 apartments between 1998 and 2004. On the most recent figures, the speed of the munching doubled between 2003 and 2004.[3] Things have been going on this way for seven years now, and will most likely continue. It is a huge, large-scale undertaking, but a quiet one. Only at the start was there any big outcry. The atmosphere at the first residents' meeting in Schwedt was like in a witch's cauldron, as Ingeborg Beer, the local commissioner for the Soziale Stadt (Socially Integrative City) program recalls. The idea that one's own apartment, where the children grew up, was just going to be thrown away—that was hard to take. But the extent and constant progress of the demolition ultimately surpassed the residents' capacity to be infuriated or shocked. "Demolition goes like this," a woman from Schwedt puts it: "In the morning I go to the office, and when I get back, the building's no longer there."

No big bang, no rite of passing. There is nothing cathartic or liberating about the mood in the shrinking cities, which seem to be packed in cotton. It is not explosions that are taking place here, but implosions. The lack of activity and city gossip is felt to be oppressive; those who stay just withdraw to their own four walls, where the way the world looks still lies in their power.

But experts on the social significance of shrinking urgently recommend the establishment of parting rituals. A retreat with "decorum and dignity" is what is needed, as the housing politicians from Hoyerswerda put it early on. The death of a city needs to be given a setting, just as people receive their final blessing, this author was told by Simone Hain, a historian of architecture and urban planning. Since the church has nothing to say here, Hain sees artists in the role of priests administering blessings. And why not stage demolition as a ritual? With dramatic music, beer, and bratwurst, some suggest, so that the crashing of the demolition balls could provide the kind of background music Knapp rhapsodizes about.[4] Such considerations culminate in rituals that are carried off for better or for worse in places where a whole lot of world has disappeared: 44 days of the "Superumbau" (Giant Reconstruction) project in Hoyerswerda, a facade gallery in Schwedt, demolition art in Hattingen. But dignified parting can only take place if it is clear what this parting means, what dimensions it has, and, most importantly, what a new beginning might look like.

But neither the extent nor the significance of this retreat have been accepted in a way that means we are fully aware of the consequences. The shrinking of some cities makes it clear that within the coming years a critical population threshold will be reached, rendering the maintenance of communities impossible.[5] The operation of local transportation networks, wastewater systems, and garbage services will become unprofitable, and public institutions will be called into question. Whether this then means that cities will have to be abandoned and resettled in a planned fashion, or that ways might be found to sustain such shrinking communities, is something that can hardly be foreseen. And then there's the countryside. Is anyone talking about the fact that villages will quite certainly disappear from the map?

In any case, shrinking means much more than "less" of something that remains constant in and of itself. It is no surprise that this does not get talked about much, for desettlement touches on a sensitive cultural taboo—the abandoning of a homeland. In the biblical sense, settling is something good. Giving up a place, in contrast, is seen as something catastrophic. When in 1908 the absolutely unimportant and tiny Brandenburg village of Schiedlo was relocated because it sat on a sandbank on a bend of the river Oder and was flooded nearly every year, an almost spooky aura developed around this abandoned piece of land. An entire book mourns the downfall of Schiedlo. As written in the foreword, it was not considered appropriate for a Prussian king to allow an old, familiar cultural site to simply disappear: "No Schiedlo child can ever again visit his childhood home, and if he comes to the beloved place, a strange oak tree will stand there."[6]

At its core, the retreat at issue here is not just the demolition of buildings and the fall of entire cities. At the heart of the issue is the loss of a sacred cow—labor, which the American philosopher Frithjof Bergmann describes as modern society's "buffalo."[7] Like the buffalo herds for native North Americans, for the West labor stands at the center of society. A life without work remains unimaginable. It thus seems logical that Wolfgang Kil experiences an "almost reflexive refusal to discuss any topic,"[8] as he tours through the country describing the increasingly empty eastern Germany as a laboratory whose residents can do nothing but attempt life under changed paradigms. Kil especially sees a shocking refusal to face reality among older listeners and local elites.

A corresponding lack of security can be traced in the staged rituals of parting. The lack of a name for the departed leaves most attempts strangely vague, as if there were no real agreement on what was to be done. In Schwedt, young people decorated buildings being torn down with banners: "I love Schwedt," one read. Readings were held in empty buildings, with the audience looking in from the outside through the windows. Picnics were held before demolitions. This was an "eventlet" rather than "event," as one of the organizers put it, because for her a large event seemed entirely inappropriate. She questioned whether any kind of parting was really taking place here. In Leipzig, a first bite out of a building by an excavator was staged, but of course this did not have the expected dramatic impact. In Berlin the architect Cornelius Mangold wanted to hang colorful cloth on the first apartment blocks facing demolition, to show that some happy memories were tied to the precast concrete high-rises typical of the German Democratic Republic, but his idea did not get past the authorities.

"Forster Tuch" (Forst Cloth), a project held in the Brandenburg town of Forst before the apartment buildings at the town center were torn down, treats the question of lost labor, but somehow the event did not quite hit the nail on the head. The Spacewalk group had the residents of Forst, a town that had depended on its textile industry, design a huge cloth with visions of the future. This cloth was then divided up and auctioned off during a huge show. While the parting from the textile industry was thus translated into a clear, simple sign, and creativity with respect to alternative future projections was at least mildly stimulated, the hippie-esque, futuristic weaving had an air of harmlessness that stood in a strange, almost eerie contrast to the everyday atmosphere of Forst with its dark windows and factories grown over with birchwood. The performance took place, and Forst remained definitively without a future.

"Superumbau Hoyerswerda 2003"—where the demolition of a five-story building became part of an art action—was ambivalent from the very get go. On the one hand, the demolition was to become a model case for approaching the dissolution of cities, the

Blasting the Hotel Europa investment disaster, Troisdorf, Germany, May 13, 2001.

The Background Muzak of an Epochal Change_*Tina Veihelmann*

organizers wrote. But elsewhere it was said that the project sought to make the shrinking of cities the object of artistic commentary. The entire project was marked by this indecisiveness, constantly oscillating between two levels. Somehow the event of demolition itself is the artwork, and it is staged via the floodlights of a demolition site or the daily illustration of the ongoing process of demolition in the daily press. At the same time, artists placed artworks that seemed appropriate in front of this dramatically charged backdrop, art that circled around remembering: appearances of the Schwarze Pumpe mine in films, a filmic reading by Brigitte Reimann, photography on the melancholy of disappearance, and a theater director who had residents act out parts of their life stories. After 44 days, this program accompanying the dramatic shrinkage of Hoyerswerda came to an end. The five-story building is now a wasteland, and the clearing process is continuing as before, with patches of green beginning to surface here and there. If you ask the residents today, they puzzle over whether "Superumbau" took place here, nearby, or somewhere over there.

Despite all the indecisiveness, these attempts to give a shape to parting should not be sneered at, for they have not remained without consequence. The memory theater of "Superumbau" provoked residents to spray the slogan "We can think for ourselves" as a defensive reaction against the pedagogical occupation. At the same time, this reaction also points to a strong inner participation. Two years later an old woman from Hoyerswerda remembers the event exactly, and says, "That was important to me, yes. I'm almost blind, but I still followed everything closely. I'm just like that, I have to talk about it when things are torn down. I took part in building each one of these buildings, there was so much hope then."

Nonetheless, these rituals of demolition, carried out by artists in the role of ritual masters, medicine men, or priests administering the last rites, can do nothing about the anxiety that reigns in the towns and cities themselves. But the artists are not at fault for not giving their all in trying to give this parting some kind of formal framework. Instead, the form of these parting rituals corresponds to the formlessness of the retreat. How can the parting be given a form if no retreat is being undertaken? As long as a shrinking city is nothing more than a city that has become less, with empty buildings and ruins that cause phantom pains like an amputated leg, the ritual masters can do nothing but treat the pain. For what counts is evoking the memories that are linked to the gaps and voids so that they at least are given a language.

Parting requires leaving together. But usually, only those buildings are torn down that have become unprofitable, and the people remaining find themselves increasingly living on a terrain that is neither maintained nor abandoned. The collective decision would have to be made to pack up and abandon a whole district, a neighborhood, or maybe even a small town, when staying becomes unbearable. Then, a parting ritual could accompany a withdrawal in "decorum and dignity." A clear step in this direction would allow for a clear sign that respects the honor of what is left behind. A ritual of purification before departure could be such a sign: perhaps as in the Soviet film *Farewell to Matyora* (directed by Elem Klimov), in which a Siberian farmer cleans her wooden house with sand, freshly whitewashes the oven, decorates the table with flowers, and closes the shutters before the entire village is flooded following the erection of a dam. "What are you doing, how does that help now that you're leaving?" ask the others, who like her have to burn down their houses. The artists suggested a similar ritual of purification as a solitary event for Hoyerswerda, but the curators of "Superumbau" rejected it, saying that it seemed at the time to be too brutal.

Perhaps it is mostly the lack of a new beginning that impedes the happy destruction found in Gottfried Knapp's big bang. We must become more conscious of the changing times so that the voids and the peripheries that are no longer marginal can be seen as possible points of departure for a new beginning. Then it would be easier to celebrate—with perky Herta, bratwursts, and perhaps the first blow with the wrecking ball as a raffle prize.

Translated from the German by Brian Currid

Notes
1. Gottfried Knapp, "Am Anfang war der große Knall," in *Detonation Deutschland: Sprengbilder einer Nation,* ed. Julian Rosefeldt and Piero Steinle (Munich: Orangerie, 1996).
2. Other techniques to carefully dismantle the buildings, such as removing prefabricated elements for reuse, were tried out on an eleven-story building in Cottbus, but not adopted because they proved economically infeasible. The extensive downsizing of large apartment blocks into terraced housing, as done in Leinefelde, would also be too expensive on a large scale.
3. Personal communication from press office at GdW Bundesverband deutscher Wohnungsunternehmen (National Association of German Housing Enterprises).
4. See Achim Schröer, "Stadtumbau und Spaß dabei," *Planungsrundschau* 5 (Summer 2000); http://www.tu-harburg.de/sb3/objekt/planungsrundschau/planungsrundschau_05/frsets/start05.html.
5. Personal communication from press office at GdW.
6. Otto Eduard Schmidt, *Schiedlo: Die Geschichte eines untergegangenen deutschen Dorfes* (Leipzig: Grunow, 1908). This book has been repeatedly reprinted in light of its regional popularity and can be purchased today at Neuzelle Abbey in Brandenburg.
7. See the conversation with Frithjof Bergmann in this volume.
8. Wolfgang Kil, *Luxus der Leere, vom schwierigen Rückzug aus der Wachstumswelt* (Wuppertal: Verlag Müller und Busmann, 2004). Also see Kil, *Keine Baukultur ohne Rückbaukultur* (Potsdam: Brandenburgische Landeszentrale für Politische Bildung, 2004).

PALAST DER REPUBLIK: RE-DECONSTRUCTION
Berlin, 2002
Eric Tschaikner

The project proposes to stage the planned demolition of Berlin's Palast der Republik (Palace of the Republic) in radical slow motion, transforming it into a collective, participatory process. Bit by bit, beginning on the inside, every six months one-sixth of the 18,279 floorboards will be dismantled and used to test models of urban planning by stacking them in various constellations outside the building. On the inside, ever larger spaces will be opened up (aisles, chimney, slabs, courtyard, theater, rifts), spaces that can be rented and used by individual initiatives following certain rules. After three years, the external form of the building will also begin to change drastically. First, the removal of the facade will expose the building's steel skeleton. As this is dismantled, the buttressing reinforced concrete towers will come into view, and after these are demolished all that will remain will be an imprint on the ground. For over the course of the five-year process of demolition, all of the building's mass will have been buried within its own foundation; this is not least a technical necessity—to keep the foundation from flooding. (Ed.)

The original German title of this project is "Wiederabbau."

Transforming the building's stories one by one is part of a long-term process of deconstruction.

THE SOLUTION: VIBACH IN 2042
Johannes Touché

What really happened to Vibach?[1] There's nothing about it on the Internet, just the occasional anonymous flames that get blocked after a few hours, and—more professional perhaps, but just as unbelievable—the advertising material from DCS, "DeutscheCity-Solutions." That's who holds the monopoly on information when it comes to Vibach. Vibach is DCS Town, and DCS is the Vibach company. And DCS has only one thing to say: the crisis is over, the problem of Vibach has been solved, or "soluted," as the DCS jargon puts it.

We decide to visit the local history museums created by DCS. Rumor has it that they're going to be closed. There are three: the "Industrial" in the old train station, the "Citizen" in Vibach's old town hall, and the "Village" in the old village church of Alt-Dürfeld. Neu-Dürfeld, which once had 20,000 inhabitants, didn't get a museum—the history of the *Plattenbau* apartment project, according to DCS, is sufficiently documented in the Industrial.[2]

It's already evening when we find the Industrial, but there's still a light on. The director meets us in the foyer; we're familiar with that from the other museums. But while in the other museums we only met smooth "urban representatives," here the man standing before us—well over seventy, gnarled, and grumpy—seems to fit no known marketing concept. Hobbling and grumbling, he leads us past looms and mining carts, streetcars, cafeterias, and living room interiors, clicking his way through the accompanying explanations as if he were alone.

Only after the tour do we dare to ask what he thinks of the Vibach "solution." He looks at us questioningly, then he points at the ceiling, where there are pink balls hanging from the steel beams, and whispers warningly, "Mood meters! They're supposed to measure visitor satisfaction, but you can see," the old man points to the deserted hall, "how much there is to measure here. If anyone evaluates the data at all, then it's only to check up on the employees." We can see as few employees as we can visitors, but we don't want to contradict the old man. He pulls us behind a screen and says in a normal voice: "Here they're broken. Water damage," he grins. Clearly he spends quite a lot of time here. Data chips are piled up on several tables, along with books, DCS brochures that have been used as scrap paper, and numerous cigarette packs. He sits down and lights a cig.

He then begins to speak, using old-fashioned language and taking long breaks in which he pensively follows the path of the smoke. "You know, in order to understand the 'solution' you have to know the prior history. But it works the other way, too: only now that I know the result do I truly understand the prior history." He smiles at our quizzical looks. "But first things first ...

"The beginning of the end came after the 2008 crisis with the establishment of the Special Economic Zones—the most brutal kind of local economic policy directed at attracting investment. Reduced ecological and social requirements, tax-free status for ten years, wage supplements, strike bans, truly everything that a company could ever wish for. I have a poster around here somewhere: 'East Thuringia Investment Zone: Almost for free, never for nothing,' a horrible ad put out back then by the state government. But it wasn't just the marketing that failed. There were simply always other regions that had more to offer. It was impossible to keep up with the deregulation. Brussels had lowered the standards so quickly. Then came the 2015 crisis, which took out the last remains of industry, small retailers, construction, and of course the housing authorities, who were abandoned by their last solvent renters. The banks pulled out, and the local government was bankrupt for at least a year. You probably know what happened on the federal level, new elections, grand coalition, the arrival of 'project governing.' The federal government no longer distributed money according to the needs of each region, but on a project-by-project basis on application—a way of governing they picked up from the EU. It was clear who could offer the better yield estimates: for the Rhine Main area or Munich, for example, project governing was a blessing. But here … The Great Economic Crisis in 2022 was the final blow. The towns and cities went bankrupt, one after the other. And what did the coalition do? It thought up a nice new expression: 'municipal controlling,' better known as compulsory administration by the federal government. Vibach's local politics in the hands of Berlin strategists. No local democracy, no local opposition, no local checks and balances. Municipal controlling—what a joke!" But the old man isn't laughing. While we're trying to work out how many economic crises there are left to go, he quenches his cigarette in the DCS cup he's using as an ashtray.

"After the economic crisis of '29, the state cut down its guarantee to provide utilities. Suppliers of water, electricity, and local transport were able to choose freely where and at what price they wanted to offer their services. Very practical: fewer renters, higher costs, leading to even fewer renters again, and so on. The town was half empty anyway, and now real ghost towns were springing up. So they leased the hamlets and commercial zones, the so-called villages, to developers. Two years later that was incorporated into 'project governing,' too. What was it they called it again? 'Municipal outsourcing,' that's it. The developers were able to apply for state subsidies, so they kept on revamping their villages to beat the band, while the rest of the town, still under compulsory federal administration, decayed. We called it a fedslum."

The old man bangs his fist on the table and looks around at all of us. "But then things got really serious! It's 2035 and we're more or less in crisis again, but we can handle that! We know the ropes. The federal and state governments agree on a new strategy: 'government outsourcing.' The German Development Bank, a few foundations, whose names I forget, and a consortium of banks and large developers found DCS, the world's first company for urban liquidation. And we became a pilot project, or a guinea pig, whichever you prefer.

"Vibach was truly a good choice, for the most important developments had already been completed. The industry and workers had disappeared forever, the local administration was dead, all the town services privatized, half of the town was a slum, the villages were entirely self-sufficient. And the people from DCS thought, well, it works, but it looks shit. So they founded a propaganda division, DCS Image Control, which bought the information rights and hung up these mood meters everywhere." We look, frightened, towards the ceiling, but he continues, undaunted.

"The second measure affected the old town: you'll have seen it already. The DCS has that fully under control, unlike the state way back when. A lot of greenery and fresh paint, three malls, a few senior citizen residences, pretty weekend houses for the exiles. But don't be fooled: most of the facades are dead, just screens behind the windows, with grass growing behind them. The old town is just an obsession of those who are nostalgic for the days of the burgher town. Small, but pretty, now they have what they always wanted."

CRETTO
Gibellina, Italy, 1981 (1985–1989)
Alberto Burri

In 1968, an earthquake destroyed several towns and villages in Sicily, including Gibellina. The village was abandoned and rebuilt 20 kilometers away as Gibellina Nuova. Thirteen years later, the Italian artist Alberto Burri turned the remaining ruins of the town into a monumental artwork memorializing the disappeared town. In a 300 x 400 m area, the remaining streets and ruins are sealed in a layer of concrete, and thus preserved. The structure of the former town lingers in the impression of the pattern of streets, where traces of the place's history are legible. For this project, Burri used the concept of *cretti* (fissures), a concept he developed in his painting, where monochromatic works change over time due to the random cracks that emerge in the thick layer of paint. (Ed.)

Now the old man really gets going. "And the fedslums, the high-rises, and the inner suburbs? There had been lots of depopulation already, but there were still people left, and they resisted. Sabotage in the administration, compensation litigation, street protests, campaigns on the Internet. Since the abolition of the guarantee to provide utilities, a few houses had their own wells and generators. There were initiatives for school bussing, senior citizen care, and street repairs. As long as the state was responsible, the people still believed they had a voice. They thought that all the outsourcing was just an interim solution, that it was still their town, and their state." The museum director seems to have forgotten us. Grimly he crumples up an old DCS brochure.

"But once the state had withdrawn completely, there were no holds barred. The slums were to go, period. The generators and wells—gone. Supposedly for ecological reasons. Self-helpers were hassled with fees and regulations. But the greatest trick they pulled off was the 'New Security.' You can imagine what happens in a slum like this when citizen's defense is outlawed. Especially when the place is full of arsonists and looters, and skinheads—no one knows if they are protesting against the DCS or working for them ...

"Eventually, the only people left in there were the DCS explosives experts and landscape planners. Officially their task was renaturalization. And then there was nothing left to do. Why bother with the work if no one will see it anyway? A fence is much cheaper. Since then, Vibach has become three-quarters off-limits. That, gentlemen, is the solution."

The old man gave us a penetrating look. "Sometimes I still go in there, I have a special permit to find exhibit material. But I don't just collect old junk, I also take pictures." The old man points to the data chips on the table. "I've documented everything. And not just the ruins, but the people, too. You won't believe it, but there are still people living there. I even think that there are more and more of them. Ultimately, an off-limits zone has its advantages. It doesn't just have no services, it also has no controls. Lots of people that have set up home there have no official papers, others simply no money for a house in one of the villages. And some just want to get out of here. Sometimes I think I might be better off there myself."

We look at the dusty exhibits and the mood meters above us, and ask ourselves why he hasn't been fired long ago. As if he had noticed, he snarls, "They still leave me alone. Me and my exhibition." Tired, he lights a final cigarette. "Maybe you think I'm an exhibit myself."

It's gotten late. We are not yet out the door before the old man has already turned off the light.

———

Translated from the German by Brian Currid

———
———
———
———
———
———

Notes
1 Names changed to protect the innocent.
2 *Plattenbau* (literally "slab structure") is the name given to the prefabricated concrete apartment blocks built throughout the former East Germany.—Ed.

EVOLUTIONARY CITY

Cities and buildings are subject to a constant process of construction and decay, the course of which rarely can be anticipated. Planning means creating spatial structures that are open to various future developments and that thus become spaces of potential. Their specific indeterminacy generates architectonic and urban qualities. Design also can consist of making processes of transformation visible and thereby challenge our perception of permanence.

ROBERT SMITHSON AND THE ARCHITECTURE OF ABSENCE
Kai Vöckler

Cities emerge and then pass away. They give an impression of duration and security, and yet without question they are in a constant process of being reshaped and will one day disappear again. If nothing is permanent and everything is only temporary, then all housing is only something provisional, its future absence already inherent. This is the gap, the blind spot of architecture and urban planning, for it points literally to the de-forming that is inscribed in every forming of urban space.

The Provisional Structure

The image of construction that has been dominant for centuries has its origins in the myth of the Tower of Babel.[1] This mythical mammoth construction site was considered the greatest construction project of human history, an architectonic fantasy that can still be found in architectural visions today. To recall the legend: the image of the Tower of Babel blends the written reports of early authors on the city of Babylon with the biblical myth; the stories have been read as one ever since the early modern period. Since then, Babylon has stood for the enormity and vastness of a city that, according to Herodotus, contained the highest construction ever built. The biblical myth adds a utopian dimension—the vision of a construction project that offers all of humanity a home after completion. As Genesis 11:4 reads, "Go to, let us build us a city and a tower, whose top may reach unto heaven; and let us make us a name, lest we be scattered abroad upon the face of the whole earth." It was this striving towards unity that incurred God's wrath. The plan failed, and the mythical dispersion of the first society into the languages and peoples of the world became the source of the calamity of world history.

This mythical construction project has set afire the fantasy of planners and artists alike ever since the sixteenth century.[2] The many depictions dating from this period present a reinterpretation of the biblical myth: no longer are humanity's presumptuousness to build as high as the heavens and the subsequent divine punishment placed in the foreground, but rather the unfathomable technical achievement and the act of construction itself. While the building of the Tower of Babel remains an emblem of punished arrogance and a symbol of *vanitas,* at the same time it is read as the utopian architecture of an ideal city. One depiction of this scene, interesting for the way it subtly combines and reflects upon these contradictory interpretations, is that of Pieter Bruegel the Elder, which today hangs in Vienna's Kunsthistorisches Museum.

Although I cannot explore Bruegel's complex depiction in detail, a number of unusual aspects of this painting created in 1563 should be mentioned. Although the monumental building is not yet completed and construction is still in full sway, an amazingly small number of the (already tiny) construction laborers can actually be made out in the picture. The process of construction seems to take place all on its own. Since Bruegel has the tower emerge from a rock, which serves as both foundation and construction material, it gives the impression of a quasi-natural growth process. The construction seems to grow out of the rock, rising like an artificial mountain over the landscape. The partially ruined state of the new construction also shows the impact of natural forces. Whereas the left side is close to completion, the right side of the tower seems, on the

The simultaneity of construction and decay: *The Tower of Babel* by Pieter Bruegel the Elder, Antwerp, 1563.

one hand, incomplete and, at same time, about to disintegrate. Emergence also meets disintegration at the top of the tower as it stretches into the clouds: this takes on the form of the Roman Coliseum, the most famous antique ruin in the sixteenth century. The combination of the Babylonian building with the ruins of the "Eternal City" could be interpreted as a warning regarding the fleeting nature of all human activity. But as Ulrike Wegener has pointed out, the process of decay has come to a halt: there is scaffolding on the ruins, indicating their potential restoration and the possible completion of the construction project. The motif of decay becoming emergence seems paradoxical since it reverses the temporal perspective. There seems to be another, nonlinear understanding of time at work here. One clue is provided by the Old Testament story, which points to the presence of God. In his essence, the before and the after, and the beginning and the end coexist. While religious time also has a beginning and an end—the Creation and the Last Judgment—from a religious point of view coming to an end means returning to the beginning; the irreversibility of time is but a misleading perspective. As a ruin striving towards completion and a new building simultaneously in a state of decay, the Tower of Babel here stands for an incompletable process, for the eternal impossibility of completing such an undertaking under worldly conditions. For only when the "great whore of Babylon" has perished can the thousand-year reign of God be established, followed by eternal salvation. The Tower as a utopia uniting humankind is uninhabitable: it remains provisional.

The Architecture of Transition

Bruegel's representation of the failure of all construction projects maintained the transcendental perspective of overcoming the cycle of growth and decay that is inherent in the Christian promise of eternal life. But what is the use of images depicting the hope of eternal life to which a belief in the continuance of personal existence can cling? Taking leave of an anthropocentric perspective, we are left with an imageless eternity, an end state with no change or development. The artist Robert Smithson saw an analogy in entropy: this concept from the world of physics refers to the irreversible process of the collapse to which all order is subject, with the result "that in the ultimate future the whole universe will burn out and be transformed into an all-encompassing sameness."[3] In a 1972 lecture to students of architecture at the University of Utah in Salt Lake City, he thus proposed living in the provisional, moving beyond any eschatological final solution. The point of departure for this proposal was the unspectacular Hotel Palenque that Smithson had discovered in 1969 during a trip through the Yucatán. To the students' surprise, the object of architectural focus in his lecture was not the world-famous Maya ruins, but this decaying building. For Smithson, notable here was that the hotel's architecture was constantly in flux: construction materials lying about indicated that some kind of building was going on, but at the same time there were also traces of decay. The hotel was simultaneously construction site and ruin. In his slide show, Smithson then showed numerous details of the fragmentary construction: piles of rubble, half-finished walls with protruding iron reinforcements, crumbling floors, free-standing columns supporting nothing, the remains of an older hotel that had clearly been overlain by the new construction, piles of cement blocks, roofless interiors. Freely associating, in this parody of an academic lecture he compared these found details with contemporary artworks or interpreted them as echoes of pre-Columbian culture; at the same time, he was bewildered by the unknown creators of this chaos. The individual measures seemed to follow no internal logic, inside and outside were in permanent exchange with one another. The inadequacy of this Mexican hotel that was neither completed nor abandoned inspired Smithson to his notion of "de-architecturization," which confronts the longing for permanence and protection that inheres in architecture with processes of decay and disintegration.[4] Smithson developed the notion of an architecture of the temporary that thematizes its own disappearance; his architectural event is permanent transition, the ambivalent relation between renewal and decay.

Sites and Nonsites

But this masterpiece of Latin American improvisation only turned into a reflection on the essence of architecture from a position of aesthetic distance, by way of the ironic comments made during a slide presentation—which Smithson declared an artwork. Smithson took this very seriously, commenting elsewhere that his point was not "building a better tomorrow. I posit that there is no tomorrow, nothing but a gap, a yawning gap. That seems sort of tragic, but what immediately relieves it is irony, which gives you a sense of humor. It is that cosmic sense of humor that makes it all tolerable. Everything just vanishes. The sites are receding into the nonsites, and the nonsites are receding back to the sites."[5] With the concept of "nonsites," Smithson developed in 1968 an artistic strategy that makes absence a sculptural theme. The nonsite as a work form confronts the problem of how to represent an (absent) place. All the same, at issue are not various sites, but

Robert Smithson and the Architecture of Absence_Kai Vöckler

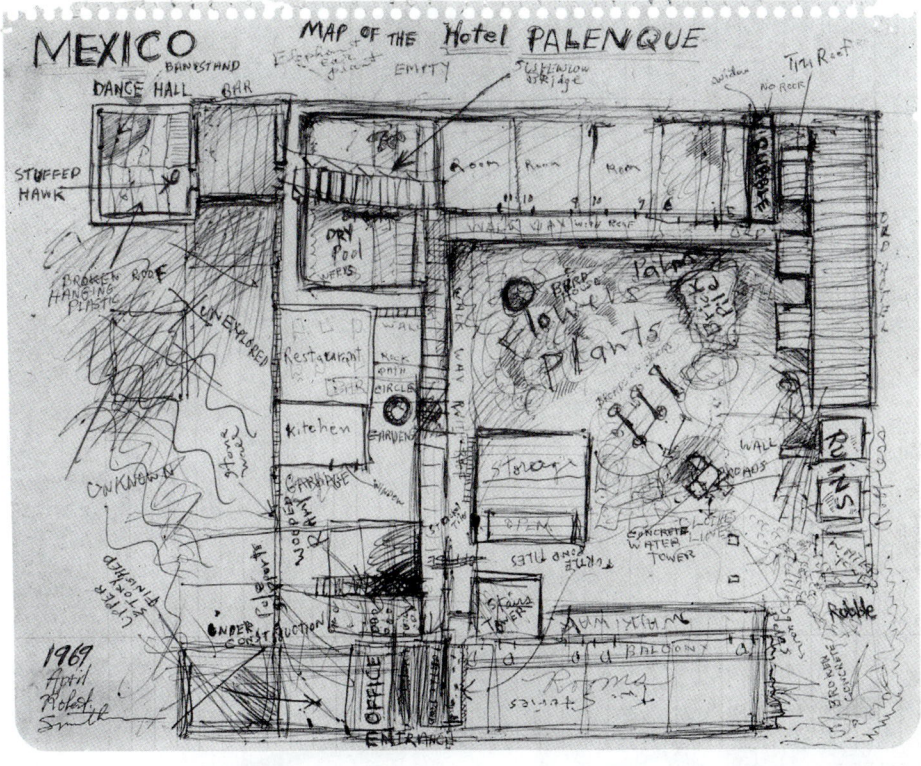

In his study of an unremarkable hotel on the Yucatán peninsula in Mexico, Robert Smithson illustrates the simultaneity of construction and decay and, hence, the building's constant metamorphosis—observations on which he bases a new architectural theory of instability. *Hotel Palenque,* 1969/70.

Evolutionary City

Robert Smithson and the Architecture of Absence_Kai Vöckler

those that lie outside our attention, that are in a sense already absent. Smithson sought out peripheral sites like quarries, abandoned airfields, or slag heaps—sites that for him "show an effect of time, a kind of sinking into timelessness."[6] He there collected stones, gravel, bed ash, and soil, which are then presented in exhibitions in open containers like those used for shipping along with photographs and topographical maps of the territory as well as descriptions of the site. The heterogeneous arrangement of these various references to the site make it unmistakably clear that it is something different than the place itself. Smithson termed nonsites "three-dimensional logical pictures" that create a relationship between the artificial and the natural, the virtual and the real, without this connection being readily subsumed in a representation of the site. This construction is for him the continuation of "logical two-dimensional pictures," like charts or maps that might describe a place, but are not like them.[7] The summation of various references to the site produces a complexity that at the same time underscores the impossibility of representation. The "nonsites" not only engage in a dialogue about presence and absence, but are also a structure of lines and letters, images and descriptions, and material and containers that forms a space of its own: "In a certain sense, my nonsites are rooms within rooms."[8] It is a sculptural-architectural-topographical construction that forms a space that for Smithson represents a confrontation with a "very ponderous, weighty absence" resulting from the endless back and forth between site and nonsite.[9] In this process of dissolution, the beholder is also implicated, for Smithson intends that the beholder approach the nonsite "in terms of its own negation, so that leaves you with a very raw material that doesn't seem to exist."[10]

The Experience of Things Disappearing

In his earlier sculptures based on mirrors, Smithson also constructed a spatial experience that develops independently of a beholding subject and provokes a disturbing experience of a space that is slipping away, ungraspable, inaccessible. The mirror is one of his preferred materials; with it, the closure of surfaces and bodies can be opened; the virtual can be intersected with the real. And nested inside one another, reflecting one another, these spaces no longer confirm the narcissistic presence of a beholder, but reflect an absence. An example of this is the lost 1965 work *Enantiomorphic Chambers,* where the crystalline structure dissolves the beholder's perception into countless mirror images. Interestingly, in his 1969 article "LAWUN (Locally Available World Unseen Networks)," David Greene of Archigram refers to an article published by Smithson that same year, "Incidents of Mirror-Travel in the Yucatan,"[11] in which Smithson describes what happens when twelve mirrors are placed in nine different sites in the Mexican landscape. The landscape and the image of the landscape, he writes, melt together, for the mirrors simply reflect everything that comes into their horizon.[12] In a delirious description of this experience, Smithson allows time and space to collapse, opposing the apathy of material to identity and existence. Greene uses the photographs of the nine *Mirror Displacements* as illustrations for his article, and quotes Smithson as saying that "only the dimension of absence can still be found," which is the starting point for his considerations on an "architecture of absence."[13] But Greene ultimately misunderstands Smithson's *Mirror Displacements,* albeit in a productive way: he sees in them a technical material that is inserted into a landscape and then removed without a trace. He is fascinated by the camouflage effect of the mirror, which allows it to virtually disappear into the landscape, leading him to ruminations about an infrastructure that would fuse with the landscape, about an invisible environment freed of architecture. Here, he notes that it is odd "that time in recent years has played such an important role in the arts, with the exception of architecture," and adds prophetically, "Perhaps the architects have always known that they are robbing themselves of business if they entertain the temporal dimension."[14]

Self-Questioning and Self-Dissolution

For the artist and architect group SITE (Sculpture In The Environment), the concept of time would become the starting point for their questioning of architectural values. The head of the group, James Wines, took up the concepts of "de-architecturization" and "entropy," and in 1973, referring to Smithson, developed the notion of an "architecture of indeterminacy."[15] Famous here is the *Indeterminate Façade* of the Best department store—where decay was planned into the construction in 1975—as a brick facade from which a cataract of bricks pours down onto the entrance canopy. But this temporariness is not part of an architectural program, but a symbolic critique of the sterility of the purportedly timeless architecture of consumption. The precarious relationship of architecture to the forces of nature is also thematized in the 1980 *Best Forest Building,* where nature is allowed to penetrate the building and spread out in it, but only in a limited sense. SITE, like Smithson, thus explores the relationship between presence and absence, emergence and disappearance. More strongly bound into functional contexts, this relationship can only be represented on a symbolic level. The most impressive example of this is the 1978 *Ghost Parking Lot,* where in the corner of a department-store parking lot twenty cars disappear beneath the surface of the asphalt. Between them, parking can go on as usual. The present-absent cars, "buried" under asphalt, evoke an alienating sense of a state of immobility, accompanied by fears of mortality. That the "good life," the promise of the department store, one day will slip away is a variation of the *vanitas* theme; the reminder that all earthly things will pass becomes a moral call to take stock of oneself.

Smithson, in contrast, was interested in self-dissolution, as shown in his most famous work, *Spiral Jetty,* in Utah's Great Salt Lake. This sculpture, which has become an icon of Earth Art and for whose realization 6,650 tons of mud, salt crystals, and rocks were poured onto a spiral-shaped dam, is not famous so much due to actually being seen, but rather thanks to Gianfranco Gorgoni's famous photograph of the work. Less well known is the fact that due to the puzzling variations of water level in Great Salt Lake, the spiral jetty disappears for long periods of time underwater. It has reemerged only recently. This repeatedly returning absence is part of the concept. Smithson shows the site and the work in a film that is an equally important part of the artwork. In a delirious montage of images and words, combining geological descriptions, quotations from Beckett's *Molloy* and science-fiction novels, the medical definition of a sunstroke with red-toned images of dinosaur skeletons or shots of Robert Smithson himself rushing across the jetty, pursued by a camera shooting from a helicopter, and also a shot of the cutting room, the sculpture and the beholder are drawn into an insoluble, unending process of perception and reflection, without a goal: "The helicopter maneuvered the sun's reflection through the *Spiral Jetty* until it reached the center. The water functioned as a vast thermal mirror.... A withering light swallowed the rocky particles of the spiral, as the helicopter gained altitude. All existence seemed tentative and stagnant. The sound of the helicopter motor became a primal groan echoing into tenuous aerial views.... I was slipping out of myself

Evolutionary City

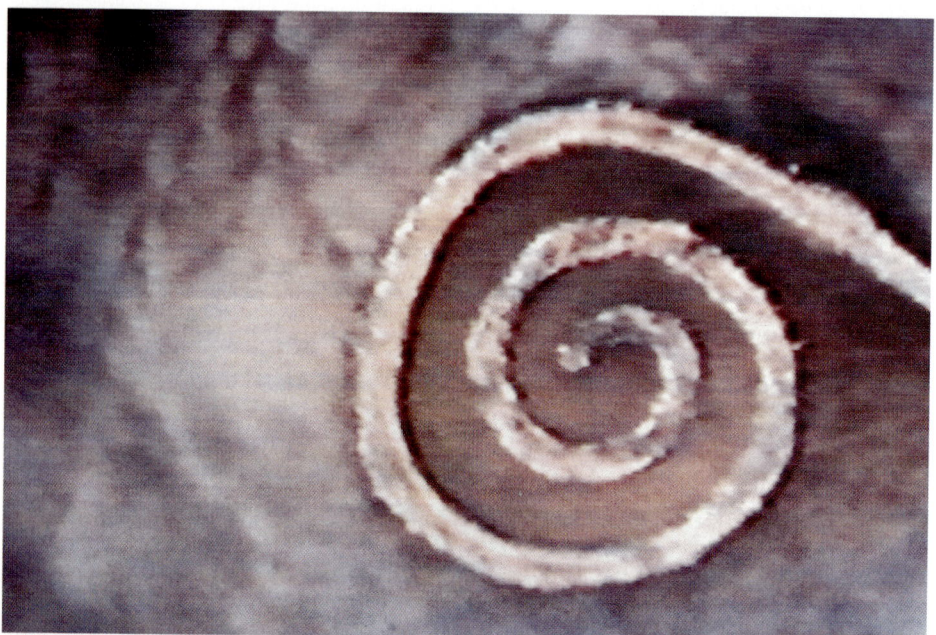

The idea of entropy and long-term transformations in geological time-frames lies at the core of Robert Smithson's artistic work. These not only affect natural metamorphoses but are also the basic theme of many of his projects.

Spiral Jetty: In 1970 Robert Smithson created a 500-meter-long spiral out of basalt, grit, and salt in Utah's Great Salt Lake, whose water level is subject to gradual fluctuations.

Robert Smithson and the Architecture of Absence_Kai Völcker

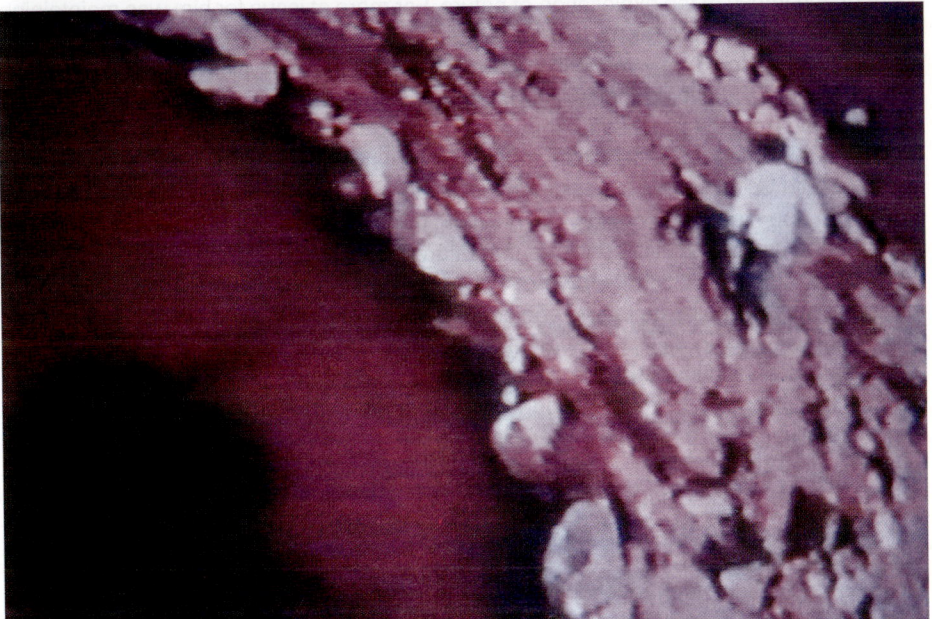

This artwork is subject to constant transformation. If the lake's water level rises, the spiral is submerged and disappears. It reappears after a few years when the water level sinks again. In addition, the salt crystals themselves alternate between an organic and a crystalline state.
Processes of entropy are constitutive for the artwork, despite the artist being unable to control their form.
(Stills from the film *Spiral Jetty*, 1970.)

Robert Smithson and the Architecture of Absence_Kai Vöckler

In 1972 the commercial enterprise Best Products commissioned the SITE group to erect a series of retail outlets in several cities in the United States.
The *Indeterminate Façade Showroom* in Houston (1975) simultaneously epitomizes modern development and dereliction. The architecture draws, among other things, on the artistic work of Robert Smithson. It is a critical commentary on the typology of department stores and consumer society and at the same time an eye-catching and effective sales location for the retail chain (left and above).

In 1980 the *Best Forest Building* in Richmond, which lies in a lush and luxuriant suburb, was carefully integrated into existing vegetation. The forest grows into the showroom, creating the illusion of a romantic and overgrown ruin (pp. 128/129, 130).

Evolutionary City

Robert Smithson and the Architecture of Absence_Kai Vöckler

CONTINUOUS CONVEYOR BELT CITY
1972
Superstudio

Like an enormous snake, this city of eight million residents devours its way across the landscape, progressing at a speed of 40 centimeters an hour. The Grand Factory at its head consumes what is left of useless nature and from its rear end expels fully equipped and operational city districts. From childhood onwards, the longing of the city residents is focused on these buildings with all their technical innovations. Those who can afford to move once a month, in accordance with the Grand Factory's rhythm of production.

But luckily, it isn't even possible to stay in one place for more than four years, since the buildings' supporting elements as well as their furnishings begin to disintegrate after this length of time. In a continuous process of growth and decay, the city continuously reproduces itself. Only social outcasts dare to remain among the ruins and waste that the city leaves behind. (Ed.)

"Continuous Conveyor Belt City" is one of Superstudio's *Dodici città ideali (Twelve Ideal Cities,* 1972).

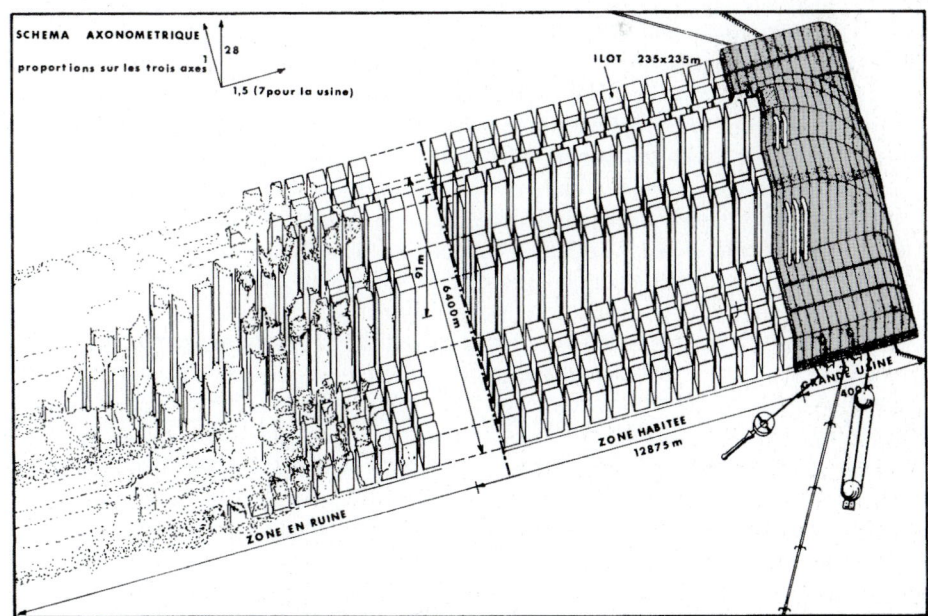

The "Continuous Conveyor Belt City" reproduces itself in a constant process of growth and decay.

STRUCTURES OF POSSIBILITY
Pierre Huyghe
—
—

In Mediterranean countries one frequently comes across unfinished poured concrete houses that have been under construction for years, or even for decades, and that are partly inhabited, while additional stories are present only in skeleton form: iron core rods suggest the possibility that construction will be continued shortly. It is a kind of building-in-progress that lays little claim to being representative or purposely designed. It is the result of a growth process that is often very protracted and also erratic, and is hence also an interesting prototype of any construction that remains partly vacant for long periods, or that is only marginally used; one that can develop over time relatively unencumbered by classical notions of architecture. The following text elaborates the particular qualities of this type of building, and thereby opens up, among other things, new perspectives on how partially vacant properties might be used. (Ed.)

A Note of Intent

The construction bears witness to the choices and processes that comprise it. What went wrong, became redundant, was forgotten, or took a new direction is inscribed in these strata. Each layer tells its story. Nothing has been planned. It is not a linear construction but one that extends in multiple directions, open to possibility, to transformation: its potential for change and its accessibility are permanent features.

It is a construction with potential. Each layer is an omen of a virtual world. What can be seen is less than what can be imagined. It is nothing final, but a route, a starting point. It is the necessity of now. What is present is a manifestation of what is possible. Here, what is present emerges from the future to which it is leading. A habitat is conceived in terms of its ultimate state, from its structure to its public face, its facade: one completes it then inhabits it. Here the process is reversed; one starts, one moves in; completion is a term that has yet to be defined. Let us be done with completion! An indeterminate habitat means living with transience, as if on a permanent construction site, interrupted or, rather, expectant. How can a state of incompleteness become a rule of conduct?

The construction will develop in accordance with, and for the purposes of, whatever it leads to, in order to be able to adapt to constraints, to remain supple, to respond to situations in flux. It is a construction that responds without stating its needs, and that therefore eliminates any idea of completion: everything must remain possible and compatible at all times. One can conceive this in terms of a parallel and nonlinear patchwork process: in neural terms. The construction responds to the unpredictable with incompleteness, to situational instability with transience. Time integrates space, transforms it into multidirectional movement. To work with space as in Judo: to transfer energy not by resisting it to preserve energy but by going with it, recycling it by absorbing the tension, responding to the flow.

The construction is modern, basic, made of concrete, with the potential for optimal implants. It is a fixed structure with changing variables. It is open to complexities elaborated by time and necessity; it is open to different levels, these additional expanding structures, to implants, to transformation. The unstable conditions of the Mediterranean basin (as much political as social, legal, or conflictual) provoke corresponding architectural decisions. These are precise, which is to say, necessary or contingent—necessary to what is there, contingent on what will be. Futures spaces: the maximum number of possible locations for diverse scenarios, for virtual and therefore polyvalent space.

Narrative Structures

Construction is carried out over a long time, unfolding parallel to what is lived. It is a slow house or, more precisely, a house with several speeds. The process is interwoven with family history. Its structure must be able to accept this, to make it possible. It tells us private stories. The structure evolves and becomes a biographical narrative, becomes inscribed with a series of facts, of events. Its form is a fact of relatedness, a nonlinear narrative, an evolution lasting for multiple concurrent periods of time, where stories create spaces.

Constraints produce palliative systems applicable to different constructions depending on their situations; architectural form therefore has little relevance. These mechanisms are not predetermined. The singularity of these constructions does not rest on a predetermined form, it is not contained by the parameters of a model that can be reproduced. Its transposition could take the form of a text, of a story. It is a model without formal, specific representation. It is not an object but the principle on which it itself rests and that makes it change over time.

This mechanism is not in any way a parasite insofar as it does not live on an existing body. It emerges in the course of constituting itself, but independently of any architectural form. In a (politically, socially, etc.) stable system, conservatism, logically enough, reproduces a past form, barely changing it. Conversely, here the present is not determined by an overly unstable past and it therefore establishes itself in the future. The effects of this determine the present. The virtual determines the present. The construction is the starting point of an instrumentality. It evolves. It is not a key object on hand, an object of representation, or contemplation. It is practical, a tool for daily use; an instrument that responds, that calls out. Its function is clear, its practice changes. Its singularity does not lie in technology or in the use of certain materials but in the way it is articulated, put together, and in the nature of its relationship to the future. It is fluid architecture in which one can intervene at any moment, select new functions, make choices, pass from one state to another. A mobile home moves without changing; this is a variable home with nomadic immobility.

Translated from the French by Jill Denton

This is an abridged version of "Note d'intention", in *exposé* 3 (1998). Reprint with kind permission of the author.

Evolutionary City

Concrete skeleton buildings photographed by Pierre Huyghe in Lazio, Italy, 1993.

Structures of Possibility_*Pierre Huyghe*

SPECIFIC INDETERMINACY: WITZNITZ BRIQUETTE FACTORY
Borna, Germany, 1996–1999
Florian Beigel Architects and Architecture Research Unit, London Metropolitan University

———

We seek an approach that can respond to changes in the economy and the building market, to changes of program, and to the diversity of future lifestyle aspirations that no one can predict. Like a bricoleur, we create design strategies that can cope with incompleteness and can transform a situation of multiplicity of styles and expectations into a pleasure.

We are not interested in soulless flexibility or in technocratic infrastructural planning. What are needed are tools that can bring a sense of communality to an urban design and a sense of belonging to a place. There must be a glue that connects this diversity of private interests. The shared realm should feel like a gift. It should be well chosen. The question concerns how much needs to be fixed, and what should be fixed and what left open. So designing for us is often a question of how much and how little to fix.

In our age of diversity, uncertainty, rapid change, and open-endedness, we are looking for structures that make these instabilities enjoyable.

The first project that gave us an opportunity to test and develop strategies for working in situations of economic and social uncertainty was carried out in the post-industrial former coal-mining region found south of Leipzig in eastern Germany. Our objective was to find an architectural space that left room for the unfolding of human imagination. It would be characterized by a specificity of context, place, and materials, and it would be indeterminate with regard to a predetermined set of uses. In this sense, one can speak of a specific indeterminate architecture. It is determinate in that it is site-specific and has strong materialities. It is indeterminate in that it is programmatically open-ended.

Specific indeterminate space has an enigmatic emptiness. It is a space that is waiting for something to happen, a space where one can be alone or in a crowd. It is a space that attracts temporary proximity of different uses, densification of use, and change of use. In its basic form it has similarities to a stage in either a house or a city, or to a stage between cities. Many scenarios can be acted out on it. Stages are typically indeterminate with respect to program, and they are often empty, without vertical structures. To varying degrees they have service structures around them or above or below them, and their theatrical potential increases with the size and capacity of these structures.

Specific indeterminate space is formed in the first instance as an *architectural infrastructure*. To be both specific and indeterminate seems to be a contradiction in terms. If use is not the main factor that determines the design of a space, one usually assumes that the design must be general, multipurpose, and nonspecific. Herein lies a possible danger. The exclusion of specificity has tended to create out-of-place, characterless buildings or black boxes, like suitcases left standing on a platform, uncollected, not belonging.

This specificity of space comes from the place. A heightened awareness of a situation must be created. Attraction and charge can come about by generating a new view of an adjacent large or small space, a landscape or a piece of town, perhaps as a momentary glimpse. Giving measure to an existing topography, making new connections within a given place, offering a safe degree of danger or excitement, revealing lost information: these are all ways of giving attention and specificity to the space.

Such a space might also give rise to reflection and contemplation, providing some distance and perspective to the flowing or chaotic movements that we experience in everyday life. The new perspective might also generate a sense of beauty in an observer who is contemplating situations that are usually considered to be necessary evils, or one might simply be made more aware of the sky, the clouds, the weather, or raindrops falling into a puddle. In a metropolitan context, Cedric Price designed what he called "Magnet" projects to attract activity and condense life. "Magnets" generate new forms of use, safety, information, views, spectacles, and contemplation.[1]

Specificity can also derive from the materiality of the location or, to be more exact, from the authenticity of the material. As the Irish theologian William Fitzgerald put it, "That is called authentic, which is sufficient to itself, which commends, sustains, proves itself and hath credit and authority from itself."[2] Material choices for architectural infrastructures can be further informed by the materiality of the site—in the case of the Witznitz project, by the materiality of the mining landscape, a kind of "second nature."

The concept of specific indeterminacy has also been well described by Rem Koolhaas: "If there is to be a 'new urbanism' it will not be based on the twin fantasies of order and omnipotence; it will be the staging of uncertainty; it will no longer be concerned with the arrangement of more or less permanent objects but with the irrigation of territories with potential; it will no longer aim for stable configurations but for the creation of enabling fields that accommodate processes that refuse to be crystallized into definitive form."[3]

Transitional Territories

Uncertainty is closely associated with places in transition, disused places, places that have become partially wild, that are cracks in the fabric, holes in the landscape. These places occur between or at the periphery of cities. Increasingly, transitional places are being found even within the traditional centers of cities that have become mere tourist stage sets.

Designing in these transitional territories requires a complete reassessment of the accepted ideas of city public spaces in the European tradition: the street, the square, the park. Nostalgic urban forms or idealized landscapes as in the paintings of Caspar David Friedrich are not applicable in the context of these holes. They freeze the temporal potential, they destroy the wildness. These ideas are insensitive to the notion of the holes having a second nature. This character and identity needs to be sensitively revealed, responded to, and strengthened.

The question that arises is how strong should the intervention should be. We would like to avoid an overdetermined response. We subscribe to Mies van der Rohe's attitude of "doing almost nothing," making a response that is elegant, clear, and generous, and revealing it with ease in the spirit of the genius loci. Another source of inspiration is Carl Andre, the sculptor of horizontality and abstracted place: "I don't like works of art which are terribly conspicuous. I like works of art which are invisible if you are not looking for them."[4]

The Witznitz Project

Witznitz is in the process of becoming a prototype or generator for a postindustrial regional city landscape within the Halle–Leipzig–Dresden axis. In approximately fifty years from today, the mining excavations in the Südraum (south region) of Leipzig will have turned into lakes. Witznitz is characterized by uncertainty brought about by the sudden decline of the brown-coal mining economy of the region sparked by its exposure to worldwide competition following the reunification of East and West Germany in 1990. This caused a reduction of the mining workforce from 60,000 to 6,000 overnight, and almost wiped out an eighty-year-old regional lifestyle.

The region is in a situation of rapid economic transition. Large industrial sites continue to operate, but there is increasing uncertainty about their future use. There is an unknown potential for attracting new companies to use the existing industrial settlements and to build new industries. The urban planning competition brief (first phase) summed up the situation as follows: "In this ambivalent regional spatial situation, the possibilities and the risks are equally balanced. This uncertain transitional state will persist for several years. This state creates the temporal scope for the development of new regional spatial models and a new regional spatial identity."[5]

An Architectural Landscape of Activity Fields

The main idea of the design is to cultivate an architectural landscape of "activity fields"—a kind of "mining garden" at the outskirts of the city—in order to considerably enhance the attractiveness of the site before the buildings are regenerated. This concept of activity fields is a response to the uncertainty of the situation and to the need to increase the attractiveness and enjoyment of the site. If no development ever takes place, the town will still have a mining garden.

Activity fields are fields that have the power to attract various activities and to unify them. They are designed to make the variety and uncertainty of this postindustrial condition enjoyable. Their power of attraction and unification is generated by the existing natural and manmade landscape. These fields can be described as "carpets in the landscape."

The garden is composed of a variety of materials and activities, mostly as they are found on the site. They range from railway marshalling yards, traces of lost buildings, pavements constructed of demolition material, ash basins with ecological test beds, and clay covers, to contaminated soil deposits, a wild meadow of long grass, dense groups of birch trees, fields of allotment gardens, and market gardens. The construction of this mining garden represents the preparation of the ground for the new community of Witznitz, where people will work, live, and enjoy themselves.

Short-Term and Longer-Term Use Scenarios

For both land territories and existing buildings, the design provides for initial, interim, and long-term uses and activities. Temporality is essentially the most important design consideration for this project.

Specific Indeterminacy_*Florian Beigel Architects*

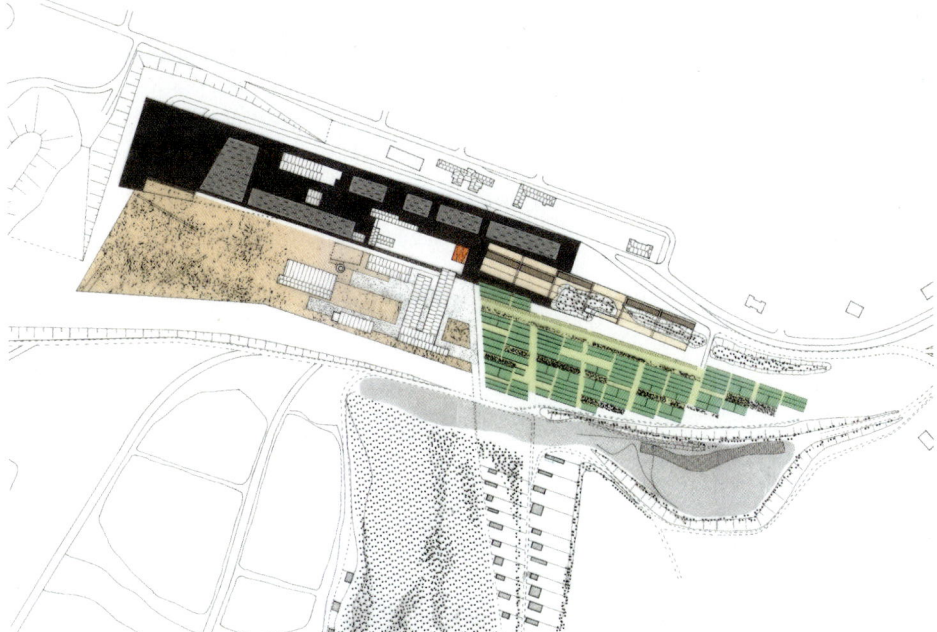

▲ Theater stage in Colombé-les-deux-Églises, France. Plans for Witznitz envisage that both space and the development program might freely unfold, as on a stage.
▼ Overall concept: the project anticipates various areas of activity on the site of the Witznitz briquette factory, each of which offers scope for indeterminate programs to develop.

In the face of programmatic uncertainty, ideas of final form in the sense of the urban tradition of the European city are problematic. The idea of activity fields is at odds with the idea of a fixed and final urban form. The former is open, the latter is closed in character.

The following activity fields were proposed, and have since been partially realized:
- an area paved with black ash and initially used as playing fields, which will be transformed in time into a site for new trading companies;
- a horticultural field with market gardens and apple orchards, which will become a carpet of approximately one hundred patio houses built between long garden walls; the orchards will remain;
- a field of allotments, which will later accommodate workshop houses within the plot divisions;
- a large field containing an ensemble of industrial monuments will start out as a field with tall grass, wild flowers, and large glacial boulders unearthed during mining; in time, several of the old buildings will be adapted for cultural events;
- a field for ecological testing on the former ash basins.

The Witznitz project tested the idea of a gradual metamorphosis of landscape carpets into building carpets. The discovery of a "second nature" in the existing mining landscape gave rise to the desire to strengthen and emphasize the differences between this artificial topography and the natural topography, rather than wiping it out and replacing it with a romantic imitation of the "natural." Essentially we endeavor not to overdetermine the design programmatically, neither at the level of the buildings nor at the urban level. The design proposals test the idea of a metamorphosis over time from carpets in the landscape, as we like to call these fields, into building carpets, a tapestry of houses, trading buildings, and reprogrammed industrial buildings.

Text by Florian Beigel and Philip Christou

This is an abridged version of an essay published in *arq: Architectural Research Quarterly* 2, no. 2 (Winter 1996): 18–38.

Participants in the project: Suresh A'Raj, José Aquilar-García, Mathew Barton, Florian Beigel, Ulrike Brauer, Philip Christou, Eamon Cushnahan, Max Daiber, Francis Henderson, Jonathan Hendry, Rex Henry, Dan Jones, Mernoosh Khadivi, Mareike Lamm, Daniel Mallo, Costantino Meucci, Philipp Misselwitz, Ellen Monchen, Susanne Müller, Soo In Oh, Yong Ho Shin, Chris Snow, Taro Tsuruta, Sylvia Ullmayer, Georgios Vavelos; consultants: Ellen Bottcher, Jonathan Cook, Uve Ferber, Doreen Grauman, Wolfgang Heinichen.

Notes
1   Cedric Price, "Magnetism Personified," *Building Design*, May 24, 1996, 12–15.
2   William Fitzgerald quoted in Will Crutchfield, "Fashion, Conviction, and Performance Style in an Age of Revivals," in *Authenticity and Early Music: A Symposium*, ed. Nicholas Kenyon (Oxford, UK: Oxford University Press, 1988), 24–25.
3   Rem Koolhaas and Bruce Mau, *S,M,L,XL* (Rotterdam: 010 Publishers, 1995), 969.
4   *Carl Andre, Sculptor 1996*, ed. Eva Meyer-Hermann (Stuttgart: Oktagon, 1996), 48.
5   City of Borna, *Städtebaulicher Ideenwettbewerb Nachnutzung der Brikettfabrik Witznitz, Auslobung Erste Phase* [Brief for First Phase of Urban Planning Ideas Competition on Reuse of Witznitz Briquette Factory] (Leipzig: Stadt Borna, 1996), 10.

Specific Indeterminacy_Florian Beigel Architects

▲ The foundations of former industrial buildings will be exposed and the remaining buildings gradually converted into venues for cultural events.
▼ The former turbine hall, for example, will be converted into an open-air theater.

FERAL CITY

Urban withdrawal creates vacant spaces. Wasteland, forests, and fields creep back into the city and increasingly determine its look and its structure. Typical landscapes thereby undergo change and absorb urban elements and functions. Urban agriculture or community gardens can generate new social networks or the basis for local economies.

NATURALLY DETERMINED URBAN DEVELOPMENT?
Jörg Dettmar

Wastelands, wilderness in the city, industrial forests, dark forests, succession areas, urban nature zones—there is certainly something happening in German cities. City shrinkage and redevelopment are creating new open spaces, and in light of the general shortage of public funds there is a certain helplessness as to how these areas should be developed and used.

It would be shortsighted to limit our attention solely to shrinking cities. Shrinking and growth are two sides of the same coin, even if in the postwar period we in Germany have been almost exclusively programmed to think in terms of growth. Seen over a larger time frame, growth and decay are not such unusual elements in the history of the city. This is a fact that is much more readily accepted in the United States or in parts of Asia, for example.

In our urban growth zones, too (e.g., the *Zwischenstädte,* or "intermediate cities," of the Rhine-Main area, and the belts around Stuttgart and Munich), some scenarios are conceivable in which the share of land that remains unused at least for a certain period of time increases very rapidly. For example, what would happen if what remains of urban agriculture were to reach its limits, what if it became impossible to maintain all undeveloped areas imposed by way of the compensatory regulations under environmental protection law, and what if this also resulted in partial crises in certain economic sectors?

It is thus quite forward-looking to see wastelands with naturally determined growth as urban building blocks. But what does this mean in concrete terms?

Using the example of the "Industriewald Ruhrgebiet" project (Industrial Forests of the Ruhr), I would like to present the details of one approach. A few years ago, in association with the Emscher Park "International Building Exhibition" (IBA), an experiment was begun on how to use wastelands in a sensible way with little financial investment. This "Restflächen" (Leftover Land) project has now completed its test phase. In 2001 it was established as a long-term project under North Rhine-Westphalia's forestry administration. The forestry administration will now further develop and extend the project (now called "Industriewald Ruhrgebiet") with the support of the Recklinghausen forestry commission and the Rheinelbe in Gelsenkirchen ranger station, which has since been expanded.

The idea was to not redesign wasteland elaborately using new planning, but to allow natural development, or succession, to freely run its course. All the same, these areas were not to be entirely left to their own devices, rather a form of social control was to be established that sought to prevent negative developments like misuse for trash disposal and vandalism and to make the areas accessible to all segments of the population.

The starting point was also the realization that succession offers ecologically valuable as well as aesthetically appealing elements in all of the phases that lead up to that of a growing forest. At issue was thus not redesigning the areas, but opening them up to the population as far as this was possible. A kind of "caring development" in the form of foresters stationed in the area, or at least coming at regular intervals, was set up. A total of four employees of the forestry administration now look after around 200 hectares of industrial forest, largely in central urban sites in the Ruhr district. Other areas are currently being prepared for inclusion; the target size for the project is around 1,000 hectares.

The core areas belong to the North Rhine-Westphalia land reserve and were integrated on the basis of a foresting contract with the Recklinghausen forestry commission in accordance with the State Forest Act. In the meantime, areas held by private owners such as Thyssen-Krupp and Deutsche Steinkohle have also been included in the program. Here, a conventional leasing contract has proven to be a suitable basis.

The foresters develop their own ideas for the use of the areas, always under the guiding principle of "let it grow." Simple paths are laid out, serious safety risks like pits and the like removed, and regular guided tours of this "industrial nature" are offered.

In addition, as part of the IBA, sculptures were placed in a few areas (by Ulrich Rückriem in Zollverein Essen, and by Herman Prigann in Rheinelbe Gelsenkirchen), in order to give them some additional artistic value. But there are also areas with no accompanying artistic use. Some areas were integrated into the program only temporarily— a section of the Rheinelbe in Gelsenkirchen colliery, for example. Now, as originally intended, a further component of a commercial zone is being developed here.

Judging by the regular numbers of visitors and the number of tours in recent years, all this has functioned well. The forestry administration has gained important public recognition and visibility in the cities of Gelsenkirchen and Essen. The free(dom) spaces, which are much larger than other open urban spaces, are very attractive to children and young people, in particular. Here, a truly direct contact with nature takes place.

So what from this experiment can be applied to other cities or regions? Of course, a godsend like the Emscher Park IBA as a catalyst that provides the initial funding is rare indeed. While the foresters of course generate personnel costs, the development and maintenance of the areas in this way is many times more affordable than for conventional landscaping.

It is conceivable that looking after and/or guarding the areas can also be organized by way of employment schemes, citizen groups or nature conservation associations, residents, or other volunteers. All the same, a coordinating and supervisory authority is necessary, and forest or park authorities are well suited to this task. Prerequisites for this, however, are employees who are enthusiastic about the project, and further training in how to treat succession, where employees would be taught how to let an area go wild and hold the instinct of immediate intervention in check. Principles in terms of access and danger prevention must be set, although forest areas would require less safeguarding with respect to public liability.

Perhaps the most important future task for landscape architecture is to develop suggestions and solutions for the use and design of remaining open spaces. How can a sustainable and attractive urban landscape be developed from the leftovers found in seemingly endlessly suburbanized metropolitan areas? Is it possible to create a sustainable and attractive urban structure in the context of city shrinkage with its emerging wastelands in perforated city structures?

Of course, the conditions in suburban growth zones and in shrinking cities are at first glance quite different from one another. While on the one side there is high economic pressure and demand for space, the other side is characterized by shrinkage and retreat. But seen in structural terms, both conditions result in urbanized spaces consisting of a patchwork of vacant and built-up areas.

If one conceives of processes of urbanization in a more fundamental way, growth and shrinkage go hand in hand. The further development of urban industrial society has produced a kind of "total landscape," as the historian Rolf Peter Sieferle has put it.[1] It is marked by a constantly growing flow of information and the universal availability of materials on the basis of increasing energy consumption. What results is an apparently individual and temporary pattern of differentiation, a combination of variety and monotony on the basis of identical, universally available fashions, building styles, architectures, and landscaping, outfitted with the appropriate commodities, building materials, and garden-center products. In contrast to the old cultural landscapes, however, no new lasting or truly recognizable style emerges. That would require much more time to develop and a certain regional insularity. The only true characteristic thus remains constant change. This mobilized lack of style is the only generally valid characteristic of our urbanized landscape: "the only constant is the permanence of change."[2] As a functional principle, this applies everywhere, be it a region of suburban growth or urban shrinkage. This is also true regardless of the degree of settlement; regardless of whether we are dealing with city or countryside, to use the historical categories.

We are attempting to control these processes, using planning to arrive at a design that ultimately results in economically viable, attractive, livable, functioning urban and landscape structures. Most experts would argue that this has up until now not succeeded with respect to the *Zwischenstadt* structures of suburban areas. Here, architects and urban planners are placing their hopes in the possibility of proceeding from the open spaces to give order to the *Zwischenstädte,* to organize them, and to grant them new identity. Here, again, open space plays a central role in urban planning.

The various approaches to regional parks in Germany—for example, the Emscher Landschaftspark (Landscape Park) in the Ruhr, the Rhine-Main regional park, the Grüne Nachbarschaft (Green Neighborhood) in Stuttgart, the Filder Raum regional park—follow this strategy. And in practice it is usually linked to plans for green stretches of land at regional level and for systems that join together open spaces. In so doing, the planning usually follows familiar goals of securing, preservation, order, and design.

If one follows Sieferle's analysis, the attempt to order the chaos, though understandable, is doomed to failure from the very start. Permanent change ultimately precludes any stable ordering patterns. The recourse to typical landscaping elements from the pre-industrial phase (Rhine-Main regional park) or the aesthetic staging of the former industrial landscape (Emscher Landschaftspark) form an integral element of a mobilized landscape, where museumified or symbolic islands only underscore the entirely constructed nature of this landscape.

Attempts at creating order ultimately derive from fear and a need for harmony; the recourse to the known is understandable. But what happens if this goes wrong? Since we still have no clear notion of the structure, function, design, or qualities of the mobilized and urbanized landscape of the Age of Information, at the moment a great deal of energy is being spent on examining and trying to understand the existing state of affairs and the mechanisms of its development. But to what extent is a perception molded by historical images and notions truly able to see the possible qualities or ordering patterns of new structures?

In processes of shrinkage, too, the attempt is being made to plan an orderly retreat, to keep chance alone from determining the formation of the new city structure. Planners want to control where and to what extent demolition is undertaken, where new green spaces emerge, and how they can be meaningfully linked.

Naturally Determined Urban Development?_Jörg Dettmar

Regardless of whether it is urban structures from the Wilhelminian era that are shrinking—for example, in bgmr landscape architects' East Leipzig "Dunkler Wald" (Dark Forest) project—or large housing projects on the city limits (like Berlin-Marzahn), the new open spaces are supposed to give everything a sense of order. Forest borders and tree clusters form the new spatial limits when the buildings are gone. Lurking behind this is again fear, in this case a fear of the loss of urban structures that one has come to love, a fear of the end of the traditional European city.

Letting open lots grow wild is only accepted as long as it takes place in prescribed frameworks, as long as it integrates itself into the planned pattern of new open spaces. This can clearly be recognized in the plans for East Leipzig. "In many places, the open space in the dissolving city will be given the task not of bringing wilderness into the city, but of maintaining the urban and social-space continuum. In other words, using landscape design for urban planning."[3] Ultimately, the goal of these approaches as they are realized in Leipzig is extensively designed, economically maintainable green areas of the old kind. The underlying fear is of slum formation, the dilapidation of city areas, and further social decline. This is all understandable, but in this way nothing really new emerges, and instead the status quo of our notion of city is preserved.

Seen historically, cities were places that had liberated their inhabitants from the dangers and risks of nature. The cultural separation of town and country begins with people's alienation from direct production of food and the discovery of the countryside by "liberated" man. Countryside becomes a synonym for nature and increasingly loaded with aesthetic symbolism. When "nature" finds its way into the city, then only in a civilized, aesthetically staged form in the way of gardens and parks, with very different visions of nature predominating in various cultural epochs. In any case, a "wild," spontaneous "nature," not adjusted to urban conditions, is not the expression of a symbolically ideal nature, but rather the banal expression of urban reality. In addition, it is the expression of a city that is precisely not in perfect working order.

At least in Germany, derelict areas with wildernesses generate massive psychological fears when they surpass a certain level. In the cities, this certainly has to do with their cultural and historical origins, with the history of wars, from the Thirty Years War with its devastation to the destruction of the Second World War. This should all be taken into account if one considers naturally controlled development in derelict areas as an integral component of urbanized landscapes, and not just as an unavoidable evil. Derelict areas are available at much more affordable prices than other public green areas. Reuse or redevelopment, if the social and economic conditions should change, is certainly possible.

Under certain conditions they offer wonderful qualities in terms of ecology, aesthetics, and social aspects. As islands of naturally determined development in constant flux, they can provide a different kind of permanence of change in the total "urban landscape" and are always site-specific originals. This is all the more true the more time they have to develop. For children and young people, especially, an available, usable, uncontrolled, wild experience of nature seems an important component of development.

Wastelands can also provide reservoirs for establishing cyclical processes for energy, water, and nutrients in urban landscapes, such as for example the near-natural use of rainwater in urban spaces. In terms of sustainability, decentralized wastewater cycles with biosewage plants, biomass production, and biogas usage would constitute sensible

In the "Industriewald Ruhrgebiet," former industrial areas are largely abandoned to natural succession. Minimal interventions create distinctive attractions and open them to the public; here a temporary art installation at the site of the Hansa cokery by Tamer Serbay, Dortmund, 2002.

Naturally Determined Urban Development?_*Jörg Dettmar*

uses of urban landscapes in such open spaces. The adjacent placement of traditional green areas, succession forests, wetlands, and plant sewage plants is conceivable.

With the end of the industrial age, we need to question the function, perception, and also the design of open space in a completely urbanized society and landscape. Central here is the question of our understanding of the relationship between nature and humanity in the Age of Information.

A core element of a new understanding of nature seems to be the stronger focus on natural principles of development as opposed to specific states of development. In this sense, wastelands could become sites for learning about and experiencing natural development in a mobilized landscape, and perhaps also for learning about "naturally determined urban development." This means departing from familiar notions of stable urban structures and from the permanence of the European city, which in fact only ever existed as an idea. The image of cities in a mobilized society is marked not so much by constancy as by dynamism. This should not simply be seen as a threat, for it also offers opportunities. One such opportunity could lie in thinking about city, landscape, nature, and humanity as part of one whole, which would mean no longer seeing them as apparently antagonistic products of the industrial age. In other words: "cities as nature."

Translated from the German by Brian Currid

Notes
1   See Rolf Peter Sieferle, *Rückblick auf die Natur: Eine Geschichte des Menschen und seiner Umwelt* (Munich: Luchterhand, 1997).
2   Ibid.
3   Carlo W. Becker and Undine Giseke, "Wildnis als Baustein künftiger Stadtentwicklung?" *Garten + Landschaft* 2 (2004), 22–23.

Literature
Bächthold, Hans Georg. "Landschaft—die neu entdeckte Dimension der Raumplanung?" *DIS* 123 (1995).
Dettmar, Jörg. "Wildnis statt Park?" *Topos* 26 (1999): 31–42.
———. "Forests for Shrinking Cities? The Project 'Industrial Forests of the Ruhr.'" In *Wild Urban Woodlands: New Perspectives for Urban Forestry,* ed. Stefan Körner and Ingo Kowarik, 263-276. Berlin: Springer-Verlag, 2005.
Giseke, Undine. "Urbane Freiräume in der schrumpfenden Stadt." *Der Architekt* 8 (2002).

DUISBURG-NORD LANDSCAPE PARK
Duisburg, Germany, 1990–2002
Latz + Partner

The Duisburg-Nord landscape park, one of the largest projects created as part of the Emscher Park "International Building Exhibition," makes a 200-hectare area around the Duisburg-Meiderich blast-furnace plant, which was closed in 1985, accessible to the public. In designing the landscape, the interventions made into the remains from the industrial past were limited to the bare essentials. Acupuncture-like insertions of elements like stairways, paths, ground coverings, lighting elements, plants, and walls connect the existing industrial fragments and also enable new usages. The ruins of the old smelting works have become the "Hochofenpark" (Blast Furnace Park), which has a sport complex and large open-air event venues for up to 50,000 people. The web of train tracks has become the "Bahnpark" (Railway Park), whose numerous pathways provide access to the site and which offers a wide variety of views from the railroad embankments. The Emscher Canal, freed of sewage, is now the "Wasserpark" (Water Park), an artificial ecosystem. And the bunker gardens today offer spaces for retreat called the "Horti Conclusi" (Walled Gardens). Numerous groups and associations organize leisure, sport, cultural, and educational activities on the site. In addition to several formal plantings, for example of orchards and gardens, spontaneous ruderal vegetation also dominates the character of the park grounds. (Ed.)

The original German title of this project is "Landschaftspark Duisburg-Nord."

View of the former sinter bunkers, a new footbridge, and an abandoned rail-mounted crane.

Duisburg-Nord Landscape Park_*Latz + Partner*

▲ The former ore bunker is now a climbing wall for amateur and professional rock-climbers. ▼ Behind the amphitheater runs the formerly contaminated Old Emscher Canal, which has now been transformed into a water park.

Duisburg-Nord Landscape Park_Latz + Partner

▲ The Piazza Metallica, used as the main event venue, consists of weather-beaten metal plates from the former iron-ore foundry. ▼ The Bunker Gardens are part of the former sintering plant and now offer peaceful retreats or "Horti Conclusi" within the extensive park grounds.

URBAN AGRICULTURE
Holger Lauinger

> Who will save the city? The land will save the city ...
> Create urban land!
> The cities must embrace their own land.
> Hundreds of thousands of hectares lie bare:
> Construction land, barracks land, street land, wasteland ...
> Take it in hand.
> Plant: public gardens, for the youth bound to the city.
> Plant: rental gardens, for the tenants bound to the city.
> Plant: settlements, for the labor bound to the city.
> Plant: model gardens for those not provided for! Plant!
> ...
> Not an acre of urban land can be left longer derelict.
> That will secure 100,000 new city livelihoods.
> That will ease millions of existing city livelihoods.
> That, and more besides, will preserve city life.
>   Leberecht Migge, *The Green Manifesto*, 1919

Leipzig-Plagwitz during the summer of the EXPO 2000 exhibition. A scene to disturb our sense of well-being: against a backdrop of vacant buildings, a farmer pulls his horse and plows through derelict city land. What he sows grows into a field of wheat: the Millennium Field. The residents of the neighborhood learn to bake bread from the harvest.

This event performed by the Schaubühne Lindenfels theater in the middle of what was once an industrial urban area is reminiscent of images from times of crisis that were thought long past. Will we in our shrinking cities experience a shift from industrialized "urban" production to agrarian "rural" production? What is the significance of urban agriculture for our notion of the city?

Urban agriculture is the production of agricultural goods within city limits. The phenomenon of agrarian elements in the city is nothing new, not even in the history of development of European cities. Modernist urban utopias and city planning concepts for decentralizing the old "compact" city in favor of a "looser" city sought solutions to resolve the opposition between city and countryside. Experiences of urban crises because of overpopulation in industrialization phases and of hunger crises in postwar years gave a special significance to self-subsistence by way of urban agriculture. The utopian urban conceptions of the "Garden City"[1] from 1898 and "Broadacre City"[2] from 1932 emblematize the visions of urban planners in times of crisis.

Utopias of a Rural Urbanism
The Garden City as conceived of by the English court stenographer Ebenezer Howard was a regional network of small cities and towns. Around a central town (58,000 inhabitants) he grouped a number of smaller towns (32,000 inhabitants). The cities were surrounded by an agricultural belt; the agrarian use of this land was to be organized in

Vegetable gardens for self-sufficient production on Clapham Common, London, during the Second World War.

decreasing intensity towards the outskirts: gardens were followed by dairies, grazing meadows, and fruit groves, then forests and large-scale agriculture. The Central City was to form the "social city." Here, a central park was surrounded by a glass-covered arcade. The Crystal Palace was to be the public space and site of direct marketing. The adjacent residential and work districts were structured on the basis of radial streets and parks. Each family was to have a house with a garden. Autonomous and organized as collectives, the advantages of urban life were to be linked in this way to a free rural existence. Howard wanted agricultural production to be seen as an integral component of urban culture.

For the American architect Frank Lloyd Wright, the industrial city was also a symbol of the exploitation of humanity. In 1929, the year of the Great Depression, he developed a de-densified city with no urban center, which he allowed to be absorbed by a rural system. Broadacre City, he said, "will be nowhere, yet everywhere." The land itself would come to life as a truly great city. Wright integrated the traditional American principles— individualism and a love of nature—into the famous grid structure that has marked America ever since colonial times. In a decental system of adjacent lots, agriculture and industry were to be interwoven with one another. In the homesteads, each citizen was to have access to around 4,000 square meters of land. On this he was to build his house, using the surrounding land for gardens or small-scale farming. Agricultural production was to supplement the industrial wage. Like Howard, Wright was convinced that true democracy is only possible if everybody is a landowner.

In modified form, Howard's Garden City also influenced social-democratic urban planning during the Weimar Republic in Germany. It became the ideal model for many suburban developments centered around open space and bearing the same name. Even if this model was ultimately reduced to "houses with large gardens," the latter did help to ease urban overcrowding.

Productive Open Spaces and Urban Agriculture

The gradual widespread arrival of suburbanization processes in urban modernity rendered possible the introduction of agrarian usage in the development of open spaces. In the years following the First World War, it was the German garden architect Leberecht Migge, especially, who saw decentral urban planning as a chance to create "productive green areas": "Open space should not be an unaffordable burden for the city, but the opposite—its safety valve!" The slogan "Everyone self-sufficient!" also found its political fulfillment. In 1919, the year in which Migge's *Green Manifesto* appeared,[3] the Weimar Republic introduced the *Kleingarten- und Kleinpachtverordnung* (Allotments and Small Tenure Act). The law stipulated that in times of need all citizens should be allowed to till 600 square meters to supply their own nutritional needs. The "strength-giving soil" was supposed to restore a sense of identity. Dominant in these years for the planning of unused spaces in Germany was the model of the "productive landscape" *(Fruchtlandschaft)*.[4] In many places this remained valid until the 1950s. Hans Scharoun's idea of an urban landscape for redesigning Berlin after the Second World War was also marked by a partition of urban space to include agrarian usages. The image of potato and vegetable production in Berlin's Tiergarten forest—which had been almost completely harvested for timber—or on traffic islands is symbolic for the destitution suffered at the time. But it also is a sign of a revaluation of open spaces born of need, and something that could return with the phenomenon of shrinking cities.

The Trier sociologist Bernd Hamm predicts for major European cities conditions approaching those of the "third world": massive informationalization of the economy and high unemployment rates. Seen in this way, the model of a compact city with no space for collective agrarian production could even be termed a social outrage. For a realistic fight against poverty, he argues, the myth of the rich city must be abandoned, and urban agriculture must be strategically included in communal planning.

If we accept this hypothesis, agriculture should soon be interpreted as a facet of urban life and given shape. Beyond the cultural realm of the European city, it is already understood as an important part of the urban economy.

The Global Dimension of Urban Agriculture

In 1987, the Brundtland Commission report entitled *Our Shared Future* stated that "publicly supported urban agriculture could be important for urban development and improve the nutrition supply of the urban poor." According to reports published by the Food and Agriculture Organization in 1996, today over 200 million urban farmers provide food for more than 700 million people. In the Chinese metropolis of Hong Kong, 45% of the vegetables needed are farmed in the city, in Shanghai the share is a hefty 85%. Dakar covers 80% of Senegal's food needs. In Cuba's capital city Havana, 27,000 collectively run *huertos populares* (public gardens) have been supported by the state since the beginning of the 1990s to combat the food-supply crisis. In the former Eastern Bloc, the collective models

Urban Agriculture_*Holger Lauinger*

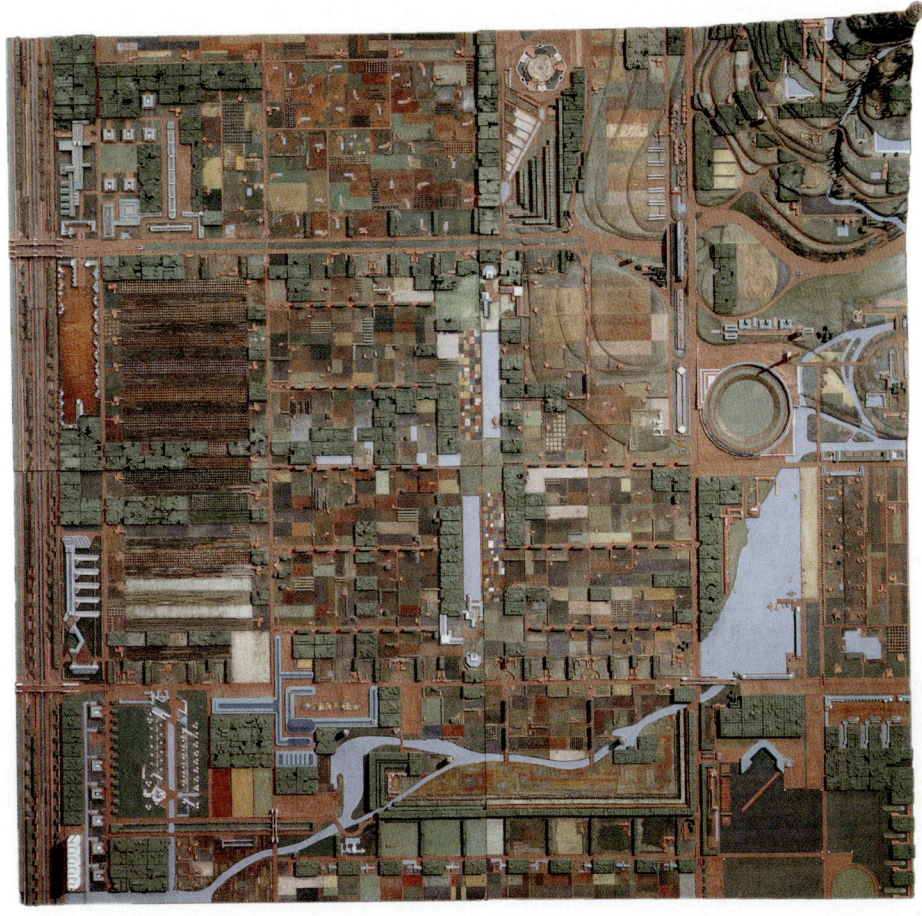

In Frank Lloyd Wright's "Broadacre City" (1932), the city unfolds as an urban agrarian landscape. Each citizen is allocated a plot of tillable land with which to supplement his industrial wage.

were always supplemented by individual small-scale urban agriculture. For example, fruit and vegetable gardens in the small towns of the German Democratic Republic served to qualitatively supplement the food supply. After reunification, most fell victim to their inefficiency. During the economic supply crisis in Russia between 1989 and 1992, around 65% of Moscow families engaged in growing their own food at their dachas. Detroit today has around 600 community gardens, which are sometimes organized as farms given the large surface area the plots cover. Post-urban Detroit thus already exhibits initial structural characteristics like those of Wright's Broadacre City.

Nonetheless, there is no organized mass movement worldwide that openly proclaims the demand for an urban agriculture. However, New York's community gardens represent a model that European cities are also beginning to learn from.

Fight for Your Right to Garden: The Community Gardens in New York City

The battle cry could not have been more cynical: "This a free-market economy, welcome to the era after Communism!" With these few words, Rudolph Giuliani, mayor of New York City, made clear who he saw as the enemy at a 1997 press conference with the Community Farmers. His strategy of zero tolerance is difficult to combine with what in 1973 led to the founding of the first community garden in the Global City. Many empty lots in the ghettos were occupied by residents, freed of trash, and turned into arable ground.[5] The aim of the activists was to "reclaim the commons" so as to secure individual livelihoods and preserve social peace. In the villages of the Middle Ages, the commons guaranteed collective property rights for the landless to engage in farming and cattle-grazing for subsistence. In this spirit, the gardens are collectively run. Vegetables, for the most part, are planted on both communal and individual beds. The gardens are fenced in to protect them from vandalism but open to the public during the day. Run primarily by local groups of residents, like the residential neighborhoods they are therefore organized more along ethnic lines than in a multicultural way. Their presence has led to a noticeable decline in violence and an enhancement of the immediate surroundings. In 1978, New York had around 25,000 derelict areas. After more than three decades of fighting for their right to exist, today there are around 700 member gardens on which around 70,000 people are actively engaged in subsistence farming. The distribution of the produce from these ecological vegetable gardens takes place by way of 28 local farmers' markets and a vegetable-subscriber system named Community Supported Agriculture. It is estimated that 250,000 citizens are fed in this way.

But this economic sector is informal and dependent on the power relations in American civil society. From the start, the community gardens have been supported by the 800 members of the Green Guerillas citizens' initiative, who have organized fund-raising, networking, educational programs, and material donations. At the beginning, the movement defined itself as a "militant pacifist self-help action" for the appropriation of land. Since the mid-1990s it has been working to orient the gardens towards self-sufficient supply by way of vegetable production and to establish new markets for direct sales.

Due to growing public pressure, the urban program Operation Green Thumb was launched at the end of the 1970s to facilitate mediation between the gardeners and the city authorities. Green Thumb is seeking legalization, allowing the gardens to be maintained with symbolic leases—a conflict-ridden, in part paradoxical position. When in 1998 Mayor Giuliani suddenly terminated all the leases in order to sell the property, the limits

Urban Agriculture_Holger Lauinger

In 1999 a former industrial site in Leipzig-Plagwitz was transformed into the *Jahrtausendfeld* (Millennium Field). The nearby theater, Schaubühne Lindenfels, used the inner-city cornfield for two years as a venue for diverse cultural events.

faced by the Green Thumb Organization became all too clear. One hundred of the community gardens that were to be sold by auction were bought by the private cooperatives New York Restoration and Trust for Public Land and with the aid of donations from wealthy New Yorkers. At the moment, 114 gardens are still illegal and at risk.

The need to organize the struggle for land in a solidarity network has lead the community gardens to develop from what initially was a movement with a more social and ecological bent into what today is more a politico-economic pressure group. Accordingly, the activists see themselves not as radicals who want to revolutionize the system, but as complementary to the system. The New York community gardens are a strategy for people forced to live on the outer margins of the free-market society.

Rurbanity and Civil Society
To "gain ground under our feet" is also the civil-society concern of the German initiative Interkulturelle Gartenprojekte (Intercultural Garden Projects). Since 2003, the Stiftung Interkultur (Intercultural Foundation), a nationwide network of 26 community gardens, has been fostering the integration of migrants and other marginalized persons. Prominent examples of gardens involved in the initiative are the Internationale Gärten Göttingen and the Bunte Gärten Leipzig. These bodies not only offer training in horticultural subsistence economy, but also educational programs. It is notable how often these projects have been awarded prizes by public institutions and foundations. Increasingly, civil society is recognizing and supporting the socially integrative power of urban agriculture. Thus, in the new states of eastern Germany, nine projects have already joined the network, and a further eight are in the process of being set up. Stiftung Interkultur's support encompasses financial help and consulting services. The acquisition of property must be achieved by initiatives cooperating at local level. "Neustadtgärten" (New Town Gardens), a project initiated by the Kulturblook group in Halle-Neustadt, was the first project from an urban reconstruction zone to join the network. After two years of intensive and dedicated work on site, following negotiations with the local city planners, the local park authority, and the Leuna housing company, the land where five apartment blocks had been demolished was handed over to the citizens. The initiation and activation phase was completed with funds provided by LOS (Lokales Kapital für soziale Zwecke—Local Capital for Social Purposes). It will be exciting to see what design the residents will give to the area. In Greifswald, a second project group currently wants to join the network.

"Social activation" and efforts to harness the potentials of civil-society involvement are increasingly being considered by local administrations with declining financial capacities as a way out of their own inability to act. For example, the Berlin city government has recently started to recruit "pioneers of space" to make interim use of urban wastelands. Urban gardens are thus seen as a way to stimulate more community involvement among residents. An oft-cited example is the Samariterviertel—a Wilhelminian-era neighborhood where the STATTBAU reconstruction agency has initiated interim uses for derelict lots. It seems that urban agriculture is found latently in communal strategies for open spaces.

But is the potential offered by urban agriculture limited to the neighborhood garden? Surely not. Urban planning appears to be still stuck in the small-mindedness analogous to building-block structures, and this at a time when imagination and new ideas for the future of shrinking cities are needed. Cows in parks and noise protection provided by fruit-bearing hedges also used for jam production were serious suggestions in the days

The "Sixth Street and Avenue B Community Garden" in New York's Lower East Side has blossomed on an abandoned lot since 1982.

when Scharoun was planning the city landscape. Would it not be feasible to plant the oft-visited rural labyrinths of wheat, corn, and hemp in devastated urban areas as well? Which city plays host to "strawberry fields forever"? In searching for solutions, we also need to think big. Oceans of flowers blowing in the wind can be seen as a new facet of urban life, truly allowing "blooming landscapes" to enter the cities. Why not use carefully selected seed mixes and have cities glow in different colors three to five times a year?

The search for means to blend urbanity and rurality is just beginning. The aesthetically tedious large-scale maintenance of green areas or even the helpless abandonment of open spaces by local governments must be countered with the principle of "rurbanity." The shrinking city does not have to be gray; it should be green. With a little more idealism, it could flow with milk and honey. At the moment, we still have the time and the money to explore in socioecological experiments what might later become vitally necessary in socioeconomic terms. Or, as the self-proclaimed "Spartacus in Green" once put it, "Create urban land!"

Translated from the German by Brian Currid

Notes
1. Ebenezer Howard, *To-morrow: A Peaceful Path to Real Reform* (London: Swan Sonnenschein, 1898).
2. Frank Lloyd Wright, *When Democracy Builds* (Chicago: Chicago University Press, 1945).
3. Leberecht Migge, "Das grüne Manifest," in *Funktionalität und Moderne: Das neue Frankfurt und seine Bauten,* ed. Christoph Mohr and Michael Müller (Cologne: R. Müller Verlag, 1984).
4. Frank Lohrberg, *Stadtnahe Landwirtschaft in der Stadt- und Freiraumplanung* (Stuttgart: Libri, 2001).
5. Elisabeth Meyer-Renschhausen, *Unter dem Müll der Acker: Die Community Gardens in New York City* (Königstein/Taunus, Germany: Ulrike Helmer Verlag, 2004).

TILBURY PARK
Tilbury, UK, 2003–2005
muf architecture/art
www.muf.co.uk

In early 2003, the architect group muf was commissioned to plan a community garden for Broadway Estate, one of the most socially disadvantaged housing developments in Tilbury. Surprised by the presence of ponies on the barren green areas of this 1970s apartment complex, which were taken for granted by the residents and not even mentioned in the official information, muf first initiated a research and art project—"A Horse's Tale"—to find out more about the special meaning of the public space for the residents and this rather unconventional utilization. A group of schoolchildren created a photographic inventory of the life of the ponies, which belonged to several residents, and collected their stories in a digital archive. Another group donned homemade horse costumes and reenacted these stories in the urban space. Photographs of this performance, hung as posters at the bus stops, called on passersby to think about their relationship to their own surroundings. In each of these actions, the horses symbolically represent the residents' desire for a more personal relationship to their immediate environment, one that goes beyond conventional modes of utilization or possession.

But this investigative research not only made the history of the area playfully available to experience, helping to give it a new self-confidence, but also facilitated the development of Tilbury Park together with the residents.

The result is a subtly designed park landscape. Slightly terraced levels of varying gradients divide what had been an undifferentiated landscape into sections with different characteristics. A meadow, a playground, amphitheater-like stairways, and an arena for equestrian events were hewn into the landscape. As archetypes, they form elements that are readily understandable. The limited space offers a range of possibilities for various uses and also allows for further elaboration based on the individual needs of the residents. (Ed.)

Tilbury Park_*muf architecture/art* 167

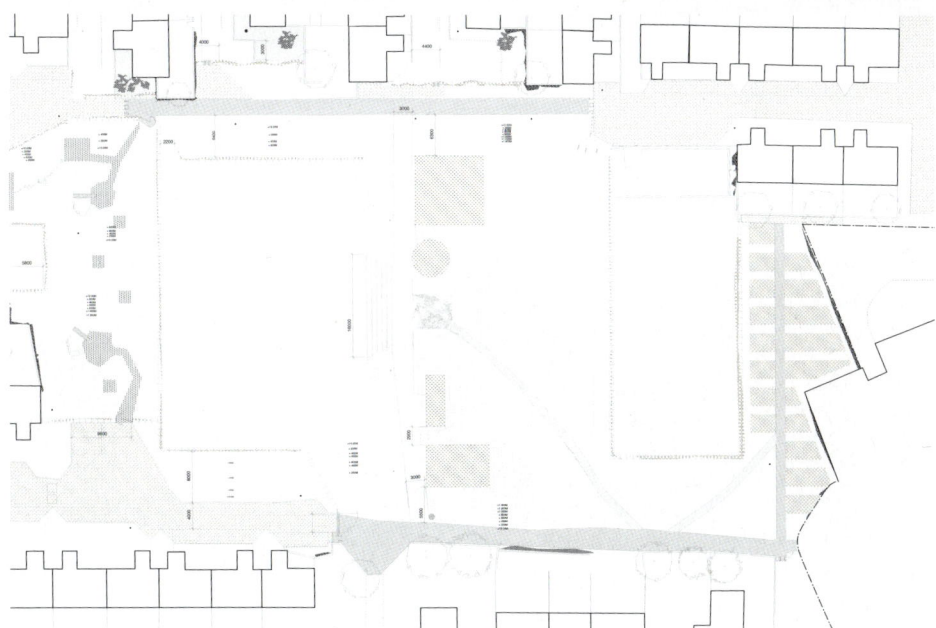

The research and art project "A Horse's Tale" (left) accompanied the development of the Tilbury Park community garden (right).

APPLE TREE COURT: AN URBAN OASIS
Salford, UK, 1996
The Residents of Apple Tree Court, with Anthony Milroy and the Arid Lands & Sustainable Communities Trust

Apple Tree Court is one of three apartment blocks in a once run-down 1960s development in downtown Salford. To be better able to influence the design of their own living environment, in 1988 the residents of this sixteen-story high-rise formed their own residents' association, and as a result in 1994 were able to secure the transfer to them from the city of responsibility for the administration of their building and the neighboring plot of land. Shortly afterwards, the Urban Oasis initiative was founded in partnership with Anthony Milroy, the head of the Arid Lands & Sustainable Communities Trust. This collaboration made it easier to gain access to monies from primarily private sources and to collect the donations needed to finance a community garden. Based on Milroy's experience with a Yemenite garden tradition that allows intensive land use in the tightest of urban spaces by way of vertical stacking, a green oasis now emerged step by step. The richly varied garden landscape in the midst of modernist architecture was created solely by volunteers. The different areas of the garden do justice to the diverse needs of the residents, at the same time providing them with fresh vegetables and fruits and granting the place as a whole a new identity. (Ed.)

COW—THE UDDER WAY
Liverpool, UK, 2004/05
Ulrike Steven, Paul Cotter, Gareth Morris, Heidi Rustgaard, Eike Sindlinger, and Susanne Thomas
www.theudderway.info

Walking down Park Street towards St. Gabriel's Church in Toxteth, a Liverpool neighborhood, a thrilling vista suddenly emerges. Expansive lawns generously open up among the individual rows of houses. The view looks down on the broad Mersey river, whose opposite bank houses harbors and industrial plants. This bank, by contrast, is home to an impressive montage consisting of an old gas tank, a towering industrial plant, and terraced houses. The landmarks of the city center can be seen on the horizon.

But what use is a poetic view that overlooks the facts behind the forms? Toxteth is one of the poorest and most disadvantaged parts of Liverpool. What this means—beyond the familiar, disturbing statistics—becomes evident when one encounters the masses of children on the streets and witnesses a six-year-old sniffing cigarette lighter fluid out of patent boredom and a few teenagers breaking a windshield just as a female driver is leaving her vehicle. Over the past few decades, Toxteth has increasingly become the reality of life for an underclass that began to form in Liverpool as it declined in economic importance after the Second World War; today, there are families here who are dependent on state support for the second or even third generation.

In this area dominated by urban problems, an experiment was set up that was remarkably simple. "COW—the udder way" consisted of no more than placing a small herd of cows in one of the many public spaces of Toxteth for nine days, and waiting and seeing what would happen. The action was characterized neither by broad networking with local actors beforehand, nor intensive public relations, nor initiatives or workshops for the residents, nor even a socially educative drive for sustainability. The initiators speculated (successfully) on the local dynamic that would develop spontaneously when a herd of cows suddenly turned up in the middle of Toxteth.

Historical and performative reasons provoked the choice of cows as protagonists. Small-scale dairy farming had been widespread in the area for some years after the Second World War, and many older residents remembered this immediately upon seeing the cows. In addition, the effect of the restfully grazing cows, their massiveness and apparent vulnerability should not be underestimated. This addressed a sensory aspect of experience that in light of the obviously difficult behavior of many Toxteth children could already be seen as a value in and of itself. Being able to touch and smell the cows meant especially communicating about their presence, using a comprehensible and strong sign language, without making a clear and transparent statement. Bringing cows into this context was a strong and at the same time a playful gesture. The conscious focus on this simple gesture and its physical and sensitive qualities, the emphasis on the symbolic content, as well as the planning background disengaged the intervention from any burden of striving towards social change.[1]

With this action, the initiators inspired reflection as to whether self-organized urban farming could be an option for Toxteth, and with it the question as to how empty lots could be used beyond the standard strategies of improvement. This exemplified the potential that lay in the vacant lots, making it available for experience for just a brief time. It is now up to the residents to draw their own conclusions.

Text by Gregor Harbusch

Translated from the German by Brian Currid

This project was developed for the *archplus* competition "Shrinking Cities: Reinventing Urbanism."

Participating in the action in Liverpool were Mark Davis, Neil Pinguenet, and Mark Saunders, Westcott Farm, Devon.

Note
1   On this point, see "Governmentalizing Planning" by Nikolaus Kuhnert and Anh-Linh Ngo in this volume.

On June 18, 2005, five cows, five calves, three cowherds, and a dairyman descended for nine days on the Toxteth district of Liverpool. Every day the cows were taken to one of four meadows on formerly built-up sites, and were grazed and milked in this strange environment as they normally are on a farm.

GROW!
Gera, Germany, 2004/05
anschlaege.de: Christian Lagé, Steffen Schuhmann, and Axel Watzke, with Johannes Touché and others

———

———

The promise of "blooming landscapes" in eastern Germany has become stale. Where investment assistance has not born fruit, now the demolition of apartment buildings is being subsidized.

What a waste of wonderfully arable terrain, for these now-vacant prefabricated high-rises offer space for practical utopias. If the abandoned spaces were transformed into farms instead of rubble, then sites could be developed where over the long run profits could be made. What would emerge is what is still lacking in eastern Germany: employment and self-produced added value.

A start should be made with farming higher-priced mushrooms. As it happens, the most common type of high-rise built in the German Democratic Republic—the WBS 70—is just ideal for mushroom-farming. Perfect growing conditions can be established without making the slightest change to the six-by-six basic plan underlying this model. A few details even seem to have been included specifically with mushroom-farming in mind. The utility duct between the kitchen and bathroom, for example, facilitates the installation of the necessary ventilation. The modular structure of the buildings can also be easily adapted to industrial farming. Nonetheless, without investment, without capital, no one can build up a functioning high-rise mushroom farm. We recommend that the prospective farmer either found a collective or release bonds.

Basically, any WBS 70 on a north-south axis could be a potential location for a mushroom farm. We carried out an economic feasibility study using Gera in East Thuringia as an example. Not only does this town offer a stock of highly qualified unemployed inhabitants and vacant residential housing, but it also has a very good transport infrastructure. This is a decisive advantage when it comes to distributing the easily perishable mushrooms.

Mushrooms are just one possibility. They are perhaps only the beginning of a seasonally independent, lucrative, and employment-intensive foodstuffs industry.

So a mushroom farm would not only be welcome in Gera, but the idea of using urban spaces for agricultural purposes would then also seem less absurd in general. Nothing is inconceivable: fruit, vegetables, and flower gardens in vacant lots, Christmas-tree or timber farms on abandoned industrial sites, or even a carp farm in the construction pits left behind by bankrupt investors.

———

This project was developed for the *archplus* competition "Shrinking Cities: Reinventing Urbanism." The original German title is "Bau an!"

———
———
———
———

175

Feral City

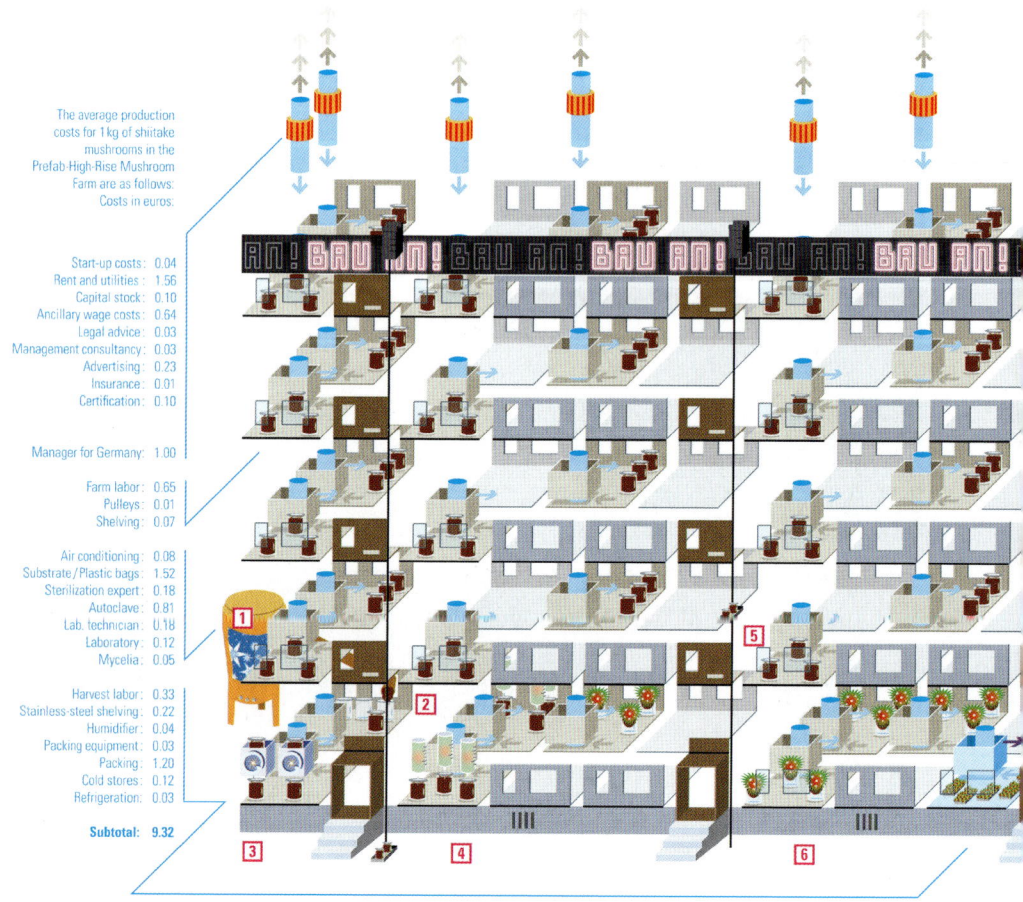

The average production costs for 1 kg of shiitake mushrooms in the Prefab-High-Rise Mushroom Farm are as follows:
Costs in euros:

Start-up costs: 0.04
Rent and utilities: 1.56
Capital stock: 0.10
Ancillary wage costs: 0.64
Legal advice: 0.03
Management consultancy: 0.03
Advertising: 0.23
Insurance: 0.01
Certification: 0.10

Manager for Germany: 1.00

Farm labor: 0.65
Pulleys: 0.01
Shelving: 0.07

Air conditioning: 0.08
Substrate/Plastic bags: 1.52
Sterilization expert: 0.18
Autoclave: 0.81
Lab. technician: 0.18
Laboratory: 0.12
Mycelia: 0.05

Harvest labor: 0.33
Stainless-steel shelving: 0.22
Humidifier: 0.04
Packing equipment: 0.03
Packing: 1.20
Cold stores: 0.12
Refrigeration: 0.03

Subtotal: 9.32

Diagrammatic illustration of an agrarian production process in a standard WBS-70 high-rise block; here, a shiitake mushroom farm. Water, calcium carbonate, and beechwood shavings are mixed together[1] and inserted into plastic bags.[2] These are sterilized in the autoclave.[3] Then they are inoculated in the laboratory with mycelia.[4] Every day 1,092 kg of mushroom substrate are produced. Kept in the dark at a temperature of 20°C, mycelia require around three months to grow through the substrate. They are stored for this purpose in one of 36 growing units. Each unit comprises a standard WBS-70 living room, kitchen, and bathroom, and has a surface area of 6 x 6 m. Shelving can be used to extend this surface area to a tillable surface of 66 m². [5] The units require good air-conditioning: the ambient air must be completely exchanged on an hourly basis. Air-conditioning technology is installed in existing duct shafts between the kitchens and bathrooms.

Grow!_anschlaege.de

9.32 : Balance

0.29 : Management
0.18 : Secretarial
0.14 : Travel costs
0.02 : Office furnishings
0.06 : Telephone/Internet
0.01 : Accounting

0.18 : Sales personnel
0.25 : Distribution manager
0.65 : Distribution personnel
0.07 : Vehicle hire
0.07 : Gas
0.11 : Miscellaneous

11.38 : Total

The average cost of producing 1kg of shiitake mushrooms in the Prefab-High-Rise Mushroom Farm Collective is 11.38 euros. The average retail price for 1kg of shiitake is 24 euros.

* Costs of converting offices for management (216 square meters) are not yet included in the above calculation.

Once the mycelia have completely grown through the substrate, they can be placed in cold stores for up to one month. Alternatively, they can be taken directly to a harvesting unit. [6]

Here, the plastic bag containing the substrate is removed. The substrate is placed on stainless-steel shelving at a temperature of 18°- 20°C, in humidity of 85% - 95% and lit by 200 lux. Ambient air must be exchanged on an hourly basis with sterile air. One square meter of shelving can accommodate a maximum of 16kg of mushroom substrate. After three days in the harvesting unit the first mushrooms can be harvested. [7]

Fresh mushrooms can be stored in a cold store at a temperature of 2°- 4°C for around one week. One kilogram of substrate yields approximately 225g of mushrooms. [8] With a staff of fourteen and optimal capacity usage of the harvesting units, a moderate crop of 3.6kg of mushrooms per square meter of shelving can be obtained. It would be possible, therefore, to market 237.6 kg of mushrooms daily. [9]

CONTRACTION CITY

Shrinkage stirs hopes that cities might be reduced to their essential core and in this way make qualitative gains. Depending on the respective viewpoint, the aim of such controlled shrinkage is to develop a compact city, an urban archipelago, or a reticular strip city. Even when, given the open property market and a mobile society, such comprehensive spatial concepts cannot be realized, they do mold perceptions of the city and influence where spatial interventions are located.

THE COMPACT CITY: A MODEL FOR EASTERN GERMAN CITIES?
Markus Hesse

Among the dominant visions of urban planning in Germany, the compact city is undoubtedly considered the most important model. Many urban-planning programs and policies are explicitly or implicitly conceived with reference to this idea. It represents a strategic countermodel to the reality of the postwar era: processes of suburbanization and dispersion are to be reversed in favor of a dense, urban settlement structure or multifunctional mixed-surface usage.

The compact city is at the same time the morphological building block of the "European city" model—an all-inclusive term that covers various political, cultural, and sociological conceptions of the urban.[1] In this context, the concept of the compact city not only gives consideration to the goals of urban planning, but also focuses on open space, infrastructure, traffic, and social cohesion: in the end, "urbanity."[2] This holistic character has made the model very attractive. At the same time, the openness has also been obtained at the cost of a concrete statement of what the compact city is truly able to provide.

The compact city derives its advantage from the tendency inherent in spatial artifacts (cities, industry) towards concentration. What Alfred Marschall called the "industrial atmosphere" resulted from internal and external savings based on agglomeration.[3] Agglomeration also largely serves to explain the nature of the city as such.[4] The progressive decentralization of urban functions due to lower energy costs and modern mobility has now weakened spatial ties, with no sacrifice of internal and external savings. The rest of the story is well known: the compact city came to be replaced by the dispersed urban landscape or city region.

Practice and Critique

In terms of urban planning, the compact city has manifested itself in two ways. First, the objective of the planners was the positive revaluation of the city centers—at least since the 1990s not only in the context of historical conservation strategies, but also as an approach to planning. The goal here was to strengthen functions other than only tertiary uses in urban centers (like housing), and thus to shore up the urban structure. Second, urban expansion was not to take the form of dispersed, low-density areas of single- and two-family residences, but compact, dense outlying quarters oriented towards the principle of suburban towns.

Although the model of the compact city in the context of the European city had indeed achieved a kind of hegemonic status, it was increasingly criticized in urban-planning discourse. On the one hand, there was a doubt that compact cities were still a *realistic* vision under the conditions of property markets and mass motorization. Indeed, in the growth conditions of the postwar years, urban development was dominated by processes of suburbanization. Contrary to the model doctrine, the growth of residential areas took place primarily outside the core areas and axes preferred by planners. On the other hand, the *effectiveness* of the model was called into question: the greatest problem of the model lies in the transformation of the character of space from a behavior-structuring prescription into an option. Short distances and attractive neighborhoods *can* be used, but no longer *need* to be used as was the case in the age of the pedestrian city. Transport, information, and communication systems as well as the growth of affluence have replaced the "logic of geometry," according to which the compact city had operated, with a "logic of choice." In brief: the compact city was at best a vision based on the old, but never a convincing plan for the new.

In light of these limits on realization and problems of effectiveness, the model of the compact, European city was declared no longer in line with contemporary needs.[5] Thomas Sieverts spoke in this context of the effective impact of images of the historical center, of industrial-era housing and city walls, and so forth. These images, he argued, are one-dimensional, and blind to the strengths and weaknesses of today's structures of settlement. This debate is still going full force; all the same, the critique has at least contributed to a pluralization of the debate. The orthodoxy with which the model was defended in the 1980s and 1990s has today given way to a more easygoing attitude, since beside centrists and de-centrists, there are also compromisers who see advantages in a mix of compact core-city forms and loose settlement structures.[6]

A Shrinkage-Induced Shift in Perspective: Back to the Compact City?

Can the compact city serve as a model under the transformed conditions of urban development and, if so, should this even be aspired to? As a mode of interpreting and predicting future development, shrinkage has indeed changed the frame of debate, and inevitably therefore also the way in which models are used.

Before the phenomenon of population decline leads us to immediately expect the renaissance of the compact city, we should examine a few assumptions. For it could well be that the importance of the issue of "shrinkage" is overestimated in current urban-planning discourse. All the same, the growth of settlement has indeed come to a halt for the time being in many areas all across Germany. In eastern Germany, the pressure has in fact almost been entirely reversed. But we still cannot be sure whether what is happening is a pendulum swing or some kind of secular change, that is, a general departure from city expansion and suburbanization via growth. There is much to suggest that growth in prospering regions will remain on the agenda, but this will no longer apply everywhere.

For the eastern German regions, where it is quite certain that the population will continue to stagnate or even decline and also age for some time, a second point is far more important: the reorganization of settlement structures will by no means necessarily take place according to the plan of the compact city. It would be too simple to interpret shrinkage as a physical-geometrical "retreating of the city to the core." This would underestimate the fundamental mechanisms of urban development in the same way as had been the case with growth-driven city planning. The real estate market will continue to localize land use according to the law of supply and demand, not necessarily according to the conceptions of the planner, even if the supply is quite significant indeed. Traditional location theory has already shown out that the availability of space and its qualitative appropriateness are two different issues. This leaves a significant potential for uncertainty.

Freedom of mobility will continue to exist in the future, as will the compulsion to be mobile. This will take place in a growing space and in larger radii, and will probably involve a great deal more long-distance travel. In terms of behavior, it should be expected that the ratio of local mobility—based on the rudiments of a compact city—to long-distance travel (work, consumption/culture, vacations) will be remixed entirely. More complex networks are forming. This means, de facto, that urban development will amplify the

Sixteenth-century Nuremberg epitomized the ideal compact city.

tendency already observed for some time towards the formation of fragmented, perforated city landscapes.[7] The compact city will be a part of this urban region, just like suburbia, the "Zwischenstadt," or urbanized villages. In the future, a more or less precarious coexistence might result, depending on the decline or growth, the contraction or extension of urban space.

This process challenges our traditional notion of the city, but that notion has basically been following a continuum since industrial-social urbanization. What role can the compact city play here? Until now, the model has been more a vision than a real plan, and this will change little in the future. But it can provide a rough guide, and identify certain channels for directing planning priorities. The compact city will nonetheless not be a one-to-one model of reurbanization. Urban development will continue to follow similar rules to those it followed in the industrial age, but it will take place under different conditions. We should thus be cautious and avoid any euphoria about our ability to control this process. Even in the days of growth and affluence, urban planning was only able to realize the European concept of the city in a limited sense. It thus seems all the more absurd to assume that planning will now be more successful in the context of competition, globalization, and the erosion of the welfare state. Nonetheless, the compact city does offer some concrete points of departure:

- First, nodal points must be created in the urban landscape, where principles of density and compactness can certainly play a dominant role. But the result will be something new: the old form of the city will mix with the usage structures of the postindustrial urban region.
- Second, every society needs "points of identification," including those that take the form of space or architecture. These need not only include the market square, late nineteenth-century ensemble, and church tower, but could also be a former steel plant,

The Compact City: A Model for Eastern German Cities?_Markus Hesse

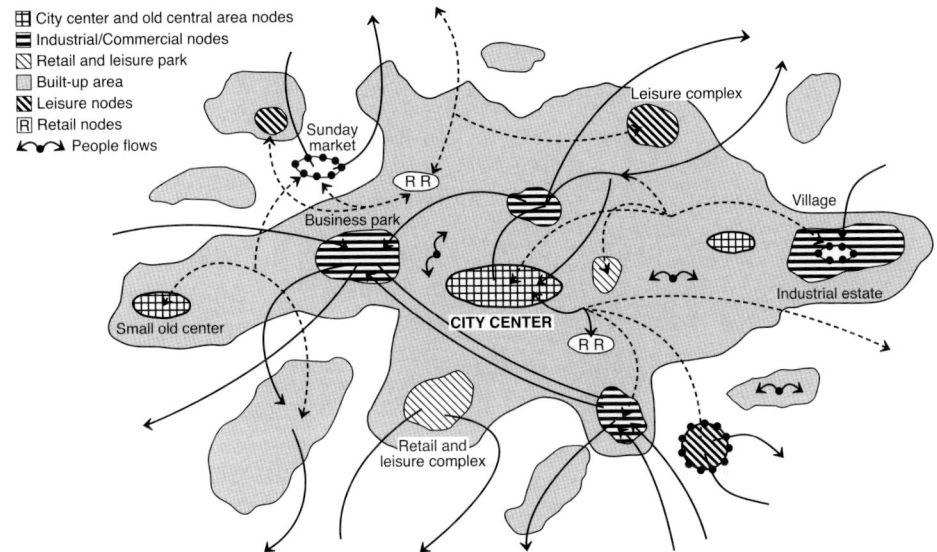

Today's urban landscapes lack clear spatial borders; instead, they organize streams of activity in space (diagram based on work by Patsy Healey, 1999).

old mining equipment, or what was once a factory. The more city landscapes will have to be accepted as a fact, the more sensible ways of designing these nodal points will emerge.

The compact city is then no longer a center and a point of crystallization, rather just one building block among many in the mosaic of the urban landscape. But it is also more than just a backdrop or a monument.

Translated from the German by Brian Currid

Notes
1   See Walter Siebel, ed., *Die europäische Stadt* (Frankfurt am Main: Suhrkamp, 2004).
2   See Martin Wentz, ed., *Die kompakte Stadt,* Die Zukunft des Städtischen 11 (Frankfurt am Main: Campus Verlag, 2000).
3   "Internal savings" are an effect of scale. The more produced of a certain good, the lower the price per unit, and the higher the profits (presuming the existence of a market). "External savings" rest on advantages of urbanization or localization, that is, when one has many similar companies in one place, as once was the case in the mining industry in the Ruhr and Saar regions, for example, or in the cutlery industry in Sheffield or Solingen. This density lowers production and marketing costs. The chance of obtaining both types of savings is of course much greater in cases of agglomeration—that is, in urban areas—than in the countryside.
4   See Gerd Held, *Potentiale der kompakten Stadt: Eine institutionenökonomische Studie über die spanische Schuhstadt Elche,* Dortmunder Beiträge zur Raumplanung 87 (Dortmund, Germany: Institut für Raumplanung der Universität Dortmund, 1998).
5   See Thomas Sieverts, *Zwischenstadt: Zwischen Ort und Welt, Raum und Zeit, Stadt und Land,* Bauwelt Fundamente 118 (Braunschweig, Germany: Vieweg, 1997).
6   Mike Jenks, Elizabeth Burton, and Katie Williams, eds., *The Compact City: A Sustainable Urban Form?* (London: E & FN Spon, 1996), 13.
7   See Markus Hesse and Stefan Schmitz, "Stadtentwicklung im Zeichen von 'Auflösung' und Nachhaltigkeit," *Informationen zur Raumentwicklung* 7/8 (1998): 435-453.

REMAKING BARNSLEY
Barnsley, UK, 2003–2033
Alsop Architects

———

Alsop Architects have developed new models of urbanism in consultation with the local residents of several cities in northern England affected by deindustrialization. For the next few decades, these are to form the basis for further urban development. The idea for Barnsley picks up on its past as an important trading city. Now, only the historic marketplace bears witness to this age: the coal industry and suburbanization have fundamentally transformed the once compact town. The concept relies on the strength of the marketplace in the town center and includes a new city wall; all future development is to concentrate on the area inside the latter.

While outside the city wall the urban sprawl will be scaled back so as to assume village-like structures, within the wall a dense, lively center is to emerge, with new businesses, offices, living areas, and leisure and cultural facilities providing the entire city with a sense of identity. The wall itself—a ten-story mixed-use construction—will represent a new interpretation of the medieval town wall, for its roof will sport a public park that offers a view of the city from a new perspective.

For the duration of the project's lengthy execution period, a halo of the same diameter as the planned wall will be projected over the city, depicting Barnsley's potential future. (Ed.)

———

BRADFORD CITY CENTRE MASTERPLAN
Bradford, UK, 2003–2020
Alsop Architects

—

—

The strategy for the former textile city of Bradford is exactly the opposite to that for Barnsley. The numerous empty postwar buildings in the town center are to be torn down to make way for a spacious park landscape with a lake. In this way, the original topography of the city with its two riverbeds will again be made available to experience. At the same time, the park will create a new bridge between once separate areas of the city. In the middle, where the two valleys meet, an artificial lake will form the empty center of the new Bradford, providing the basis for a sense of identity. (Ed.)

—

Contraction City

The master plan for Bradford—a city made up of several boroughs that have merged together—foresees both the creation of a new center and the reinforcement of the city's polycentric structure. Alsop Architects divided the city into 64 squares, each measuring one square kilometer and, as the conceptual model shows, assigned each of them a specific identity.

OSWALD MATHIAS UNGERS'S URBAN ARCHIPELAGO FOR SHRINKING BERLIN
Jasper Cepl

Berlin as a green urban archipelago: Oswald Mathias Ungers's vision is undoubtedly one of the most important planning concepts of the twentieth century for the ideal city. For a long time, his work was given little attention, but today, in light of the city shrinkage taking place in many parts of the world, interest in his vision is growing. Nonetheless, when it comes to actual details, practically nobody is familiar with his concept.

The idea was developed in 1977 during a summer academy that Ungers—then teaching at Cornell University—had organized with his students in Berlin. While they were busy designing "urban villas," Ungers and his collaborators—who included Rem Koolhaas and Hans Kollhoff—developed the concept of the "city within the city," which was then reworked and presented by Ungers as an "urban planning concept for Berlin's future development."[1]

The occasion was the discussion concerning the "International Building Exhibition" planned for the early 1980s in Berlin. Initially, following the model of the 1957 "Interbau" exhibition, a clearly demarcated demonstration area like the Hansaviertel was also planned for the "International Building Exhibition." But in the course of the preparations, the viewpoint won out that the aim should not be an exhibition of exemplary architecture but rather the repair of the city itself. In 1977, in what they called their *Morgenpost* campaign (after the newspaper in which it appeared), Josef Paul Kleihues and Wolf Jobst Siedler began insisting on revising the concept in this sense.

Ungers took a stand against the calls for urban repair with his concept of the urban archipelago. West Berlin was shrinking in 1977, and Ungers asked how this city marked by the war and the demolition craze of the postwar years could ever be "repaired." At best, Berlin had been rebuilt in a fragmentary way, and empty lots dotted the whole city, so that often it was very difficult to recognize continuity between the remains of the original perimeter development. Ungers saw room for an interpretation that allowed, indeed demanded, quite different perspectives.

As he remembered later in an interview, his impressions of Berlin in the postwar years would decisively influence his way of seeing things over the long term: "When I came to Berlin for the first time, I saw in Friedrichstadt a huge landscape in which stood individual monumental objects. Like a landscape with missing teeth. I experienced this reality, and not a historical reality that no longer existed."[2] Based on this experience, Ungers hoped to look ahead and provide the city with a new orientation. He wanted to work with the forces of shrinkage, not against them, so as to develop an exemplary image of how the city might look in the future.

Ungers's concept is presented in the form of eleven theses.[3] The starting point and first thesis is that of "the decline in population." Ungers cited estimates that predict a decline "during the 1980s equal to more than 10% of the present figure which is between 2.0 and 1.7 million inhabitants." If Berlin had been intact, the shrinkage alone would have hardly led to the considerations presented in the following. But in light of these conditions, Ungers demanded a new approach: "Since Berlin occupies a limited territory and political reality is such that it can be neither reduced nor increased, future strategies have got to be devised that will take into account a controlled decrease in the population density, without jeopardizing the general quality of the urban environment." With this plea,

Ungers was certainly the first to take this development seriously and look for new concepts of urban planning to meet the challenge.

Thesis 2 is a "critique of design theory to date," which takes the notion of urban repair as its starting point and has nothing to offer when confronted with the problem of shrinkage. In light of the fact that there was simply no need for building measures to remedy deficits, Ungers saw the idea of urban repair as a false nostalgia that did more harm than good. He was of the view that new qualities needed to be created on the basis of the shrinking itself if the further destruction of the city was to be avoided.

For, according to Thesis 3, "the problem of the population decline" concerns not only Berlin. Other large cities also have to contend with an increasing "exodus to suburban areas.... The consequence of this constant efflux is a general impoverishment, and, in a broader perspective, a partial decay of the city center." As a reason for this urban flight, Ungers named the increasing attractiveness of country living, which thanks to the car and television was no longer tantamount to a "flight from society.... With the improved means of transport both the spatial and the psychological distance has been considerably reduced."

Ungers pointed out that not only Berlin, but "most of the big cities of the world" were affected by the shrinkage problem. In New York, the population decline in some areas was "more than 60%," with the result that "entire districts have virtually been wiped off the map." Urban land was even being transformed back into farmland. In one "once highly populated district in Brooklyn" one thousand "urban farms" were to be built, Ungers wrote of one project that was certainly a great inspiration to him.

Ungers saw this and other examples of shrinking cities as "signs of a much more general tendency" that he and other urban planners had never expected. At the beginning of the 1970s, an incipient population explosion was taken as a given. At that time, Ungers was focused on planning whole new cities with his students for New York State. He had organized his entire teaching around the goal of preparing the future architects for "building for large numbers."

Then came the oil crisis. The Club of Rome warned of the "limits of growth," the birth control pill brought about a sudden drop in the birthrate, and the direction of history suddenly changed. Soon, the news of shrinking cities spread across the Western world. For Ungers it was like waking up from a bad dream. Now he took on the challenge of the opposite scenario. The city that seemed almost made to measure for working out a strategy for this new problem of shrinkage was West Berlin, an island artificially kept alive by the West. Although constantly losing inhabitants, the city could not shrink in size, because its borders were fixed immovably by the Wall.

The fourth postulate, central to Ungers's thesis, is "the concept of the city in the city."[4] During the same period, Léon Krier, a close associate of Ungers, was propagating a concept with a similar name: the notion of "cities within the city."[5] The demands of the two architects were basically quite similar. But in one decisive respect Ungers took a different approach. Krier's ideal city was a city that did not consist of zones, but of small quarters, each with its own core and identity, but similar in structure and appearance. For Krier, all cities within the city were the same, while for Ungers—as becomes clear in the next postulate—each urban island was to be different.

On the one hand, Ungers declared smaller, unified, and manageable cities to be more human and livable, but on the other he believed that contradiction was a key characteristic of urbanity. In his view, a city is characterized by the "overlapping of many opposite and divergent conceptions," in contrast to "villages, rural populated areas, urban districts, and small or medium towns [whose] chief characteristic is expressed in the predominance of a single principle or, if there are more than one, these will nevertheless be complementary to each other."

Ungers arrived at a conclusion that basically summed up the entire concept: "These considerations lead one to ask whether within the context of a selective programme for the reduction of urban over-population, or even of a partial demolition of those districts that are superfluous and work badly, the reduction of the population of Berlin might not perhaps provide an outstanding opportunity to redevelop zones that no longer satisfy technical, social and structural demands. Simultaneously, those zones that deserve to be preserved should be identified, or, at the outside, their characteristics should be underlined, and if incomplete, completed. These enclaves liberated from the anonymity of the city would in their quality of quasi islands form a green urban archipelago in a natural lagoon." What Ungers imagined as a synthesis was basically an encyclopedic collection of all possible ideal cities.

Thesis 5, "the differentiated urban structure," explains according to which selection criteria those urban islands worthy of being maintained should in a first step be named and in a second step prepared, that is, unified and thus individualized, so that Berlin could become a "federation [of] single towns with different structures, developed in a deliberately antithetic manner. A decisive factor in the choice ought to be the degree of clarity and comprehensibility of the existing basic and design principles." The first step thus consists in finding urban areas with already recognizable characteristics that are worthy of being maintained and accentuated.

Aesthetic questions or personal preferences for this or that city form should play no role in determining "so-called identity-spaces.... The architectural and planning intentions for the future consist solely in enucleating the true configuration of each single island-in-the-city on the basis of which it was first chosen." In contrast to Krier, for Ungers different urban forms were equal in value: "Substantially, therefore, the Märkische Viertel, Westend, Kreuzberg, and Lichterfelde are included in this project and should be regarded as complementary elements with different characteristics having the capacity to raise the supply and hence the freedom of choice."

Ungers found this new freedom of choice appropriate for the individualistic society of the time. "The pluralistic project for a city within the city is in this respect in antithesis to the current planning theory which stems from a definition of the city as a single whole. This corresponds to the contemporary structure of society which is developed more as a society of individuality with different demands, desires and conceptions." Ungers thus envisioned not only an open urban system in which many different sites combined to form a multiple and complex urban environment, but also a pluralistic concept in political and social terms, where numerous, ideologically differing views existed alongside one another.

And so to the execution of the plan. Thesis 6 outlines "the establishment of the area of city-islands." This phase is "both the result of a programme and a formal and urban design job." The islands are not only characterized by their morphological structure, but also by their programs for use, which are varied and should also be specified.

For filling out the fragments, Ungers believed that structural comparisons with other cities or urban areas should serve as a guiding principle. In this way, the "ideal project

Contraction City

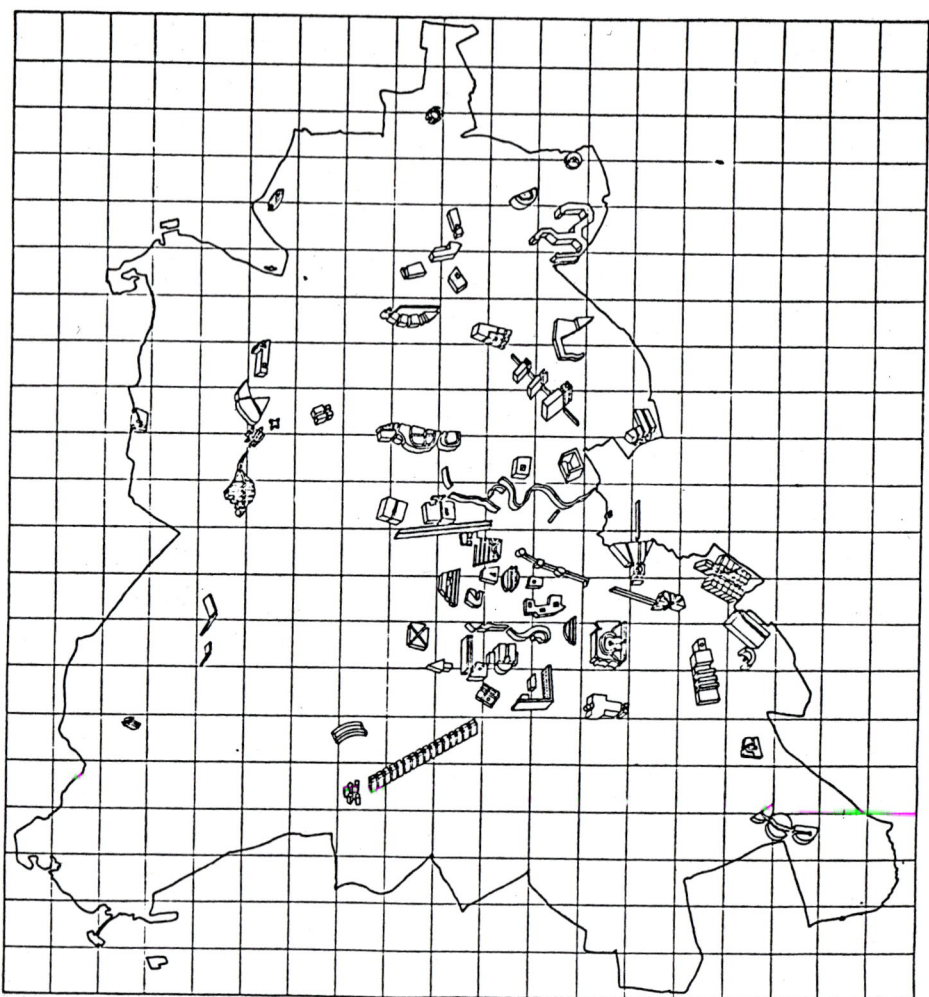

▲ The existing city is deconstructed so as to become a series of selective urban islands, each with a specific identity. Oswald Mathias Ungers, 1977.
▶ By comparing structures with other cities or concepts of cities, individual morphological structures are elaborated for each urban island in Berlin: Southern Friedrichstadt/Karlsruhe (top), Görlitzer Bahnhof/Central Park, New York (center), and Unter den Eichen/Leonidov's urban concept for Magnitogorsk (bottom).

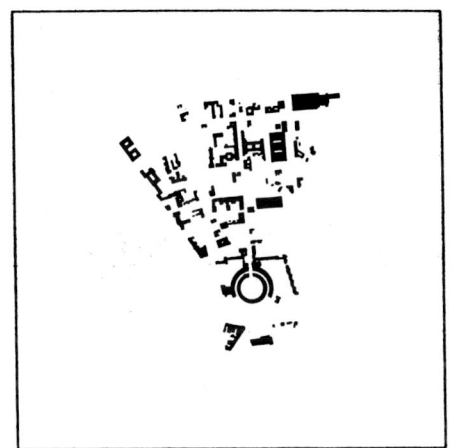
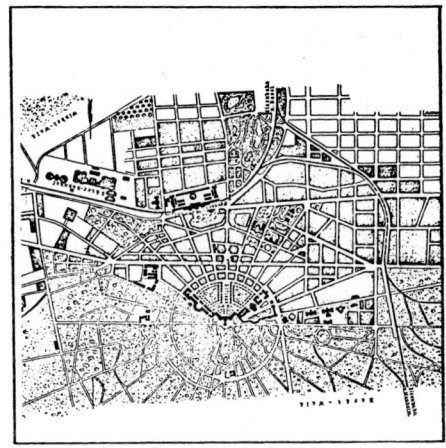
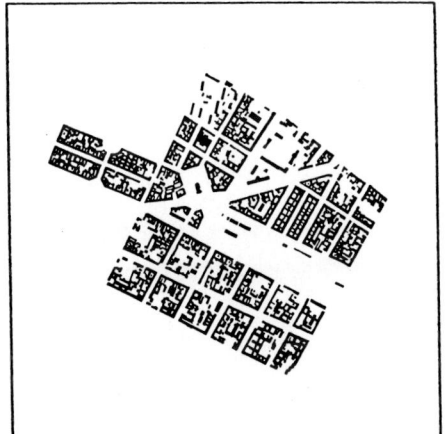
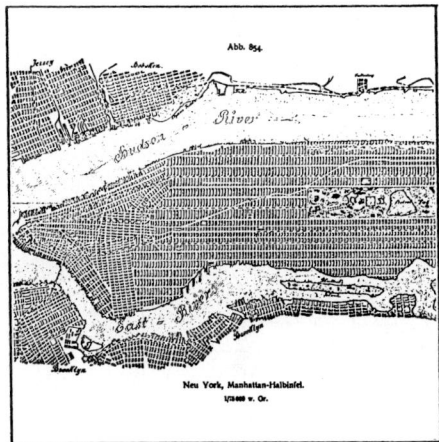
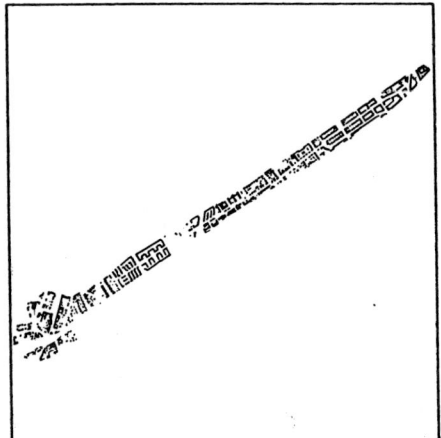
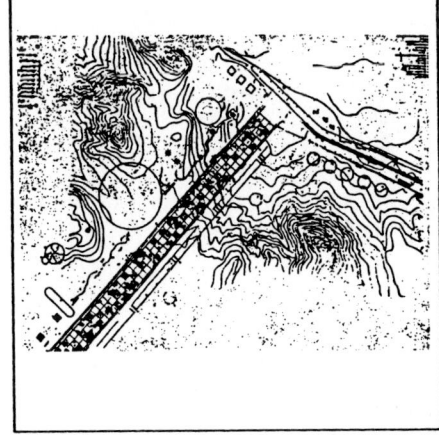

Contraction City

A plan by OMA/Rem Koolhaas for the city of Melun-Sénart (1987) takes up Ungers's concept of an urban archipelago—to which Koolhaas previously contributed—for the shrinking city of Berlin. This analogous concept foresees the creation of a new town on the greenfields at the gates of Paris. The project defines programmatic belts with collective functions interspersed with open green zones that—irrespective of how future architecture might develop nearby—are intended to guarantee the city identity and beauty. The islands between the belts have their own individual development structures and are otherwise initially undefined. Their characters will thus be able to freely unfold over the twenty-year construction period, depending on their respective locations, architects, and proposed development programs.

of Karlsruhe with its radial axis," for example, "might serve as an example for a configuration of the southern part of Friedrichstadt." Similarly, Manhattan's Central Park could serve as a model for the area around Görlitzer Bahnhof (railway station), and Leonidov's linear-city concept for Magnitogorsk might provide a model for the street Unter den Eichen. Not only Leonidov's concrete plans for this city, but the regional-planning concepts of Soviet revolutionary architecture in general were of great significance for Ungers. The plan presented by Mikhail Barshch and Moisei Ginzburg for transforming Moscow into a "Green City" also served as a model for the concept of the urban archipelago; in this plan, only a few characteristic islands would remain in an ocean of green.[6] (For more on the Russian disurbanists, see the following essay by Christiane Post and Philipp Oswalt.)

In a similar way, if on a larger scale, areas of Berlin with a more defined structure were to be chosen so that their "extremely different" structures could then be developed further. For Ungers these included "buildings in blocks but also single, radial, linear and reticular forms, open and closed systems, a network of regular and irregular streets, and different graphic, spatial, functional and social characteristics."

Thesis 7, "the green archipelago," now explains how the concept of the city in the city "is completed antithetically by the surfaces in between the islands-in-the-city.... The structures here, by now valueless, ought to be allowed to be gradually retransformed into natural zones and pastures, without any rebuilding." It is here that the weakness of the concept becomes clear, for Ungers failed to come up with many superfluous structures: he named in particular the areas around Kemperplatz, Görlitzer Bahnhof, and Potsdamer Bahnhof, and at a later point in time Tempelhof Airport. There was in fact precious little that could be sacrificed without much ado, but it was just as necessary to name what was to be eliminated as it was to say what was going to be built. Nonetheless, as Ungers explained: "These islands-in-the-city would, in other words, be divided from each other by strips of green, thus defining the framework of the city in the city, and thereby explaining the metaphor of the city as a green archipelago."

In this way, a new kind of synthetic, "modified nature" emerges, that in its rich contrasts heightens rather than diminishes the experience of the city, not least because of the anti-urban uses that find their place here. "The natural grid ought also to welcome the infrastructure of this technological age in which we live, that is to say, it should embrace a motorway network to link up the islands-within-the-city to one another, it ought also to include supermarkets, drive-in cinemas, drive-in banks and similar services connected with the car just as any other typology of the twentieth century which depends not only on space but on mobility."

As a professor at Berlin's Technical University, Ungers had already been very interested in motorways and the like, and had explored the architectural use and exaltation of these large infrastructures in the United States with his students. These considerations now found their way into his concept of the ideal city; the perfect form here has a place just as does the formless. Here, the essential parts of modern urban life that cannot be combined with the traditional closed city are given the space they need, and short-term uses are also integrated into the plan. "Next to suburban zones with a different density, wooded areas, shooting preserves, natural parks, gardens, family allotments, urban agriculture, and infrastructural services of the modern age, it should also be possible to rely on green zones for 'parking' temporary mobile facilities."

This makes all sorts of new, alternative, transitory lifestyles and forms of entertainment possible. This includes "mobile homes" as an alternative to "living in green areas," "amusement zones of the Disneyland type and national parks for the friends of nature," and the "setting aside of production areas in the 'industrial parks' style of American cities with leisure time facilities and amenities for play and sport for the workers."

It is here that the true value of this conception reveals itself, not so much in the idea of deconstruction—the shrinking of Berlin just made it possible to think further. Ungers really had no answer to the question as to how deconstruction should actually take place, he only envisioned the final state: an ideal city that integrated the experience of the American city with its extensive highway networks and endless suburban spaces with the ideal forms of the European city with its dense public spaces.

The significance of the concept lies in its attempt to develop a notion of the urban that orders the wild chaos of cities, but in so doing freely recognizes the contradictions—in contrast to the plans for the "International Building Exhibition," for which the concept was developed. The International Building Exhibition took a different approach: the shrinking of Berlin was not considered a grave problem and hardly played any role at all in the planning of this project.

Ungers, who had originally been entrusted with the projects for the southern part of Friedrichstadt, decided not to sit on the International Building Exhibition management board after all and returned to building after many years of teaching. He was now interested in making his own contribution to the contrast-rich city architectures inherent in the concept of the "city in the city," with its juxtapositions of formal visions. This probably also explains the subsequent development of his architecture, especially its severity.

The concept of the urban archipelago was pioneering; it was a clear presentation of Ungers's understanding of the urban and still counts as one of the essential elements of his work. But as Rem Koolhaas also admitted in 1086: "The green urban archipelago project became for me the absolute model of the European metropolis."[7] This was made very clear in his design for the new town Melun-Sénart in France (1987), which was based on a system of urban islands and green corridors. His descriptions of cities like Atlanta or Singapore also clearly take the ideal of the urban archipelago as their standard.

Koolhaas has also turned to the question of how the demolition of urban areas might proceed. For the design of Paris-La Défense, his studio OMA proposed a strategy of orderly retreat: over a period of 25 to 30 years, parts of the area should be "freed" of buildings, not in order to create an urban archipelago, but ultimately to make room for a grid city. But this vision of the gradual development of an ersatz Manhattan is of course just as unrealistic as Ungers's vision for shrinking West Berlin. More recent suggestions, like the "core and plasma" strategy inspired by Ungers's urban archipelago and introduced by the architects of the Leipzig initiative L21, are also more valuable as ideal plans and less useful for the actual formulation of practicable policy.

So, ultimately, the question remaining is how the concept Ungers introduced can help us today, even if cannot be realized and—like most modernist urban visions—would ultimately fail due to the fact that land cannot be as easily disposed of as Ungers suggests. Urban building land is largely in private hands, and its owners would surely find a concept of selective disurbanization quite arbitrary: what could justify the fact that one property owner is allowed to benefit from an intensification of use, while the property of another is obliterated and made worthless? The only solution would be to take the entire city out of private hands.

At any rate, it is basically irrelevant for the concept itself whether the city is shrinking or growing. This is not an actionistic, but a contemplative utopia—an attempt to provide the existing heterogeneous city with a concept; and in this sense, Ungers's urban archipelago is also an ideal for the twenty-first century.

Translated from the German by Brian Currid

Notes

1. Oswald Mathias Ungers, Rem Koolhaas, Peter Riemann, Hans Kollhoff, and Arthur Ovaska, "Cities Within the City: Proposals by the Sommer Akademie for Berlin," *Lotus International* 19 (1978): 82-97. This is a revised translation of the manuscript "Die Stadt in der Stadt: Berlin das grüne Stadtarchipel; Ein stadträumliches Planungskonzept für die zukünftige Entwicklung Berlins." (Unfortunately, the translation is in part quite poor indeed. Nonetheless, since this is the only published version of the material, I have chosen to use the translation basically as is, with a few minor alterations.—Trans.)
2. Oswald Mathias Ungers in conversation with Armando Kaczmarczyk, "Reparatur ist reaktionär: Die Stadt ist kein Dorf," *werk und zeit* 4 (1985), 3.
3. The first seven theses explain the concept and are explored in detail in the following. The subsequent theses are less important for our purposes and will not be discussed here, but let us at least list their titles: Thesis 8: "The urban villa as a form of residential building"; Thesis 9: "Transformation of the city in the course of history"; Thesis 10: "Standards and definition of objectives for the future"; and Thesis 11: "Scheduled project times."
4. The titles of Theses 4 and 5 were erroneously switched around in the Lotus International version of the text (see note 1).
5. See Léon Krier, "Cities Within the City," *A+U* 84, no. 11 (1977): 69-152.
6. Of course, Ungers must also have been inspired by older planning concepts for Berlin, like Scharoun's idea of an urban landscape. For more on this and the model character of the constructivist designs, see Oswald Mathias Ungers, "Berlin: A Morphological History," *Urban Design International* 2, no. 6 (September/October 1981), 20-25, 40.
7. Rem Koolhaas in conversation with Patrice Goulet and Nikolaus Kuhnert, "Die erschreckende Schönheit des 20. Jahrhunderts," *ARCH+* 86 (August 1986): 34-43, here p. 36.

RUSSIAN DISURBANISM
Christiane Post and Philipp Oswalt
—
—

Revolution and civil war had a significant impact on urban development in Russia. Beside a general economic crisis and drastic supply shortages, the initial years following the October Revolution were also marked by the destruction, depopulation, and unstoppable decay of Russian cities. Millions of people fled the cities to settle in the countryside. St. Petersburg had a prewar population of 2,440,000; Petrograd (St. Petersburg's name from 1914 until its change to Leningrad in 1924) had only 706,000 inhabitants by 1920—a decrease of 71.1%. Gorky described the decline of the capital as follows: "Petrograd is dying. Everyone is leaving the city, by foot, by horse, by train. There are dead horses lying in the streets, the dogs eat them. The city is unbelievably filthy. The Moika and the Fontanka are full of garbage." The population of Moscow was cut in half, while in other Russian cities the number of residents decreased by an average of 30%.

Against this backdrop of drastic urban depopulation, triggered by ever-worsening supply shortages that forced the population to begin small-scale agriculture on land just outside the city or to move entirely to the country, Russian urban planners turned to the idea of the "garden city." Areas on the city limits and suburban zones became more attractive for construction. Settlements called "vegetable garden cities" developed spontaneously on the outskirts of the larger cities. The theory of the garden city was declared official urban-planning doctrine in the early 1920s. New workers' housing developments were to be constructed according to this model, and older cities redesigned by a policy of deconcentration and greening.

A key turning point in urban planning, which stagnated in the 1920s because of the Civil War and economic crisis, came with the first Five-Year Plan in 1929. This plan, which had the goal of building up socialist industry on a large scale, included a radically new organization of the productive forces in the country. But the plan did not contain any stipulations regarding the settlement patterns that were to be linked to this spatial transformation. This points to the secondary importance given to urban planning in an economic policy focused on accelerated industrialization and the forced collectivization of agriculture.

The debates among experts regarding a form of housing that would be appropriate to the new developments began in 1929. Inspired by Marx and Engels, they were essentially targeted at overcoming the opposition of city and country and implementing a collective way of life. Beside the planning of new cities, the other issue was the remodeling of existing cities, and especially of Moscow, the new socialist capital.

The search for an alternative to the "outmoded" city played a central role in this debate, which also found some resonance in the media. At first, the party leadership did little to influence the discussion, as was typical of the relative freedoms that characterized the beginning of the first Five-Year Plan.

In 1929, the debate on the construction of new socialist cities was marked by two contrary positions: on the one hand, the conception of the "socialist city" *(sotsgorod)* developed by the economist Leonid Sabsovich; on the other hand, the "socialist mode of settlement" *(sotsrasselenie)* developed by the sociologist Mikhail Okhitovich.

Sabsovich believed that the decentralized distribution of industry across the entire country and the concentration of agricultural production in large farms would soon dissolve the opposition between city and country, blurring the differences between urban and village settlement. The reorganization of the settlement structure would then render necessary an entirely new type of socialist city. This new type was to be based on the "radical socialist reformation of everyday life," and a "total redesigning of life on the basis of complete socialization." Expanded green zones, efficient roads, and large, standardized "dwelling combines" were to form the basis of the new, radically modern city under socialism.

Sabsovich's sotsgorod concept, which initially found general acceptance, met with opposition in late 1929 in the form of the disurbanist vision of the dissolution of the city. Okhitovich fundamentally rejected any retaining of city structure, even in the radically new form proposed by the "urbanists." He was also convinced that the new way of life required immediate implementation, but not in the shape of urban concepts and large apartment complexes. He thus proposed the dissolution of the cities in favor of linear settlements along existing or planned traffic routes or electricity transmission lines. The architecture for this entirely new type of settlement structure was to consist of standardized, prefabricated, and demountable living units. The reference model for Okhitovich's "socialist settlement" was Henry Ford's decentralized "anti-city." However, with their linear model of the city the disurbanists were seeking to establish a balance between the individual and the collective, between the individualist urbanism of single-family homes in North America and the model of forced collectivization proposed by the Russian urbanists. These linear settlements were to consist of autonomous, minimal dwelling units for each individual complemented by community facilities.

These two basic positions—*sotsrasselenie* versus *sotsgorod*—then underwent further elaboration in urban-planning competitions, which represented an important medium for the debates of the period. While their aim was to pave the way for concrete, practicable plans, in actual fact they also served to clarify fundamental positions and attempts to implement them. Exemplary for this controversy between urbanism and disurbanism were the biddings held for Zelenyi Gorod (literally "Green City"), northeast of Moscow, and for Magnitogorsk, the most important model city of the first Five-Year Plan. In the context of the debate on shrinking cities, the plans for the Green City near Moscow are especially interesting, given that the disurbanist model proposed a radical strategy of deconstruction for the capital.

The Green City near Moscow was inspired by the idea of making the concept of the dacha accessible to all. The initial idea of a weekend housing settlement was followed by that of a model workers' colony, a forest spa, and a proletarian country sanatorium. Against the background of the urban-planning debate and the accompanying demand to "already" build a "socialist city" in 1929, it was asked whether the Green City should only be a "city of relaxation," or whether it could not also serve as a model for the new forms of socialist settlement.[1]

At the end of 1929, an architectural bidding competition was held for the Green City. The most radical entry was submitted by the architects Moisei Ginzburg and Mikhail Barshch. Both took a stand against any kind of pure leisure zone, changed the task at hand, and proposed the complete disurbanization of Moscow and its surroundings. Ginzburg and Barshch wanted to "redesign Moscow in a socialist way" and dissolve the entire city in "greenery." In their vision, living was to mean rest and relaxation. A linear ribbon settlement along the main traffic arteries seemed in line with their ideas. They

Contraction City

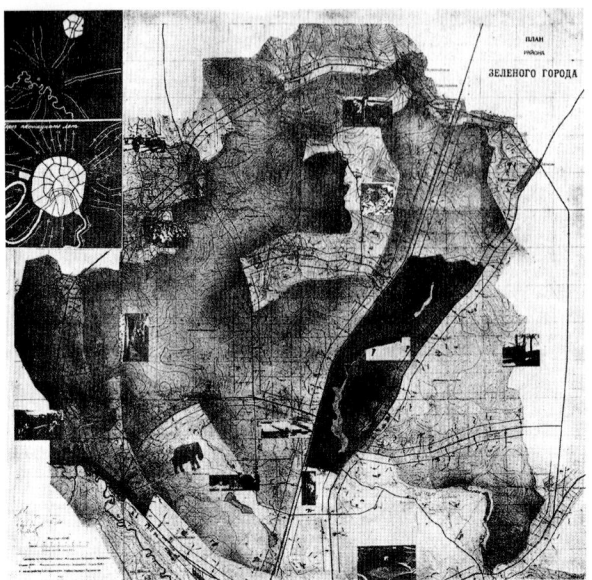

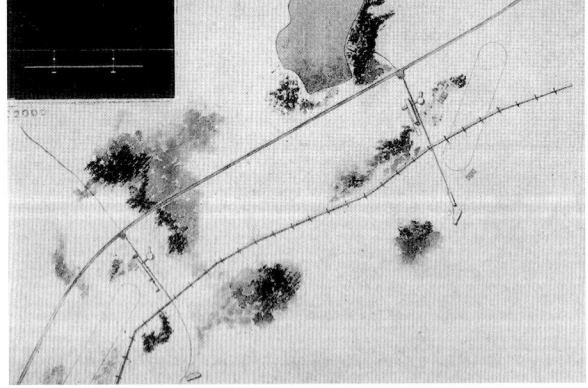

The proposal submitted by Ginzburg and Barshch to the architectural competition for the recreational settlement "Green City" outside Moscow (1930) foresaw not only construction that runs parallel to utilities, in line with the principles of disurbanization (above), but also an analogous deconstruction of Moscow itself. The belt of housing runs parallel to the streets; the communal facilities lie in between.

considered their planned Green City (for 100,000 inhabitants) a part of the socialist reconstruction of the capital. According to them, Moscow should be allowed to decay completely into Green Cities by way of "passive" renovation: decay and demolition of the existing housing stock.

In their article, Ginzburg and Barshch described the "gradual lessening of the settlement of Moscow" as the "emphatic and insistent systematic withdrawal from Moscow." This first step was to be followed by the "resettlement of Moscow's working population, not within Moscow but along the arteries that link Moscow with other centers in the vicinity." The third measure was based on "the broad dispersion of most of Moscow's industry and its academic and administrative institutions," and consisted of "a ban on all building in Moscow and the systematic greening of all free spaces." Specifically: "All construction in Moscow is to consist in landscaping new green spaces, with the goal of transforming the city into a central park of relaxation and culture towards which its lines of socialist housing settlements will lead and converge. In economic terms, this process should take place in an entirely painless way. We are namely still compelled," Ginzburg and Barshch wrote, "to use the surface area of existing buildings. But we will not invest any more in new construction. We will patiently wait for the old buildings to decay on their own; we will wait for their amortization. Then the demolition of these buildings and neighborhoods will be a painless process of purifying Moscow. We will keep the characteristic old parts of Moscow and carefully preserve them: the Kremlin, parts of aristocratic Moscow with the streets and palaces around Arbat and Povarskaya, part of Prechistenka, the Zaryad'e shopping and business district, Zamoskvorech'e, Myasnitskaya, and the proletarian quarter Krasnaya Presnya. We will turn all the other parts into a huge park."[2]

The increasing saturation of the city with parkland opened the opportunity to develop completely new ways of living, a mix of urban development and nature. The "need for spatial expanses," according to Ginzburg and Barshch, is "so important that it is the basis of the entire solution to the housing question. The dwelling unit is characterized by good ventilation and light on two sides. Only this provides a feeling of distance and closeness to nature.... The windows take up the entire wall from floor to ceiling: the sun saturates the entire living space. These folding windows transform the accommodation unit into a covered terrace, surrounded by green. The room thus loses its closed character. It dissolves into nature, becoming a horizontal surface.... The entire organization of the settlement is such that beyond the folding windows lie the wide spaces of gardens, parks, and collective farms."[3]

Walkways would connect the accommodation units to stations placed at regular intervals along Yaroslavl Highway. These stations or highway stops, which would also be equipped with garages, were to be the endpoints for private and public transport to the Green City. According to the planners' conception, no noise or dust from the highway was to penetrate the residential area. Community supply facilities were to be placed halfway between the stations and the accommodation units, no more than five to ten minutes away. These supply stations, which were to be accessible by covered walkways, were to include cafeterias as well as collective and individual rest areas linked to a small sport complex. Daycare centers, schools, technical academies, and cultural institutions were to be placed in the "virgin countryside" on the other side of the highway.

Ginzburg and Barshch emphasized that their proposed solution was only one of several possible variations, and that even if the same principles were adhered to, the

Contraction City

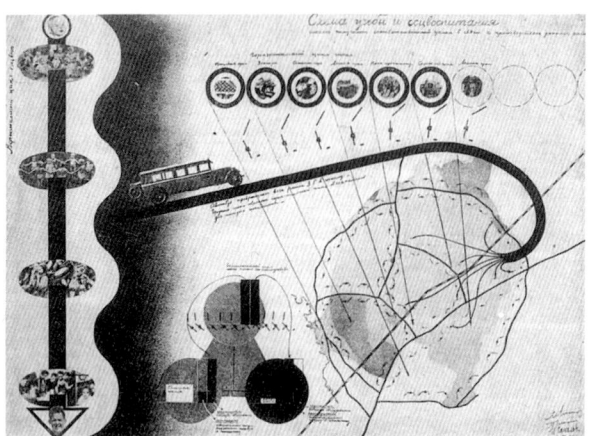

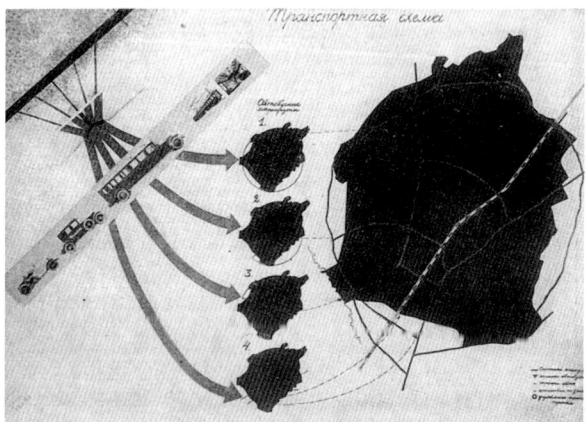

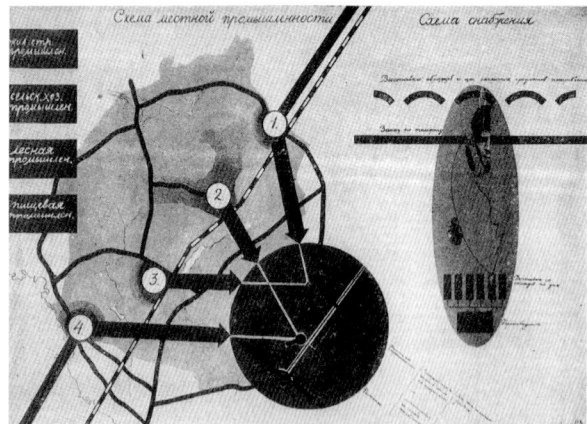

The spatial organization of the urban functions of education (top), transport (center), and industry (bottom) was designed to optimize their respective traffic flows and interlink them as much as possible.

variations remained numerous. "The better we succeed in freeing Moscow, the easier it will be to resettle it. The more complicated it seems, the denser the settlement belt will become. But we will also follow the principle of unrestricted construction, whose density will be regulated by the possibilities offered by the cheapest construction materials and the shortest possible amortization periods."[4]

At almost the same time as the competition for the Green City, a competition was held for the construction of Magnitogorsk, a prototypical socialist city that was to house the largest steel plant in the world. In the collective project presented by Barshch, Okhitovich, and others, the ideas of disurbanism were concretized in a very different way than in the Moscow competition. Here, the focus was more on concrete architectural, programmatic, and functional ideas.

In the disurbanists' plans, settlement was not to be long-lived: it was conceived as light, mobile, and temporary. Not only were the old cities to be abandoned to gradual decay and dissolved into linear settlements, but new construction—in the Magnitogorsk project—was to consist of impermanent, small wooden houses that could be erected and dismantled on site in a few hours, and—for the time an unbelievably modern idea—that were to be equipped with telephones. "For a long-term sinking of costs, it is necessary ... to shorten the amortization period. This in turn will allow the use of cheaper materials" and thus avoid an "unnecessarily long life span."[5] Construction and settlement were to be only short-lived and were to disappear if they hindered the development of new modes of living. At the same time, they should be very easy to alter, which is why the "construction elements must be made of local resources and secondary raw materials" that "ensure the undisturbed expansion of the living space 'upwards and outwards.'"[6]

The emphasis on "local" raw materials was a response to the existing economic shortages and at the same time offered opportunities for local self-help and the beginnings of local autonomy. These aims are also supported in the disurbanist settlement model. Large areas of the Green City consist of forests, which are at the same time the basis for urban forestry and construction, and thus a supply of construction materials. Exemplary for this vision is also the plea against a centralized water system and for decentralized sewage disposal. Here the same concept of an ephemeral, resource-saving, and mobile settlement was formulated as that found 65 years later in MVRDV's "Light Urbanism" project—a concept that today has still lost none of its currency.

The disurbanists' approach was so innovative and radical that it even included the opportunities offered by today's telecommunications technology for this form of settlement, describing the idea of teleshopping—today an important way of furnishing sparsely populated, shrunken regions. In the design of the Green City near Moscow, the park between the linear settlements features "a network of model exhibitions, where the various articles and their prices can be displayed. Every resident of the Green City can order the required item by telephone and have it sent from the warehouse."[7]

In the designs for Magnitogorsk, something analogous was proposed: "The goods must be brought to the consumer.... The commercial network must be broadly spread out, that is, it must be mobile.... But not just commodities should be delivered to the customers, rather representatives from the delivery companies and if necessary workmen will also come to the customer's home.... Each dwelling should have a radio, and, if possible, a telephone. Each bus station is to be equipped with a public telephone. As long as it is not possible to place a telephone in each dwelling, communication between

Contraction City

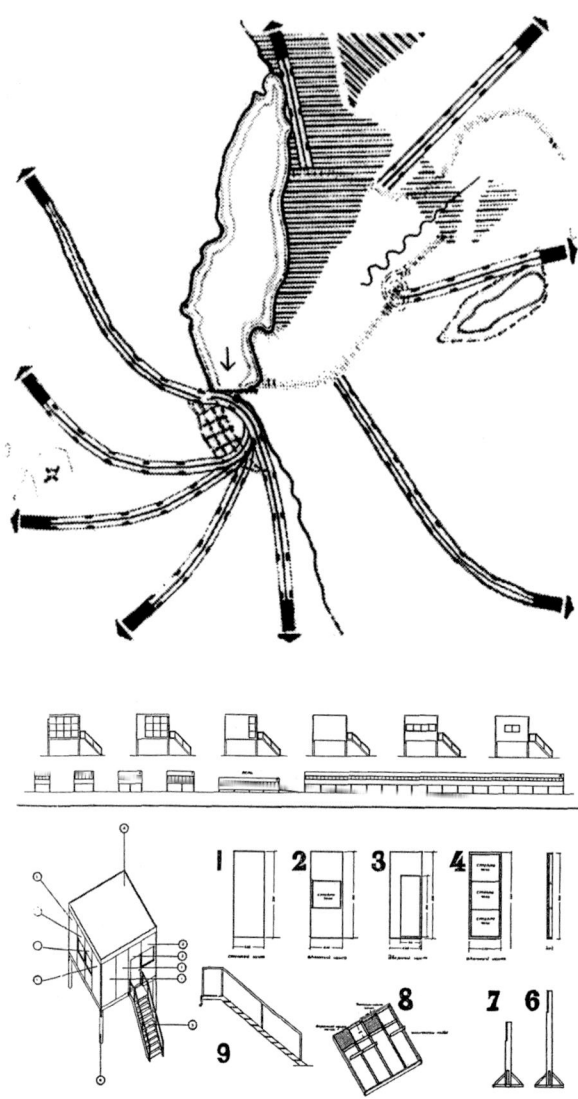

The master plan for Magnitogorsk by Barshch, Okhitovich, and others (1930) was based on the idea of ribbon development along the axes of primary utilities. The proposed dwelling units were lightweight wooden constructions that could be rapidly assembled and disassembled.

bus stations and apartments will take place using signals." And consumers should use "cashless transactions wherever possible."[8]

Although the designs of the disurbanists never became a reality in the Soviet urban planning of the 1930s—after the political shift of 1931, which brought a rejection of experimental urban planning, the disurbanists were considered anarcho-individualists and thus anti-socialists—they are a crucial element of the overall history of urban development. They were a source of inspiration for Ivan Leonidov's theory of city expansion and Le Corbusier's "Cité linéaire industrielle," a confirmation of Bruno Taut's "Dissolution of the Cities," and the point of departure for Frank Lloyd Wright's vision of "Broadacre City." In the current debate about shrinking cities, the works of the disurbanists represent an important position, especially with respect to the formulation of urban models and concepts, that can help us to grasp current urban changes and to elaborate their unique characteristics and potentials.

Translated from the German by Brian Currid

This article is based on research presented in Harald Bodenschatz and Christiane Post, eds., *Städtebau im Schatten Stalins. Die internationale Suche nach der sozialistischen Stadt in der Sowjetunion 1929-1935* (Berlin: Verlagshaus Braun, 2003).

Notes
1. The union of older industrial centers with new Green Cities was also planned at the end of the 1920s for other cities such as Ivanovo, Leningrad, and Khar'kiv.
2. Mikhail Barshch and Moisei Ginzburg, "Zelenyi Gorod," *Sovremennaia arkhitektura* 1/2 (1930), 18, 22.
3. Ibid., 31.
4. Ibid., 18.
5. See Mikhail Barshch et al., "Magnitogor'e. K sheme Genplana," *Sovremennaia arkhitektura* 1/2 (1930), 41.
6. Ibid., 45.
7. Barshch and Ginzburg, "Zelenyi Gorod," 28.
8. Barshch et al., "Magnitogor'e," 56.

FIBER CITY, TOKYO
Tokyo, 2003–2005
Ohno Laboratory/University of Tokyo

———

———

The Japanese city has a number of serious problems. One of them is a declining population. If the birthrate remains at the present level, by the middle of the twenty-first century the current population of 1.26 billion people will have fallen to 90 million, and it will have been halved by the end of the century.[1] Although in Japan the metropolitan areas will probably be less affected, the entire nation will be unable to escape the effects of the declining population and the extreme aging of society.

At the same time, the people of Japan have the longest life expectancy of any nation in the world. Fifty years from now, senior citizens will make up one-third of the population. As for the aging of the population from a social point of view, due to the decrease in the ratio of the working to the total population, companies will not be able to employ a sufficient workforce, and it will become impossible to maintain the conventional quality of life within individual family budgets. Bringing in workers from abroad has been discussed, but as it would be impossible to compensate for the total decrease in population in Japan by foreign workers, the Japanese themselves will have to work more. Simply put, elderly people and women will be required to fully participate in production. In an "aged" society, economic independence will also be demanded of the elderly. Women will no longer be able to remain full-time housewives, and a diversification of labor types, for example in the form of job-sharing, will be required.

In the future, as elderly people and women are urged to work more, it can be easily predicted that demand for residences in the downtown area will increase. For example, commuting for two hours is uneconomical if one only works in the morning. If the children must be entrusted to others before going to work, a lengthy commuting time is also inconvenient. A conspicuous characteristic of recent purchasers of inner-city apartments is that they tend to be either dual-income households or senior citizens. Why senior citizens? The reason is that is impossible to achieve anything in the suburbs without a car, especially in the newer suburbs. As the physical abilities of elderly people deteriorate, driving a car becomes difficult. After their children move out, they tend to sell their detached houses in the suburbs and live without a car by moving to an apartment in a downtown area equipped with cultural facilities and other amenities.

Some shrinkage will also be inevitable if the environmental problems are to be resolved. If we succeed in halting the system of over-production that stimulates endless consumption in the industrialized countries as well as the technical improvement of the facilities used to produce commodities, then we will reduce global greenhouse-gas emissions. If we can successfully manage our lives without automobiles, we will reduce the consumption of fossil fuel.

It is time for us to steer our ship towards an era when shrinkage will continue for a longer period than we have ever experienced in modern times, quite distinct from a temporary recession, and we must have our hands firmly on the helm. In such an era, we cannot navigate without a nautical chart. The problem is that the only charts available are old ones. Our intention is to take on the challenge of drafting a new chart. This

The present distribution of Tokyo's population (top: satellite photo, 2005) will be compacted into the catchment area circumscribed by local transport systems, whose accessibility will be improved by the construction of more stations. The result will be a lattice-shaped urban structure consisting of settlement belts.

means we will do more than merely accept a difficult situation; I believe it is an opportunity to improve the environment of Tokyo.

The Ideal of the Compact City
Since the beginning of the 1990s, (mainly European) urban planners and architects have been proposing the "compact city" as the ideal city image. This is a city without an excessive dependency on cars, where one is able to walk, and where public transportation is profitable because of its high density. It is also an efficient city requiring a minimal investment for the construction of urban infrastructure, and has low maintenance costs and moderate energy consumption. The compact city is not simply environmentally superior in every technological respect; the small city is also considered to be preferable in terms of quality of life.[2]

Looking at the way human beings endlessly attempt to enlarge their range of movement, it is doubtful whether the idea that a small city = utopia, which has captured the hearts of so many contemporary urban planners, is really supported by the populace. In most of the world only the big cities are thriving, even though most goods are available even in medium-sized cities, where living expenses are also lower than in large cities.

Urban Planning between Modernism and the Atomic City Model
In the twentieth century, many metropolises were afflicted by huge population increases. In response, one twentieth-century method of tackling urban planning was to use the satellite-city paradigm, based upon Ebenezer Howard's *Garden City,* to restructure growing cities. In other words, new towns were constructed in suburbia, which became the dormitory towns for people working in the downtown areas. The paradigm of the satellite city may also have a metaphysical connotation. As can be understood from the word "satellite," it is analogous to the solar system. A similar model is also used when explaining the structure of an atom. In other words, this is a model in which small planets or electrons revolve around a larger mass like a star or an atomic nucleus, and it can also be applied in relation to cities. It may therefore be considered to be a paradigm for describing the world. This paradigm can be called the Atomic Model. Might it be possible that the image of an urban area comprising a "mother city" and several satellite cities is able to combine the economic appeal of a big city and the humanistic environment of a small city?

This is the structural image that should be deployed when expanding cities generate new cities in vacant land. If such model is applied to an area that is already fully urbanized and the increase in population is held in check, it will not succeed because of the large discrepancies between the model and reality. The theories and images of space applied to existing cities will probably take another, more flexible form.

For organizational structures, modern architecture and urbanism used the image of a machine. The anticipated goal was to be achieved using precisely crafted components in intricate relationships. However, a real city is a coexistence between indefinite elements where interventions can only ever be partial, making such a precise assembly exceedingly difficult. A flexible and powerful model is required, one that permits contingency and heterogeneity among the components, and allows a variety of relationships between them without the loss of overall coherency. In areas such as those Japanese cities that completed their basic structures and necessary amenities during the twentieth century, the most important aspect of city planning has shifted from new development to the preservation of existing facilities, and it has become essential to reinterpret these in a new context. In a word: the role of city planning has shifted from creating a city to editing a city.

New city planning ought to edit surfaces by manipulating lines. Focusing on the manipulation of lines is also a natural outcome of the desire to edit the context without denying the existing environment. In other words, in considering the suppression of development costs for land purchases and attempting to minimize the destruction of the existing environment, one logically arrives at a linear intervention. In concrete terms, various strategies may be conceived, such as inserting a new border into an existing domain, substituting an isolating boundary with one that encourages exchange, or relaxing the opposition between domains by blurring their boundary. Examples of this approach have been implemented in real cities: the insertion of a public passage covered by a glass roof into a block to connect two major streets, the construction of a road which enables people to overlook the city from the edge of a cliff, the transformation of a road into a promenade, and the reduction of dependency on cars through the introduction of streetcars.

From Machine to Fiber

As a result, a model based on fabric can be developed. Fabric is different from a machine in being both soft and supple. Fabric is made of threads, each of which is entangled with other threads. It is not necessary for each of these threads to span a sheet of fabric from one edge to the other. Each scrap of thread is interlinked with others by means of tiny fibers projecting from its surface, and even when there is a hole in one part of the fabric, this does not mean the entire piece will tear. Partial repair is simple. Depending on the choice of thread and type of weave, the possible variety of fabric textures is infinite. Fabric has the characteristics of cushioning and of insulation thanks to the air trapped between the fibers.

If a linear urban intervention is attempted based on the machine image of the Atomic Model, the result will be unconvincing and haphazard. That is to say, an intervention based only on logical parts will ruin the consistency of the overall system. However, if an intervention is based on the fabric image of the Fiber Model, simply changing the texture of the fabric will not upset the overall system. My prediction is that the Atomic City will probably be succeeded by the Fiber City as an urban paradigm.

The Importance of Railways

Apart from the period spanning the Second World War, the scale of both the population and the economy has consistently increased. Suburban Tokyo has developed in accordance with the expansion of the railways. The railroad companies display a great deal of power in suburban development: the framework underlying Tokyo suburbia is the railway network. Both downtown and in the suburbs, the railway stations have become local centers and representative of their respective areas.

In big cities, particularly in Tokyo with its dense web of subways in addition to the above-ground railways, it could be said that the number of stations itself indicates the number of communities or districts. The cross-shaped space created by the perpendicular intersection of a shopping district and a railway line becomes the nucleus of a community. A map-like image of a city as large as the Tokyo metropolitan area, with its 80-kilometer diameter and its 30 million inhabitants, is impossible to understand geometrically; it can only be grasped topologically. Although difficult to understand when walking, it becomes comprehensible at the speed of a train. Because the railroads are lower in density than the roads, they are very convenient as structural elements for organizing extremely large expanses of urban space. These cross-shaped structures can be understood as the intersection of two fibers corresponding to two scales of the city: on the one hand, the shopping districts—local, linear, central, public open spaces—and, on the other, the railroad arteries—points of reference positioning a community within the spatial structure of the metropolis.

Such a high-density railway network is unattainable in the low-density cities of the United States. It is only supportable in densely populated Japanese cities. Therefore, if the population density of Japanese cities continues to decline, and this smaller population becomes dispersed, the fear is that the railways will become impossible to maintain. In fact, in the suburbs of Japanese regional cities, some areas have already begun to appear in which it is difficult to profitably continue public transportation services (mainly bus lines, but also some railways). Not only does "suburbanization" progress further in regional medium-sized and small cities than it does in big cities, the former also undergo a decrease in population earlier than the big cities because of the phenomena of social migration and the rising share of elderly people. They portend the future of Tokyo.

Consequences of Shrinkage

The declining birthrate and the aging population will render places that are inconvenient to transportation routes increasingly unpopular to live in, and the wealthy will move to suburban residences where transportation is near at hand, or to the downtown areas with their proximity to amenities and cultural facilities. The civic centers of the big cities, which are able to fulfill these two conditions, will probably continue to attract people. In this way, the residential density will drop in suburbia, particularly in distant suburbs, and before long it will become economically difficult to maintain the various "infrastructures" of life such as roads, retail stores for daily commodities, and bus services. On the other hand, because land prices will also fall in places where conditions are poor, it will become difficult to sell residential land, and the social class that cannot escape the suburbs will surely be stuck there.

The Compact Fiber City

If we are to conceive of compact cities in the Japanese context, they should make use of existing railways, maintain their world-class high-density network, be sensitive to the environment, and ensure suitable mobility for an aging society.[3] First of all, because it is fundamental to sustain the existing railroad network even as the cities shrink, maintaining passenger levels on the suburban railways is a priority. Concentrating residential areas along the railway lines is therefore necessary. More stations should be built on the existing lines in order to shorten the intervals between stations in such

Fiber City, Tokyo_*Ohno Laboratory / University of Tokyo*

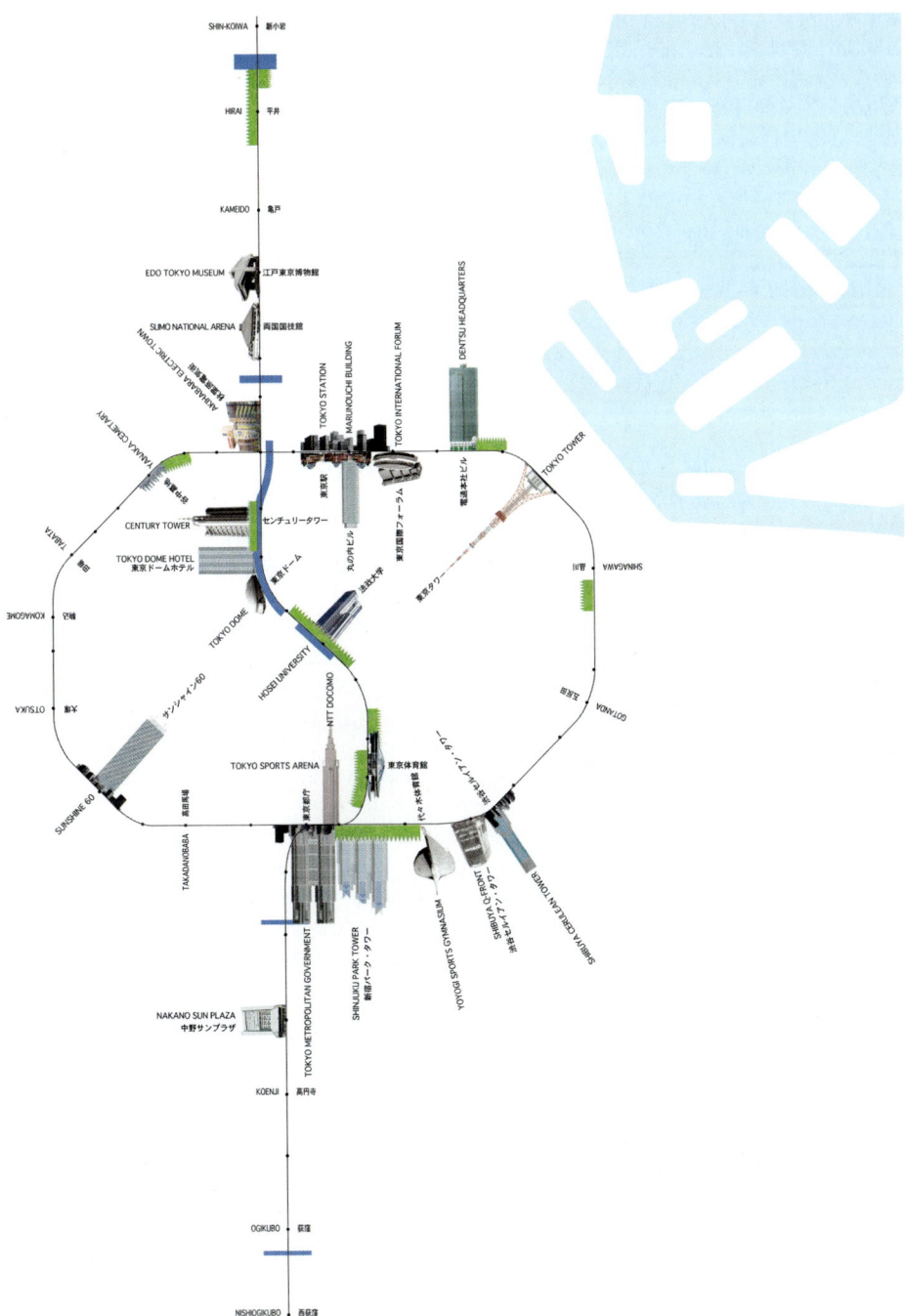

Tokyo's important monuments are already concentrated around the stations on the Yamanote railway line.

a way that they come to resemble streetcars. If this were achieved, train use would become more attractive and many people would prefer it to their cars.

We therefore should consider altering our axioms: increase the number of stations, enlarge the residential areas from which one can walk to the stations, and create residential areas only in such places. A package of policy measures must be used to persuade people to move to residential areas adjacent to the railway lines.

Advantages of the Compact Fiber City

Fiber Cities make it possible to reduce car dependency. If a policy of increasing the number of stations—aimed at improving accessibility by foot from home to station—is extended to all residential areas, this will greatly contribute to reducing the environmental impact. Because in a Fiber City the suburban residential areas are grouped along the railroad lines, vacant land will then become available. The weakest aspect of the current suburbs of Tokyo is the fact that although they are called suburbs, the residential areas are located a long distance from green tracts of land. If this vacant land were converted into parks or agricultural land, it would be possible to provide nature in close proximity to the residential areas. Even if these areas were defined as residential areas for the wealthy, a positive effect on the environment could be anticipated from the greenery of their gardens. For similar reasons, the use of schools and cultural facilities is also possible. Depending on their location, these areas also lend themselves to facilities needing a very large site, such as factories or research institutes.

The Fiber City has high mobility in multiple directions. In the Atomic Model, travel time towards the preestablished center of the tree-shaped transportation network may be short, but going to other destinations takes far longer because of the necessary detours. A society with a declining birthrate and an aging population has diverse modes of living and working. It is a society in which it is difficult to establish a single center, which is why a semilattice network is necessary.

A Fiber City is not only aimed at following and reproducing a cross-shaped neighborhood community similar to those along the Inogashira line, but is also an attempt to allow the security of a small city to coexist with the fluidity of a big city.

The Fiber City possesses a high level of redundancy, which allows it to cope easily with urban transformation over long periods of time. The busiest streets of Tokyo have shifted to the west, from Asakusa and Ginza in the prewar period to Ginza, Shinjuku, and Shibuya after the War. Precisely because a Fiber City is structured like a piece of fabric comprising mutually entangled fibers, it may easily respond to changes in urban metabolism. A tree-shaped system of transportation is an attempt to anchor hierarchical urban relationships. The Fiber City enables varied development of a city on the basis of its semilattice structure. This is the alternative image of a compact city—a new organizational model that attempts to meet the demands of citizens in the twenty-first century.

This text is an abridged version of *Towards the Fiber City: An Investigation of Sustainable City Form*, by Hidetoshi Ohno (Tokyo: MPF Press at the Ohno Laboratory, 2004).

Notes
1   National Institute of Population and Social Security Research, "Population Projections for Japan: 2001–2050," http://www.ipss.go.jp/pp-newest/e/ppfj02/ppfj02.pdf.
2   See Mike Jenks, Elizabeth Burton, and Katie Williams, eds., *The Compact City: A Sustainable Urban Form?* (London: E & FN Spon, 1996).
3   Fiber City was conceived as a generic idea. The notion of fiber in urban design does not mean only the railway lines discussed in this article. Fiber could equally refer to shopping street, river, canal, boulevard with a row of trees, architecture, embankment, forest, lane, and so forth. Every linear space and structure can be a fiber that contributes to the organization of urban space.

DEPLETED CITY

Shrinking cities have reduced density, yet spill over into surrounding areas despite the decline in urban substance. Depleted cities are characterized by older populations, for it is usually the young who leave. In areas with decreasing densities, spatial interventions, urban planning strategies, new organizational forms, and digital technologies help ensure that existing urban qualities can be retained and new ones can be created. The parameters of time, mobility, and access take the place once held by physical presence. Pendular migration and tourism turn places into part-time towns.

THE SHRINKING AND PERFORATED CITY
Marta Doehler-Behzadi

—
—

> *Growth is good, said the balloon, and burst ...*
> *Growth is bad, said Death, and laughed.*
> *I have no idea what you're talking about,*
> *said the caterpillar and became a butterfly.*
>   brandeins *47 (2003)*

Contraction, Segmentation, and Perforation

The city is in transformation. It is difficult to predict where the current situation of falling, stagnating, or at most very slowly increasing demand accompanied by a surplus of space might lead. And the big question is whether the vacancies will continue by and large to be widely dispersed, or whether specific areas of the city will be abandoned by large numbers of occupants. Two urban planning responses as to how to deal with a surplus of urban space immediately come to mind. On the one hand, one could envisage deconstruction from the city outskirts inward, as if the cities were to undergo a process of contraction and concentrate their functions in the smaller space. This is the intention of the "compact city"—a concept that in its association with that of the "European" city and its remembrance of the historical urban structure is related to qualities of spatial closure, functional and social mixing, and shorter distances. The distance between the perimeter and the center of the city would shrink again. On the other hand, one could seize the opportunity to modernize the public system of space, for example enlarging public and private open areas in the urban center so as to create playgrounds, green areas, parking spaces, or "air corridors." The result would be a more structured city, and new partitions, new borders, and inner perimeters would emerge.

However, in circumstances where the land has been divided into small parcels since the Wilhelminian era, where the ownership structure is heterogeneous, and where the economic and psychological needs of the many different actors are multiple, it can never be expected that all owners can or will want to all work together towards one goal. Against this backdrop, it is clear that the localization of the processes of contraction and segmentation will have to be unambiguous and the urban planning decisions unequivocal. Moreover, these processes will entail a very high intensity of intervention, while in the case of housing surpluses and free choice, the power of urban and spatial planners to control developments will be reduced.

It is interesting to compare Rabet and Rietzschkeband—two green areas in eastern Leipzig—in this light. Rabet was built "in one go" in 1975 after the complete demolition of a nineteenth-century city quarter. In Rietzschkeband, in contrast, based on a plan from 2001, the deconstruction of older housing stock in favor of more green areas was set as the general goal, but the execution of the plan has been more responsive to the various requirements of the respective ownership structures, the actual state of renovation, and other factors. The Berlin landscape architects Becker, Giseke, Mohren, and Richard thus created a new kind of urban space for what they called "on-site change" that not only considers the structural demands of urban reconstruction but also integrates them into the design. In this way, beside contraction and segmentation, a third strategy—perforation—

is introduced, which pragmatically makes reference to the reality of the late nineteenth-century city and the accidental collaboration of its fellow players in urban restructuring.

The Perforated City: A Regenerative Form and a New Variation on the European City

The historical city exists in various degrees of preservation. There are largely intact, authentic, compact, and coherent city cores and neighborhoods, but there are also considerably fragmented areas. In this sense, the perforated city is a model of reality that depicts a disruption in the program of the European city, which, according to André Corboz, is marked by substantial architectural cohesion and the dual principle of buildings that are clamped together and of one height. To perceive the perforated city as a reality also means, as Corboz sees it, taking leave of a "pathos-laden, restrictive notion of the [European] city" and opening ourselves to a realistic vision and understanding of the city in flux.

The perforated city is the result of various sudden events or long-term influences: wartime destruction or natural catastrophes, or lack of economic strength over long periods and the sudden abandonment of older relations of use and ownership. Small gaps are simply overlooked in people's perception of these urban areas and hardly affect their conceptual scheme. It is only when large gaps and wastelands appear that it becomes impossible to ignore the fact that the settlement structure has been disrupted. The vacant urban lot is the first indicator of perforation.

The positive accompaniment to perforation is a form of loosening. The perforated city is a loose type of urban space in that it is accompanied by an extensification of usages; in once quite densely used stock, smaller households now fulfill their need for significantly larger living space. This takes place in an architectural-spatial context with many gaps and voids. People live further away from one another, and the distances sanctioned by the social standards of the city increase. There is hardly any lack of free space, at most there are deficiencies in terms of quality. This leads to an improvement in the quality of life and living surroundings, indeed an almost luxurious state of affairs in terms of the consumption of private and public spaces compared to the construction and use densities found in western German cities and even more so in American cities, not to mention Asian metropolises. This is the enormous opportunity offered by the empty, perforated city: it is potentially more user-friendly, more bearable to live in, and more healthy than cities have ever been at any time or any place. The residents no longer feel the need to flee this city for the country.

The downside is marked by decay. The perforated city indicates past, current, and thus also future emptying. It means a lack of demand and lost profits for the owners; it means a decline in economic value and the resulting physical loss of building substance. The perforated city is a latent form of the urban. Weak areas and bad stock are excluded from valuation by the demand market and threatened with gradual abandonment. Of course, all cities also have robust urban structures, attractive housing, and good neighborhoods with excellent prospects of regenerating themselves as subsistent and vital urban quarters. But it is equally clear that the future prospects of the weakest and poorest areas are quite different. The physical decay of apartments in multistory apartment buildings and their declining attractiveness are clearly most pronounced in those areas historically marked by especially high densities of construction and use. The traditional working-class districts are more subject to emptying than areas built in a looser, more generous fashion.

The situation threatens to reach tipping point where demolition has already begun and the gaps begin to converge. Firewalls make their way into our image of the city and begin to dominate the facades, whose size appears reduced by the new perspective. The gaps in the housing blocks also destroy the near uniformity in the height of the buildings. The rear walls and courtyard facades of the blocks behind the gaps are exposed, and these are just as little a part of the city's historical structure as are fences, sheds, or garbage cans. The city begins to take on a restive appearance as courtyard life becomes public. Only rarely and occasionally do we grasp that this reduction could also bring benefits—in the form of changed spatial opportunities to pause and "respire" in the middle of the "corridor street." Usually, all that is perceived is the reciprocal incursion of public and private space, and no new landscaping concept will be able to separate them in a way that draws its meaning, form, and status from the contrast between them.

In this way, the perforated city reproduces in its own way the social mix of late nineteenth-century architecture, characterized by more gradual distinctions between main street and side street, front wing, side wing, and rear wing, bel étage and garret, and park lane and slaughterhouse street. The differences between buildings, streets, and districts are not glaring, but gradual. In eastern Germany, this pattern is still quite hidden by the renovation boom of recent years. The buildings, renovated often for tax purposes by absent and (as far as the local conditions are concerned) astonishingly ignorant capital investors, exhibit a remarkably unclear distribution of vacancy: economically weak areas also have renovated buildings, and the more affluent areas also have ruins. It is difficult to predict whether these scenarios will lead to more dispersion or more polarization.

Compared to the economically driven behavior of coalitions of housing companies in the large housing developments, the owners in the perforated city act in a more unpredictable fashion. Either they act rationally in accordance with economic criteria, or unconsciously in a hazily defined space, or they do not react at all. This means that rational, strategic decisions cannot be expected of "the owner" of small parcels of stock in historical structures built in the nineteenth and twentieth centuries. Entirely new strategies are required to be able to deal with a random spectrum of intentions, possibilities, and options for urban reconstruction. The fact that game theory has recently been applied to the urban context of the shrinking cities with frequent reference to the famous prisoners' dilemma might indicate that in our understanding and practice of planning we should take a closer look at the agents involved in architectural processes of reproduction and urban transformation. This means that against the backdrop of degressive development, spatial processes of redistribution take place unsystematically, that is, by chance and in an almost anarchic fashion, and this presents a stark contrast to the kind of planning we are familiar with from the era of growth and in the context of a morality of assistance based on the welfare state.

Normative accents in the sense of planning as we know it can easily become pipe dreams in a perforated city with limited public funds and high risks for private investors. This means that our plans must focus on those areas where intervention should and actually can take place. But this also entails that other parts of the city will have to be left alone. Planning will probably have to be done in a much more descriptive way than has been the case up until now, while computer technology will allow for entirely new approaches (using geographic interpretations, complex data linkages, databases that can be accessed by the general public, and the like). Planning will come to mean collaborating and rendering visible.

Under these conditions, perforation is a new urban answer to processes of urban structuring in the post-growth era. But what the concept stands for is a new, lower density, including a greater or lesser share of gaps. As a new type of urban space, it is marked by a growing incidence of surplus lots of sizes and distributions that cannot be precisely determined in advance. Because this does not represent the other side of the coin to a densely or even excessively occupied city quarter (as conceived by our current planning mindset), traditional concepts of planning and design have become obsolete. These empty lots then go unused, and the financial means to structure and maintain them are not available. This renders necessary a reinterpretation of the empty spaces in the perforated city, innovative planning concepts, and the acceptance of more modest standards that ultimately will lead to changed forms of appropriation.

Translated from the German by Brian Currid

This is an abridged version of "Die schrumpfende und perforierte Stadt," in *Integration und Ausgrenzung in der Stadtgesellschaft (Zukunft von Stadt und Region* 1, Beiträge zum Forschungsverbund "Stadt 2030"), ed. Deutsches Institut für Urbanistik (Wiesbaden: VS Verlag für Sozialwissenschaften, forthcoming). Abridged preprint with the kind permission of the author.

Literature
Corboz, André. "Die Schweiz, Fragment einer europäischen Galaxie der Städte," and "Die vier Phasen der theoretischen Auseinandersetzung mit der Stadt im 20. Jahrhundert." In *Die Kunst, Stadt und Land zum Sprechen zu bringen,* 45–54 and 65–74. Basel: Birkhäuser Verlag, 2001.
Lütke Daldrup, Engelbert, and Marta Doehler-Behzadi, eds., *Plus Minus Leipzig 2030: Transforming the City,* 32–48. Wuppertal: Müller und Busmann, 2004.

CHEMNITZ-BRÜHL
Matthias Grünzig

—
—

At the last national German conference of the ministers of buildings and public works in June 2005, Federal Minister of Buildings and Public Works Manfred Stolpe gave a positive summary of Stadtumbau Ost, the large-scale urban replanning program for eastern German cities. The cities in eastern Germany have been strengthened, he said, and many city quarters have become more attractive. But he could hardly have meant Brühl, a district of Chemnitz. This listed area, built between 1820 and 1900, today resembles a ghost town. It has shopping streets where almost all the businesses are empty and housing blocks where all the apartments have been abandoned. In Mühlenstraße, demolition teams are already at work, tearing down one house after the next.

On first glance, images like these recall the pervasive decay and the demolition in the 1960s and 1970s of historical city quarters in both the German Democratic Republic (GDR) and the former Federal Republic of Germany. Some people are reminded of the days when planners dreamed of "driver-friendly" cities while citizens' initiatives protested against the demolition and squatters occupied the empty buildings. But many things are very different in Chemnitz, which makes the situation all the more complicated.

For Brühl was by no means neglected during the GDR period, quite the contrary. The entire area was carefully restored in the early 1980s and transformed into a lively area with cafés, bars, and shops. There were solidly built-up street fronts, Wilhelminian-era buildings with elaborate plaster facades, corner towers, and shops on the ground floor. Brühl's decline only began after 1990. Then, the residents either moved to new single-family housing developments on the city margins, or to western Germany, where there were more jobs. Chemnitz became a shrinking city. While in 1989 the city still had 310,000 residents, today the population is only 250,000, despite recent annexations of surrounding communities. And the retailers also moved from Brühl to the new shopping centers. Left behind are vacant shops and apartments.

Chemnitz's city planners cannot be branded as demolition-happy enemies of older architecture. Their early planning for the shrinking process actually intended to reinforce the older parts of the city. To meet this goal, the city was to shrink from the outside in. This was very much the target of the integrated urban replanning program drawn up in 2001. The plan was to fully dismantle Hutholz-Süd, the most outlying GDR-era high-rise development, in order to strengthen areas like Brühl near the city center. The residents, the city planners thought, would eagerly move from the high-rises to the city center.

But the residents proved anything but enthusiastic about the planners' plans. The residents of Hutholz-Süd, for example, protested vehemently against the demolition of their neighborhood, declaring that by no means did they want to move to Brühl. At residents' meetings, it became clear that many could not care less about the urban environment and pretty facades. They were much more interested in whether they could park their cars directly outside their front doors. In addition, they pointed to further positive qualities of Hutholz-Süd, like its proximity to green areas and the views of the Erzgebirge mountains offered by this area, which is located on a hill.

For city planners committed to the principles of "gentle" urban renewal and the co-participation of residents, this situation presents quite a dilemma. Should they decide to

Chemnitz-Brühl, demolition in Mühlenstraße, 2005.

go ahead and revitalize the older areas and, if necessary, force the residents to live there? The situation is made even more difficult by the fact that it is practically impossible to implement unpopular measures because the responsible parties are then immediately punished by the electorate. In Chemnitz's local elections last year, the vote shared by the governing parties (the center-right CDU and center-left SPD) was reduced to 42%, while a radical right-wing party won 10% of all votes, and the PDS, the successor organization of the former East German communist party, became the strongest political force at 27%.

In light of these constraints, it is no surprise that the demolition plans for Hutholz-Süd were abandoned. On top of that, several of its apartment buildings have already been converted into condominiums and sold with no difficulty. Demolition is out of the question here. The other side of this development was a long-term vacancy rate in Brühl that finally led to the tearing down of the block between Hauboldstraße and Mühlenstraße. In one fell swoop, sixteen buildings were torn down. And the demolition in Brühl is not an isolated case. In Zwickauer Straße and in the Sonnenberg and Schloßviertel quarters, larger-scale demolition projects have already been carried out; next, part of the Humboldthöhe development, built by Chemnitz city planner Fred Otto between 1928 and 1932, will disappear.

But demolition is not an unavoidable fate. Instead one could imagine concepts that address the real issues underlying depopulation, such as strengthening the economy or more child-friendly family policies. But as long as shrinkage is taken to be a law of nature, then the demolitions will probably continue.

Translated from the German by Brian Currid

CORE & PLASMA
Eastern Leipzig, Germany, 2001
L21 – initiative zur förderung zeitgenössischer planungskultur

---

In response to a call for proposals for the future development of eastern Leipzig, the architectural initiative L21 developed the Core & Plasma concept as a model for this area characterized by a 50% vacancy rate.

L21 defines "plasma" as those spaces that have lost most in terms of significance and functionality. This type of urban region represents an area of improvisation in the broadest sense, marked by dynamics, contradiction, and low density. Plasma underscores the freedom of the individual as the bearer of processes of social change and is able both to grow and to shrink.

Abandoned plots in "loud plasma" (areas with a high volume of traffic) are planted with dense forest; similar plots in "soft plasma" are used as gardens until demand grows again and the green disappears. Peripheral, space-intensive uses such as commercial applications can also be absorbed by plasma.

"Cores," in contrast, are stable formations that represent point of social concentration. They are dense islands of the "European city" with valuable, historically evolved urban structures. They can be found wherever great potential is already at hand or is needed to stabilize part of a city. The communal activities of retail, culture, education, and communication are concentrated in the core areas. (Ed.)

The original German title of this project is "Kern & Plasma."

In response to the expected reduction of the settlement by 50%, building stock is divided into three categories: "core areas" that are to be completely preserved, areas that are to be completely demolished, and the "plasma" in between, which will absorb fluctuations of growth and shrinkage in the city.

◀ Diagram. ▶ Structural plan for eastern Leipzig. Between core settlement zones and parkland zones lie "loud plasma" (brown) and "soft plasma" (yellow).

WALL IT UP. AND TAKE A BREATH.
Halle, Germany, 2004/05
Peter Arlt and letzelfreivogel architekten

In the debate about shrinking cities, two contrary developments are apparent. On the one hand, an attempt is being made to activate the last remaining "local potentials." And after all capacity for self-healing has been fully exhausted and can no longer be reactivated, then an attempt is made with the help of artistic-architectural "advisers" to breathe some life into the now desolate area. The reanimation efforts are undertaken ambitiously and energetically, but are only ever truly effective in a limited and temporary way. In the end, this well-meaning traveling circus runs out of steam in the face of overpowering forces of emptiness and lethargy. Left behind are the frustrated remaining residents of the area, who have already lost all hope of better times to come.

The second strategy is a less gentle but ultimately more sustainable approach: total demolition. Here there is no clinging to the illusion of salvation through all kinds of miracles. Instead, what is relied on is funding from the "big pot"—the Stadtumbau Ost program for urban restructuring in eastern Germany—which provides the hefty sum of sixty euros per square meter of demolished building. And choosing to rely on this solution is a good idea, for 90% of the monies from Stadtumbau Ost go into demolition and only 10% into improvement measures. The empty urban lots are filled with parks and parking lots, but these uses are also only finite; their maintenance and care often can no longer be financed.

The "third way"—the alternative to demolition and sprawling urban wastelands—is a solution that nurtures no false hopes and looks reality straight in the eye. It proposes walling in those areas (and the buildings on them) that will not be needed in the foreseeable future.

Areas with high vacancy rates and at risk of demolition, and wastelands with no medium-term prospects will be closed off by a wall lacking any kind of entrance. The wall will be huge (around four meters high) and too high to scale without auxiliary equipment. It will be impossible to access or even to see what lies behind the wall. There will be no planned date for the removal of the wall and thus no fixed duration.

What will this achieve?

1. Economically speaking, this solution will consolidate the real-estate market, as is also the case with demolition. Residential and commercial space and urban plots will be removed from the market. In addition, there will be no significant follow-up costs (except for wall maintenance).

2. The physical removal of space will trigger a concentration in the remaining space (for the urban planners as well!). The slogan of demolition programs, "More city through fewer buildings," will actually be fulfilled with the walling-in solution: the shrinking city will be densified by way of subtraction.

3. At the same time, the proposal will counteract the ruralization of cities. The wall is an urban entity and will provide a sense of urban continuity. The interior space will be a subtrahend and be protected by the wall: it will not be usable and will be impossible to look into.

Walling in derelict areas (as proposed here for Halle city center) removes them from consciousness. The illusion of a high-density city is restored.

4. In the course of time, biotopes will emerge independently in the walled-in spaces (as in abandoned military no-access zones) and this will positively influence the ecology of the surrounding city (the air, for example).

5. The real beauty of "walling in" lies in the continuing existence of the original city in the minds of the residents. The mental city will remain in existence and will continue as an individual memory.

6. The negative aura (downward spirals that also spread to surrounding areas) of abandoned lots will be counteracted by walling in. The broken-down city will be out of sight, and out of mind. The physical release will be accompanied by a psychological one.

7. The areas will be improved—in part thanks to the wall itself.

8. The city will be given mysterious, quiet spaces. On first glance, they might be "white spots" or "black holes," but in the minds of the residents these "silent grounds" will develop a life of their own, thus remaining a part of the city.

9. While other cities frantically simulate activity, this city will take a moment to catch its breath.

Translated from the German by Brian Currid

The first version of this proposal, entitled "Stille Gründe" ("Silent Grounds"; 2001), was elaborated together with Tom Hobusch, André Schmid, and Dirk Stenzel. This project was commissioned by the Bauhaus Dessau Foundation in the context of "Shrinking Cities." The original German title is "Einmauern. Und Luftholen."

Depleted City

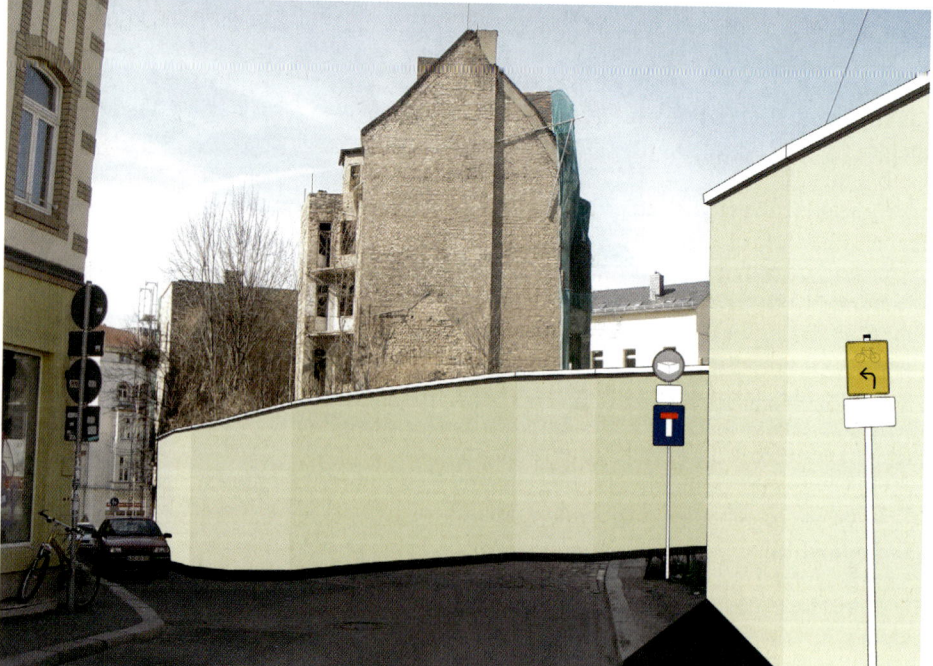

The construction of a wall removes the empty lots from view.

THE SUBURBANIZATION OF INNER CITIES
Walter Prigge

The exodus of segments of the population and of jobs from the core cities to outlying regions is commonly criticized as constituting suburbanization. Suburbanization is indeed a source of shrinkage that can be observed around the world. The core cities are losing people and jobs and therefore also potentials for centralization and financial allocations, which instead are going to the regions characterized by urban sprawl: shrinkage in one place corresponds to growth in another. But the more serious assault on European core cities is taking place in the reverse direction: I mean the encroachment of suburban principles of lifestyle and spatial structures into central urban cultures. The suburban triangle of *mall culture, automobility,* and *single-family housing* is increasingly also peripherizing everyday life in the inner cities.

    The shopping mall is replacing the functions of the city center; indeed in smaller cities like Dessau it itself is becoming the city center. It centralizes consumption and combines it with entertainment cultures. In this combination of consumption and culture, the centrally located shopping mall is so successful that it has also become the model for standard shopping streets and for their design; only by adapting in this way have they a chance of standing up to the competition. Combined with other uses such as housing, culture, and services, the more complex shopping mall has now become the valid urban-planning model for fragmented and densified production of urban space: apart from the "Urban Entertainment Center" there is no other private or public model for urban production. Tied into the value-added chains of goods and services, these centers have become nodal points in a global network of logistical spaces and it is they that now determine the significance of the city centers or the city limits where they are located. On the margins of the city center, highly reduced and decentralized forms of shopping center are increasingly dominating daily, close-to-home shopping. The competition is harsh, for every 700 meters a new supermarket of the familiar rural typology is being built, each with its own bakery and some form of newspaper kiosk, and each with a large parking lot (see Aldi, Lidl, Penny, and so forth).

    Mall culture is peripheral spatial culture, but it is not only typical of city outskirts: it has also long since taken over the city centers and their mix of consumption and entertainment culture. It is based on *automobility,* which under conditions of shrinkage, especially, is experiencing a revival as the dominant culture of mobility. Shrinking cities quickly slip below the critical masses for maintaining culture and infrastructure, and this is also true for public transportation. Increasingly it will become necessary to offer infrastructure in a mobile fashion, with central stations at nodal points in ever-looser supply networks. Gas station urbanism is a good illustration of this development: open around the clock, the gas station is a symbol of the 24-hour city—a social location with an urban selection of commodities and services that goes far beyond just gasoline and magazines. This fits together well with the high-speed return of the automobile as an appropriate instrument of social differentiation. In the lower social classes, it is indeed the sole means for representing an individual lifestyle: widespread tuning or "pimping" (e.g., the current hubcap fever) and inner-city cruising illustrate the return of the automobile as a social cult object.

Construction of private homes by a municipal owner-occupant initiative in the middle of a densely built Wilhelminian-era district in Leipzig-Gohlis, Germany, 2005.

The Suburbanization of Inner Cities_*Walter Prigge*

Depleted City

In the South Bronx (178th Street and Vyse Avenue) there once stood a tenement building with 64 apartments (top, June 1980). Photos by Camilo José Vergara, New York.

Empty after being burnt out (center, January 1983), it was then demolished (bottom, January 1986).

The Suburbanization of Inner Cities_*Walter Prigge*

The barren lot (top, March 1988, and center, May 1991) was eventually filled with four town villas housing eight families (bottom, October 1994).

GAS STATION URBANISM, OR WHAT'S LEFT OF THE CITY
Orange Edge: Stefanie Bremer and Henrik Sander

> Watch the little gas station.... In our present gasoline service station you may see a crude beginning to such important advance decentralization; also see the beginning of the future humane establishment we are now calling the free city. Wherever service stations are located naturally these so often ugly and seemingly insignificant features will survive and expand. [The new city] ... is all around us in the haphazard making, the apparent forces to the contrary notwithstanding. All about us and no plan. The old order is breaking up.
> Frank Lloyd Wright, The Living City

Frank Lloyd Wright's model of "Broadacre City" is not a model of a shrinking city. And yet, with its emphasis on broad expanses and looser development structures, it does in a certain sense describe the characteristics of shrinking regions. Settlement areas today are changing, shifting, dissolving, shrinking. But what are the constants in this process? On which building blocks of the urban can planning continue to rely?

An essential feature of the shrinking city is a well-developed street network and a higher demand for transportation among residents. Whatever else changes, the network of streets, the traffic, and the gas stations will remain. Especially in the shrinking city, gas stations take will on a new significance as functional and urban nodes.

An average gas station today sells between 1,500 and 3,000 different products a range similar to that of a small supermarket. These are then supplemented by beverage markets, online shops, lottery points, bookstores, and video stores. Postal service shops and package pick-up points make the gas station also a post office. Commercial customers, in particular, and salesmen take advantage of this opportunity to have round-the-clock access to their packages. And the food service industry at gas stations is also growing rapidly. Gas stations now have bakeries and coffee shops and often work together with chains like McDonald's and Segafredo. BP Global's Aral brand has now become the seventh-largest fast-food chain in Germany.

It is true, however, that the network of gas stations is also undergoing a process of shrinking. While in the 1970s there were 46,000 gas stations in Germany, today only 14,000 remain. But gas stations, in particular, are places that constantly reinvent themselves. The outstanding quality of a gas station is that it combines a variety of services and products in the most compact space possible, uniting local and passing demand, for the gas station caters both to those passing through and to local residents. This mixed basis for calculation renders them very versatile and thus resilient. Today, only around 25% of the profit at gas stations is still made with gasoline. The real profits are made in the shop and in services. For a gas station to make the most of its potential between brand names and local needs, an intense engagement on the site and also with the local area is required—an engagement for which the oil companies with their global perspective do not have the necessary personal touch. The local niche is thus as a rule occupied by independent gas-station operators and individual leaseholders. With each expansion in

The gas station as an urban node by Frank Lloyd Wright (1966) and Aral (2005).

the range of products, the gas station increasingly becomes a decentralized local supplier and a place where a broad range of social groups spend their time.

For example, in Sandau, a town in Saxony-Anhalt, a group of pensioners has been meeting every morning in the gas station for several years. Here, they exchange news, useful addresses, and family gossip. In warmer weather, they meet in the beer garden. It is important to the group that those who cannot make it let the others know. If not, their companions follow up with a phone call or even a house call. For those without a car, the station's leaseholder takes care of shopping or errands in the next town. In this way, the gas station has become the most important service provider in the area.

In the northern Bavarian town of Geiselwind, a gas station has become the largest highway stop in Europe—a meeting point for vacationers, motorcycle freaks, and fans of country music and German folk music. Some kind of large event is held at the gas station almost every month—anything from biker meets to concerts on the station's own stage. At night, the atmosphere can get quite wild at the bar, especially on the weekends. It is full to bursting point inside, and outside it is impossible to find a free parking space. Groups of friends meet up here before going out to the local disco, and between three o'clock and six o'clock in the morning, many drop in again on their way home.

In Putbus, a town on the Baltic island of Rügen, the gas station has become a small tourist attraction. Tailored to the appearance of this residence town, which was designed in neoclassical style in the early nineteenth century, the gas station gleams in white steel, fitting perfectly into the historical ensemble.

Has the gas station thus become a replacement for the urban wherever the normal city no longer can be reproduced? Would the corner store regain its importance if only Esso Oil, blessed with the endurance of a multinational and the possibility of liberal opening hours, were cut back in size and became a simple gas station again? But the gas station as a nodal point in a mobile society is not a peculiarity or a wrong turn. Anyone who believes this has not understood modern settlement structures. The gas station is neither better nor worse than a traditional market square. It is only new and has not yet found its definitive form.

The gas station has needed around eighty years to be perfected as a marketing machine for selling gasoline and to come into its own as a building. With the current transformation of the urban, the gas station is again in an embryonic state, and on the way to becoming Frank Lloyd Wright's equivalent for the city. The standard box is changing into a local service provider, a tourist attraction, a place for events. Shrinkage processes will accelerate this process. One thing will remain: the little outpost of the urban on the arteries of our residential landscape.

Translated from the German by Brian Currid

Literature
Bremer, Stefanie. "Jenseits von Benzin." In *Stadtraum B1: Visionen für eine Metropole,* ed. Michael Koch et al., 18–23. Wuppertal: BUGH, Arbeitsgruppe Herbstakademie, 2002.
Polster, Bernd. *Super oder Normal: Geschichte eines modernen Mythos.* Cologne: DuMont Reiseverlag, 1996.
Wright, Frank Lloyd. *The Living City.* New York: Horizon Press, 1958.

ON-DEMAND INFRASTRUCTURE FOR SHRINKING REGIONS
Florian Böhm

—

—

The term infrastructure is often associated with fixed, constant institutions like networks for communication or transportation, or indeed centers where, for example, medical services are provided. From a technical point of view, however, this permanence and constancy are by no means an absolute necessity. An extreme example are the thinly populated desert and grasslands of the Australian outback, which have had an almost entirely airplane- and radio-based medical-care system since 1928. The heart of this system, known since the 1940s as the Royal Flying Doctor Service (RFDS), is the combination of radio communication with small airplanes that are able to land in a variety of terrains. When the system was established, both technologies had a range of approximately 500 kilometers: oral communication was possible over this distance by means of the available radio stations, and a doctor could reach a patient at 500 kilometers' distance within 90 minutes' flight time. The older technologies of telephones and automobiles were not well suited to the expansion of the system, for the necessary fixed infrastructure in the form of roads and telephone lines would neither have been affordable nor sufficiently efficient in view of the surface area that needed to be covered and the long distances. The dynamic infrastructure of the RFDS, which largely does without any fixed bases and provides medical services quickly where they are actually needed, makes it possible to provide care to extremely thinly populated areas.

Each of the RFDS support points is outfitted with an airfield and hospital quarters and is responsible for an area of around 250,000 square kilometers—a territory almost the size of Poland. Today, the RFDS has 22 support stations distributed in four regions, which are manned by 400 employees flying 50 small airplanes. Each of the outposts catered for by the RFDS, including farms or mines, is equipped with a radio station, a few hundred meters of landing strip for the airplanes, and a depot of medicines stocking the most important drugs. The medicines are numbered according to a standard system and are prescribed by radio by a doctor. Consultation via radio is the main approach in the case of minor illnesses. For more serious complaints that require the physical presence of doctors, they will come by airplane to the outpost and treat patients on site or take them to the base hospital by plane. The RFDS thus provides the population with a "safety net," giving outback dwellers the security that they are not alone in an emergency.

It is remarkable how the RFDS system has developed over the decades. And especially interesting are the new functions that have been added to it. Originally, the system was exclusively intended as a provider of medical care, and thus represents an early form of today's telemedicine. But it later evolved into a sophisticated communication and educational system.

The Schools of the Air use the radio stations to teach the widely dispersed population of schoolchildren. Since the low population density would not justify establishing permanent schools, education takes place by radio, with the teaching material being distributed by mail or airplane. The only time the pupils congregate in one fixed place is for exams. Radio channels are also kept free at certain times for general conversations between neighbors, who sometimes live hundreds of kilometers away from one another. Of course, new developments in communication technology have been integrated into the system.

Depleted City

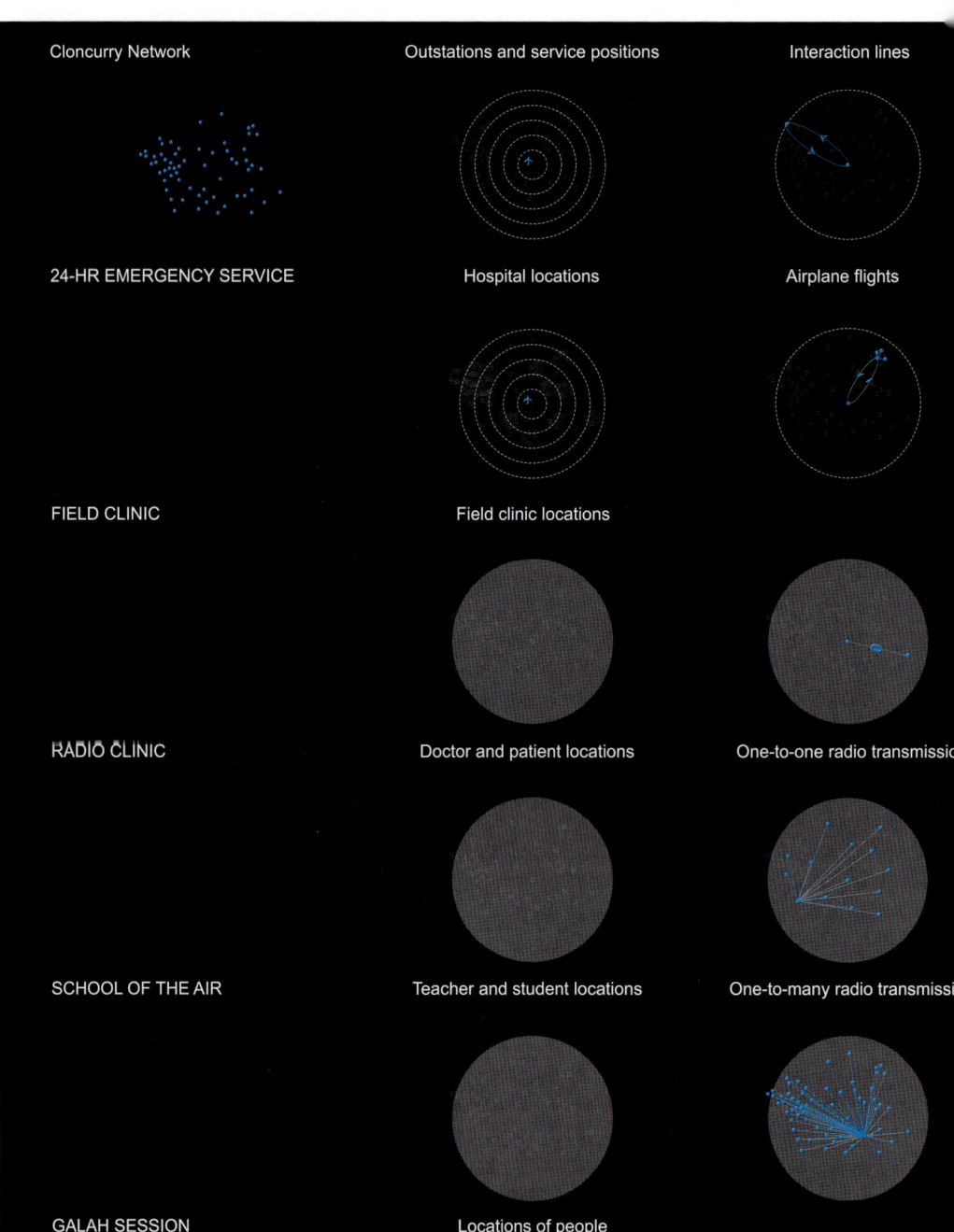

The Royal Flying Doctor Service (RFDS) in Australia is a prototype of an efficient, mobile infrastructure for thinly populated areas that now not only guarantees basic healthcare but is also used for education and communication. From the research project "Time-Sharing Urbanism" by Peter Trummer (Berlage Institute, Rotterdam), 1998.

On-Demand Infrastructure for Shrinking Regions_*Florian Böhm*   237

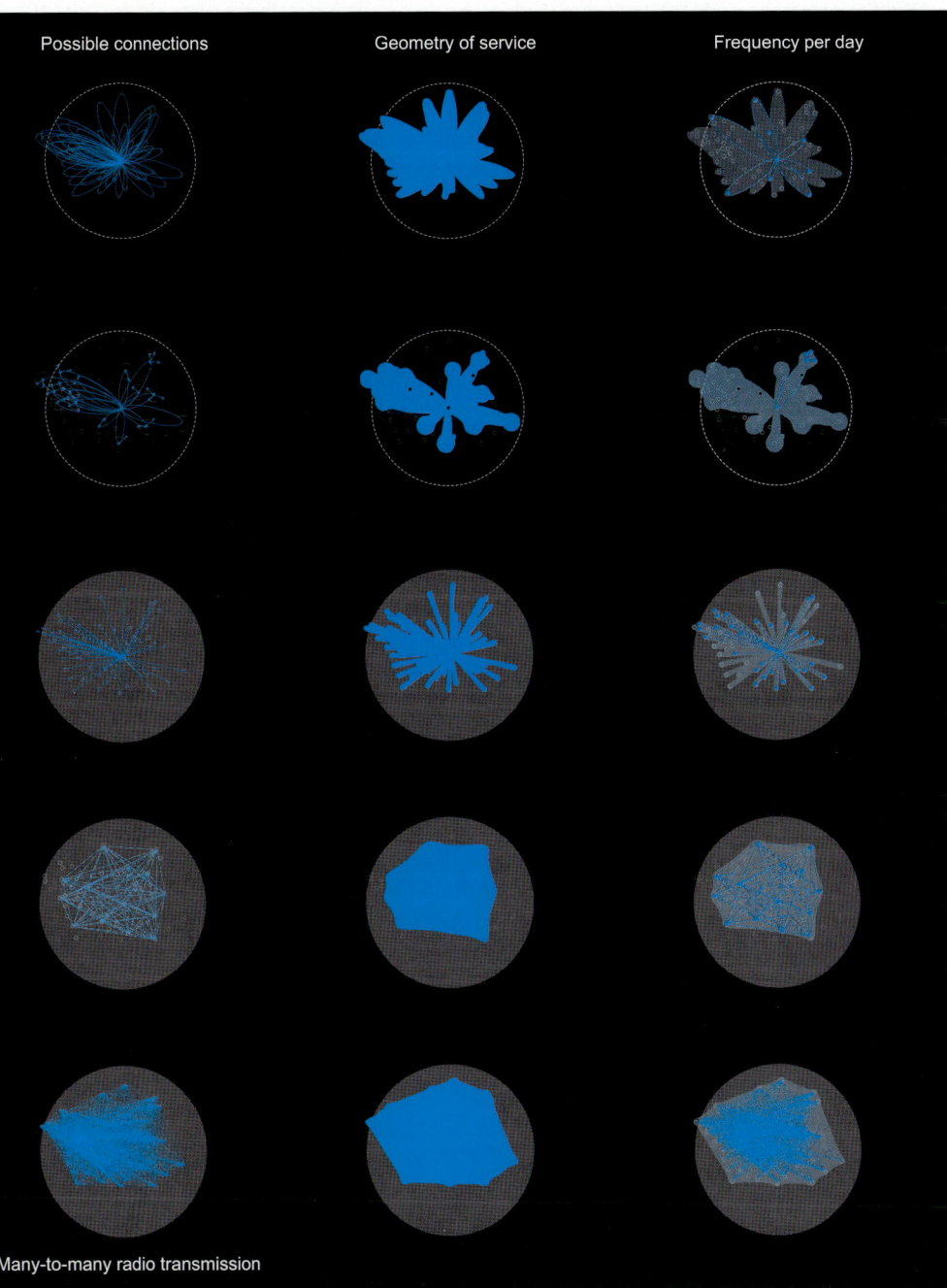

The illustration depicts various spatial structures for respective network usages (from top to bottom): service bases (blue) and clients (white), patterns of interaction by radio and airplane, possible points of connection, distribution of RFDS services, and the number of clients per day.

For example, solar-powered shortwave radio links have been hooked up to Australia's transcontinental fiberglass cables, which has provided even the most remote outposts with telephone and Internet connectivity. The linkage of radio technology to high-speed data lines significantly increases communication potential and bandwidth. The landing strips for the RFDS also serve as the foundation for an air-based transportation system: several air-taxi companies make it possible to supply outlying posts with goods and enable travel between neighboring towns and settlements. Considering the large distances involved, it is not surprising that the airplane has become an everyday means of transportation in Australia. Because of the relatively high cost of acquisition and operation, coordination of schedules and efficient route planning are of great importance.[1]

Dynamic Infrastructure for Shrinking Regions

The example of the RFDS may be an extreme case, but it still illustrates that it is possible to provide services to thinly populated regions using technologies that have been available for some time. How to deal with shrinking regions is thus less a technical problem than a political and a planning issue. It has been important to realize that due to the falling population figures in many areas of eastern Germany, for example, infrastructure facilities cannot be maintained at their current levels. Nonetheless, a minimum in terms of supply and quality of life should be maintained in these shrinking regions, and the right to equitable living conditions (which is guaranteed by the German constitution) should not simply be surrendered. Another desirable aim would be if suitable measures could guarantee an acceptable quality of infrastructure despite the shrinkage process. And finally, the infrastructure must remain cost-effective over the long term, without users or suppliers being overly burdened. This means that the costs for infrastructure for thinly settled regions should not dramatically exceed those for densely populated regions. In practice, the political goal of securing equitable living conditions cannot be realized without additional costs.

These goals can only be realized in a cost-effective way by using new approaches to infrastructure planning. This includes the creation of a dynamic or on-demand infrastructure. The idea at the heart of this approach is that infrastructural services do not need to be constantly available at fixed points, but only at the time and place needed. On the one hand, meticulous planning is required to see how extensive this dynamic infrastructure must be so as to fulfill all service needs. On the other, the communication and transportation systems needed will enable the request for services and the real or virtual provision of the services to take place in the desired place at the desired time.

Communication Infrastructure

A basic requirement for any dynamic infrastructure is a high-capacity communication network. Without the telephone or Internet, services like on-call buses or e-commerce are useless. While landline and mobile-phone networks are currently available almost everywhere and, given the low maintenance costs, will remain available in more thinly populated regions, broadband Internet connections are still limited. The DSL technology widely used in Germany has only a limited range, so users may only be at limited distances from their Internet providers. For commercial providers, it is often not worth the investment to provide a thinly populated region with effective broadband networks. As a rule, satellite links either depend on a technology that is still not powerful enough or is still too expensive.

The same is true of the mobile communication system UMTS, which due to the costs of the network is still mainly only available in metropolitan areas.

As an affordable alternative to centrally organized infrastructure, in many places local, decentralized wireless networks using WLAN technology have been established, where the range can be extended up to 20 kilometers using point-to-point transmission. With this affordable and uncomplicated technology, each participant acts as a node in the network and therefore contributes to increasing the network's size. In this way, a network can be built up on an immense scale and the residents of a region can establish a citizens' network on their own initiative. The set-up and operating costs of a communally organized citizens' network are minimal—currently less than those for a commercial DSL connection. Examples like the djurslands.net network in Denmark show that the collective construction of a largely virtual technical infrastructure also enables a communicative link to emerge among the people of a region.[2]

The region of Djursland, northeast of Århus on the Kattegat strait, found itself cut off from the main traffic flows by the construction of bridges over the Great Belt and the Öresund. The volume of traffic in the ferry harbors of Grenå and Ebeltoft declined dramatically, and with it the number of jobs fell and the hospital and the local newspaper were closed down. To maintain a basic infrastructure despite these structural changes and to encourage the remaining companies to stay in the region, the residents founded self-help organizations that built up the largest wireless citizens' network in Europe: now djurslands.net links over 3,500 households. By linking the connection at the hospital in Grenå, now closed, to the Danish fiber-optics network, the citizens' network can be operated cheaply using high-speed broadband Internet connections. Local interactive Web portals have now taken the place of the former regional newspaper.

Official services are increasingly offered online, and Internet-based visual telephony is currently being installed. In this way, the region, which seems cut off from information and transportation, now has access to a highly modern and serviceable communication network. This new network makes it possible to maintain relationships despite lower population densities and the resulting increasing distances. New communicative structures enable participation in social life.

With the wireless citizens' networks, Cedric Price's 1990 concept of the "Digital Halo" became a practical reality. In this project, developed for a run-down, partially depopulated mountain village in Croatia, the British architect suggested modernizing and enhancing the location by giving it a hovering electronic infrastructure without changing the architecture of the town. But in a citizens' network like that created in Djursland, this digital halo providing a means of communication is now largely invisible because of the further development of radio technology. And it has not been established by a well-meaning government, but by the users themselves.

Transportation Networks

Physical accessibility also needs to be secured in regions affected by shrinkage, for not everything can be done virtually by Internet. A functioning transportation infrastructure will be necessary to keep residents mobile inside and outside their region, and is also required to bring commodities and services to residents. Due to this double function, the design of transportation infrastructures in these regions takes on considerable significance. Transportation is one of the most important and one of the most difficult components of

Depleted City

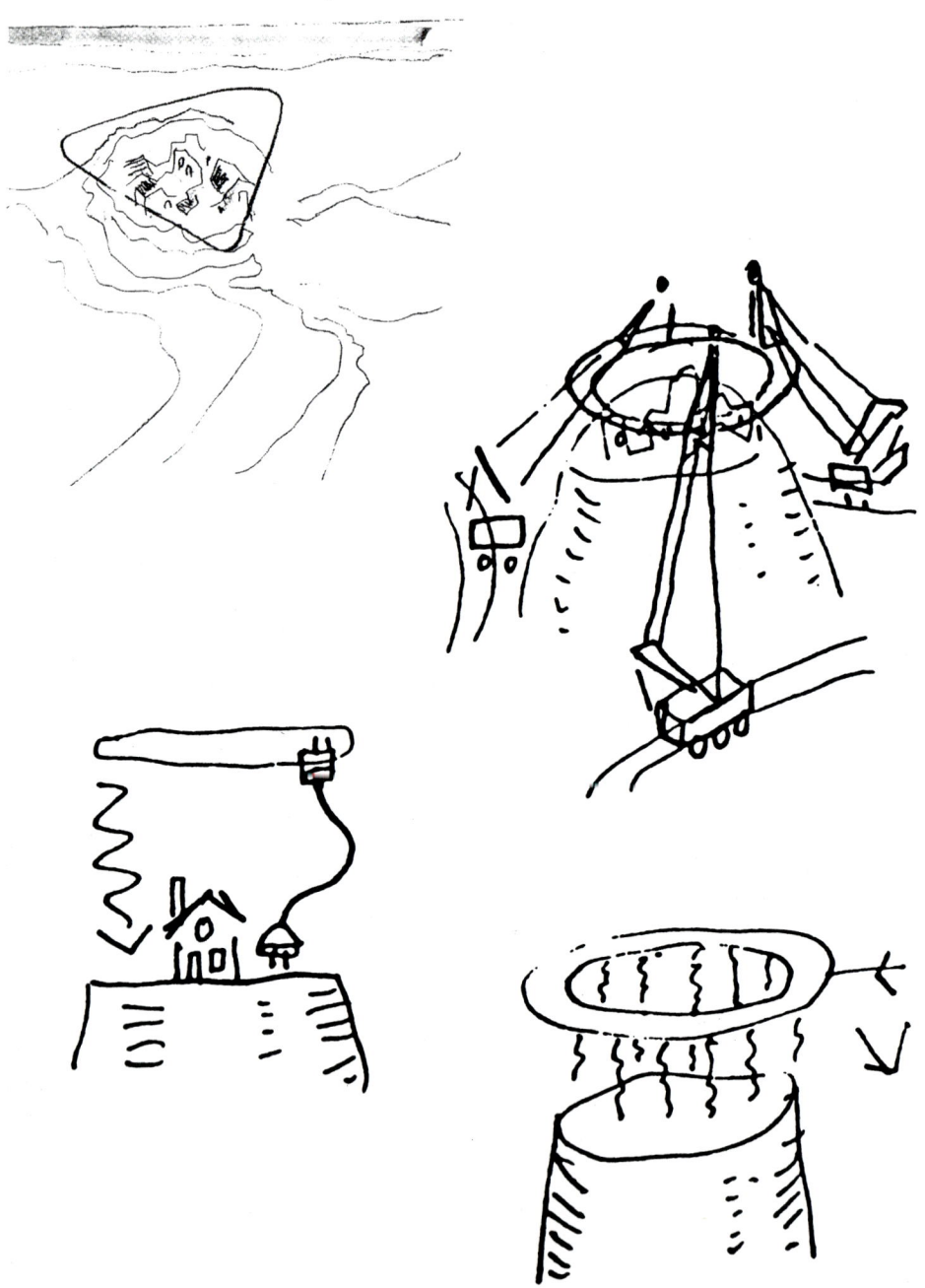

To modernize and enhance an old, partially depopulated mountain village in Croatia, British architect Cedric Price in his project "Digital Halo" (1990) proposed a floating electronic utilities infrastructure, which could be created without having to adapt existing buildings.

infrastructure to plan and operate. Private transportation is the smallest problem, for almost everywhere a network of roads is available. The more difficult task is providing transportation for those without a car. Especially in light of the demographic shifts in shrinking regions that bring a significant increase in average age, providing local transportation which is appropriate for the elderly is crucial. To do this, new concepts are needed: bus transportation systems, which are often inflexible, can only fulfill the mobility needs of the population in a very limited sense. The low population density means only a few trips a day are worthwhile, and then usually at times that do not correspond to the needs of elderly persons (e.g., in the early morning, when children are taken to school). Accordingly, only a transportation system that is flexible and adapts itself dynamically to transportation needs can guarantee long-term mobility in regions affected by shrinkage.

Individualized local transportation systems like on-call buses have been in discussion since the 1970s but have often failed because of the lack of the necessary coordination. Today, much larger computing capacities and networks are available which can process numerous different requests simultaneously. Extensive studies on this issue were undertaken in ten related projects funded as part of the Personennahverkehr für die Region (Short-Range Regional Transportation) program run by the Germany Ministry for Education and Research (BMBF). One emphasis of these projects was rendering local transportation services more flexible. Thus, a study investigated why on-call bus systems had still not been established. The greatest problems proved to be the high labor costs, the complexity of personnel coordination, and the legal framework. It is unclear under Germany's transportation laws whether on-call buses represent regular services, which would be eligible for public support, or merely occasional transportation, which would not be eligible. The founding of citizens' bus associations represents one solution to the problem. While the establishment of such associations has been funded for some time in the state of North Rhine-Westphalia, the Gransee association in Brandenburg is the first of its kind in the new federal states of eastern Germany. The purchase of the bus itself is funded with state support, but the service is operated voluntarily by the members of the association on a rotating basis. The citizens' bus thus represents a further development of the idea of the car pool, which already represents an important form of mobility for people without cars in thinly populated regions.

Another approach to the operation of individualized local transportation might be cooperation with taxi companies or logistics providers. The latter, in particular, already deliver packages almost everywhere in Germany. Combining a package service with on-call transportation could help to avoid empty trips and optimize the use of vehicles and staff. Instead of delivery vans, small buses could be used that provide and charge for both transportation and delivery services. This innovative idea was explored in the "MultiBus" project, also funded by the BMBF. Here, in the western part of the Heinsberg district near Aachen, a highly individualized transportation service was offered using a low-riding small bus. The services provided and the profits made by the project are to be improved in the future through cooperation with a transregional delivery service. Initially, packages will be collected or submitted by the passengers; later, the service will also deliver packages and passengers' shopping.

In rail transportation as well, there are possibilities for developing services that cater to low-density areas. A prominent example is the Karlsruhe city railway, which connects the railway lines of the region with the city center using streetcar tracks. By using special multisystem city-railway wagons that can operate both on streetcar tracks and mainline train tracks, on the one hand the operating costs compared to the former train service can be lowered, and at the same time the number of passengers can be increased through the provision of an attractive service. The Karlsruhe example has in the meantime found imitators. It now serves as a model for similar projects in Saarbrücken, Kassel, and Chemnitz. Interestingly, residents identify highly with such local transportation networks.

Shopping

A fixed location for a supermarket or sales point in a region with a declining population is often simply no longer worth the investment. All that are left are gas stations. Although these are only a service component of the road-traffic infrastructure, their round-the-clock shops have often taken on the function of general store and local meeting point. Disadvantages here include their location—usually on the outskirts of settlements—and the limited inventory at comparatively high prices. A well-known alternative is the option of on-demand sales utilities such as vending trailers that have a range of stock limited by the reduced space available inside. The other possibility is for customers to be brought to a large shopping center or to have their goods delivered from there. These options can be ideally combined with e-commerce. Since it is no longer possible in such cases to maintain extensive stocks locally, the Internet enables users to choose from a large set of products on offer. The goods ordered are then delivered by a service that could be easily combined with a flexible minibus system or a rolling sales point. If functioning communication and delivery infrastructures are present, today almost any kind of good can be ordered by Internet: daily groceries, books, even a complete prefab house. The latter might be an extreme example, but basically all products for which the buyer does not require extensive advice can be ordered on the Internet and delivered "just in time."

Education

The availability of affordable broadband Internet access already represents an important prerequisite for participation in a dynamic educational infrastructure. While comprehensive opportunities have been available in the area of higher education for some time (e.g., the Fernuniversität Hagen in Germany or the Open University in Great Britain), this is not yet the case for elementary or secondary education. In addition, today's e-learning systems offer new possibilities for the presentation of the teaching material and the interaction of students with one another and with the faculty. In light of the rising average age of the populations of shrinking regions, virtual adult education or, more conventionally, theater buses and mobile libraries are worth considering. Especially in thinly populated regions, virtual, on-demand adult education renders attractive and extensive opportunities possible that otherwise would not be feasible because of the meager local demand.

On-Demand City

The examples described above show clearly that the shrinking of regions or low-density settlement need not be linked to a decline in infrastructure services. Crucial here is that planners and policy-makers adjust to the processes of change that are under way and organize or support appropriate dynamic infrastructures. On-demand transportation services such as citizens' or on-call buses need to be supported in the same way as classical regular services. In the same way, cost-free frequencies need to be made available for non-commercial citizens' networks. Furthermore, the bundling of functions like transportation and delivery services or communication infrastructure and educational opportunities needs to be given public support. The technology is available and need only be applied.

A prerequisite for many services in a dynamic infrastructure is serviceable communication networks. These can, as shown by the example of citizens' networks, be affordably built up using personal initiative. Important here is that such initiatives be given political support, allowing for the establishment of a legal framework and free frequency use for citizens' networks. Comparable conditions apply to individualized public transportation. Here, the regional authorities can directly support the establishment of flexible service utilization and the coordination of the various types of mobility—individual and public as well as local and interregional. The same can be said when it comes to education, e-commerce, and delivery services.

In the context of shrinking regions, conventional urban standards like density and proximity need to be replaced with simultaneity and virtuality. Density only exists in the presence of urban attractors. Where they are not present, we need to cope with the newly emerging forms of settlement. The changes need not be considered a loss, as shown by those tourists who in their quest for rest and unspoiled nature travel to Sweden or Australia. What is important is avoiding the feeling of not being provided for. Here, the appropriate technology can help to provide the required infrastructure "on demand" when necessary. Scandinavia's dispersed settlement structure led to the rapid development of the mobile telephone industry (Ericsson in Sweden and Nokia in Finland, for example), which then became a key sector in these countries. The essential, on-demand infrastructures used in thinly populated regions can of course also be used in other regions; the investment can pay off.

All of this results in new approaches for the planner, who now needs to confront the specific characteristics of dynamic infrastructures. How many urban planners are familiar with the practical applications of queuing theory, for example?

Translated from the German by Brian Currid

Notes
1   For a presentation of air-rescue services in Germany and Australia, respectively, see http://www.rth.info and http://www.flyingdoctor.net.
2   Information on virtual citizens' networks is available at http://www.freifunk.net.

Literature
Bundesministerium für Bildung und Forschung (BMBF), ed. *Personennahverkehr für die Region—Innovationen für nachhaltige Mobilität.* Bonn and Berlin: BMBF Referat Publikationen, 2004.
Dean, Penelope, and Peter Trummer. "Time-sharing urbanism." *Daidalos* 69/70 (December 1998/January 1999).
Kocks, Martina, ed. "Demographischer Wandel und Infrastruktur im ländlichen Raum—Von europäischen Erfahrungen lernen?" *Bundesamt für Bauwesen und Raumordnung: Informationen zur Raumentwicklung* 12 (2003).
Larson, Richard C., and Amedeo R. Odoni. *Urban Operations Research.* Englewood Cliffs, NJ: Prentice-Hall, 1981; http://web.mit.edu/urban_or_book/www/book/.

TOURISM IN A LUXURY OF VOID
THE PRODUCTION OF DESIRE, CULTURAL TRANSFER, AND UNINTENTIONAL SIDE EFFECTS
Michael Zinganel

Tourism is a market that lives on hope, all the world over. It is a substitute for potential income sources thwarted by deindustrialization, or a chance to get at least a slice of more prosperous societies' buying power. Tourism strategies in Germany's new federal states have also "followed the decline of industry like a shadow.... And the less promising the chances of economic revival, the more audacious speculation has been."[1] The Lausitzring is the most bizarre example: a newly built racing track into which the state of Brandenburg pumped €123 million to create, in the end, only 44 permanent jobs, instead of the promised 1,500. This amounts to a subsidy per job of €2.8 million.[2] Another example is the proliferation of "fun pools" that were built as "a means of extending the season" at a time when tourism was still practically nonexistent.[3] Eastern Germany hence soon had the dubious reputation of being "the region with the greatest density of fun pools in Europe," and its local authorities risked being eventually crippled by the maintenance costs of such sumptuous and yet little-used facilities.[4]

Wolfgang Kil sees little hope for major tourism projects in eastern Germany—not even for ambitious attempts to transform redundant industrial sites into adventure parks. The Emscher Park "International Building Exhibition" in the Ruhr District has probably already exhausted the interest of a wide—and sufficiently solvent—public in "industry as a leisure factor."[5] The widespread practice of transforming historical towns into picturesque jewels is no solution either, according to Kil, and especially not for towns that are off the beaten track of major sight-seeing routes. Not even an exceptionally attractive and consciously prettified town like Görlitz on the German-Polish border seems to interest anyone any more. It has, despite its prettiness, reached the stage of functional irrelevance.

Tourism as Utopia?
As there are no signs of demand warranting expensive tourist developments in the foreseeable future, Kil suggests instead that the expanding void be reserved as a state-subsidized experimental laboratory for "gardeners and tinkerers, thinkers and dreamers, explorers and connoisseurs: for people looking for a wholly new way of life"; or, more specifically, that self-determined alternative lifestyles be consciously developed in this "restrained urbanity" with the help of state "closure premiums."[6] He sees this idea not as an alternative to tourism, but as an indispensable motor for a range of civic activities that could, in turn, help stem the menacing introversion of people left behind in peripheral regions and their slide into radical right-wing ideology.[7]

The development and experience of tourism could likewise be an antidote to menacing introversion—as long as local people are not excluded from decision-making regarding concepts, potential contacts, and the ensuing profits; and tourists do not merely drive through and look at the locals as if in a zoo. It is less a question of optimizing profits and growth and more about creating at least a minimum of spaces and opportunities for some social exchange.

To achieve this one would have to stop demonizing tourism across the board. For a start, there are different types of tourist industry, some of which definitely have more in common with Kil's glorified "visionaries and tinkerers" than with global capitalist enterprises: small-scale businesses with roots in farming, for example, or "parasitic" mini-businesses that eke out an existence selling niche products at or near tourist destinations.

Artifacts of Longing: Tourism and Art
Since the 1990s, tourism has been understood as the consumption of symbols and images, that is to say, as the active reconciliation of images experienced personally at a particular location with images produced by the tourism industry that create the desire to go there. Besides prospectuses and catalogs, other media such as literature, films, and artworks play their part in the creation of desire as well as, not least, travelers' personal photos and souvenirs: the proof that they have fulfilled their desire—"been there, done that," in popular parlance—helps reproduce such desire in their immediate circle of acquaintances. John Urry writes that this process—professional production of images and text about locations, and tourists that follow the prescribed itineraries, thereby recreating the professional images as personal snapshots that they can show their friends back home—is of major significance for the construction of new tourist attractions. His conclusion is that, theoretically, any place can be marketed as a sight worth seeing, as long as images appropriate to creating desire exist and can be verified by tourists who return home and perpetuate the aforementioned process.[8]

It is not a stable cycle, however. Even travelers can to some extent disrupt, refuse, or subvert the consumption of prescribed imagery, for example, by producing and distributing their own counter-imagery. Moreover, should the latter prove to be acceptable to tourists, it will be integrated into the cycle of desire production, initially by elite and subcultural circles, in the main; but, geared as it is for diversity, the extremely flexible tourist market generally follows hard on their heels.

Media theory instructs us that the expanding "void" in the inner periphery of eastern Germany can be transformed in the medium term into a distinctly competitive edge for alternative "marketing concepts." The very absence of established imagery or values pre-empts any need to deflate or reassign them. The void, the "emptying," and the depreciation of property prices that have all ensued from functional irrelevance offer chances for rediscovery, not only in the semiotic but also in the spatial sense. The region will become affordable—not only for investors but, above all, for groups with minimal capital. Tinkerers and visionaries have always played a considerable role in developing and running segments and sites of the tourist industry that require only minor investment. The long-term slump that local citizens now have to come to terms with is in itself an opportunity for alternative strategies, precisely because the prospect of low profit margins is causing larger investors to withdraw.

The alternative production of desire, the reassignment of images, has been one of the major contributions of the "Shrinking Cities" project and its ambassador "imagists," for art and tourism are related mechanisms. It is the desire for "something other," for the supposedly authentic—or at least the deconstruction of any fabrication of the authentic—that drives the protagonists. Such production of desire is effected primarily by images and, historically, artists, visionaries, and dropouts have contributed considerably to their production for tourist purposes. It was writers and painters who turned the no-go areas of the Alps and the seaside into must-sees. Perhaps it will again be the artists who manage to ascribe new functions to vacated landscapes—with state subsidies, of course, as Wolfgang Kil insists.

From Authentic Experience to Extraordinary Ordinariness

Alienated living and working conditions in metropolises are putting the masses to flight in search of the promised "authentic" experience. And although such "authenticity" has been deconstructed and revealed to be a production staged by local people and the professional service sector in a landscaped set, it nevertheless continues to function as an essential motor behind *all* types of "trip."[9] Tourists' longings might consequently be described as the need to regress, either to certain periods in their own lives or to historical epochs. The significant factor in each case is that these belong in the past or are in the process of vanishing, and can consequently be romantically endowed with more authenticity than one's own current experience.[10] Grown men building sandcastles at the beach or drinking and flirting in bars like adolescents epitomize the former, for instance, whereas the latter is evinced by pilgrimages to historical excavations, monuments, or industrial sites. In reality, however, only one's own body promises the "truly" authentic experience, be this contemplative immersion in wellness or the excesses of extreme sports.

Whether something is seen as being extraordinarily ordinary depends on the habits and perspective of the person looking. Astonishingly, Tue Halgreen could note that many of his—typically middle-class—students would spend study excursions to cities roaming about suburban high-rise housing estates, many of them distanced and ironic, others in wide-eyed admiration.[11] While some were critical of inhuman living conditions and interpreted the buildings as proof of tragic sociocultural developments in the modern period—as the unfortunate result of an unconditional faith in progress—others argued from a primarily aesthetic perspective that the housing blocks were fascinating simply because of their huge dimensions and because they were reminiscent of visions of an egalitarian age. Their brutal appearance simply reflected brutal planning processes—the more brutal the better.[12] They thus served the students as an object of nostalgic longing for a bygone age in which society still believed in grand theories, made far-reaching plans for the future, and also had the courage to implement them.

Target groups with an interest in prefab housing, abandoned villages, and renaturalized industrial landscapes do then actually exist. Their consciously ironic fascination with "extraordinary ordinariness" is precisely what makes them "space pioneers." They will hardly open up a viable mass market, however; at most a minor niche segment for postmodern culture vultures who find signs of the decay of the modern period just as attractive as picturesque historical towns, castles, and palaces.

"Dark Tourists," "Diaspora Tourists," and "Inverse Tourists"

Their motivation is similar to that of travelers who seek authenticity "on the dark side" of "tragic" social developments. This form of tourism is hence described as "negative sightseeing," or "tragic" or "dark" tourism.[13] But there are also other tourists who are susceptible to the pull of eastern Germany's expanding void: the people who grew up there but then moved away to regions with better employment prospects. They regularly return with their partners and children to visit relatives in a region increasingly inhabited by pensioners.

Tourism in a Luxury of Void_Michael Zinganel

Signs of cultural transfer in eastern Germany as a result of the experiences abroad of both tourists and migrant seasonal workers. Collages by Hans-H. Albers.

[INVERSE] SEASONAL CITY
Eastern Germany / Tyrol, Austria, 2004/05
Hans-H. Albers, Michael Hieslmair, Maruša Sagadin, and Michael Zinganel

—
—

Since 1999/2000, when private German job agencies, working with the Austrian employment services center, began an aggressive campaign in eastern Germany to recruit personnel for the winter season in Austria, more and more Germans have been rushing to the Alps—no longer as holidaymakers, but as seasonal personnel, working where other people go on vacation. The reproach that recruiting primarily skilled young people could in the medium term further accelerate the economic demise of their native region is countered by the job agencies' emphasis on the singular opportunities for both personal development and professional experience that the young people can put to good use once they return home. For the majority of those concerned, however, seasonal work is simply the only way they have of earning any money and surviving the limited period they can still spend at home.

For this project a fictitious shrinking city in eastern Germany (a source region for tourists *and* seasonal labor) and an actual booming major tourist center in the mountains of Tyrol are contrasted associatively like vessels that reciprocally empty and fill each other.

Target Region/Source Region

The target region is Sölden in the Ötz Valley, *the* top tourist destination in the Austrian Alps, and yet one that is characterized by extreme seasonal swings, despite having two seasons and direct access to a glacial skiing area. The entire infrastructure is geared to maximum capacity, which is actually attained for only two weeks in February, when 24,000 tourists descend on the 3,500 locals. Maintenance and repair of the huge surplus of hotel rooms, cable lifts, ski buses, water and electricity supplies, and so forth, must consequently be financed by profits from the winter season's peak periods. Seasonal swings in Tyrol are much greater than in the potential source regions in eastern Germany, which are characterized by a high incidence of commuters and seasonal employment. Temporary vacancies in the low season are accepted by inhabitants of Tyrol as part of their culture, just as, in eastern Germany, exceptionally high levels of unemployment in the low season are not perceived as a social problem at all, but as a well-earned and state-subsidized rest from the daily grind in the service sector.

The source region is a typical small town off the beaten track of eastern Germany's major thoroughfares, with remnants of an historical town center, rows of family homes, redundant industrial sites, and high-rise prefab housing; it is a place where the local gas station has become a social hot spot. The town is characterized by unemployment, mass migration, and a high incidence of commuters. Our projection of an unusually high share of seasonal labor commuting between this remote backwater and an equally remote Alpine valley, whose rhythms and experiences will trigger far-reaching changes, is entirely fictitious.

The example of a small bar opened by a former seasonal worker in her hometown demonstrates how the transfer of cultural know-how and capital accumulated during seasonal work, and the use of the social skills and transnational social networks that emerge from tourism's subcultures, can complement each other productively; and how people's heterogeneous experience of tourism can offer unexpected opportunities for self-empowerment.

Actors/Alter Egos

The project is based on interviews with jobseekers, employment agencies, and employers in Leipzig, Gera, Jena, Dessau, Bad Liebenwerda, and Tyrol. Interviewees were asked about their personal experiences in and of the new "care drain" of seasonal workers from eastern Germany to the Alps. For our projections, their actual micropolitical visions were temporally and spatially compressed and exaggerated to the point where they culminated in an optimistic outlook with respect to the range of available personal options.

Artists and architects, aged 30–45, engaged in research; "dark tourists"; artists in residence
- begin by circulating images and statements about the decline of eastern Germany. They then attempt to document social and technical infrastructures in datascapes. In every small sign, however unimposing, they perceive indications of significant changes that legitimize the creation of a utopian vision.

Family of hoteliers in Tyrol, culture-vulture tourists
- have managed to satisfy their need for seasonal workers from eastern Germany with the help of a private job agency. They are so surprised to learn that the workers' native country is in economic crisis that they spend the low season driving the length and breadth of it, discovering a little-known and peaceful refuge.

Former placement officer, 44 years old, diaspora tourist
- has trained some of the seasonal employees and arranged their placements. Visits the partner hotels and local employment services offices in Austria every year. She relocates to Austria herself when Germany's private job agencies hit a slump. She starts a new family in Tyrol and regularly visits her parents and her children from her first marriage in eastern Germany.

Skilled seasonal worker, 24 years old, "inverse" tourist
- was taken along by a colleague who had acquired a job in Tyrol through a private agency. Was able to find another job in Kärnten for the following summer. He now works for two relatively long seasons, earns good money, and spends the low season as a tourist at "Hotel Mama." In return, every year he brings her souvenir wood carvings from Tyrol.

Unskilled seasonal workers, a couple aged 60 and 55, seasonally unemployed, own a small house
- have an emotional and financial investment in their hometown. She went to Tyrol as a chambermaid while he manned the home. The following season she found her husband a job as a caretaker in another hotel where she was able to work as a chambermaid. They now spend the winter season in a double room at the hotel and the rest of the year scrape by in their own little house.

Depleted City

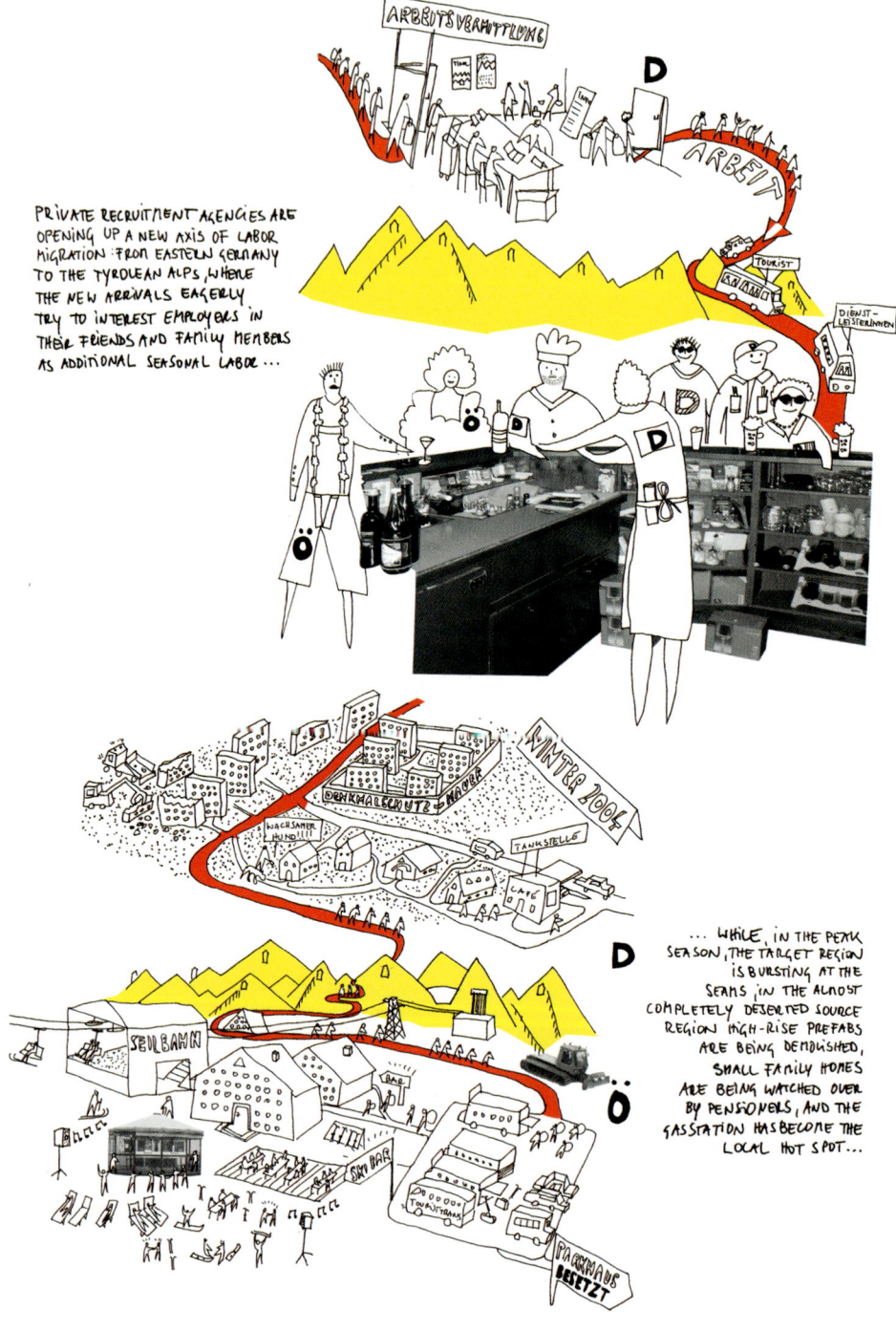

Private recruitment agencies are opening up a new axis of labor migration from Eastern Germany to the Tyrolean Alps, where the new arrivals eagerly try to interest employers in their friends and family members as additional seasonal labor...

...while, in the peak season, the target region is bursting at the seams, in the almost completely deserted source region high-rise prefabs are being demolished, small family homes are being watched over by pensioners, and the gas station has become the local hot spot...

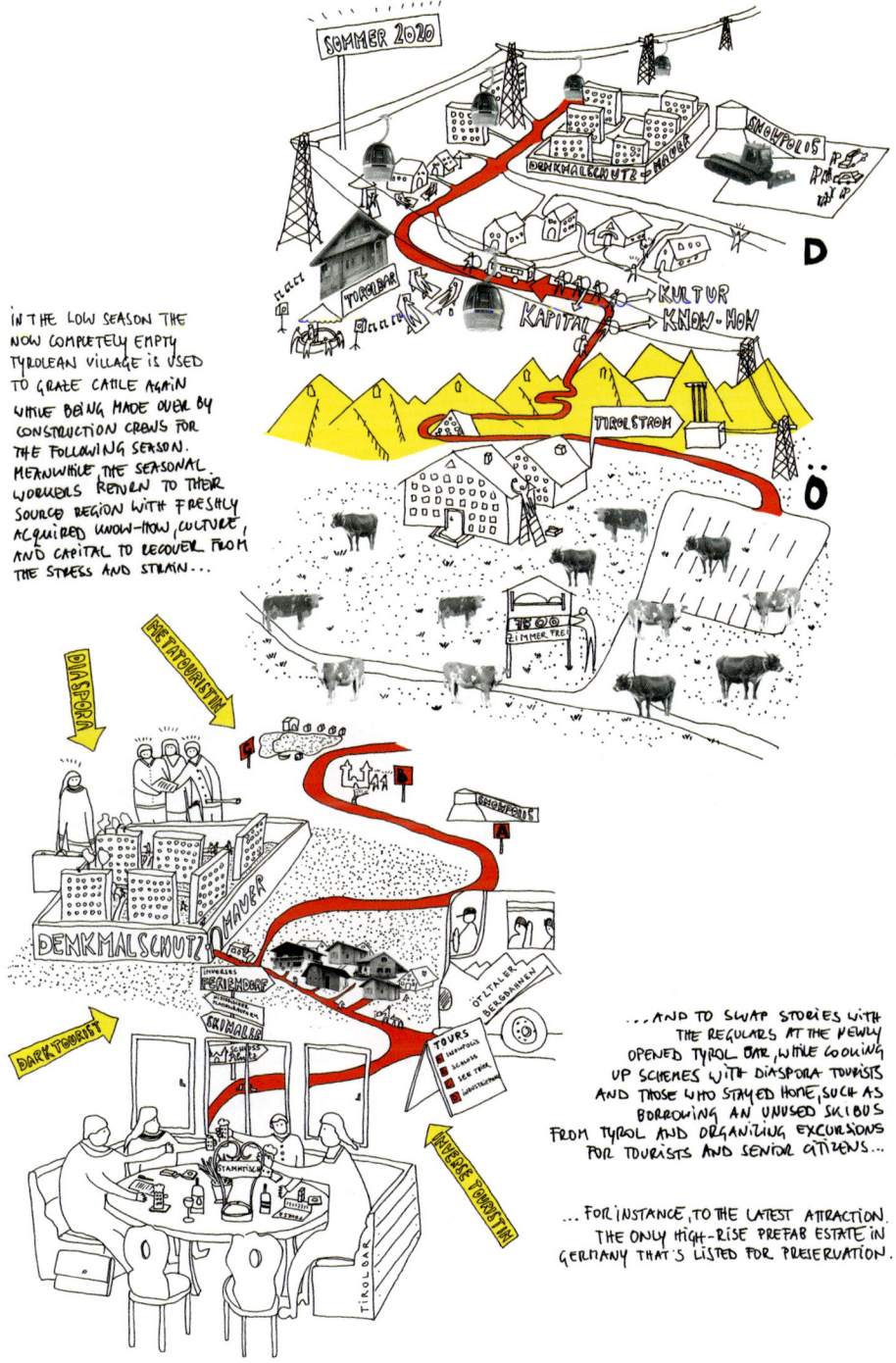

Depleted City

Inverse Low Season
Vacated eastern source region during peak season in Tyrol

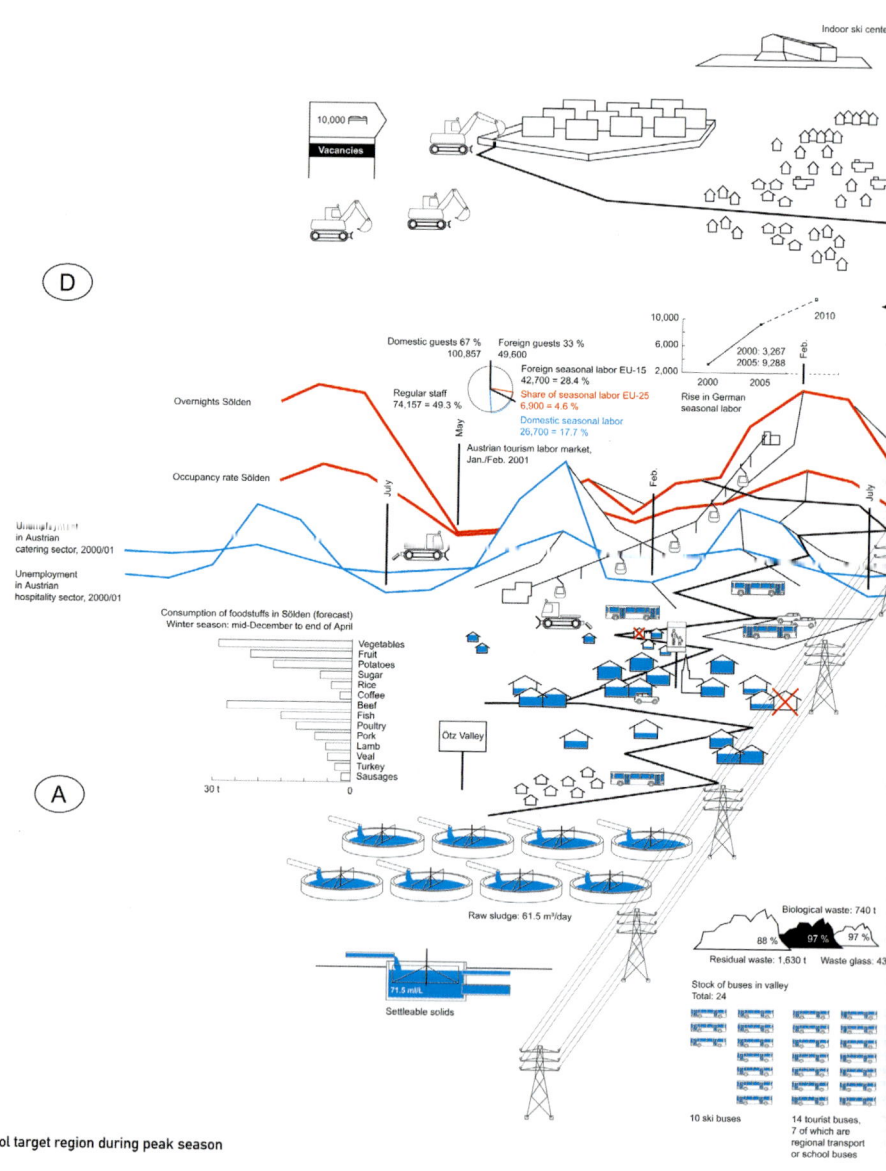

Full Tyrol target region during peak season

[Inverse] Seasonal City_Hans-H. Albers, Michael Hieslmair, Maruša Sagadin, Michael Zinganel

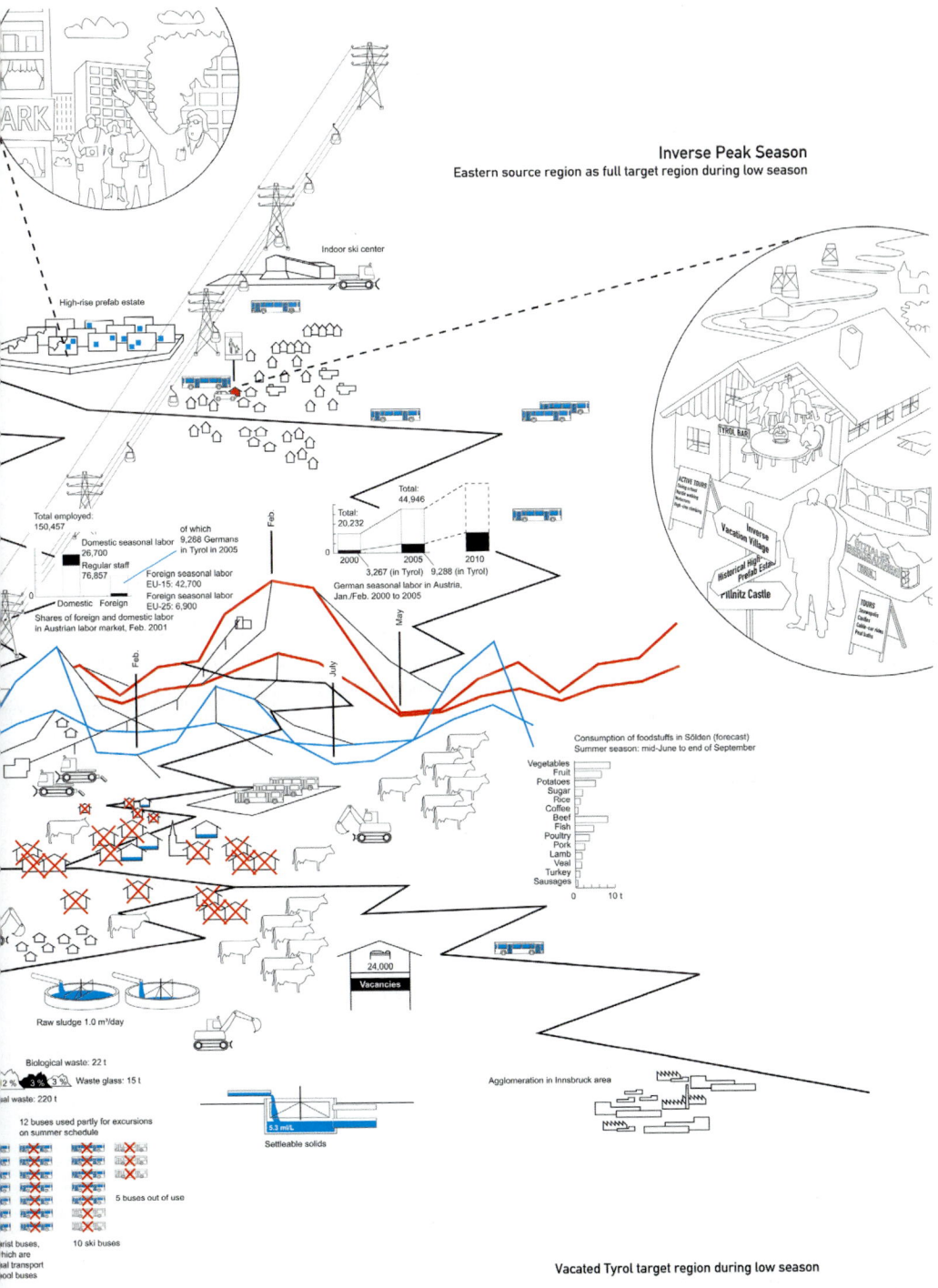

Skilled seasonal worker, chef, 35 years old
  - after five years she has had enough of seasonal work and wants to become self-employed at home. She trains new job applicants at a private agency for seasonal work in Tyrol. She will later take over one of the kitchens used by the agency for training purposes and set up in business. In memory of her years traveling and working abroad, the former cook will name her new small business the "Tyrol Bar."

The Regulars' Roundtable at the Tyrol Bar, Eastern Germany

The Tyrol Bar is where the transfer of culture and know-how and the transnational social networks of tourist subcultures are consolidated. In Tyrol, the major tourist ventures and perhaps also other schemes used to be cooked up over a schnitzel by the local mayor, the cable-lift boss, and the barkeeper. In eastern Germany, such a gathering can also serve as a place to find business associates and as a pressure group in co-operative schemes. The bar is consequently a restaurant, an informal travel agency, a job center, and an NGO rolled into one. Goods and services are exchanged without money changing hands, jobs in Tyrol are filled, there is a library, and children and old people are taken care of—all under one roof.

When it is low season in Tyrol, diaspora tourists and well-heeled seasonal workers taking a vacation descend on the people who never left. Views from beyond mix with views from within … and foreign networks become interwoven with local networks.

The new local company offering tourist excursions, for example, borrows the bus that the Ötz Valley mountain railways have no use for in the low season. When the seasonal workers return to Tyrol, they not only bring the bus back, but also tourist brochures from their hometown, while the tinkerers and visionaries from the urban cultural scene—who have worked here as artists in residence—return to the big cities with their new, reinterpreted images of what longing can mean.

―――

Translated from the German by Jill Denton

―――

This project was commissioned by the Bauhaus Dessau Foundation in the context of "Shrinking Cities." The original German title is "[Inverse] Saisonstadt."

CITIES IN AN AGING SOCIETY
Matthias Grünzig

Germany's Aging Future
A specter is haunting Germany. This time, it is older people who are alarming politicians, economists, and urban planners in equal measure. All demographic forecasts predict increasing numbers of older citizens in Germany and almost all other European countries. The "empirica" research institute in Berlin has calculated that the number of people in Germany aged over 65 will rise by almost 20% by the year 2015.[1]

Yet what does this development really mean for the future of cities and towns? "Older people" do not constitute a single homogenous group, so this is a difficult question to answer. For the same reason, it is almost impossible to create a "one-size-fits-all" urban model that takes account of older people's needs. Yet current research and trends already offer some clues as to how cities can expect to change in an age characterized by aging.

Comfort
One of these changes concerns accommodation. As physical health generally worsens with age, comfort is a major issue for older people. Their concern focuses on quite practical aspects, such as having an elevator or an easily negotiable environment.[2] Their concept of comfort also encompasses being able to satisfy daily needs in or near their home. Having a terrace or balcony is important, at best with a nice view,[3] while stores, restaurants, medical centers, leisure facilities, parks, and local transportation close at hand are equally desirable neighborhood factors.[4] Last but not least, desire for more comfort is mirrored by the increasing demand for care and support services, on which older people will have to rely more heavily in the future, when the increasingly "individualized" society will leave more and more of them without a family network.[5]

These needs are already giving rise to unexpected consequences. In many places, high-rise tenements and large housing estates that had long since been pronounced defunct are benefiting from the upturn in demand from older people. In Michelangelostraße in Dresden, for example, two somewhat dilapidated seventeen-story tenements were remodeled—incorporating medical practices and communal spaces—to suit the needs of older people. A shopping center, leisure facilities, and a streetcar stop nearby make these apartments very popular with older people, to say nothing of the fantastic view they have over Dresden.

Similar trends can be seen elsewhere: in Halle-Neustadt two eleven-story traditional tenements were remodeled to accommodate older people and upgraded as the "Katharinen Estate" and the "Albertinen Estate"; a twelve-story tenement in Rostock-Evershagen was transformed into the "Rasmus Estate," which is particularly user-friendly for older people; and two tenements in the Hans-Loch district in Berlin underwent a renaissance when they were remodeled to suit the requirements of older people.

The need for nearby facilities can also benefit the historical centers of smaller towns. Köthen, Bernburg, and Ballenstedt are examples of historical towns that have experienced an upsurge of older residents in recent years. Particularly appealing for older people are locations surrounded by beautiful countryside, such as Weimar or the coastal areas of Mecklenburg-Western Pomerania.[6]

Security

One important point that older and younger people perceive very differently is the need for security. Surveys attest that security is a much more significant factor for older citizens than for younger people. This need for security is related in part to traffic issues. There is a demand for traffic-free streets set back from major highways that should intersect with the latter at as few points as possible.[7] This requirement is mirrored to some extent by the increased demand for accommodation in housing estates built in the postwar period, which successfully separated traffic-free streets, quiet access roads, and thoroughfares. Quiet estates built in the 1920s and pedestrian zones in inner-city areas are also benefiting from this trend.

But more important again is the question of crime protection.[8] The effects of concern about security can already be observed in many places. By way of example, closed-circuit television, (semi-)sheltered housing with an on-site concierge, and partnerships between landlords and the police have significantly increased in recent years. The pioneers of such complex security schemes are often postwar housing estates. The limited number of landlords here makes reaching agreement on a common security strategy easier than when many landlords are involved.[9]

How such security strategies might look in practice has been demonstrated by Rostock's municipal housing agency, WIRO, which has responded to the needs of older people with a policy called "3 S" (Security, Sanitation, Service). It was in this context that closed-circuit television and concierge services were extended. The result was not only a below-average crime rate but also remarkably well-maintained estates with barely any pollution or graffiti.

Manageable structures characterized by a high degree of social control also benefit from demands for better security.[10] The winners on this front are small towns and manageable estates from the 1920s that are frequently characterized by traditionally stable populations with the capacity to exercise forms of social control, when necessary.

In addition to all that, the lower delinquency rate among older people also contributes to safer cities. For older people commit crime less frequently than younger people. This is the other reason why one finds below-average crime rates in districts with a predominately older population.

Urban Culture

The demands being made on urban centers with respect to cultural life are also undergoing a transformation. Studies of older people's needs have crystallized two major messages. On the one hand, many older people wish for a town that is suited to their age group. They expect that leisure facilities, businesses, restaurants, and the city as a whole cater to the needs of the elderly by offering convenience, peace and quiet, and comfort.[11] On the other hand, older people are not at all inclined to live in an "old people's ghetto" inhabited exclusively by senior citizens. There is a demand for more diversified accommodation that appeals equally to older and younger people.[12] How intergenerational culture might look can be experienced already in the town of Bad Elster. Here there are well-kept parks with colorful flowerbeds and idyllic ponds that invite residents to take a stroll, and sporting facilities ranging from tennis to cycling tours to Nordic walking. The theater, the spa hotel, and the Hotel Sachsenhof offer drama, concerts, readings, and film screenings. And culinary tastes are catered to by numerous cafés, whose comfortable armchairs, discreet charm, and varied menus consider the needs of young and old equally.

Above all, Bad Elster is characterized by a quite particular joie de vivre. The whole place seems to be surrounded by an imperturbable calm, miles away from any hectic endeavor. This peace and quiet surrounds the strollers in the park and the cafés where the young and old meet to have an ice cream or homemade pie. Everywhere one is met by a culture of consideration and discretion that must without doubt make life easier for young and old in equal measure.

Vacant Property

Demographic change will not only generate winners, however. Districts that are unpopular with older people will have to battle with considerable vacancy levels. Rising vacancy rates are forecast for housing estates in peripheral areas with poor infrastructure.[13] Inner-city areas in major cities also number among the frequently overlooked problem areas. Here one finds not only densely built-up areas, noise, and a lack of elevators and recreational parks, but also conflicting interests regarding the use of property for residential, gastronomic, or entertainment purposes. The latter uses frighten older people away. Furthermore, many such districts suffer from splintered property relations that hamper the realization of coherent development and security measures. Various inner-city areas, for example, Berlin-Mitte, Leipzig-Südvorstadt, and Dresden-Äußere Neustadt, have experienced a substantial withdrawal of older residents in recent years. At the moment, younger people moving into the districts compensate these losses. This will not suffice in the long term, however, for it is already foreseeable that demand from young adults will fall by around 2010.[14]

In neighborhoods where older people have left and younger people have failed to replace them, one can get a picture of how such districts will look in the future. Examples are Wurzen's Oststadt, the Brühl and northern Sonnenberg districts of Chemnitz, the historical town center in Limbach-Oberfrohna, the Packhof and Jahnschul districts in Wittenberg, and Crimmitschau-Südstadt. All of these are centrally located "ghost-town" districts with vacant apartments and boarded-up stores, and a recipe for their regeneration has not yet been found.

Urban Development

The preferences of older citizens have been making themselves felt in the context of the Stadtumbau Ost (Urban Restructuring in Eastern Germany) program. In the past, many redevelopment schemes failed to accommodate the interests of older citizens. Districts popular with older people were even frequently condemned, while youth-friendly districts were maintained. A comparative survey of districts in the city of Halle an der Saale registered a high proportion of older residents not as a plus, but rather as a disadvantage.[15]

The result was an embittered fight between older residents, the city authorities, and housing companies, which finally led to a revision of the urban development plans in favor of districts that were more compatible with older people's needs.

Plans to demolish the Hutholz-Süd residential area of Chemnitz provoked a wave of protests and the plans were abandoned. A residential area in Brühl is being demolished instead. Similar conflicts raged recently in Cottbus-Sandow and Naumburg-Mägdestieg,

US OLD FOLK
Eastern Germany, 2004/05
L21 – initiative zur förderung zeitgenössischer planungskultur

Germany is both aging and shrinking. But the two processes are not uniformly distributed across the country. While some western German conurbations are still growing, there are signs that eastern Germany will represent a "retirement belt" by 2020, in the sense that every third person will be aged over 60. The typical migrant leaving the belt today is a young, well-educated woman. The area is thus losing its regenerative humus for new generations and its conventional economic foundation, for this retirement belt is in a sense also a belt of the poor and undereducated. All known parameters of shrinkage are present here in the extreme.

A by-product of the paradigm shift in urban planning policy towards the planned withdrawal from extreme-impact areas is the opportunity to develop new social models that go beyond standard ways of thinking. Might the retirement belt become a haven for those who refuse to conform to society, a laboratory for new "sociotopes" and informal economic models? The retirement belt fluctuates between the extremes of social utopia and social downfall, coupled with uncontrolled political developments and criminal activity. In addition, a purely pragmatic problem is presented by the necessary adjustment of the oversized technological and social infrastructure. Solutions must therefore be developed both for the micro level of sociospatial and political problems and for the questions of spatial order and infrastructure found on the macro level.

Even just to guarantee the supply of such areas with goods, services, and utilities, a reorientation is required between the priorities of autarchy and concentration. There are three conceivable urban residential models that can facilitate life in areas that are breaking up in this way:

- One model is the "regional anchor" as a miniature conurbation. It represents the new, concentrated infrastructure systems of the state and is at the same time responsible for the mobile supply of goods and services for neighboring areas.

- The island model of the "cultural city" is based on the maintenance of cultural assets and a stable population by attracting the elderly. This European version of a kind of Sun City can already found in the work of the Fundus group in Heiligendamm. This model implies both concentration and autarchy, and a tendency towards extreme social segregation.

- As a third model, "regional autarchy" will be concerned with self-administered and regionally limited infrastructure systems. Here it is the existing solitary or networked structures that need to be strengthened.

The spaces that remain will be left to their own resources: new landscapes will emerge, regions will turn to wasteland, and our fear of the wolf will melt away. (Ed.)

This project was commissioned by the Bauhaus Dessau Foundation in the context of "Shrinking Cities." The original German title is "Wir Alten."

where older residents once again thwarted plans for demolition. And current conflicts in Halle and Leipzig also indicate that urban development concepts will increasingly take older people's interests into account.

The Older Avant-Garde

A further phenomenon in an aging society is a mentality that can be described as the "older avant-garde." Many older citizens do not consider their age to be a reason to retire, but become extremely involved in civic and cultural activities. In the eastern German federal states, in particular, it is mainly older people who are behind numerous initiatives and associations, and they develop an astonishing amount of discipline and perseverance in attaining their goals.

What miracles this older avant-garde can perform can be seen in Prignitz, one of Germany's most thinly populated areas. Here there are solitary expanses, country roads onto which a car rarely strays, abandoned granges, and villages that have lost most of their young populations in recent years. What one finds in the small locality of Mesendorf is therefore all the more astonishing. A railway station suddenly appears, with a narrow-gage locomotive and carriages. It seems like a mirage in the middle of this area. And when a passenger comes along, then the train really does start moving. It chugs through the fields at a leisurely pace, and stations like Klenzenhof and Brünkendorf slip by behind the carriage windows, as deserted as everything else in the area. But in any case, this railway has nothing to do with satisfying transportation requirements. Here one travels not to get from one place to another, but to enjoy a little contemplativeness and dilatoriness. And, on the journey from Mesendorf to Vettin, the passenger really does land in a world beyond frenzy and celerity, and his or her experience of the landscape is accordingly much more intense.

The railway is sensational, anyhow, for reason of it being, in a certain sense, a newly built facility. For the section between Mesendorf and Vettin was only opened between 2002 and 2004, thanks to the Prignitz association, Kleinbahnmuseum Lindenberg e.V. (Lindenberg Narrow-Gage Railway Museum), which is run mainly by older people. The enterprise was prompted by memories of the old Prignitz narrow-gage railway that served the local area until it was closed down in 1969. But because the locals were not willing to put up with their little railway being gone forever, they founded the association in 1993 in an effort to bring at least a part of the railway network back to life. There followed a bitter struggle for reconstruction. Members of the association got hold of and restored old carriages, fought the local job center so as to acquire funding for community jobs for the unemployed, applied to Brandenburg's federal government for grants, and finally began laying the tracks. And they are not finished yet: a further section is already under construction between Vettin and Lindenberg, where the association has transformed an old locomotive shelter into a narrow-gage railway museum.

There are numerous associations run by older people in Germany. Railway buffs have reopened abandoned narrow-gage railways in Jöhstadt, Schönheide-Süd, Schwichtenberg, and Bad Muskau. Other associations concern themselves with the maintenance of railway stations and depots and with the restoration of old locomotives and carriages. In addition there are associations with military and technical interests that restore disused bunkers, airfields, and factories. Exemplary among these are the former bunkers at

Falkenhagen, Kossa, Harnekop, and Wollenberg, the airfields at Merseburg, Cottbus, Borkheide, and Eberswalde-Finow, and the former Total fire-extinguisher factory Apolda. A broad spectrum of associations exists—for motorbike and model-railway fans, old-timer enthusiasts, and local historians—that breathes new life into vacant buildings and puts its stamp on urban and regional culture. These associations achieve much more than merely filling up leisure hours. For it is through them that, beyond the constraints of market forces and commercial importunities, a quite singular culture emerges that opens up new vistas for idealism and self-realization.

The Return of Politics
An important consequence of demographic change will be an increased significance of politics for all aspects of life, for older people are much more affected by policy decisions than any other age group. One issue is basic living standards for older citizens, as they are particularly dependent on benefits (such as pensions) that are significantly influenced by politics. A second aspect is the healthcare system, whose provisions are much more relevant for older people than for the young. And on top of all that, civic initiatives and associations are, of course, also affected by policy decisions, for almost all of them depend on public funding.

It is still entirely unclear how politicians will deal with these issues. On the one hand, the dominant demand is for more denationalization and therefore policies aspiring towards lower labor costs, taxes, and welfare benefits. In addition, economic researchers point out that the increasing number of older people may exceed the capacity of the constantly falling number of employed adults to support them.[16] The consequence could be a reduction of pension levels. Yet even if the current pensions system can be maintained, the menace of a dramatic fall in pension levels remains, in particular in the eastern German states. Pensioners in eastern Germany now can mostly look back on a long career of full-time employment, which assures them a relatively good pension. Future generations of pensioners, whose employment histories will often be characterized by long periods of unemployment and poorly paid jobs, would, under the current pension system, have to get by on a meager minimum pension. The consequence of such a development would be an enormous reduction of spending power, the closure of stores, restaurants, and leisure facilities, and, finally, the desolation of whole regions.

On the other hand, there are other trends. Pensioners are also voters and their increasing numbers could bring about a reshuffle of political priorities. For policy-making today is really only a reaction to the interests of the middle classes, who are demanding reduced taxes and insurance contributions and measures against unemployment. More political weight in the pensioners' camp could, by contrast, make guaranteed pensions and better healthcare provision—even at the cost of higher taxes and contributions—the central political issue.[17]

Furthermore, the economic power of a country depends not only on the number of people employed but also on its productivity rate. Thanks to this interrelation, it has been possible to successfully overcome previous phases of reduced employment and rising pensioner levels by increasing productivity.[18] Due to the fact that fewer employees are now capable of producing a greater amount of distributable goods, both employees and pensioners dispose of a higher income today than their counterparts one hundred years ago, although at that time it was much more common for employed people to support a pensioner. There is no reason why such an increase in productivity should not also ensure prosperity in the future, despite the demographic transformations.

Translated from the German by Jill Denton

Notes
1   Stephan J. Bultmann, Eckhard Feddersen, and Marie-Therese Krings-Heckemeier, *Wohnen im Alter, Teil 1: Komplexe Lösungen für den Wohnungsbestand,* empirica paper no. 76 (Berlin: empirica, 2003), 5.
2   Stephan J. Bultmann et al., "Wohnen im Alter, Teil 2: Im Bestand: Umbaumaßnahmen als kalkulierbare Kostenbausteine," *Die Wohnungswirtschaft* 3 (2003), 62-63.
3   Bundesministerium für Familie, Senioren, Frauen und Jugend, ed., *Zweiter Bericht zur Lage der älteren Generation in der Bundesrepublik Deutschland: Wohnen im Alter* (Bonn: BMFSFJ, 1998), 145.
4   Christian Holz-Rau, "Alte Menschen, Raum und Verkehr," in *Mobilität älterer Menschen,* ed. Antje Flade, Maria Limbourg, and Bernhard Schlag (Opladen: Leske und Budrich, 2001), 141-154; Gerrit Köster, "Betreutes Wohnen ohne Umzug," in *Service-Wohnen als zukunftsorientiertes Wohnkonzept,* ed. Heike Engel and Dietrich Engels (Cologne: ISG Sozialforschung, 2000), 61-80.
5   Bultmann et al., *Wohnen im Alter, Teil 2,* 5.
6   Paul Klemmer, "Demographische Entwicklungstrends der Kreise und kreisfreien Städte Deutschlands" (lecture, "Stadtumbau West" conference, Gelsenkirchen, November 27, 2003; http://www.mswks.nrw.de).
7   Klaus Friedrich, *Altern in räumlicher Umwelt* (Darmstadt: Steinkopff, 1995), 96-97.
8   Ibid., 89-90.
9   Bundesministerium für Familie, Senioren, Frauen und Jugend, *Zweiter Bericht,* 150.
10 Klaus Friedrich, "Wohnen und Wohnumfeld älterer Menschen," in *Die Gesellschaft braucht die Alten,* ed. Peter Borscheid, Hermann Bausinger, and Leopold Rosenmayr (Opladen: Leske und Budrich, 1998), 132.
11 Friedrich, *Altern in räumlicher Umwelt,* 96-97.
12 Rolf G. Heinze, Volker Eichener, Gerhard Naegele, Mathias Bucksteeg, and Martin Schauerte, *Neue Wohnung auch im Alter* (Darmstadt: Schrader-Stiftung, 1997), 5.
13 Deutsche Bank Research, "Demografie lässt Immobilien wackeln," *Aktuelle Themen* 283 (September 2003), 17.
14 Bundesministerium für Verkehr, Bau- und Wohnungswesen, *Bericht der Kommission "Wohnungswirtschaftlicher Strukturwandel in den neuen Bundesländern"* (Berlin: BVBW, 2000), 42.
15 Stadt Halle (Saale), *Stadtentwicklungskonzeption Wohnen Phase 1,* May 2001.
16 Deutsche Bank Research, "Die demografische Herausforderung," in *Demografie Spezial,* special issue, Aktuelle Themen (July 2002), 35ff.
17 Charlotte Höhn, "Demographische Probleme des 21. Jahrhunderts aus deutscher Sicht," *Zeitschrift für Bevölkerungswissenschaft* 3/4 (2000): 375-398.
18 Klaus Bingler and Gerd Bosbach, "Kein Anlass zu Furcht und Panik," *Deutsche Rentenversicherung* 11/12 (2004): 725-749.

Whereas Detroit's wealthy citizens have moved to the suburbs, its socially deprived groups, which include very many elderly people, remain in the inner city. Niagara Apartments in Detroit's Cass Corridor (above). Lawrence G., a tenant, 1978 (right). Photos by Bruce Harkness.

Cities in an Aging Society_Matthias Grünzig

In the United States, the wealthy frequently retire to the southern states. This gated community in Sun City, Arizona, is reserved exclusively for retired people (2003). Photos by Peter Granser.

Cities in an Aging Society_*Matthias Grünzig*

POLARIZED REGIONAL CITY

The ideal of equitable development is being eroded. Provocative models propose that spatial development should be polarized: compaction of urban agglomerations vis-à-vis the depletion of peripheral areas. Can regional disparity be turned into a productive force? Can peripheral regions develop qualities beyond traditional growth scenarios? The potential for taking action is increased through the creation, within present agglomerations, of regional administrations that encompass zones of shrinkage and growth in equal measure.

METROSACHS
ON THE HISTORICAL DEVELOPMENT OF A YOUNG METROPOLITAN REGION
Eastern Germany, 2004/05
Friedrich von Borries and Walter Prigge

"MetroSachs" is today an outstanding twenty-first-century model of urban compaction.[1] A prosperous agglomeration situated between Berlin, Prague, and the Rhineland-Main region, it assumes an important role in the Central European economic network. This is all the more astonishing given that moves to create this young metropolis began only in 2012. It emerged from the former Saxon Triangle and now extends from Dresden to Erfurt. Today, sixty years after German reunification, there seems nothing unusual in the fact that the German Democratic Republic has dissolved into two prosperous regions. At the beginning of the century, however, such a development was not yet a realistic political option, for the ideal of a homogenous national territory was still held to be inviolable. Yet the reality of eastern Germany looked quite different even then.

Paradigmatic change became evident around 2012, when neoliberal locational policies, formulated in the preceding decades in response to "globalization," were seen to have failed. It became increasingly difficult to overlook the fact that eastern Germany had lost its economic, and hence also its political standing in the global market. Joint programs launched by the federal and state governments to "promote acceptance of social and regional inequality" failed to fulfill their promise of boosting the eastern German economy; likewise, calls from all sides for increased mobility and competitiveness failed to elicit the emergence of a more autonomous and active civic society. And this despite the fact that when it came to changes in their lifestyles and their readiness to be mobile and to work for wages amounting to self-exploitation, the inhabitants of eastern Germany had proven to be vastly more accommodating than their counterparts in western Germany.

This kind of societal demand for more flexibility, which aspired to make every individual "fit for action" in twenty-first-century globalized societies, had failed. Neoliberal locational strategies demanded and indeed funded globalization, yet individuals failed to come to terms with it either socially, culturally, or economically. This changed only in 2012 when the all-party federal government voted to found, in addition to Berlin, a second metropolitan region in the southern "corridor of expansion" between Dresden and Erfurt. It was only then that eastern Germany, shrunken and simultaneously compacted in these two core regions, became a genuine part of international relations and the global economy.

Until that point, ongoing decline in the material and social quality of life had led to the exclusion en masse of the losers generated by a radical shift to a market economy orientation, which also had repercussions for policy pertaining to social services, education, and healthcare. The underclass was thus robbed of the material and cultural basis for successful individuation and its inherent advantages: personal risk-assessment and a guarantee of social support regarding issues of employment, living standards, old age, and health. The prerequisites for the social integration of the underclass were particularly lacking in those regions of eastern Germany that had fallen through the net of Germany's socioeconomic development. The state had withdrawn from the margins of such regions as much as it possibly could as early as 2006, and its subsequent allocation of subsidies exclusively to clustered sectors did nothing to change structural economic problems. For, notwithstanding investment in the infrastructure of supraregional transportation that integrated eastern Germany in the network of European metropolitan regions, neoliberal strategies failed to establish an independently viable economy within eastern Germany.

At the latest by 2012, therefore, it had become apparent "that all conventional political concepts and realism in urban planning are doomed to failure in shrinking regions cut off from the global economy."[2] This insight marked the end of an era for what had come to be called globalization policy—a modernization strategy that had propagated uneven development patterns as a spatial motor for economic dynamism since the 1990s, and that had culminated in the increasing marginalization of extensive areas of eastern Germany. This strategy was complemented by a social policy that liberated individuals from social welfare and state imperatives, and aspired to animate them as responsible members of an economically streamlined civic society by recourse to empowerment strategies and the promotion of cultural identity. The failure of this policy also put an end to those realistic approaches to urban planning that had renounced political governance and, instead, promoted market forces and their inherent self-regulating competitiveness in urban and regional matters. The end of image cultures and urban marketing (policies for image creation), on the one hand, and mediation and presentation (discourse and negotiation strategies), on the other, marked the end of an era for sociocultural placemaking. In brief: with the demise of a culture of communicative planning, which had been a constitutive element of neoliberal locational policy, regional hardware and the structural problems of shrinking regions began to occupy center stage in the planning and political arenas.

However, the end of neoliberal policies did not by any means indicate a return to the twentieth-century welfare state and its comprehensive social infrastructure. Implementation of Europe's mandatory Social Charter in the whole of eastern Germany was unrealistic, and bidding farewell to (the concept of) homogenous space subsequently became inevitable. It was thus initially in eastern Germany that those concepts of social and spatial compaction were implemented that would shortly afterwards also characterize regional development in western Germany. Founding MetroSachs as a "metropolitan region" was in this respect a realistic anticipation of a process of social and regional polarization that was in reality already unfolding—albeit, in this case, cushioned at the sociopolitical level and carefully geared to political and economic targets. All investment and funding programs in eastern Germany have since then focused on the expanding corridor region in the south: a consistent implementation of federal Germany's commitment to "metropolizing" its regional development. This new agglomeration was put on a par with other European metropolitan areas with the aid of two European Union (EU) programs for economic regeneration: the Special Economic Zone ensured, among other incentives, deregulation and tax relief, while the Special Welfare Zone provided for child and unemployment benefits at twice the usual level. At the same time, the state successively withdrew from neighboring regions. Ever since the population of the southern half of eastern Germany relocated to the new

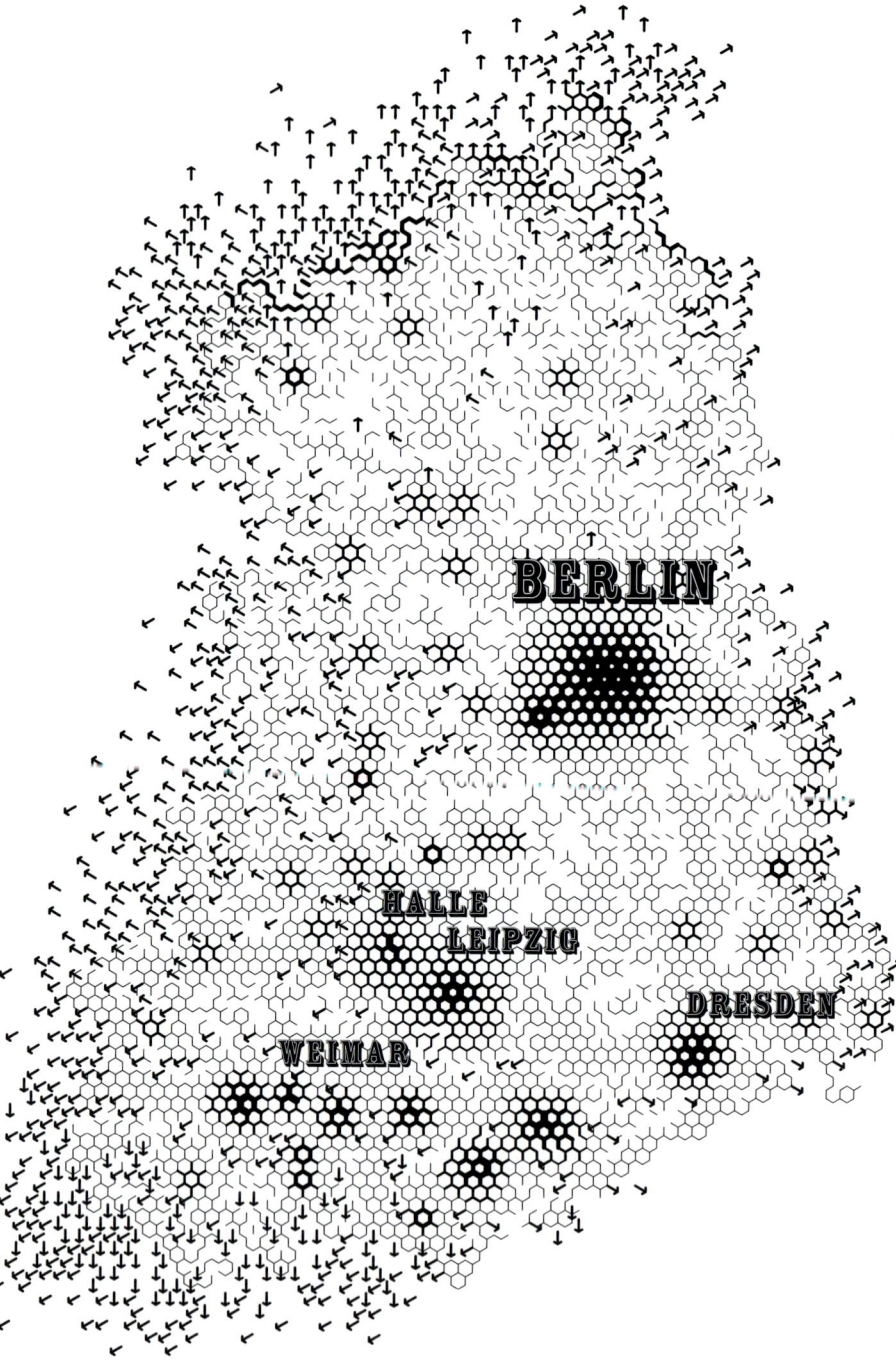

Migration (either abroad or to western Germany) and regional depletion in a context of ongoing shrinkage (1990–2050).

Domestic migration and regional compaction following the foundation of a metropolitan region (2015–2050).

metropolitan region between Dresden and Erfurt, MetroSachs has been developing as a viable entity, no longer dependent on state subsidies.

The flip side of domestic mass migration and the subsequent regional concentration of growth is the great expanse of abandoned renaturalized land, which the EU has since designated as a national ecological factor that can balance the ongoing sealing of land in western Germany, where, for example, 40% of Bavaria and Baden-Württemberg had already been sealed by 2015. Today, in 2048, the state has completely withdrawn from these areas, which are reminiscent of America's Wild West or the Australian outback. People who choose to live there (tax-free) are obliged to organize all their own foodstuffs and facilities, for public administrations, hospitals, schools, and so forth are now available solely in MetroSachs.

The foundation of MetroSachs put an end to the idea of a homogenous national territory that had held sway in Modern Europe. Given the realities of a "two-speed Europe" (global prosperity, local poverty), this Modern concept of space could no longer be upheld. On the contrary: following 2012, the division of eastern Germany into two metropolitan regions was considered to be a successful model for countering the entrenchment of regional polarization and social tensions between the prosperous corridors and those socially and economically deprived areas beyond the metropolitan network into which foreigners, the impoverished, the elderly, and other misfits had been shunted. MetroSachs countered this development by integrating the southern half of the eastern German population in an urbanized region that guaranteed all its inhabitants the advantages of metropolitan life. With hindsight it can be seen that this regional concentration of the population was a prerequisite for the maintenance of an acceptable material and social quality of life for all.

And so the growth project MetroSachs also marked the end of the German debate on shrinkage that had taken place throughout the century's first decade. But which urban planning models were to be used to densify the expanding MetroSachs region following the era of shrinkage? If planners and architects indeed had to reinvent European urbanism, they could not fall back on traditional European, U.S., or Chinese patterns of urban development. In addition, sealing the fate of shrinking cities by phasing them out and consciously promoting growth at other locations was an idea that initially appeared quite paradoxical to many observers. Yet this was by no means a new concept in urban development: it had been implemented consistently under eastern German shrinking policies until 2010. The demolition of vacant housing and the liquidation of unviable districts had concentrated urban development in those districts considered to have optimal chances of growth. Limited budget funding for demolition (which covered a mere third of housing stock), the renewed increase in the number of vacant properties after 2010, and the definitive economic collapse of rural regions in eastern Germany all contributed to putting the structural problems of whole towns—the "dying towns"—on the planning and political agendas. It was because of this that the vision of MetroSachs could win over politicians, public administrations, and experts by 2012—and it had the population's support from the get go (MetroSachs's popular nickname in the early years, "DD-ER," was a combination of Dresden and Erfurt's vehicle registration codes).[3]

The historical cultural entity "eastern Germany" is today comprised solely of the two metropolitan regions of MetroSachs and Berlin, in a way similar to former West Germany, which is comprised solely of the metropolitan regions of Hamburg, Munich, Ruhr District, and Rhineland-Main. Life for everybody in these metropolitan areas meets the standard level stipulated by the EU's Social Charter. The renaturalized landscape of ruins between the eastern metropolises might be reminiscent of centuries-old settlement strategies for "the German East"—and yet, since the EU was annexed by the global superpower, India, the geographical significance of Old Europe is rapidly dwindling and, with it, the memory of what was once "East Germany."

Translated from the German by Jill Denton

This project was developed for the Bauhaus Dessau Foundation in the context of "Shrinking Cities."

Project contributors were Nicolas Bourquin, Hannes Gieseler, Nina Gribat, and Johanna Leuner.

Notes
1   The name "MetroSachs" is the brainchild of Nina Gribat, an architect based in Berlin and a contributor to the project.
2   Werner Sewing, "Vom Schrumpfen des Politischen," *archplus* 173 (2005), 60.
3   DD-ER is also reminiscent of DDR, the German acronym for the German Democratic Republic.—Trans.

THE LAST BASTION
DUTCH STRATEGIES IN A NEOLIBERAL AGE
Bart Lootsma

———

———

Two issues dominated international debates on architecture throughout the 1990s: first, the computer and its consequences for architectural practice; second, and above all, the issue of growth. We realized that the majority of the world's population lives in cities, and that growth in some of these cities is rapid and unchecked. While social geographers had long since forecast this trend, it was Rem Koolhaas who first addressed it as a major issue in architecture and urban development. By drawing on examples, such as the Pearl River Delta in China or Lagos in Nigeria, he demonstrated spectacular and chaotic processes of growth, and the way that inhabitants and planners dealt with this phenomenon. Koolhaas considers urban growth in the context of economic expansion, the increase in world population, and migration from rural to urban areas. Despite the euphoria that accompanied the New Economy, we have had to recognize that recession can reoccur at any moment; and that migration nowadays tends to mean not an influx from rural areas, but a drift from one urban region to another. This leads us to the underlying causes of shrinking processes, which have emerged particularly in Germany. The question is, to what extent are typological solutions to the problems of density and growth applicable to situations of shrinking and inverse densification?

Koolhaas's actual influence at international level is difficult to assess. There is, however, no doubt that he profoundly influenced Dutch architecture and urban development in the 1990s. Koolhaas's interest in the issue of growth largely corresponded with the self-perception in the Netherlands at that time. The country underwent enormous expansion in the twentieth century, the greater part of which occurred after 1945. More than 75% of the country's built-up areas were created in this period. During the early 1990s, the government was still reckoning on the basis of 16 million inhabitants, who would require between 800,000 and 1,000,000 new housing units by the year 2005. These new housing units were to be created under new conditions, for the 1990s brought the extensive deregulation and privatization of construction and planning. No wonder that Dutch architects and planners were interested in growth processes in Asia and South America! Many of them undertook study trips—sometimes in groups and with state funding—to precisely those places that Koolhaas had investigated. The idea, formulated by Koolhaas, "that architecture could directly influence how issues are formulated in a culture founded on density, technology, and significant levels of social instability" filled them with pride and inspired them to develop new typologies.[1] Deregulation and privatization were not only widely accepted but were sometimes even supported or even funded. Growth, density, and instability in the Netherlands are of course not comparable with conditions in many Asian, Latin American, or African cities. The latter are often considerably more exciting than their European counterparts, as Rem Koolhaas also remarked: "When one compares Shenzen with Almere, the question poses itself as to why Almere, with so much more architectural input and so much more money, is so much less of a city."[2] In order to wield more cultural influence, Dutch architects demanded more freedom. But the opposite occurred, and the influence of Dutch architects declined.

Point City

Existing Dutch population
at Los Angeles density
population: 15 million
diameter: 87 km

Existing Dutch population
at Manhattan density
population: 15 million
diameter: 27.6 km

South City

Existing Dutch population
at Los Angeles density
population: 15 million
area: 6,000 km2

Existing Dutch population at Manhattan
density along Dutch/Belgian border
population: 15 million
area: 345 km x 1.75 km

In order to improve the Netherlands' competitiveness on the European market, OMA's project "Point City/South City" (1993) proposed two concepts for regional reorganization in this densely populated country. By successively concentrating the whole population in the green heart of Point City and in the southern provinces, namely, South City, economically buoyant metropolitan growth zones would emerge as a balance to the rest of the country, which would be reserved for renaturalization, the agrarian economy, and recreation.

Perhaps the only counterposition to this view in the 1990s was that taken by MVRDV. Projects such as "Metacity/Datatown" (1999) show how the future of the Netherlands might look with a population density four times greater than today's. The Netherlands is conceived as a single, 400 square kilometer metropolis and is intended to be completely self-sufficient. Experiments based on collective behavioral shifts or on commonly agreed laws are conducted in a real-time computer simulation—a classic vision of Utopia. Metacity/Datatown was intended as a forewarning of that which is taking effect today. The project sees itself as a didactic political instrument. For this reason, the collective risks (of a quadrupled population density in a situation of complete autarchy) have to be magnified to the extent that they become barely imaginable and difficult to grasp—something Slavoj Žižek also describes in his critique of the risk society.[3] What remains is irrational fear, even when the project is enthusiastically taken up by politicians and even when a prototype is built, for example, the Dutch pavilion at the EXPO 2000 exhibition in Hannover.

The "Shrinking Cities" project can hence also be seen as a reversal of the Dutch obsession with growth. And it is perhaps no coincidence that its chief curator, Philipp Oswalt, worked in 1996–1997 first with Rem Koolhaas and OMA, and then with MVRDV—in the very period when interest in explosive growth, density, and instability reached its apex in Dutch architecture. The question was obvious: might not perhaps the typologies and methodologies developed by Dutch architects for growth scenarios be simply reversed?

One 1990s project in Dutch architecture corresponds perfectly to the situation in Germany, and appears in retrospect to have been almost visionary. It was for a long time considered improbable and frivolous, however. OMA's "Point City/South City" was created in 1993 for the international colloquium on architecture, "Alexanderpolder: Where the City Continues."[4] Two of MVRDV's founders, Winy Maas and Jakob van der Rijs, were major contributors to the project. Point City/South City addresses the question as to how the Netherlands might approach regional development at a moment when the country is on the verge of missing its chance to become part of a European economic core zone—the "Blue Banana" that extends from London to Milan. In attempts to become integrated in this core zone, the Netherlands has already been implementing infrastructural schemes such as high-speed trains (HSL) and railway freight networks for some years now, but such ventures have been interminably held up. Point City/South City is another project that builds on the Dutch population's fear of becoming marginalized.

The project proposes two different concepts. One is to concentrate all construction projects in the Netherlands in the empty heart of the Randstad conurbation (consisting, among other cities, of Amsterdam, Utrecht, Rotterdam, and The Hague) in the west of the country (Point City): a phased development, intended to create a new metropolis with genuine urban qualities. This metropolis would lie directly on the border of the Blue Banana and consequently attain a critical mass that could easily hold its own with Paris or London. The other concept, South City, proposes concentrating all construction in the southern provinces of the Netherlands. In both cases the rest of the country would be reserved for renaturalization, the agrarian economy, and recreation.

However incredible this project may appear, a glance at a current map of the Netherlands reveals that both developments are already taking shape. The northern part of the Netherlands is shrinking—albeit at not quite the dramatic rate seen in other countries. Years of investment in a city such as Groningen—to where, for example, the headquarters

The Last Bastion_Bart Lootsma

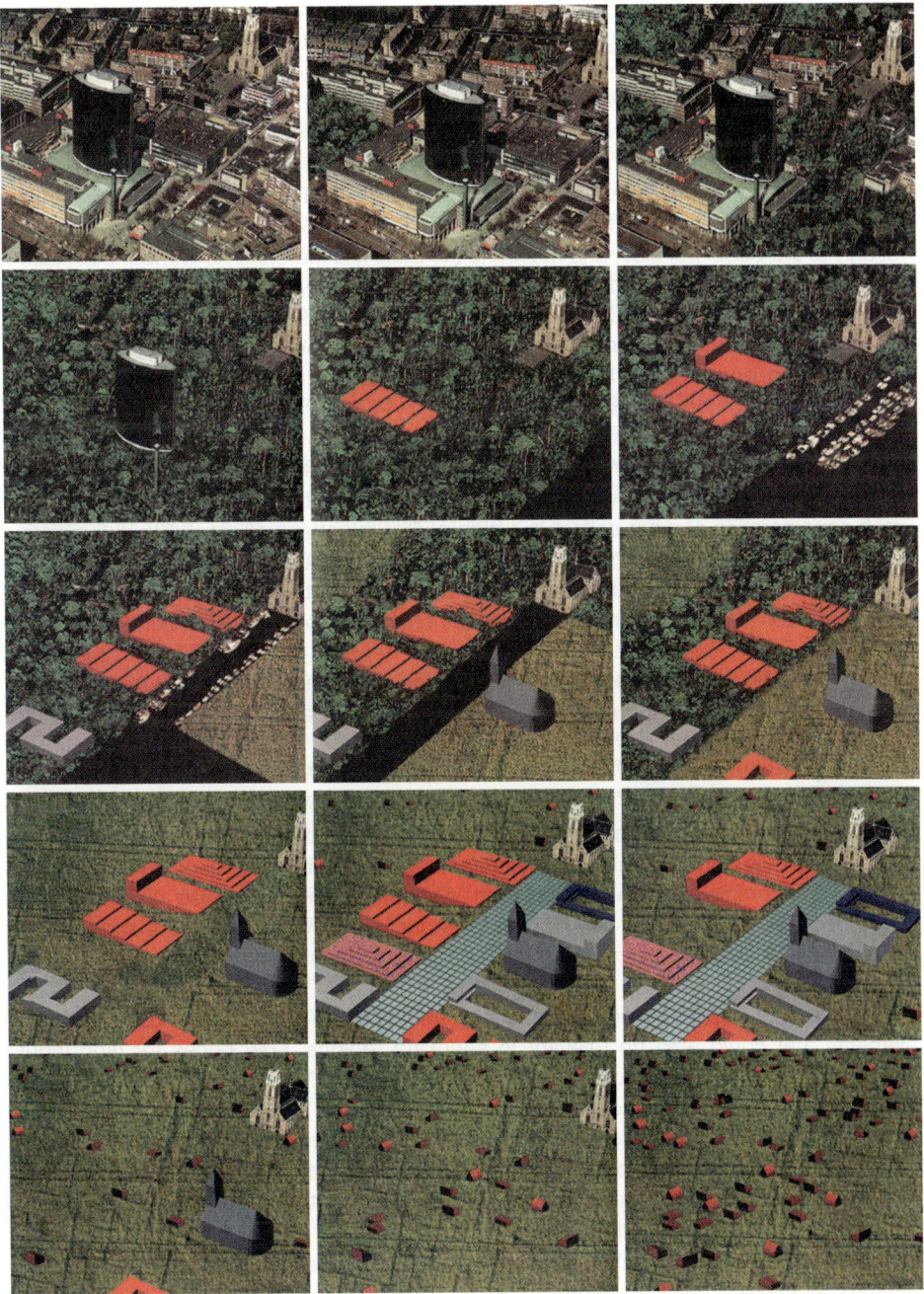

The concept of "Light Urbanism" (MVRDV, 1995) challenges the apparent permanence of urban substance and instead proposes a more playful way of dealing with constructed elements. Temporary infrastructure and uninhibited demolition offer cities the opportunity to completely dissolve into the landscape, and yet also to recompact, as required.

TERRITORIAL RETREAT
ON THE DIFFICULTIES OF DELIVERING PUBLIC SERVICES IN PERIPHERAL REGIONS
Hans-Joachim Bürkner

Ongoing regional economic crises and population declines are having a severe effect on the public budget in eastern Germany. Important sources of tax revenue are drying up, while the costs of providing and maintaining urban infrastructure and public amenities are rising due to lack of demand and resulting below-capacity usage.

The public budget crisis now obliges both municipal and federal bodies to try and invest their ever-dwindling resources more efficiently—an aspiration that is having considerable regional repercussions. It has already led eastern German states—albeit to different degrees—to abandon traditional welfare-state targets, such as balancing regional disparity, for example. The motto now is, "Sprinkler-style funding is over!" Such a fundamental shift in funding policy can amount to the state completely withdrawing from a region. Some states are already planning to compact regions and urban areas into those locations or core settlements that have development potential, to cut urban infrastructure and facilities for which demand is low, and to reorganize the functions of certain central locations. Some of these schemes have already been implemented. While their effect on "strong" locations is still difficult to forecast, a relative devaluation of less competitive locations can already to be reckoned with. In all probability these will suffer further losses of both people and commercial enterprises.

The logic underlying current policy shifts at first seems quite plausible. Funding that yields neither structural nor political benefits is considered to be money down the drain; its allocation is politically barely justifiable. From the perspective of the local authorities and the population affected, however, such strategies of retreat may be grounds for considerable conflict. Ultimately it is a question not only of how local living standards will be affected by these new targets, but also of how local authorities will manage at all to deal with the state's changing role. Funding policy that seeks to "strengthen the strong" is perceived by a relatively strong, successful person as being consistent with the "enabling state," yet it can amount to a "disabling" policy for relatively weak or endangered citizens, or even to political "disempowerment," namely, to political exclusion and a reduction in opportunities for taking local action.

Is Basic Provision in Danger?
Shrinkage processes fundamentally foil the logic underlying the principles of traditional welfare-state distribution. A decline in population means there is less demand for schools and daycare centers, hospital beds, and other public services. Individual institutions have larger catchment areas and thereby become less easily accessible for certain clients. New disadvantages arise for people with limited mobility. Below-capacity usage dramatically increases the costs of maintaining transportation systems, leading to cuts in services and reduced maintenance budgets; Brandenburg has for the first time axed some rural highways, for example.[1] Loss of life quality and the increasing dysfunctionalism of formerly viable infrastructures and facilities are a real menace. One need name only a few examples in order to illustrate the extent of new problems regarding service provision. And it is not only among public, but also among private service providers that one can find such examples.

State Provision Policy

Classical state provision policy (infrastructure policy, for example, but also superordinate policy areas such as regional policy) is targeted in Germany at creating generally equitable living conditions. To this end, the state had developed a mandatory model that was intended not only to guarantee high-quality service delivery but, in addition, to lay the foundations for the identification of broad classes or population groups with the state and to ensure their participation in society. While this model of mandatory provision functioned relatively smoothly during former West Germany's phases of growth, in the new eastern German states the economic basis for it was lacking from the start: lack of growth and blanket shrinking processes left the state model high and dry. In federal states such as Brandenburg, investments in infrastructure to the tune of millions have literally gone up in smoke. Against all hopes, they failed to regenerate the economy and tended rather to result in more radical retreat. They made it easier for the mobile population—whose employment chances in Brandenburg itself are slim—to move or to commute to other states for work. Such investments in eastern Germany's peripheral regions practically created the material basis for a substantial "brain drain," or migration of qualified labor. Well-educated locals are now in short supply there, which considerably detracts from the state's appeal as a business location. In relatively successful states such as Saxony, only those metropolitan regions experiencing partial economic growth (Leipzig, Dresden, and Chemnitz) were able to benefit from upgraded infrastructure.

Debates on whether or not to abandon the principle of equitable distribution resulted in a far-reaching discussion of minimum standards and legally enforceable vested rights. It has never before been precisely stated who in which place has the right to demand which goods or services. This could turn into quite a battle. The Brandenburg government is currently attempting to cluster important service provisions (e.g., supplying local authorities with a general education system) as part of its reform of the "central location system." Analogous discussions are also under way in Saxony and Saxony-Anhalt.[2] Brandenburg's current concept is premised on radically reducing the number of central locations. In particular, the number of basic centers in peripheral areas is to be drastically reduced. The remaining central locations are seen as "anchors" for their respective micro-regions and are expected to cater particularly for the rural population that is otherwise tending to migrate.[3] Such plans have already been protested, above all in rural areas. Critics fear that the planned reduction in the number of central locations and subsequent enlargement of the remaining centers' catchment areas will lead to lower-quality service delivery and tend to isolate the rural population.

Private Provision

Population decline is also putting the private service sector under growing pressure. Medical provision in thinly populated areas (e.g., the Uckermark region of Brandenburg) is increasingly threatened by lack of demand and the sinking viability of practices and institutions. Attempts have been made to counter this trend by guaranteeing a minimum income to doctors willing to take on a rural practice—but with only moderate success to date.[4] New organizational models such as ambulant solutions have not yet been sufficiently tested and, without flexible funding that can be tailored to specific needs, their practical use is rather limited.

The Uckermark region also made changes in its transportation system, introducing the model of on-call minibuses to maintain services for thinly populated areas. Passengers can order a minibus by phone or online, as required. Yet this model is incompatible with transportation services legislation, which often hampers prospective providers in developing attractive and viable services.[5] In this case, too, more flexible subsidies and licensing laws are required before practicable solutions can be reached.

"Strengthen the Strong" – Economic Policy's New Credo

Regional disparity of living standards was discussed in eastern Germany at a very early stage. Legitimate fears that radically deindustrialized regions and rural areas might be left far behind general development were countered in the 1990s throughout most eastern German states by recourse to the policy of evening out disparity. The underlying logic of this policy was that directly funding the least developed locations would have the greatest positive effect and, above all, positive spin-off effects for the location's immediate vicinity. Equality and funding efficiency would thus be achieved in one. In the 1990s, Brandenburg had hoped, for example, to promote development in peripheral areas by highlighting and exploiting endogenous potential.[6] In practice, however, it has become evident that economic growth has failed to transpire in peripheral areas, in particular. Here, on account of shrinking demographics and dwindling human resources, a reversal of this trend can now no longer be expected. Indeed, any funding earmarked for evening out disparity is currently considered by politicians to be money down the drain.

Even revamped political concepts for regional development can already be seen to have failed. Once again, Brandenburg has come up with an impressive example, namely, a planning concept developed in the 1990s and called "decentralized compaction." By defining "regional development centers" in the vicinity of Berlin as well as in some more distant corners of the state, it was hoped to create engines of regional development that would stimulate growth and stability in "their own" surrounding areas. Yet, as economic growth has failed to transpire (above all in Berlin), the regional development centers in the peripheral areas are today a downright disaster. In most of these towns, spillover or evening-out effects are now considered highly improbable.

Experiences such as these have led to policy shifts in those states that were formerly oriented towards removing disparities. Recent debates on reforming and realigning funding policy now follow a completely reversed logic. The basic premise today is that strengthening locations that are already strong will bring the best results. Given that shrinkage and budget crises have already decimated the available funding, what is left can legitimately be used only in places where it really will contribute to growth and stability.

Brandenburg, for Instance

In the case of Brandenburg, this approach looks in practice as follows. The concept of regional growth centers formulated by the State Ministry of Economics expressly aims to develop sectoral centers of excellence that have a promising future. These centers of excellence are very specifically located, in recently established "priority sector-specific locations." Any location with more than 20,000 inhabitants that also has a scientific institution or two as well as potential for economic development is awarded the ancillary status of "regional growth center" and receives preferential funding.[7] In this way, growth centers

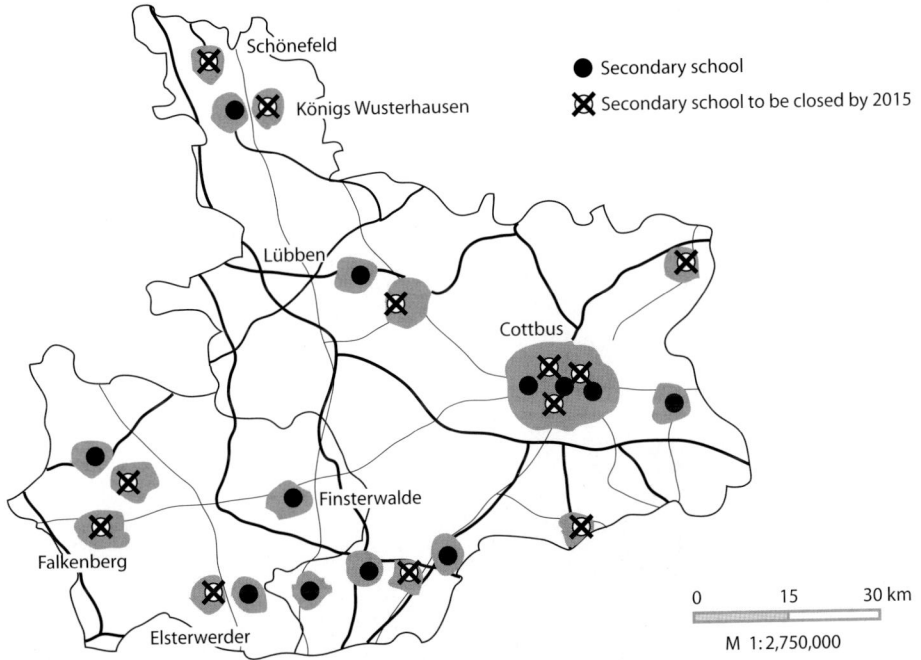

The decline in population often makes it impossible to retain public amenities. As early as 2002/03, the Lausitz-Spreewald region of Brandenburg therefore planned the closure of numerous secondary schools by 2015.

acquire, among other things, the means to develop and extend soft locational factors, which primarily means specific local strategies for locational marketing, networking, and so forth. The aim is to help the respective locations position themselves well in global competition and also to create spin-off effects for their surrounding areas.

This logic is not new. It was already implemented in states such as Brandenburg in the 1990s, although at that time it was called "clustering." Funding innovative clusters—whereby small and medium-sized businesses in fields requiring a high level of technology and knowledge were concentrated in certain locations, integrated in global networks, and generally networked at a local level—at least in some cases helped establish local hubs of flexible production, knowledge-based service industries, and sometimes even research and development. Nonetheless, those small clusters created in Brandenburg—microelectronics, biotechnology, vehicle construction, and aviation and space technology—have created very little employment. Their spin-off effect on the surrounding regions has also been negligible.

The number of growth centers that can be identified as such is still low. Most places are characterized by the wave of deindustrialization that hit former East Germany's mono-structural manufacturing centers. Independent, neo-Fordist reindustrialization—whereby subsidiaries of western German and multinational companies are rapidly established in traditional sectors or in labor-intensive, low-tech manufacturing—are much more typical of the everyday regional economy here than are highly technological and globally competitive clusters.

In outlying areas, modernization—of the railways, for example—is nowadays frequently synonymous with peripheral regions' loss of vital infrastructure. The closed-down railway station in Friesack, Brandenburg, 2005.

In general, Brandenburg's policies promoting global integration have barely got off the ground. The repercussions of a political drift that in the 1990s (when Manfred Stolpe was premier of the state) mistakenly took a whole string of unsuccessful prestige projects to be the spearhead of modernization can still be felt today. This accounts for the fact that new innovation strategies tend to be approached only halfheartedly. In any case, new policies of clustering will barely manage to fulfill traditional hopes for a return to old-style mass industrial employment, though these are clung to by Brandenburg's government and municipal authorities and its inhabitants. Formulating and publicly communicating an economic policy that is committed to creating, supporting, and globally integrating innovative endeavor is extremely difficult under these circumstances.

For the time being, political regard for peripheral regions that are now demographically and economically up against the wall continues to wane. The new policy of compaction primarily benefits the metropolitan area of Berlin.[8] In the "bacon belt" on the outskirts of the city, one finds important clusters and service-sector industries with good growth prospects. Apart from some vague hopes still for the spin-off effects of growth centers, nobody has any idea what to do about peripheral regions that are falling ever further behind, and the suspicion remains that a new period of laissez-faire could well cause problems to accumulate—a potential time bomb that could result in social and political upheaval in the near future. The outlook for areas such as Uckermark, Prignitz, and Oberlausitz is hence none too rosy.

In Saxony-Anhalt, too, there are calls for a reform of funding strategies. Debates consciously take account of the fact that discrepancy between development rates in new growth centers and rural regions will become more acute.[9] The latter are casually advised to "lean on" their nearest large town for support. Here, too, a readiness to simply accept potential disadvantages for "weak" regions and to wait and see what the effects of new compaction policies will be is evident. Given the enormous social and political repercussions of this transparent political turnaround, the policy incentives accompanying it are of a decidedly experimental nature.

Saxony, for Instance

Saxony is the only eastern German state where the allocation of funding to growth centers and industrial agglomerations has had positive results. Shortly after the fall of the Berlin Wall, industrial core zones in Leipzig and Dresden and their respective infrastructures were identified as being favorable prerequisites for the further development of research and manufacture. These have transpired in the Dresden area thanks to relatively concentrated investments by multinational companies and the development of new economic clusters, for example in microelectronics. It was possible in both cases to draw, at least in part, on Dresden's long-standing industrial tradition. The comprehensive spatial concentration of companies specialized in semiconductors around leading concerns such as Infineon or AMD is practically the only original cluster formation of global importance in eastern Germany—that is, one that emerged without the aid of massive state funding. The regional strategy of funding industrial compaction has in any case proved successful here, not least because it also contributed at an early stage to developing and stabilizing the cluster and, hence, to its economic momentum. Such "flagship policies" spurred on the vital development of networks, in particular in the semiconductor industry, which in turn allowed a critical mass of viable economic activity to establish itself in a way that was not possible in Brandenburg or Saxony-Anhalt. The industrial base was renewed by intelligently mixing policies that supported innovation with clever marketing of the city's historical assets.

This process was supported by Saxony's regional development policy, which, as part of the overall concept for the "Saxony Triangle" European Metropolitan Region—a development alliance linking Leipzig, Dresden, and Chemnitz—seeks to create the structural base that will, in the long term, guarantee and also extend this agglomeration's leap forward in regional competition.[10]

Yet notwithstanding its booming metropolitan regions, Saxony still has marginal regions such as Oberlausitz-Niederschlesien and Westerzgebirge that have no part in the state's general economic fortunes and are severely hit by shrinking demographics. Former mining regions and centers of heavy industry have suffered the same decline as their counterparts in Brandenburg. Official flagship policy has long since stolen the limelight in public debates from questions of regional disparity. The "model regions" policy recently announced by the state government and expressly designed to find solutions to problems posed by shrinkage appears in this context more like a strategy of retreat. Its core purpose is to render the effects of global modernization more socially palatable. Mobile public administrations and attempts to mobilize civic resources, such as voluntary work and community self-help, are noted here initially as isolated threads, and loose threads at that, in the absence of any overall economic strategies.[11]

The Federal Government's Finger in the Pie
Germany's federal government recently decided to intervene in these still virginal debates. In line with its proposal to allocate future funding to specific sectors, innovative centers of excellence, and networks at locations with promising prospects, it is currently recommending that all eastern German states adopt Saxony's renowned flagship policy, for example by creating regional cluster administrators.[12] With the exception of Brandenburg, whose approach is being endorsed by the latest federal funding policy, several states appear to oppose this idea. Regional politicians in Saxony-Anhalt have spoken of "compaction imposed by the federal government" and censure the centralizing and quasi planned-economy impetus behind this policy shift.[13] And it is true that innovation might be hindered if funding is allocated only to those places where something already exists. This policy would therefore thwart any chances of instigating new networks and clusters at hitherto unknown or insignificant locations.

The latest controversy shows that this funding policy has not been thought through to its logical conclusion. There is widespread doubt as to whether eastern Germany's development dilemma might realistically be resolved by funding general, sectoral, and regional targets. On the contrary, it appears as if a general search for new, sustainable strategies has only just begun. Economic research therefore currently counsels keeping a careful eye on small-scale developments and funding economic core-development areas or clusters not only in a flexible manner but also on a small scale, for example at the municipal and district level.[14] Nevertheless, there appears to be a distinct trend towards more state-imposed compaction.

Differentiated Funding Policy: An Alternative?
This whole debate barely touches upon the question of the future of peripheral regions. Amid all the compaction hype, this threatens to pose a huge problem that is quite simply

being suppressed by new hopes for development. Given the fact that eastern German politicians were until recently still vehemently defending the idea of regional equality, this issue is all the more worrying. In the light of current predictions, it does appear as if policies that address growth alone will accelerate the isolation of peripheral areas from general development trends. Policy amendments that fail to prevent negative effects on peripheral areas, even while they may at least alleviate them, will presumably have to entertain a minimal notion of how disparity might be removed. Without a differentiated funding policy that accommodates growth as well as demands for regional equality and that, in considering the shifts in everyday requirements, comes up with a flexible definition of what basic provision in the towns and villages of marginal regions might look like, it is hardly to be expected that the desired goals—of creating regional "anchor towns," for example—will be attained. Simply offering "mercy killing" to towns that fail to hold their own in regional competition, or assigning new functions to marginal regions—as recreational or renaturalized areas, or as biotopes for alternative lifestyles—will not suffice; even less so when one takes the stubborn entrenchment and emotional ties of the remaining local population into consideration. Politicians and planners will consequently continue to be confronted with the problem of providing adequate prospects for the population "left over" from shrinkage processes in marginal areas—a population that is elderly, has restricted mobility, and is increasingly poor. Unless, that is, they fall back on a draconian directive such as resettlement—a measure that is, however, scarcely compatible with the basic principles of a democratic society.

Any Way Out for Peripheral Towns and Regions?
Consideration of peripheral regions' actual strengths and potential to improve their situation has been lacking in the debate to date. Future realignments of pertinent funding policies will therefore have to be judged not only on the extent to which they implement massive cuts in services for the leftover population, but also, and at the least, on their draft policies for complementary guarantees (of certain living standards) and for mobilizing resources. Some of the planned items and pertinent themes are briefly summed up below.

• *Creating an image and identifying strengths.* New, differentiated funding policy should be primarily oriented towards the actual local strengths, image, and talents of respective towns and local authorities. The conditions of shrinkage mean that strength can no longer be defined merely in terms of a town's or region's economic power (as it was under traditional funding concepts), but also in terms of the capabilities of local actors to valorize available resources and to identify new resources and potentials. Clear incentives are required to get people involved in the search for a local identity and for social, economic, and cultural strengths: local creativity and personal initiative must be rewarded.

• *Promoting complementary economic sectors.* Funding policies in eastern Germany were hitherto primarily oriented towards industrial growth sectors, large projects, and scientific and technological research. While such measures may well increase a federal state's overall competitiveness in the global economic context, the local and regional effects of such policies are minimal. Peripheral regions are particularly in need of funding concepts that stabilize complementary economic sectors at the regional level. These are essential for small and medium-sized low-tech production companies, for consolidating small businesses with limited capital, and for developing local and regional networks—all of which can at least partially cushion the risks inherent in regional and urban competition in a global market.

- *Civic engagement and accessing social resources.* Faced with drastic reductions in the public budget, the state will soon no longer be able to finance public welfare as comprehensively as it has in the past. Nor, furthermore, will it be able to define public welfare across the board. Any services beyond an adequate basic provision for the population regarding infrastructure and public facilities, social services, and so forth therefore increasingly lie beyond the state's competence. Demands for civic engagement, as a contribution to maintaining decent living standards, are consequently increasing in importance. The negative aspect here, namely, that the state thus places part of its financial responsibility for social and regional equality onto its citizens, is not all that should be seen. Inherent opportunities for participation and the development of self-determined lifestyles in shrinking cities and regions are more positive aspects.

Learning from Sweden? An Outlook

In order to guarantee a minimum of regional competence and flexibility in the midst of restructuring crises and rampant inequalities, the state will find itself increasingly obliged to cooperate with numerous actors from other sectors, in other words, engage in governance. Ensuing forms of regionalism are new to the extent that they aim for flexible cooperation and creative compensation strategies, and thereby challenge the traditional allocation of duties and responsibilities at the political and administrative levels.

In the context of such political debates, "Scandinavia" is a popular catchword. Its example of providing goods and services to thinly populated regions has made achieving high standards of provision based on complementary structures and mobile services appear viable, at least on paper. Admittedly, this particular example has also shown that regions' ability to take independent action is clearly limited, and that respective development policies' viability still depends on state directives and initiatives.[15] Sweden, for example, introduced municipal tax adjustments, improved access to public institutions by rescheduling the transportation system and investing in modern communications and IT, promoted cooperation between neighboring communities, and initiated a coordinated series of regional development programs. The key here to creating feasible and flexible systems for service provision was not government standards but each local population's own needs. Top-down policies and bottom-up initiatives had to be effectively combined in order to create structures that really work.

"Eastern Germany, the special case," still seems to be avoiding this dual task. On the one hand, the tendency to follow its traditional "five-year plan" approach, characterized by rigid organizational structures and distribution mechanisms, remains dominant; on the other, bottom-up initiatives, particularly those based on civic engagement, are currently in short supply. A direct transfer of models that have emerged in other regional development contexts and other state frameworks hence appears doubtful. One must also consider that Sweden's initiatives, in particular, were backed up by a prosperous state that adheres to highly efficient funding policies, two prerequisites that, on account of the currently critical economic situation, are unlikely to be able to establish themselves in eastern Germany in the foreseeable future.

For the time being, eastern Germany finds itself politically constrained to take small steps—away from its old planning mentality and towards new, flexible ways of assessing demand, identifying and promoting individual local strengths, and calculatedly funding a new culture of cooperation at the municipal and regional levels. This is necessary if the state's withdrawal is to be somehow compensated—by innovative, high-quality solutions that will be able, from case to case, to ensure not only losses but also new win-win situations.

Translated from the German by Jill Denton

Notes

1. See Martin Klesmann and Jens Blankennagel, "Das Land will Straßen loswerden," *Berliner Zeitung*, January 24, 2005.
2. See CDU-Landtagsfraktion Sachsen-Anhalt, *Bürgerland Sachsen-Anhalt: Thesen einer Strukturpolitik für zukunftssichere Städte und Dörfer,* http://cdu.eckpunkt.de/images_downloads/pdf_66.pdf (accessed July 2, 2005).
3. See Ministerium für Infrastruktur und Raumordnung des Landes Brandenburg, *Überarbeitung des Zentrale-Orte-Systems in Brandenburg,* www.mir.brandenburg.de/cms/media.php/2239/presse-02-03-05.ppt (accessed April 1, 2005).
4. See Katrin Bischoff and Jürgen Schwenkenbecher, "Trotz Garantiehonorar—der erste Landarzt gibt auf," *Berliner Zeitung,* April 11, 2005.
5. *VDI nachrichten,* "Der öffentliche Nahverkehr in ländlichen Regionen soll verbessert werden," June 3, 2005.
6. See Rudolf Woderich, "Chimäre oder Chance? Endogene Entwicklung in Brandenburg," *Deutschland Archiv* 7/8 (1998): 605-616.
7. See Ministerium für Wirtschaft des Landes Brandenburg, *Branchen-Kompetenzfelder, Branchen-Schwerpunktorte, Regionale Wachstumskerne,* www.wirtschaft.brandenburg.de/cms/media.php/gsid=lbm1.a.1312.de/Charts_Pressekonferenz.pdf (accessed April 1, 2005).
8. See Klaus-Peter Schmid, "Nehmen, was kommt: Der Bund will im Osten nur noch bestimmte Länder fordern—die Länder wehren sich," *Die Zeit,* May 4, 2005; www.zeit.de/2005/19/Ostf_9arderung (accessed July 2, 2005).
9. See Jens Bullerjahn, *Sachsen-Anhalt 2020: Einsichten und Perspektiven; ein realistischer Blick auf die Entwicklung von Bevölkerung, Arbeitsmarkt, Wirtschaft und öffentlichen Finanzen,* http://www.spd-sachsen-anhalt.de/files/zukunft1_2020.pdf, 49 (accessed April 1, 2006).
10. See Freistaat Sachsen, Sächsisches Staatsministerium des Innern, ed., *Landesentwicklungsplan Sachsen 2003* (Dresden), 8.
11. See Reiner Burger, "Silberbergwerke, Braunkohletagebau, Brachland," *Frankfurter Allgemeine Zeitung,* April 27, 2005.
12. Schmid, "Nehmen, was kommt."
13. Ibid.
14. Peter Franz and Martin Rosenfeld, "Fertigstellung der IWH-Studie 'Innovative Kompetenzfelder, Produktionsnetzwerke und Branchenschwerpunkte der ostdeutschen Wirtschaft,'" (Press Release 37, Institut für Wirtschaftsforschung Halle, 2004), 7.
15. See Bärbel Winkler-Kühlken, "Voneinander lernen—Bevölkerungsrückgang und Strukturanpassung in ländlichen Regionen Europas," *Informationen zur Raumentwicklung* 1 (2003): 779–787, here p. 780.

EMSCHER PARK INTERNATIONAL BUILDING EXHIBITION
A TRENDSETTING MODEL?
Arnold Voß

The Emscher Park "International Building Exhibition" (IBA) was conceived as a laboratory for economic, social, and ecological structural change and selected as its "experimental subject" an area that urgently needed this kind of integrated approach: the former industrial conurbation of the Ruhr District. As early as the 1950s, this region, whose importance since the nineteenth century had derived primarily from coal mining, was driven by the more competitive energy sources on the global market to the brink of economic disaster. In attempts to stem the region's decline, the state promptly initiated various restructuring and funding programs: subsidies for traditional industries, subsidies for capital investment throughout almost the whole region, the promotion of small and medium-sized businesses, and the costly purchase of abandoned and often highly contaminated land by a regional development company set up specifically for this purpose. Yet, against all hopes, none of these produced the decisive breakthrough to structural change. Only the foundation of a string of universities in the 1960s, as well as the technology transfer that ensued from new funding measures for innovation and research, showed initial signs of success, at least in the university towns.

In the light of this history, the idea of implementing the first IBA project that would cover a whole region can be seen as a consequence of the failure of previous growth and subsidization strategies. In comparison with the sums that had been spent up to that point, and considering the IBA's ten-year time frame (with a projected DM 4 billion to DM 5 billion for mobile investments, in addition to around DM 8 billion for the Emscher redevelopment itself) the actual costs of around DM 30 million for the IBA organization must have seemed to the state government to be a veritable policy bargain. This was possible because the quite considerable amounts of public money allocated to IBA projects came from existing public or European funding programs.

The Emscher Park IBA focused in particular on the northern part of the region, the former Emscher Valley, with its circa two million inhabitants—still, at that time, the part of the region most strongly characterized by the base-metal and mining industries. Once a natural river, the Emscher and all its tributaries had been abused since the beginning of the twentieth century as an almost 400-kilometer sewer and quasi-canalized industrial river that had become a major focus of endeavor for change. Its renaturalization, initially required by new European Union guidelines on water and then pushed through by the Emscher Cooperative (an association specialized in matters of sewage organization and comprising concerned local authorities), was the starting point for the IBA's second major scheme, the creation of a continuous regional landscape park along the east-west axis of the "new Emscher." New workplaces and residences in and around the Emscher Landscape Park were planned, along with the conversion of an increasing number of vacant cathedrals of industrial architecture into cultural centers. At its inception at the end of the 1980s, therefore, the Emscher Park IBA corresponded perfectly to prevailing concepts of urban development, architecture, and regional planning. A "brain-storming" appeal, aimed at professionals in all conceivable social fields, and launched by North Rhine-Westphalia's Ministry for Urban Development and Transportation in 1989, marked

Polarized Regional City

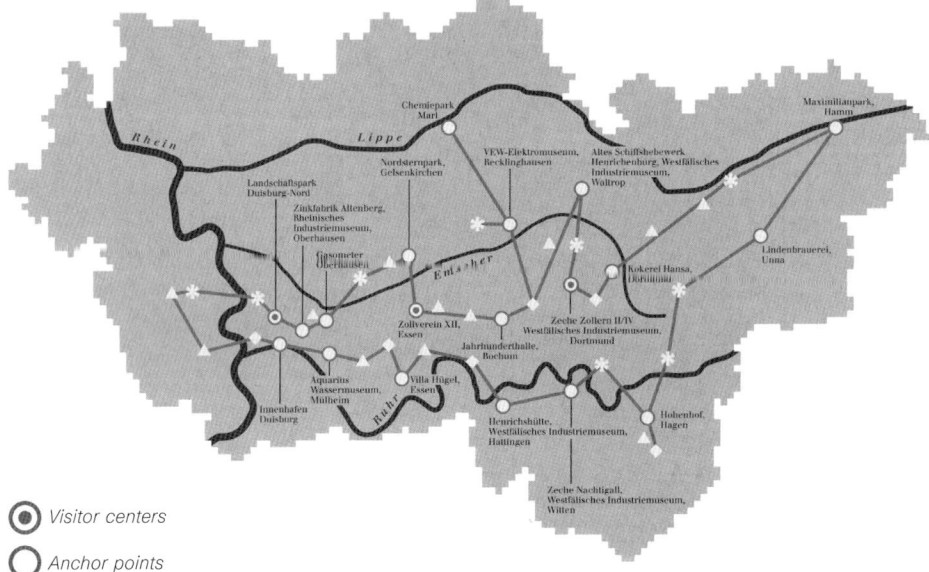

◉ *Visitor centers*

○ *Anchor points*

△ *Important settlements*

✳ *Panorama of industrial landscapes*

◇ *Supraregional museums*

The "Industrial Culture Route" consists of nineteen anchor points in a network of prominent, formerly industrial locations, and encompasses industrial monuments, museums, viewpoints, and important settlements.

the start of this long-term project. Over the course of the following ten years, 120 projects on six major themes were carried out.

- The proposed aim of the *Emscher Landscape Park* was to recoup nature and exploit its recreational, regenerative, and constitutive potential for the urban context. The green corridor, almost 70 kilometers long and several kilometers wide, with an industrial forest, open landscapes, waste heaps with landmarks, and residential and commercial properties, offers a broad spectrum of typologies for space and usage.
- The *ecological regeneration of the Emscher* was aimed at sustainable regional development by means of a new approach to hitherto neglected, natural basic materials in urban development. The river was renaturalized and freed of effluents by the construction of new sewage plants.
- The concept of *new industrial culture* created a framework for the new historicity of urban planning under the slogan "Regeneration by Preservation." The conversion, primarily for cultural purposes, of industrial ruins and the attendant review of local history, were intended to help the region find a new identity.
- The concept of *working in the park* reflected aspirations that structural change would create fewer, yet more highly qualified, workplaces, which were integral to the city.
- The concept of *new accommodation and neighborhood structures* was based—at least as far as experimental architectural approaches were concerned—on the expectation that lifestyles and the constitution of the family would change. DIY options for homeowners or renters, along with purchase assistance and amortized loans, were intended to guarantee the provision of accommodation for people from a wide range of social backgrounds.
- The goal of numerous *social initiatives* was to include the local population in the redevelopment process and especially to integrate young, long-term unemployed people by means of job-creation schemes and training programs.

The IBA saw its role as being that of facilitator, engine, and quality controller. It put its seal on the project, thereby rendering the real investors "fit for funding," provided that these were not themselves public bodies. Investment projects, in turn, saw themselves as flagships of creative design, as islands of innovation in the morass of regional planning. The underlying idea here is "perspective incrementalism," whereby, in the context of a still vague, long-term overall perspective, concrete single steps are formulated and implemented. The projected investment sum of DM 4 billion to DM 5 billion was, if one can believe the official statistics, chalked up by the more than one hundred projects. The greater part of this sum had, however, once again flowed from public funds and, by the end of the IBA project an overall concept for future redevelopment—a kind of master plan—was still nowhere in sight.

The Reversal of Social Trends: Regeneration without Growth
Before the ball even got rolling, however, growth rates in Germany began to fall. In the Ruhr district the pendulum even shifted to partial stagnation or below zero—and this against a background of demand-deficient unemployment caused by the onset of regional structural change some considerable time earlier. Applied to the IBA area itself, that is, to the northern part of the region, these figures indicate a social structure that was already characterized by an above-average proportion of older and less-qualified

long-term unemployed. An ongoing decline in population and state revenue at both regional and federal levels was already foreseeable, too, as the process of structural change overlaying economic problems continued to accelerate.

Insofar, the central slogan of the Emscher Park IBA project, "Regeneration without Growth," was perfectly suited to the social landscape. But only on the face of it. In reality, the slogan belonged to a period when growth had been largely a matter of course, and an ecological critique of it arising from newly won political awareness was hence almost inevitable. Now the threat of too much growth had been deprived of the "growth" part. The Emscher Park IBA was planning de facto with a yesteryear slogan for a move into economic and social tides of change that, despite all its successes, were bound to overwhelm it in the end. None of the people in charge could have imagined that, in less than ten years, the trend would completely reverse and that shrinking would constitute the major threat; and not only from an economic viewpoint.

If one takes a closer look at the lead projects, however, it is clear that the IBA, and likewise the state government behind it, were hoping, at least in the medium term, for fresh economic growth, or at least to raise the regional growth rate to the state and federal average. The *working in the park* concept, which solely because of its regional political implications had been established in almost every town in the Emscher zone, demanded as much. The extension of landscaped recreational areas, likewise foreseen in the *park* concept, was also pursued quite halfheartedly, although the need for more forceful action was clearly signaled by all demographic forecasts. The region's political players understandably considered the growing expanse of available land not as an opportunity for more recreational areas, but as potential locations for new investors, which it was imperative to keep in reserve. And, when it came to the crunch, the IBA—despite knowing better—did not contradict them.

From Idea to Ideology: The Emscher Park IBA as Regional Design

Declining growth rates were found in many other locations as a result of German reunification, which at least in its ultimate form was quite unforeseeable, and of the subsequent opening of Europe to the east. This heralded the start of harsh competition for growth opportunities and, above all, for funding—a trend that was to be reinforced throughout Europe by the new wave of globalization that began at the same time. The foreseeable regional shrinking process was thereby exposed to additional pressure from external forces. This by no means led to acceptance of the increasingly hopeless prospects of regional growth but, on the contrary, to a veritable do-or-die promotion of redevelopment as a means to new growth. The Emscher Park IBA thus not only found itself obliged to conduct a considerable, additional marketing campaign; it also bade its antigrowth slogan a final farewell.

Instead, an image change for the Ruhr district took center stage in all of the Emscher Park IBA's endeavors for a regional upturn. Regional regeneration and—more than anything else—the iconic potential of its media representation were in practice esteemed much more highly than any real exposure to the shrinking process in all its pertinent creative, social, and urban aspects. Beyond its economic causes, no further interest in the issue of shrinking was expressed at all. Not a single project dealt seriously with its inevitable consequences for urban design and sociocultural developments.

From Self-Marketing to Self-Deception
From this point onwards, the IBA was much too preoccupied with the regeneration part of its strategy to have any willingness to see that the general situation around many of its flagship projects was continuing to deteriorate and, in fact, at a more rapid rate than ever since structural change had begun. It did not see that the people who were supposed to be animated by aesthetically top-notch islands of innovation, inspired by a new culture to enter the old halls of industry or, at least, to take pride in it all, were growing constantly poorer, collectively older into the bargain and, above all, fewer and fewer. When, on top of everything else, the strategy based on *perceptions* of structural change marked up its first media successes, nobody gave even a moment's thought to changing the underlying priority ranking of so-called soft locational factors. Criticism initially voiced in this regard by some economic experts and by the Christian Democratic Party also evaporated.

In the grand, euphoric phase of the image change, nobody wanted to admit that the Ruhr District had been at its most successful when it had neither a blue sky nor postmodern architecture, when there had been fewer cultural highlights and no tourists. Nor was anyone inclined to listen to those who said that the region, although indisputably more lovely, more ecologically sound, and culturally more diverse, was constantly losing more jobs and more people.

History as a Limited Endogenous Force
This corresponded with the IBA's notion of the "endogenous forces" that were earmarked for funding. For want of any explicitly trendsetting poles of economic growth, and in blind loyalty to its "post-material ideology," it perceived the Ruhr District's inner strength primarily in its architectural industrial heritage, which it radically reinterpreted in a radically regional style. The last vestiges of traditional industrial production were very successfully imbued with a new mythical history and identity and declared to be a unique selling point. While the segment of the Ruhr's capital that was either leaping into position as a global player or planning its getaway engaged in a purely economic and often (for residents and local authorities) negative disposal of the remains, the IBA's distinctly alternative way of dealing with "the leftovers" gave people something lasting, in the truest sense of the word. The psychological effect of ensuing regional self-confidence should therefore not be underestimated. Yet in the long term, unless regional potential for an economic leap forward is strengthened, this kind of strategy ends up going nowhere. It certainly proved less capable than ever of slowing down the shrinking process, let alone stopping it. However important a detail for the region it might be, the growth of architectural and cultural tourism—which was later boosted by the highly subsidized "Ruhr Triennale"—cannot trigger any fundamental reversal.

Regeneration Begins with Policy Structures
That the regional political and administrative apparatus was, given the hitherto unstoppable downward spiral, no longer adequately equipped to deal with the problems and, indeed, was itself one of the problems, was something that the IBA failed to address either in its program or practically. The theme of a "Ruhr city" or regional city was not even hypothetically discussed. The IBA was too entangled with existing political structures to ever think

of challenging them, even verbally. Yet the organization of regional shrinking and regeneration processes emphatically requires both widely networked decentralized structures and centralized structures that can draw the various threads together and take effective action. To this day, the Ruhr District has neither one nor the other, even though the central side was potentially strengthened by the creation of a new regional alliance in 2005.

An extremely inflexible, overly bureaucratic municipal system composed of thirty local councils that all compete at the regional level is still in charge, and of course hampers attempts by all nonmunicipal initiatives to regionalize their own endeavors. Intermunicipal cooperation, if it occurs at all, is limited purely to win-win constellations and, for this reason alone, is incapable of effecting comprehensive structural change throughout the whole region.

Shrinking in the Ruhr District Is Only Just Starting

Considering this almost systematic refusal to look problems in the face, it is little wonder that the Emscher Park IBA has not found an official successor to this day. And yet, from a purely demographic viewpoint, shrinking in the Ruhr District is only just beginning. All estimates reckon with a population decline of between 350,000 and 400,000 by the year 2015. That represents 6% or 7% of the population, admittedly with an uneven distribution. There are towns like Dortmund that have not yet registered any losses, or like Bottrop that have even made small gains. Altogether, however, the trend is cutting across the board and hitting the communities in the Emscher zone, that is to say, in the former IBA area, particularly hard. As this development is mainly due to the falling birthrate and the aging population and as, in the short term, a radical change in Germany's immigration policy is highly improbable, population decline is irremediable. Even the region's political caste is beginning, albeit belatedly, to accept and to take account of this fact. For the first time, local authorities are prepared to retract their option on land they had reserved for prospective job creation and cede it to the new Emscher Landscape Park 2010, which was developed by Projekt-Ruhr GmbH as the continuation of the IBA's master plan. Even the demolition of residential areas is under discussion.

An Historic Moment

In reality, the Ruhr District has no other choice but to finally make a virtue out of necessity. The decline of its population—an irremediable fact in the medium term—is therefore to be seized as an historic moment. This ties in very closely with two other equally momentous regional schemes. First, the further regeneration of the Emscher sewer, which during the IBA period was restricted to its tributaries and, second, the systematic extension and integration of the Emscher Landscape Park as stipulated by the new master plan. The redevelopment of the main course of the Emscher, for which the Emscher Cooperative submitted an alternative master plan, foresees, in addition to the Rhein-Herne canal, a second waterfront with public access that will provide the ecological backbone for a sustainable extension of open parkland and recreational areas. This resolves one of the region's largest and oldest structural problems, namely, the internal disparity between north and south, which has accelerated alarmingly in recent decades.

There are two further developments to be borne in mind here that affect the Emscher zone, in particular, and that the latest master plan has largely ignored: the increasing poverty of the population, and the growing share of ethnic minority residents. Together these trends make a fatal brew, for the unemployment level for immigrants is even now almost twice as high as for the German population. Considering that, parallel to population decline, sociostructural changes are ensuing now from social conditions that were created in the region some considerable time ago, the opportunities presented by shrinkage must be evaluated differently for the Emscher zone than for the rest of the region. It is important to differentiate in this regard between short-term (until 2015), medium-term (2030), and long-term strategies.

Shrinkage and Impoverishment
In the short term the Emscher zone will have to continue to play, and even strengthen, the role it has had, at least at its most densely populated core, since structural change began: it is the region's dustbin for modernization's losers. The fall in property prices and rents that will accompany population decline will—particularly in the case of second- or third-level locations—be advantageous both to this group and to the local authorities, who frequently have to cover their rent expenses. Another parallel consideration is whether the trend towards lower rents (and the resulting possibility of being able to afford a larger apartment) might relieve the daily stress faced by children of people on social welfare or low-level unemployment benefit.

That the demolition of accommodation should not be permitted at this phase goes without saying. It stands to reason that market forces should also apply when they are unfavorable to landlords, and lead to rents that young entrepreneurs, artists, and other creative people or, in a word, anyone with lots of ideas but little money, can afford. Furthermore, the subsequent devaluation of real estate could lead groups that previously had no chance of buying to become owner-occupants.

No Demolition Until the Worst Is Over
In the medium term, the trend towards devaluation and revaluation must be countered, or rather complemented, by a new valorization scheme. An essential economic prerequisite for this is a reduction in unemployment that will occur automatically in the Ruhr District in the next ten to fifteen years as a result of the low number of children currently living there. In addition, the effects of urban development strategies for valorization based on the regeneration of the Emscher and the Emscher Landscape Park will begin to be felt throughout the region at that time. It is only then, it seems to me, that there would be any point in systematically demolishing completely devalued properties and infrastructures in order to extend recreational areas, mainly in the urban areas of the Emscher zone, particularly because population decline will continue for some time after 2015.

The close interrelation between built and unbuilt areas, very typical for this part of the Ruhr city, should in this context be further accentuated and integrated by means of a gradual extension of the Emscher Landscape Park. In this way, the prevalence of Turkish gardens could increase, alongside the allotments with their orientation towards self-sufficiency, the leisure pursuits in and around industrial monuments, and the recreational use of the banks of the old canals and the new Emscher. Altogether, this would mean a huge, sustainable, and—above all—family-friendly augmentation and improvement of the residential environment, combined with real-estate prices that, compared with those in the Hellweg area and—even more so—those in other densely built-up areas, are relatively low.

Urban Peacefulness and Self-Organization as a Long-Term Locational Advantage

Abundant green recreational spaces and multicentered, small-town or village-like development structures in the Ruhr city, so untypical of conurbations, together with a long tradition of neighborliness and immigration have, in spite of increasingly acute social problems, not yet led to any notable rise in crime or violence. In the coming decades, when towns that are still flourishing today will be dragged into the global maelstrom of unemployment, poverty, and brutality, this structural plus will prove to be an additional and sustainable locational advantage. The IBA, by supporting the Ruhr District's garden-city tradition, has accomplished good groundwork.

In this context, the Emscher Zone does not need state-financed demolition but the low-level refurbishment that its impoverished residents can afford. This means more use of flexible mortgages and neighborhood support schemes, more cooperative elements, such as community partnerships between landlords and commercial enterprises, and—above all—more legislative protection from large-scale property speculation. In these areas, too, the Emscher Park IBA has demonstrated some approaches that are well worth adopting.

Translated from the German by Jill Denton

Literature
Hermann, Rita A., and Sebastian Müller, eds. *Inszenierter Fortschritt: Die Emscherregion und ihre Bauausstellung.* Bielefeld: AKP, 1999.
Internationale Bauausstellung Emscher Park, ed. *Katalog der Projekte.* Gelsenkirchen: IBA, 1999.
Kreibich, Rolf, Arno S. Schmid, Walter Siebel, Thomas Sieverts, and Peter Zlonicky, eds. *Bauplatz Zukunft: Dispute über die Entwicklung von Industrieregionen.* Essen: Klartext-Verlag, 1994.
Wachten, Kunibert, ed. *Wandel ohne Wachstum? Change without growth?* Braunschweig: Vieweg, 1996.
Wissen, Markus. *Die Peripherie in der Metropole: Zur Regulation sozialräumlicher Polarisierungen in Nordrhein-Westfalen.* Münster: Westfälisches Dampfboot, 2000.

SCHKREUTZ CITY MAP: 1ST EDITION
Halle/Leipzig, Germany, 2004/05
SMAQ – Sabine Müller and Andreas Quednau

In the years following 1989 the Halle/Leipzig area underwent a profound transformation. While both cities suffered a loss of population and jobs, a new settlement area sprang up between them. This was due partly to local suburbanization, which led to shrinking city centers. At the same time, it was also a consequence of the mechanisms of a global economy that ignores local conditions. This new urban development is to be named Schkreutz after the Schkeuditz freeway interchange at its center.[1] Schkreutz has not yet been incorporated into either city's dominant urban image policy. It at best appears as the periphery of different centers. The "city" of Schkreutz has not yet found its image.

The region is still characterized by competition between various core areas that each advertise themselves as "complete" cities, thereby suggesting that they exist independently in an open landscape. The problematic issue of Schkreutz itself is ignored, namely, that following a much further-reaching logic it is actually an interregional urban arrangement in which single towns play a lesser role than do the strategic positions of the interchange, the airport, and the national highways. The "Schkreutz City Map: 1st Edition" project seeks to intervene in this urban image policy with the aim of rendering the urban fact visible as a "city."

Schkreutz City Map: 1st Edition places the periphery at the center and draws on the traditional linguistic terms and ciphers of city maps. Place-names are based on catchwords taken from billboards in the region and on key concepts from publications. The new "city limits" lie 5 kilometers away from the freeway and it is there that Schkreutz's promoters can be found: supraregional logistics enterprises, car manufacturers, and hotels. In keeping with its function of linking various shopping malls, the freeway is labeled a "pedestrian zone." The river meadows become a recreational "city park." The old cities are depicted, from the "Schkreutz" perspective, as sightseeing destinations with weekend shopping malls. Schkreutz effects a comprehensive realignment of urban organization. The large-scale shopping malls with their time-based catchment areas underlie the area's division into new "administrative districts." Schkreutz is a logistical location, a market outlet, and an investment interest dependent on decisions made outside the area. Accordingly, western German centers of capital and leadership are an integral part of the "Schkreutz environment."

The decidedly global context and one-dimensional economic structure of Schkreutz give rise to conflict and fractures that are articulated by its fragmented appearance and are particularly apparent in local opinion and practice. An explicit case is City Center Neumarkt (see the detailed map). Here, a maintenance tunnel under the A9 freeway has become an underpass to the shopping mall for pedestrians and cyclists from the surrounding villages, which have been deserted by their small retailers. Here, public utilities emerge as a side effect.

This project was commissioned by the Bauhaus Dessau Foundation in the context of "Shrinking Cities." The original German title is "Schkreutz. Stadtplan. 1. Auflage."

Note
1   The name plays on the German word *Kreuz* (here "interchange").—Ed.

Polarized Regional City

Schkreutz City Map: 1st Edition_SMAQ

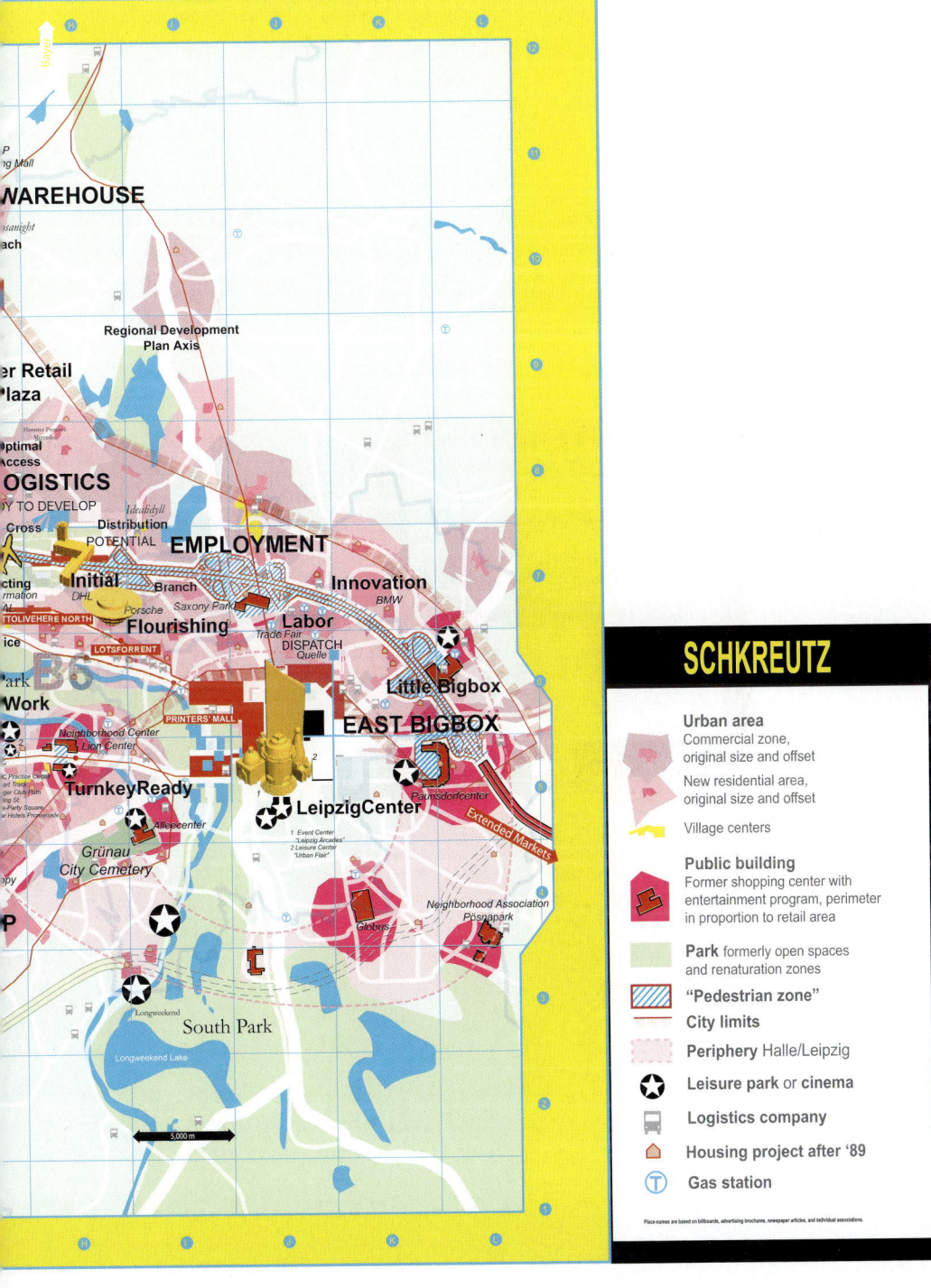

Polarized Regional City

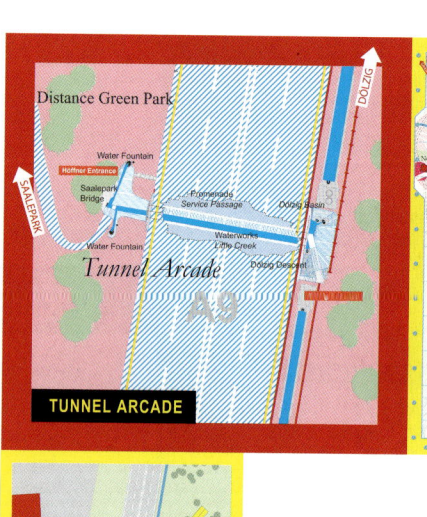

The TUNNEL ARCADE

The **Tunnel Arcade** lies right in the center of Schkreutz-Neumarkt. As the latest thing in shopping arcades, it isn't actually used for shopping but as a passageway for shoppers on their way to shop.

Modest in appearance, this is an architectural jewel of civil engineering. It was poured in brut concrete in the classical modern tradition. A cross-section of the passageway shows a perfectly balanced square that is the necessary 2.26 meters high and has the same width. The upper corners, chamfered at an angle of 45 degrees, are an historical reference to recent architectural history (the 1970s), and speak eloquently of the burden of the individual, national, and trans-European freight haulage that crawls continuously across the roof, which is formed by the A9 freeway. The width of the passageway, which has been designed with a view to spatial intensification, is apportioned in accordance with the Golden Section rule: the wider part is accounted for by a gully, while the actual promenade width is reduced to a compact 86 centimeters.
After the Saale Park mall was built in 1989, the Tunnel Arcade rapidly became a veritable magnet for the surrounding area. Its patrons often have to wait until cyclists entering the passageway from the opposite direction have passed through before they can mount the narrow steps to enter

themselves. Yet, when they emerge on the western side and see the wide expanse of retailer Höffner's delivery area spread out before them, they know it was worth the wait. The Tunnel Arcade is extremely popular, in particular among the residents of Dölzig, many of whom meet here. Small retailers have become almost extinct in Dölzig and the village is now a practically homogeneous residential area. When doing their daily errands, many Dölzig residents save the bus fare to the Saale Park and reach it—the largest mall in eastern Germany—by traversing the passageway on foot or by bike.

Many parties invested disparate energies into creating the Schkreutz success story of the Tunnel Arcade. Who would have thought that what began as a technical measure to conduct a little trickle of water under the freeway would become so wildly popular? The state, responsible for the construction and maintenance of the freeway, laid a gully for the trickle of water. Extrinsic sectors of the private economy concentrated resources here, thereby depriving retailers in the surrounding area of their means of existence. The administration failed to coordinate activities beyond regional borders, with the result that there is neither a pedestrian route nor a cycle path from Dölzig in Saxony to Günthersdorf in Saxony-Anhalt (the location of the mall). And, last but not least, residents responded to the circumstances by locating gaps and penetrability potential.

Public life as a side effect.

The lively activity in the passageway suggests that vendors will soon be found at its access points and that—when night has fallen—perhaps even a bar or a club will be set up for the summer months in the Tunnel Arcade.

BITTERFELD: A TRANSLOCAL REGION
Bitterfeld region, Germany, 2004/05
Urbanista
www.urbanista.de

The spatial identity of cities is not (any longer) tied to their territorial location, rather they are defined in terms of translocal, social, and economic reference points. Operating on this premise, the Urbanista architects group came to the following conclusions about Bitterfeld:

- Bitterfeld is not shrinking but becoming more diffuse; migration therefore means simply that Bitterfeld residents, ergo Bitterfeld, relocate to places beyond the city limits. These locations constitute the first level of the translocal region—Bitterfeld is the center of an "atomized homeland."
- Bitterfeld is a global city; the new enterprises with headquarters in distant locations network the city with the rest of the world. This gives rise to the second level of the translocal region, namely, a new "economic operational area" (François Perroux).
- Bitterfeld is conquering the world; cities such as Halle and Leipzig have long since been part of Bitterfeld's everyday life, providing consumer goods, leisure opportunities, and services. This third level is the city's extended, fragmented "everyday space."

As well as changing perceptions, the concept of the translocal region is intended to counter regional polarization. The underlying principle is that of return benefits: Bitterfeld is compensated for the fact that, as a part of the translocal region, it puts its assets at the disposal of other actors and locations. "Assets" are in this sense its consumers, workforce, taxpayers, and commercial outlets. The return benefits are organized at the three regional levels.

The balance between disadvantaged "giver cities" and the "taker cities" is to be regulated by means of a financial alliance. To this end, a portion of the income tax lost to Bitterfeld due to migration will be transferred back in the form of a homeland tax. The "economic operational" level will guarantee local value added by means of shareholding or "locational dividends," whereby Bitterfeld will co-own local businesses. And, via a "consumer card," a part of the value-added tax spent in the wider area will flow back to the core city. An alliance for image presentation and transportation will create additional surplus value for the region.

This project was commissioned by the Bauhaus Dessau Foundation in the context of "Shrinking Cities." The original German title is "Translokale Region Bitterfeld."

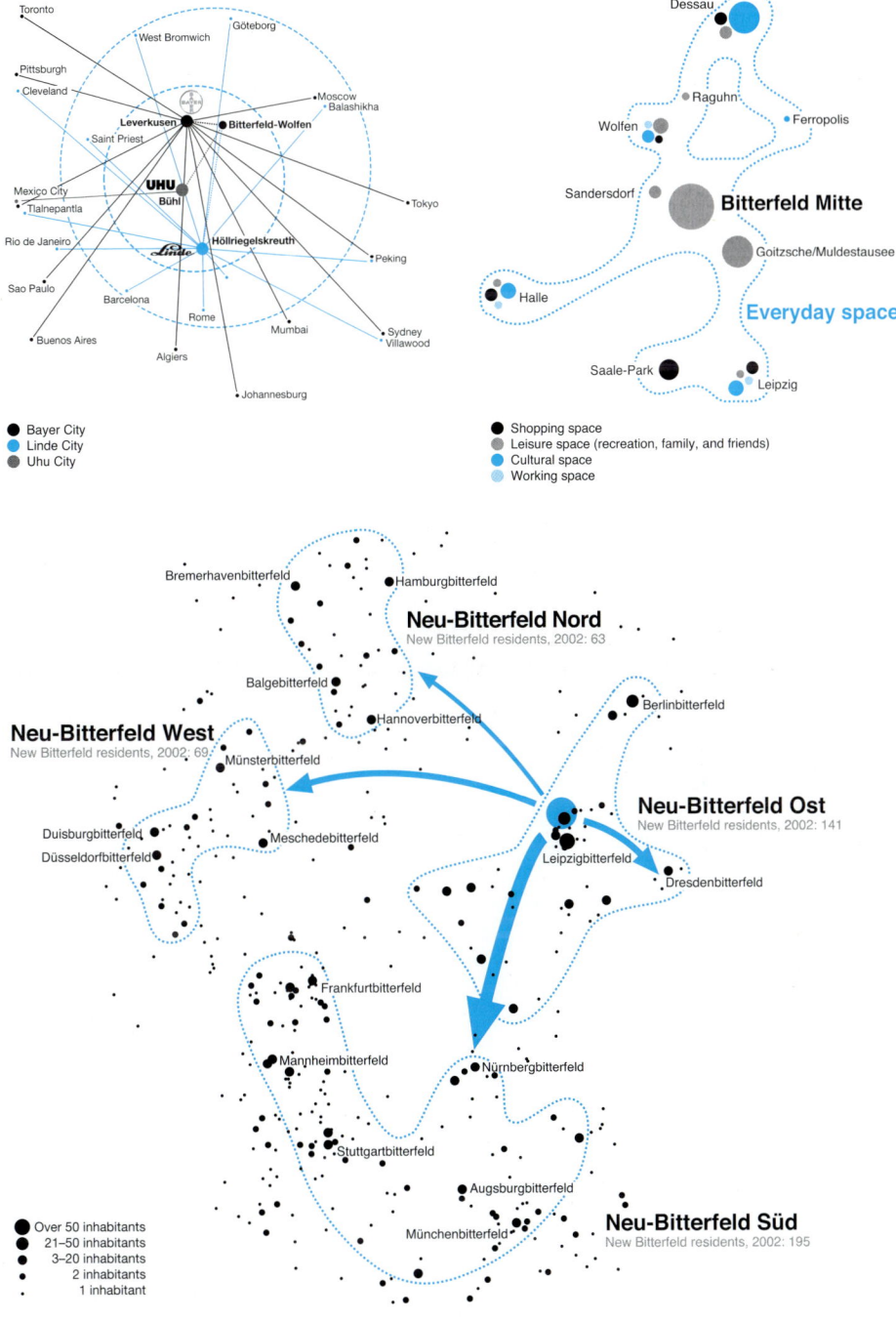

Trading networks of companies located in Bitterfeld (top left), everyday venues of residents' activity (top right), and migration patterns (bottom) constitute the translocal region of Bitterfeld.

HOLLOCORE
Region between Amsterdam, Brussels, and the Ruhr Valley, 2002
AMO

While the cities in the developing world are exploding into bigger, less containable metropolitan areas, urban Europe is in a state of entropy. No longer energized by growth, cities and towns are drifting into a muddle of provincial sameness, leaving an urban vacuum behind them. But, of course, modernity abhors a vacuum, and an infinite multiplicity of new forms of urbanity is emerging to take the place of what has become redundant.

The HOLLOCORE© is emblematic of Europe's new urbanity. The amorphous super-region that links Brussels, Amsterdam, and the Ruhr Valley is urban Europe's nonevent: it is home to 32 million people, or 9% of Europe's population, yet has no city larger than one million inhabitants. Two-thirds of its population live in cities of less than 200,000 inhabitants—in places no one has ever heard of.

The Hollocore has had one of the highest concentrations of cities and towns in Europe since the Middle Ages. Despite explosive population growth during the industrial revolutions, the Hollocore is not dominated by a single center. Instead, it has swelled into a cloud of atomized subcenters and peripheries. Every center claims its own identity, history, and centrality, while numerous peripheries offer space for new cultures and identities to unfold.

In the Hollocore, all that is urban is losing ground. Over the past decades, overall population growth has dropped to –0.2%. Within this static condition, inconstant population movements ensure that metropolitan density recedes: established cities lose residents while thinly populated areas gain them.

In the name of identity, city centers are stripped down to their historic pedestrian shopping streets and appear more village-like than ever—frozen in a time that never was. Meanwhile, the periphery fills up with a mix of business parks, commercial parks, leisure parks, industrial parks, logistics parks, villa parks, office parks, and brain parks—generic urban matter embedded in massive inversions of green. In the Hollocore, the city has become the void left in the wake of its own expansion.

The Hollocore stretches across three countries with three legal systems and their cumulative loopholes, all combining to form the most progressive legislative ecology in the world. The Hollocore is a loophole culture: within its ambiguous borders, prostitution is legal and taxed, marijuana an official medicine, euthanasia legal, highways (in Germany) are free of speed limits, and gay couples can marry. Conversely, the combined progressive politics seem to have created Europe's ideological black hole. In the Hollocore, tolerance and freedom have become Janus-faced. Populist rhetoric of intolerance, as exemplified by murdered Dutch politician Pim Fortuyn, has found a steadily growing audience. Freedoms blossom next to extensive corruption, whether it is the massive fraud within the Dutch Ahold concern, the alleged network of pedophile politicians surrounding serial killer Marc Dutroux in Belgium, or the large number of Al Qaeda members residing throughout the region prior to 9/11. The Hollocore's culture of tolerance balances on the verge of anarchy.

Text by Nanne de Ru (AMO)

In the amorphous super-region of Hollocore, no city has more than one million inhabitants, yet in total the region has 32 million inhabitants.

THE CITY TURNED INTO A REGION
CONCEPTS FOR ACTION IN AGGLOMERATIONS
Robert Kaltenbrunner

The city has left its "container." A comparative glance at modern literature may help to illustrate just how far-reaching the city's structural changes ultimately are: "Up to the Age of Enlightenment there were cohesive pictures of the world into which literature could be written and from which it could be understood. By the twentieth century, at the latest, that had changed decisively: in literary work the illusion of an inherently ordered world was destroyed in order to avert the false conclusion that the world outside literature might be similarly intelligently shaped. Modern literature is thus 'difficult' because incomprehensibility and the inability to understand not only became important as subjects, but also because they found expression in the form."[1] Incomprehensibility and the inability to understand also characterize the form of the city of today, with suburbanization and sprawl playing a decisive role. Overflowing settlements beyond the city, industrial parks, cheap supermarkets, entertainment and logistics centers crowd their way into the picture. Patchwork structures, areas on the margins, and in-between spaces that are neither center nor periphery are part of the reality of today's city.

As a result, however, the "city" is no longer the semantic space that could embrace all the empirical observations it is used to describe. At best, and however it may be delimited, that space would be the region, of which the city is, in turn, the integral part. Understood in a positive light, "region" describes the plexus in which an area is connected with other areas in manifold ways; the term also suggests, however, that the autonomy of the individual subareas initially blinds them to the consequences they have outside their borders, and in relation to the larger whole.

Of course the individual's experiential and living space extends over broadening areas, embracing them, however, only selectively. The emerging social structures can no longer be smoothly projected onto images of geographical ordering. Rather, the social differences and relationships and their sociogeographical projection onto the settlement pattern represents an elaborate plexus that can only be explained on a higher level of abstraction which no longer can be represented geographically. The networks of relationships overlap, but in a given urban region they have little left in common; circles of family and friends turn out to be widely ramified geographically. Thus our cities have long since joined with the surrounding communities to form large agglomerations, and today's city dwellers move about in these agglomerations as naturally as generations before them did within the walled old town.

At the same time, however, it must be said that there is a fundamental incongruity between the areas of responsibility at the political and administrative level and functional spaces, and that within regions there is a simultaneity of the nonsimultaneous, that is to say, partial growth and extensive decline. And when, at present, the basic conditions are, essentially, (a) demographic shrinkage, (b) economic stagnation, and (c) sociocultural crises, then these naturally find expression in an intensification of municipal-regional battles over the distribution of funds, in competitions for settlement through aggressive supply-oriented policies of individual local authorities, as well as in disparities—not least between the regional urban center and its surrounding communities. Few examples illustrate this better than Detroit: the depopulation of "Motown" went hand in hand with the rise of its surrounding suburban belt.

Increasingly something similar is beginning to manifest itself in eastern Germany, although it has a different character: "The increase in value, both physical and social, of the suburban space is simultaneously accompanied by the structural and social decline of other urban subareas, as currently expressed in the increase in urban fallow land, vacancies, and building demolitions in eastern German cities."[2] The conflicting processes are at the same time mutually dependent; they are two sides of one coin. The key political difficulty is that today there no longer is anyone who could mold the structure and changes of these spaces even though their statistical status as "agglomerations" suggests possibilities of geopolitical ordering and hierarchy. However, viewing "city regions" as simply economic units for the realization of economic growth—as seems to frequently be the case in times of "neoliberal consensus"—falls decidedly short. Rather what is needed is an understanding befitting of the sociogeographical complexity as well as its intrinsic contradictoriness. A central desideratum is to ensure in a constitutive way that there is interest and participation in what is happening in a region.

The Problem

There is a certain ambivalence inherent in the regional: who or what determines what a region is? Can the regional be explained in its departure from the supraregional norm? Does the regional in turn define itself via its centers, or is it really a network of places with related features that slowly alter until they tumble over into the characteristics of another region? Or is region a concept of selective perception in a very concrete framework of interests that experiences collective validation through focusing on certain regional problems or conflicts?[3] Nevertheless, and independently of such questions, the basic units in the competition of locations worldwide are more regions and less individual cities, or even communes, as it is only at this level that infrastructural conditions for economic vitality are capable of being produced. The spaces for everyday action of private households and individuals become differentiated and are constantly expanding geographically, thereby paving the way for a parallel regionalization of ways of living. Thus even though the central level of action is no longer the commune but the region, the point must be made that we are not prepared for this—and this is not limited to the Federal Republic of Germany—not institutionally, not mentally, and not even conceptually.[4] Regional planning and administrative tasks are fragmented among state ministries, regional and local associations of governmental bodies, special purpose associations, district governments, special administrative boards, administrative districts, as well as informal alliances, regional structure conferences, development agencies, initiatives, and so on. In the end, however, not one of these institutions offers a basis for a strong regional policy that could constitute a counterbalance to both the local egoisms as well as to the partial interests of individual actors.

This makes integrative approaches to action all the more necessary at the regional level. Admittedly, this also involves very different logics of action, at least three of which are relevant in this context: the economic logic of action of businesses and enterprises, profit-oriented and controlled via the markets and thus to a large extent spatially independent; the political-administrative logic of action of the public authority in all its divisions, power-oriented and controlled locally via elections as well as regulations; and finally the social logic of the population, geared toward self-development and controlled via personal solidarity networks.[5]

The cultural and local-political binding effect of the commune as a community defined by location is crucially weakened by the loss of geography and tradition as factors in many economic and social relations and by an expansion of the spaces for daily or weekly action well beyond the local commune. Many communal governments are reacting to these developments by seeing themselves increasingly as "service enterprises" whose political substance is evaporating more and more and whose unwelcome political side effects are seldom even addressed. And thus, in the end, the core of the commune's political sovereignty is eroded.

An essential question in the control of regional processes is cost-benefit regulation, particularly in view of overall geographical functions as well as geographical polarization processes. The current financial system of communes discriminates against the larger urban centers, which are forced to maintain central infrastructures and yet are confronted with bigger and bigger social problems owing to social polarization. It must be said, generally speaking, that though the role fiscal aspects play in the debate over regionalization is difficult to understand, it is decisive: the suburbanization process in particular is characterized by an unraveling of microeconomic cost-benefit relations and the cost-benefit relations that concern society as a whole.

For the individual it may make perfect economic sense to settle in the distant outskirts of a city. The lower price for building land compensates for potential commuting costs, and the polity provides for schools and other infrastructure. The communes, for their part, designate building sites and support the private acquisition of property for residential building because they expect positive results, even financial gain (for example, via the residency principle for the collection of wage and personal income taxes and proceeds from business taxes). It is true that from a regional perspective this leads to unwelcome side effects. For one, the regional urban center receives a smaller allocation of personal income tax from the federal state in question, even though it provides and maintains a large part of the nonlocal, regional services (universities, schools for continuing education, hospitals, cultural institutions, etc.); the outlying communes, on the contrary, receive more of this money. Moreover, it is more the "good risks" who move to the outskirts, while it is the "bad risks" (the elderly, asylum seekers, job trainees, the homeless) who remain.

That regional sharing of burdens and benefits has not worked to this day—and this despite all the compensations provided based on financial calculations—can hardly be cause for astonishment. A small example: Frankfurt has a business tax assessment rate of a handsome 490 percentage points; in contrast, the neighboring city of Eschborn has only 300 percentage points and is as a result—through its proximity to the city, autobahn interchange, and airport—a formidable rival in attracting new residents and wooing away businesses. Thus when making a plea for regional development, the prevailing fiscal policies relating to regional approaches to action and the significance of systems for equalizing tax revenue and fiscal burdens cannot be disregarded; rather, it seems, they form the solid core of all geography-related structural problems.

At the same time the striking advantages of an integrated regional policy are quite obvious. The many existing examples of single-purpose associations already point up the territorial dimension. Just imagine local public transportation that is not organized into an integrated transportation system, as is the case in Detroit, for example: streetcars or buses will take you, if you are lucky, to the city limits, but there are no connections to buses in the neighboring county and, anyway, timetables are completely different there—and on top of all that you need a new ticket. Such considerations, and similar ones like wastewater and garbage disposal, are comparatively well regulated in Europe. If, however, municipalities A, B, and C form an integrated transportation system, B, X, and Y a wastewater association, A, C, and Z have decided to join forces, on the other hand, for the provision of electricity, one gradually begins to suspect how complex things could be and how difficult, or even impossible, it becomes to push through higher goals in the interest of the common weal.

Concepts for Action

Happily the "region" is currently experiencing a real boom in the professional discourse of developmental planners, while receiving far less attention among politicians or urban developers. But the devil is in the details. For all the understanding over how significant an expanded framework for action—and hence the region—would be, there is little agreement as to how this would be organized and constituted. Whereby the crux of this supposed detail turns into a cardinal question: for a corporate region means, first, real losses of authority for communes; second, under constitutional law it was never intended to be a state unit. There is evidently no place for the corporate region between the commune and the federal state.

Today the "region" is propagated for the most part as a sort of "network of actors" that is heterogeneously, flexibly, and regionally adapted—or should be. Underlying this is the reservation that, given an "institutionalized region" with the status of a regional administrative body, the process of the administration would be more difficult, more complicated, and more confused. Now it is probably not really surprising that in times of deregulation there is a prevailing fear of excessive administrative apparatus. But neither can it be denied that, beyond a certain measure of interconnections and dependencies, but also of permanent conflicts of interests, it becomes necessary to create public institutions on the communal level that go beyond networks of actors. Some have, of course, had good experiences with "simple" political marriages of convenience (transportation or wastewater associations, for example). But voluntary cooperation at the communal level quickly reaches its limits when it is no longer a matter of monocausal considerations or allocating growth. Dealing with shortages, with simultaneous shrinkage and sprawl, with the coexistence of winners and losers calls for more binding basic conditions than those given when a terminable association is in place. What is needed is "region" as public corporate body, ideally one that is democratically legitimized via its own elections, with political and administrative apparatuses that, though they are based on cooperation, are able, when push comes to shove, to carry measures through—even in the face of resistance.

How Can a Region Be Formed?

The problem with urban development today is that the regional dimension must first of all be recognized and appreciated and must find its way into the thoughts and actions of the parties involved. Then one has to decide between voluntary cooperation and a corporately conceived region as a type of new "large commune." Expression of this is found in the decades-long—and in the end unresolved—issue in the Rhine-Main region around Frankfurt,[6] the diverse networking in the Stuttgart region,[7] the not inconsiderable instances of incorporating neighboring communities into Leipzig in 1999, as well as the current discussions in Mecklenburg-Western Pomerania about forming five regional districts.[8] But elsewhere as well the decisive question centers around this very point.

"Glattal-Stadt" in the agglomeration area of Zurich constitutes neither a local authority with binding political borders nor a homogenously circumscribable region.[9] The institutions and communities that shape and attend to this area have spheres of action of varying sizes and with different responsibilities and tasks. But these spheres of action overlap, at least in part, and influence one another. Glattal is in this respect an area that is being perceived more and more as a cohesive structure, even though institutionally it is not. For when it comes to controlling settlement development, the individual cities and communities play a dominant role thanks to their jurisdiction in planning issues. Their goals are geared toward the local, and they compete to attract businesses, which are to help boost the tax substratum. "Although the operating competencies of the actors involved are regulated, their individual activity fails to produce an integrated whole. There are insufficient incentives for orientation toward a superordinate spatial development that benefits most of those involved. The existing framework is not coherent or binding enough either. The federal subsidiarity principle increasingly creates situations in which an insufficient competency becomes entrenched with regard to a successful spatial development."[10] All the same, Glattal-Stadt has been able to sell itself to the outside world as having a certain regional unity, which is gradually developing a common outlook. The eight Glattal-Stadt communities have banded together to form the association glow.das Glattal in order to develop joint projects in the areas of economy, sports, and culture. A further step, as the most important infrastructural measure, is the planning of the light-rail system Stadtbahn Glattal. All the same, the communes remain competitors—for example, the municipality of Opfikon is using the most advantageous position between the airport and the city of Zurich to carry out an ambitious plan for development, the heart of which is the Glattpark, measuring approximately 12 hectares.

There is noticeably more administrative and political commitment in Greater London. When in 2000 the Greater London Authority (GLA) was institutionalized by the Labour government of Tony Blair, the model was a holding company: a strong and democratically legitimized level of decision making for the entire city region that largely decentralizes, however, the operational implementation into different (public and private) legal and organizational forms. The GLA carried on the tradition of the Greater London Council (GLC), which was founded in 1973 and had itself evolved from the London County Council (LCC), an association of 32 independent communities that had originated in 1900. The task of the GLC was to coordinate physical planning as well as environmental and transportation policy in the municipal region. Under the Tory government of Margaret Thatcher the GLC, which had largely been shaped by the Labour Party, was dissolved in the mid-1980s and not replaced. Today, under Ken Livingstone, the directly elected "regional" mayor of London, the GLA keeps a certain amount of distance from the government. Like its predecessors, however, the GLA has thus far barely been able to launch sustained, municipal-regional development.[11]

The cooperation of the American twin cities of Minneapolis-Saint Paul, which covers roughly the same territory, has often been praised as exemplary. In particular, emphasis has been placed on its policy of tax revenue distribution; property and business taxes first end up in a common pool in order to then be paid out on a per capita basis to the municipalities. This has reduced the fiscal disparity of 50:1 to a ratio of 12:1—which is still an alarming figure, from a German point of view. The Minneapolis–Saint Paul Metropolitan Council covers seven counties with 25 cities and 105 towns; its central instrument is the Metropolitan Development and Investment Framework. The task of the council is, however, more to work out strategic guidelines than to function as an executive enforcement-oriented body; it has no direct authority over its member municipalities and as little direct democratic legitimization. For that reason, the governor of the state of Minnesota is the central figure; moreover, there is apparently a certain amount of dependency on the benevolence of the central government: federal grants under the Carter administration made up approximately 67% of the council's finances; this then fell, however, to a mere 20% under Reagan.[12] It is still quite a long way from its goal of a official regional city, with stronger support being displayed in the recent past under Governor Jesse Ventura.

But in Germany as well there is a current example of regional cooperation: Region Hannover, which covers an area approximately the size of the state of Saarland. It has existed by law since November 1, 2001, when the previously existing Kommunalverband Großraum Hannover (Greater Hannover district association) as well as the administrative district were dissolved and made an integral part of Region Hannover. It is financed from special assessments; there is a regional parliament and a president of the region. Some district tasks that were previously fulfilled by the district government have been delegated to the Region.[13] It is still too early, however, to assess the actual effects of the official institutionalization of Region Hannover. But it does have a historical forerunner whose success is beyond question: the fusion of a series of autonomous cities and administrative districts with the imperial capital in 1920 in order to form a de facto regional city with the name Greater Berlin.[14]

An even more comprehensive step has been taken in the meantime in the People's Republic of China. Beijing, Shanghai, and Tianjin—these three large metropolises reveal that already a half a century ago territorial administrative sovereignty was understood as a key factor in urban-planning strategy in China: the large-scale expansion of municipal areas on the occasion of the territorial reorganization of local government between 1957 and 1959 was unprecedented in international history. It was based on the conviction that the expansion of a rural area under the jurisdiction of a city into a city region ultimately represented the sine qua non for an actively pursued and planned decentralization of urban agglomerations. The use of the concept of the "city region"—introduced by K. I. Fung in 1979, in relation to the urbanization process in China—is an attempt to understand the city and its outskirts as one urban-oriented socioeconomic unit. Without administratively secured control over their hinterland, none of these cities would have been in a position to meet their needs for usable raw materials for industry, water, foodstuffs, and reloading points for goods near to the city. The expansions of the areas themselves were carried out in several steps. In Shanghai, for example, the city limits experienced a multistage "stretching"; the two largest stages stemmed from the year 1958 when, to begin with, three districts were incorporated in January and then later, in December, seven more. The area subject to integrated municipal administration expanded from 636.18 square kilometers (in 1949) to 1,713.23 square kilometers (in January 1958) to 5,910 square kilometers (in December 1958)—so, an increase of a good ninefold (by way of comparison, Berlin covers approximately 880 square kilometers). A similar situation applies to Beijing: Beijing Shi, that is, the metropolitan region of the city, today covers an area of 16,800 square kilometers (the original, developed area of the city in 1981 made up approximately 340 square kilometers of this) thus exhibiting three times the expansion of Shanghai. All three metropolises—but Shanghai especially—have always known to make the most of the strategic advantage of their regional structure in their overall planning, and in defiance of all occasional setbacks, like, for instance, those during the Cultural Revolution. Unlike in Europe or the United States, however, the issue is also not so much stemming sprawl, but rather decentralizing economic policy and ensuring basic agrarian supply.

A unanimous judgment can hardly be drawn from these examples—the respective political climates and the specific circumstances are too varied. In both the positive and negative sense, they all demonstrate, however, that if a region is to "function"—irrespective of whether it is an association or a corporate body—it must be given clear jurisdiction over tasks and revenue. An organizational solution does not by itself inevitably lead to a consistent regional policy. For that something more is needed.

What Makes a Region?

Independent of how a region constitutes itself formally is the question of what it "makes of it" and what it undertakes—not least by means of developmental planning—in order to reconcile disparities, to establish priorities, or to generally become "fit for the future." In this respect, for approximately fifteen years now, Barcelona has played an important role. The city region (Corporación Metropolitana de Barcelona) took its lead from the London example, was at the mercy of similar ups and downs,[15] and never achieved a resounding success. But the city administration was—in particular via the push for development provided by the 1992 Olympics—very successful in its approaches to reurbanization. Thus in Catalonia it is not so much regional planning categories but rather urban development strategies that are considered exemplary: on the basis of massive investment in infrastructure, putting public space to use, and revitalizing unutilized industrial regions in the periphery and along the fringes of the city, Barcelona set standards even internationally.

Some observers believe the renaissance of a far more comprehensive approach can be identified in the United States. They see a "new regionalism" drawing near, understood as integrated planning that attempts to be based on and to do justice to the irresolvable interweaving of economic, social, and environmental systems.[16] Portland, Oregon, is generally cited as an example; it is said that regional planning in Portland has attained uncommon prominence as a policy tool as well as an unusual acceptance as an expression of the representation of community interests. Portland Metro regional government represents a cooperation of the existing local governments, while due to the strong position of the state, land management in Oregon is organized as a top-down system—the latter strongly supporting the Metro planning association, also with regard to the respective municipalities. Portland's planning efforts are concentrated—quite successfully—on (a) stemming sprawl by means of an established "Urban Growth Boundary" and (b) improving the local public transportation system (e.g., a Metropolitan Area Express was inaugurated at the end of 2002). That the preservation and redevelopment of a user-friendly downtown represents an essential component of the strategy also demonstrates, however, how dominant the core-city perspective is. Nevertheless the teamwork seen in the Portland city region is considered to be a "remarkable constellation—and cooperation—of far-sighted politicians, dedicated environmental organizations, and an enlightened and politically active public."17 Though Portland cannot be compared with European standards (in the categories of local public transportation systems and population density, for example), it is very much exemplary in the "overcoming of competition between cities and surrounding communities for people and jobs."18 With its Regional Growth Concept 2040 for the long-term development of the region, Portland Metro presented four spatial scenarios for settlement and transportation development in the agglomeration; from this it extracted a binding development plan. This is considered, and not without good reason, to be a classic example for the planning of the sustainable utilization of land and transportation, and has been summed up as "smart growth." Admittedly, there is a sour note: the ecologically oriented concept of smart growth also provides more affluent communities with a pretext to prevent the influx of low-income households.

Precisely because this approach to planning does not start out from the perspective of an urban core but rather occurs in a more intrinsically decentralized manner, a comparison with the Ruhr region comes involuntarily to mind. As the "largest German city," the Ruhr region has neither strictly delimited boundaries nor clear centers. Even though the Siedlungsverband Ruhrkohlenbezirk (Ruhr-Coal District Settlement Association) was founded as early as 1920, intercommunal and extracommunal collaboration established along the Ruhr and Emscher Rivers is still resolutely more sporadic and focused on single projects than truly cooperative—as the shifting role of the Regionalverband Ruhrgebiet continues to illustrate. Nevertheless, the Emscher Park "International Building Exhibition," (IBA) has had a large impact at the conceptual level. It stands for a determined attempt to focus on the whole again. Seventeen sovereign cities gathered under a common roof in order to advance their goals. But, in retrospect, this was temporary and then only thanks to a strong axis: Karl Ganser, a powerfully persuasive spiritus rector of the enterprise, and strong support from the relevant minister in the state government.

Today there is little sign of either the spirit of optimism or the regional cooperation that the IBA generated. That does not mean, however, that the conceptually decentralized approach must have been wrong, just as conversely—in a given concrete regional situation—the more classical, urban center oriented concept of Portland can be right. And what we learn from the example of Barcelona is that the complementary relevance of urban planning activity cannot be forgotten in any comprehensive course of action for regional planning.

Critique of Regionalization

The discussion now taking place in the United States of the "regional city" is quite instructive in the international context. Against the backdrop that the word "city" in the United States long ago became synonymous with everything that the more affluent sections of society sought to flee—city districts falling into ruin, crime, minorities—by taking refuge in the suburbs, the new regionalism actually reveals new qualities. But by being styled as a successful counter-idea to the city now in disrepute, it has formed a breeding ground for a further problem area. Silicon Valley became the main symbol of the exurban parkland settlement, the "megalopolis unbound." It also provided the reference model for the French science (anti) city, Sophia Antipolis, which—quite logically, you might say— explicitly bears the anti-urban program in its name.19 Aside from a virulent anti-urbanism, the new regionalism, however, holds yet another danger: such spatial constructs for agglomeration and conurbation spaces (or conurbations like the Randstad Holland or the

Ruhrstadt) tend, in some circumstances, to deny or abolish all existing interregional disparities, competitions, identities, and differences in favor of a greater spatial unity.[20] Manuel Castells even goes a step further: he believes that because individual action and orientation space stretch far beyond urban spaces, that because there is no longer an urban focus, but rather just disperse locations for work and living as well as supply centers with uniform public spaces, there is an underlying "new spatial logic" that he describes with the label "space of flows."[21] The space of flows in post-Fordism replaces the old logic of the "space of places," according to Castells. But the latter, as practical life experience shows, by no means gets lost in the process. Dieter Hoffmann-Axthelm logically laments the "leveling and smoothing plane of regionalization" and interprets the construct of the regional city as an attack for the purpose of dissolving the city: "I maintain that the city region is the Trojan horse by means of which regional planning finally seizes hold of the city from within."[22] If, however, what lies behind such assumptions is more fear over whether certain disciplines will lose out or over the struggle for interpretative sovereignty in the urban discourse and less the real dangers, then creating a regional identity space is indeed appropriate—without neglecting such aspects in the process.

Summary

The reinterpretation of the relationships between the city and its surroundings requires an intellectual feat: "a 'region'—this is the output of an activity that can be called 'regionalization,' and 'regionalization' means manufacturing ideas and images of regions and filtering these with more or less success into social communication. In any case, there are major advantages to understanding regions in this manner not as physical-material realities on the earth's surface, but to considering them first as constructs and integral parts of social communication—or also as signs in texts."[23] It is true that the administrative, political, and interpretative juxtaposition of urban centers and the districts surrounding them actually perpetuates outdated city-country differences, polarizes the region, and prevents necessary benefit and burden sharing. But such an analytical approach must be accompanied by one that is emotional and contributes to the formation of identity.

Regionalization is not a set of instructions as to how to act under conditions of growth alone but also—and especially—remains necessary under shrinking conditions. The region has to become a basic joint structure for understanding in which planning, policy, economy, and population are "resident" in equal measure. Territorial and administrative and economic-geography and urban-development oriented interpretations of concepts, among others, must be made to coincide persuasively.

That the region may be the city constitutes a claim that is as correct as it is noble, but that still is not suitable for daily use. Changing this will require a sort of double step: (a) a regional constitution that—in whatever form—provides for a sharing of benefits and burdens would have to be created as an institutionalized prerequisite; this would then be the basis for (b) a conceptual and integrative overall planning and steering. For though legal, organizational, and financial aspects alone could perhaps constitute a city region, they would hardly establish it as a space of identity. For that it also has to be "shaped." Planning and conception are necessary, though it may be said that at the level of regional planning today, usually—as for example in the case of the Emscher Park IBA—a sum of the projects "makes up the plan"—a sum which under better circumstances is guided by an overarching strategy. Projects are, of course, merely points on the regional map, locations in the extensive regional plan. But these activities are at least intended—particularly in their presentation—to dominate the dialogue. And for that an impressive image is necessary. An image that is not arbitrarily and vociferously formed by agencies but is actually built with an obligation to regional identity.

This innovation-oriented, activating regional planning, once it has found a stabil organizational-political form in individual regions, is perhaps the most effective means to a principled debate on shrinking regions. Activating regional planning becomes necessary in precisely those regions where the once familiar, self-running regional growth processes are absent. In this situation it is no longer sufficient that regional planning merely present a rough land-utilization grid thereby sharing out where one is allowed to build and where one is not, and which sites are to be developed with which infrastructure. For it is no longer to be expected that sooner or later these plans will be "filled out." Now the activating regional planning may not under any circumstances lead to the landscape area and culture area being arbitrarily available to the actors and their activities. In accordance with the principle that "the main thing is that something happens" there may not be—as central groups in current politics argue—any limitations resulting from geographical guidelines. On the contrary, for the future development of a regional economy that is no longer self-sufficient, the landscape and culture-area qualities of a region are a location factor whose significance is growing. Thus a considerably more assertive "security planning" must be put in place as a complement to activating regional planning, thus preventing the reduction in value of the landscape area and culture area from being larger than that which is added through new activities. And this too belongs to a holistic, multidisciplinary, and integrated planning, as it is required today—and not just for the region. At the same time it should be clear that classical planning tools and softer, consensus-oriented approaches to control—for instance via contractual regulations—are required in parallel in order to shape regions.

In 1952, P. H. Chombart de Lauwe proclaimed that it was not a matter of knowing whether people adapted to the new demands of urban living or not. Rather the true problem, he claimed, lay in creating cities that adapted to the new society and to the new people. And more than a half a century later this problem persists—only now the concept of region has replaced that of city.

Translated from the German by Steven Lindberg

Notes
1   See the introduction to Horst Steinmetz, *Moderne Literatur lesen: Eine Einführung* (Munich: Beck, 1996).
2   Manfred Kühn, "Regionalisierung der Städte: Eine Analyse von Stadt-Umland-Diskursen räumlicher Forschung und Planung," *Raumordnung und Raumforschung* 5/6 (2001), 410.
3   See Friedrich Achleitner, *Region, ein Konstrukt? Regionalismus, eine Pleite?* (Basel: Birkhäuser Verlag, 1997), 102, 164.

4   Alain Touraine, for instance, diagnosed this in principle as follows: "In whatever context one places urban development, the conclusion is always that the city is fragmented and can no longer control its own parts. The city is no longer the symbol of triumphant modernism, rather is that of the disunity of a society in which the economy is less and less social"; Alain Touraine, "Das Ende der Städte?" *Die Zeit,* May 31, 1996.
5   See Dietrich Fürst, "Stadt und Region: Schwierigkeiten, die regionale Selbststeuerung nachhaltig zu machen," *Deutsche Zeitschrift für Kommunalwissenschaften* 2 (2001), 87.
6   A good deal of solid thinking went into a Rhine-Main regional district, though it was not put into practice. A conurbation law, initiated by the Regional premier of the Federal State of Hesse, Roland Koch, entered into effect in the spring of 2001 but with little practical relevance.
7   The 1994 formation of the Verband Region Stuttgart (Association of the Region of Stuttgart) on the basis of a state law generated a fair amount of attention across Germany; noted with particular and intent interest was the strong commitment on the part of the government of the state of Baden-Württemberg, whose primary concern was an improved competitive position for its economic core region, as well as a tightening of the region-planning apparatus (with a planning law). Since then, however, things have, comparatively speaking, quieted down.
8   According to the plans thus far the intention is to completely integrate the (large) towns not currently administered within districts (i.e., including Rostock and Schwerin) into such regional districts. Because all communities would then be "regionally affiliated," it would become possible to improve the balance in the sharing of needs and burdens.
9   In connection with this the FOCJ (Functional Overlapping Competing Jurisdiction) model has been under discussion for some time in Switzerland, in particular with respect to the example of the "Greater Zurich Area." Under the FOCJ certain tasks, for cost and efficiency reasons, can be passed on to an entity between the local and the cantonal, or between the cantonal and the federal level.
10 Alain Thierstein, Thomas Held, and Simone Gabi, "Zurich/Glattal," trans. Mark Walz, in *Urbanscape Switzerland: Topology and Regional Development in Switzerland; Investigations and Case Studies,* ed. Michel Schneider and Angelus Eisinger (Basel: Birkhäuser Verlag, 2003), chap. 10, pp. 283, 287-288, and 295-296, esp. 296.
11 In any case, it must be said that Greater London has, almost traditionally, operated more in a city-oriented manner than in a region-oriented one. For example, the LCC visibly kept its distance both from backing of Patrick Abercrombie's Greater London Plan of 1944 and from A. G. Powell's plan for a New London Region from 1960, and instead focused on the issues of residential construction.
12 See Urlan Wannop, *The Regional Imperative: Regional Planning and Governance in Britain, Europe and the United States* (London: Jessica Kingsley Publishers, 1995), 294-304. See also Peter Calthorpe and William Fulton, *The Regional City: Planning for the End of Sprawl* (Washington, D.C.: Island Press, 2001).
13 Region Hannover did not come out of nowhere; its emergence was preceded by years of discussions, reports, and political debates. A central factor certainly was that the leaders of the city, district, and local association administrations virtually all retired at the same time. Last but not least, the region corresponds to a large extent to the "regional city" that had already been developed as a planning model in the 1960s by the then head of city planning in Hannover, Rudolf Hillebrecht (a model that Calthorpe and Fulton [see note 12], for instance, recently drew upon).
14 The new municipality of Greater Berlin with 3.8 million inhabitants—which included formerly autonomous cities like Schöneberg, Charlottenburg, and Spandau—was founded via a law dated April 27, 1920.
15 Corporación Metropolitana de Barcelona (CMB) was founded in 1975 and is modeled on the Greater London Council—established a year before—and its responsibilities. Just a year later a "metropolitan master plan" was adopted. CMB did not have directly elected representatives; for the sake of simplicity the mayor of the city was also the president of the CMB. Similar to what happened in London, party-political dissonance was the decisive factor in the dissolution of the CMB in 1987. Two smaller special-purpose associations took the CMB's place: the Entitat del Medi Ambient for the supply of water, and the disposal of wastewater and garbage, and the Entitat Metropolitana del Transport for transportation. Ultimately a third organization was added that assumed planning coordination responsibility from the CMB, the Mancomunitat de Municipis, and which is comparable to, for example, the Gemeinsame Landesplanung von Berlin und Brandenburg. All three associations taken together "constitute" what is known as the Área Metropolitana de Barcelona (AMB) but which ultimately has no institutionalized form.
16 Stephen M. Wheeler, "The New Regionalism: Key Characteristics of an Emerging Movement," *Journal of the American Planning Association* 68, no. 3 (Summer 2002), 268. Calthorpe and Fulton, in their oft-quoted book, *The Regional City* (see note 12), also argue for a new synthesis of physical, social, and economic planning—with specific reference to the metropolitan region.
17 See Michael Wegener, "Portland: Rationalistische Planung im deregulierten Amerika," in *Going West? Stadtplanung in den USA, gestern und heute,* ed. Ursula von Petz (Dortmund: IRPUD, Institut für Raumplanung, Universität Dortmund, 2004), 224, 227-228; Carl J. Abbott, "The Capital of Good Planning: Metropolitan Portland Since 1970," in *The American Planning Tradition: Culture and Policy,* ed. Robert Fishman (Washington, D.C.: Woodrow Wilson Center Press, 2000).

18 Wegener, "Portland."
19 See Dieter Läpple, "Stadt und Region in Zeiten der Globalisierung und Digitalisierung," *Deutsche Zeitschrift für Kommunalwissenschaften* 2 (2001), 26. In the choice of corresponding reference regions, there is also definitely—and repeatedly—a note of such resentment in the discussion of regionalism here in Germany.
20 For example, one result of the incorporation of communities into Leipzig was that the "single-family home building in the open countryside" was no longer suburbanization—problematic or not—but still simply a migration within the commune.
21 Manuel Castells, *The Information Age: Economy, Society and Culture,* vol. 1, *The Rise of the Network Society* (Oxford: Blackwell, 2000), 378.
22 Dieter Hoffmann-Axthelm, *Anleitung zum Stadtumbau* (Frankfurt am Main: Campus Verlag, 1996), 37.
23 Gerhard Hard, "Regionalisierungen," in *Region: Die Zukunft des Städtischen,* ed. Martin Wentz, Frankfurter Beiträge 5 (Frankfurt am Main: Campus Verlag, 1994), 54.

THE UPPER CALDER VALLEY
Yorkshire, UK, since 2003
John Thompson & Partners, the Yorkshire Forward Agency, and Calderdale Council
www.ucvr.com

As the former textile and market towns in the Upper Calder Valley lost their economic base in the course of deindustrialization, Calderdale Council, in cooperation with the Yorkshire Forward Agency and the urban design and architecture practice, John Thompson & Partners, developed the "Upper Calder Valley" project for the five most important towns situated along the river: Sowerby Bridge, Mytholmroyd, Hebden Bridge, Todmorden, and Walsden. Under the project, production of knowledge and concepts is to replace textile manufacture. In order to optimize opportunities for cooperation, particular value has been placed on linking the towns with one another, both in a physical sense, by extending the network of public amenities; and at the conceptual level, by strengthening regional identity. The intermunicipal art project "The Flying Shuttle," for example, envisages stations at exposed spots along a route through the valley, which both draw attention to change in the region and offer visitors the possibility of communicating from station to station. It is planned to extend local networking by installing a common broadband server, setting up multimedia centers, and extending public amenities.

Foodstuffs have been identified by various initiatives in the region as a decisive catalyst for the Upper Calder Valley's reemergence as a market center. The agrarian economy unit of the project cooperates with the Grass Roots Food Network and the local Farmers' Association in developing strategies to promote local produce and local suppliers. Retail is dominated by large supermarket chains, yet interest in local produce is rapidly growing: one of the first organic food stores opened in Hebden Bridge, for example, and Cleakheaton hosts a Farmers' Market. Local production combined with direct marketing make the provision of high-quality and specific products a viable option. So, on formerly abandoned land in the Upper Calder Valley, Asian immigrants are now growing coriander, fenugreek, and (Caribbean) spinach to meet local demand.

At the start of the overall project, efforts were made to integrate a maximum number of interested parties in the planning process: invitations to attend public workshops and other events were taken up by over 2,000 people. The most diverse participants, from specialists to local organizations, came together for a five-day planning workshop. Citizens' participation meetings were chaired and strictly structured according to the Charette method. As a result, a charter was formulated that sums up the resolutions agreed upon, and establishes targets for the next fifteen years. Eight working groups on issues such as the economy, housing, and tourism, along with the supervisory Valley Steering Group, then set about developing intermunicipal approaches and solutions as well as financial proposals appropriate to their implementation. (Ed.)

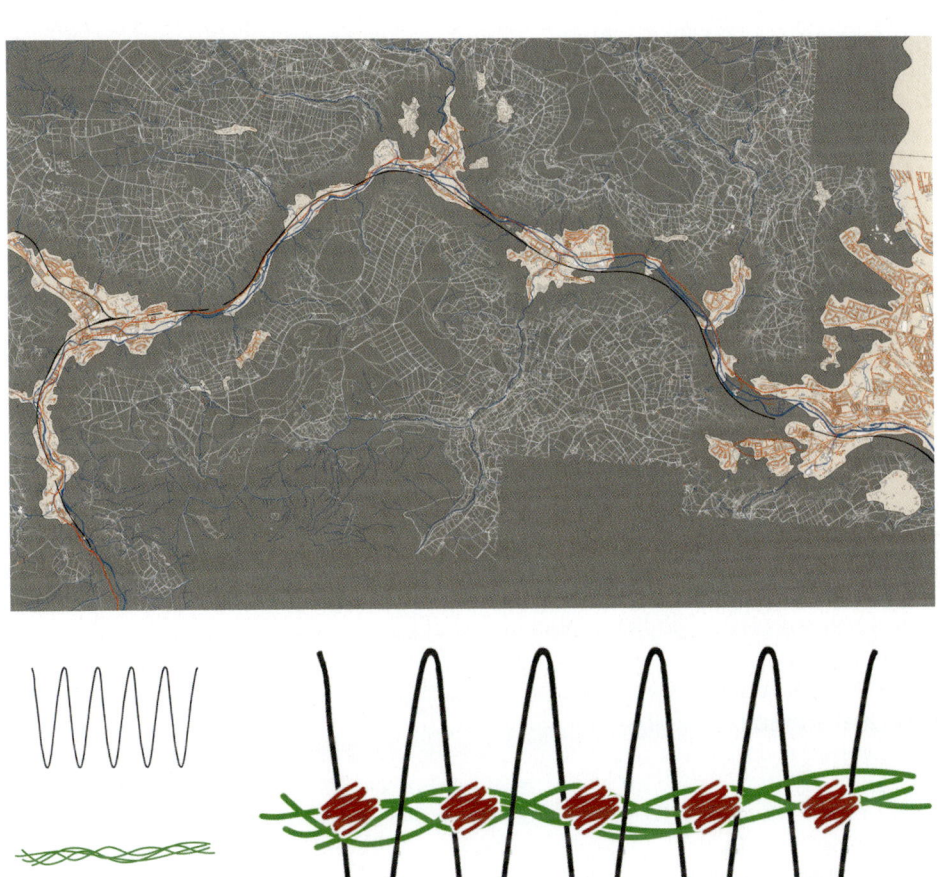

The towns of the Calder Valley in Yorkshire, a former textile production center, are to be linked with one another at various levels in a manner analogous to weaving techniques.

HOWEVER UNSPECTACULAR: THE NEW SUBURBANISM
Detroit, 2004/05
Interboro: Tobias Armborst, Daniel D'Oca, Georgeen Theodore, and Christine Williams; Center for Urban Pedagogy: Damon Rich and Rosten Woo
www.interboropartners.com
www.anothercupdevelopment.org

Forget the romantic theories. Despite the stated wishes of some, Detroit is not returning to nature. Detroit will never return to nature; it will return to the suburbs. Today it is the suburbs, not the indigenous landscape, that you can count on to fill in whatever hole civilization has created. Simply put, they are the most ravenous, opportunistic force around.

And there is no lack of evidence of this in Detroit. As we document in our project, whether masterplanned or homegrown, much of Detroit's new development is happening at lower densities than before. When the city's mayor, Kwame Kilpatrick, recently took government officials on a tour of new housing in Detroit, almost all of his exhibits were the sort of thing you would expect to find outside the city.

Would the continued suburbanization of Detroit be a bad thing? Potentially. If it follows the national trend, then the outlook is bleak. Whites will increasingly repopulate the city, blacks will be relocated to inner-ring suburbs, and a period of exacerbated racial tension accompanied by pious hand wringing over gentrification will precede the final outcome: a low-density white city, rich in services and opportunities and surrounded by an impoverished ring of black suburbs.

"However Unspectacular" stems from our conviction that the suburbanization of Detroit does not have to follow national trends, but can do better.

Detroit Today: Three Premises
Our proposals are based on three premises:

1. *Detroit is not a shrinking city, it is a growing region.* While the core city of Detroit has steadily lost population since 1950, the population of the three interdependent counties that make up the Detroit metropolitan area has steadily grown in the same period of time.

2. *Detroit's real problem is that it is growing unevenly; moreover, it is characterized by segregation and extreme inequality between the central city and the suburbs.* Metropolitan Detroit today is characterized by hypersegregation; the core city is 80% black, while the suburbs are 80% white. Central Detroit is most definitely not a bleak tabula rasa of abandoned buildings and vacant lots. It is a municipal ghetto, where residents have little money and less mobility. Although the current state of Detroit is frequently portrayed as the inevitable result of abstract forces like "economic shifts" and "market trends," we believe that Detroit's decline can be explained in much more concrete terms. The shrinkage of Detroit must not be understood as the death of a city. Instead, we should ask how the central city was transformed—politically, economically, racially, and spatially—into a receptacle for risk, while the suburbs became a citadel of wealth and opportunity.

3. *This strategy of uneven development has failed. Detroit has accrued all of the liabilities of both suburb and city: sprawl, poverty, traffic, sterility, and crime. It is neither convenient nor idyllic nor "cool."* For the last thirty years, Detroit has been a victim of all manner of centralized schemes designed to resuscitate the dying inner city with high-dosage injections of capital. Our proposal is not to revive the "inner city," but to spread the assets of the suburbs throughout the region.

Detroit's Future: Two Strategies
Many of the negative symptoms of shrinkage found in Detroit today—vacant land, low property values, lack of access to credit, and generally uneven development—result from failures to evenly distribute resources among all residents of the metropolitan area. While the best hope to correct these failures would be an effort to assert a social and governmental role in the operation of the market, today's climate of "big government is the problem" poses a significant challenge. For example, Detroit today is immediately surrounded by other municipalities—municipalities created by residents in order to avoid annexation by Detroit. By incorporating themselves as independent entities, they avoided having to share their resources through taxes with the often lower-income residents of the central city. Over the past twenty years, the political climate of the United States has led to dramatic slashing of taxes and a corresponding retrenchment of the welfare state. Less government revenue means less potential reallocation of resources. At the same time, the idea of government intervention has been increasingly demonized. How does one even introduce progressive ideas about regional revenue sharing into a culture that has come to think of market intervention as "tampering" or as an "interference" with a mechanism that is efficient only when it is free and unbridled?

With these difficulties in mind, our project uses two mutually complementary strategies for countering uneven development. A pragmatic, self-interested, "bottom-up" New Suburbanism, on the one hand, and long-term education, on the other: two strategies—at two scales—that share the same goal: a better, more vibrant, and more equitable city.

The New Suburbanism
The New Suburbanism can be characterized as a smaller, more immediate strategy. If increasing social and governmental involvement in the operation of the market is one way to address uneven development, another might be to encourage people to take advantage of opportunities that are already available to them. Beyond the typical story of Detroit's decline, and in the face of low property values, a lack of access to credit, and other such unfavorable conditions, one can nonetheless identify a number of ways in which individual Detroit residents—acting out of self-interest, and often with little formal education—"make do" and actually *take advantage* of shrinkage by increasing their space, thereby improving their "lot."

The New Suburbanism is happening all over Detroit. Ten years ago, Jorge Toral of 4930 Wesson Street owned one house on one 30 x 90 foot lot. Today, the same Jorge Toral owns one house on three 30 x 90 foot lots. The extra space enabled him to put an extension on his house, build a garage for his trucks, and erect a jungle gym for his

Polarized Regional City

Administrative structures in Detroit today (top left), which pit the city (red) against almost one hundred autarchic suburbs, entrench inequality regarding access to opportunities and resources. Redefining the city limits (top right and bottom) could alleviate such structural inequality.

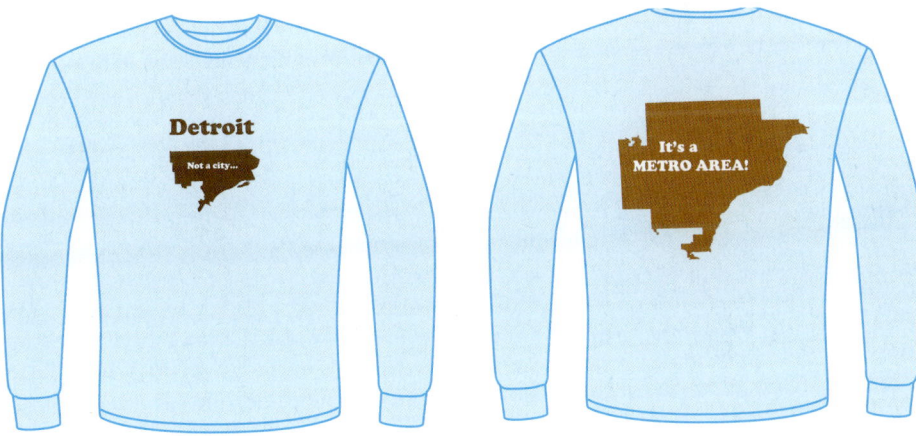

The project's marketing campaigns are aimed at strengthening people's identification with the region as a coherent entity.

children. Eventually, bottom-up efforts like these will change the genetic code of the city. We documented some of these practices and looked at ways in which they can be strengthened through specific interventions.

Implicit in the New Suburbanism is a new attitude towards urban redevelopment. Instead of emphasizing the spectacular new developments that are helping to gentrify Detroit's downtown, we take as our inspiration the small-scale individual efforts that are already under way to improve one's lot and increase one's space.

Education as Urban Design

By introducing the resources of architecture and planning into the classroom, we hope to support a regional political will to undo the ill effects of uneven development. Our project follows a long line of demands for a regional approach to the problems of U.S. cities. In the face of entrenched opposition, long-term education must be seen as an integrated component of the practice of radical urban design. This thinking was shared by Daniel Burnham, who drafted a curriculum to accompany his 1909 Plan of Chicago, and required it be taught in elementary schools throughout the Windy City. By opening up the disciplines of architecture and planning to the general public through education, decisions about development, oftentimes obfuscated by technicalities, can become part of the everyday discussions of democratic politics.

Our curriculum kit, "Detroit Do Your Thing!" is for use in schools throughout the Detroit metropolitan area. It is designed for teachers and students interested in using their city as the basis for required lessons in local history and social studies. We ask Detroit high-school students to investigate five aspects of their metropolitan region: its water system, transit systems, municipal boundaries, and racial and economic demographics. Each of these systems tells a complex story about Detroit's development and about how the city is governed. Students examine each topic through stakeholder interviews and interactive maps. The interviews, conducted with nonprofit organizations, businesses, and government agencies, present the views of various stakeholders, and help students learn how decisions are made in a complex society. The maps, made using census data, visualize the patterns in infrastructure, demography, and political organization that shape physical reality. The new civics education must link everyday life to the complex and abstract systems that shape it—economies, ecosystems, and polities. Encouraging residents to contribute to the making of their communal physical environment is a critical component of a democratic society. Despite attempts to decentralize planning authority over the twentieth century, granting a say to the broad population remains a political challenge. Democratic planning and design do not mean that everyone goes to urban design school, but it could mean that urban design goes to everyone's school.

This project was developed for the *archplus* competition "Shrinking Cities: Reinventing Urbanism."

However Unspectacular_Interboro, Center for Urban Pedagogy

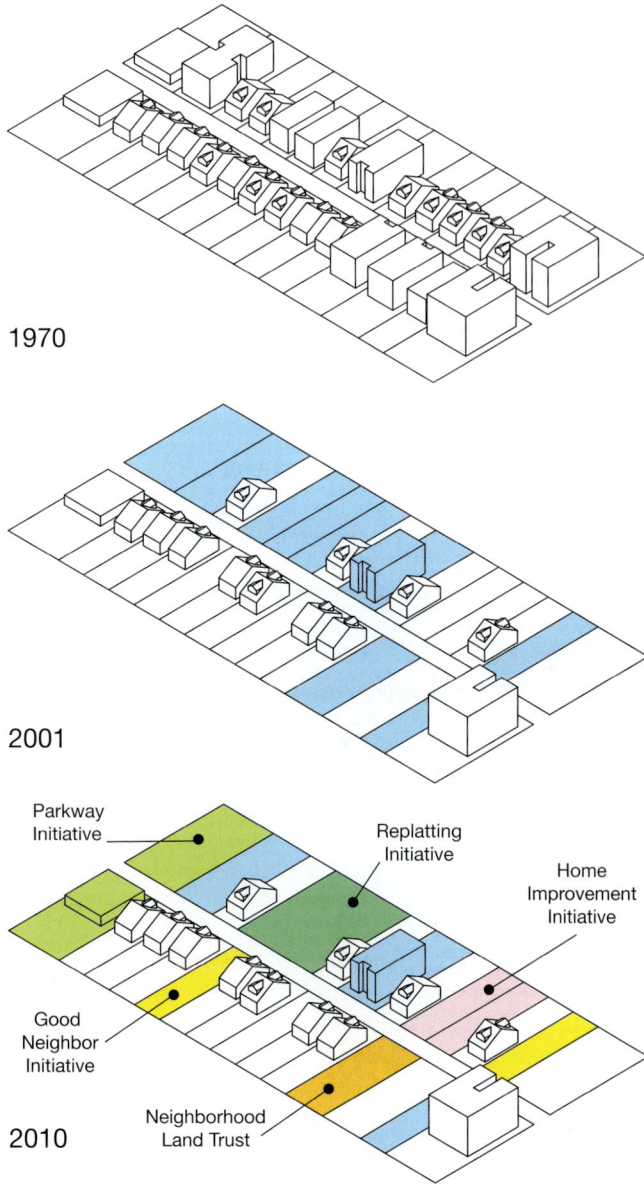

New Suburbanism is a "bottom-up" suburbanization of the inner city. Vacant lots are bought and used by the owners of the adjacent properties or by local initiatives. The results are inverse urban densification and "reparceling," which redefines property boundaries and hence creates new lot formations. This has been practiced in Detroit, almost unnoticed, for many years now. By rendering this activity visible and by supporting it through the development of new tools and typologies, we hope to establish it as a recognized form of urban design and thereby illustrate the advantages that can derive from shrinkage processes.

STRATEGIC PLANNING
Manfred Kühn

The Revival of Strategic Planning

Since the 1980s, western European planning experts have assumed that general trends toward globalization, liberalization, and deregulation will increasingly reduce the ability of governments to control urban and regional planning. During the planning euphoria of the 1970s, the model of "comprehensive planning" was still founded on faith in comprehensive planning works, in the ability to integrate various areas of responsibility and political spheres into a "master plan," and in stability and uniformity of planning goals.[1] During the 1980s and 1990s, the technocratic rationality and statism of this model became clear. It dominated the skepticism about planning in critique of problems of control and deficits of implementation found in integrative total planning. The conception of planning now began to be oriented instead around the model of "disjointed incrementalism," characterized by a gradual approach that is open to results, by selective solutions for limited areas, and by short-term actions.

In planning theory, the new paradigmatic approaches of the "communicative turn" and "collaborative planning" abandoned the model of the public planning authority by thematizing instead new forms of cooperation and processes of negotiation between the official state sector and private parties.[2] At the same time, at the end of the 1990s, several European cities and regions had a "revival of strategic planning."[3] Public planning adopted principles of strategic planning developed for the management of private companies. Although a uniform conception of strategic planning has yet to emerge, in the context of urban development it is primarily associated with the following characteristics:

- *Cross-departmental and area-based approaches*

A cross-departmental approach is intended to be adequate for the complex overlapping of physical, social, and economic problems of cities, and to manage urban change. The "comprehensive" approach also requires an "area-based" approach to selecting and demarcating target areas in cities. This approach is followed in Germany by the "Soziale Stadt" (Socially Integrative City) program, among others.

- *Cooperation of public and private actors*

Limits on controlling by means of state planning are often accompanied by an institutionalization of public-private partnerships, especially in countries with a strong free-market orientation. Frequently, this is tied to a hope that public funding will attract subsequent private investment.

- *Implementation of visions in strategic projects*

This is the core of strategic planning. Particularly at the start of planning processes, visions (or *Leitbilder* in German) play an important role in creating consensus and guiding activities for a shared future when integrating various actors and departments. Unlike staged image campaigns, strategic visions are based on social processes of negotiation between the parties involved in the city. Visions determine long-term goals or visions on the level of the city as a whole. They require a local political consensus on determining location factors or a city's economic base (e.g., a "city of culture," "university town," or "sports city"). In deindustrialized cities confronted with the need to determine their postindustrial identity, one often finds conflicting visions operating in local politics. Projects should generate visible and symbolic successes for the parties involved and thereby avoid the implementation weaknesses of integrated master plans. Projects are designed to be short-term, to intervene in specific places within the urban region, and to have clearly defined connections to the actors involved, the financing, and the measures taken. Strategic projects are called "key projects" when their effects are intended to radiate outward. In the case of the regeneration of shrinking cities, these effects are often expected to spread geographically (metastasizing) or accelerate in time (catalyzing).

- *Learning capacity*

A strategy is, ultimately, a kind of planned action that analyzes the requirements for achieving a certain goal and selects the necessary instruments on that basis. Consequently, in lieu of rigid planning goals and fixed durations of plans, openness and flexibility are important characteristics of strategic planning.

All in all, strategic planning attempts to find a third way between the large master plan and small steps. This is done to avoid both the lack of results of vision-based discourses, on the one hand, and the actionism of projects, on the other. In Germany this hybrid type of planning became famous thanks to the example of the Emscher Park International Building Exhibition (1989–1999) and has been labeled "perspectival incrementalism."

Strategies of Urban Regeneration in Great Britain

The theory and practice of urban regeneration in Great Britain is based substantially on the concept of strategic planning as a cross-departmental approach that integrates the physical and architectural goals with social and economic ones.[4] In Great Britain, public-private partnerships or local strategic partnerships are the most important institutions for funding regeneration projects.[5] In the name of such partnerships, many British cities since the 1990s have institutionalized their own development companies to carry out regeneration projects. Several Urban Development Corporations in the 1990s were followed by the first three Urban Regeneration Companies in Manchester, Liverpool, and Sheffield since the year 2000. As so-called quangos (quasi-autonomous nongovernmental organizations), they implement strategic projects in precisely defined areas of the cities ("area-based"). These can be, but do not have to be, inner cities.

With reference to the two core elements of strategic planning, the practice of urban regeneration can be outlined as follows:

- *Visions*

The local planning partnerships elaborate models ("visions") for the cities. In the case of the city of Manchester, which had to cope with a prototypical structural change from an industrial city to a service-based city, long-term visions are evaluated in retrospect as having been an important part of the regeneration strategy.[6] In Manchester these visions centered on repopulating the city center by capitalizing on the sporting prowess of the city, promoting the city's cultural, high-tech, and scientific base, and emphasizing the role of the airport to attract international investments.[7]

The strategic visions of other former industrial cities in northern England were also based on establishing a service- and knowledge-based economy. In addition to universities, science parks, sports, tourism, and banks, the revival of inner cities was increasingly pushed by means of cultural services, restaurants and bars, and the image of "party" or "nightlife" towns. The "shrinking city" is not the vision anywhere in Britain (by contrast, Halle in eastern Germany used that phrase as the title of its application to become a

European cultural capital). On the contrary, nearly all the visions for cities in northern England are solidly based on growth and place their hopes in such familiar "engines of growth" as airports and global players. In Newcastle, for example, the strategic vision is explicitly called "Going for Growth." In the former industrial area of east Manchester, the strategy of the Urban Regeneration Company is to double the population by attracting 30,000 new residents and creating more than 10,000 new jobs.[8]

- *Projects*

Anglo-Saxon regeneration policies are strongly oriented around implementing large projects in shrinking urban areas. The most popular large projects are sports stadiums, shopping malls, international events like the Olympic Games or world fairs, and spectacular museums and bridges. The competition between cities over large events and projects is escalating. As symbolic policies, so-called flagships are supposed to result in a change in image that will provide the basis for making the cities attractive again. One early cautionary example of such a large project was the Renaissance Center in Detroit, which was constructed in 1977. Although the present world headquarters of General Motors provides approximately 15,000 jobs and thousands of parking spaces and hotel rooms, as well as theaters, restaurants, and shops on the edge of Detroit's fallow downtown, due to the fact that in terms of both urban planning and function it was incorporated into the city like some sort of an autistic citadel, this project never contributed to an urban renaissance. On the contrary, many offices moved from downtown to the Center, draining the city even more. Such "oasis effects" of large projects can also be assumed for sports stadiums, as they are scarcely embedded at all into their surrounding neighborhoods and are used only on a temporary and exogenous basis.[9] Moreover, many publicly funded large projects produce resulting costs that are completely underestimated beforehand or produce problems for later use. No one has yet evaluated the metastasizing or catalytic effects that large projects in fact radiate, or the extent to which support for many small projects might not represent a more effective alternative for regenerating shrinking urban areas, and hence it is difficult to answer the question.

The revival of the severely depopulated inner city of Manchester since the 1990s has been based only in part on a series of strategic large projects. The Commonwealth Games, the Millennium Stadium, the Bridgewater Concert Hall, the Imperial War Museum, the Urbis Centre, and other large projects primarily target exogenous users and symbolically transform the image of the city. But the real regeneration process of the city was no less the result of an invasion—not initially intended by city planners—of pioneers from creative milieus in specific districts of the city: trendsetters who discovered the Castlefield district in the 1980s and the Northern Quarter, among others, in the 1990s. Clearly, in Manchester, planners were able to learn and adapt in order to integrate these endogenous projects into their strategies. Thus it would seem that a mixture of exogenous and endogenous stimuli, of large projects and processes in limited areas, produced the oft-cited success of the urban regeneration of Manchester.

- *Strengths and weaknesses*

The strengths of regeneration strategies in northern England lie above all in the partnerships between the public and private sector and in the ability of the institutions responsible to bring together national funding programs across departments and to implement them in strategic projects. Growing disparities between sections of the cities are tolerated by an "area-based strategy." One weakness of the regeneration strategies of northern England lies in their highly exogenous dependency on national funding. For example, the institutionalization of the Local Strategic Partnerships and Urban Regeneration Companies was essentially initiated by funding programs from London. Empirical studies suggest that in many cases they are not self-sustaining but remain dependent on the support of national funding.[10]

Stadtumbau Ost in Eastern Germany: A Strategy for Urban Regeneration?

Coupling strategic discourses on visions with the operative implementation of key projects is something that has only been practiced in a few of eastern Germany's shrinking cities. Urban research and planning in eastern Germany is focusing its attention on the federal and state development program Stadtumbau Ost (Urban Restructuring in Eastern Germany). But Stadtumbau Ost is not a strategic plan to regenerate shrinking cities, for the following reasons:

- The Stadtumbau Ost program's measures for tearing down empty apartment buildings and improving the value of districts are restricted to the departments responsible for urban planning and housing policies. Socioeconomic approaches to regeneration that would support employment and the local economy of urban neighborhoods are not the goal of this urban renewal project (in contrast to the Socially Integrative City program).
- The urban renewal is essentially carried out by public or semipublic planning authorities. The integrated concepts of urban development were worked out in a collaborative process with the city planning agencies and communal housing companies or cooperatives. Private-sector actors from companies, banks, and households were and are only marginally involved.
- By placing the political focus on demolishing existing buildings, there is a lack of strategic projects that could produce a sense of new departure in the cities (instead of one of destruction). The target areas of urban renewal to which most of the funding flows are the large but shrinking residential areas on the periphery. It remains doubtful whether self-sustaining regeneration processes can be developed in "consolidation areas," as defined by planners.

Prospects

Strategic visions and projects cannot simply reverse long-term demographic and socioeconomic shrinking trends in cities. They can, however, contribute to a symbolic transformation of shrinking cities and regions by opposing the resigned images of decline with positive images of regeneration and thus embody postindustrial structural change. The earlier experiences of cities in northern England in coping with processes of shrinking and in testing regeneration strategies suggest, however, that the spatial disparities in eastern German cities will increase in the future, since only certain areas of the cities can be regenerated, while other areas continue to shrink.[11]

Translated from the German by Steven Lindberg

Notes

1   See Hartmut Häußermann and Walter Siebel, "Wandel von Planungsaufgaben und Wandel der Planungsstrategie: Das Beispiel der Internationalen Bauausstellung Emscher-Park," in *Jahrbuch Stadterneuerung 1993,* ed. AK Stadterneuerung (Berlin: TU Berlin Universitätsbibliothek, 1993), 141–154.

2   See Patsy Healey, *Collaborative Planning: Shaping Places in Fragmented Societies* (Houndsmill, UK: Macmillan, 1997).
3   See William Salet and Andreas Faludi, eds., *The Revival of Strategic Spatial Planning* (Amsterdam: Royal Netherlands Academy of Arts and Sciences, 2000).
4   See Peter Roberts and Hugh Sykes, eds., *Urban Regeneration: A Handbook* (Thousand Oaks, CA: Sage, 2000).
5   See Michael Carley, "Urban Partnerships, Governance and the Regeneration of Britain's Cities," *International Planning Studies* 5, no. 3 (2000): 273-297.
6   See Brian Robson, "Mancunian Ways: The Politics of Regeneration," in *City of Revolution: Restructuring Manchester*, ed. Jamie Peck and Kevin Ward (Manchester: Manchester University Press, 2002), 34-49.
7   Ibid.
8   See New East Manchester Limited, ed., *New East Manchester: The New Town in the City; Annual Report and Accounts, 2002-2003* (Manchester, 2004).
9   Häußermann and Siebel, "Wandel von Planungsaufgaben."
10 See Jonathan S. Davies, "Conjuncture or Disjuncture? An Institutionalist Analysis of Local Regeneration Partnerships in the UK," *International Journal of Urban and Regional Research* 28, no. 3 (2004): 570-585.
11 See Gordon Dabinett, "Uneven Spatial Development and Regeneration Outcomes in the UK: Reversing Decline in the Northern City of Sheffield?" *Städte im Umbruch: Online-Magazin für Stadtentwicklung, Stadtschrumpfung, Stadtumbau und Regenerierung* 2 (2004): 18-22; www.schrumpfende-stadt.de.

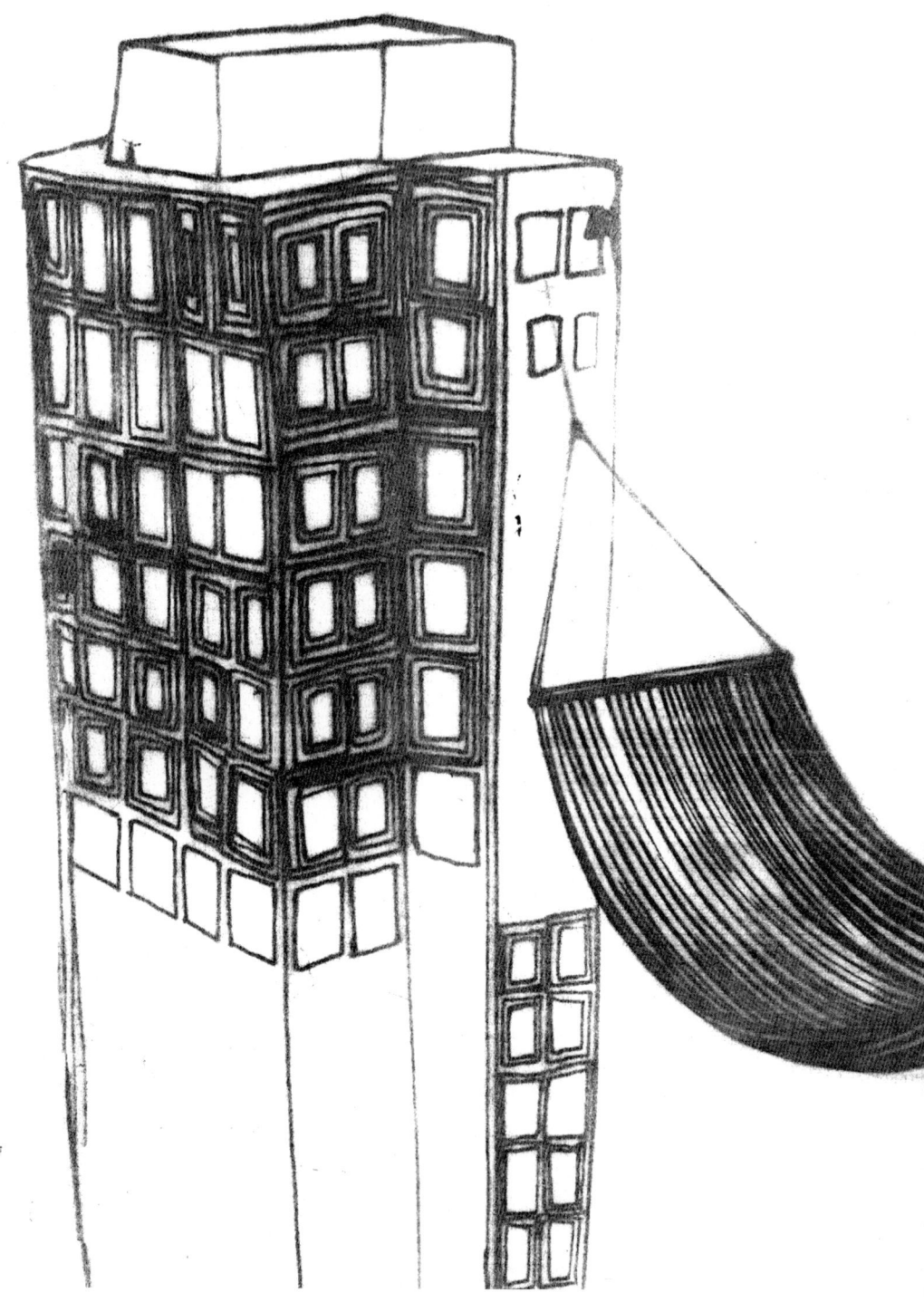

TEMPORARY CITY

A surplus of freed-up space provides new possibilities. A dearth of long-term options for repurposing is replaced by the ephemeral activities of interested parties who have little capital to spare. They experiment with new uses and forms of co-operation, create social interactions, and give new cultural meaning to what was found there. Not every vacant space will find interested parties, and the fleeting actions are of limited duration. Still, sometimes they represent seeds for longer-term developments.

VACANT LOTS AS INCUBATORS?
INTERIM USES IN SHRINKING CITIES
Klaus Overmeyer

Helle Tempo is located in the Berlin district of Hellersdorf, not far from Helle Mitte. Helle Tempo has not been around for very long. It was created after some houses had been torn down and even green areas in this neighborhood of prefab concrete buildings went unused. Several of the buildings are still completely rented out, but the gaps can scarcely be overlooked, especially those between the buildings.

What immediately strikes one about Helle Tempo is the wide variety of provisional uses, which are found on nearly every corner. It all began because the increasingly overgrown state of the abandoned properties was causing a growing number of residents to abandon the neighborhood. Fearing that the dilapidation and vacancy could spread to the new shopping district Helle Mitte, which is right next door, the district authorities decided without delay to employ unconventional but very effective measures.

First, they issued a public invitation for bids for Helle Tempo as a district for interim uses. The district authorities had the curbs along the neighborhood's boundaries painted yellow; whirlwinds were placed on all of the vacant lots to indicate that interim uses could settle here spontaneously and without bureaucracy. Since then special rules have applied for Helle Tempo which make it considerably easier for temporary uses to be established here. Following the slogan "Space in exchange for ideas," the district hired a local agent to ensure that everyone in Helle Tempo who needs space for his or her own initiatives can obtain it on short notice and under favorable terms. For example, all of the vacant lots were made available for free if the users would pay for the maintenance of the lots. If someone wished to establish a company in an unused public building, he or she was charged only for operating costs. Even building inspections were granted more free play in Helle Tempo. The stipulations had to be met, of course, but many of the requirements for obtaining permission could be satisfied gradually. The administration made a special arrangement for private owners: the property owners permitted the temporary public use of their property; in exchange, property taxes and the obligation for liability insurance were waived. Even existing building permits were preserved, and the district provided donations of materials to those using vacant lots who were also taking responsibility for their maintenance. One condition for all such uses, however, is that a time limit be set. If there is an interested buyer for a building or lot, a new location must be found for the interim use.

In the meanwhile, with the agent's help, a wide variety of use typologies has located here. Several young people are keeping ponies on the land that once belonged to a day-care center; recently a children's merry-go-round museum opened in a former warehouse; the old gymnasium has been adopted by a boxing club; and an Austrian woman intends to offer ski courses for children on an artificial hill.

What sounds like an El Dorado for pioneers of free space of every shade is, for now, just a fiction. The district of Marzahn-Hellersdorf has not yet identified an "urban laboratory" with its own rules as a way of deliberately attracting the establishment of interim uses. That can be attributed above all to the existing laws and building codes, which one community cannot simply repeal. In 2003, however, Marzahn-Hellersdorf was one of the first communities in Germany to establish an office for the coordination of interim uses.

The background behind that decision was the increasing vacancy of social infrastructures, which represent an immense potential in terms of space (approximately 250 acres over the medium term), remain unused for long periods, and have high maintenance costs. The coordination office has meanwhile established itself as a connecting link between potential interim uses, government offices, planners, owners, and residents. The pioneers of space are spared time-consuming research and visits to government offices.

The local agent of the coordination office, who as a former school board director is very familiar with the structures of the bureaucracy, takes on the role of a guide. From a pool of unused public lands supported by a geographic information system, interested parties are offered appropriate spaces on the basis of their use profile. With the help of user questionnaires and checklists, the agent investigates beforehand whether the use requires a permit and unbureaucratically helps interested parties realize their ideas. In addition, the coordination office organizes public forums where use proposals are gathered, contracts are established between individual initiatives and public bodies, and the merger of networks is encouraged.

The coordination office sees itself more as a catalyst than as a body responsible for interim uses. It has no official powers, but it does have great potential in terms of contacts and knowledge about available spaces and users. The acquisition of free space takes place far more quickly than would have been possible by means of a development plan. During the past two years the coordination office has primarily supported voluntary garden projects in Marzahn-Hellersdorf. Subsidized by the municipal redevelopment program and facilitated by local agents, community vegetable plots and multicultural gardens for immigrants have been created on former school grounds. The use of vacant public buildings in Marzahn-Hellersdorf usually falls through because the interim users often wish to use only part of a building and are not prepared to pay the operating costs that would be incurred for the whole building.

In the meanwhile, all of the communities and lot owners in shrinking urban districts are feverishly occupied with the question of how at least temporary uses can be found for vacant spaces. Interim uses seem to be the miracle cure for bankrupt districts, space surpluses, vacancy, and reduced budgets. In addition to the goal of saving the fees and operating costs incurred even by unused vacant lots, the governments of shrinking cities are hoping above all that interim uses can stop the trend toward perforated spaces and social segregation. Because lack of demand rules out the options of selling or building on unutilized properties, interim uses often represent the only opportunity to stop the feared downward spiral—vacancy, the departure of residents, and vandalism, until entire districts are abandoned—so that the urban network and public life can be preserved, at least temporarily.

Not every vacant lot or every empty building is suited for interim use, however. In every shrinking city the available space far exceeds the needs of potential users. In agglomeration areas in large cities with limited available space and yet a high fluctuation of young people, the density and spectrum of interim uses is far higher than in small and medium-sized cities where the younger people have moved away and the population is aging. As a result, unutilized inner-city areas with good transportation connections and high population density will no doubt more easily be converted into creative milieus for new kinds of event and leisure cultures, start-up economies, and new trends in sports than will abandoned school and daycare sites in peripheral sections of large residential areas or vacant areas in small rural towns. In addition, even for interim uses, such strategic factors as a site's location and transportation connections, synergies with existing interim uses, relations with neighbors, and basic financial arrangements are crucial.

Unlike trendy neighborhoods in the inner city, in which unused spaces can easily become fertile soil for spontaneous and unplanned uses, interim users for vacant spaces in shrinking milieus often can only be found, if at all, through long-term efforts and lucrative offers from communities or owners. Whether it is youth projects in former daycare centers, art actions in buildings marked for demolition, vacation camps for children on playgrounds that no longer can be maintained as public spaces, sports activities sponsored by newly founded associations in vacant school gymnasiums, exhibitions of refugee projects in vacant storefronts, children's farms and the keeping of animals on vacant lots, or projects to create temporary residential space, most of the temporary projects in shrinking contexts serve to stabilize social structures and are dependent on state programs or the support of private owners. The initiation and support of interim-use projects by district administrators or delegated sponsoring companies lowers the inhibitions of many citizens about becoming active themselves. Many examples demonstrate, however, that the users leave the sites when the public programs run out as a result of budget cuts.

The communities cannot, however, retreat to classical supply-oriented planning. Urban development in shrinking cities has long since had to get by without urban construction, so interim uses are one of the few options that communities still have to play an active role in shaping the processes of transformation. One example of the proactive management of space by the city of Leipzig shows how interim uses can be strategically integrated into urban development, despite limited funds.

For several years now the municipal government of Leipzig has made a point of negotiating with owners of unutilized properties and vacant lots for temporary use of these sites as public green areas. The private owners and the city agree on a temporary change of ownership by means of a use agreement. The property owner is subject to no further costs after the property is handed over. The property taxes and the obligation to ensure traffic safety (for a maximum of two and a half years) are waived, while the right to build and any existing building permits remain valid, and the planting of trees is done in a way that will not prevent any future construction measures. The city makes available fifteen euros per square meter (ca. 11 square feet) from city development funds for a redesign of the site, and either undertakes that work itself or passes the funds on to interested users. Since the inauguration of this model, more than 150 of Leipzig's 1,000 vacant lots have been made available for public use or gardening. These green reserves do more than just create an integrated ecological system for the inner city. The image of the late-nineteenth-century district of the city has seen lasting change: even suburbanites are finding it attractive to move to the city again. Structures that were once built closely together are now fused with open meadows, garden enclaves, small forests, and refuges for leisure activities, creating a heterogeneous urban character whose fissures and niches permit new forms of urban life.

Improving the stability of interim uses is desirable even in Leipzig, under certain conditions, given the long-term nature of the low utilization levels. Property owners' fears that they might not be able to get rid of the interim users when demand rises have given way to deliberate incentives to attract interim users and offer them prospects for long-term development. Even if the use agreements do not permit the construction of new buildings, the coalition of communal initiative and private engagement has paid off over the long term for all the interested parties. Those who discover opportunities to try out and experiment with individual ways of life that had not previously been possible in their surroundings, those who can drive by car to their own garden garages in an unutilized industrial area in the middle of the city, those who can take their ponies for a ride in stables from the late nineteenth century, those who can live rent free for several years in exchange for renovating their apartments—they will not abandon that opportunity over the long term but rather stay.

The range of interim uses in shrinking cities is large. In addition to the volunteer initiatives that are usually dependent on state aid, entrepreneurial interim uses can create mixed use structures, especially in monofunctional residential complexes in large housing developments. As a rule they are concentrated around the more heavily frequented cores of such housing developments and are geared toward local needs. Interim-use entrepreneurs sell everyday necessities: used cars, auto tires, and repair work on vacant municipal lots; remnants sold in old market halls; pet salons in temporary buildings; nail salons in ground-floor apartments; massage salons in former daycare centers. Sometimes the locations and strategies of established economies are taken over or copied: Marzahn-Hellersdorf recently saw the opening of its twelfth store of the "Gut und Billig" chain. The business idea follows a simple principle: an individual entrepreneur rents a convenience store, usually one approved for demolition. It is furnished as simply as possible, with folding tables and shelves, and the food and stationery are sold by temp workers until the owner has made a final decision about the property.

Other entrepreneurs form use clusters with a correspondingly broad spectrum of offerings. For example, there are auto repair shops in buildings that once belonged to collective farms, and old industrial grounds often have automobile-related businesses offering everything from car sales and painting to junkyards and do-it-yourself repair shops. In addition to easy accessibility, one important prerequisite for such uses is the presence of heterogeneous structures that can be used flexibly.

In the ideal case, the engagement of the interim entrepreneurs results in its own dynamic even without stimulation from the communities. In an abandoned industrial area in Berlin's Marzahn district, a prefab concrete building that once belonged to ORWO-Filmfabrik but was vacant for years has been rented since 1998 as a storage area for a real estate company. Soon a curious mix of businesses had established itself in the building: Vietnamese florists stored dried flowers between rehearsal spaces for bands. In the years that followed it grew to be Germany's largest cluster of rehearsal spaces, with nearly eighty bands. Four hundred musicians enthusiastically built their rehearsal spaces and studios themselves, one after another. The easily accessible and intact structure was attractive to them primarily because there were no apartments in the neighborhood. After the building department discovered substantial fire code violations in the building in the spring of 2004, the owner responded by canceling the leases on short notice. The florists looked for alternative sites, but the musicians stayed. Their investment in building their

BUILDING GUARDS
Leipzig-Lindenau, Germany, since 2005
HausHalten e.V.
www.haushalten-leipzig.de

In order to protect from dilapidation those late-nineteenth-century buildings in Leipzig neighborhoods that are worthy of preservation, the association HausHalten e.V. looks for users who are prepared to live or work in parts of vacant buildings and keep them in good repair. To that end, the association contracts with the property owners for permission to use their buildings for five years.

Since May 1, 2005, Lützner Straße has had the first such "guarded house" ("Wächterhaus"), with two apartments with ateliers shared by several occupants, a food cooperative, and an art workshop for children. The users share only the costs for utilities and building services and pay a small contribution to the association. In return, they renovate their spaces themselves, make inspection rounds, and handle small repairs. The intention is not to offer residential space at dumping prices but to maintain the building fabric while keeping the number of users to a minimum. (Ed.)

COMMUNITY GARDENS ON JOSEPHSTRASSE
Leipzig-Lindenau, Germany, since 2004
Lindenauer Stadtteilverein e.V., with citizens of Leipzig
www.josephstrasse.de

When a family-friendly residential project was completed on Roßmarktstraße in the Lindenau section of Leipzig in 2003, the interest and demand was enormous, not least because of the immense gardens and green spaces that had been created on razed sites formerly occupied by industrial buildings. The district association of Lindenau decided to make additional unutilized properties on Josephstraße available for use as private gardens near existing residences. Private lease agreements with the property owners were signed, which allowed users to clean up the sites, plant on them, and use them without a fixed term. When there is a plan to develop the properties, however, the use agreement can be terminated on short notice.

During two construction parties of several weeks each in 2004, the lots were adapted by the future users and a number of volunteer helpers. The result was several private gardens to be kept by families from the neighborhood as well as collective plots maintained by the district association and used for public events.

In the meanwhile the district association of Lindenau has extended its commitment. It supports the temporary use and maintenance of conservation-worthy old buildings under its "Haushalten" project. In addition, the association gets involved in the urban development process as a representative of local interests by acquiring private funding to be used as the local matching contributions necessary to receive funds from the urban development program, which are used for demolition or improvements. (Ed.)

Vacant Lots as Incubators?_*Klaus Overmeyer*

An unutilized industrial plot on Josephstraße in Leipzig is converted into community gardens.

rehearsal spaces argued against moving. In response, the building was closed off by guards and a fence; locks were changed.

Only now are the young people, who initially responded as individual renters, forming an association. Just before the building was to be evacuated, they spent three weeks living in the building and formed the Orwohaus Association. By means of demonstrations, concerts, conversations with politicians, and effective publicity work, they succeeded in mobilizing prominent figures from the music business and district councils as well as the senator for culture, who negotiated with the owner and achieved a temporary solution. A city-run company will manage the building for six months. In the meantime, the young people, with the help of a management consultant, are putting together a proposal for use and financing of the building, which covers nearly two acres, and are beginning to implement the required changes to meet the fire code. The young musicians purchased Orwohaus in the spring of 2005 and are planning to run it themselves as a "music factory," with integrated platforms for music-related services like Web studios, photographers, CD production, and booking agents. Orwohaus is a clear example of the possible coordinates of a future urban development that is not a long-term consequence of urban planning but the result of a successful interplay of individual initiative, modifications to legal and economic conditions, and a proactive community.

Temporary uses are certainly not a panacea against shrinking. They do, however, represent in many respects a new culture of use and urban development that can essentially be traced back to the collapse of traditional planning instruments and models for investment. Suddenly individual citizens are in the limelight of urban development, if only temporarily, until new demand for construction is anticipated; even so, all hopes are on them. They are supposed to reactivate plots that are no longer utilized, to draw attention to neglected sites, to explore new uses, to awaken creative potential, to found companies in niches, and to enhance the value of desolate sections of the city. Their role is undoubtedly ambivalent. Are communities merely shifting all the responsibility to citizens, or are they truly opening up new fields of action by allowing them to appropriate unused spaces? The question can be put into perspective by examining daily life in shrinking cities. Most of the open spaces are not suitable for an interim use in the first place, because they are too large, too inaccessible, or inappropriate for other reasons. The second deficiency stems from the citizens themselves. There are simply too few people who are prepared to become pioneers by taking advantage of excess space. The young, the creative, and the well-educated are still those most likely to take a risk on unutilized spaces that cities have long since forgotten. Thus, the potential for temporary uses in shrinking cities should not be overestimated.

Nevertheless, communities will have to do everything they can to reduce substantially the inhibition thresholds to acquiring space—not as planning authorities but as mediators and facilitators. If communities in growing metropolises are sometimes stepping in to protect interim users against property owners and their interest in utilizing their property, then in shrinking milieus a crucial role is played by changes in land-price policy, agreements on limited-term public use of private lots, the mediation of interim uses by agents, minimal construction interventions to open up spaces, and political discussion and support.

One essential precondition, however, is that the potential of existing resources and the status of the sites need to be realistically assessed for their suitability for use. On plots with existing use potential, it may be possible to attract a cluster of users through active communal management, which compensate for the deficits in terms of social space and influence the development of other sites in a positive way. Other spaces that are not suitable for either construction or interim uses will drop out of the urban spatial context entirely and can, at best, be turned into forest or meadows again.

The consequence is a radically polarized urban development that stands the previous image of that process on its head. For most shrinking cities, there will be no return to the homogeneous, concentrated city. Interim uses offer an opportunity to become familiar with the polarized city, to explore it and develop new cultures of use. Test it.

———

Translated from the German by Steven Lindberg

DIETZENBACH: DEFINITIVELY UNFINISHED
Dietzenbach, Germany, 2002/03
Dietzenbach City Planning Office, Social Studies Department of the Johann-Wolfgang-Goethe-Universität Frankfurt am Main, Urban Design Group of the Technische Universität Darmstadt, Büro Topos, Büro mwas—martin wilhelm architektur/städtebau
www.100qm-dietzenbach.de

Dietzenbach is a planning ruin from the 1970s. Planned as an ideal city for ordinary people, West Germany's largest urban development measure ever now consists of unutilized and underutilized areas right next to large housing complexes. Because it is located directly in the booming Rhine-Main region, the properties are so overvalued on paper that there is scarcely any flexibility for planning and use.

In view of this situation, the strategy of "100 qm dietzenbach" was to encourage the residents of Dietzenbach to put the unutilized areas of their city to new use. Ten thousand copies of a brochure depicting particularly conspicuous vacant lots were distributed, but without saying whether any of these areas had been made available. A large installation with several thousand large posts was set up in the city center to symbolize the opportunity to stake a claim. More than a thousand citizens registered, three hundred of them with concrete ideas such as gardens, art and small crafts projects, playgrounds, and public parks. Only after demand had been created did the project team try to establish some sort of legal basis for such use. The community developed a use agreement called "Fläche gegen Verantwortung" (Plots in Exchange for Responsibility). The fear that chaos would ensue when the lots were occupied proved unfounded. The users, sometimes with the help of plans from the project team, simply staked claims using the posts taken from the installation and immediately began revamping the lots or building on them—in the case of the most successful and best-known project: a chicken farm for children.

The difficulties ultimately came from the city: there were fears of loss of control, and so they began to try to scare off the citizens with requests for security deposits or with prohibitions. Issues of site development were particularly significant in choking off the do-it-yourself dynamics and in making parcels prohibitively expensive. The biggest success of the project is that, despite these problems, citizens of the city founded the Association for International Gardens and finally, in early 2006, freed one large plot for gardens for long-term use. For future projects, it would seem advisable to anchor the self-help nature of the project in the urban social context from the outset through clear communication of its advantages and to give the community mechanisms as much free play as possible.

Text by Claudia Becker and Martin Wilhelm

This project was part of the research and support program "Stadt 2030" of the German Federal Ministry of Education and Research (www.stadt2030.de). The original German title is "Dietzenbach – definitiv unvollendet."

 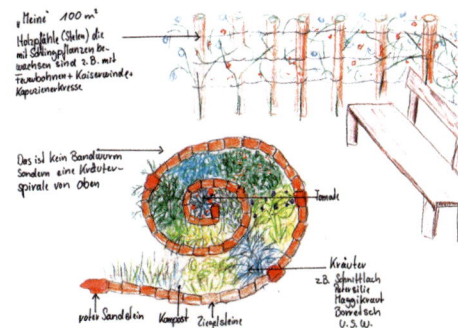

The residents of Dietzenbach were able to present their ideas for unutilized areas on postcards. Later they were given an opportunity to use stakes to symbolically mark off desired plots in the city. A chicken farm for children was one example of a space transformed in this way.

SPORTIFICATION
Halle, Wolfen, Berlin, Dessau, et cetera, Germany, since 2003
complizen Planungsbüro
www.sportification.net, www.complizen.de

Anke Hagemann: What is "sportification"?
complizen: Sportification is events in urban space for fun and extreme sports. We're interested in a playful approach to the recreational potential of vacancy, large housing developments, and abandoned sites. How much fun, sports, and individual initiative can urban planning permit, and how much of the city and architecture can be integrated into new kinds of sports? We don't want to just present "our thing": we want to tailor the program to the needs and interests of those involved and develop appropriate use concepts in dialogue with the athletes.

How did the project come about?
Halle's joint Olympics bid with Leipzig in 2002 was the catalyst that got us to look at sports and the city critically. From the outset we concentrated on "other" types of sports as a way of distancing ourselves from the dominant Olympics euphoria. Sportification as an urban development concept was later refined for Halle-Neustadt in the summer of 2003. In cooperation with Hotel Neustadt and the Thalia Theater Halle, we presented a "new sports event" in and around an eighteen-story high-rise. When this pilot project met with great enthusiasm, we pursued the concept for other sites. Since then we have been active in finding and trying out new locations.

What kinds of sports have you invented?
The High-Rise Frisbee Race, for example, which takes advantage of the urban setting of four abandoned high-rises, from whose roofs the disk is thrown. It's a game of passing and catching, with several teams playing against one another. The athletes literally play through the city. In Tag-Master Biathlon we used the uniform, structured interiors of the PY prefab concrete building. In the parallel stairwells and long halls we turned a 1970s video game à la Pac Man into a running game and combined it with an aspect of contemporary youth culture: graffiti. In Halle-Neustadt we also had a Downstairs Competition for Mountain Bikes, Concrete Climbing, and a Paper Airplane Contest. Like-minded agencies ran the Balcony Triathlon (Peanutz-Architekten) and the Trial Parcourse for BMXers on doors from prefab concrete buildings (Raumlabor).

What effect does sportification have on the city?
Sportification sees urban space in a positive way and helps to transfer the image of sports and youth to built structures. Recreational and individual sports represent a great potential for identification, and not just for young people. These images demonstrate an innovative approach to supposedly problematic urban spaces.

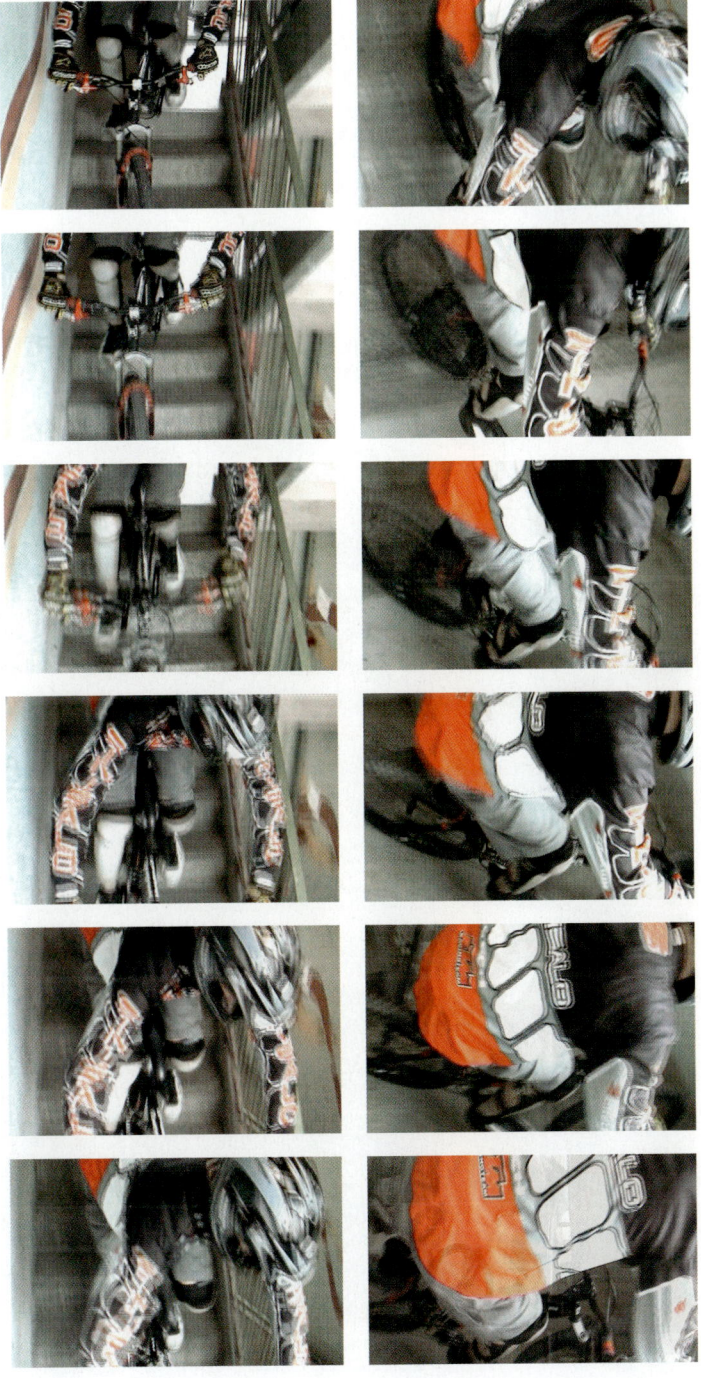

The "Downstairs Competition" in the stairwell of Hotel Neustadt, Halle, 2003.

Facade-climbing during a "sportification" event in Wolfen-Nord, 2004.

UTILIZATION OF VACANT SPACE IN DESSAU-WEST
Dessau, Germany, circa 2000 to present
Anonymous users

A housing development from the 1930s on the western end of Dessau's city center, consisting of multistory ribbon buildings among railroad yards, community gardens, and commercial areas, stands completely empty. As is clear from occasional press reports, the empty buildings are—despite the general perception of them as unused spaces—a resource for many activities, though not all of them are in line with usual ideas of use:

"There is a search underway for people who were staying illegally in the dilapidated buildings.... After consultation with the building owners, a large-scale operation was undertaken. In addition to some abandoned sleeping spots, one homeless person was found and handed over to the social welfare office."[1]

The police had been receiving tips for some time "that people were staying illegally in the vacant buildings, consuming drugs and storing stolen goods. In other spaces, equipment such as video recorders was found, some of it in its original packaging."[2]

"Under the motto 'Urban development—a work in progress,' the International Building Exhibition office is presenting an exhibition in 39 apartments by the 39 cities in Saxony-Anhalt that took part in the national competition Stadtumbau Ost (Urban Restructuring in Eastern Germany).... A vacant building is appropriate for this exhibition, as it represents ideas for treating this subject.... A light installation will show how vacant living spaces can be temporarily enlivened through art."[3]

"Experiences on Elballee, where residential blocks have already been demolished, have shown how quickly feathered lodgers can put vacant buildings to use for nest building. In such cases, it is said, the Dessau housing department cannot begin short-term demolition measures but is required under nature conservation laws to wait out the hatching season. In addition, the housing department has to provide nesting aids to replace any nests destroyed."[4]

"These measures were necessary to prevent theft and vandalism. The manager referred to actions of unknown perpetrators in Dessau-West who specialize in removing modern windows and other reusable installations from buildings."[5]

"Members of Dessau's professional fire department practiced in vacant residential blocks yesterday. Fires in apartments and basements were simulated for this purpose."[6]

Text by Friedrich von Borries and Walter Prigge

Notes
1 Offener Kanal Dessau, November 5, 2002.
2 Ibid.
3 *Mitteldeutsche Zeitung,* October 8, 2003.
4 *Mitteldeutsche Zeitung,* March 12, 2004.
5 Ibid.
6 Ibid.

WHAT IS ART UP TO IN DISUSED BUILDINGS?
Elske Rosenfeld

—

—

Abandoned or temporarily disused buildings provide artists with much-needed space as well as freedom from economic, physical, or institutional constraints. In expanding cities, finding, getting access to, and holding on to these spaces is an ongoing struggle against the interests of city councils and landlords alike: every square meter must first be claimed, then continuously defended. The temporary use of buildings or land by artists, musicians, and (other) squatters bears witness to different, nonconformist types of urbanism. Yet the appropriation of these places by artists against the will of city officials, owners, and investors is often followed by their reintegration into the prevailing economic logic—as attractors for other, more commercial users in the inevitable process of gentrification.

In shrinking cities, by contrast, art projects often are not only tolerated but actively encouraged or even commissioned by public bodies as a way of dealing with the growing confusion surrounding the future of these places, which have gone from being an economic asset to being a liability. In such environments art is looked to more and more to provide tangible solutions, but confusion about what art can actually achieve and how it goes about it tends to prevail. The cities' hopes for new ideas about how to deal with shrinkage may not be compatible with the artists' intentions to establish their work as tools for the negotiation of alternative urban identities.

Many art projects also fall short of their self-proclaimed aim of achieving a real social impact. What exactly constitutes this sought-after social effectiveness and how it can be measured can, however, only be discussed in relation to each concrete case: there are no objective, external factors by which a project's social effect can be measured or planned. None of the many possible and contradictory strategies—such as either engaging with local institutions or refusing to do so; either using pop culture in order to reach a wider public or using a more complex, intellectually challenging language; using either a participatory or a traditional approach to producing and presenting art—can guarantee to automatically make a project subversive or emancipatory. Instead, these different strategies provide a set of possible tools that must be chosen and combined to achieve the desired social effectiveness for each concrete artwork and in each concrete social situation—and not just on the level of its stated objective and underlying artistic concept, but right down to the concrete conditions of its production, presentation, and reception.

A remarkably high number of the projects that have taken place in different contexts of shrinkage took place in modern housing estates: in eastern Germany—where they are known as *Plattenbau Siedlungen* (precast housing developments)—as well as internationally. The estates have attracted artists for a number of reasons: they are seen by some as providing an interesting formal or conceptual context for artistic interventions, by others as rich visual landscapes—as a treasure chest of past utopias that can be brought to the attention of others through art, if not back to life. Others again come to these concrete estates in search of the "real world," a reality beyond the perceived artificiality of the gentrified city centers—a last site of true artistic inspiration. Or they come here to carve out a niche for themselves in a place that has not yet been completely submerged in the laws of the market.

Temporary City

▲ In summer 2002 *Dostoprimetschatjelnosti* brought 53 international students from various creative fields to a building in Berlin-Hellersdorf to live and work together.
▼ The project "Blockbuster Weißwasser" brought together artists from Saxony working in various fields to perform for one month in a prefab concrete building in Weißwasser which was slated for demolition.

What Is Art Up To in Disused Buildings?_*Elske Rosenfeld*

▲ ▼ The association Kultur/Block e.V. has declared vacant properties a social resource and is trying to create a forum of contemporary art in Halle-Neustadt. One example is the exhibition "Neustadt/Niedersachsenplatz," which took place in 2003 in a vacant eleven-story building.

Society, on the other hand, is also looking to this "housing estate art" with ever-higher hopes and expectations: not so much out of a newfound love of the arts, but rather because of the lack of or failure of other ideas for dealing with these parts of town, with their declining populations, economic marginalization, and rising social tensions. Art is being looked to for concrete solutions, as a means of strengthening local identities and providing a conceptual framework for change, and sometimes simply as a way to provide some sense of positive development.

Projects with a critical or emancipatory approach find themselves in something of a minefield, as any attempt to strengthen local bottom-up perspectives for courses of action automatically runs the risk of performing the cultural groundwork for the neoliberal retreat of the state: the artists' talk of "empowerment" translates all too easily into the New Deal values of "flexibility" and "self-initiative," whereby people are asked to find their own resources to compensate for the ongoing cuts in social spending. In housing estates, artists find themselves in precisely those areas where people are worst affected by these cutbacks.

One of the first projects to "discover" the precast housing estates in eastern Germany was the Berlin-based project *Dostoprimetschatjelnosti* (Russian for "landmarks"—a nod and wink to everyone who benefited from the East German school system's pro-Soviet curriculum as much as a tongue-twisting nightmare to everybody who did not). Invited by three communication design students from the Berlin-Weissensee School of Art and Design, 53 young art, design, and architecture students from 17 different countries came to Berlin in the summer of 2002 to move into two abandoned tower blocks in the Hellersdorf district, where they lived and worked together for three months. The idea was to involve the residents of the neighboring estate in a joint cultural effort to develop ideas for new uses of the abandoned buildings.[1]

The project was generally regarded as a success, especially in terms of the media attention it managed to attract, which helped move "housing estate art" into the limelight of the local and national media. However, the story that was told here was very much the artists' and not the residents' view of life in Hellersdorf: it was a story about "the real world" of sausage stalls and bag ladies, of abundant hunting grounds for aficionados of retro design. And it was a story about creative freedom—the story of the new housing-estate chic. The story of the everyday life of an eastern German community undergoing the dramatic changes caused by Germany's reunification and the subsequent social disorientation and economic marginalization went untold. Despite the project organizers' best intentions and their explicit goal to involve local residents, it proved almost impossible to generate any sort of local interest in the project, let alone get anyone actively involved. One event that was regarded as a success in this context was the distribution in neighboring housing blocks of handwritten invitations to a party marking the end of the first half of the project: as a result of this effort, a notably higher number of people showed up than on previous occasions. Was the neighbors' previous disinterest really down to the lack of handwritten invitations, or was it simply that events tailored to the needs and interests of an urban art crowd had nothing to offer them?

Beyond its ambitions to be an integrative project with some tangible social impact, the project was seen as an experiment in praxis-oriented, noninstitutional learning in an international setting. It was praised for setting a precedent for the temporary or even permanent use of abandoned housing blocks. In this respect, too, it could be argued that the project would have been more interesting and convincing had more of its character as a social experiment—with all its conflicts and compromises—and more of the joyfulness of living and producing art together filtered into the "artistic end product": the exhibition. Instead, the final exhibition presented "pure art," that is, those products of individual creative self-expression that the artists had been able to wrench from the chaos of living together. As a result, the "art school outpost" was doomed to be perceived as an intrusion in a neighborhood like Hellersdorf, causing irritation to neighbors who remained firmly seated on their own balconies, binoculars in hand, observing the goings-on in this alien enclave with its noisy inhabitants, who would no doubt disappear, returning to their refurbished flats in the trendier, central parts of town as soon as winter set in.

It is not only in postsocialist countries that the housing estates of the 1960s and 1970s tend to be the urban areas where shrinkage shows first and most dramatically, and it is not only there that they attract the attention of artists. In Liverpool, for example, the project series "(FURTHER) Up in the Air" was initiated in a demolition-fated tower block by artists Leo Fitzmaurice, Neville Gabie, and Kelly Large in cooperation with the Liverpool Housing Action Trust and the residents.[2] An initial twelve artists were invited for the first project "Up in the Air" in 1999/2000. Its follow-up, "FURTHER Up in the Air" (2001–2003), brought eighteen artists—some from Liverpool, some from other cities—to live and work in the building for between four and six weeks each. In contrast to *Dostoprimetschatjelnosti*, this invitation was not connected to any explicit social or political aims; instead, there was an underlying assumption that interesting questions and frictions would arise from the everyday confrontation of the artists' perception with the realities of the half-empty housing block. Because there were never more than a handful of artists in the building at any one time, the residencies never developed the festival-like character of the Berlin event. Instead, the coexistence of the visiting artists with what was left of the estate's community gave rise to a very unique social environment—one which enabled both parties to meet and interact on equal terms. The previously unconnected worlds of artists and residents not only met through the everyday processes of artistic production and living together; in doing so, they also contributed to the "artistic end products," changing everybody's perception both of life in the tower blocks and of art. Moreover, the exhibition was not simply designed as a platform for the artists to present their work to a visiting art crowd, but was used by the residents as a way of reflecting their own situation and presenting it—as something worthy of attention—to the outside world. The project, then, achieved an empowerment of local actors that was chosen by them and not predefined by the logic of a political art discourse. Likewise, many of the visitors to the exhibition did not come for the art itself, but came in order to catch one last glimpse of their or their neighbors' old homes and the glorious views from them. This did not compromise the quality of the project; in fact, its true strength lay not so much in any explicit political, emancipatory ambition, or a participatory approach involving local actors, but in its willingness to allow itself to be appropriated by them—on their terms.

Vacancy is a problem that is, of course, not limited to peripheral housing estates; it increasingly affects residential and commercial areas in city centers as well. Here empty shop windows and crumbling facades really hit cities where it hurts, as they threaten to scare off tourists and potential investors alike. Many cities have started experimenting with different ideas for the temporary use of these buildings—often involving cultural and artistic strategies—in order to breathe new life into these parts of town. Here, too, cities are looking to art to achieve a whole range of possible effects, from stimulating direct commercial activation (e.g., through commercially oriented projects in abandoned shops, such as the two Berlin initiatives Boxion and Wrangelei) to improving the image of the neighborhood or providing fresh "impulses" and a new sense of self-worth for local communities.

The project "Making It 2" was initiated in Vienna in 2005 with similar goals—as a follow-up to its more architecturally oriented predecessor "Making It" (2000).[3] Vienna is not a shrinking city, but Making It 2 nonetheless dealt with the localized processes of shrinkage that can occur in growing cities, just as shrinking cities can contain zones of growth. A jury selected nine projects, each of which was then given an empty shop in Vienna's Fifth District to use rent-free for the duration of one year. Much like FURTHER Up in the Air, the project aimed to decode the local "language of the street" (the project's subtitle) through a confrontation of the artists' perception with local realities—through the process of living and working in the shops. And like *Dostoprimetschatjelnosti*, the project aimed to achieve concrete, permanent changes—a "sustainable activation," as stated on the project's Web site. Cultural interventions in disused buildings are increasingly confronted with questions about their sustainability. Organizers or funding bodies as well as the artists themselves are keen to avoid producing festival-like events that may be accused of being too media- or marketing-friendly or of frittering away public funds. In the case of Making It 2, the initiators hoped to establish the project's cultural initiatives as permanent uses for the shops or at least to set precedents for future uses by "creative entrepreneurs" and cultural workers.

One of the projects selected by the jury was *Ballesterer*—a soccer magazine and a fan club that aim to promote and document local soccer culture. The project used soccer as an accessible format to strengthen local traditions and to initiate a discussion about the sport's emancipatory potential as well as its more exclusionary aspects. Other projects, such as Sammer/Steeruwitz's collected portraits of local living rooms, Studio Margeriten's portraits of residents, and in between: architecture's *Dictionary of the Street*—a collection of texts and a writing workshop, pursued a similarly integrative approach.

What makes Making It 2 particularly interesting is that it combined these locally accessible formats with a number of more discursive projects aiming at interdisciplinary knowledge production for a predominantly external audience. Among these projects were "framework," a platform for new architectural positions, and "raumspray," a research project about the communication between spaces and their users. This strategy of addressing both local and external audiences may have helped residents perceive the project as "theirs" rather than as an intrusion. Many similar cultural interventions in disused buildings limit local involvement to a mere incorporation of local realities: they encode local concerns into an artistic language that remains unintelligible to local actors, turning them into ethnographic objects. The success of cultural interventions with an emancipatory intent must ultimately be measured by the extent to which they manage to integrate precisely those people who have the least access to dominant social discourses.

Socially engaged projects in vacant buildings are judged as artworks and as models of social change alike; by choosing to highlight their political implications, they make themselves accountable in both areas. So-called autonomous art foregoes this kind of social accountability by hiding behind the myth of an aesthetic reference system existing outside social constraints. The great strength of engaged art projects is that they consciously reflect their own unavoidable political and social involvement. Beyond any immediately recognizable, quantifiable, or "sustainable" results, these projects can contribute to gradual change of the social and cultural patterns and strategies that they choose to position themselves in.

Translated from the German by the author

Notes
1   For more information on the project, see http://www.anschlaege.de.
2   See http://www.furtherafield.org.uk.
3   See http://www.making-it.at.

Literature
Bourriaud, Nicolas. *Esthéthique relationnelle*. Dijon, France: Les Presses du reel, 1998.
Domela, Paul. "Further Up in the Air." In *Contemporary Art: From Studio to Situation*. Edited by Claire Doherty, 123–132. London: Black Dog, 2004.
Further a Field. *FURTHER Up in the Air*. Coventry, UK: 2003.
Grünzig, Matthias. "Wünsdorf – Hilft die Kultur gegen den Leerstand?" *Kunst und Raum: Informationen zur Raumentwicklung* 1 (2005): 43–46.
Schuhmann, Steffen, Christian Lage, and Axel Watzke. *Dostoprimetschatjelnosti* (catalog). Hamburg: Junius Verlag, 2003.
Steiner, Barbara. "Protest, Resistance, Usurpation: Value Generation in Art and Culture." In *Shrinking Cities, Vol 1: International Research*. Edited by Philipp Oswalt, 438–441. Ostfildern-Ruit, Germany: Hatje-Cantz, 2004.
Turner, Victor. *From Ritual to Theatre: The Human Seriousness of Play*. New York: Performing Arts Journal Publications, 1982.
Willats, Stephen. *Art and Social Function*. London: Ellipsis, 2000.

FURTHER UP IN THE AIR
Liverpool, UK, 2001–2003
Leo Fitzmaurice and Neville Gabie
www.furtherafield.org.uk

The project "FURTHER Up in the Air" was developed and managed by artists Leo Fitzmaurice and Neville Gabie. It built on the success of a previous project, "Up in the Air," which was based on the same site and conceived in 1999 by the same artists, together with Kelly Large.

The focus was Sheil Park in northern Liverpool, an estate of three 22-story tower blocks from the 1960s, which were due to be demolished and then replaced with a new estate of semi-detached houses and bungalows. Each block was no more than half-occupied, offering plenty of scope for the empty flats to be used by artists. Up in the Air was based in Kenley Close; FURTHER Up in the Air was located in Linosa Close, the last remaining block on site. Over a five-year period some 25 artists were a part of these projects.

FURTHER Up in the Air involved eighteen artists who lived in and made work in response to Linosa Close for month-long periods over its last two years prior to demolition. Each artist was given accommodation in one flat and a further empty flat for use as a studio. At regular periods throughout the project, the tower block was opened to the public: visitors were able to view a continuously evolving number of works in flats from the twenty-first floor down to the ground-floor lobby. In all, some twenty flats containing work were open to the public by the time the project was completed. The entire project involved the development of a very close working relationship with the residents of Sheil Park, without whose support the project could not have been carried through. Because the buildings remained occupied throughout the project, residents were very much involved in practical aspects, such as opening the buildings, as well as in the selection of some of the artists involved. The project also received significant support from the Liverpool Housing Action Trust, which is responsible for the redevelopment of the estate.

Artists involved in Up in the Air and FURTHER Up in the Air: Will Self, Tom Woolford, Vittorio Bergamaschi, Jordan Baseman, Julian Stallabrass, Anna Fox, Marcus Coates, Stefan Gec, Bill Drummond, Lothar Gotz, Gary Perkins, Greg Streak, David Mabb, Leo Fitzmaurice, Catherine Bertola, Neville Gabie, Paul Rooney, Elizabeth Wright, Gernnan & Sperandio, Dirk Konigsfeld, Kelly Large, Becky Shaw, Philip Reilly, George Shaw, Chloe Steele.

The projects "Up in the Air" and "FURTHER Up in the Air" were organized in two of three tower blocks that were to be demolished in succession. In each case, the project office was located in one of the vacant apartments. Many of the participating artists managed to establish communication with the residents, as Marcus Coates did in his performance.

Temporary City

For his installation for the project "FURTHER Up in the Air," Neville Gabie removed all of the remaining elements in a vacant apartment—such as floor tiles, the built-in furniture, and the plumbing fixtures—and stacked them to form a cube.

FURTHER Up in the Air_*Leo Fitzmaurice, Neville Gabie*

THEATER AS URBAN INTERVENTION
Andreas Hillger

—

—

The moment when shrinking eastern German cities were powerfully made part of the public consciousness as a place and subject of the dramatic arts can be dated quite precisely: in the summer of 2003 the projects "Niedersachsenplatz" and "Hotel Neustadt" in Halle an der Saale and "Superumbau" in Hoyerswerda were staged at nearly the same time on their chosen sites: the once model prefab housing developments of the German Democratic Republic. Even if one recalls that this new change in direction was boosted both by the Federal Cultural Foundation and its "Schrumpfende Städte/Shrinking Cities" initiative and, in part, by the planned International Building Exhibition in Saxony-Anhalt, the concepts of the three projects were astonishingly alike in terms of both content and form. Indeed, it appeared as if very different players—ranging from an autonomous artists' group to the municipal-funded children's and youth theater, from those immediately affected to independent observers—simultaneously felt a need to confront creatively the growing depression in communities affected by emigration and demolition. In order to understand the aesthetic systems of reference that they could rely on in that process, it is necessary first to call to mind the perception of the city in the history of East German literature. In it one finds motifs that recur, in mirror reverse and transported in time, in these present-day projects.

The socialist city was—as the visible model of a society made egalitarian in both positive and negative senses—a source of enormous pathos in the East German realist literature of 1960s and 1970s. This is evident not only in novels like Erik Neutsch's *Die Spur der Steine* (The Trace of Stones) or Brigitte Reimann's *Franziska Linkerhand*, which found their genuine models in those who built Halle-Neustadt and Hoyerswerda. Dramatists like Alfred Matusche also viewed the housing communities in prefab concrete buildings as compressed images of society, as is evident, for example, from his play *Prognose* (Prognosis), which premiered in 1971. The circumstance of a writer recording and commenting on the first move into a high-rise was indebted to a real-life model. The book *Städte machen Leute* (The City Makes the Man), whose very title conveys the desired pedagogical effect of the built surroundings on the residents, was a kind of collective diary from 1968 in which the authors Werner Bräunig, Peter Gosse, Jan Koplowitz, and Hans-Jürgen Steinmann followed the emergence of Halle-Neustadt. When the curator for Hotel Neustadt, Benjamin Förster-Baldenius, handed out flower seeds to passers-by there some 35 years later, he was alluding directly to an episode from this book: the brigade of authors had begun by sowing sunflower seeds on the unutilized plots as their symbolic contribution to the growth of the new city.

A process accompanied by that kind of empathy and burdened with the symbols of many artistic testimonies also provokes a creative echo with its about-face. So after the fall of Communism, the neglected, dying city became a dramatic metaphor for the loss of social connections and biographical perspectives. In Dirk Dobbrow's play *Legoland*, which received the Kleist Prize of the city of Frankfurt an der Oder in 2000, a group of young people choose the roof of the high-rise as the place to flee from amputated families. And Fritz Kater's play *Vineta (oderwassersucht)* does not just describe the slow decline of a city on Germany's eastern edge. In Markus Dietz's staging of the premiere

When the Thalia Children's and Youth Theater in Halle had to switch to other performance venues as a result of the desolate condition of its original building, it made this move part of its program: for example, a prefab concrete building, a streetcar, and, as seen here, the abandoned Karstadt department store on the market square were used for performances.

at the Schauspiel Leipzig, the actors even performed on the facade of a prefab concrete building that had been tipped to form a steep plane.

After reunification, those working in theater in eastern Germany generally saw public space as a specific challenge, and the experience of the street as a forum of the fall of Communism in 1989 surely played a role in that. The primary trailblazers in this direction were the Freie Kammerspiele Magdeburg, which under the artistic directorship of Wolf Bunge chose a new urban venue for each event in its "Summer Spectacle" festival. In addition to idyllic sites like the banks of the Elbe and the cathedral square, from very early on they employed as backdrops unutilized industrial areas like Magdeburg's industrial port and the former grounds of the Ernst Thälmann Machine Building Combine. This had consequences for the subject matter as well: by producing the plays on-site, local history was approached head on; the projects brought in contemporary witnesses and documented the disappearance of work—a process of showing an interest that set an example for other locations.

Hotel Neustadt—which, owing to its complexity, will be discussed here as representative of other projects—also developed from an intense effort to come to terms with urban space. The move from the safe haven of traditional, institutionalized space in Halle's Thalia Theater, which set these efforts in motion, was initially the result of external necessity: when Annegret Hahn took over as artistic director of the children's and youth theater, its regular venue was seriously endangered because it was in a dilapidated state; a complete

Temporary City

From June 6 to July 6, 2002, the Halle an Salle children's city, an initiative of the Thalia Children's and Youth Theater, was erected in an abandoned exhibition hall. Children designed and decorated the houses and infrastructure, elected a mayor, established laws and rules, and introduced their own currency (www.kinderstadt-halle.de).

renovation required a temporary relocation into an empty department store. However, the opening of this interim venue already made clear that this imposition had been seen as a liberation. Under the transformed conditions, the ensemble not only redefined the technical coordinates of its work but also discovered new aesthetic challenges. A department store and a cinema as a trading center and a factory of dreams were invitations to whimsical journeys by foot. They helped young students from Halle build their own city, which they ran themselves, and offered a streetcar ride through history. All these experiments ultimately led, long after they had returned to their original venue, to the hotel project, which once and for all exploded the coordinates of all traditional theater work.

Concealed behind the playful arrangement was pure provocation: an accommodation for tourists and business travelers, of all things, would be created in the very problem zone that had long since declined from being a self-confident younger sister to being an invalid in need of expensive aid from the city of Halle. Accommodation was, in fact, the only thing available in surplus after the fall of Communism. Even so, in this seemingly nonsensical offering lay the symbolic value of the enterprise: just as the ancient philosopher Diogenes walked about the busy marketplace in Athens with a lantern in broad daylight in order to find honest men, the demonstrative reanimation of already sealed-off residential space was intended to provoke curiosity and contradiction as a doubling of what was already there. A functioning hotel, after all, asserts a need by its very existence and is dependent on a location that is attractive to business or tourism.

This step already created the beginnings of a utopian reservoir that counteracted the effect of the true loss of significance of this concrete-slab housing development. The choice of the so-called Scheibe A—an eighteen-story building of gargantuan scale—as a site was enough to mobilize a considerable nostalgic interest. After all, in East Germany the building had served as a boarding house for thousands of students, which meant that it had facilities that would simplify its conversion into a hotel. One important argument for acceptance by the locals seemed to be artistic engagement with (and under) real living conditions: in lieu of interchangeable reserves for shopping and amusement of the sort that had been built in Halle-Neustadt, too, since the fall of Communism, there would be an area of authentic experience that could endow the apparent rubbish of shrinkage processes with new meaning. To that end, Thalia activists worked well in advance of the actual opening with young people from Neustadt to develop creative concepts, using rap contests and workshops in its organizational office "Fernost"—a former railway station—to attract participants.

As an intervention into the public vacuum that was both sensitive and energetic, this long-term preparation in itself provided a counterproposal to the fleeting experience of the conventional theater evening; but only with the opening of the hotel did the comprehensiveness of this approach really become clear. In addition to a classic accommodation business—with individually designed rooms built to a minimum standard and an average occupancy rate of 80%—the Hotel Neustadt was also a "tuning workshop" that worked out proposals for the everyday lives and leisure time of the residents. And it was this aspect that left behind the most lasting disturbance: whereas the unambiguous theater actions of the guests of the international festival—from the Grotest Maru stilt theater to the art guerillas Club Real—could be dissected relatively unproblematically with the terminological instruments of the trade, the confusing invitations to participate eluded common perception. The theater people had stepped out of their roles and thereby counter-

The international theater festival Hotel Neustadt took place in September 2003 in an abandoned high-rise in Halle-Neustadt. Balcony-tuning by Peanutz-Architekten Berlin (top); entrance portal of the Hotel Neustadt (center left); audience of the interactive evening show (center right); walk-in installation by the Syntosil action collective (bottom left); the performance *Bahnsteig wischen (Cleaning the Station Platform)* by the Schutzhaus-Zukunft Task Force in the Neustadt railway station (bottom right).

manded their agreements with their public, who had been freed of passive consumption and animated to join in actively.

What means were employed to achieve such effects? First, the artists around Annegret Hahn as well as the project curators Cora Hegewald, Benjamin Förster-Baldenius, and Matthias Rick had reflected on one original function of theater by transforming the hotel into a collective storeroom of memories. Through her continuation of the above-mentioned chronicle *Städte machen Leute,* the artistic director herself ensured that the many memories of Neustadt which had been silenced in resignation would be articulated again. Petra Spielhagen developed a tour of the city called *Zwischen Hochhausgipfeln* (Between the Tops of the High-Rises), which showed the residents of Neustadt their own community, with long-forgotten anecdotes and superlatives and surprising points of view. For her thesis film *Scheibe A: Porträt eines Hauses* (Scheibe A: Portrait of a Building), the film student Carolin Ernst interlocked the past of the student dormitory with the present of the art project.

Another group of works dealt directly with the "recycling" of high-rise accessories and with the rededication of the larger architectonic structure. For example, Christoph Brucker created a miniature golf course from found objects, which gave new value to the abandoned relics in the hotel by using them for recreational activities. For the project "Sportification," the planning office complizen conceived its own athletic disciplines which were tailored to competition in the Scheibe environment. Peanutz Architects disseminated proposals for "balcony-tuning" as a way of designing one's individual venue within a standardized framework. Kyong Park designed *The Slide,* a slide through the floors and windows of the high-rise; though the plan was not realized, its simulation of a downhill ride for recreational purposes was nevertheless filled with symbolism. All of these approaches, which could be located at the intersection between theater and design, had one thing in common, which Förster-Baldenius accurately captured when he described himself as an "acting architect."

The strategy of taking an area that is increasingly stripped of meaning and function and filling it with new semantic and aesthetic content could also be seen in the "Superumbau" of the Spirit of Zuse Association in Hoyerswerda and the culture block project "Niedersachsenplatz" in Halle, though the emphases and focuses of attention were different. All of the projects profited from the traditional understanding of East German New Towns as a worthy occasion for artistic engagement. They also confronted the unambiguously optimistic messages of the East German art in prefab concrete housing developments—whose state of conservation reduces such decor to the absurd—with a scenography that addressed the problems in a way that showed an openness about the results. This did not replace the old truths with new certainties but instead encouraged the audience to take the responsibility of confronting their own living conditions. That did not happen without conflicts, as demonstrated, for example, by the public discussion of the funding granted "Superumbau" in Hoyerswerda. But aggression and anger are also emotions that can lead to a new perception of surroundings that were once familiar but are increasingly felt to be alien. Thus, such poetic interventions provide the courage to take up self-initiative, even when they only function as temporary art hotels and leave behind a vacancy that is perceived as all the more painful when they close.

Translated from the German by Steven Lindberg

PIONEER CITY

Many people are leaving shrinking cities and regions; for others, this opens up new perspectives on life. Pioneers of space—whether entrepreneurs, dropouts, or cultural producers—are moving into shrinking areas in order to build new lives, and bringing with them great motivation and a willingness to invest. The unutilized and cheap space in interesting buildings and landscapes offers opportunities for alternative lifestyles. In larger cities, there are efforts to put such practices to use for placemaking.

SPACE PIONEERS
Bastian Lange and Ulf Matthiesen

———

The number of activities, projects, and networks that try out new functions and forms of use for the depopulating regions of eastern Germany is larger than is commonly recognized. The Leibniz Institute for Regional Development and Structural Planning in Erkner has been using the search term "space pioneers" since 2003 for such network activities.[1] With this phrase we address a wide variety of mixed forms of activities from fields such as commerce, art, culture, education, handicrafts, ecology, science, research, and development. These approaches are contextualized somewhat by manifold forms of reinvention of traditions and communal lifestyles. At the same time, as a rule they are also trying out interesting couplings of urban and rural activities. All these activities operate in micronetworks that thus far are hardly networked themselves. Moreover, they have been ignored in both state and regional development plans.

From West to East
What attracts a well-educated native of Munich to Görlitz an der Neiße, to a city and a region characterized primarily by emigration, brain drain, an unemployment rate of over 25%, and population aging? What tempts him to buck the trend? In this case, it is a founders' center being established in an old factory building on Leipziger Straße, near the train station. The building is one of the oldest on this street. The surrounding station district has a residential vacancy of over 75%. And yet the project with the motto "People, Space, and Material: Not Otherwise Needed" is intended as a place for precisely the sort of people in Görlitz who want to remain and therefore must quite literally take their future into their own hands. This building was converted from industrial to residential use but has remained empty ever since, and the future users are going to determine what happens to it. The concept is to be developed during the project: "research" and "application" go hand in hand. Curiosity, experimentation, and the search for workable solutions are also part of the project. The initiator considers it a possible prototype for the urban renewal of parts of the city with high vacancy rates.

Christoph Bayer is still the only person to have moved into the former machine tool factory in Görlitz's station district. His idea is to couple surplus building materials found elsewhere with the underutilized labor power and creativity here to produce "jobs." The building will be renovated primarily through the participants' own planning and work, and recycled construction materials will be used in the process. Friendly assistance and solidarity shown by interested parties who help to bring the building into shape will be rewarded not by capital but by the right to use the finished building or to participate in future profits. The architect Christoph Bayer intends to acquire building materials—window frames, doors, parquet floors, sanitary equipment, and other materials that are no longer needed at their current location—in the places he lives and works, which include Karlsruhe, Mannheim, Heilbronn, Würzburg, Nuremberg, Hof, Chemnitz, Dresden, and Görlitz. The special appeal for him is "living in the project."

City/Country
Into the early 1990s West Berlin was a well-funded microcosm of West Germany, an island,

parts of which embodied freedom and an eagerness to experiment. It would be nice to think it was an ideal creative biotope, but the artist and curator Christine Hoffmann knowingly moved from an up-and-coming Berlin to what the writer Ludwig Tieck called "one of Germany's sorriest regions": Steinhöfel-Buchholz in eastern Brandenburg, halfway between Frankfurt an der Oder and Berlin. It is one of Brandenburg's many small villages built around a common, though this one also has a large castle and a village inn designed by David Gilly, with open paths and small front gardens that are only partially enclosed by thuja hedges. The association LandKunstLeben (LandArtLife), founded there in 2001, has made it its goal to couple regional and international cultural work and to combine them with local and regional developments. The association took part in European cultural projects, applied for European Union project funds for conferences and art projects, and became a member of several European networks of cultural centers.

In a historic former seat of the aristocratic von Massow Steinhöfel family, the LandKunstLeben association is creating a "Kunstlehrgarten" (art didactic garden). On the dilapidated grounds of the former castle gardens and in a space on the edge of the landmark castle park, the garden combines traditional elements of a didactic garden with the presentation of international contemporary art. Situation-specific and temporary events address structural instabilities and emerging regional identities. This art institution in a rural space also acts as a networking partner for interested local citizens and is working to establish a new home for art as part of the Global Village Garden in Steinhöfel that opened in 2003. An important aspect of that project is to try out new horizons for itself and for others while not forgetting the space, the landscape, and its population. The garden combines rural culture with international discussions on current, efficient, and sustainable use of rural space.

The central idea of the newcomers is thus to attract to the new Steinhöfel location the Europe-wide connections of the association's members and their networks with art and learning institutions, while also integrating the people who live there—who until now have been poorly networked—into the process of discussion and change. Without this local potential, the "artists" would, sooner or later, essentially be burying their projects like lonely satellites in the sands of Brandenburg. Artists invited to Steinhöfel thus actively engage with the changes in the region. In this way, one of the sorriest places in sorry Brandenburg has developed an innovative laboratory at the interface of art and local projects, of international discourse and regional networking practices, which addresses questions of sustainable local and regional development.

In doing so the members of the association and their local and global networking partners explore how nature and art can be experienced and make their mark in one location and how the garden can be enhanced to become a green, outdoor art space. The reevaluation and enhancement of such a specific regional space of culture and nature is carried out in a way that is exemplary and experiential. The international orientation of this pioneering project of artistic space ensures that its key participants will take international curatorial and artistic tasks beyond their activity in Steinhöfel. This step toward improving the image of eastern Brandenburg, an area undergoing transition and upheaval, could help to weave this difficult place into a network of interaction that spans Europe. At the same time, a whole spectrum of use options for spaces that have lost their utility and function is explored and invented via the project networks—a task that creates space in the truest sense.

Redesign Places

The graphic artist Ulrich Lange is from Dessau. After his studies he spent several years moving about as a "journeyman" in his profession before deciding to return to his native city to open a graphic design office. Dessau is a difficult place for the owner of a graphic design and advertising office. He found appropriate space in the renovated former brewery, so he "joined in with the brewery adventure." He knows and admires the actors and organizers of the association responsible for it. His customers and partners in joint ventures were surprised by the location at first. After two years, however, Ulrich Lange has found that his customers no longer refer to his "graphic design office in Dessau" but rather to his "graphic design office in the brewery." The "brewery" location, which is being converted and gaining in attractiveness, has also been associated with new uses, fields of activity, and actions in the mental topography of the residents of Dessau, the region, and even beyond.

An interim conclusion: this site in an industrial area that was virtually stagnating was initially unclear and ill-defined, but it has gradually transformed itself thanks to the activities and networks of Lange and others located here. Times are hard for those providing services to companies, however. Tough competition results in immense pressure to be creative and to innovate. Lange offers interns, students, and other "searchers" and "freelance creative people" from nearby institutions of knowledge (technical colleges, professional academies, etc.) the possibility of temporary work. More formal cooperation, such as between the technical college of Anhalt and his office, has yet to happen. As someone whose profession it is to make codes, paths, and images visibly intelligible, Lange is helping to place the brewery in various analog and digital media. In this way he encourages its initiators, operators, and organizers to become more professional. This demonstrates a desire both for greater identification by those on the outside and for increased recognition for customers and guests.

Cells, Micronetworks, Networks, Soft and Hard Networks, Milieus

Small cells of space pioneers in the crisis regions of eastern Germany are supported by micronetworks that are in turn extraordinarily well networked with the outside. They demonstrate that an activity that is initially individual can only be realized and become stable with the help of newly generated local and (supra)regional structures of relationships and interactions. Self-organized, at great risk, and using communication methods that are often controversial or even rejected locally, individual pioneers practice new uses and functions "for good reason" and contradict a broad trend. In his book on exit and voice from 1970, Albert O. Hirschman presented his theory of voice, defining it as "any attempt at all to change, rather than to escape from, an objectionable state of affairs."[2] Seen from this perspective, the pioneers of space have not decided, despite the most difficult conditions, in favor of the "exit" option, avoiding a situation that is difficult and suboptimal for them. Others have, however, decided in favor of other spaces. According to Hirschman, exit is based on a clear "either-or decision"; whereas the essence of voice is the art of developing constantly in new directions. Skillful refinement of broadly defined and newly discovered prospects of achievement at the local level must thus be seen as one central "reason" and hence as a starting point for a participant-centered approach to regional redevelopment that deserves to be taken seriously, especially under conditions of shrinkage.

Against the backdrop of dramatic population migrations, of loss of function, and of brain drain particularly in the peripheral cities and regions of Brandenburg and other flatlands of eastern Germany, we have seen that space pioneers who quietly trickle into the countryside with new solutions that they have tested themselves and found practicable can survive but also can fail. The most important thing is that the emigration of human resources from shrinking cities, which in the meantime has become chronic, necessarily leaves behind homogenized milieus. Space pioneers thus play an important role as innovators by providing heterogeneity in homogeneous urban milieus, without abandoning their contact with the place in question (as in the case of Steinhöfel).

In practice pioneers of space pursue and develop a wide range of activities, ranging from networks of competence in the crafts by way of agricultural specializations (e.g., ostrich raising, organic farming in Brodowin), forms of light tourism (skating in Luckenwalde), and youth and recreation cultures that emphasize physical activity to (temporary) workplaces for actors in the fields of information, communication, design, and media. Space pioneers frequently come from lifestyle milieus with explicit ambitions of autonomy, from transitional fields between economics, ecology, art, culture, and the media. Precisely because of their transfer of knowledge and their insight into local networking structures, they are able to function as incubators and stimulators of new ideas.

Territories that have dropped out of the functioning circulation of geographic, economic, and social systems as a result of population loss and economic decline can provide free space for players in a wide variety of fields related to production, creativity, and communication in a way that is both sustainable and rich in options—if they make themselves more attractive by reducing the number of regulations. Examples include pioneering "new reconquerings" of unutilized areas by family members of the old nobility east of the Elbe. What all the new forms of use have in common is that they are committed appropriation of spaces that are no longer functionally integrated and that they connect in succession, sometimes only temporarily, the new micronetworks with the existing potential of city and country found there. One important side effect of such "invasive" techniques is the importation of information in terms of technology, competence, and culture potential into peripheral regions that are increasingly unstable in economic, demographic, and social terms.

Depletion of Areas or Pioneering Options through Shrinkage?
Against the backdrop of dramatically weaker socioeconomic performance, there is a risk of new peripheries emerging in the center of an expanded Europe. In Brandenburg, for example, this situation is leading to crass developmental disparities between the so-called outer developmental area (and its cities) and the new "power area" of the wealthier suburbs. Here and there "played" cities and islands (economic clusters, centers of information and competence) alternate with landscapes that have fallen fallow, resulting in historical cultural landscapes turning into a patchwork with no clear settlement structure. The sobering continuity of the processes of demographic, economic, and sociocultural change in urban regions in eastern Germany seems to have made it onto the political agenda slowly and only after a bizarre time lag, beginning in 2004, notwithstanding the fact that the scale of the processes of depletion and shrinkage has been known for several years.

Most likely the cause is not so much ignorance and incompetence as a lack of practical and dependable options for responding and learning, which also makes it difficult to readjust, for example, municipal and state policies. Now that many large industrial projects have failed, or survive thanks only to top-down planning and immense state subsidies, a turn to developmental strategies using a pioneering, more intelligent mix of top-down and bottom-up approaches is not yet on the horizon of state policies, even though it would appear to be more urgently needed now than ever. The search for countermeasures and new approaches is gradually beginning, and, predictably, it is shaping up to be controversial. Instruments for controlling economic and urban planning that have been induced from above for the whole region have proven to be detrimental precisely because the problems and options differ so greatly from place to place. At the same time, Brandenburg (like all the other federal states) has for several years now had to find its place in at least two ways: first, within the context of expansion of the European Union to the east, and then within the framework of the dynamics of competition of the knowledge society, which has intensified extremely the regional competition for the best thinkers. Traditional planning and fiscal investment instruments of control have not yet been able to induce a change of direction.[3]

Necessary Options for Action and Proposals for Proceeding

Especially in the smaller cities of eastern Germany and their peripheries, pioneers of space have to generate new networks—without giving up their old, translocal ones—in order to establish knowledge-based structures of communication and relationships in social spaces that are thinning out. The points of departure are often small micronetworks, some of which already exist. Markus Bretschneider and Ekkehard Nuissl distinguish between "nets" as existing structures and "networks" as a work process within netlike structures.[4] This networking work is by no means simple: competition has to be negotiated and balanced with dependable forms of cooperation, commitments have to be instituted, and transparence and trust established. A continuous and measured importation of knowledge and methods to emerging networks can help shrinking city regions avoid the massive risk of isolation, decoupling, and forced homogenization.[5]

The precarious side should be mentioned as well: the "positive" networking effects that space pioneers expect are in some places and for many micronetworks countered by the constant pressure of coping with existential problems, by multitasking in the area of entrepreneurial practice, by the need to maintain the existing social interactions, by the sometimes segmented and diverse worlds of "different" pioneers of space, and above all by the lack of networking among themselves. To pull these things together now as a homogeneous "unity" and sharply defined type would overlook the attractive heterogeneity of these worlds, each with its own culture of knowledge and communication. Heterogeneity can promote creativity, but it also can prevent the generation of focused, forward-looking effects as part of network-building.

Translated from the German by Steven Lindberg

Notes

1. The term "space pioneer" *(Raumpionier)* was first coined in the context of shrinkage and urban renewal by the landscape architect Klaus Overmeyer of Berlin. See Klaus Overmeyer, *Raumpioniere in Berlin* (Berlin: Senat der Stadt Berlin, 2004). A more regionally oriented conception of space pioneers, and one that is more closely related both to regional politics in Brandenburg and to heuristic research issues, may be found in Ulf Matthiesen, "Das Ende der Illusionen: Regionale Entwicklungen in Brandenburg und Konsequenzen für einen neuen Aufbruch," *Perspektive* 21 (May 2004): 97–113.
2. See Albert O. Hirschman, *Exit, Voice, and Loyalty: Responses to Decline in Firms, Organizations, and States* (Cambridge, MA: Harvard University Press, 1970), 30.
3. See Matthiesen, "Das Ende der Illusionen."
4. See Markus Bretschneider and Ekkehard Nuissl, "'Lernende Region' aus Sicht der Erwachsenenbildung," in *Lernende Region: Mythos oder lebendige Praxis?*, ed. Ulf Matthiesen and Gerhard Reutter (Bielefeld, Germany: Bertelsmann, 2003), 35–38.
5. See Ulf Matthiesen, "Guben/Gubin: Im Sog von Schrumpfungsdynamiken," in *Lernende Region,* ed. Matthiesen and Reutter, 89–114.

The Brauhaus Verein Dessau has been gradually renovating the former Schultheiss-Patzendorfer brewery since 1999; in the meantime it has attracted independent entrepreneurs and small businesses, restaurants and bars, concert promoters, artists, and social projects.

Space Pioneers_Bastian Lange, Ulf Matthiesen

▲ Chris Pyka and Tobias Schönemann are members of the association Von der Rolle e.V., which plans a 13,000-square-foot skating hall in the cellar of the former Schultheiss brewery. ◀ DJ Thomas Sittrich performs at events in the Kesselhaus, which has a capacity for 1,800 visitors. ▶ Volker Bretschneider is chairman of the climbing association IG Klettern, which is creating Saxony-Anhalt's largest climbing tower in the brewery's old sugar tower.

Space Pioneers_Bastian Lange, Ulf Matthiesen

▲ The architect Dieter Bankert of the architectural office Bankert & Lohde played a leading role in the renovation of the former Schultheiss brewery. ◀ Thomas Busch, manager and chairman of the Brauhaus Verein Dessau, initiated the building's reoccupation. ▶ The director of the Bauhaus Dessau Foundation, Professor Omar Akbar, is responsible for the storehouse; the foundation's collection has been stored here since 2005.

ALTERNATIVE INVESTMENT IN SHRINKING CITIES
Birgit Schmidt

In times when cities are shrinking, the real-estate market seems to stand still. Because demand is lacking, buildings are no longer renovated, and vacant lots remain empty, as they probably would have to be sold for less than the owner would like. Yet vacancy also represents an opportunity for new users and investors. The reality does in fact show that new, alternative investors become active in urban regions that are abandoned by the normal market. These uses include those by squatters (who have existed and continue to exist in growing cities as well), interim users, and owner-occupants, as well as everything from initiatives and civic action projects to cooperatives, foundations, and "progressive" investors who acquire vacant buildings, facilitate new uses, and invest money and labor in a shrinking market. What is the difference between the people involved in such projects and classic investors that leads them, even in shrinking and incalculable markets, with demand falling and uncertain economic perspectives, to acquire, take over, and renovate property, investing money, time, and work to do so, and thus set new directions for the neighborhoods, districts, and cities in question? Several new premises are crucial.

1. Use Values Rather Than Returns
One central quality of such new players is that they pursue values and goals other than purely monetary ones. The goal of alternative and new investors is use values, not returns. The specific use values are defined by the people and groups in question. Highly individual expectations of use result in a great variety in the specifics of renovation, construction, and use when vacant buildings and lots are acquired and restored. What matters is the individual quality of a given project rather than quantity in the form of standardized mass-produced goods.

2. Rights of Disposal Rather Than Property
One central theme of alternative investments is rights of disposal for properties and buildings. Increasingly, creative forms of rights are applied alongside the usual property rights. Therein lies one essential factor in overcoming the economic blockade that results from a lack of demand and falling rents and incomes. Traditional property rights are supplemented or replaced by rights of disposal in the form of models based on leasing and inheritance law, use agreements, models of interim use with limited-term rental agreements, rents that cover only operating costs, and rights of use in exchange for maintenance and upkeep of spaces, buildings, or lots.

3. Users as Investors Rather Than Investment for Anonymous Users
It is the users themselves who acquire the living and working space in the city and renovate it according to their needs. The direct connection of the user-investors means that not only money as a means of exchange is invested for a finished product or service (e.g., an apartment, office, space, or use right) but also time, work, commitment, and materials as well as individual and social resources.

At the same time, this means that citizens as users take on a new role and position in the market and in society. They are no longer just (passive) purchasers, renters, and users of finished products and services that are offered but themselves investors, property owners, and contributors to the form of the city and to economic, social, and cultural relationships.

4. Concrete Places Rather Than Arbitrary Properties

The specific local circumstances play an essential role in the decisions of users as real-estate developers. For example, the particular qualities and the specific ambience of a given place—such as historical buildings, integration into the surrounding urban areas or neighborhood, or a particular potential for use—are important criteria in the decisions of users to adopt a particular location. The new investors also see the acquisition and renovation of such places as a contribution to the identity of the city and its image. In that spirit, the value of the site, neighborhood, and city are increased in symbolic ways as well as functional and constructional ones.

5. Use of Existing Instruments

The innovative aspect of alternative investments consists not in the invention of new instruments and models for real-estate development or new legal and financial constructions but rather in the combination and application of existing opportunities that are logically connected to the interests and opportunities of the partners involved.

6. Cooperation Rather Than Competition

Models based on owner occupancy and renovations by renters represent new forms of cooperation between property owners and users or renters in the "normal" market structure of rented and owner-occupied apartments. Their positive effects on shrinking cities result from the rediscovery and utilization of inner-city life and residential qualities in new forms of organization that are economically viable. The win-win nature of such models makes both existing inner-city buildings and sites for new construction more attractive to the new target groups.

Three essential groups of initiators and participants in alternative investments are interim users, owner-occupants, and civic projects. Interim users seek opportunities for the limited-term use of spaces, buildings, or lots, for example for locating new businesses, independent entrepreneurship, cultural or commercial initiatives, or art and media projects. Owner-occupants are primarily important in urban residential situations. Civic projects implement new uses as a group. Owner-occupants and civic projects are described more fully below on the basis of experiences in Leipzig and Dessau.

Owner-occupants

Under the banner "the last third of the Wilhelmine era," a variety of models for the renovation, protection, and reutilization of vacant late-nineteenth-century buildings in Leipzig were realized. When the term of the special depreciation allowance ran out, many buildings dating from the Wilhelmine era were still left unrenovated, because renovations financed by the usual means led to high rents, which no longer were feasible as demand was decreasing. There was not enough financially strong demand for the "last third" of such buildings.

Models based on the renter doing the renovation represent a form of cooperation between property owners and renters that under such circumstances can benefit both: the property owners need only renovate the building shell and the shared areas; the renters pay for the rest of the renovation themselves, doing much of the work themselves and renovating their apartments and the interior decorations according to their own wishes. As a result, rents are lower because the owners need to finance only the renovation of the building, not that of the apartments. The renters feel much more closely associated with the building because they have contributed to the look of their apartments with their own efforts, which means that the owner can count on comparatively stable renters. On the one hand, renters can in principle afford larger apartments, such as those, common in the late nineteenth century, occupying an entire floor. On the other hand, the renovation of entire buildings can be financed gradually, apartment by apartment.

Similar ideas are behind the "Selbstnutzer.de" model. Families are sought for vacant buildings that they can occupy themselves and eventually own. They form owners' or construction associations to purchase and renovate both the building itself and its apartments.

The city assisted both models with advisory services (consulting architects), information, and aggressive publicity work; initiated the necessary cooperation among the partners (the Leipzig Housing and Building Association, private property owners, interested occupants and renters, and experts); and improved the programs on the basis of its experience.

The owner-occupant program has since been expanded to include new construction, specifically, the construction of town houses in unutilized areas of the inner city by and for private families and construction associations. Among other things, the city sponsored an architectural competition to provide initial examples and stimulus for the new types of construction and living under this model.

There is now an agency that is responsible exclusively for spreading information about this program and its conditions, publicizing new offers, and mediating between parties interested in a given project. Measured in terms of the ratio of public funds spent to the private investments they stimulate, the owner-occupant program is one of the most successful public subsidy programs.

Civic projects

A second group of examples of alternative investment are civic projects engaged in urban renewal. I researched such projects in Saxony-Anhalt in 2003 for the International Building Exhibition "Urban Redevelopment Saxony-Anhalt 2010." These projects and initiatives are supported by civic groups and either are devoted to specific buildings or are committed in a broader sense to such themes as municipal history, urban development, and marketing of the city. Cooperative residential projects are another form of such civic projects. Examples include the Kochhaus in Dresden, described below, the Schwabehaus, and the former brewery discussed in the preceding essay by Ulrike Steglich.

The Kochhaus is a landmark residential and office building from the Wilhelmine era that was purchased and renovated by the housing cooperative DAKSBAU, which now manages it. It is a mixed-use building with residences, offices, and cultural offerings. It houses initiatives, associations, research projects, offices, and independent entrepreneurs, and there is an informal network of ideas among the members and the renters. As a sociocultural and commercial initiative, the influence of the Kochhaus extends into the neighborhood. Tours and lectures, the annual Hermes Festival, and other events organized by the renters take place here and attract the interest of both ordinary citizens and experts.

The former Koch ironware store was vacant and had been up for compulsory auction since 1997. A group of individuals and associations looking for residences and offices was interested in the building, so it founded a cooperative and purchased the building at auction. The first repairs and use began in November 1998 (the "pioneering occupation"); the basic renovation of the main house and the west wing followed in 2000–2001. In autumn 2001 the last apartment was occupied. Today there are sixteen units rented in the Kochhaus.

The housing cooperative DAKSBAU now has 27 members and is property-oriented. It is administered by volunteers and has no paid employees. The financing of construction investments is obtained through shares in the cooperative, loans from its members, self-help (in the form of construction assistance), private loans, labor market funding, residential modernization loans from the German Development Bank (Kreditanstalt für Wiederaufbau), advance payments of rent, and bank loans, secured by small guarantees and by the Guarantor Bank for Social Economy (Bürgschaftsbank für Sozialwirtschaft), as well as by funds for landmark buildings from the city of Dessau. About half of the cooperative's members received funds from the state subsidy for home ownership for their shares in the cooperative. That helped bring supporting members to the project. Altogether, the cooperative invested one million euros in the project. Current operations are supported by rental income (the housing cooperative).

The project also received support from many friends (guarantors), the community bank GLS Gemeinschaftsbank Bochum, the authorities for historic monuments in Dessau, and the cooperative auditing association PkmG. Problems were encountered with many agencies and institutions on account of the "unknown" legal form of a cooperative, especially because the project wanted to make investments of this scale as a small, newly founded cooperative. Nor did the cooperative's mix of residential and commercial use fit into any of the "models" for public funding and jurisdiction. The high fixed costs for administration that resulted from the cooperative's obligations to prepare a balance sheet and audits are difficult for small cooperatives to afford. The lack of regional and local networking among (residential) projects meant that many more experiences and expenditures had to be dealt with. At "Stadtumbau 2002" in March 2003, the Kochhaus won first prize in the competition for exemplary renovation solutions in Saxony-Anhalt.

In Summary, Alternative Investors ...
... are new economic players
They take up where classic investment theory and practice fail to materialize due to lack of returns. The projects are models for new forms of ownership and acquisition of vacant buildings and lots in cities. As a result of their legal and financial structure, their investment volume, and their economic effects, many projects have become new economic players in the economic structure of medium-size entities in cities. They make private capital accessible and open up new sources of and paths to financing for urban development projects, in addition to acquiring public funding, market capital, and even international support. The parties involved provide organizational and management services for

urban development and urban renewal tasks and problems. The projects' investments bring contracts for regional firms, and jobs are created through the civic projects and interim uses.

... contribute to the quality of a city
A central theme of many projects is the preservation of historically valuable buildings, which are often vacant and in poor structural condition and usually important to the image of the city. The restoration of such buildings (or complexes) helps create an identity for cities and neighborhoods. By providing new and supplementary functions in (inner) cities that are offered neither by public nor by commercial ventures, the projects contribute to functional variety. Among other things, they contribute to urban culture and tourism as features of the city that not only have economic effects but also strengthen and develop so-called soft location factors. Alternative investments thus improve the value of their locations in many ways.

... represent social capital for cities
Alternative investment projects activate and bring together people and personal commitment for urban development and municipal politics. They counteract the brain drain that occurs with shrinkage. This civic commitment takes the form of projects in public space, at both the political and the technical level, and thus also counters boredom with politics. Participation in civic projects is in keeping with current ideas of voluntary commitment (project-related, limited-term) and addresses all ages and generations. Civic commitment to such a project and the skills gained through participation in it can justly be considered building blocks of a civil society.

Alternative investors create interest in and attention to cities and locations, not just within those cities but beyond (sometimes even internationally). They link up new networks of participants, and build up and take advantage of networks of citizens, municipal administrations, and political and technical experts. They thus have an integrative function in society as well. They are part of the social capital of their cities as well as a contribution to development. This social capital is an important potential for processes of urban development when exogenous potential is lacking.

What can cities do to turn the positive effects of investment more directly to the renewal and development of shrinking cities? The first goal would be to achieve the necessary acceptance, to take seriously the new players and their investments in policies and administration at all levels.

To that end, communities in particular have a whole series of opportunities and instruments that could support this aim, such as providing publicity for alternative investment projects and maintaining registers of vacant lots and buildings that contain basic information (e.g., owners, size, price, building permits). Equally helpful are advice centers that collect information and make it available to interested users and investors: everything from opportunities for funding to the relevant governmental authorities and advisers. Professional forms of such support would include running use and site management, which would bring together uses and available sites. In addition to such advice, institutional consulting infrastructure can also provide focused incentives for new investments.

Examples include Selbstnutzer.de in Leipzig, Stattbau GmbH in Hamburg, the Runder Tisch for residential projects in Wiesbaden, and the consulting office Wohnen im Alter in North Rhine-Westphalia. The state program "Initiative Ergreifen" (Take the Initiative) in North Rhine-Westphalia combines support of start-up investments for projects with advice on developing and implementing viable concepts. The criterion for subsidizing projects is that they must be economically viable after four years of decreasing start-up financing. There the state functions as an activist government in support of civic projects.

Translated from the German by Steven Lindberg

ALTERNATIVE INVESTMENT IN SHRINKING CITIES: INTERNATIONAL MODELS
Manchester, Liverpool, Boston, Detroit

Architect and Property Developer Model: Urban Splash (Liverpool, Manchester)
In the early 1990s the property developer Urban Splash invested in Liverpool's and Manchester's inner cities, in places where the real-estate market had effectively ceased to exist and where conventional investors never would have risked such a strategy. Its extremely successful and profitable concept was to seek out run-down industrial buildings with potential, purchase them cheaply, and convert them into offices and residential lofts through the use of various sorts of public financing—at a time when the higher-earning target groups in question were just beginning to form in inner cities. (www.urbansplash.co.uk)

Cooperative Urban Renewal Model: Homes for Change (Manchester)
In Manchester's Hulme district, which had a reputation as a problem area but also was known for its subculture, a development of houses with access balconies dating from the early 1970s was torn down; the area was then partially rebuilt in a postmodern block style. The Homes for Change cooperative, which had been founded in the late 1980s by residents of the district, attempted to put into practice its own ideas for the reurbanization of the district. It picked up on the idea of the access balconies of the old buildings as an architectural expression of communal living. It linked ecological, social, and participatory principles with models of communal living and working. It was able to obtain public funding to construct 75 public housing units. The building block, which is still partially surrounded by unutilized areas, was designed in a joint process by residents and architects.

Community Development Corporation Model: Greater Corktown Development Corporation (Detroit)
So-called community development corporations, development companies of specific neighborhoods that are run by residents, local business, and organizations in the United States, are proof that people no longer count on help "from above" to solve urban problems. One such entity is the Greater Corktown Development Corporation (GCDC) in the shrinking district of Corktown, one of the oldest sections of Detroit's inner city. The GCDC was founded in 2002 through the merging of a nonprofit residential construction cooperative with a corporation for the economic development of the district, with the intention of producing a dynamic, diverse, and socially compatible "urban village" there. Its concrete goals are to renovate and construct affordable owner-occupied homes, to improve infrastructure, and to revitalize commercial streets. Whereas Corktown's center has already seen appreciable, autonomous improvements—including bars, restaurants, and loft apartments—the GCDC is currently concentrating on North Corktown, which is more problematic. (www.corktowndetroit.org)

Resident-Supported Development Model: Dudley Street Neighborhood Initiative (Boston)

The Dudley Street district is one of the poorest neighborhoods in Boston and for decades has been marked by disinvestment, decaying buildings, arson, and large unutilized areas. In 1984 citizens, businesspeople, and district initiatives got together to do something about it and to protect the area from outside speculators. The Dudley Street Neighborhood Initiative was the only nonprofit organization of its kind to receive from the city of Boston the right to expropriate abandoned lots and transfer them to communal trusteeship funds. The expropriated land is leased to (nonprofit) construction companies and then to building owners or cooperatives. More than a hundred affordable new apartments have been created thus far. This instrument enabled civic representatives to develop a "shared vision" and a comprehensive plan for revitalization together with the residents and to redevelop in a socially acceptable way. (www.dsni.org)

Nonprofit Volunteer Initiative Model: Motor City Blight Busters (Detroit)

An initiative run primarily by Afro-American volunteers, Motor City Blight Busters has been active since 1988 in run-down and even abandoned sections of northwestern Detroit. By renovating 157 apartment buildings and constructing 112 more, living space has been created for more than 1,040 people, and artists' studios and spaces for neighborhood initiatives also have been established. In 2005 it began to develop a "culture mile" on the main street, Grand River, which will include an art gallery, workshops to provide art classes for young people, and an Internet café. The project is funded mainly by donations. Motor City Blight Busters activities include the safeguarding or demolition of abandoned buildings, youth and student projects, and patrols during Devil's Night, the night before Halloween, to prevent arson. (www.blightbusters.org)

Private Company Model: Midtown (Detroit)

Although Midtown Detroit still lacks adequate infrastructure for residential purposes—grocery stores, for example—an astonishing upturn has taken place here since the late 1990s. Not so much large investors but rather small investors with a private obsession for the central district and its rich tradition, which since the 1970s has been known as a neighborhood for artists and alternative living, have renovated the massive historic buildings, one by one, as high-quality residential units. The developer Joel Landy, for example, who has been active in Midtown for decades, took on the Charlotte-Peterboro neighborhood and transformed the Addison Hotel, with its high ceilings and oak floors, into apartments. Problems and crime were reduced; restaurants and bars were opened. A large part of this development is based on an initiative by the University Cultural Center Association of Wayne State University, which is located in northern Midtown. (Ed.)

Translated from the German by Steven Lindberg

LEIPZIG-PLAGWITZ: THE DARK LAND BEHIND THE MARSH
Kathleen Liebold and Heidi Stecker

For some time now when we open a newspaper or magazine and read a report on Leipzig, there is a good chance that the Leipzig district of Plagwitz will be mentioned. It would, however, appear that Plagwitz consists of a single site: the former spinning mill. The photos illustrating such articles are astounding. They show utopian scenes of socialist communal life: artists in proletarian work clothes sit together on weather-beaten roofs and eat something they have cooked themselves, with views into the distance over Leipzig. Colorful paintings are schlepped across idyllic factory sites; super chic, spacious lofts in a morbid ambience of rusty steel beams and bricks darkened by time promise unconventional living.

The site of the former cotton-spinning mill has brought Leipzig-Plagwitz closer to the center of national and international attention. The fuss over the so-called New Leipzig School of painters has created a large audience for the area. Atoll-like, it rises up out of the sea of shrinkage. The depression that weighs heavily on eastern Germany is illuminated by a bright spot here; art adds pleasing accents. Aesthetes and sensitive spirits find abundant spoils. The artists who work and sometimes live here are attracting the world's gaze and suggesting, "It works if you want it to and you have exciting ideas!" The impression that Plagwitz is made up of exclusive and successful places is, however, deceptive.

One can of course just follow the path of the wealthy art collectors, traveling only to the spinning mill to purchase trendy art and overhearing remarks like, "Honey, how much do you want to spend today? Not more than €17,000, I hope."[1] But one can also take many roads and explore a section of the city that is particularly diverse. The memories of unbreathable air, foam-flecked bodies of water that stank of phenol, streets blackened by decades of soot, rotting buildings, gray streams of people who trudged exhausted through the factory gates during shift changes—in short, unbearable circumstances that scarcely can be recalled today. For some, such memories might still evoke a certain nostalgia, out of mourning for their lost jobs. But such impressions are detrimental to the romanticism of industry that is propagated today.

After the fall of Communism the extreme environmental damage and the utterly unacceptable living conditions were one focus of the discussion. The closing of the factories quickly reduced the environmental pollution. In the early 1990s the site for "living on the water" that is being extolled today was not yet on the horizon. Naturally, people still assumed that the working and living situation would improve along with industrial production and full employment.

The Plagwitz district of Leipzig is a textbook example of the activities of investors and developers in the industrial and postindustrial ages. Plagwitz struggles with the legacy of a part of the city that was notorious for decline and pollution as a result of excess industrial exploitation under the German Democratic Republic (GDR) as well as with the new, unforeseen developments between population loss and vacancy. In that sense, the district is being discovered again. Its location, which has not traditionally been as trendy as other neighborhoods and is not directly near the city center, has made it financially attractive. Image politics and revaluations are supposed to be an oasis and anchor in the face of the devastating outcome of rapid social change. Different groups certainly employ different strategies to deal with shrinkage, with different results.

It begins with those who want to live here. They often look for an apartment in the remote district of Schleußig, which is experiencing an upturn. More than ever, Plagwitz consists of many islands: enclaves of people with higher incomes and active cultural lives are located amid desolate areas and proletarian-looking street fronts with remnants of the architecture of poverty, which look very calm. It takes a bit of effort to make out the traces of a once strong culture of celebration, such as the very large number of bars and restaurants that grew out of the large breweries and represented the initial spark of the district's development.

Walking through Plagwitz, one bumps into economic, social, and cultural projects and with them into omnipresent processes of upheaval. For example, there is the Gieszer 16 cultural center on Gießerstraße, which tends to leftist anarchism, and the nearby Plaque or the Volxxküche on Industriestraße, where the punks are organized. These projects were frequently targets of attack by the extreme right wing. On an evening walk it is not uncommon to encounter right-wing extremists. Then, suddenly, the district no longer feels so charming. For security reasons, Gieszer 16 has converted its former factory into a fortress. Sauntering along the new paths that run through Plagwitz these days, which run alongside the old rails, one notices this and may be surprised by the martial gesture amid all the hominess. Walking paths and playgrounds now surround the site: the city is trying to defuse this particular clientele and these political conflicts by means of beautification efforts.

Near the Business Innovation Center, on Karl-Heine-Straße, one finds the technology museum Garage—or, rather, found it, for it had to close down (perhaps only temporarily). It represented the history of industry through a collection of apparatuses that have since become exotic; children and young people were allowed to try them out. The Schaubühne Lindenfels offers theater, lectures, discussions, festivities, and, along with Cineding, the best cinema. Other locations were used for temporary performance, such as an empty transformer hall that was used for Ulrich Hüni's staging of the play *Golem* in 2002. The thread factory along the Karl-Heine-Kanal, on the side of Nonnenstraße that leads to the city center, was converted into lofts. They are supposed to attract high-income residents to the district, but they recall a gated community with a rather disappointing interior. With their many cell-like apartments, these luxury lofts look more like a prison.

Spinning and Dederon Overalls

The history of Plagwitz during the nineteenth century was intertwined with that of capitalists like Karl Heine and Carl Ernst Mey. The brutal industrialization of the late nineteenth century had a massive influence on this district and Leipzig's development generally. Textile, metalworking, and other industries, publishers, and commerce made their way into the marshes of the Auewald and the village of Plagwitz, which is evident from the parks that make the sections closer to the city center more attractive. Industry shaped Plagwitz right down to the locations of streets and backyards. The families of the factory owners did not locate their villas separately in privileged neighborhoods but right next to working-class families, alongside the rental barracks and farmers' shacks; and between them the homes of the upper- and lower-middle classes proudly claimed their place. The social contrast was concentrated in a confined area.

Capitalism in Plagwitz showed all its faces: miserable living situations, horrendous working conditions, child and female labor, revolutionary movements, a culture of excessive festivities, educational endeavors, and social commitment. There are only a few remaining public indications of this past.

Much of it was already lost under the GDR or at least ideologically reinterpreted: child labor took place in the context of school courses in the name of "education day in the productive facility" or "productive labor," and there were many forms of voluntary labor. Female labor was considered evidence of equal rights and emancipation. At the "spinning wheel," women could produce piecework for sale in Germany and abroad. The past of these people, even that of the workers' and socialist movements with their rich culture of associations, has been forgotten. History seems to be dominated by the great cultural achievements of the wealthy bourgeoisie.

The New City Will Glow

The current identity and image politics in Leipzig picks up on figures like Karl Heine and the now strange- and morbid-looking industrial real estate, but it reinterprets them in a positive way. The images of a new city should function suggestively both outwardly and inwardly. The protagonists of industrialization are glorified like heroes of the Christian conquest. As if they had brought civilization to the desert, or at least to mosquito- and malaria-infested swamps, they are celebrated as resourceful men with visions. Such romanticizing is intended to encourage identification with the neighborhood, to draw potential investors as well as old and new residents of Plagwitz into its spell. It is hoped that hectic activity will paper over the stillness that has been imposed all around.

The pioneers of the present are not, however, occupying empty spaces but rather locations that have been occupied many times. The history that is told is thus a very limited one, so that it will not scare off said investors and residents of Leipzig. The areas that tell of industrial history were often converted to significant, sought-after, and expensive residential and commercial locations. They are both the old and the new face of Plagwitz, which can be seen along the Karl-Heine-Kanal: the Stelzenhaus was converted from a contaminated factory building into a respectable location for a restaurant, a beer garden, offices, and apartments.

The Karl-Heine-Kanal was reactivated as a local recreation area, with walking and bike paths in place of the old barge paths and tracks, and it truly does represent a kind of oasis. Boats and a small ship make the area along the water inviting; here one can admire several of the sites in the middle of the industrial architecture and fallow landscape. The public broadcaster Mitteldeutscher Rundfunk constructed a ship-like building above one of the bridges for its talk show *Riverboat*.

"Gentrification ... Just Say NO!"[2]

Leipzig had already recognized and responded to the problem of shrinkage by the early 1990s. Facilities like the Business Innovation Center were expected to revive this section of the city, with benefits that would in turn spill into the city. The effects have remained limited, however. The program URBAN II adopts a rather traditional view of "prosperity and growth." The city's fathers hope that highly subsidized settlement of new business structures will result in an entrepreneurial boom, but the results thus far have been dubious: residents continue to move away. All that is flourishing is call centers: they offer new low-wage jobs for women. Yet the hope is fed by an influx from other parts of the city, the region, and elsewhere in Germany.

The discussion revolves primarily around the many unutilized areas, which in some cases are problems inherited from the Second World War or the GDR but also include relics of recent deindustrialization. Fear of vacant lots is spreading, for a vacant lot symbolizes disorder and a lack of growth or of socially approved use. Eliminating them is the goal of city planners. The project EXPO 2000 was also supposed to function as a driving force and a catalyst of urban renewal, and the program "Grüne Gleise" (Green Tracks) and the district park for Plagwitz aimed at revitalization, or at least beautification. Fascinating industrial relics and their fallow lands are always places for cultural uses. Actions like the "Jahrtausendfeld" (Millenium Field) of the Schaubühne Lindenfels brought attention to shrinkage and the failure of growth, which had not yet been adequately treated in the public discourse. The temporary venue for the children's and youth theater, Theater der Jungen Welt—a brightly lit tent—and the extension hall of the association Archleague provide pretty, if not necessarily coherent, metaphors, but they represent only ephemeral masking.

Unutilized areas are not empty places but rather locations with multiple connotations that are certainly used, if not by the sections of the population on which everything is focused. Children, young people, elderly persons, the so-called socially weak, dog owners, and others are crowded out of vacant areas and brought under control, as if self-determined uses were not permitted. Wild adventure playgrounds and sites of unplanned activity and communication are at risk of disappearing. People and history are removed from sight and the city is vacated, even if there is some resistance to such processes. The islands of the protected and of culture stand amid hopelessness and loss of jobs. Characteristically, there is a "Leipzig Table" in Plagwitz that distributes food to the needy. Its clientele is growing.

"From Cotton to Culture"[3]

The formation of images and legends around the former cotton-spinning mill, which was founded in 1884, has been absurd and highly effective in the media. In the 1990s artists, several galleries such as Kunstraum B/2, projects such as "Tangofabrik," and small businesses moved into the factory area or first established themselves there. Because of its primitive and dilapidated condition, the old spinning mill was a cheap place to live and work, and for a long time it remained something of an insider tip, as it is located rather inconveniently on the periphery and public transportation connections are poor. No one could have suspected that several of the artists located there, like Neo Rauch, would go far. The spinning mill became a cultural reference point for the district and the city of Leipzig as a whole. As the fame of the artists grew, so did interest in the location. In 2004, Galerie Kermer moved in; the galleries Eigen + Art, Kleindienst, Dogenhaus, and others followed in 2005.

The operators are hoping that the mixed cultural and commercial use will flourish under the primacy of art. The revaluation employs the argument of authenticity: artists can get by here well as bohemians, creating important things while living under the most primitive conditions, shaping the genius loci with their creativity. The bad reputation of grimy drudgery lingers, but not in an insistent or disturbing way. The odium of art production infuses the visitors who now come here for big events. These spaces are conceived for those who are flown in specifically to consume art. The advertising campaign

▲ The former spinning mill in Leipzig-Plagwitz has developed from a site for alternative culture into a location for art galleries, and hence made the site commercially important as well. ▼ Open house at the galleries on April 30, 2005.

Leipzig-Plagwitz: The Dark Land Behind the Marsh_Kathleen Liebold, Heidi Stecker

▲ The exhibition "Passion des Sammelns" (The Passion of Collecting), Hall 14, in 2005. ▼ Opening of the exhibition "Xtreme Houses," Hall 14, 2004.

"Leipziger Freiheit" (Leipzig Freedom) picks up on this, and seduces with photographs, for example, of a student in an elegant loft that might be in the spinning mill, as if to say that anyone can live like a prince here for next to nothing. There are reasons to fear displacements of less commercial uses. The area certainly helps to keep the district from becoming even more barren. A strong upswing should not be expected, however, since there is little potential on which to build. And so it is prophesied that the excitement will be limited to events like the gallery open houses. For how long will collectors and tourists from wealthier countries make the pilgrimage to Plagwitz by the busload to be in the presence of famous artists? What will happen when everyone has had enough of painting? The next set of artists will look for other places that are cheaper and less chic.

Translated from the German by Steven Lindberg

Notes
1 Overheard in a conversation of a couple strolling on the site.
2 Graffito, quoted in Universität Leipzig, "Leben in Plagwitz: Hintergrund einer Studie," http://www.uni-leipzig.de/~kuwi/studie_plagwitz.html.
3 Slogan of the owners of the cotton-spinning mill property.

Literature
Gormsen, Niels, and Armin Kühne. *Leipzig: Den Wandel zeigen.* Leipzig: Edition Leipzig, 1999.
Michael, Klaus, Günter Behnisch, Peter Kulka, and Engelbert Lütke Daltrup. *Leipzig: Probleme der Stadtentwicklung unter besonderer Berücksichtigung des EXPO-Standortes Leipzig-Plagwitz.* Dresden: Sächsische Akademie der Künste, 1999.
Pro Leipzig e.V. *Plagwitz: Ein Leipziger Stadtteil im Wandel.* Leipzig: Pro Leipzig e.V., 1999.
Stadt Leipzig, Dezernat für Stadtentwicklung und Raumplanung, ed. *Workshop Leipzig-Plagwitz.* Beiträge zur Stadtentwicklung 5. Leipzig: Stadt Leipzig, 1992.
Stadt Leipzig, Amt für Umweltschutz, ed. *Ökologische Altbausanierung: Modellbeispiele und Möglichkeiten für Plagwitz.* Leipzig: Stadt Leipzig, 1993.
Weissbach, Wolf-Dieter, ed. *Vision Plagwitz: Der Gründer- und Gewerbehof; Beratungsstelle für arbeitsorientierte Strukturentwicklung in Sachsen e.V.* Leipzig: 1993.

STRUGGLING WITH THE CREATIVE CLASS
Jamie Peck

Creative Class, Rising

"Be creative—or die" is how *Salon* writer Christopher Dreher summarized the new urban imperative: "cities must attract the new 'creative class' with hip neighborhoods, an arts scene, and a gay-friendly atmosphere—or they'll go the way of Detroit."[1] The occasion was an interview with Richard Florida, whose newly released book, *The Rise of the Creative Class,* was already on the way to becoming both an international bestseller and a public-policy phenomenon. The book's thesis—that urban fortunes increasingly turn on the capacity to attract, retain, and even pamper a mobile and finicky class of "creatives," whose aggregate efforts have become the primary drivers of economic development—has proved to be a hugely seductive one for civic leaders around the world. From Singapore to London, Dublin to Auckland, Memphis to Amsterdam—indeed, all the way to Providence, Rhode Island, and Green Bay, Wisconsin—cities have paid handsomely to hear about the new credo of creativity, to learn how to attract and nurture creative workers, and to evaluate the latest "hipsterization strategies" of established creative capitals like Austin, Texas, or wanna-bes like Tampa Bay, Florida: "civic leaders are seizing on the argument that they need to compete not with the plain old tax breaks and redevelopment schemes, but on the playing fields of what Florida calls 'the three T's [of] Technology, Talent, and Tolerance'."[2] According to this increasingly pervasive urban-development script, the dawn of a "new kind of capitalism based on human creativity" calls for funky forms of supply-side intervention, since cities now find themselves in a high-stakes "war for talent," one that can be won only by developing the kind of "people climates" valued by creatives—urban environments that are open, diverse, dynamic, and cool.[3]

Hailed in many quarters as a cool-cities guru, assailed in others as a new-economy huckster, Florida has made real waves in the brackish backwaters of urban economic-development policy. As the conservative critic Steven Malanga has observed, the "notion that cities must become trendy, happening places in order to compete in the twenty-first-century economy is sweeping urban America.... A generation of leftist policy-makers and urban planners is rushing to implement Florida's vision [just as] an admiring host of uncritical journalists touts it."[4] In the field of urban policy, which has hardly been cluttered with new and innovative ideas lately, creativity strategies have quickly become the policies of choice, where they license both a discursively distinctive and an ostensibly deliverable development agenda. No less significant, though, they also work with the grain of extant development agendas, which are framed around interurban competition, gentrification, middle-class consumption, and place-marketing.

Clearly tapping into many of the same "cultural circuits of capitalism" as its new-economy predecessors, the creative-cities script has found, constituted, and enrolled a widened civic audience for projects of new-age urban revitalization, anointing favored strategies and privileged actors and determining what must be done, with whom, how, and where. And the tone is appropriately declarative and direct: "I like to tell city leaders that finding ways to help support a local music scene can be just as important as investing in high-tech business and far more effective than building a downtown mall."[5] This is a script that gives urban actors significant new roles, while prodding them with talk of new competitive threats. And on recent evidence a strikingly large number of cities have willingly entrained themselves to Florida's creative vision.

Creative Juices

Florida argues that we have entered an age of creativity, comprehended as a new and distinctive phase of capitalist development, in which the driving forces of economic development are not simply technological and organizational, but *human*. In essence, the book seeks to describe a *new,* new economy, in which human creativity has become the "defining feature of economic life ... [It] has come to be valued—and systems have evolved to encourage and harness it—because new technologies, new industries, new wealth and all other good economic things flow from it."[6] Creative types have always been critical to capitalist growth, of course, but in the past few decades, so the argument here goes, they have grown both in number and influence, such that they now account for some 38 million U.S. workers (or about 30% of the workforce), and therefore justify proper-noun status—"the Creative Class has become the dominant class in society."[7] This discovery having been made, the challenge is to understand what makes the members of this class tick, how they like to spend their money and their (precious) time, what they *want*. As the source, apparently, of all good economic things, the Creative Class must be nurtured and nourished, its talents must be harnessed and channeled.

Glimpses of the kind of society the creatives might build are to be found, we learn, in the distinctive locational decision-making of the talented, the revealed preferences of whom are quite unambiguous. The Creative Class seeks out tolerant, diverse, and open communities, rich in the kind of amenities that allow them precariously to maintain a work/life balance, together with experiential intensity, in the context of demanding work schedules. Uniquely suffering from a relentless "time warp," creatives gravitate toward "plug and play" communities, where social entry barriers are low, where heterogeneity is actively embraced, where loose ties prevail, where there are lots of other creatives to mingle with, where they can "validate their identities."[8] One of the primary indicators of these diagnostically critical conditions—of openness and tolerance—is the conspicuous presence of gays and lesbians, characterized here as the "canaries of the creative economy," due to the way in which they signal a "diverse, progressive environment," thereby serving as "harbingers of redevelopment and gentrification in distressed urban neighborhoods."[9] Should these avant-garde economic indicators somehow be overlooked, more concrete clues—which have not been lost on urban planners and consultants—include "authentic" historical buildings, converted lofts, walkable streets, plenty of coffee shops, art and live-music spaces, "organic and indigenous street culture," and a range of other typical features of gentrifying, mixed-use, inner-urban neighborhoods. Creatives want edgy cities, not edge cities.

Biscotti and Circuses

Florida's principal method is to rank cities according to multiple direct and stand-in measures of these phenomena, both in isolation and in combination—a calculated but also highly effective means of popularizing the creative-cities thesis. Urban regions are ranked on everything from the number of patents per head to the density of bohemians and gays, on their respective shares of immigrants, credentialized knowledge-workers, and even "fit versus fat" residents—the endlessly manipulated combinatorial outcome of which is Florida's "Creativity Index." The declared winner in the big-city race is San Francisco, followed by Austin, Boston, and San Diego; atop the midsize-cities category are Albuquerque, New Mexico, Albany, New York, and Tucson, Arizona; and at the next level down in the new urban hierarchy come Madison, Wisconsin, Des Moines, Iowa, and Santa Barbara, California. "Nothing," Paul Maliszewski observes, "can quite guarantee a book national media attention, reviews in local newspapers, and a shot at becoming a best-seller than a list like this, declaring authoritatively that some stuff is better than other stuff, but only one is best of all."[10]

The fairly obvious appeal of cities like Seattle and San Francisco is translated into a new kind of currency in Florida's rankings. Rather than plodding through a complex causal argument, the mobilization and manipulation of extant urban images function here to great effect. Positive urban images are crudely quantified, then recast as objects of deference— as places to be emulated. Almost at a stroke, a new dimension of urban competition was constituted by Florida's league tables (which are periodically revised, just to maintain attention). They allow some city leaders to congratulate themselves on a job well done, even if this had been achieved subconsciously, whereas the rest all have something, or somewhere, to aim at. Playing to this newly constituted gallery, Florida confidently asserts that *any* big city, with the right political will, "can turn it around," and that most of the other urban centers at least have a shot, if they possess the essentials—like a good university, some "authentic" neighborhoods, and a handful of high-tech employers.

In a fashion that recalls the way in which a few "turnaround" entrepreneurial cities, like Cleveland and Baltimore, were celebrated during the 1980s for pioneering property-led and partnership-facilitated downtown revitalization,[11] a new set of extant and aspirant creative cities has quickly risen to prominence on the back of the work of Florida and his followers. San Francisco and Austin are continuously invoked, and are subject to instrumental practices of "case study," as these are the places that define the new urban genre. Typical of such emulative efforts was the response of Memphis, Tennessee. Spurred into action by its near-bottom location on the Creativity Index, the chamber of commerce and several local government agencies commissioned a study of the city's image among "young urban knowledge-workers," benchmarking themselves against "high-performing" creative cities, and dissecting Austin's experience in order to identify "hopeful signs of what happens when a city actively fosters creativity."[12] Similarly, Portland, Oregon, also has been promoted as a "compelling case study" of urban creativity; the replication-friendly lessons for other cities include identifying creative leaders, building new systems of communication within the local community, promoting the adaptive reuse of buildings, supporting festivals and other street-level events, and, above all, being "authentic."[13]

The reality is that city leaders from San Diego to Baltimore, from Toronto to Albuquerque, are embracing creativity strategies not as *alternatives* to extant market-, consumption-, and property-led development strategies, but as low-cost, feel-good *complements* to them. Creativity plans do not disrupt these established approaches to urban entrepreneurialism and consumption-oriented place promotion, they *extend* them. Florida implicitly concedes as much when pointing out, in response to his critics' axe-grinding attacks, that he works with "civic leaders from both sides of the aisle on economic development issues," disarmingly observing that "whatever pundits might say about our findings, business and civic leadership in city after city has taken them to heart."[14]

Fast Urban Policy

More than fifteen years ago, David Harvey called attention to the rise of "entrepreneurial" urban strategies, pointing to emergent features of the city-political terrain that have since been, to all intents and purposes, normalized.[15] Describing the responses of deindustrializing cities in the 1980s, where the accelerating retreat of the Fordist economy was compounded by diminished urban fiscal capacity and a political turn against redistributive spending and social programs, Harvey portrayed the rise of interurban competition as a disciplining and coercive force. Confronted by an extremely limited repertoire of politically feasible options, cities threw themselves into a series of zero-sum competitions for mobile public and private investments, thereby inadvertently facilitating (indeed subsidizing) the very forms of capital circulation and revenue competition that were major sources of the problem in the first place. In this climate of beggar-thy-neighbor competition, cities turned to a restrictive suite of supply-side and promotional strategies, which were serially reproduced and emulated in the scramble for mobile investment, jobs, and discretionary spending. None of this, of course, increased the aggregate amount of available investment, though it certainly contributed to its increasing rate of circulation.

The creative cargo cults of today are little more than retreads of some very familiar local strategies. Urban creativity strategies facilitate and extend the "third generation" forms of gentrification in which the (local) state assumes an increasingly active role in "retaking the city for the middle classes."[16] Discourses of creative competition, moreover, serve to enroll cities in more far-reaching forms of cultural commodification and artistically inflected place promotion, which is targeted at a new audience. Creativity strategies, even as they promptly have become clichés in their own right, are in many ways tragically appropriate for late-entrepreneurial cities like Baltimore, the cities that already have tried practically everything, including, of course, building stadiums and offering corporate inducements. Today, hopes are pinned on "an increasingly standardized narrative of 'creativity-led urban economic development,'"[17] one which nevertheless reorganizes the stakes, sites, and scales of urban competition—around creative individuals and their favored neighborhood habitats. The "Creative Baltimore" strategy, for example, includes a long list of existing programs, while launching some small-scale initiatives with a creative-cities feel: building bike paths; establishing a mentoring scheme for creative wanna-bes; converting unused industrial buildings to art studios and live/work spaces; setting up a city-wide music festival and arts parade; placing chess tables outside city hall; promoting offbeat and eccentric events that are unique to Baltimore, including the American Dime Museum, John Waters, and Edgar Allan Poe.[18]

Rather than "civilizing" urban economic development by "bringing in culture," creativity strategies do the opposite: they commodify the arts and cultural resources, even social tolerance itself, suturing them as putative economic assets to evolving regimes of urban competition. They enlist to this redoubled competitive effort some of the few remaining pools of untapped resources; they enroll previously marginalized actors for this elite effort, enabling the formation of new governance structures and local political channels; they constitute new objects of governance and new stakes in interurban competition; and they enable the script of urban competitiveness to be performed—quite literally—in novel and often eye-catching ways. And they do all of this within the framework of an inherited complex of new urban "realities," which variously contextualize, channel, and constrain "creative" urban politics. In the short run, at least, the discursively privileged actors on this stage are not the (distracted and self-absorbed) members of the Creative Class itself—since these are the ones who must be catered to—but those "regional leaders" with the vision and the determination to adopt "aggressive measures."[19]

Creative-city strategies are predicated on, and designed for, this neoliberalized terrain: repackaging urban cultural artifacts as competitive assets, valuing them (literally) not for their own sake, but in terms of their (supposed) economic utility. In order to be enacted, they presume and work with gentrification, conceived as a positive urban process, while making a virtue of selective and variable outcomes, unique neighborhood by unique neighborhood. They provide a means to intensify and publicly subsidize urban consumption systems for a circulating class of gentrifiers, whose *lack* of commitment to place and whose weak community ties are perversely celebrated. In an echo of the Creative Class's reportedly urgent need to "validate" their identities and lifestyles, this amounts to a process of public validation for favored forms of consumption and for a privileged class of consumers. In fact, indulging selective forms of elite consumption and social interaction is elevated to the status of a public-policy objective in the creative-cities script.

The notion of creative cities also extends to the urban domain the principles and practices of creative, flexible autonomy that were so powerfully articulated in the libertarian business ideologies of the 1990s,[20] for all the knowing distinctions that creativity advocates ritually draw with their new-economy forebears. As Lehmann has noted, "the core values that Florida charts as the key to the 'creative ethos'—individuality, meritocracy, diversity, and openness—are all by now slogans of first resort for the same corporate economy that [he] claims is being displaced by high-tech innovators in no-collar workplaces and edgy neighborhoods."[21] Discourses of urban creativity seek to normalize flexible labor-market conditions, lionizing a class of workers that can not only cope with, but positively revel in, an environment of persistent insecurity and intense, atomized competition, just as they enforce modes of creative governmentality based on "compulsory individualism, compulsory 'innovation,' compulsory performativity and productiveness, compulsory valorization of the putatively new."[22] This is achieved, in part, by the suggestive mobilization of creativity as a distinctly positive, nebulous-yet-attractive, apple-pie-like phenomenon: like its step-cousin flexibility, creativity preemptively disarms critics and opponents, whose resistance implicitly evokes creativity's antonymic others—rigidity, philistinism, narrow-mindedness, intolerance, insensitivity, conservativism, *not getting it*.

The contemporary cult of urban creativity has a clear genealogical history, stretching back at least as far as the entrepreneurial efforts of deindustrialized cities. The script of urban creativity reworks and augments the old methods and arguments of urban entrepreneurialism in politically seductive ways. The emphasis on the mobilization of new regimes of local governance around the aggressive pursuit of growth-focused development agendas is a compelling recurring theme, but whereas the entrepreneurial cities chased jobs, the creative cities pursue talent workers; whereas the entrepreneurial cities craved investment, the creative cities yearn for buzz. The tonic of urban creativity is a remixed version of the entrepreneurial-cities cocktail: just pop the same basic ingredients into your new-urbanist blender, add a slug of Schumpeter lite for some new-economy fizz, and finish it off with a pink twist.

So packaged, creativity strategies were in a sense preconstituted for this fast policy market. They empower, though only precariously, unstable networks of elite actors, whose strategies represent aspirant attempts to realize in concrete form the seductive "traveling truths" of the creativity script. They give license to portable technocratic routines and replicable policy practices that are easily disembedded and deterritorialized from their centers of production—at least in a shallow, essentialized form—for all the talk of local "authenticity." They reconstitute urban-elitist "leadership" models of city governance, despite their ritual invocation of grassroots efforts. They foster experimental and mutually referential policy development processes, framed within the tight parameters of urban fiscal capacity, and manifest in the form of the serial reproduction of an increasingly clichéd repertoire of favored policy interventions, the value of which is eroded in the very act of their (over)construction. They legitimate new urban development models and messages, which travel with great speed through interlocal policy networks, facilitated by a sprawling complex of conferences, Web sites, consultants and advocates, policy intermediaries, and centers of technocratic translation, the combined function of which is to establish new venues and lubricate new channels for rapid "policy learning." And they discursively and institutionally select subnational scales, highlighting in particular gentrifying urban neighborhoods as the preeminent sites for both privileged forms of creative action and necessary modes of political proaction, the places that *can and must* act. As such, creativity strategies subtly canalize and constrain urban-political agency, even as their material payoffs remain extraordinarily elusive. The cult of urban creativity is therefore revealed in its true colors, as a form of soft law or lore for a hypercompetitive age.

This is an abridged and revised version of the article "Struggling with the Creative Class," which appeared in *International Journal of Urban and Regional Research* 29, no. 4 (2005), 740-770. Reprint with the kind permission of Blackwell Publishing.

Notes
1   C. Dreher, "Be Creative—or Die," *Salon*, June 6, 2002, http://www.salon.com (accessed January 27, 2005), p. 1.
2   O. Ohoa, "The Road to Riches?" *Boston Globe*, February 29, 2004, p. D1.
3   R. Florida, "The New American Dream," *Washington Monthly*, March 2003, 26-33, here p. 27.
4   S. Malanga, "The Curse of the Creative Class," *City Journal*, winter 2004, 36-45, here p. 36.
5   R. Florida, *The Rise of the Creative Class* (New York: Basic Books, 2002), 229.
6   Ibid., 21.
7   Ibid., ix.
8   Ibid., 304.
9   R. Florida, *Cities and the Creative Class* (New York: Routledge, 2005), 131.
10 P. Maliszewski, "Flexibility and Its Discontents," *The Baffler* 16 (2004): 69-79, here p. 76.
11 See T. Hall and P. Hubbard, eds., *The Entrepreneurial City* (Chichester, UK: Wiley, 1998).
12 Memphis Talent Magnet Project and Coletta & Company, *Technology, Talent, and Tolerance: Attracting the Best and Brightest to Memphis* (Memphis, TN: Coletta & Company, 2003), 8.
13 See B. Bulick, C. Coletta, C. Jackson, A. Taylor, and S. Wolff, "Cultural Development in Creative Communities," *Monograph*, November 2003.
14 R. Florida, "Revenge of the Squelchers," *Next American City* 5 (special feature; 2004): i-viii, here pp. ii, v.
15 D. Harvey, "From Managerialism to Entrepreneurialism: The Transformation in Urban Governance in Late Capitalism," *Geografiska Annaler B* 71 (1989): 3-17; or see abridged version in this volume.
16 N. Smith, "New Globalism, New Urbanism: Gentrification as Global Urban Strategy," *Antipode* 34 (2002): 434-457, here p. 443.
17 C. Gibson and N. Klocker, "Academic Publishing as a 'Creative' Industry: Some Critical Reflections," *Area* 36 (2004): 423-434, here p. 431.
18 City of Baltimore, *New Ideas for Promoting Baltimore City* (Baltimore: Mayor's Office of Community Investment, 2004).
19 Florida, *Cities and the Creative Class*, 151-152.
20 See T. Frank, *One Market Under God* (New York: Doubleday, 2000); N. J. Thrift, "'It's the Romance, Not the Finance, That Makes the Business Worth Pursuing': Disclosing a New Market Culture," *Economy and Society* 30 (2001): 412-432.
21 C. Lehmann, "Class Acts," *Raritan* 22 (2003): 147-167, here pp. 163-164.
22 T. Osborne, "Against 'Creativity': A Philistine Rant," *Economy and Society* 32 (2003): 507-525, here p. 507.

WERKLEITZ GESELLSCHAFT E.V./CENTER FOR ARTISTIC VISUAL MEDIA IN SAXONY-ANHALT
Werkleitz, Germany, 1993–2004; Halle, Germany, since 2004

In 1993, in the restaurant Zur Post in the small village of Werkleitz, near Magdeburg, the association Werkleitz Gesellschaft – Verein zur Förderung und Realisierung von Film-, Kunst- und Medienprojekten (Association for the Support and Realization of Film, Art, and Media Projects) was founded, two years after three film students had discovered and renovated a former brickworks near Werkleitz as a place to live and work. The idea of an annual presentation of the artists and filmmakers involved in the association developed into a small interdisciplinary festival in 1993, with films, performances, concerts, and an exhibition area. Its first recurrence in 1996 led to the Werkleitz Biennale. The "documenta of the East," which brought international (media) artists to the small village as well as an interested public, took place for the sixth time in 2004, and it is now the largest festival of its kind in eastern Germany. Each time it has a specific cultural-political theme (e.g., *real[work]* in 2000 or *Zugewinngemeinschaft* [community of accrued gains] in 2002).

In addition to the biennial art festival, the association built the infrastructure for regional film financing in Werkleitz, setting up a fully equipped media workshop and the first nonuniversity Internet server in Saxony-Anhalt (1994). It also has established supraregional and international cultural networks. Since 1996 there has been international funding for what is now the official "state media center."

In 2004 the Werkleitz Gesellschaft moved its seat to Halle and located a park there as the new site for the Biennale *(Common Property/Allgemeingut*, 2004). As before, there is a media workshop and postproduction technology available, as well as stipends and workshops in the areas of recording, postproduction, and film and media theory. (Ed.)

Project by Nils Normann for the Werkleitz Biennale 2000.

CHINATI FOUNDATION
Marfa, Texas, USA, since 1986
Donald Judd
www.chinati.org

In Marfa, a small town in Texas, the American artist Donald Judd's idea and dream to develop a different model for a contemporary art museum has been realized. Beginning in 1975, Judd purchased together with the Dia Art Foundation 350 acres of land, along with fifteen buildings from a former military base. His aim was to install his own work, as well as that of artist friends like John Chamberlain and Dan Flavin, far from the commercial art market of New York. After a falling-out with the Dia Art Foundation, Judd established his own foundation, the Chinati Foundation, and transferred to it the property rights for the land, the building, and the artworks.

Here he could realize his idea that artists should themselves create the conditions under which their works are presented. He renovated the ruins and fragments of buildings using simple architectonic means so that they could be used as exhibition and living spaces.

Judd, who questions museums as a place for art, was particularly mistrustful of transporting artworks from exhibition to exhibition. His criticism was that the artworks had to be followed—only to see them set up under poor conditions. When the Chinati Foundation opened in 1986, its mission was described on the invitation as the uniqueness of its installation, in which art could be encountered in the context of its architectural and natural surroundings, not isolated in the anthology of a museum.

Judd has succeeded in Marfa at inseparably combining art, architecture, and natural surroundings. In at least one respect, however, it is doubtful whether he has done complete justice to his original intention: the permanent installation in this remote site in the Texas desert is visited by more than ten thousand international art lovers annually—a flow of visitors that is certainly comparable to large commercial successes on the international art scene. As a result, there has been a considerable real estate boom in Marfa. Old houses are being converted into second homes with modern designs. The price increases have clearly affected established residents, and the delicate ecosystem of the surrounding landscape is threatened by tourists. The search for autonomy and happiness in a remote location far from the culture industry has turned into its antithesis. (Ed.)

▲ The Chinati Foundation in Marfa is located on a former military base. ▼ Donald Judd walking east of the Chinati Foundation's Arena.

The Arena, one of the Chinati Foundation's three large halls, was originally an airplane hangar and was later used as a riding hall. Donald Judd renovated the building simply and transformed the space and the architecture by means of specific interventions like removing material, adding openings, or supplementing them with furniture designed for the space.

Chinati Foundation_*Donald Judd*

LOS TOPOS
Berlin and Halle, Germany, 2004
Club Real and Peanutz-Architekten

———

———

"Los Topos" is an as yet unrealized project proposal for a play about urban development. It proposes constructing in different variations and for various peripheral locations in eastern Germany an Old West town with an interactive play about pioneers. The visitors slip into the role of pioneers and practice antiurban rituals along various routes, such as a hunting course, a stag fight, or ritual burials. "We do not intend to present a historicizing parable of the pioneers of civilization," its authors wrote, "but rather to bring to life—and depict in their diverse forms—the idea of a carefree new beginning and a moderate to ruthless reshaping of the landscape as part of a character drama." The play accompanies and comments on urban transformation processes in which places are sometimes cut off from civilization and returned to the wilderness. At the same time, existing foundation myths are evoked by the figure of the pioneer. (Ed.)

———

This project was developed for the *archplus* competition "Shrinking Cities: Reinventing Urbanism."

———
———
———

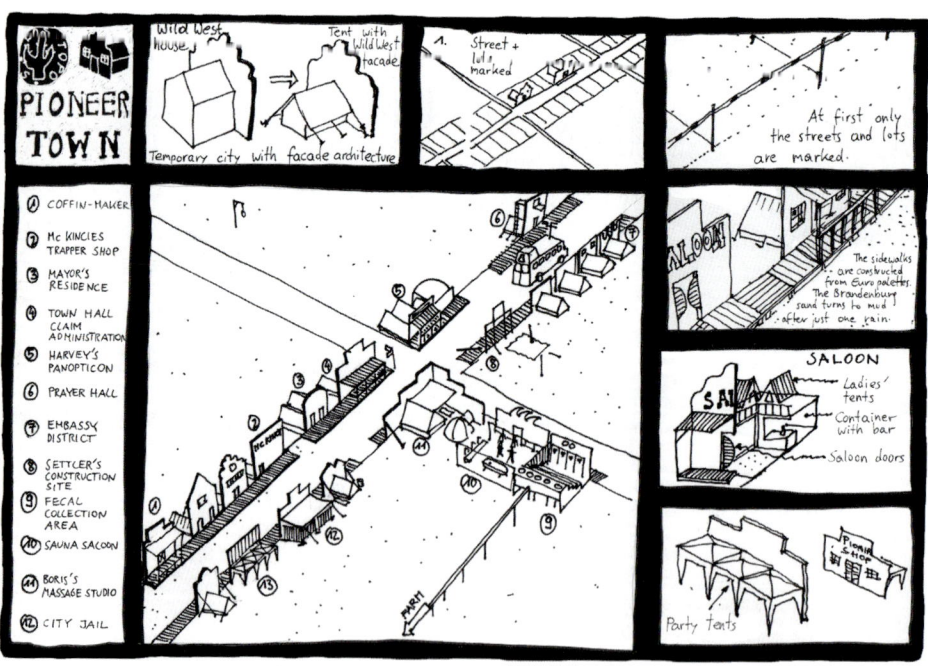

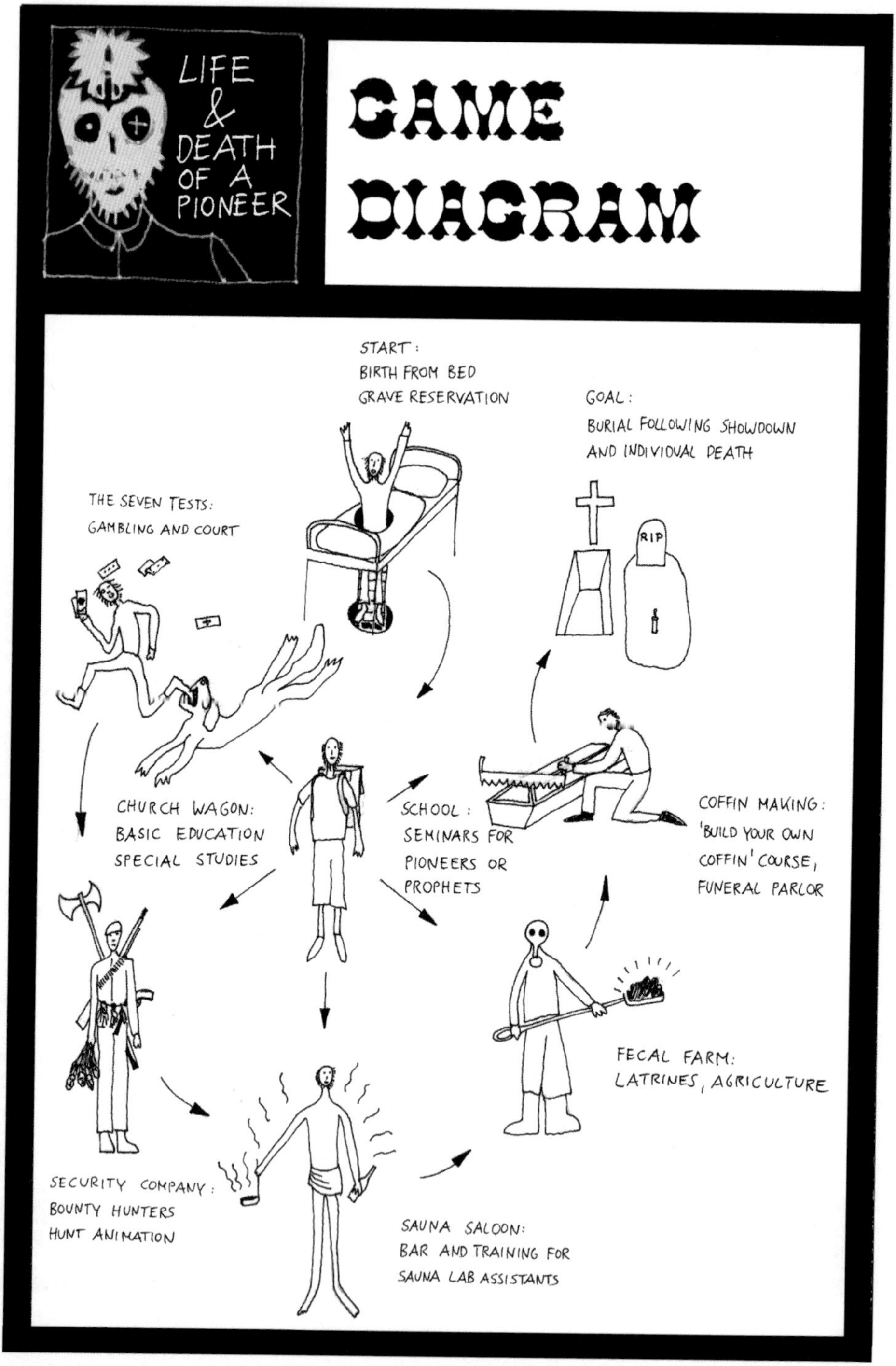
LIFE & DEATH OF A PIONEER
GAME DIAGRAM
START: BIRTH FROM BED GRAVE RESERVATION
GOAL: BURIAL FOLLOWING SHOWDOWN AND INDIVIDUAL DEATH
RIP
THE SEVEN TESTS: GAMBLING AND COURT
CHURCH WAGON: BASIC EDUCATION SPECIAL STUDIES
SCHOOL: SEMINARS FOR PIONEERS OR PROPHETS
COFFIN MAKING: 'BUILD YOUR OWN COFFIN' COURSE, FUNERAL PARLOR
FECAL FARM: LATRINES, AGRICULTURE
SECURITY COMPANY: BOUNTY HUNTERS HUNT ANIMATION
SAUNA SALOON: BAR AND TRAINING FOR SAUNA LAB ASSISTANTS

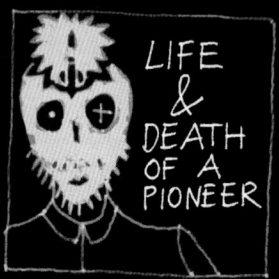

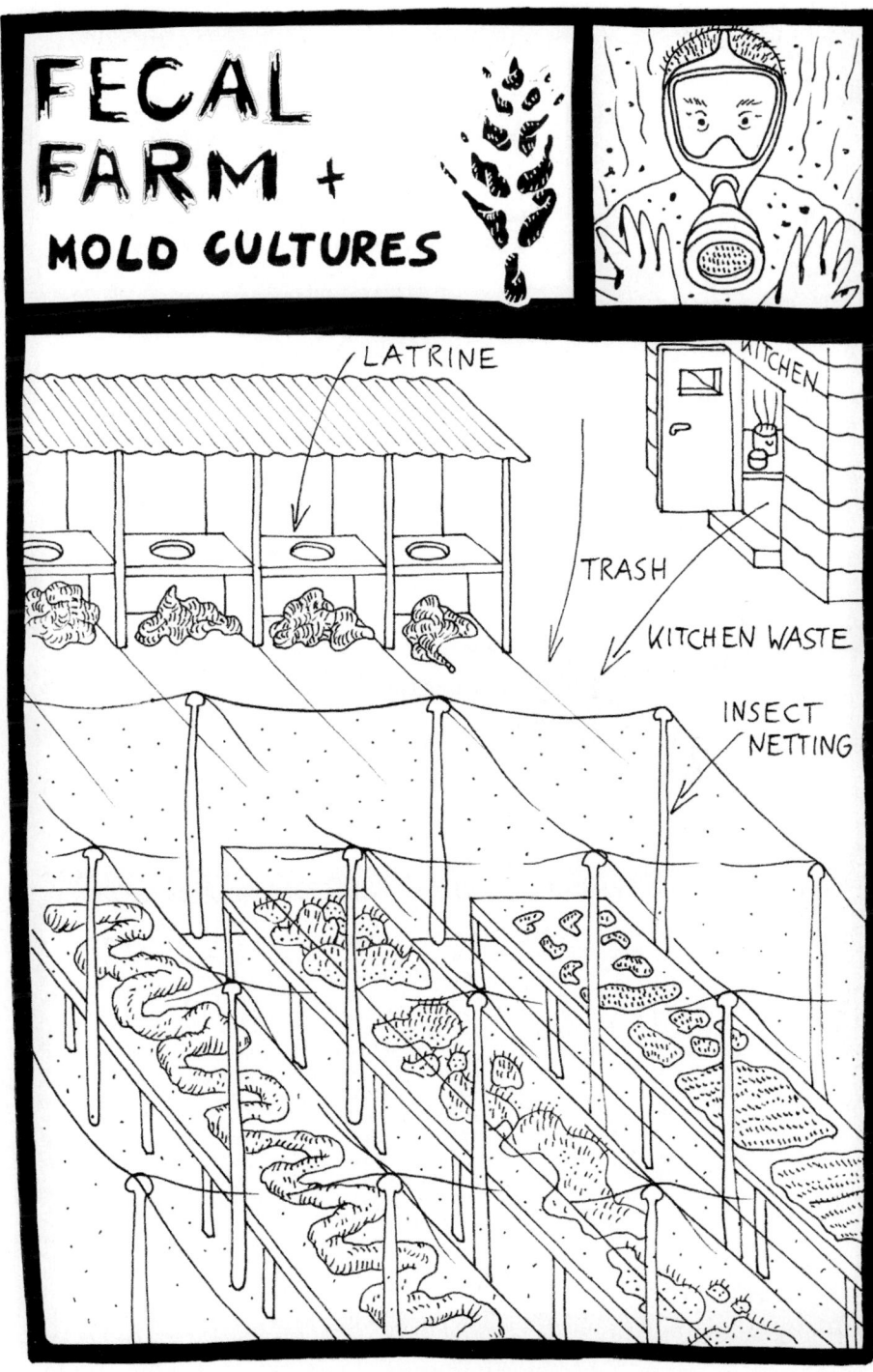

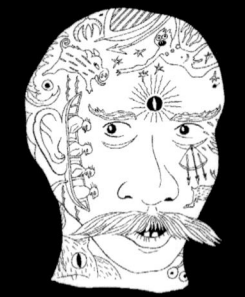

LOS TOPOS
PIONEER PLAY

THE TOPIC OF THE PLAY IS THE NOW-FORGOTTEN BREED OF THE PIONEER: HIS WORLDVIEW AND HIS SUCCESSES AND CATASTROPHES. IN THE NINETEENTH CENTURY THE TERM 'PIONEER' TOOK ON A NEW MEANING IN ADDITION TO ITS PURELY MILITARY SENSE, SO THAT THERE WERE ALSO PIONEERS IN SCIENTIFIC, ECONOMIC, AND SOCIOPOLITICAL FIELDS. THIS WENT HAND IN HAND WITH A HOPEFUL AND SOMEWHAT CAREFREE SENSE OF A NEW BEGINNING, WHICH FOR MANY MEANT A NEW HOMELAND, WEALTH, AND IDENTITY, BUT FOR OTHERS EXPULSION, EXPLOITATION, AND DEATH. BUT WE DO NOT INTEND TO PRESENT A HISTORICIZING PARABLE OF THE PIONEERS OF CIVILIZATION. RATHER, WE AIM TO BRING TO LIFE THE IDEA OF A CAREFREE NEW BEGINNING AND A MODERATE TO RUTHLESS RESHAPING OF THE LANDSCAPE AS PART OF A CHARACTER DRAMA AND TO DEPICT THESE IN THEIR DIVERSE FORMS. THE BACKGROUND MATERIAL WAS DRAWN FROM THE TEXTS OF VARIOUS PIONEERING OR REVIVAL MOVEMENTS, SUCH AS THE PROPHECIES OF THE FOUNDERS OF VARIOUS RELIGIONS (JOHN SMITH et al., BOOK OF MORMON, 1827-1829), INDIVIDUALIST PHILOSOPHICAL TREATISES (H.D. THOREAU, WALDEN, 1854), AND NOVELS ABOUT ECONOMIC OR OTHER BORDER CROSSING PROJECTS (J.F. COOPER, THE PIONEERS, 1823; J. IBARGÜENGOITIA, THE DEAD GIRLS, 1977).

THE SETTLERS … IN THE BOONDOCKS
Germany, 2004
Claus Strigel
www.siedler-film.de, www.denkmal-film.com

Claus Strigel has called his film "a documentary Western in the German East." It sketches the history of a commune, the Lebensgemeinschaft Klein Jasedow, which moved from Switzerland in 1997 to a nearly abandoned village in the eastern section of West Pomerania in order to establish a media company, an organic herb garden, a project for a "European Academy for the Art of Healing," and a new existence in accordance with its own ideas of life. In the "only municipality in the eastern section of West Pomerania that is now growing" (according to the film description), dilapidated buildings were renovated, various projects were initiated, and jobs were created. Just a few years later, however, a controversial herbicide accident in the adjacent factory farm brought to the surface the conflicts between the locals and the "newcomers." In the film the protagonists express their different points of view, as the following dialogue excerpts and stills show:

Matthias Andiel (former mayor of the municipality of Pulow)
In 1996 there was an article in *Der Spiegel* that discussed the problems that we in rural areas faced at the time. When confronted with the question "What does it look like in a rural community?" it was clear to me the answer was that it looks like the boondocks. It was clear that people move away, that they go to the money, and the only people who will come here are artists or crazy people who are truly prepared to work in muck. That is, creative people.… Then I got a call from Switzerland. Johannes Heimrath introduced himself. He explained that they had something to do with music, that they were a media company, and that in any case they were a large family, some fifteen people. And that they were searching for a new center for their lives.

Klaus Holsten (Lebensgemeinschaft Klein Jasedow)
I came here and had a strong feeling of the devastation that prevails here. We moved into abandoned buildings, after all.… To the left of the entrance to Klein Jasedow there is an old corn silo that is supposed to be converted into an inn at some point. On the right there is a large stall, which is supposed to be converted into a seminary some day. To the left is the upper village, with two families. From there you see the sound studio that is being built. And here the office, glimmering yellow in the sunlight. It was once the assembly room and kitchen for hundreds of workers in the collective farm. So what we are doing here is truly an extensive conversion.

Paul Martschinke (neighbor of the Lebensgemeinschaft Klein Jasedow)
So a guy comes here and has long hair—people criticized that. I said, look, folks, try going to Berlin or anywhere else; people just go around like that there. If they come here, it means something new for us, but I can live with that. I admire them for taking this step. I respect it very much. None of the locals would have done that anymore. Because the village had been run into the ground.

 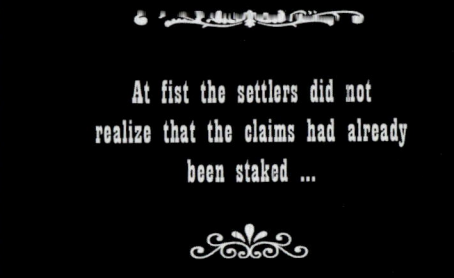

Stills from the film *Die Siedler—Am Arsch der Welt* (The Settlers … In the Boondocks).

The Settlers ... In the Boondocks_Claus Strigel

For the settlers, West Pomerania was terra nova.
A place where everything or nothing would be possible ...

The settlers not only had brought work for themselves:
new jobs also were created ...

Ausschnitte NDR-Bericht Sept. 2001

Philipp Graffam
der Pastor

Hans-Joachim Enke (neighbor and employee of the Lebensgemeinschaft Klein Jasedow)
From the first day, we got along well. They are people just like me: I too want to have my own chickens and peace in the country.... We started to talk. I was an unemployed autobody worker, so Johannes Heimrath proposed that I could build musical instruments, make repairs, fix vehicles, if I wanted. I said yes, and I've been doing it for nearly six years.

Christiane Wilkening (Pommerland Herb Garden Co-op)
We are the strangers, I have to say that. We all come, as they see it, from western Germany—though in fact I am the only one—and are the ones who arrive here with money and know-how to get something going. And I think they find that very threatening. Nor does it happen the way they imagine, but rather in accordance with our ideas, and I think that conflicts arise for that reason.

Mr. and Mrs. Bliese (Waschow Regional Association)
We are the local citizens. We have the right to remain. That has to be accepted by the other side as well. We feel ... pressured ... and also pushed out.... We heard that the new people had arrived, and that they dressed a little strangely. It was supposed to be a sect, that's what people said at the time. So we were surprised to find that they were so sociable, that they came to us and organized a joint celebration. We genuinely thought that was very good.... Then time passed, and people got along with one another. Until the accident with the spraying in Brasan occurred. They knew that there was large-scale agriculture here, and that they could not have organic farming in the middle of conventional agriculture. That led to conflicts; that was bound to happen. And probably that's how it should be.

Johannes Heimrath (Lebensgemeinschaft Klein Jasedow)
On September 15, 2001, suddenly our many green leaves were white. Herbicide had gone astray—it was from the one factory farm that dominates around here and was intended for their canola fields. The lemon balm fields that the herb farm had worked so hard to establish here were destroyed. The feeling that many years of preparation were in vain was enormously painful. That pain was then expressed spontaneously.... The herb gardeners filed a complaint that damage had been caused. And that was exploited by interested parties to accuse the newcomers of wanting to destroy the conventional agriculture here, and in general to destroy everything. From one day to the next they had conceived a perfectly organized method for destroying our reputation. A pamphlet literally called for us to be driven out.

Philipp Graffam (pastor in the village of Pulow)
Anyone who moves to a new place brings his or her history, interpretations, and plans for life. That this doesn't happen without tension is inherent in the matter. First, there is a questioning of our situation, that is, of the people who live here. Now people come from outside and suddenly say that it's better to live like this. This feeling is spreading.

Translated from the German by Steven Lindberg

GO EAST: ON THE WILD-WEST RHETORIC OF SHRINKING CITY PROJECTS
Anke Hagemann

A herd of cows is driven to vacant urban lots; "claims" are marked off with wooden stakes; a pioneer drama conducts shamanistic rituals of decivilization; and the history of a rural community is staged as a Western documentary, accompanied by Ennio Morricone's famous theme music. Concepts for reoccupying areas that have fallen into disuse and empty buildings in shrinking cities often make use of ideas and images that are borrowed, consciously or unconsciously, from the context of the opening up of the American West: new "settlers" are to "colonize the Wild West" with "pioneering spirit." As a rule, such transported connotations are viewed positively: adventure, a new beginning, the opening up of unknown terrain, and the conquering of wilderness.

But even within this terminological system of reference—the historical example of colonialism (which meanwhile has been significantly reshaped culturally)—the unintentional side effects are part of the structure of any such action. The act of resettling and acquiring space bears features of anarchy and adventure, of idealism and utopia, but also of colonization and individual appropriation. Thus a reoccupation of places in shrinking areas, whose basic motivation ranges from the idealistic to the subversive, is often accompanied by an attitude toward the local situation that ranges from elitist to ignorant. The Western rhetoric reveals both the ambivalence and the potential for conflict in the "pioneering" attitude toward eastern Germany.

The Frontier of Shrinkage

The "frontier" in the American West marked the extent of settlement within an area that had not yet been settled—the borderline between civilization and wilderness, as it were. In the nineteenth century, for example, the frontier was determined statistically, on the basis of population density.[1] The Wild West rhetoric in shrinking contexts also makes use of the opposition of nature and culture, which can be interpreted in two ways. First, the "frontier of shrinkage" is advancing, and the wilderness is reconquering places abandoned by civilization. In "Claiming Land," a proposal submitted to a competition, this process is described as follows: "Deserted urban row houses, neglected playing fields, abandoned schools, forsaken churches, disused factories, emptied neighborhoods, and (nearly) forgotten districts ... that essentially characterize the image of cities like Liverpool and Manchester are the results of a decades-long process of transformation that has turned broad swathes of the historical city into a 'new frontier.' Paraurban zones have resulted that have largely lost their previous identification as 'cities' and in many places have a rural character again, though without being able to redeem the promises of the countryside: security, health, prosperity."[2] The pioneers of this wilderness thus opt out of civilization, frequently proposing or even implementing a return to agrarian forms of production, for example. In the project proposal "Los Topos," anti-urban practices were intended to make that step easier: "Long live the shrunken urbanites! They are pioneers of a self-run urban existence relieved of the tetanus of civilization through a therapeutic bloodletting. Yes! These pioneers are content with the natural uselessness of a landscape and live in it like players who dig the earth around them for their own pleasure."[3]

The term *frontier* is used in another way for another pioneer movement that opens up land that has been abandoned, recycles it, and returns it to civilization. At the Urban Drift conference in 2002, the project-development office D:4 presented a "proposal to resettle Lausitz with an agro-urban society" that recalls "above all archaic ways of settling land." "However, today the point is not to wrest untouched land from nature for economic uses. Rather, this land must ... be cultivated for a second time."[4]

No-Man's-Land and the Wild East

Such calls to reoccupy shrinking regions often carry connotations of a no-man's-land or an area bereft of civilization. This strategy is not new; it legitimized both the settlement of land in the American West and the gentrification of inner-city neighborhoods in recent decades. In *Die Stadt als Beute* (The City as Booty), the urbanologists Klaus Ronneberger, Stephan Lanz, and Walther Jahn refer to the American urbanologist Neil Smith, who describes the terminology of wilderness and frontier as borrowings from the pioneering frontier of the nineteenth century intended to legitimate the process of conquering inner cities at the expense of those already living there, and find similar metaphors in urban development in Germany in the 1990s. "Either these areas are declared no-man's-lands or compared to dangerous jungles.... A classic example is Berlin after the fall of the Wall, when elements of the subculture claimed they were turning the 'Wild East' into 'Western civilization.'"[5] The corresponding idea of shrinking areas as "virgin lands," as vacated no-man's-lands, decontextualizes such spaces, strips them of their histories, and thus makes them available for reoccupation.

Occupying Land and Privatization

The settlement of the American West was the result of individual processes of appropriation, some of which had an anarchic character. In his essay "Der Siedler" (The Settler), Stefan Kaufmann emphasizes this by quoting the American historian Frederick Jackson Turner: settlers would turn to lynch justice without hesitation when it came to their individual rights with respect to the wilderness. Property was established by actually taking possession of it and justifying this action through using it properly. "Those who did not place visible markings on their land, did not drive in stakes, did not build houses and churches, did no more than plant the land, without improving it or cultivating it, cannot claim property rights.... In precisely that sense, the rights of an Englishman are far ahead of the rights of nature."[6] In shrinking cities, too, there exists an ideal image of an individual adding value to a space—that is to say, the only resource that exists in surplus. In times when public funds are lacking, private initiative is seen as the only opportunity to increase value and provide new stimulus. As the "Claiming Land" proposal puts it, "These ill-defined, hybrid, and uncertain zones represent land that should only be given to people with entrepreneurial spirit, a desire to do things, and the ability to combine pioneering concepts of use directly with their own perspectives on life."[7] The acquisition of unutilized areas free of charge is mentioned in many project proposals as either an incentive ("Die Chance der Fläche" – The Opportunity of Expanse), a gift ("Land for Free"), or a justified claim of the users ("100 qm Dietzenbach"). The symbolic acts of surveying land and appropriating space often play a significant role. In "Claiming Land," for example, the "unutilized areas are not awarded in their original configuration but resurveyed and reparceled with the active participation of pioneers."⁸ In the project "100 qm Dietzenbach," the land is awarded through an interactive ritual: "The stelae symbolized the opportunity to stake a claim. The residents could take the wooden posts, by agreement with the project team, and mark the 100 square meters of land that they wanted to use and maintain."⁹

Pioneers and Settlers
John Mason Peck's *A New Guide for Emigrants to the West* (1836) describes the role of the pioneer as follows: "Generally, in all the western settlements, three classes, like the waves of the ocean, have rolled one after the other. First comes the pioneer, who depends for the subsistence of his family chiefly upon natural growth of vegetation, called the 'range,' and the proceeds of hunting…. It is quite immaterial whether he ever becomes the owner of the soil. He is the occupant for the time being, pays no rent, and feels as independent as the 'lord of the manor.' The next class of emigrants purchase the lands, add field to field, clear out the roads, throw rough bridges over the streams, put up hewn log houses with glass windows and brick or stone chimneys … and exhibit the picture and forms of plain, frugal, civilized life. Another wave rolls on. The men of capital and enterprise come. The settler is ready to sell out and take the advantage of the rise in property, push farther into the interior and become, himself, a man of capital and enterprise in turn."¹⁰

In the field of urban development, the term *pioneer* was first used for a sociological model to explain gentrification. In a process astonishingly similar to that discussed above, it characterized those who paved the way to the revaluation and development of an urban area by a population group with a higher status. The negative implications of such developments, which result from an appropriation and valuation of spaces that comes from outside, seems to have posed no problem in shrinking contexts—after all, there is more than enough space. Instead, the pioneers are described as independent and inventive interim users, as the hope for new stimuli for growth. Klaus Overmeyer, an expert on temporary uses, described it as follows at the symposium "Raumpioniere" (Space Pioneers) in Berlin: "Pioneers are and have always been—like the foot soldiers of earlier times—those who explored unknown terrain and thus prepared the field for those who would later settle there…. Frequently, they created establishments in these places and thereby made them attractive for other users…. Interim users make dirty places clean."¹¹ By contrast, in "Land for Free: Die Stadt der Pioniere," a project proposal for the Ruhr Valley, pioneering becomes a fantastic permanent state: "A new city, provided with the power of the informal, whose social climate is determined by the cultural ur-action of settling…. The land left over is the natural ground of this city of pioneers; open, disparate, often ill-defined land that people appropriate, with their families, their ideas, their dreams, and their desires for new homelands…. The pioneers build summer colonies on disused tracks, inventors' garages on asphalt deserts, working lofts in abandoned public swimming pools, radio stations on slag heaps, pile dwellings in the swamps of old mining pits, temples in offset areas, Japanese-style minihouses in birch forests."¹²

The proposal "Die Chance der Fläche" foresees a method of awarding land that is less anarchic; the project is intended to initiate a settlers' movement for Lausitz, in a sparsely populated region near the Polish border. "The free awarding of land and start-up capital will attract as many as six thousand young people who have completed their education to settle here.... The settlers' first task will be to renovate the area they have been awarded, roughly two hectares per person, and arrange for places for themselves and their families to live.... In a second phase of development they will then use their land to produce yields for sale."[13]

Colonization with Idealism
The opening up and appropriation of the North American continent was determined not solely by motifs of power politics and economics but often by the idealistic intention to live a better life, found new communities, and cultivate the land according to Puritan beliefs. Not only for Protestants and sectarians, but also for deviationists, outsiders, and utopians, the American West offered new lebensraum: "We are all a little wild here with numberless projects of social reform. Not a reading man but has a draft of a new Community in his waistcoat pocket"[14]—Lieselotte Ungers and Oswald Mathias Ungers quote this letter by the American writer Ralph Waldo Emerson from 1840 and comment: "In the period from 1800 to 1900 there were more than one hundred utopian communities, with some one hundred thousand members in America."[15]

In the shrinking regions of eastern Germany, too, dropouts and alternative communities are often the only ones who dare to make a new start. "Since the early 1990s numerous communes and communal projects have been founded in Brandenburg. Above all, it has been the low price of real estate in the partially abandoned countryside of Brandenburg that has contributed to this.... There are ecological, religious, and psychosocial projects as well as others from the feminist or gay movements."[16] Idealist intentions do not, however, always spare the new residents from feelings of mistrust and rejection, as demonstrated by Claus Strigel's film *Die Siedler—Am Arsch der Welt* (The Settlers ... In the Boondocks), which is about an alternative rural commune that had been established in a deserted village in West Pomerania. "But the emptiness was deceptive; the claims had already been staked: factory farming had the place firmly in its grasp. The dormant conflicts exploded with all the great themes that make up the classic Westerns about settlers: an incited mob, great provocations, nasty intrigues, latent xenophobia, and bold struggles for existence."[17] The Wild West reference unintentionally suggests the colonial role of the "settlers." Those who come with investments or enough motivation can easily see themselves as the saviors in a desperate local situation. But ideas and concepts are being brought from outside into unfamiliar local contexts. "It has to be clear that one is frequently dealing with the 'losers' in these processes of transformation. Pioneers, by contrast, arrive with global biographies, academic educations, and their own plans for the world," explained Wolfgang Kil at the symposium "Shrinking Cities: Reinventing Urbanism," which accompanied the competition of the same name.[18] And Angelika Fitz warned, "In any case, precarious situations result, in which cultural differences and economic inequality enter into a difficult relationship."[19]

This cultural difference also can occur in art projects, even if they have declared participation to be their goal. "For me, this isn't art," was how the *Lausitzer Rundschau* quoted the reaction of Christian Democratic member of parliament Henry Nitzsche to the art action *Superumbau* in Hoyerswerda in 2003. "'On site the project is often met with complete incomprehension,' ... The chairman of the local arts association, Martin Schmidt, had critical remarks as well, however: 'And I think it is wrong to invite artists no one here knows and who remain strangers, while the city's associations are left waiting outside in front.' He felt that was the cause behind the distance that he felt the locals had toward the project."[20]

Translated from the German by Steven Lindberg

Notes
1 See Frederick Jackson Turner, *The Frontier in American History* (New York: Henry Holt, 1921): "What is the frontier? ... In the census reports it is treated as the margin of that settlement which has a density of two or more to the square mile."
2 Stefanie Bremer, Dirk E. Haas, Päivi, Kataikko, Henrik Sander, Andreas Schulze Bäing, and Boris Sieverts, "Claiming Land," prizewinning project proposal in the competition "Shrinking Cities: Reinventing Urbanism," sponsored by the journal *archplus*, 2004; see the project description in this volume.
3 Club REAL and Peanutz-Architekten, "Los Topos," project proposal entered in the competition "Shrinking Cities: Reinventing Urbanism," sponsored by the journal *archplus*, 2004; see the project description in this volume.
4 Thomas Herr and D:4, "Die Chance der Fläche," unpublished lecture manuscript for the Urban Drift conference, Berlin, October 2002.
5 Klaus Ronneberger, Stephan Lanz, and Walther Jahn, *Die Stadt als Beute* (Bonn: Dietz, 1999).
6 Stefan Kaufmann, "Die Siedler," in *Grenzverletzer: Von Schmugglern, Spionen und anderen subversiven Gestalten*, ed. Eva Horn, Stefan Kaufmann, and Ulrich Bröckling (Berlin: Kulturverlag Kadmos, 2002), 194; with reference to Turner, *The Frontier in American History*.
7 See Bremer et al., "Claiming Land."
8 Ibid.
9 Description of the project "100 qm Dietzenbach" in Claudia Becker and Martin Wilhelm, "Definitiv unvollendet," *db* 7 (2003), 36; see the project description in this volume.
10 Quoted in F.J. Turner, *The Significance of the Frontier in American History,* http://xroads.virginia.edu/~Hyper/TURNER/.
11 Klaus Overmeyer, "Raumpioniere," in *Stadtforum Berlin 2020: Verschenken? Bewalden? Zwischennutzen? Was tun mit der freien Fläche?* Documentation of the homonymous event on April 15, 2005, http://www.stadtentwicklung.berlin.de/planen/forum2020/de/freiraeume.php.
12 Büro für Städtereisen Boris Sieverts, orange edge – Urban Research + Marketing, and RE.FLEX architects_urbanists, "Land for Free: Die Stadt der Pioniere; Eine Kampagne für das Ruhrgebiet als Kulturhauptstadt Europas 2010," http://www.neueraeume.de/projekte/sieverts_land_for_free.pdf.
13 Herr and D:4, "Die Chance der Fläche."
14 Ralph Waldo Emerson to Thomas Carlyle, October 30, 1840; quoted in Lieselotte Ungers and Oswald Mathias Ungers, *Kommunen in der Neuen Welt, 1740–1972* (Cologne: Kiepenheuer & Witsch, 1972). The passage also can be found at the following Web site: http://humanitiesweb.org/human.php?s=l&p=c&a=p&ID=24446&c=607.
15 Ungers and Ungers, *Kommunen in der Neuen Welt.*
16 Fabian Schwade, "Kommunekarte Brandenburg," *An Architektur* 10/11 (2003), 59.
17 From the brief description of Claus Strigel's film *Die Siedler—Am Arsch der Welt; Ein dokumentarischer Western im deutschen Osten* (Germany, 2004), http://www.siedler-film.de; see the project description preceding this contribution.
18 Wolfgang Kil, lecture at the symposium "Shrinking Cities: Reinventing Urbanism," sponsored by the journal *archplus*, Berlin, January 21, 2005.
19 Angelika Fitz, lecture at the symposium "Shrinking Cities: Reinventing Urbanism," sponsored by the journal *archplus*, Berlin, January 21, 2005.
20 *Lausitzer Rundschau*, August 28, 2003.

REINTERPRETED CITY

Materials and buildings that are no longer used take on new functions through reinterpretation and reorganization. This helps save resources. Through the reforming of existing material, social transformation is assimilated culturally. A productive tension results from the difference between the given and the new situation desired. This tension produces new typologies, programs, and connections, and also reveals unexpected qualities in the seemingly obsolete large housing developments of the postwar era.

FORTY YEARS OF HETERODOXY
ON CEDRIC PRICE'S POTTERIES THINKBELT
Juan Herreros

———

———

PTb is the common name by which we know the Potteries Thinkbelt,[1] a project conceived in the 1960s by Cedric Price, with the aim of searching for a new meaning for industries in a process of decline. This region (North Staffordshire) saw its main activity—the production of pottery and porcelain—crumbling, and together with it its own character, memories, and reasons for existing. Nevertheless, PTb should not be understood as a "rehabilitation project," nor, of course, as a project conceived exclusively from the patronizing morality of preventing a catastrophe or the disappearance of a rich tradition. It is about taking advantage of change in order to generate a different industry, another community, another way of life, which can recycle what is still useful after ruthlessly throwing away what is not. Architecture then becomes a critical instrument capable of redescribing the world and uncovering new opportunities in places where all seems lost.

The idea is simple, and other authors have already explained it quite well:[2] take advantage of the unused railways, which connect the area's factories and warehouses, and superimpose a residential and educational program. In this way, there will be not a main function for the region but a hybrid enriched by industry and teaching, production and living, knowledge and mobility. The supporting infrastructure organizes and steers the project operationally, but its strong presence and its ingenuity should not eclipse its exploration. In this project Price linked or superimposed with optimistic curiosity throo simultaneous events of differing magnitude: the local crisis in the porcelain industry; the necessary educational reform of technical universities at the national level; and the new global configuration through the onset of the "third wave of industrialization," the precursor to globalization.

A number of central themes of Price's oeuvre emerge in this project; two are of particular interest here. On the one hand, there is teaching, or—as he preferred to call it—the adventure of "learning"; the learner is given center stage, and he or she should experience learning as a pleasure, as a recreational and creative activity. On the other hand, there is "shelf life," or, more generically speaking, "change," which is understood as the new material and the prime mover of architecture. For Price, "change" was not a more or less attractive phenomenon through its vitality alone. Rather, he perceived it as made up of physical aspects relative to the differing durability of materials and technical systems, as well as to operative aspects associated with the obsolescence of activities and the mobility of people.

Cedric Price also attempted to answer a need—linked with the de-urbanization and dispersion of the city—for a new idea of community. The most attractive aspect of the project from today's perspective is the richness of the plan as a landscape. He encouraged us to look at it as a real landscape on which to work: an unnatural landscape, an inherited result of action and change, in constant fluctuation. The second process of change, initiated by PTb, also creates a new nature, which is detached from all sentimental ideas about paradise and poetically takes root in the ruins of the industrial city. This innovative concept from Price anticipated artistic currents that years later would come to be known as *land art*.

According to Price, when something loses its function because its original use is outdated or no longer relevant, there is no point in forcing adaptations or in pursuing sentimental conservation. When its time comes, change takes over; in the best of cases, there is total change by means of reuse, substitution, or destruction of the original thing. It makes no difference whether this is an object, a building, an idea, a place, or a tradition. The death of the modernist movement was an accepted fact at the time, but it was not easy to dispose of those heavy categories choking the discipline. Great Britain was without a doubt the most active in this redefinition, thanks to successive generations of innovative architects, who were well connected among themselves but whose leading protagonists nonetheless were characterized by their individuality: Stirling, Price, Archigram, Smithson, and the mediatory figure of Reyner Banham. Price appears to have been the most radical among them. His method seemed to consist of setting aside one by one those old myths, and then observing what happens with the remainder—in the same way that one proceeds with the analysis of a system in order to test how the remaining whole reacts when faced with the absence of an omitted element. In most cases, the outcome proved the triviality of some of the major truths that are supposedly inherent in architectural practice: location, permanence, and confidence in predictive planning or in the design process as a formal or organizational means of clarification or purification. All this can be forced into a state of crisis, and in this way force architects and planners to invent new tools to manipulate a context whose potential will remain hidden as long as their tools are not adapted to its reality. This ever-changing and fleeting reality is a hybrid of physical and immaterial conditions, pushed forward by energies that have little to do with necessity, balance, or any other traditional form of order.

For Price, nothing was absolute, and each item dissolved into what was already there: education into industry, industry into transport, housing and living conditions into everything. A comparison with Buckminster Fuller's heterodoxy (as opposed to modern heterodoxy) is obvious but not sufficient, as Price did not fall for technological fascination and always took as his starting point a specific reading of the subject and its reality. Fuller took on big subjects in an abstract way, as theories to prove (e.g., the home, the geodesic dome, the automobile), for he was still prisoner of the idea that technology has more to do with the material nature of invention. Fuller did this with the epic dimension of a man bringing the future to the present: a nostalgic future whose fundamental achievement would be well-being, harmony, and equality; a homogeneous future stimulated by the competition of science and its exact and indisputable methods. Price, on the other hand, was aiming for democratic access not to production and products, but to information. By means of the latter, the main achievement of a postindustrial society would be to do without what is useless, including unnecessary architecture. This rejection of the superfluous was not existentialist but instead pursued the simplification of a world imprisoned by a culture of overabundance.

Indeed, in view of the damage inflicted by the over-exploitation of resources, the production of a climate of threat, and worries about the environment, Price's work makes us aware of the inherent contradictions in all dreams of a better future that are constructed on a generalized model. In the face of these contradictions, PTb is concerned with the recycling of a specific enclave, not with a universal model, and it aims to show how a great part of what is needed to achieve this is already there. One only needs to identify it, change its name or the way in which it is used, and add some new elements, which in their turn will also have a limited useful life span. This confidence in not doing more than what is necessary lucidly points to the hidden face of globalization, the one that frenetically looks solely for consumers who will satisfy imaginary needs, including architectural ones, needs which they actually do not have.

Translated from the Spanish by Isabel Giesler

Notes
1 The name "Thinkbelt" is Price's own invention. In this context "belt" makes a dual metaphorical reference to both "region" and "transmission"—like that for an engine. Thus, the combination "Thinkbelt" alludes to the creation of a support mechanism for the transmission of thought or, more precisely, to the generation of thought as a result of a productive process.
2 See, for example, Stanley Mathews, "Potteries Thinkbelt: An Architecture of Calculated Uncertainty," in *Arquitecturas Silenciosas: Thinkbelt de Cedric Price* (exhibition catalog; Madrid: Fundación COAM, 2001), also available at http://people.hws.edu/mathews/potteries_thinkbelt.htm; and Royston Landau, *New Directions in British Architecture* (New York: George Brazilier, 1968).

POTTERIES THINKBELT
North Staffordshire, UK, 1963–1966
Cedric Price

—

For the unrealized project Potteries Thinkbelt, which was directly connected to his work on the Fun Palace and which he developed on his own initiative without a commission, Cedric Price went beyond the dimensions of a building and sketched a new concept for an entire region. The traditional porcelain industry around Stoke-on-Trent in North Staffordshire, which was based on the natural presence of coal and clay, had been in decline since the Second World War. In addition to an abandoned industrial wasteland of factories, limekilns, pit mines, and slag heaps, it left behind an extensive network of rails on which the Potteries Thinkbelt concept was built.

Price proposed implanting a radically new industry of applied education for twenty thousand students; above all, it was to serve as an alternative model to Britain's ossified elite university education, and it also would be open to the local workers for continuing education. Price used the existing rail system as an infrastructure to plan this education industry in a mobile and flexible way and to distribute it throughout the region: three large transfer areas, connected to one another by tracks, form the outer corners of the project area as well as connecting points to the national transportation system. These transfer areas have cranes for loading mobile units (e.g., teaching and seminar rooms, work cells, folding and inflatable lecture units) onto flatbed railway cars, which can be combined according to the relevant requirements and then transported via the railway network to the desired location, such as one of the four faculty areas. Railbus shuttles transport the students between stations.

In addition to cybernetic infrastructure for the teaching program, there were also modular residential buildings for the students, which were not restricted to the campus but rather integrated into the region.

The overall goal was to interlock teaching, living, and industry closely and productively and to regenerate the economy of the region on the new basis of a postindustrial knowledge society. (Ed.)

—
—
—
—
—
—
—
—
—
—
—
—
—

Reinterpreted City

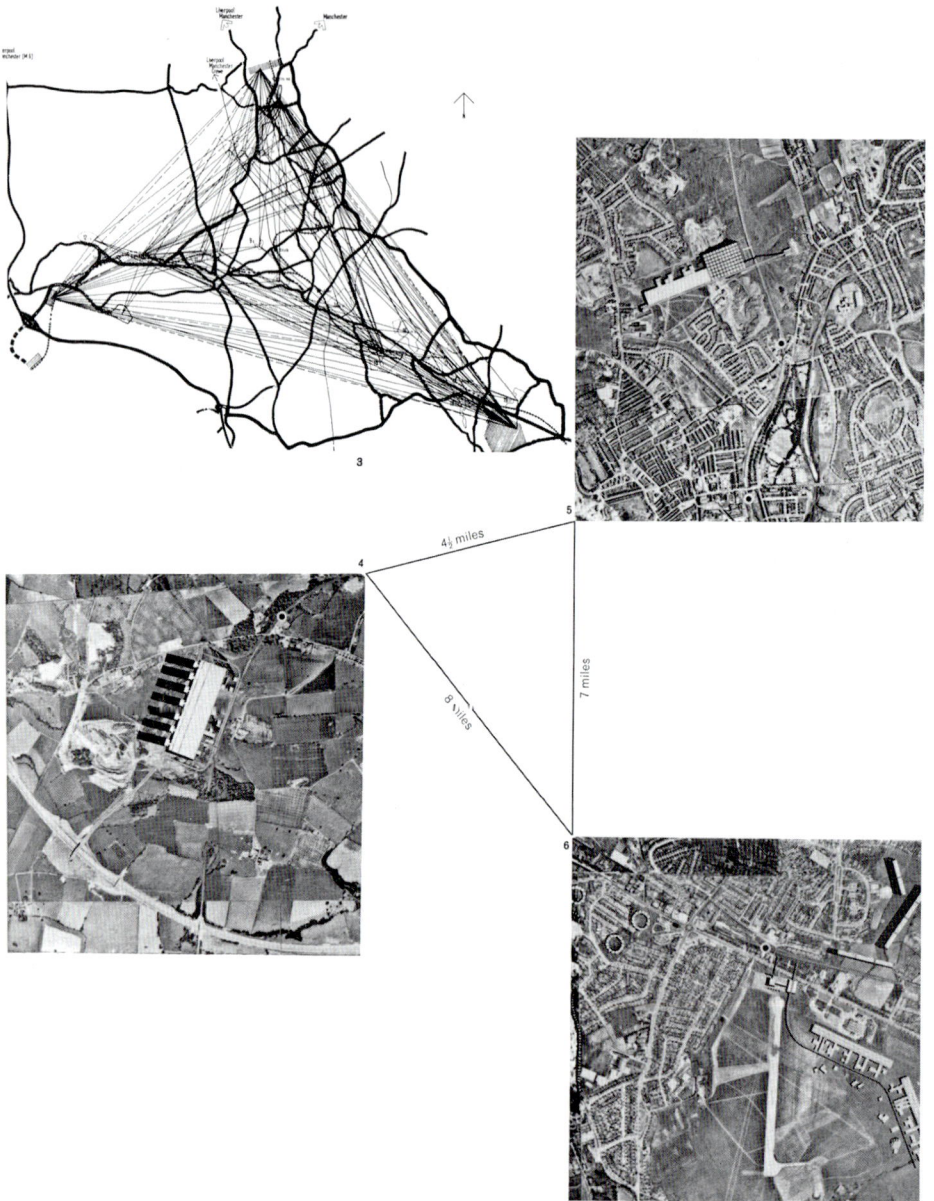

The three transfer areas Pitts Hill, Madeley, and Meir, with a connecting network of rails and streets and a mobile university on tracks (Silverdale, Hanley, Tunstall/Pitts Hill, and Fenton/Longton), make up Potteries Thinkbelt.

Potteries Thinkbelt_*Cedric Price*

▲ Madeley, the largest of the transfer areas, connects Potteries Thinkbelt to the M6 motorway and has facilities for the construction, storage, and loading of mobile teaching and living modules. Seven hotel towers offer residential space for those employed on a short- or medium-term basis. ▼ New residential typologies ("Battery," "Sprawl," and "Capsule" housing) among the slag heaps in Hanley.

Potteries Thinkbelt_*Cedric Price*

AGAINST NECROPHILIA
Stephen Mullin

———

———

Where a building, or an agglomeration of buildings, had effectively ceased to perform a useful function, it should be removed. Cedric Price's celebrated response to the fire that devastated York Minster cathedral—"Pull it down"—is perhaps the most extreme example of this approach, though it contains more than a touch of self-parody.

Quips like this made him an easy target for earnest conservationists, who berated him for his advocacy of "wasteful" limited-life buildings. But, as Price pointed out, buildings that do not serve their users well are themselves wasteful of human and material resources, and the longer a building lasts the more likely it is to function inefficiently. Furthermore, they can be recycled effectively by exploiting existing structures for that proportion of functionality that they still retain, just as new extraction methods have made it economically viable to exploit the waste dumps formed by old industrial processes.

In his Bat Hat project, Price argued that the only useful part of the redundant Battersea Power Station was its striking profile: its "hat" of four chimneys rising from a rectangular base. Why not slice it off and support it on a new structure? And in the OCH project, the existence of the London Hydraulic Main next to the large, derelict cafeteria building that he had been asked to remodel provided the key to an economic solution: it could be used to power a series of movable floors for an immensely flexible entertainment center.

These were single interventions in the urban fabric. In the Thinkbelt, however, the scale was so large, and the opportunities so diverse, that it was possible to realize a whole new landscape quite unlike the patterning of city structure offered by orthodox thinking at that time. It was a landscape constantly in transformation, renewing itself in response to changing demands: messy, crumbly, lively, and never static. Even the large, quasi-permanent structures proposed—the three transfer areas and the Crate and Battery housing developments—were merely frameworks for evolving uses.

Price himself freely admitted that it was impossible—and dangerous—to guess what form the Thinkbelt might take in the future. Once he had started up this huge generator, who knew what new industries, what new enterprises might come out of it?

Price's projects in urban areas questioned the continuing need for built fabric. For Glasgow, he felt that a major food-growing complex would be "a more valid regenerator of beneficial city-centre activities than a marina or opera house." And when he prepared competition proposals for the redevelopment of the Department of the Environment headquarters in Central London, he seized with delight on my information that the three existing towers encased wartime concrete static water-tanks that had themselves been recycled from prewar gasholders. He proposed reusing these concrete cylinders, which were situated on highly valuable government real estate, as public swimming pools and water gardens.

The models put forward by Price in his projects are becoming increasingly relevant to the requirements of a postindustrial society like England. Like it or not, we in Europe are living in the ruins of our past, and the choice is ours as to whether we will allow our lives, and those of our descendants, to be warped by undue reverence for these artifacts.

Sir John Soane, whom Price greatly admired, famously chose to exhibit at the Royal Academy his masterpiece, the Bank of England, as a ruin. I sometimes wish that when I was drawing the Madeley Transfer Area for the Potteries Thinkbelt project, I had made a similar study of those buildings in ruins.

―

The author worked in the office of Cedric Price from 1964 to 1970.

BAT HAT: REDESIGN OF BATTERSEA POWER STATION
London, 1984
Cedric Price

The architect Cedric Price proposed to leave just the four iconic smokestacks of a decommissioned power station on the banks of the Thames and to tear down the brick walls of this industrial monument in order to reduce the high maintenance costs. The steel-frame construction produces an astonishing optical effect: the smokestacks seem to float, while the silhouette of the building, which contributes so much to the image of the city, is retained. The space freed up under the structure is left undefined by Price, creating a gigantic experimental field for ambitions and interventions. (Ed.)

"URBAN RENEWAL": NOT JUST DEMOLITION APPROACHES TO PREFAB HOUSING DISTRICTS
Wolfgang Kil

Large residential areas, New Towns from the conceptual and formal repertoire of modernism, are no longer popular in most West European countries. In the countries formerly governed by "really existing socialism," the change in system was followed by a rush to adopt the Western culture scheme as quickly as possible and to be "ashamed" of the mass construction of large ensembles of social housing. But that is not enough to shed this unpopular legacy: too many apartment buildings were constructed in this supposedly "monotonous, anonymous, and soulless" type of building to simply get rid of them. Even if one does not appreciate this type of housing, it cannot be dispensed with.

Consequently, the most frequently asked questions are of necessity: What can large residential areas mean for a city? For whom are they important? Today? In the future? Can they be made suitable for the future, whatever it may look like? The questions imply that we are dealing with a kind of city especially designed for a particular, or particularly problematic, group of residents. But here it is necessary to insist on the opposite position: large housing developments—that is to say, residential districts planned as a whole (referred to in East Germany, in a phrase as abbreviated as it is disparaging, as *Plattenbau* [a prefabricated concrete construction])—are, in the long run, entirely normal urban situations. All that is necessary is to not deny them their normalization.

The *normalization* of industrially constructed mass housing, and its adoption into the stratifications of natural urban history, was a process that required functional corrections and overlapping uses. The word *urbanism* was never projected onto drawing boards. On the contrary, "The space as a living creature withdraws itself from total planning and design control and sooner or later will be nothing like the plans, perspectives, and pictures that were once developed on the landscape architects' computer screens or the artist's sketchbook. Even the most elaborate computer simulations cannot get anywhere close to keeping up with the liveliness and atmospheric density of the real space."[1]

How one might avoid the inevitable one-dimensionality of master plans can be considered in view of the process of diversification in which the residents of a development appropriate it in practice (usually to the horror of the planners involved): at some point the artificially created urban form faces a structural crisis. The ideal conceptions of the plan are exhausted, and from that point on "real life" determines how things will progress. Spaces and lots are reoccupied; connections among paths are established anew; and places obtain new significance. Businesses move into residential areas that were originally monostructural: agencies, ateliers, workshops, and medical and legal practices. Rooms once used to dry laundry are now used to sell bananas, tea, or insurance. The space once occupied by a large restaurant now has fitness equipment; the former storeroom for the caretaker was occupied first by a passport photo studio and then by a copy shop. At the crossroads of public transportation, the kiosks become as numerous as in a bazaar. To the extent that these kinds of new structures of use become stable, they result in construction measures to meet their needs; sooner or later, functional variety will lead to changes to the built form, and hence bring an end to abstractly, clearly shaped figures of space.[2]

The redesign of a public housing development in Alençon in Normandy, France, by the architect Lucien Kroll and the sociologist Paul Wallez in 1978 is one of the first and best-known examples of how monofunctional postwar developments can develop new urban qualities when converted. The goal was to shake off the negative image of a "poor neighborhood." On the basis of surveys of citizens, a plan was developed that took the residential structure of the 1960s and transformed it into a varied urban landscape by reducing the size of outer areas, employing an assortment of building styles, and combining different uses.

For variety and stimulating complexity to emerge at all, time must pass. But the New Towns of eastern Germany do not have time. Dramatic declines in population mean that most of them have to reduce the available housing, and the primary method for achieving that is to demolish precast concrete buildings. Hence most of the New Towns in eastern Germany do not last long enough for the process of normalization to take place. On top of that, the demolition of buildings that are visibly intact—well before their construction begins to show wear and tear—reinforces the tiresome cliché that prefab concrete buildings represent an unsuitable method of construction or an impracticable building type.

There is, of course, plenty to criticize about the types of buildings that were constructed en masse. But who is it who decided that, as they stand now, their possibilities are exhausted? "Precast concrete buildings are entirely normal building types that simply were occupied too soon, in a raw state of construction, so to speak. All that is necessary is to bring the building process to a conclusion, to give them a solid finish, to show off materials of respectable quality, and then these buildings are totally OK." The architect Frank Zimmermann of Cottbus knows what he is talking about, because he has already received numerous prizes for his various reconstruction projects.[3] His projects are never about cosmetics for the facade, which create a superficial illusion of "individuality" and "variety" without really addressing the heart of the matter—the similarity of the apartment types. In his projects, it is often the case that little remains of the old building but its basic structure.

In the meantime, the Cottbus architect is no longer a lonely pioneer. His approach has found imitators in Dresden-Gorbitz, Magdeburg-Neustädter Feld, Schwedt, Templin, and even tiny Eggesin in West Pomerania. The state program Stadtumbau Ost (Urban Restructuring in Eastern Germany) spurred this change in attitude by indicating that it is not sufficient to demolish residential space; the quality of life has to be improved in the neighborhoods that remain. Often enough, this can be achieved simply by reducing the number of floors, and because the real-estate companies are plagued by vacancy rates that force them to court renters, they are more open to creative modernization. In the Südstadt section of Leinefelde, Thuringia, a real "architecture exhibition" has resulted, with a wide variety of reconstruction approaches. It is probably the most effective advertisement for a true *Rückbau,* or "deconstruction," as an alternative to an urban transformation policy that is based exclusively on demolition: "reducing within the housing stock," not destroying that stock. Certainly the costs for such improvements in quality are *within* the realm of "cost-efficient new construction," but they are beyond the reach of many property owners facing bankruptcy. Even more problematic is the decision about how many residents need to have moved away to justify offering alternative living spaces of greater value.

The twelve-story buildings in Berlin-Hellersdorf, which have not been modified externally, now have new maisonette apartments which are striking for their unusual window formats. The sculpturally rich forms and holiday-like colors of the once eleven-story, now three-story, buildings of the Ahrensfelder Terrassen in Berlin-Marzahn immediately make the improvements in quality evident to the passing viewer. The appearance contradicts stubborn prejudice about such buildings. Concrete need not be a building material for eternity. The precast concrete structures that are supposedly so rigid are in fact flexible and just as suited for repurposing as any traditional brick building from the late nineteenth century. They finally are being treated accordingly: when the first phase of the building's

▲ Zimmermann + Partner Architekten recycled an eleven-story precast residential building in Cottbus-Madlow in 2000–2002 by using the concrete slabs to create five urban villas. ▼ The architect Thomas Hillig transformed a two-story precast building in Berlin-Hohenschönhausen in 2002–2004, in no small measure by enlarging the wall openings and creating new ones.

"Urban Renewal": Not Just Demolition_*Wolfgang Kil*

As part of the "deconstruction" of Leinefelde-Worbis in Thuringia, between 1998 and 2004 one of the first architecturally ambitious attempts was made to partially deconstruct East German precast concrete buildings, transforming a once quite monotonous construction method by means of architectural and functional diversity.

▲ Muck Petzet, for example, was able to circumvent the complete demolition of a building by creating a renters' center on the ground floor of the partially deconstructed high-rise and using materials from the demolition to modulate the exterior grounds. ▼ Stefan Forster Architekten deconstructed a 650-foot-long precast concrete building to create eight urban villas, whose floor plans were adapted to the individual preferences of the future renters.

use has run out, the creativity of a second generation of designers comes in to produce new forms of living and take into account higher expectations of quality,[4] or to find room in redesignated ground floors for facilities that previously were lacking. Maisonettes and roof terraces, elevators, concierges, and social stations for the elderly—when such advantages are read off, who is still reminded of the "raw forms" of the buildings that once bore abstract abbreviations like WBS 70 or P2?

This also makes clear what really matters in redesigning prefab concrete buildings: the conversion of buildings is a normal process, and every single building develops its individual "social biography" as it is adapted to suit changing needs. In doing so, it becomes an example of the great cultural project that urgently needs to be confronted: the *historical normalization* of modernism's planned worlds.

The widespread critique of that era is too simplistic when it presumes that the initial plans are irrevocably rigid. After all, the late-nineteenth-century neighborhoods that are considered superior today were originally "planned cities," artificial forms based on a master plan,[5] and hence for their contemporaries, and even more so for the generation that followed, a pure expression of contempt for the human race and of sheer greed for profit. It took about eighty years for this bogey of urbanism to give way to the idealized model for today's city. And if one then compares the original state of these "barracks for rent" with the standards for how they are used today, it is clear that it is only possible to love these old houses because they are no longer what they once were.

The normalization of modernism's planned worlds—of industrially produced buildings as well as of functional urban development—is the next challenge coming up, throughout the world. As long as precast concrete buildings are considered to be merely "demolition reserves" in favor of historical city centers, the global perspective of the problem will be lost. For the global dimension is the *ecological* one: even modernist buildings represent a resource! Those who believe an unpopular phenomenon can be dispensed with simply by "blowing it up" have not yet considered the actual, purely physical dimensions of the reality of modernism—not only in eastern Europe but especially there. That cannot be thrown away. That has to be transformed, and so it has to be brought into the future.

Translated from the German by Steven Lindberg

Notes

1. Udo Weilacher, "Ecological Aesthetics in Landscape Architecture Today?" trans. Michael Robinson, in *Ecological Aesthetics: Art in Environmental Design; Theory and Practice,* ed. Heike Strelow (Basel: Birkhäuser, 2004), 118.
2. Unfortunately, strict regulations in Germany make spontaneous and informal urban activities enormously difficult. Characteristically, the biggest progress in the "urbanization" of social housing areas in eastern Germany occurred during the period of anarchy: that is, during the largely lawless periods before and after German reunification in 1990.
3. For example, the Bauherrenpreis of 2003 for his modest dismantling of a twelve-story building in Sachsendorf-Madlow: its concrete panels were reassembled in the same location to create six small "urban villas."
4. One of the most important points of criticism with respect to the P2 series of apartments—namely, the kitchens located in the interior of the apartment—was corrected in a wide variety of floor plans.
5. Consider this for comparison: at the end of the nineteenth century, the Wilmersdorf district of Berlin, which today is considered the ideal of bourgeois urbanism, was an enormous construction site on the far edge of the city limit, where within ten years residential space for roughly one hundred thousand people was created. The circumstances and figures are approximately the same as those for Marzahn about a century later.

WIMBY! (WELCOME INTO MY BACKYARD!)
INTERNATIONAL BUILDING EXHIBITION ROTTERDAM-HOOGVLIET
Rotterdam, The Netherlands, 2001–2010
Crimson Architectural Historians

Green pastures surface on both sides of the subway line, willows mark the course of narrow country roads, sheep graze the banks. Then, all of a sudden, one of the new housing estates appears and we arrive at Hoogvliet Station, lined with high-rise blocks and large apartment buildings. It is Rotterdam's farthest outpost, 12 kilometers away from the center. Hoogvliet is a veritable New Town, an autonomous urban unit designed in the late 1940s according to the principles of the English New Towns near London.

The small medieval village of Hoogvliet, situated in the immediate vicinity of the Shell refinery, was singled out as a "nucleus of growth," suitable for housing the labor force needed by the expanding port. Gradually, the old village was to be replaced by a completely new Hoogvliet. The drawings of Hoogvliet, made by architect and town planner Lotte Stam-Beese (who had been associated with the Congrès Internationaux pour l'Architecture), radiate a mundane, urbane atmosphere—Hoogvliet was to be a proud and independent urban core next to Rotterdam.

Successes and Failures

The architecture of the houses, schools, and shops was sober and homogeneous. The functionalist feeling was greatly enhanced by the industrial building methods that were applied in Hoogvliet. Apart from that, it expressed one of the great ideals of the time: social equality. An abundance of open spaces and collective gardens compensated for the small houses; the transparency and openness of the public greenery represented a new, open urban society. Naturally, traffic was organized according to the latest ideas on efficiency. Cars, bicycles, and pedestrians were provided with their own special lanes. These were combined to create wide traffic arteries provided with ample greenery: a modern version of American parkways. All components of the urban structure were endowed with the qualities of modernism and efficiency, and at the same time manifested an idealistic social model.

Like most postwar utopias, the ideal New Town of Hoogvliet soon experienced serious difficulties. Instead of fostering social cohesion, the neighborhood units promoted a feeling of contingency. The size of the houses was seen as too small. Lacking an extra room that could be used as a study, the houses offered in Hoogvliet were bound to have a devastating effect on the development of individual personality, and at the same time hampered opportunities to have a harmonious family life. Furthermore, what had been conceived as one of the blessings of Hoogvliet, its situation at a stone's throw from the Shell refinery, turned out to be a major setback, as a series of accidents and the continuously polluted air demonstrated. On January 20, 1968, an explosion shattered most of the windows in Hoogvliet, dramatically changing its image from a friendly, efficient, and modern city to a place better avoided.

Planners and public alike forgot the idealistic project that Hoogvliet was meant to be, and the ambitious public center was realized only in small part. Terraced houses were built on the area that was left open. Even today, the area near the old village church gives the impression of a suburban wasteland, used for parking only. Instead of the urban, even semi-metropolitan character originally meant to single out Hoogvliet's housing estates, the last ones that were built have a typically suburban character, defined by small, meandering streets lined with single-family homes. Hoogvliet has become a mutant: half New Town, half suburb.

Ghetto

It may be true that Hoogvliet failed to live up to its promises of a New Town, and it is hard to deny that the dream of the modernist city became discredited here even before half of the project had been realized. Even so, Hoogvliet does exist and is here to stay. In the mid-1990s, over thirty thousand people lived here, some of them the middle-aged "pioneers" of the 1950s and 1960s. They liked Hoogvliet because to them it was a quiet place at a comfortable distance from the increasingly problem-ridden metropolis of Rotterdam. Many of the former inhabitants of Hoogvliet—those who could afford to move—had left the tiny, noisy homes and settled in the bigger houses of the surrounding cities. The inexpensive houses of Hoogvliet attracted new inhabitants: Hoogvliet became a refuge for immigrants, many of them from the Dutch Antilles. They took up residence in the northern parts of Hoogvliet, where their different lifestyles soon caused trouble. It did not take long for a schism to develop between the suburban, well-to-do southern parts, which were mainly inhabited by native Dutch people, and the northern parts, which were increasingly dominated by socially weaker groups. The housing blocks in this area were especially small, built in sombor brick and located in the least desirable part of Hoogvliet: close to the oil refinery and alongside the highway. In the 1990s, these streets were transformed into what soon became known as a ghetto. Junkies, drugs dealers, and vandalism made the area an ideal topic for a documentary on Dutch television, which further strengthened the image of Hoogvliet as a sad and lost neighborhood.

Revitalizing Hoogvliet

To stop the downward trend, Hoogvliet proclaimed itself a disaster area in the mid-1990s. First of all, the problematic residential areas in northern Hoogvliet were raided by the combined forces of the police, the public health service, tax collectors, and bailiffs, who combed out all the apartments in an attempt to stop all illegal activities. Drugs dealers were imprisoned, defaulters indicted, illegal tenants chased away. The apartments were demolished. Thus, the most disgraceful part of Hoogvliet had been dealt with in a mettlesome manner, in part to set an example for the projects to come. The local authorities worked together with two housing corporations, which recently had been privatized and owned most of the housing stock in Hoogvliet, in an attempt to improve housing conditions. No less than five thousand homes, 30% of the housing stock, were to be demolished, mainly apartments of 56 square meters or less, which no longer could live up to people's expectations in the 1990s. Marketable homes were to take their place. By creating a more diverse palette of housing types and reducing the rate of subsidized tenement housing (which used to be 70%), a more diverse and more affluent population was expected to be willing to move to Hoogvliet.

▲ The "Heerlijkheid" project by FAT takes up observable trends in Hoogvliet, such as "do-it-yourself applications" that compress things and events in space and time. ▼ The new community center Heerlijkheid next to the freeway. The story of Hoogvliet is told in the hall.

The revitalization campaign for Hoogvliet was clearly an answer to concrete needs, but it also reflected fundamental changes in the Dutch welfare state. The state withdrew from public life, a strategy that led to almost complete privatization of public housing. The housing corporations shook off their traditional role as social organizations and were run as semi-commercial companies. This led to strategies determined more by administrative and commercial concerns than by social ideas. This is why they chose a generic approach for all reconstruction projects, no matter how different the original situation may be. Everywhere, low-rise, mostly single-family homes took the place of high-rise buildings and apartment houses; private gardens replaced collective greenery; and small neighborhood shopping centers disappeared, leaving large central shopping malls in their stead. Low-cost tenement houses were suppressed, while expensive owner-occupied houses were strongly promoted.

To correct the negative image of Hoogvliet, it was decided to replace most of the urban structure, the public spaces, and the housing stock with something with a more "contemporary" outlook. The characteristic composition of elementary blocks floating in space, so typical for the modern city, was considered out of date. They were replaced by enclosed spaces and traditional urban motifs: the inner-city street, the return of the building line as the main organizational principle, the square, the boulevard. Collective spaces, a fundamental principle in postwar town planning, had to make way for private gardens. From now on, the individual and his personal lifestyle were to determine Hoogvliet.

In short: the most characteristic feature of the 1990s revitalization scheme was the urge to eradicate the modern model on which the original plan for Hoogvliet had been based. The town planners' main aspiration was to reinvent Hoogvliet. Even though they returned to tested, traditional models, their ambition to bulldoze most of the existing New Town out of the way is reminiscent of the tabula rasa mentality of those who built Hoogvliet in the 1950s.

WiMBY!

The WiMBY! movement—Welcome into My Backyard!—began in 1999 as a brave attempt to counter the prevailing currents in urban politics and the town-planning profession, which were entirely focused on spectacular and highly prestigious projects in Rotterdam's inner city. It aimed to instead direct attention to the slum-like conditions in many of the postwar housing estates. Felix Rottenberg, former chairman of the Dutch social democratic party, has led the management team since 2001. The themes of the movement are defined by two architectural historians from Crimson, Michelle Provoost, the author of this article, and Wouter Vanstiphout.

What could WiMBY! possibly add to a planning machinery that was already in full swing? Its specific tasks were to improve the quality of the revitalization scheme, to introduce innovative concepts on the social, economic, urban, and architectural levels, and—most important—to make these proposals really happen. We chose to concentrate on the existing planning machinery's blind spots, and decided to cause a coordinated series of incidents that should have a marked effect on Hoogvliet. The projects that we embarked upon were to set an example for similar projects in postwar reconstruction areas elsewhere. Apart from engaging in concrete projects, we also aimed to change people's mentality. Our focal point was the existing substance of Hoogvliet, both in physical terms (the buildings) and in social terms (the people).

As in so many reconstructed housing estates, there had hardly been time to reflect upon the object of so much planning fervor: the New Town of Hoogvliet. Nor had the results of research by sociologists, traffic experts, and town-planning historians been properly assessed. WiMBY! identified the need to correct this as a prerequisite for reinterpreting the worn-out New Town. It aimed to rediscover its now hidden qualities as an unknown, captivating urban entity with its own peculiarities. The guiding principle of a reconstruction process should be to reinterpret and reuse what is already there. As a consequence, some projects—the "Estate Hoogvliet," "Hoogvliet Inside Out," "WiMBY! Week"—were on the verge of becoming social community work. Sometimes initiatives that bore no direct relation to architecture were most effective in presenting alternative approaches for over-ambitious, large-scale reconstruction projects. Temporary interventions, cultural reprogramming, or a onetime event facilitated a rediscovery of the New Town's hidden positive qualities. Above all, they brought to light unexpected urban potentialities, which can inspire future strategies. This potential is located both in the inhabitants and in the existing urban fabric.

Anti–Tabula Rasa

We were absolutely sure that if Hoogvliet was to become a new, vital, and attractive city in ten years, nothing could be more counterproductive than to start from scratch. The tabula rasa mentality may have been useful in the postwar reconstruction era, but in this case it was totally useless. The use of existing qualities can help prevent a New Town from becoming generic. While the planning machinery set in motion by the corporations continued to prepare the demolition of thousands of homes, postulating the values of a new, quiet, suburban, and middle-class Hoogvliet to be created in its place, WiMBY! worked on an entirely different concept for the city. Hoogvliet was to resemble itself and not try to emulate other cities. It was to find ways to deal with its green, village-like character and the ethnic make-up of its inhabitants, and to cherish what positive opportunities manifested themselves. This approach called for a thorough analysis of Hoogvliet, focusing not only on problems and difficulties but also on the positive aspects. Nobody had mentioned the profuse greenery, and public gardens were regarded only as wasteland waiting to be developed. Nobody drew attention to the potentialities of the large Antillean community; the problems of recent years had only left room for negative feelings. Thus, many qualities that could have inspired the revitalization process were simply disregarded—an approach that seems inherent in Rotterdam's "progressive" tradition.

The analysis had distinct therapeutic features because it showed the residents how unique their New Town really is. Thus, their ingrained inferiority complex could begin to heal. We hoped to promote a change of mentality that might help to curb purely negative ways of dealing with the existing situation. One of the earliest urban projects of WiMBY! seems to confirm that this strategy can be successful.

Logica

We required not an all-encompassing master plan but a different type of town-planning document, a set of instruments that could help steer the processes already at work, directing and manipulating them into a coherent policy, a joint approach. This is how "Logica, a Town-Planning Manual for Hoogvliet" came into being. Designed by

Maxwan Architects and Planners, Logica identified the qualities that can be regarded as Hoogvliet's main characteristics. Four urban features were believed to result in a consistent structure: the green buffer surrounding the New Town, the isolated situation of the individual neighborhoods, the green parkways in between, and the overall greenery of Hoogvliet.

Clear choices were then presented as each of the four structuring elements were put to the test. Were they to be respected, or could one do without them? These issues were addressed in the so-called Logica committee, which consisted of representatives from all of the parties involved: planners, local politicians, and housing corporations. Logica then shifted from being a plan to becoming a negotiation process. The outcome was a binding choice for one of the twenty-four models that could be composed through different combinations of the variables identified in the negotiation process. Remarkably, the preferred strategy was to conserve and enhance all of the existing qualities.

New Collectives

Whereas Logica addressed Hoogvliet's urban and physical qualities, other WiMBY! projects focused on its social qualities. We wanted to show what the inhabitants themselves had to offer. Working with single mothers from the Antillean community, we found that they needed forms of housing that combined the individual home with collective amenities and collective public spaces. The reconstruction campaign's implicit mantra—"collective spaces have become impossible to maintain because the contemporary New Town lacks a collective mentality"—may be true for the average Dutch family, but it does not apply to other groups. These considerations fostered two projects, which we organized in cooperation with the housing corporations. They are intended to accommodate new collective housing arrangements. For the first project, in one of the maisonette buildings—the most endangered type of housing from the 1960s—a group of single mothers from the Antilles is provided with their own individual homes as well as a collective room that can be used as a day nursery, a study, or a café. Some of the surrounding public spaces will be designated "safe collective areas" for children to play and mothers to eat or socialize together.

The second initiative attempts to attract categories of people who so far have avoided Hoogvliet. The usual single-family house with a garden can be found anywhere. As such, it cannot induce a person to move to Hoogvliet. *Cohousing*, however, is a different form of housing that combines twenty individual homes and a collective amenity that is assigned to them and managed by the twenty households living there. It can be a daycare center, an ecological garden, a car-repair workshop, or a sports facility. In this way, the oppressive connotations associated with the collective arrangements of the 1950s are replaced by self-defined contemporary forms that combine individual homes with a wide variety of opportunities to use public space.

Hoogvliet Inside Out

A rich diversity of people live behind Hoogvliet's anonymous facades from the 1950s and 1960s. They differ in income, ethnicity, and lifestyle, and express these differences in the way they dress and the way they decorate their homes. For the photo project *Hoogvliet Inside Out*, dozens of people were invited to have their picture taken in a traveling photo tent. All kinds of people showed up: elderly persons with their walkers,

The Heerlijkheid Hoogvliet park was officially opened in August 2003 with a large festival.

mothers with perms, tough-acting hip-hop boys. These portraits were complemented by interior photographs taken by the designers Gerard Hadders and Edith Gruson. The portraits and interior photos were then blown up to larger-than-life billboards, which were placed near the highway and at street crossings. They also were used during WiMBY! Week.

WiMBY! Week was held in December 2002 in a now demolished row of homes for elderly persons. All of the WiMBY! projects were presented here, and at the time half of the U-shaped row of houses was still occupied. The facades of the empty houses were used for huge billboards of the interior photos; the WiMBY! projects were presented inside the houses. In one of them, people could have their portraits taken while the elderly people living nearby provided them with coffee. In this way, WiMBY! Week showcased not only a number of different WiMBY! projects, but also the wide variety of people living in Hoogvliet.

The "School Parasites"

Educational facilities are particularly important in depressed areas. Much needed to be done to bring Hoogvliet's schools up to date. Most of them had been built in the 1960s, many according to the standard types then designed by the municipal authorities. As a result, there was a serious lack of the special rooms needed in present-day education, and there was hardly any suitable space for tutoring pupils on an individual basis or for libraries, music performances, and the like. In addition, some pupils need to be looked after during holidays or after school. To improve the facilities of primary schools, WiMBY! developed the so-called School Parasites, which were designed in cooperation with the Parasite Foundation. In three schools, beautiful facilities were created where the pupils can cook, eat, work on their own, or rehearse plays. The plans by Barend Koolhaas, Onix, and Christoph Seyferth can be industrially produced. Apart from educational purposes, the facilities also accommodate neighborhood festivities, meetings, and parent gatherings.

The Estate Hoogvliet

The Estate Hoogvliet will be the ultimate test case. All that WiMBY! has stood for the last four years culminates in this project. The Estate Hoogvliet is a summer park for recreation and entertainment. It is situated in the green buffer between Hoogvliet and the highway in the periphery of the "oil neighborhood." It comprises several components that have been developed in close cooperation with various groups in Hoogvliet: an arboretum, a graveyard for pets, a nature playground, sports fields, and the Villa. The local inhabitants initiated all these amenities and will be engaged in managing and maintaining them. In the park itself there are spaces and facilities for all kinds of activities, such as picnic tables, barbeque grills, and a pond for paddling. The Villa acts as an eye-catcher in the center of the estate. It was designed by the London-based firm FAT Architects, which also planned the park. The "decorated shed" à la Robert Venturi contains the symbols and signs of a popular and recognizable (local) visual language, which can be understood by anyone.

Even for fleeting passersby, the need for a park like Estate Hoogvliet is easily grasped, for in Hoogvliet nothing ever happens. The Villa is going to change this. There will be musical performances, plays will be enacted, and family celebrations can be held here. By keeping ourselves submerged in the wonderful world of Hoogvliet and engaging in a never-ending pursuit of the creative forces inherent in it, we believe WiMBY! can contribute to a renaissance of the old New Town. Hoogvliet's negative image of a city inhabited by a dull NiMBY! population (Not in My Backyard!) will be transformed into the positive image of a city with a peculiar mix of nature and industry, young and elderly people, and people from the Dutch Antilles. A place, that is, that makes its inhabitants proud and its visitors curious.

Text by Michelle Provoost

BATTLE OF MATÉRIEL WITH NO WINNERS
TRASH, ART, AND THE LIMITS OF RECYCLING
Claudia Wahjudi

From the used jackets and dresses that "documenta" participant Christine Hill sold in her *Volksboutique,* to the trinkets of plastic and plush that the Canadian artist Laura Kikauka auctioned in her trash house *Bauhütte Gemütlichkeit Schmalzwald,* to the *Selbstbedienungszentrale* in Berlin, a free service provided by artists for used household goods and private services; from the composting toilets of Atelier Van Lieshout to the shipping containers that Dirk Paschke and Daniel Milohnic converted into a factory swimming pool for the Kokerei Zollverein—trash, garbage, and the reprocessing of superfluous objects and materials have become natural elements and themes in contemporary art.

Since the late 1950s—that is, since prosperity moved into postwar households—trash has appeared continuously in (Western) art. It has, however, meanwhile also become clear that art's approach to trash has changed as society's attitude toward trash changed: the found object, which served only as material, has been joined by garbage as a symbolic critique of consumer society and by the idea of trash as waste material with real value.

Trash means something different in developed industrial countries than in developing countries. Trash had a very different standing under socialism than under capitalism. Worldwide developments such as oil crises or globalization have influenced its valence as well as its manifestations. Art reflects on these changes. Since the surplus of goods and materials in industrial societies has met with unemployment and impoverishment, art has opened up niches for a barter and gratis society in which secondhand goods can be traded and trash creates jobs. Since sustainability has become a topic, art also makes proposals for recycling: for the recycling of plastic as well as for the reuse of vacant buildings or entire sections of a city.

Take the works of Dan Peterman, for example. Born in the United States in 1960, the artist acquired the Resource Center in Chicago: a nonprofit center that repurchased scrap materials, served as a site for various recycling initiatives, and provided Peterman with materials for his works. The themes of the artist's work include the production and consumption of goods, environmental pollution and its social consequences, and the value of the material that he reintroduced into the production cycle. For example, Peterman created modules for utility furniture out of recycled plastic, which he employed in *Running Table* (1997): a 100-foot-long picnic table with benches placed in a Chicago park to encourage socializing. Peterman also builds objects from bottles, uses crown corks for pasta cutters, exploits horse manure to heat a junked bus that serves as emergency shelter for the homeless, incorporates bulk trash in installations, and uses soft cheese to absorb hazardous materials in contaminated areas. His methods mirror the four forms of recycling: reuse (bottles), extended use (compost as heating material), recycling (of plastic), and altered use (used glass for eyeglasses).

The Limits of Growth

The story of trash in art begins with Dada—with Marcel Duchamp's ready-made *Bicycle Wheel* (1913) and Kurt Schwitters's *Merz-Bildern*. The story continues after the Second World War with Jean Tinguely's kinetic sculptures from iron parts and the beer cans on

Jasper Johns's paintings. In the 1960s Wolf Vostell invited people to a happening at an auto dump in West Berlin. Then Dieter Roth let food rot under plastic. And in the 1980s artists' groups like Mutoid Waste Company depicted the end of heavy industry with sculptures made of scrap metal. Trash art continues to be a "celebration of the material,"[1] drawing on plentiful resources. Only when the blast furnaces had been extinguished and the miners put out of work could recycling art compete on an ideal level with wallowing in trash. In Vienna, for example, the artists' group WochenKlausur initiated a workshop in 2002 for "upcycling" used furniture and household objects: it was intended to provide employment for recovering drug addicts. *Testing the Waters* (1995–), in turn—a landscape art project by Julie Bargmann and Stacy Levy—cleaned up an entire contaminated mining site in Pennsylvania and enhanced it with culture. It was followed by works with similar aims, such as the international architectural exhibitions Emscher Park in the Ruhr Valley (1989-1999) and Fürst-Pückler-Land in Brandenburg (2000–), which used culture and architecture to transform "forbidden terrain" into public spaces for recreation.

These new approaches to trash required not only separating the concept of art from that of the object but also and above all creating a new understanding of trash. As the art historian Martin Damus wrote, "Under the title *The Limits to Growth,* the Club of Rome published its study 'on the predicament of mankind' in 1972. The recognition that natural resources were limited and the increase in petroleum prices and the so-called oil crisis of 1973, which occurred during a worldwide recession, caused profound uncertainty in industrial societies."[2] The social movements of Western industrialized countries called for environmental protection and sustainability, but roughly twenty years would pass before those topics appeared on the agendas of parliaments and corporations. Art, by contrast, in Damus's view, meanwhile pursued "individual mythologies," a withdrawal into the private sphere.[3] That did not preclude the use of trash, quite the contrary: "The enhanced status of trash and the increased admission of the unclean that began in the 1960s with art but is found in architecture and design as well can thus be understood as an attempt to counter the sterility of modernism," wrote Roger Fayet and Peter Stohler on the occasion of the exhibition "Alles Abfall? Recycling im Design" (Is It All Trash? Recycling in Design) in Zurich in 2003.[4]

A Good Business
Until the fall of the iron curtain, trash and recycling in art were a matter for the West. In the history of East European art, trash scarcely appears at all: the difference can be accounted for by the different economies. The citizens' movements of Eastern Europe criticized above all industrial air, soil, and water pollution, and not residential trash, for in their economy of shortages the leftovers of their relatively small level of consumption of mass products still had their value. In East Germany, for example, the combine Sekundärrohstofferfassung (SERO; "Secondary Resource Collection") had citizens systematically collecting and bringing in reusable material from households in exchange for remuneration. In 1988 it had approximately seventeen thousand collecting points and other facilities, most of which closed after reunification in favor of the "Dual System." In developing countries, in turn, recycling is often a question of sheer survival. Hence, the contemporary garbage art from developing countries currently making the rounds of international biennial exhibitions and exchange projects is also concerned with the relationship of poverty and ethics—as in Teresa Margolles's installations with body parts—or with the

DOOR RECYCLING
Halle-Neustadt, Germany, 2003
Raumlabor et al.

—

As part of the Hotel Neustadt festival, the interior doors of apartments no longer in use were recycled as building material that could be used in many ways. Precast concrete buildings that were vacant and slated for demolition served as the pool for materials. About 450 mass-produced P2 interior doors from Halle-Silberhöhe were converted into beds, shelves, meandering espresso bar furniture, honeycomb labyrinths (by Syntosil, see top illustration on facing page), ramps for BMX courses (by Raumlabor, middle illustration), and miniature golf courses (by Christoph Brucker, bottom illustration). (Ed.)

—
—
—

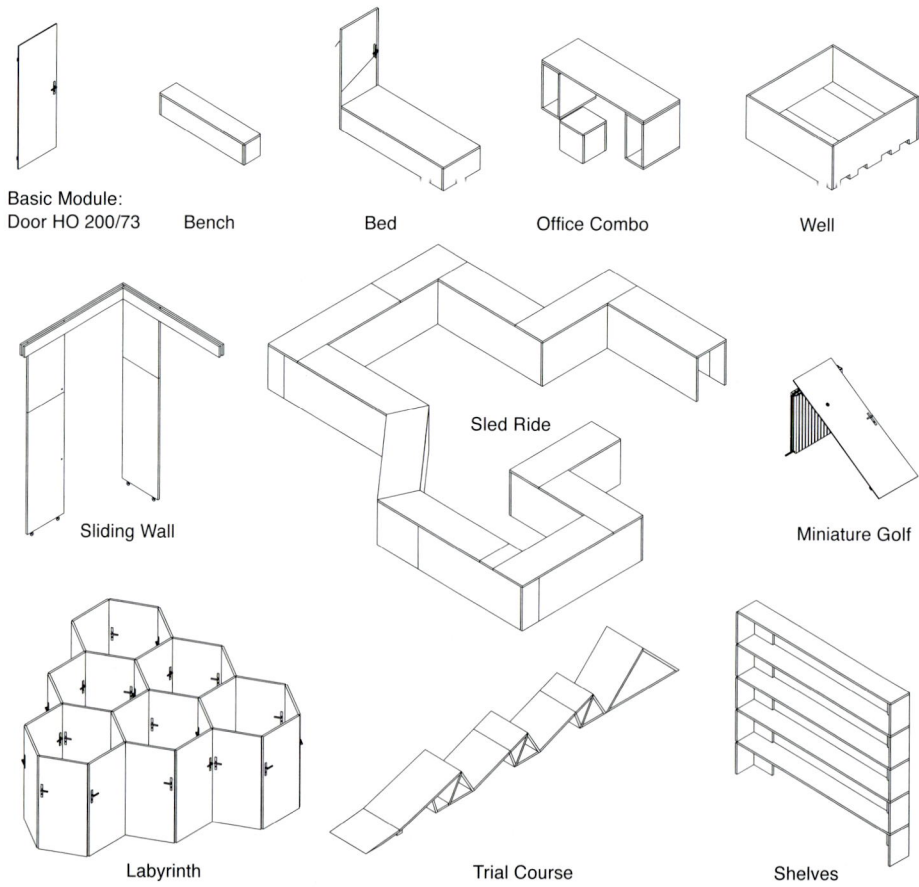

Basic Module: Door HO 200/73 — Bench — Bed — Office Combo — Well
Sliding Wall — Sled Ride — Miniature Golf
Labyrinth — Trial Course — Shelves

Battle of Matériel with No Winners_*Claudia Wahjudi* 457

tense relationship with the economy of the industrialized West—as in the ennobled (and hence expensive) corncob remains of Eduardo Abaroa and Rubén Ortiz Torres.

In Western countries, by contrast, recycling has long since become a successful branch of the economy. In Germany this sector is so omnipresent that its very tools have become artistic material, for example the curved *Kastenhäuser* of Wolfgang Winter and Berthold Hörbelt: temporary pavilions that the artists construct from the crates used for deposit bottles. Despite increases in the amount of material being returned to production, however, trash levels continue to increase: in the Federal Republic of Germany alone the figure went from 411 million tons in 1990 to 419 million tons in 2002.[5] As long as recycling promises good business, the real problem will change little: that is, the overproduction of consumer goods, which wastes energy and raw materials. Products that are less sustainable can shift some of their costs to the public at large, as Helmut Hagemann of the Wuppertal Institute has pointed out: "Many of them are therefore considerably better and cheaper than products that are more sustainable."[6] The resulting costs for a pork cutlet produced in factory farming are borne not by the supermarket customer but by the communities that have to pay for the processing of water polluted by liquid manure. The increase in trash comes in part because, as ATTAC, BUND, and Greenpeace report, "with globalization, Western models of consumption and production are on a triumphal march globally."[7] Finally, another cause is that residential trash is primarily an urban phenomenon, and in many parts of the world the cities are turning into megacities. Yet entire regions are excluded from global competition: the so-called shrinking cities and regions. The remnants of political and structural change, the bulky goods left behind by residents who have migrated, and even the dilapidating buildings themselves turn shrinking cities into giant garbage dumps.

At the End of Growth

Immediately after the fall of the Communism, artists began to recycle abandoned spaces in the eastern section of Berlin—as studios, clubs, meeting places, and stores. Laura Kikauka and Fred Rubin were among the pioneers. Kikauka came from Canada to a unified Berlin in 1992, where everything that was "made in the GDR" was virtually being tossed into the streets. Kikauka saved such discarded objects, and carried electrical appliances from hospitals, milk cans, and glass cuvettes into garages and abandoned workshops. She sorted and arranged the items into large, colorful, blinking installations that served as bars or karaoke stages. At midnight there was an auction: a competition of consumption and commodity fetishes—added value from trash. Fred Rubin removed two counters, among other things, from the Palast der Republik. He used one for a bar in a prominent Berlin music club and the other, a round one, for a motor-driven sculpture that hangs upside down "like a giant humming top."[8] He calls it "rotation recycling." As different as the two approaches are, the works of Kikauka and Rubin would have been inconceivable without the improvised nightlife culture that made the abandoned spaces of previous eras its own.

The recycling of locations, however, whether buildings of past eras or entire mining regions, pushes art to its limits. It cannot provide people with access to production and prosperity on the scale they had once known; it cannot take locations and buildings intended for a social order that has disappeared and link them one to one with the current circulation of commodities: art can neither stimulate the economy nor replace the welfare state.

Nor does it need to. Nevertheless, the artistic use of trash remains a question of economy and social order. Artists who redisplay the supposedly worthless remnants of a social order that has disappeared, like Laura Kikauka and Fred Rubin, focus our attention on their immaterial value. Projects like *Selbstbedienungszentrale* make the case for an economic system that even poor people can afford. Recycling landscape for art, as *Testing the Waters* does, can encourage us to recall regional identities, just as, for example, the sound and light installations of Hans Peter Kuhn on a gigantic, but now useless, slag conveyor bridge in a disused strip mine in Brandenburg can remind us of the pride of engineers and miners who have since been laid off—and perhaps they can also create a few jobs by attracting tourists. Sometimes art asks necessary questions. Dirk Paschke and Daniel Milohnic, for example, opened their container swimming pool at the Kokerei Zollverein at the very moment that the destitute city of Essen had to close its public pools. The art of recycling is also about a conscious retreat from prosperity in order to mitigate the brutalities of economic and social upheaval or to propose alternatives. Or simply, as the architecture critic Wolfgang Kil once expressed it in relation to the shrinking cities and landscapes of eastern Germany, to see the apparently unprofitable as "not always just ... the leftover, the 'silly remnants.'"[9] But that would already be a lot, because a way of thinking that views a renunciation of growth as an opportunity would be more sustainable than any form of recycling.

Translated from the German by Steven Lindberg

Notes
1 From http://www.uni-weimar.de/aktuelles/bogen/2002-01/flotsam.html (accessed May 1, 2005; document no longer available on site).
2 See Martin Damus, *Kunst im 20. Jahrhundert: Von der transzendierenden zur affirmativen Moderne* (Reinbek bei Hamburg: Rowohlt, 2000), 332.
3 Ibid., 333.
4 Roger Fayet and Peter Stohler, "Die Rückkehr des Abfalls: Recycling im Design oder Design aus Verworfenem?" *Kunstforum International* (special issue "Theorien des Abfalls") 167 (November–December 2003), 97.
5 Sources: Statistisches Bundesamt 1996; Bundesministerium für Umwelt, Naturschutz und Reaktorsicherheit 2004.
6 Helmut Hagemann, "Vom Kassenzettel zum Stimmzettel: Orientierungshilfen für nachhaltige Kaufentscheidungen im Massenmarkt," *Wuppertal Papers* 150 (October 2004), 13.
7 From http://www.mcplanet.com (accessed May 1, 2005; document no longer available on site).
8 See Rudolf Stegers, "Palastbartransfer," in *Berlin: Stadt ohne Form; Strategien einer anderen Architektur,* ed. Philipp Oswalt (Munich: Prestel, 2000), 195.
9 See Wolfgang Kil, *Luxus der Leere: Vom schwierigen Rückzug aus der Wachstumswelt* (Wuppertal, Germany: Müller + Busmann, 2004), 133.

Literature
Bianchi, Paolo, ed. "Theorien des Abfalls" (special issue), *Kunstforum International* 167 (November–December 2003).
———, ed. "Müllkunst" (special issue), *Kunstforum International* 168 (January–February 2004).
DeLillo, Don. *Underworld.* New York: Scribner, 1997.
Grassmuck, Volker, and Christian Unverzagt. *Das Müll-System: Eine metarealistische Bestandsaufnahme.* Frankfurt am Main: Suhrkamp, 1991.

AUTOMATENBAR
Berlin, 2001–2004
Automaten e.V.
www.visomat.com

With the changeover to the euro in 2002, many vending machines were too old to justify the expense of converting them. Gereon Schmitz/Visomat Inc. came up with the idea of an asylum for vending machines. The association Automaten e.V. was founded; a vacant storefront on Münzstraße in Berlin-Mitte was rented; and the "Automatenbar" (a vending machine bar) was installed by Fred Rubin and Michel Weinholzner, using furniture from the former foreign ministry of the German Democratic Republic.

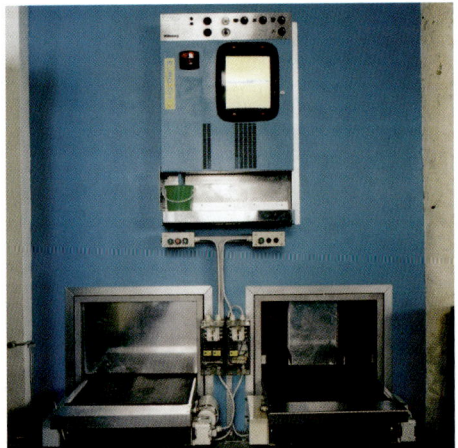

The food and drink vending machines accepted only deutschmark coins. Those who lacked the old coins could exchange euros using a machine in the bar. The bar became a kind of special currency zone where people could stop by and meet without any pressure to consume.

The room served as a kind of clubhouse for the association, which was officially established to "preserve the culture of vending machines and encourage artists to grapple with the topic of automation." Anyone could join for an annual membership fee of thirty euros, receiving in exchange a magnetic card that provided 24-hour access to the spaces. The 350 members organized lectures and various events, and even though only members were supposed to have access, the doors were usually open to nonmembers as well, especially during the summer. (Ed.)

RECYCLING PROJECTS
EXPERIMENTAL STATION, RUNNING TABLE, CHICAGO GROUND COVER, AND STANDARD KIOSK
Chicago, 1995–2004
Dan Peterman

The artist Dan Peterman combines artistic production with social practice in an oeuvre that is based on recyclable materials. In 1995 Peterman acquired a nonprofit recycling center on Blackstone Avenue, at the corner of 61st Street, right on the border between the University of Chicago neighborhood and Woodlawn, a very poor residential district. Peterman had already been running a collection center there for some time, buying back recyclable materials from scavengers. Under Peterman the two-story brick warehouse evolved into a sociocultural site with enterprises, initiatives, and projects ("Experimental Station"). In addition to Peterman's studio, the center housed projects like the Blackstone Bicycle Works, which employed young people from the neighborhood to repair worn-out bicycles; an organization for neighborhood assistance; a furniture workshop; and the editorial offices of a newspaper. In 2001 a fire gutted the building; it is currently being rebuilt.

The reuse of increasingly scarce resources, social interaction, and everyday praxis are integral elements of Peterman's installations and objects as well. For example, in 1997 he created a picnic table of recycled plastic with modular add-ons; a 100-foot-long version of it was placed in Grant Park in Chicago for use by visitors to the park (*Running Table*, 1997). He used the same material for the flooring of a dance floor that he created for Grant Park that same year (*Chicago Ground Cover*, 1997). His *Standard Kiosk* (2004) consists of two standard trash containers assembled into a house-like form and fitted out with various accessories so that it can be used as a kiosk, a bike shack, or a garden house. (Ed.)

▲ Dan Peterman's *Standard Kiosk* (2004) as an invitation to participate on the plaza of the Museum of Contemporary Art, Chicago. ◄ Dan Peterman, *Running Table*, 1997; 100-foot-long picnic table of recycled plastic, Grant Park, Chicago. ► Dan Peterman, *Chicago Ground Cover*, 1997; recycled plastic, view of installation in Grant Park, Chicago.

DO-IT-YOURSELF CITY

Crises in government organization and economic development have led to a new emphasis on the self-organization of people in urban areas. Citizens are being challenged to take economic, social, cultural, and urban development into their own hands. This has led to contradictory goals: Is the intention to reduce state spending and hand over the responsibility for public assistance and the common good to citizens? Or should the authority for decisions about resources be decentralized, with more power given to the less privileged and space for innovation created?

URBAN SELF-ORGANIZATION
A conversation between artist Marjetica Potrč and curator Hans Ulrich Obrist

Marjetica Potrč: I show examples where individuals take care of the city themselves. It's about individual initiatives. You don't necessarily have to plan to achieve results. The two most successful forms of the contemporary city, shantytowns and gated communities, are both individually initiated.

Hans Ulrich Obrist: Based on self-organization?

Yes, self-organization can work very well. Of course, nothing ever vanishes; it's just a different kind of organization. Societal structures don't disappear; they just change faces. You can compare city planning, for instance, to energy grids, electrical or natural gas, or whatever. As an individual you come into the city and you plug yourself in. Or, you can produce energy yourself and perhaps share it with others. I like that the fuel cell is becoming popular. A fuel cell is a small box that you can put in your house if you want. It produces energy. If your fuel cell runs on natural gas, your energy is cheaper than the city's energy. And then you can share your energy with the city. I'm not talking only about the deregulation of city structures, but also that as an individual you can give something back to society.

So it's no longer just about taking energy, but about reciprocity, about giving back. It leads us away from consumerism. Do you see this as a utopia?

I don't think that's utopia. If you look around, we live in a postindustrial age where nature and cities are one. Everything is processed in some way. I am not talking about original material and site-specificity. You take what is already available and use it to make something new. Whenever I do my projects, we just order material from Home Depot. I normally just transplant a situation that I find interesting in the city to the gallery as a case study.

It's a kind of do-it-yourself enterprise, which leads us to the question of do-its, the instruction, the partition.

Yes, and it's very important that that interpretation is possible.

But there is a range of interpretations because it is an open partition, not a closed partition.

Yes, it's ongoing. Twenty years ago, shantytowns were not even drawn into city plans. The planners thought that they could just erase them and relocate the population to public housing. Today, it is known that inhabitants don't necessarily want to move to such housing. Shantytowns can be upgraded and be functional communities. The perception of shanties has changed.

Venturi would say "learning from Las Vegas," but you would say "learning from shantytowns."

In a way, I take care not to put all this in a category called "shantytowns," because I think the same aesthetic is emerging elsewhere. For me, beautiful is what looks easy, light, and practical.

You were also talking about the notion of the distressed city landscape.

I look at people's taste and what they consider beautiful. Why has something become desirable? At the time of the Bosnian War, I once saw a photo which showed tourists taking photos inside the burned-out library in Sarajevo. At the time, a sniper could get you anytime. I thought this was a real desire for a distressed landscape. I found out that there are tours organized in the favelas of Sao Paulo, which would have been unthinkable ten years ago. You see the change in aesthetics happening before your eyes. In Israel, tourists can take a tour of Gaza's tent cities. Do you know about the Burning Man festival? Each summer, some people who live in San Francisco and thereabouts go out into the desert and build a temporary settlement. It's all about showing our ability to survive and conquer the inhospitable land.

Do you think that utopias can be created through small contributions to the city or society, a notion of micro utopia?

First of all, I don't feel that utopia makes sense today. For me, the present time is about self-reliability, individual initiatives, and small-scale projects. A few small-scale water turbines work better in the long term than one large dam. People still do build big dams; it's a slow process to change mentalities.

Excerpt from an interview with Marjetica Potrč by Hans Ulrich Obrist, published in *Arconoticias* 24 (Summer 2002): 55–59.

Rural Studio is an outreach program for architecture students at Auburn University; they work with the residents of economically weak, shrinking Hale County in rural Alabama to design highly personalized dwellings. Construction materials are devised from whatever is at hand in the area and usually include recycled or overlooked objects. The *Butterfly House* makes use of natural ventilation, and its roof harvests rainwater, thus making a statement in self-sustainable architecture.

▸ Marjetica Potrč's version of *Butterfly House* in the exhibition "Designs for the Real World," Generali Foundation, Vienna, Austria, 2002.

Urban Self-Organization_*A Conversation with Marjetica Potrč*

Do-It-Yourself City

Hybrid House juxtaposes structures from the temporary architecture of Caracas, the West Bank, and West Palm Beach, Florida, and shows how they negotiate space among themselves. Each of the community-based structures formulates its own language, which, in all three cases, has much in common with archetypal (and not modernist) architecture. Emphasis is placed on private space, security, and energy and communication infrastructures.

▸ The *Hybrid House* in the exhibition "Urgent Architecture," Palm Beach Institute of Contemporary Art, Lake Worth, Florida, 2003.

ADAMAH
Detroit, 1999
Kyong Park/iCUE and Stephen Vogel, with Louis Farris, Stefan Lennon, Victoria Matous, Christian Pomodoro, Rebecca Raleigh, and Shane Terpening (University of Detroit Mercy)
www.adamah.org, www.boggscenter.org

"Adamah," which means "from the earth" in Hebrew, is the title of an alternative planning concept developed for an area in east Detroit by architecture students at the University of Detroit Mercy during a four-month seminar under the direction of Kyong Park and Stephen Vogel. The planning concept is oriented around the results achieved by the many self-organized initiatives in Detroit that have filled in the gaps left by the city administration's retreat from public services, and the communities of east Detroit were also involved in its development. The wishes and concerns of those living in the area were thus taken into account, and the results were presented to the public in an exhibition held during the summer of 2001.

Using a process-oriented concept that spans a period of ten years, the project covers a wide spectrum of undertakings. The initial step of reopening a river branch sealed with concrete in order to turn brownfield sites into fertile areas again is to be followed by the introduction of urban agriculture, the establishment of collective residential and green areas, and the organization of a cooperative market. The use of alternative energy sources and the channeling of rainwater into the irrigation system are intended to promote sustainable development. In addition, in the center of "Adamah," a "Ring of Life" is planned, that is to say, a large-scale ring of hothouses with a walking trail and an information center. This will complement a variety of self-organized, small-scale projects by adding a very visible and simultaneously ephemeral element, thereby lending the entire project an overall, easily recognizable image within the urban context.

The success of the project can so far be measured not by the progress of its physical realization but by its effect as a catalyst and its ability to garner attention and positive resonance among the public. "Adamah" is no longer in the hands of its initiators; it is now being carried out by other actors in different community groups under the same name in the form of meetings and initiatives. It is an active model for the self-regeneration of an alternative Detroit. Another such plan, which will continue up to the year 2075, will follow. (Ed.)

A report on the "Adamah" project as the cover story in the Detroit weekly *metrotimes* from October 31, 2001.

CATHERINE FERGUSON ACADEMY
Detroit, since 1985
G. Asenath Andrews, with teachers and educators

In 1985, G. Asenath Andrews took over a Salvation Army school for young mothers in Detroit and developed it into a unique public school for approximately 400 girls and 200 babies and small children. The Detroit public school system is notorious for its poor quality of education and its high dropout rate. Teenage pregnancies have exacerbated the problems. Young mothers without a high-school diploma often become long-term welfare recipients. The Catherine Ferguson Academy (CFA), named after a freed slave who became engaged in education for the black community in the early nineteenth century, has set its goal in obtaining a diploma for every one of its students and then sending each on to college with the support of state grants. Each young woman is supposed to develop self-awareness and the academic and social skills needed to care for herself and her family, and to attain independence in her choice of career and lifestyle. The civil rights movement and feminism of the 1960s and 1970s represent the political background of the school's director and of many of its teachers and educators. The director promotes education and separate schools for boys and girls as strategies of empowerment because she has often seen how young women, in particular, give over power to others too quickly. Great importance is placed on accepting responsibility for oneself and one's community. Students learn this principle by tending to a small farm next to the school grounds, where they produce vegetables, dairy products, and honey. The school supplements its public funding with the sale of this produce and with persistent fundraising drives among the Detroit business community.

The student population is 94% African American and 5% Latina. Of these students, 90% are so poor that the school must supply their lunches. As a "one-stop education and social service center," the CFA offers not only instruction and personal educational counseling for its all students, but also daycare provided by fourteen childcare workers as well as courses and counseling in questions related to childrearing, vaccination, dental care, and food coupons. There is a summer school in Canada, and an internship in a Detroit organization or company is obligatory. Previous achievement is not a criterion for enrollment. Most new students have recently dropped out of another school. They are each guided through to graduation by a mentor-teacher who helps with the difficulties they and their children face as well as with their achievement in school. Despite the intense care, one fifth of students leave every year, but almost all who graduate go on to attend college. (Ed.)

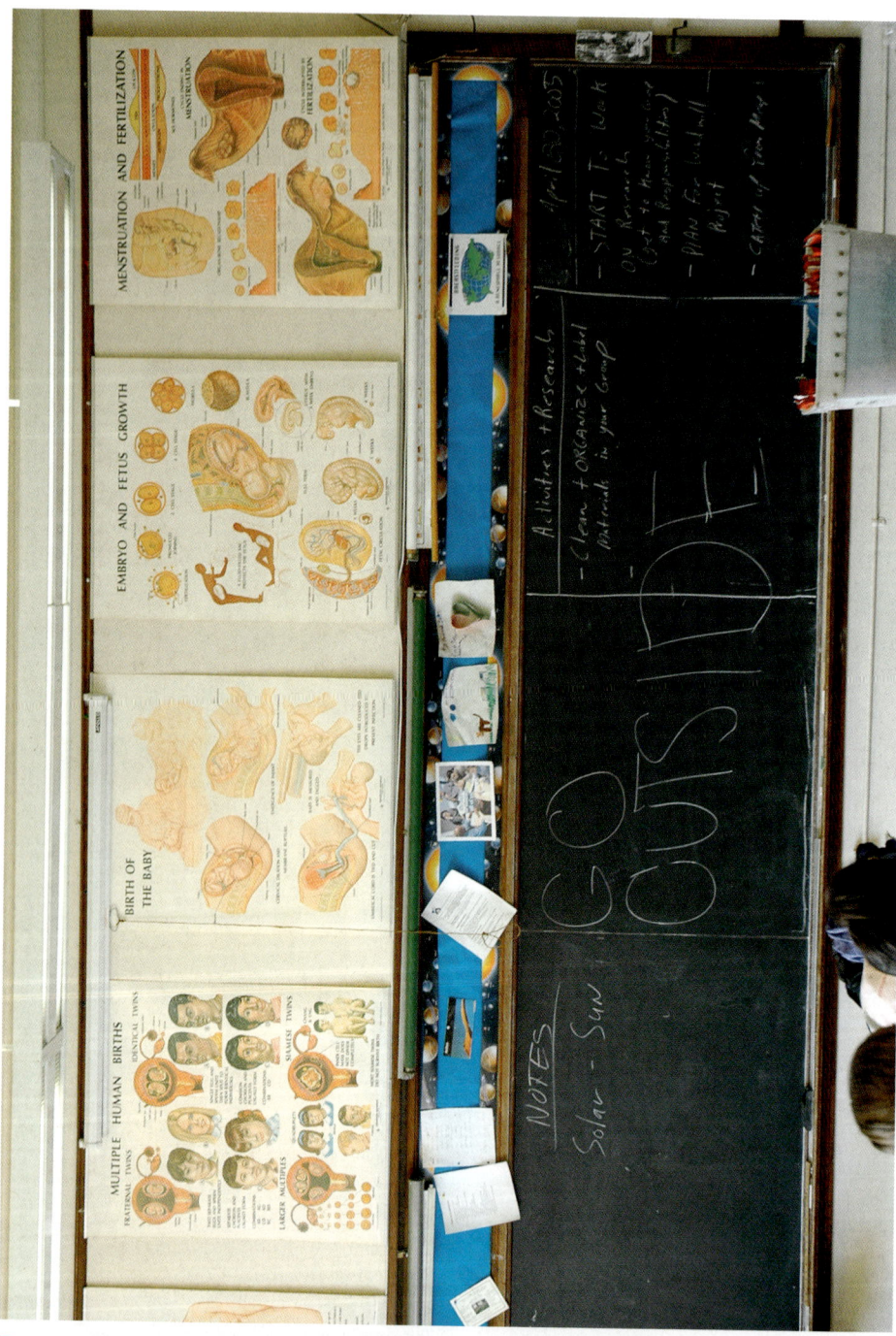

Teenage mothers finish up their high-school education at the Catherine Ferguson Academy in Detroit. The school's goal is to teach its students to be independent in all aspects of their lives.

THE ACTIVATING STATE
Thomas Knorr-Siedow

Whenever the state runs out of ideas, politicians call for people to take on more responsibility themselves. It is thus no coincidence that in the face of the dramatic phenomenon of shrinking cities, faith is placed in civil self-organization and citizen's initiatives. One could complain that this represents a declaration of bankruptcy on the state's ability to take action. At the same time, calling on citizens to take more responsibility is not merely political cynicism. As the representatives of an active civil society have maintained—most notably Amitai Etzioni and Ulrich Beck—a new balance between state and civil responsibility is necessary in order to bring the national and local levels of the state closer to the real needs of citizens and also to make them fit for a more complex and globalized world. To create the conditions for this balance, the above-mentioned protagonists, and also, in particular, Anthony Giddens, suggest that the state must take on an activating and enabling role so that both the state and its citizens can learn to make the best out of the given circumstances.

The State or the Citizens?
The key factors that indicate why things must change are the state's sustained financial troubles, the persistence of a weak economy and mass unemployment, migration, and demographic change, which culminate in an intractable polarization of social spaces. Few doubt that this misery requires changes in the relationship between the state and its citizens, in part because the state—in its many shapes and sizes, from the federal level to the municipal—has not always been particularly good at solving problems. Ultimately, the lack of flexibility and the inability to learn to address the phenomenon of shrinking cities with lasting success has led to a situation in which the state appears as both the presumed problem-solver and simultaneously as the perpetrator who is creating the next generation of problems.

Concerning the other side of the equation in striking a balance between the state and its citizens, there are barriers particularly in the shrinking regions and cities to citizens' participation in the shaping of social and spatial developments. People who have financial security and a higher level of education participate more than those who see themselves as leading a life characterized by insecurity.[1] It is not surprising that the trend toward local self-organization and residential activities is declining in the shrinking regions, given the economic realities and the social and psychological consequences there. On the one hand, there are the schools facing the threat of being shut down which are then sponsored by groups of concerned parents, or the buses driven by retirees for citizens in need of public transport. But, on the other hand, there is also resignation, the feeling that nothing can be done, and self-destructive vandalism, which drives the last remaining renters out of shrinking neighborhoods. One thing, in any case, is made clear by the mutual dynamics of economic and demographic developments, which has intensified in eastern Germany since the agreement to exit Solidarity Pact II by 2019:[2] if new responsibilities are not taken on and if certain sectors of the population who have thus far had no experience with self-help remain strangers to the idea, the municipal services that are taken for granted today will no longer be guaranteed. This will have an effect not only on care for the elderly, but also on other urban policy fields such as education, mobility, and cultural life, as well as the sociospatial management of urban districts, all of which serve in concert to hold a city together and make it attractive.

Finally a Look to the Future? An Enabling State

It has thus become evident that—particularly for shrinking cities—the "revolutionary situation" has arrived that already in 1994 led the British sociologist Anthony Giddens to his conclusion, based on developments in Great Britain, that "politics, whether as institutionalized policies of the state or the lifestyle politics of social groups, can no longer function in the traditional way." In response to the massive dismantling of the social welfare system in the Thatcher era, he suggests holding on to the goals of social equalization and social emancipation (from coercion and repression), yet adding alongside these a concept of "double reflexivity." This builds on the insight, on the one hand, that every reality is "socially constructed" and can therefore be seen from different perspectives and also be changed. And, on the other hand, it takes into account the idea that decisions can be related in a proactive way to the given possibilities and limits in order to find paths to success in a "society of clever people" that will not lead astray toward a totalitarian state or to illusory wishful thinking. Giddens sees a "dialogical understanding of democracy" as a prerequisite for this, in which the above-mentioned balance between state and civil action is actively promoted by the state.[3]

The theoretical roots of the debate on the enabling state are found in the Anglo-American tradition of the action-oriented philosophy of communitarianism—for example, in the debate on the relationship between freedom and justice/liberalism and democracy in the work of John Rawls—as well as in the political science and social-science examinations of politics in complex action contexts such as in the work of Anthony Giddens or Patsy Healey. The first of these refers to a discourse carried out almost exclusively in the United States that centers on the freedom of the individual, which in this case is ideally limited only by the minimal state propagated by Robert Nozick. While this model, characterized by Benjamin Barber as predatory democracy, may be attractive to those who are aware of themselves as active agents, it neglects the second pole—the necessity to intervene in and regulate the conflicts that arise in complex, interwoven systems. From the boundless pioneer mentality there emerges a concept of neighborly relations, in which in a Strong Democracy, civility and talking with one another become central to shaping action. This addresses both the problem of the active citizen as well as the constitution of the state in a Strong Democracy. Only when one's own interests are virtuously yielded over to the priority of the general interest—as in the fantasies of early leftists (Jean-Jacques Rousseau)—will everyone who is part of the collective make the effort necessary for the reflexivity of a Strong Democracy. According to Walter Reese-Schäfer, a question thus arises particularly in the context of the current developments, which no longer promise a generally rosy picture: "If only volunteers are to participate—how many will there be? Will they thus be allowed to have certain advantages, that is, power over the others?"[4]

Two basic problems are hereby addressed which the enabling state must consider. First, how will the state initiate the participation of those who do not engage in the regular activities of state institutions, either for understandable reasons touching on social, economic, and mental problems, or perhaps also due to social exclusion, whether real or self-imposed? And how does the state deal with the question of mentalities and the distribution of power, which is possibly a different issue in what is still a post-Bismarck German society as compared to the Anglo-American cultural sphere, where the regulative traditions in the community are based much more clearly in the self-organization of civil society, for example in the social sphere and in labor market and urban policy as part of "community development"?

Levels of Action

As always when things cannot continue as they had been before, fears arise, but also new possibilities. And in a crisis, old problems are tackled which otherwise would never have been addressed. In this sense, there is great opportunity in the drama sparked by the growing incompatibility between what the state can offer and what is socially necessary. But in what areas can the enabling state further develop itself, and what approaches can it take in order to develop and maintain the fields of learning that are necessary for reflexivity in the relationship between the state and its citizens? Two areas must be addressed as key fields: the logic of how the state supports action and the citizens' capacity for action.

From Supply-Side to Demand-Side Urban Policy

When it proves problematic for state authorities to formulate their centrally organized services in a monopolistic fashion, a countermodel emerges from the perspective of the enabling state that in effect turns this logic around to stand on its feet rather than its head. Actions are no longer defined by administrative departmental structures. Instead, political programs and projects are derived from an analysis of the given problems, and solutions are tailored to fit. For a good deal of the past two decades, this kind of approach has also shaped discourses on urban policy in Europe. The New Deal for Communities emerged under the sway of the British discussion on a third way between a predatory society and a paralyzing bureaucracy. This New Deal, assigned to the Deputy Prime Minister's office, offers the municipalities direct financial support and advice so they can devote their efforts to solving local problems in areas ranging from education and qualification to crime prevention by using intelligently integrated concepts.[5] As in almost all countries in the European Union, in the French *politique de la ville*, which has been continuously administered by an interdepartmentally acting Ministry for the Cities through several changes of government, efforts are under way to move forward with urban policies focused on problem-solving. Some structural characteristics seem consistent with this goal.

Among the policies pertaining to urban space that are under way in Germany, the Soziale Stadt (Socially Integrative City) stands out in particular—despite the overload of specific tasks—as an integrated program that itself also has the capacity to integrate.[6] Starting from analyses of problems specific to certain cities or districts, created with the explicit participation of as many as possible of those involved in and affected by the issues, those cases that were successful yielded new spaces—in a physical as well as a metaphorical sense—for communication and negotiation in which the complexity of the problems became tangible. Maintained solely with public funds to ensure communication and smaller offshoot projects, the program sought after the potentials within the given local conditions, and these were found in the repertoire of private and state actors, and in particular among the local community. This was not only about access to funds, but often also about the possibility of activating citizens' everyday knowledge for the development of the districts.[7] When, for example, mothers from ethnic minorities are inspired to apply their family-conflict resolution skills to the neighborhood at large, or unemployed youths become engaged in the upkeep of their environs, which also further qualifies them for this type of work and thus improves their job prospects, capacities for the district are activated that had previously not been understood as compatible with state action. After a long period of building trust and weighing interests beyond the strict borders of departments and organizations, often institutional arrangements and strategies for taking action were developed that were suitable for the diagnosed problems and their particular dynamics. In addition, the approach was usually to bring together funding for solving problems by dipping into all available public coffers in order to group together financial resources that had previously been doled out separately. Money was no longer simply used up, it was (as a rule) given out in a more targeted way, under close observation and following debates on committees, where it was possible to develop a new political culture for problematic city districts. Institutionalized infrastructures, time, the will to learn, and a process-oriented management are required in order to assimilate experiences.

One of the preconditions for success is also a local political leadership that is open to addressing local problems and opportunities. Wherever the municipal political leaders and other key people could identify with the codified goals of the Socially Integrative City and the various administrations were open to communicative and collaborative problem-solving, relations of partnership became the guiding model for local-state action. It could be an important step along the way to the desired enabling state action for the cities if the base structures of this constantly innovative, experimental program were brought up from the neighborhood to the citywide level and liberated from the niche of problem-solving via social measures.

Enabling, Action Capacity, and Power Relations

If a new balance between state action and citizen's self-organization is to emerge, the current, frequently symbolic level of state action will not be sufficient. There is already enough of this in the often politically cynical jargon of "sponsoring and demanding," yet without any serious institutional consequences. Instead, politics, state, and society will have to come to an agreement that the institutional prerequisites and political capacities for qualifying all partners for increased citizens' self-organization must be met.[8] This is also about—lest we forget the PISA Program for International Student Assessment—an educational task to be carried out under difficult conditions in which it is not the issue of qualification that is important but the civil aspect of education.[9]

On the one hand, state actors at all levels, from the European Union to the municipalities, will have to give over a part of their regulative power to citizens as necessitated by the task at hand. In this way, and via direction at the level on which problems can best be tackled according to the subsidiary principle, those fields of learning will be mobilized that make it attractive to citizens to accept the proposed "(new) deal" through actively "learning by doing." This can only be successful, however, when it is about real influence and material decisions that have a recognizable and direct effect on people's lives. New and moderated forms of decisions about the remaining money, available space, and opportunities will be centrally posed in order to create a link between prosperity and welfare, as suggested by experiments with citizens' budgets, new paths to acquiring real estate, or alternative models of living and experimental economic and cultural interim uses for vacant spaces in shrinking cities.

All of this belongs less in the context of neoliberal models of reducing state influence to the fullest extent possible; rather it is about a long overdue reformulation of state tasks in which the state's function of moderating, distributing knowledge, and ensuring justice are extended such that a vision can take shape of a society that is also active in crisis situations.

Translated from the German by Christina M. White

Notes
1 See www.perspektive-deutschland.de.
2 Under Germany's Solidarity Pact, the federal government and the federal states share in the special burdens borne by the eastern German states on account of the division of the country. Solidarity Pact II was passed in 2001 and ensures the continuation of financial support until 2019.—Ed.
3 Anthony Giddens, *Beyond Left and Right: The Future of Radical Politics* (Palo Alto, CA: Stanford University Press, 1994).
4 Walter Reese-Schäfer, *Was ist Kommunitarismus?* (Frankfurt am Main: Campus Verlag, 1994), 96.
5 Office of the Deputy Prime Minister, www.odpm.gov.uk/stellent/groups/odpm_control/documents/homepage/odpm_home_page.hcsp.
6 Deutsches Institut für Urbanistik, ed., *Die Soziale Stadt: Eine erste Bilanz des Bund-Länder-Programms "Stadtteile mit besonderem Entwicklungsbedarf—die soziale Stadt"* (Berlin: DIFU, 2002) (interim report on the Socially Integrative City program); Deutsches Institut für Urbanistik, ed., *Strategien für die Soziale Stadt: Erfahrungen und Perspektiven—Umsetzung des Bund-Länder-Programms "Stadtteile mit besonderem Entwicklungsbedarf—die soziale Stadt"* (Berlin: DIFU, 2003) (final report on the Socially Integrative City program).
7 Catalina Gandelsonas and Thomas Knorr-Siedow, "Lokales Wissen in der Stadt- und Quartiersentwicklung," in *Stadtregion und Wissen: Analysen und Plädoyers für eine wissensbasierte Stadtpolitik,* ed. Ulf Matthiesen (Wiesbaden: VS Verlag für Sozialwissenschaften, 2004), 293-308.
8 Heidi Fichter, Petra Jähnke, and Thomas Knorr-Siedow, "Governance Capacity für eine wissensbasierte Stadtentwicklung," in *Stadtregion und Wissen,* 309-336.
9 Gandelsonas and Knorr-Siedow, "Lokales Wissen."

Literature
Barber, Benjamin R. *A Place for Us: How to Make Society Civil and Democracy Strong.* New York: Hill and Wang, 1998.
———. *Strong Democracy: Participatory Politics for a New Age.* Los Angeles: University of California Press, 1984.
Beck, Ulrich. "Die Seele der Demokratie—Wie wir Bürgerarbeit statt Arbeitslosigkeit finanzieren können." In *Gewerkschaftliche Monatshefte* 6/7 (June/July 1998): 330-335; http://www.gmh.dgb.de/jahresin.html.
Damkowski, Wulf and Anke Rösener. *Auf dem Weg zum Aktivierenden Staat.* Berlin: edition sigma, 2003.
Etzioni, Amitai. *The Active Society: A Theory of Societal and Political Processes.* New York: Free Press, 1968.
———. *The New Golden Rule: Community and Morality in a Democratic Society.* New York: Basic Books, 1996.
Giddens, Anthony. *The Third Way: The Renewal of Social Democracy.* Malden, MA: Blackwell, 1998.
Healey, Patsy. *Collaborative Planning: Shaping Places in Fragmented Societies.* London: Houndsmill, 1997.
Nozick, Robert. *Anarchy, State, and Utopia.* New York: Basic Books, 1974.
Rawls, John. *A Theory of Justice.* Cambridge, MA: Belknap Press of Harvard University Press, 1971.

CAN SOCIAL CAPITAL SAVE SHRINKING CITIES?
Christine Hannemann

The concept of "social capital" plays a surprising role in many—particularly planning—contexts. In expert reviews and other forms of action recommendations for the precarious situations found in certain cities and regions, it is argued that strengthening social capital will contribute significantly to remedying the deficits in urban development. Some of these recommendations go so far as to suggest that, for example, limitations in providing a social infrastructure in structurally weak peripheral regions should be compensated for with citizens' engagement. Social capital is considered a resource primarily at the district level, in small towns, and other smaller areas, and it has thus far remained untapped and largely ignored in planning. The basic positive premise that a reduction in state social welfare systems can be compensated for by "social capital" is and remains questionable in many ways. But from a sociological perspective, it is significant that the presence of social capital is seen as a basic prerequisite for overcoming social dilemmas. Planning and urban development did not originally play a role in the concept of social capital as it was developed by Pierre Bourdieu, James Coleman, and Robert Putnam in debates in the social sciences. The speed with which concepts of social capital have spread from the social sciences into urban and regional planning, politics, and debates about civic engagement indicates, however, that this concept, or rather this idea, satisfies various needs. Given the present precarious social situation, the frequent and indiscriminate use of this term suggests an assumption that lifesaving qualities are readily available that allow a community to pull itself up by the bootstraps, as it were. In the following, this misleading interpretation will be contested by a clarification of the concept of social capital; then possible insights will be discussed in relation to the urban context.

The starting point for the vigorous debates about social capital since the beginning of the 1990s is the question of how integration problems can be overcome in highly individualized postmodern societies. Generally, the diagnosis is a loss of social security, which causes disintegration of stable structures in families and neighborhoods, and results in individuals living a perforated social existence. Debates in the social sciences on the concept of social capital have attempted to find at least a theoretical solution to this problem. Social capital has since entered into many different discursively related contexts such as "social networks," "civic engagement," "civil society," "social trust," and "volunteerism."

The term "social capital" is aimed at answering a question: under which conditions can social trust and volunteer engagement function as a foundation for social cohesion? Social capital has two fundamental components: on the one hand, the individual embeddedness of actors in various types of relationship networks and, on the other hand, the qualities of the relationship networks themselves. These relationships, according to the basic idea, represent an important social value for both those who are involved in them as well as for all manner of combinations of individuals who form relationships—that is, for groups that in the best case form a collective actor, which in turn has a positive effect on all types of communities.

The sociological concept of "social capital" in relation to individuals was introduced by Pierre Bourdieu in the early 1980s and referred to the whole of all actual and potential resources associated with participation in networks of social relations based on reciprocal acquaintance and recognition.[1] In contrast to human capital, social capital is not related to natural persons but instead to the relationships *between* them. Bourdieu used the concept in order to reveal the generation and reproduction of inequality effected by the power lever of social capital.

In the early 1990s, North American political scientist Robert Putnam used the concept as a political science term to describe the qualities of social networks, thereby allowing for the characterization of a key trait of communal action. This use of the term has been widely accepted in relation to the cohesion of actors. Social interaction is functionally interpreted by Robert Putnam as a factor in production, and it is interpreted as a source of economic growth. This explains why this concept as it relates to social "cementing," that is, the cohesion of actors, has been accepted both in political science as well as in research on municipal politics.

Robert Putnam defines social capital, a central concept for him, as "properties of social organization, such as trust, norms and networks, which can improve the performance of a society by making coordinated action easier."[2] He uses the term to describe an accumulation of civic qualities and virtues that he found to be unequally distributed across social spaces in the object of his observations, namely Italy, thus resulting in differences in the success rates of regional development. It is not the more favorable preconditions in northern Italy that explain regional disparities, he discovered, but instead the regional variables in factors that constitute social capital, in this case particularly variations in the quality of networks that tie into the political-administrative system and the economy; this is the decisive factor. In contrast to other forms of capital, social capital is not tied to specific individuals; it results instead from the relationships between actors.

The concept shifts attention to noneconomic, cultural factors in economic action and to the moral resources of a community that cannot be produced by political actors but are often appropriated by them. According to Putnam, norms and networks of civic engagement improve education, lessen poverty, and promote a more responsive state. On the other hand, a lack of social capital leads to deplorable social, economic, and political conditions. Putnam points to indicators such as voter participation, the numbers of newspaper readers among the population, and participation in volunteer organizations and neighborhood meetings. Social capital is formed through interpersonal contact and the social bonds it creates.

Although the concept is well recognized, it is also the focus of much critique. In particular, the twofold character of the term "social capital"—its content overlaps with areas such as "networks," "trust," and "collective assets"—limits its empirical usefulness. In addition, in the German context it is rightly argued that "social capital" is a misleading metaphor because "capital" suggests "finances." The multiple meanings of the term are also seen as a problem. According to Sebastian Braun, this is a characteristic typical of concepts that eventually become integration ideologies. He sees three weaknesses in the term: the conflation of causes and effects of social capital, the theoretically questionable stretching of the term to refer to regions and states, and the idealization of its positive effects while the negative effects remain ignored.[3]

Further, it is argued that, for example, a band of robbers or a fundamentalist dictatorship also manifest social capital, which means that the phenomenon cannot always be seen in a positive light. In addition, there is a potential danger that the concept could be instrumentally incorporated into political programs aimed at promoting sustainable development and economic growth. Civil society networks, local activities, and civic engagement are currently celebrated as panaceas in neoliberal discussions. The concept of "social capital" is thus misused as a way of anchoring a new notion of society and managing the social costs effected by it. Many critical studies have shown that state assistance programs tend to destroy rather than build up local civic networks because of their principally top-down structure.

Despite the many critiques, the Putnamian concept has become firmly established in the German debate. Admittedly, its localization in space, or rather with respect to settlement structures, has only been marginally addressed. Nevertheless, Robert Putnam and other political scientists have found a significant correlation here. One example of American research on the topic is the evaluative study by Ross Gittell and Avis Vidal from 1998,[4] which analyzes experiences with the use of the "social capital" concept in the context of "community development" during a national demonstrational program for the Local Initiatives Support Corporation (LISC). LISC is one of many national intermediary organizations that support local community development initiatives. The authors accompanied the program over three years in three different regions that had undergone considerable industrial structural transformation and had not yet developed any of their own initiatives as a means for overcoming the crisis. The goal was to explore an approach for strengthening and inducing social capital, which was—according to Putnam's theory—supposed to lead to more communication and trust in a given region and thereby promote autonomous development. Gittell and Vidal depict an overall positive image for the demonstrational program. One of the fundamental tasks, namely to fill in "structural gaps" in areas lacking their own impetus, was accomplished to a certain extent. Additionally, in each region the program was financed completely by local private funds, which must be seen as positive for the cohesion of a region. Nonetheless, the authors assert that the question remains as to whether the results support the thesis that social capital can be deliberately implemented from without.

Robert Putnam also discusses the spatial dimension of social capital in so far as he compares different types of communities. The inhabitants of big cities and the suburbs around them, says Putnam, are less organized. "In fact, even among suburbs, smaller is better from a social capital point of view. Getting involved in community affairs is more inviting—or abstention less attractive—when the scale of everyday life is smaller and more intimate."[5] German political scientists Claus Offe and Susanne Fuchs have noted the same in a study of the German states. For western Germany they found that the relationship between the size of a community and the active engagement of its inhabitants is clear-cut: the bigger the community, the smaller the rate of membership.[6]

Active engagement was noted particularly in "small town structures," where it leads to a well-developed culture of clubs and associations. This has also been shown by two empirical studies, one examining the meaning of social capital in a disadvantaged Berlin district,[7] and the other looking at attempts to overcome the phenomenon of shrinking in small towns in eastern Germany.[8] While social capital in larger cities remains limited to small-scale areas and never develops into an overall effect, in small local contexts cultures were described that are explicitly dependent upon the given sociospatial unity of this community type.

Concerning the effect of social capital, the study of small towns in eastern Germany showed that towns with strong networks of local actors that were in place early enough saw more robust economic development. The skills and competence of the local mayor also proved to be important cognitive prerequisites. A widely distributed leadership structure made it possible for towns to concentrate on a common strategic course and bring together the interests of very different groups, organizations, and individual actors.

What urban studies can learn from this is that the concept of "social capital," which has been successfully employed in political science, can be developed into a key term for analyzing the potential found in local contexts. The analytic concept of "social capital" cannot be conflated with the normative, positive assessment currently seen in the planning context. Social capital is often equated with the resources produced by its very presence. This leads to a circular, tautological argument in which cause, function, and consequences cannot be distinguished.

At the same time, the concept of social capital makes it possible to address urban social relations not only from the perspective of deficits, but also in terms of productive and constructive potentials. In the context of shrinking cities, this kind of analysis can direct attention to social qualities and make visible the positive dimensions present in a given community. This reinforces the self-confidence and endurance of local actors. Deficits in local constellations of actors can be remedied, which can lead to improved communal action without direct intervention and financial expenditure. For this reason it makes sense to place special emphasis on engaging and above all mobilizing citizens.

This raises the question of whether social capital can be increased directly through public assistance programs. Studies on the issue are unanimous in their findings that the state cannot induce social capital, let alone provide it to a community as a resource. This stands in contrast to human capital, which can be deliberately increased through assistance programs such as further education. One possibility for which there are practical examples is the promotion of volunteer work and citizens' engagement. For example, the German Ministry for Family Affairs, Senior Citizens, Women, and Youth developed a job-market program called LOS—Lokales Kapital für soziale Zwecke (Local Capital for Social Purposes).[9] In 2003, the program supported small-scale projects at the municipal and district level in regions affected by the floods in the summer of 2002; and funding remains available for micro projects up until the year 2007 in areas supported by the federal and state program Die Soziale Stadt (The Socially Integrative City) or the complementary program platform Entwicklung und Chancen junger Menschen in sozialen Brennpunkten (Development and Opportunities for Young People in Social Hotbeds). The evaluation of the LOS program arrived at the following conclusion: "In general, policies and practices in city districts in which new networks have developed since the beginning of the program are more innovative than in those districts in which no new networks emerged."[10] This result apparently indicates a successful example of how social capital can be promoted. However, the study quoted was a commissioned research project.

Whether or not the insight gained from incorporating the concept of "social capital" into municipal practice can in general be taken up in a positive way without implying a dependence upon assistance programs remains an open question, in my opinion.

I rather think this would require a much stronger autonomy among municipal actors in their decision-making, as well as sufficient funding. Both theoretically and in practical terms, it is quite plausible that appropriate activities could be developed at the civic level. There have been many examples from the shrinking cities in eastern Germany showing that despite their precarious financial situation, municipalities have supported the work of local clubs and associations, for example. The concept of "social capital" provides an analytic approach for planning practices that allows us to more precisely ascertain the difficult-to-describe "soft" qualities that are important for future developments and to formulate them in such a way as to open up possibilities for including these local cultures in urban development concepts.

Translated from the German by Christina M. White

Notes

1. See Pierre Bourdieu, "Ökonomisches Kapital, kulturelles Kapital, soziales Kapital," in *Soziale Ungleichheiten, Soziale Welt,* Sonderband 2, ed. Reinhard Kreckel (Göttingen: Schwartz, 1983), 183-198.
2. Robert D. Putnam, *Making Democracy Work: Civic Traditions in Modern Italy* (Princeton, NJ: Princeton University Press, 1993), 167.
3. See Sebastian Braun, "Putnam und Bourdieu und das soziale Kapital in Deutschland: Der rhetorische Kurswert einer sozialwissenschaftlichen Kategorie," *Leviathan* 29, no. 3 (2002): 337-354.
4. Ross Gittell and Avis Vidal, *Community Organizing: Building Social Capital as a Development Strategy* (Thousand Oaks, CA: Sage Publications, 1998).
5. Robert D. Putnam, *Bowling Alone: The Collapse and Revival of American Community* (New York: Simon & Schuster, 2000), 205.
6. See Susanne Fuchs and Claus Offe, "The Decline of Social Capital? The German Case," in *Democracies in Flux: The Evolution of Social Capital in Contemporary Society,* ed. Robert D. Putnam (New York: Oxford University Press, 2002), 189-244.
7. See Olaf Schnur, ed., *Nachbarschaft, Sozialkapital und Bürgerengagement: Potentiale sozialer Stadtteilentwicklung? Eine Analyse am Beispiel von vier Wohnquartieren des Stadtteils Moabit (Berlin-Tiergarten)—Abschlussbericht zum Projektseminar* (Arbeitsbericht 48, Department of Geography, Humboldt Universität zu Berlin, Berlin, 2000).
8. See Christine Hannemann, *Marginalisierte Städte: Probleme, Differenzierungen und Chancen ostdeutscher Kleinstädte im Schrumpfungsprozess* (Berlin: Berliner Wissenschafts-Verlag, 2004).
9. See homepage of the program LOS—Lokales Kapital für soziale Zwecke; www.los-online.de/content/index_ger.html, July 16, 2004.
10. Projektgruppe "Netzwerke im Stadtteil," *Sozialräumliche Vernetzung und Kooperation in den Gebieten des Programms E&C: Ergebnisse der ersten Phase der wissenschaftlichen Begleitung* (Munich/Halle: Deutsches Institut für Jugendforschung, 2004), 81.

CONTEMPORARY ACTIVIST ART
Stella Rollig

In 1988, the New York artists' and AIDS activist group Gran Fury developed a subject for a calendar for the media workshop "The Kitchen." One page showed a photo of a street demonstration. In the text on the reverse side, Gran Fury took a position on the question of what constitutes an adequate reaction to the devastating effect of AIDS: "With 42,000 dead, art is not enough." Almost a decade later, in winter 1996/97, the Zurich Shedhalle used the second half of this phrase as the name for an exhibition on art and activism: "art is not enough." The conviction that the beaux arts are not enough to meet the demands of the times was adopted from New York to Berlin, Los Angeles, Geneva, and Rotterdam.

Public awareness, politicization, and the demand to have an effect that reaches beyond art audiences were the declared objectives of a type of artistic practice that can be traced back to the beginning of the last century. From Russian revolutionary art to Dada and John Heartfield, a thread runs all the way through to the activist Conceptual Art of Hans Haacke and on to the Guerilla Girls, while the more playful street actionism of the surrealists as well as Fluxus and Happening delivered the prototype for a colorful, rather harmless "art into life" spectacle for their actionist successors. But the analytic, agitating, and activist art of the 1990s owes most to the 1960s, when Conceptual Art and institutional critique entered into a fruitful alliance (at least for art itself), using content and methods derived from the new social movements centering on civil rights, emancipation, and peace. Influential contributions to the art of the 1990s came from the Art Workers Coalition, Dan Graham, Michael Asher, in Europe Joseph Beuys, Otto Mühl and the AA-Kommune, and Stephen Willats, and later, from the United States again, Stefan Eins with Fashion Moda, Tim Rollins & KOS, Adrian Piper, Barbara Kruger, Jenny Holzer, and Martha Rosler.

Precipitated by AIDS and the Reagan administration's discrimination against AIDS patients, in the 1980s in the United States the art scene became connected to a purpose-driven protest movement that proved to be rather effective for a few years. In addition to Group Material, Gran Fury, and Fierce Pussy, there was also Act Up (Aids Coalition to Unleash Power)—the largest organization of its kind and operating nationwide. AIDS activism could not be separated from the struggle to gain rights for homosexuals and ethnic minorities, or from the censorship debate, the pauperization of large sectors of the population under Reaganomics, and questions about voice and representation—which in turn led to the establishment of new media collectives such as Paper Tiger TV and new feminist groups such as WAC (Women's Action Coalition). As AIDS activists, artists made reference to strategies of the grassroots movement, yet they also took up the visual language of art and advertising. In Europe all this was followed with great interest, was quoted, imported, and imitated, until the time came when action was necessary at the European end, too.

After the end of history was prematurely declared, it started up again in 1989: the collapse of the real existing socialist systems in the East, the fall of the Berlin Wall, the unification of the two German nations, which was staged as a return home for the eastern German states; then the war in Yugoslavia, migration due to war and economic depression, social tensions, xenophobia, recession, unemployment. The minimal club group, based in Munich and Berlin, spoke of a "partial suspension of art," thus referring to a political-activist practice of using the social field of the fine arts solely as a springboard. The goal of a critical intervention into society became the cornerstone of progressive artistic work, which was realized here in Germany in a more radical fashion and with a greater willingness to dispense with art(works) than in the United States, where this trend was limited from the beginning due to the market-dominated structure of the art industry there.

While the simulation theorists of French postmodernism delivered a theoretical underpinning for this art, another branch of the humanities became relevant: cultural studies as developed in England and North America. Globally and socially oriented, cultural studies satisfied a need that the structure-infatuated poststructuralists and the object-fixated art historians could not fulfill: the desire for a "real" life, a mingling with popular culture, insight, voice, action, and change.

Breviary of the Leading Concepts and Their Protagonists
Context
The modernist accomplishments of autonomous artwork are falling off their pedestals. Autonomy suddenly appears as the presumption of a special status and a veiling of the interests and dependencies within which art is produced. In this sense, the demand for contextualization means making transparent the structures and conditions under which artistic production and its presentation come into being; art is described as an "operating system" and its internal machinery is laid bare ("neoinstitutional critique").[1] What began as a critical unmasking, for example with Andrea Fraser's staged museum tours starting in 1986, ends with exhibitions such as "Backstage" (Kunstverein in Hamburg, 1993; Kunstmuseum Luzern, 1994) or "This is the show, and the show is many things ..." (Museum van Hedendaagse Kunst, Gent 1994), in which the only thing that suggests revelations about institutional exhibition practices are the titles themselves.

The word "context" as it is used in German is equivalent to the English term "site specificity," but in contrast to the English term it refers first and foremost to the socioeconomic structure of the site under consideration. Instead of the specificity of place, it is the specificity of a given situation that is necessary; this is, however, worlds away from the legacy of Minimal Art, which refers to size, proportion, and materials and which has long since degenerated into a justification for works devoid of insight and consequence.

Process, project, practice
After "context" and "discourse," the terms that have been stretched the furthest in the art of the 1990s are "process," "project," and "practice," which are largely interchangeable given that a project is about a process and vice versa, and both are about the dominant appearance of "artistic practice," as "making art" is popularly called in a general effort to demystify it.[2] The production of a work becomes more important than the product, forms of action more important than the means of expression.

Starting in 1993, exhibition venues and large exhibitions increasingly made efforts to upgrade their image as new and contemporary with so-called project art. New methods

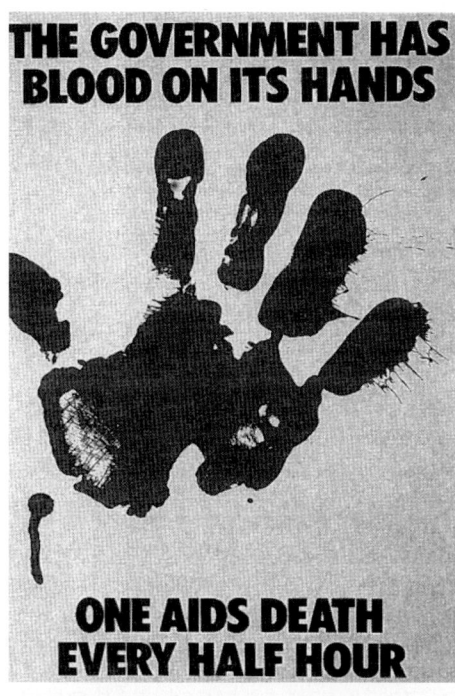 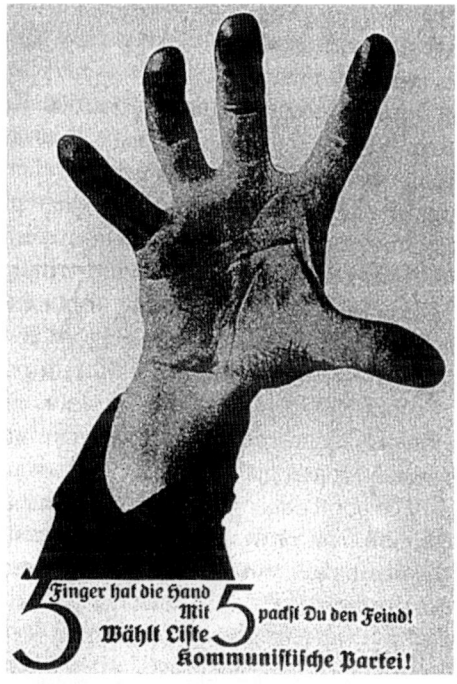

◂ The group Gran Fury created this poster in the 1980s to protest the lack of government response to AIDS.
▸ The design harks back to a political poster by John Heartfield from 1928.

influenced, for example, "Sculpture Chicago—Culture In Action" (Chicago, 1992/93), "Sonsbeek" (Arnheim, 1993), "Unité" (Firminy, 1993), "INTEGRALe Kunstprojekte" (Berlin, 1993), and then the big events of 1996: "Now/Here" (Humblebaek), "manifesta" (Rotterdam), and "nach Weimar" (Weimar). Their status as "projects" formed the least common denominator in these exhibitions, in which the individual contributions varied in purpose between analysis and amusement. In 1997, "documenta X" and "Skulptur. Projekte in Münster" ultimately brought to a head (and into the mass media) the polarization between intellectual analysis (in Kassel) and crowd-pleasing entertainment (in Munster).

Starting in the early 1990s, progressive program exhibition venues such as the Künstlerhaus Stuttgart under the direction of Ute Meta Bauer replaced the conventional display of works at least partially with conferences, lectures, workshops, and publications (e.g., the magazine *Meta* in Stuttgart) and the establishment of archives (e.g., the artists' archive Informationsdienst Kunst (Art Information Service) initiated by Bauer, which was started as a commentary on and complement to "documenta IX"). The Munich Kunstverein (under the direction of Helmut Draxler) and the Shedhalle Zurich (which after Harm Lux left was led by a shifting trio of curators, among them Renate Lorenz, Marion von Osten, and Justin Hoffmann) put their faith in politically motivated exhibitions and informational work, whereby particularly in Zurich compilations of materials, film series, workshops, and so forth largely did away with the presence of artworks in exhibition spaces.

Public sphere

As soon as artistic practice strives to have an effect beyond the borders of the art system, the "public space" becomes an important field of activity. Usually artists working on such projects are left to their own initiative because few organizations will assert in advance that exhibition spaces must not necessarily be filled or have the financial resources for nomadic projects. Among the German municipal corporate entities for art in the public sphere, there were seldom exceptions to the standard placement of sculptures. One exception was the city of Langenhagen, and another was Hamburg, where the cultural authorities entered experimental territory with "weitergehen" (going further). Private enterprises devoted to projects in the public sphere are also largely dependent upon state subsidies. In London, at least two organizations have been maintained in this way: the Public Art Development Trust (which works with artists such as Angela Bulloch and Henry Bond) and ArtAngel (whose most famous commission was a sculpture, Rachel Whiteread's *House*—the concrete mold of the interior of a house marked for demolition in East London).

The abundance of projects at the museum in progress (mip), founded in Vienna in 1989, was for many years the fruit of mip's collaboration with state sponsors, and now increasingly also with commercial partners. Operating out of a small office, mip places its "exhibitions" in the media sphere. Artists are invited to place inserts in the Austrian daily *Der Standard,* in 1995/96 the news magazine *profil* was the location of a year-long photography exhibition entitled "Traveling Eye," the television series *do it* with instructions by artists was broadcast by the Austrian television station ORF, and every year a different artist is commissioned by mip to create large-format posters as part of an advertising campaign for Austrian Airlines (the artists commissioned thus far include Gerwald Rockenschaub, Felix Gonzalez-Torres, and Rosemarie Trockel).

In publicly accessible spaces—where the media address the largest possible audience—questions about the function of art, its addressees, and its ability to carry on a dialogue become even more urgent than inside the White Cube. The works published by mip reflect the entire spectrum of artistic positions: from contextualism, that is, the illustration of a daily newspaper's media laws (for example, Heimo Zobernig's empty page, Clegg & Guttmann's translation of a Hebrew publication, Andrea Fraser's publication of readers' reactions to the project as a whole), to attempts to involve readers (e.g., Fabrice Hybert's puzzle game, Christian Marclay's invitation to crumple up the page), to references to current political issues (e.g., Martin Walde's page about the Oberwart bombers, who were still unknown at the time), and to pure imagery (e.g., Rosemarie Trockel's flowers, Christy Astuy's colorful Buddha baby).

In general, "public" art is measured today according to the conceptual position of its audience. A good work of art, so the consensus, must figure its audience as a constitutive factor in its own making, in a sense as a partner. The artist's responsibility toward his/her audience and respect for the audience's needs thus become a central demand placed on contemporary artworks. What the needs of the audience are, however, has been and continues to be defined by the art itself. Therein lies one of the most intractable dilemmas of art today, a dilemma that most attempt to ignore: what is to be done when this audience desires neither critical insight nor a call to take political initiative or any other action, but instead simply seeks aesthetic pleasure and otherwise wishes to be left alone?

As soon as a project is dependent upon the collaboration of the public—usually a well-defined segment of the public—convincing this public of the significance and purpose of the project becomes an integral part of the work involved. This inseparability of art and its reception has led to the coining of the term "mediating art." Those looking for a propaganda brochure on this subject are well served by the catalog *Culture in Action*.[3] The concept behind this city-space exhibition was represented as being socially conscious, collaborative, and process-oriented. Instead of exhibiting art objects in the streets, eight artists and artist collectives worked together over the course of a year mostly with groups of underprivileged people, including AIDS patients, Latino youths, and people living in subsidized housing. The catalog emphatically declared this public art as attributing equal significance to artists and audiences and as art that encourages dialogue through collective action, while in his introductory essay Michael Brenson raves about "real people, real neighborhoods." The abundance of life, as the art critic imagines it: the Haha group created a vegetable garden for AIDS patients, Iñigo Manglano-Ovalle founded the Street-Level Video Collective with teens from the Latino community, and Mark Dion organized a study of a park ecosystem for schoolchildren.

Community

"Culture in Action" has meanwhile been thoroughly discussed, indeed, it has become a discourse paradigm in which, depending on the respective standpoint, either model social responsibility, the absence of aesthetic pleasures, or the threat of purposive art being appropriated by municipal or social politics can be addressed. In the context of "weitergehen," the project "Park Fiction" represents the social engagement of artists who care about local needs and work hard to attend to them.[4] WochenKlausur—an artist group that since 1993 has undertaken focused social interventions from within the institutional base of the art industry—has taken up this same position in Austria. Since its first project, which organized medical treatment in a mobile clinic for homeless people in Vienna, WochenKlausur has carried out a series of social interventions in different European countries under the direction of Wolfgang Zinggl and with a changing crew of artists. But why not leave this type of thing to the experts, for example social workers and politicians?

"Artists' initiatives have a few advantages over the others. They use *their own* institutions. Because of the social and political value of culture, the media and civic capital possessed by these institutions allows for quick and unbureaucratic access to those who make the decisions. Cumbersome red tape can thus be avoided. The limited scope of these projects means that the energy required is readily available and they can be realized rather quickly."[5]

Of course, this is also about money. WochenKlausur transforms art budgets into social budgets. The fact that art institutions play along shows that the social concept has clout in the art scene. In the United States, aiming art projects toward a "community" has become one of the most powerful means for gaining legitimacy. Integrative action has become the guiding light for art in cultural administration, and private foundations organize their funding catalogs according to this principle. Cultural representation has become the most important identificatory element for ethnic, social, and political communities. The danger is that art takes the burden off social policy and is used by political actors as a Band-Aid or short-term diversion mechanism in situations of discrimination and marginalization. But also under "normal" circumstances in which social cohesion is missing, art serves a welcome role by producing a feeling of community that is lacking. This is how Clegg & Guttmann's "Offene Bibliothek" (Open Library) can be interpreted, which has been realized in Graz, Hamburg, and Mainz since 1991. Situated in an outside space, the project makes reference to the internal structure of social living units and the people who inhabit them, in other words to the "neighborhood." A shelf filled with books collected in the community invites neighbors to borrow books on the basis of an exchange for three months. If a citizens' initiative emerges by the end of the art project to support the continuation of "its" library, such as was the case in Hamburg-Volksdorf, then the artists have been successful as social animators.

A shift in emphasis from the ideal of professionalism and internationalism in the 1980s to today's focus on local intervention is what generally distinguishes the art produced in these different decades. From urban development debates to work in individual neighborhoods, artists have become involved with their immediate environs.

Self-organization

At the end of the 1980s, erecting an independent infrastructure for the production, presentation, publication, and distribution of art became a necessity for the 1990s generation, but it also constituted a programmatic battle against the establishment, which wanted to bring commodities into circulation again as fast as possible. One's "own" infrastructure was always connoted as "subcultural." Temporary home galleries and club galleries presented art as a hedonistic party accessory, collectively administered spaces were conspiratorial meeting points, events were only open to the initiated, newspapers considered themselves fanzines or manifestos, and even the factions that were serious about politics took on the fashion and drink codex of the club scene.

Cultural worker

For the project art of the 1990s, the question of its status as art was ostensibly irrelevant. As with all earlier avant gardes, it was no longer a matter of expanding the notion of art; what was at issue was a redefinition of the identity of artists. With the surrender of autonomy and with the aid of infrastructure and not least the financial means garnered from art as an institution, a space was opened up in which a sincere dialogue with the public could be developed and even concrete problems dealt with. Project artists renounced a special social status and the associated authority that always determines a hierarchical relationship with the audience.

With the dwindling belief in creative individuality, the boom for groups, collectives, and action communities seemed only natural. This development was not only explained on the basis of political strategies, but also by poststructuralist theories of the disappearance of the individual author from the collective conscience and the fracturing and shifting of stable identities. There were also very practical reasons that led to the development, such as the organizational efforts required for projects and the necessity of connecting the parallel or substitute system with the commercial mainstream. With the devaluation of personal expression and the avoidance of an artistic trademark signature, what emerged was an aesthetic of cool understatement, of the anonymous and the functional, which was represented in lapidary installations that had the atmosphere of an office, archive, information center, or club.

"We Are Not Afraid": A 1981 media campaign by Les Levine in the New York subway to combat racism.

Just like the artists, others involved in the art industry tried out new roles. Since artists no longer simply created works but also wrote texts, did research, engaged in interventions, created communication settings, offered services and political analyses, and published material compendiums, the distinction between their work and that of the critics, authors, and curators was no longer clear-cut nor did it make sense. As a reaction to this merging of professions in the cultural field, the term "cultural worker" was imported from America.

The appropriation and import of methods from academia as well as collaboration with its representatives was suited to contemporary practices. Artists were engaged with sociology (Clegg & Guttmann), biology and ecology (Peter Fend/Ocean Earth, Mark Dion), philosophy and cultural studies (Rainer Ganahl), history (Renée Green), biotechnology (minimal club), and urban studies (Yvonne Doderer), often using the same types of methods, interviews, and research as journalists. A closer look shows, however, that the change in roles was not permanent. First and foremost it was the artists who expanded their repertoire of activities—think of the many exhibitions curated by artists, or the curatorial and publishing work and the theory production by members of minimal club or BüroBert. The reverse situation, the curator as artist, usually implies the accusation of hypertrophic self-realization at the cost of the "true" creative artists. And true artists are in demand more than ever, even more than in the days of object fixation, because organizers need specific projects for each exhibition.

Commissioned artists research the history and contemporary structures of the institutions involved, the situations of local residents, local ecological problems. They install bars, cook for visitors, and work on improving the local infrastructure. As researchers and reporters, animators, social workers, designers for local spaces, or dialogue partners, they become the center point of the work. Without artists, nothing works in this business; nothing happens without their physical presence over a long period of time. Project curators thus become the directors, whose essential task is to coordinate event programs with the travel and work schedules of the artists, almost like in the opera business.

Service

The concept of service is central to the art of the 1990s given that it exposes the core of different phenomena and working methods. "Services" was the title of Helmut Draxler and Andrea Fraser's multi-part, international event that addressed strategies of collaboration with and/or resistance to the power of institutions in the art industry.[6] The objective was to draft a contract—taking into account historical precursors—that was meant to establish security for artists (not least through payment), particularly in projects commissioned by institutions. This goal was not reached, however.

Andrea Fraser's artistic development shows how critique of institutions can suddenly turn into frictionless compliance. The self-critical irony in the notion of service becomes all too apparent here: the fact that the critique of commissioned work has its own inherent contradiction, namely that artists are only accepted by institutions if they are suitable to represent the image of those commissioning and are able to fill an institutional vacuum with their project—a trap that is almost impossible to avoid, even if it is recognized as such. One example of this is Fraser's "Project in two phases" (1994/95), commissioned for the opening of the EA-Generali Foundation's new building in Vienna. For this project she researched the structure, self-conception, and internal acceptance level of the insurance company's engagement with art, thereby staging her offer of "artistic services" with the knowledge that controversial disclosures would not have been permitted.

When artists move into the role of graphic artists, designers, and so forth, this implies that they are offering a service, such as Heimo Zobernig's sketching of the musical stage for "documenta IX," his poster for "Skulptur. Projekte in Münster" in 1997, or his redesigning of the printing locations for the Vienna Secession; or, for example, Rirkrit Tiravanija's construction of a reading room in the Hamburg Kunstverein, or Gerwald Rockenschaub's musical art-party catering (Rockenschaub has a second career as a DJ). The art of the 1990s developed a whole range of working methods that can be seen, depending on the perspective, as creating new paradigms, as a welcome way of occupying the audience, or as a way of economizing in the hire of experts: from Tiravanija's Thai dinners to Christine Hill's secondhand shop Volksboutique, from Andrea Zittel's furniture modules to Christine and Irene Hohenbüchler's care of the handicapped and social outsiders, from Matta Wagnest's chanson evenings to Rainer Ganahl's reading seminars.

Counter-public sphere

In November 1992, BüroBert, along with local groups in Cologne, organized a month-long project in the CopyShop entitled "(Gegen)öffentlichkeit und Gebrauchswert" (The (Counter-) Public Sphere and Utility Value). The interconnections that were made or that were intensified there between art practices and political initiatives were later documented in a book.[7]

Artists and political groups with similar working methods were invited to participate in an informational exchange on art, the public sphere, and the economy. The insistence on relevance shaped this and other similar undertakings. The spectrum of topics included those that touched on the social phobias of the day, for example AIDS, immigration, biotechnology, and genetics—topics that seemed to desperately call for a correction of public misinformation and agitation against the interests of the economy and the reactionary press.

At the end of 1992, the Wohlfahrtsausschüsse (Welfare Commissions) were founded—a coalition of artists, musicians, and authors who opposed the strengthening of nationalism in Germany. Groups were formed in Hamburg, Cologne, Dusseldorf, Frankfurt, and Munich; events were organized—among others the "Ost-Tour" (East Tour) through eastern Germany in 1993—and a reader was published.[8] Members of the groups BüroBert and minimal club made names for themselves by specializing in producing provocative materials exhibitions; their venues were Kunst-Werke in Berlin and the Shedhalle in Zurich. In 1993 Stephan Geene collaborated with Art in Ruins and Wolfgang Winkler to organize "trap" at the Berlin Kunst-Werke, which was an exhibition and series of events on the problem of trying to defuse social and political issues from within the art world. This was followed by other projects of the same genre, including "Game Girl" (Shedhalle, Zürich, 1994) and "when tekkno turns to sound of poetry" (Shedhalle, Zurich, 1994; Kunst-Werke, Berlin, 1995)—discourses on biotechnology and genetics, feminism, gender construction, faith in technology, the youth and music scenes. At this point, the connection to relevant nonartistic initiatives was not being made on the whole, and the central problem of "counter-public sphere" art projects became evident, namely the fact that "counter-public sphere" had come to mean nonpublic and that it was hardly possible for a public that was "just" interested but not directly involved to play a productive role in the dense staging of media, materials, events, and so forth, and/or to filter out the main messages.

1998

The American collectives Group Material and Gran Fury, once the forerunners of resistance, finally succumbed to disillusionment and announced their breakup. Act Up became rather silent, and WAC became history. Communitarianism found an unexpected but welcome partner in the remnants of American goodwill art, with which local neighborhood work and citizen solidarity can be dressed up with the glamour of the avant garde. While a few years ago contemporary art was still hotly debated—with accusations ranging from obscenity to blasphemy to corruption of the fatherland—today reconciliation has arrived on the scene in the ideal of "community service."

In the German-speaking realm, the development was different. The institutions harnessed the momentum of younger artists as a hip, colorful event culture that can be talked up to the audience as avant garde. Those groups, initiatives, artists, and curators, whose critical opposition to elite institutions, to the market, and to its star system was once their strength, increasingly forfeited their ability to engage in dialogue and now manage to maintain their self-marginalization with in-fighting. It is paradoxical: the more intensely the politically motivated art scene engages with topics of urgent interest to the general public, the more hermetically sealed off it becomes. Within this closed-off sphere, in-fighting to establish the pecking order and strategies to improve one's own status led to the neglect of communication with the outside world, as if the point were dealing with the right issues rather than having an actual effect.

But content-related work, critique, and the creation of a public audience for repressed facts and unrecognized interconnections are still as badly needed as ever—this is equally true for the art industry as it is for "real life." For the latter it can at least be said that awareness about the problems and the willingness to protest globalization, neoliberalism, the tightening of European immigration policy, xenophobia, biotechnology, and so on, are growing. The art industry has had to endure a few disclosures; it continues to generously offer freedom in the choice of topics and strategies, and welcomes, if need be, assertive political positions in order to better control them and cushion their effect.

Translated from the German by Christina M. White

This is an abridged version of the article "Das wahre Leben: Projektorientierte Kunst in den neunziger Jahren" (True Life: Project-Oriented Art in the 1990s), first published in *Die Kunst des Öffentlichen: Projekte/Ideen/ Stadtplanungsprozesse im politischen/sozialen/öffentlichen Raum,* ed. Marius Babias and Achim Könneke (Dresden: Verlag der Kunst, 1998). It is reprinted with the kind permission of the author.

Notes

1. Cf. Thomas Wulffen, ed., special issue "Betriebssystem Kunst" of *Kunstforum International* 125 (January/February 1994).
2. "Making art" was the title of an exhibition held at the Kunstverein für Kärnten, Klagenfurt, in 1993. The exhibition was subtitled "Zum Rollenverständnis des Künstlers" (On the Role of the Artist).
3. Mary Jane Jacobs and Michael Brenson, *Culture in Action: A Public Art Program of Sculpture Chicago* (Seattle: Bay Press, 1995).
4. See AG Park Fiction, "Aufruhr auf Ebene p: St. Pauli Elbpark 0–100%," in *Die Kunst des Öffentlichen,* ed. Marius Babias and Achim Könneke (Dresden: Verlag der Kunst, 1998), 122–131.
5. Wolfgang Zinggl, "Die WochenKlausuren," in *Im Zentrum der Peripherie: Kunstvermittlung und Vermittlungskunst in den 90er Jahren,* ed. Marius Babias (Dresden: Verlag der Kunst, 1995), 305.
6. "Services," a materials exhibition that included discussions with Helmut Draxler and Andrea Fraser, was presented in the Kunstraum at the University of Lüneburg in January 1994 and later in the Künstlerhaus, Stuttgart, and the "Depot" in Vienna, among other venues.
7. BüroBert, ed., *CopyShop: Kunstpraxis und politische Öffentlichkeit; Ein Sampler* (Berlin: ID Verlag, 1993).
8. Wohlfahrtsausschüsse, ed., *Etwas Besseres als die Nation: Materialien zur Abwehr des gegenrevolutionären Übels* (Berlin: ID Verlag, 1994).

SOCIAL CHANGE, SELF-EMPOWERMENT, AND IMAGINATION
A conversation with artists Irene Bude, XPONA (Dmytri Kleiner, Tanja Ostojic, David Rych), Anke Haarmann, Kristina Leko, Tadej Pogacar, and Isa Rosenberger

Barbara Steiner and Kathleen Liebold: The term "empowerment" has various meanings; it is used in art contexts and it is also often found in neoliberal discourses. What does the term mean to you?

Irene Bude: Empowerment should be understood as an emancipative strategy. Our work is not about the empowerment of repressed groups or individuals. It would be naive to believe that a single artistic measure could accomplish this, if you think of the power relations that form the context in which we live and act. Emancipation is a process that takes a long time and it is not at all easy to regulate through art. Within this process we can try to produce work that allows people to explore certain experiences or perspectives.

XPONA: If we look at the original meaning of empowerment, it refers to a "development from below" in an emancipative sense, whereby vulnerable social groups restructure their potential in order to make their own decisions. We see the danger of a false understanding of empowerment in highly administrated and expensive projects that promote the social empowerment of political and/or commercial groups under a pretext and in a way that is quite apparently opposite to the actual meaning of the term.

Tadej Pogacar: If we understand empowerment as helping people find self-help, then this implies that there is knowledge on the one hand and a lack of knowledge on the other: the power of one side and the powerlessness of the other. As with other social processes, empowerment should be understood as a constituent part of power. We must always ask who gives authority to whom and to what purpose, and how the participants are socialized. In the theory of the "new parasitism," artists occupy the lowest rung on the ladder alongside other marginalized groups. If we think of the collaborative and participatory projects with marginalized social groups, we are speaking of a "weak-weak" relation that is based above all on solidarity and mutual exchange.

Kristina Leko: If I could choose between "empowerment" and "cultural revolution," I would choose—with reference to my participatory projects which are aimed at bystanders, and common and working people—"cultural revolution," even if that might sound silly. Participatory artistic projects are emancipative when they reach the right people and motivate them to take part in cultural life. Individual empowerment is a necessary process, as is the process of cultural democratization.

Isa Rosenberger: A distinction between "self-empowerment" and "empowerment" makes sense to me. I have certain difficulties with the term empowerment. Granting others power implies that one is in a position to do so and knows what others need—this smacks of paternalism. I personally am less interested in empowerment than in an (immaterial) exchange or a temporary alliance in the sense of an exchange of different experiences, competences, and viewpoints. In contrast to empowerment, an alliance refers to something that is dialogic in principle and implies that everyone potentially contributes and also receives something.

And self-empowerment, granting oneself power in the sense of Michel de Certeau, who describes the daily activities of consumers "who are allegedly condemned to passivity and conformity" and who "convert the law of this economy into the economy of their own interests and rules"—this seems to me fundamentally different than the term empowerment and it is a much more productive idea for my artistic work.

The demand for intervention in the real world is also inherent to the "Shrinking Cities" project. Often in discussions, the real and the symbolic are contrasted and action in the realm of the real is demanded. How do you understand the relationship between the two?

Anke Haarmann: I think it is all about taking the transition between the two into account—not only the transition from the symbolic to the real, but also vice versa, the transition from the real to the symbolic. In any case, politics take place in the transitions. This is where it is being decided which notion of the city should dominate and which urban reality will be asserted. And I mean "being decided" in the sense of activity. It is about the actions of those involved or the effect of things. These transitional areas in the debates cannot be overlooked and are diverse, because every individual action within them has an effect and is also significant, yet it is the accumulation of actions with similar effects and similar significance that leads to certain realities and symbols becoming permanent and thereby also uniform. It is the small things in everyday ways of thinking and the common activities that together make up the whole of the imaginary and actual reality of the city. It is precisely in these unspectacular places that the individual politics, or, if you will, the individual ethics of intervention occur. That's why our work is concerned with the particular activities of individual subjects in the city, in their conflicts with the dominant ideas and the reality of urban spaces.

Tadej Pogacar: We don't believe in a sharp distinction between symbolic action and other forms of behavior. All actions that are undertaken express something more than their mere manifestations. In our work we are interested in the actions of groups, usually isolated groups, who develop clever practices and alternative methods of survival. Symbolic rituals, as an intervention in so-called real life, can expose hidden mechanisms. A repetition of the symbolic can enable a view of true reality.

XPONA: An artistic project can only solve the problem of shrinking cities on a symbolic level. On a small scale, however, it can be highly functional. The effect of a symbolic gesture at the right time and the right place should not be underestimated; it could precipitate future transformations. A gesture alone would remain hollow; it wouldn't touch the real. XPONA's work has the underlying intention of thinking about things in functional terms—in the sense of an authentic empowerment. The guiding principle is the introduction of a combination of do-it-yourself technology, old-fashioned bartering, and antixenophobic community involvement—familiarizing marginalized groups with one of the technologies and strategies at their disposal.

Kristina Leko: Dealing with the social topoi is the only way for art to maintain its liberty and universality. This can perhaps prevent art from becoming a form of entertainment for privileged groups and intellectuals or collectors. In my art I want to bring about concrete social change, no matter how small the scale. This doesn't mean, however, that art can solve problems that should be tackled by other disciplines. Art cannot serve as a substitute for educational systems, urban planning, or other social disciplines. Social change does not take place on the material plane, rather it is about a change in relations and perceptions. And what could be more real than our perception? And what could influence our actions more than our perception?

Isa Rosenberger: "Images can eat through reality." I think that the "infiltration" and "juxtaposition" of other images can very well shift the perception of reality.

What role does the imagination play?

XPONA: It plays a big role as a motivator and as an inspiration. We can imagine a better world, better social and political conditions. The imagination allows us to think our future society. In social projects, imagination is something everyone needs. The power of the imagination, which is in constant circulation, allows us to continually reinvent our environment.

Irene Bude: Yes, well, what is imagination? I would rather speak of a sensibility for the possible, a notion of sketching the possible. An essential aspect of emancipative strategies is being able to imagine something else beyond the status quo.

Kristina Leko: Whenever I work together with a group of people, I try to introduce an unexpected and unusual situation. I call these events "little miracles" (project participants travel from Croatia to Hungary, they receive their photos printed as postcards or free plane tickets, or a cow shows up at an exhibition opening). These things are not just happenings, they intensify the group feeling among those participating.

Tadej Pogacar: Without imagination, no change will take place. Through our power of imagination we construct our own worlds, which allows us an alternative view of things and frees us from our own blindness. It has been demonstrated often enough that those who "can create fictions or have an imagination" are the true realists.

Anke Haarmann: I like to dream.

Isa Rosenberger: Imagination is very important, in the sense of having an autonomous interpretation and confronting dominant ideas with alternative ideas and images.

To what extent do you take political and economic factors and existing power relations into account in your work and in your projects?

Tadej Pogacar: At the beginning of the 1990s, we founded the P.A.R.A.S.I.T.E. Museum of Contemporary Art, a virtual institution and a critical body that among other things also analyzes institutions and centers of power in the art world as well as in other social contexts. In the era of late capitalism, the economy became the socially dominant value and discourse. We are convinced that the economy has taken over the traditional place of religion. This is why this issue plays a central role in our work.

Irene Bude: Power relations are present in the personal experiences and individual stories of those who participate in our projects. If you simply ask people about their working conditions or their living conditions, immediately the bigger political context in which they live and which directly affects them becomes apparent.

Kristina Leko: I think there is no way for me to constantly repress my own political views. The interplay between power and dominance in public spaces, on the one hand, and, on the other, the distribution of the potential in the community for work and communication—these constitute key aspects. I have worked with farmers, milk-maids, immigrants from Sarajevo, old people, and children, and I have always addressed the public. In this way, I have always tried to influence public opinion about a locally relevant issue.

XPONA: Political and economic factors are the true cornerstones at which the relevant actions in our society are anchored. Power and hierarchical structures define access and the possibility of directly affecting these factors. These are important parameters in our work and/or in the theoretical discourses that accompany it, and we take these into account as much as possible, in so far as we are aware of them.

Isa Rosenberger: Artistic action is always inscribed in the matrix of existing political and economic power relations—I try to keep this in mind. If the classical avant garde demanded the unity of art and life, I can agree to the idea that today the emancipative and political potential of art should instead be sought by investigating its genuinely artistic means and the extent to which these can be interpreted as a catalyst for a critique of the dominant relations and for a discussion of alternative ideas.

Translated from the German by Christina M. White

In 2004/05 the artists worked with project grants from the Museum of Contemporary Art Leipzig in the context of "Shrinking Cities."

THE WORLD ECONOMIC CRISIS, SUBSISTENCE ECONOMICS, AND MODERN URBAN PLANNING
Markus Kilian

On October 25, 1929, a dramatic fall in prices on the New York stock market caused the first worldwide economic crisis, the effects of which were felt well into the mid-1930s. The still rather young discipline of urban planning, whose task so far had been to give shape to the growth spurts of large cities, was now confronted with a severe recession in the areas of government finances and economic development, and, in a kind of chain reaction, also rapidly rising unemployment. In addition to the continued shortage of housing in Germany, the unemployment rate grew to 33% by 1932, which meant that around six million people were unemployed. The period known as the "home-interest tax era," during which the Weimar government subsidized the construction of large, internationally renowned housing developments, came to an abrupt end. The number of new residential buildings fell by approximately 85% within a single year.[1]

During this period of dire need, a fundamental debate started at the political level, but also among architects and urban planners. On the one hand, those who believed in developing a consequential planned economy demanded that industrial and agricultural production be rationalized and real-estate speculation checked through nationalization. On the other hand, traditionalists close to the Nazi Party declared the source of evil to be the rapid growth of the cities in the preceding decades and the moral "degeneration" this supposedly entailed. They demanded territories in eastern Europe for what they considered a *Volk ohne Raum* (a nation without space).[2]

The situation was particularly tense in the larger cities because of above-average unemployment. Besides Cologne and other cities in the Ruhr Valley, Berlin in particular experienced a population decline after a long phase of continuous growth. In Berlin, Germany's capital city, the official number of inhabitants stagnated at around 4,332,000 in 1930 and then dropped to 4,218,000 in 1934.[3] However, the actual number of people migrating from the city was considerably higher. Martin Wagner, head of the planning and construction department for the City of Berlin and a strong advocate of the planned economy, saw the shift of trade jobs into the outlying communities as a major cause of the crisis in the large cities: "Urban planners cannot just show interest in the movements from a bad location to better and even the best locations. Equally important are the movements that can be described as the effects of a concentration and fusion of industry, which also displace jobs. A large part of the local job loss in the industrial region along the Upper Spree River described above can be traced to this movement caused by concentration and fusion, and a large part of this migration is still to come."[4]

In addition to the migration of industrial jobs evident from the statistics, many unemployed people left the cities because they could no longer pay their rent and were evicted, while "ten-room apartments in the city center remained vacant."[5]

Those who had the right connections and contacts fled to small towns that were still agriculturally oriented, where they could meet their basic needs self-sufficiently. In the outskirts of the cities, "wild" (i.e., illicit) settlements without construction licenses were popping up—usually on city property—in arbors, allotments, or improvised housing. "In many cities, particularly in the West," Alexander Schwab complained as early as 1931,

"Wild" settlements in the 1920s and suburban settlements after the Second World War inspired planners to use the principles of a subsistence economy in their new settlement plans. ▲ Makeshift shelter near Düsseldorf, 1945.

"hordes of unemployed have taken possession of city property, without worrying overmuch about ownership or permission, have divided up the land among themselves and started to build primitive huts and farm a garden plot."[6] It was estimated that there were 70,000 to 80,000 improvised dwellings in Berlin alone, and 100,000 lots in neighboring areas, as early as 1930.[7]

The initiatives of the architects and urban planners were unceremoniously overridden by the politicians who in September 1931 implemented the *Dritte Notverordnung* (Third Emergency Decree) containing a program for *Stadtrandsiedlungen* (suburban settlements): The Brüning government's program proposed to legalize the "wild" settlement activities and establish new plots for the unemployed using state funds. These were meant to help settlers augment their livelihood through subsistence farming. Groups of unemployed people selected for this project were able to build houses through mutual self-help. These consisted largely of conventionally constructed homes with standardized blueprints, built on leased lots of between 500 and 2,000 square meters. Building costs ran to about 3,000 reichsmarks. To supplement their own means, they were eligible for low state loans of up to 2,500 reichsmarks. Unemployed construction workers, whose industry had crashed, had the best chances of obtaining lots due to their practical building knowledge.

Again, vehement debates broke out in all political camps. Numerous modernist architects considered the settlements on the city outskirts to be the first step toward a new symbiosis of city and countryside, as a loosely mixed cityscape of the future.[8] "The problem of the settlements," Adolf Rading wrote in 1931, "is not to keep the unemployed busy working the land, but to make the unemployed fit for work, to employ twice or thrice

In order to thin out the density of large cities, single-family units with large gardens were to be built out of the war rubble of tenements (Max Taut, 1946).

their number through part-time work, and to secure them a livelihood through additional subsistence farming and cheap housing."[9] More moderately conservative planners and politicians agreed with the Stadtrandsiedlungen because they represented the return to an agricultural lifestyle on a small scale. The apodictic right wing, however, believed that the programs promoting a return to a *Bauernvolk* (peasant nation) did not go far enough to be able to correct the "civilization tragedy of the German nation."[10]

With the help of the Stadtrandsiedlung, and above all the "wild" settlements, the housing situation at the end of the Weimar Republic returned to premodern standards, even lacking in basic hygienic and sanitary necessities. Sanitation was limited to shared wells and toilet pits in the backyard, which was also meant to allow the self-sufficient raising of crops. Provisional unpaved roads and paths were built by the residents themselves, which meant that in the event of persistent rain, settlements would sink into the mud. The Heinefeld settlement in Düsseldorf, where outlaws and people in dire need settled from 1925 onward, was reputed to be the "wildest of all wild settlements." It was considered a refuge for anarchists and criminals, a "Wild West settlement," where the police often gave up on trying to keep law and order. Besides solidly built structures, some settlers lived in improvised dugouts. Architectural journals spoke of a "Balkanization of housing."[11] Ultimately, the Stadtrandsiedlung program did not suffice to alleviate the continual hardship and misery. Berlin, for example, was allotted only 2,442 loan-subsidized settlement locations during the first phase, which was largely completed by the end of 1932. By 1935, five consecutive phases, each with its own forms of financing and means of selecting settlers according to their "political reliability," had been completed.[12]

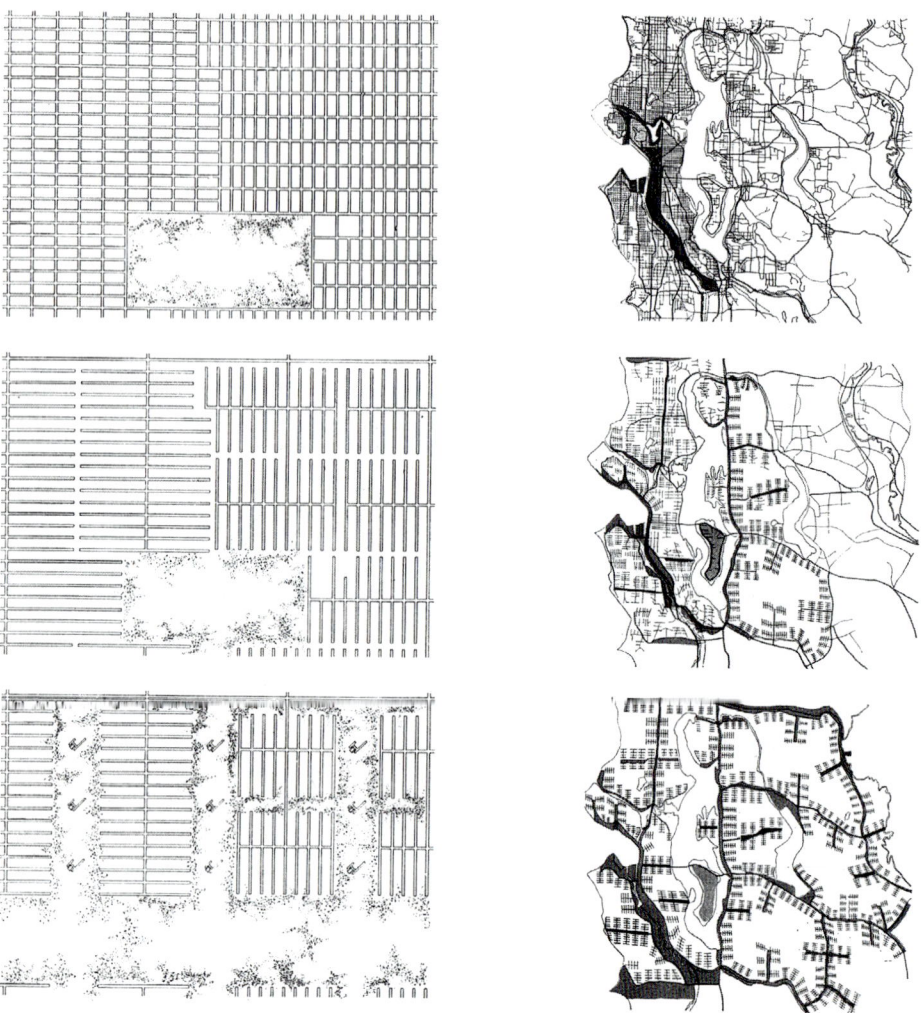

◀ The gradual transformation of Marquette Park, South Chicago (left), and Seattle (right) into the less dense, idealized settlement structures of the New City (Ludwig Hilberseimer, ca. 1950).

▶ Ludwig Hilberseimer's proposal for reorganizing the settlement of the eastern United States (1945): Congested areas of the rust belt and other metropolises are dispersed into city belts along the main infrastructure routes.

The World Economic Crisis, Subsistence Economics, and Modern Urban Planning_Markus Kilian

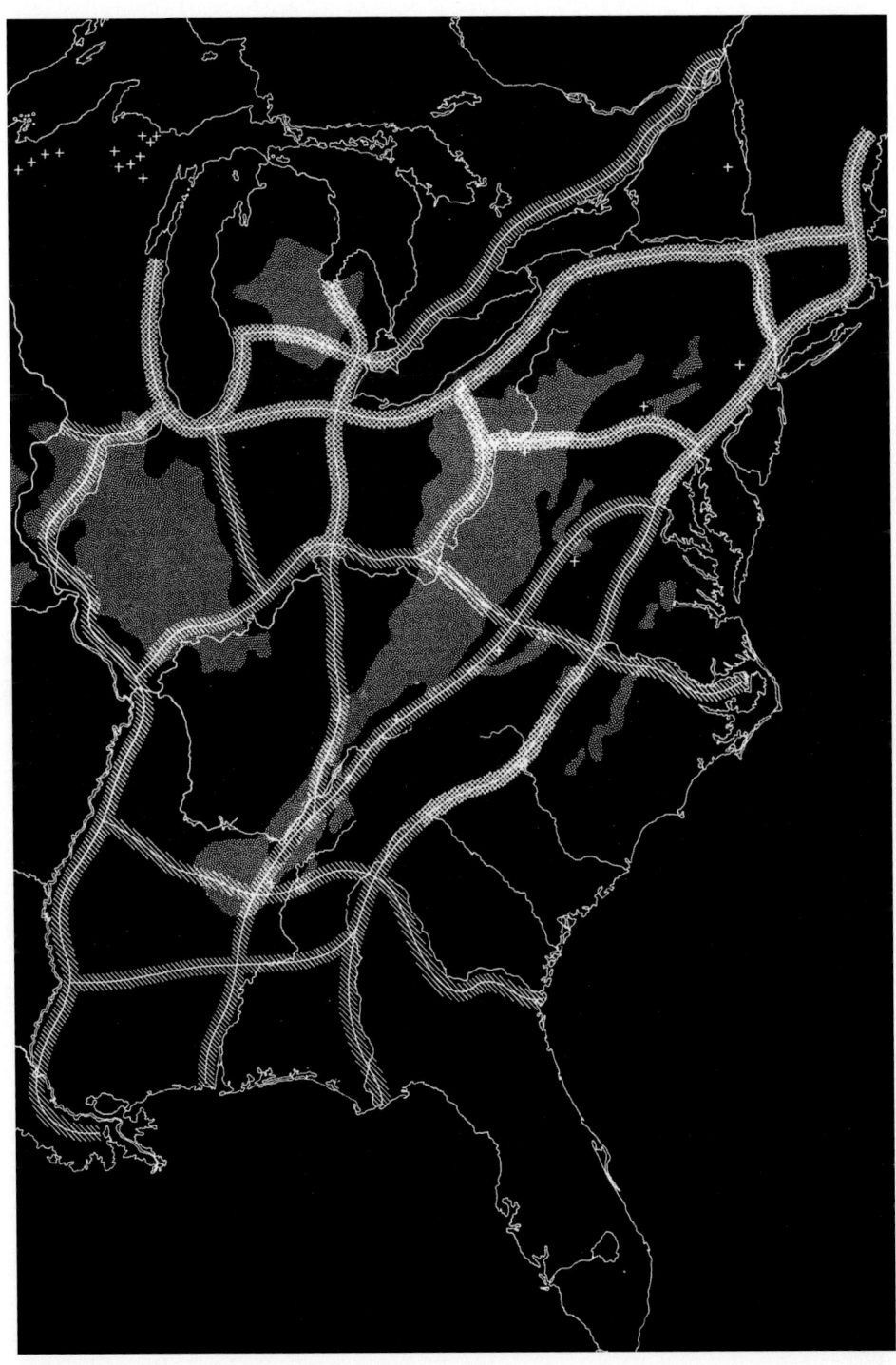

In the United States, too, the Great Depression in the wake of the events of 1929 left its mark on the cities. "With the end of the boom of the Twenties the cities slowed their rates of growth, even lost population in 1933 and again in 1938—temporary losses, but unprecedented in all the years since the land was colonized."[13] "Rural migration, regional population shifts, and urban population decline simultaneously," Robert Beauregard noted.[14]

The intermittent population decline created far fewer problems than the increasing segregation and the spread of slums in the cities. As in Germany, many planners and architects in the United States developed strategies for decentralizing and breaking up metropolises during this phase. The most famous such initiatives were the Garden City movement (whose representatives in the United States included Frederic Olmsted), the studies done by the Regional Planning Association of America, and Frank Lloyd Wright's "Broadacre City," which he contrasted with the degenerated metropolises in his 1932 publication *The Disappearing City*.[15]

A progressive architect, Ludwig Hilberseimer, had been intensively engaged with the decentralization of Dessau and Berlin since 1929 while serving as a teacher at Bauhaus Dessau. He drew the most radical conclusions from the far-reaching consequences of the world economic crisis and developed a flexible and comprehensive global settlement pattern.[16] After his emigration to the United States in 1938, he analyzed American studies on the decentralization of large cities. In addition, he made recourse to contemporary academic research in sociology (Chicago School), demography (Frank Lorimer, Frederick Osborn), ecology and economy, geography, and the regional and agricultural sciences (Ralph L. Woods, Paul B. Sears, F. H. King), using them as the starting point for his considerations.[17] He studied numerous projects by other planners to determine their potential for spatial planning and adapted them for his New City.[18] In his book *The New Regional Pattern,* Hilberseimer proved himself farsighted in addressing not only the consequences of industrialization, automation, and mass unemployment for urban development, but also the effects of an aging population: "But when this lengthening life span is accompanied, as it is, by a declining birth rate, it may create the most crucial problem of our civilization."[19] According to Hilberseimer, cities cannot reproduce themselves demographically and are therefore dependent upon migration from rural areas. He reiterates Julian Huxley's fear that after a phase of overpopulation, during the next fifty years cities will face the problem of underpopulation.[20] He repeatedly invokes the decline of Rome as a warning of the possible future direction for urban development. Hilberseimer wanted to correct the predicted consequences of industrialization and capitalism by implementing a fundamentally new concept. His goals were to ensure economic stability and to work against demographic shrinking by developing an alternative urbanism.

In addition to the typical components of modern urban planning, such as orienting buildings toward the sun, the separation of functions, fishbone-like street structures with minimal walking distances between residents' living and working places, and the positioning of heavy industry according to the prevailing winds, he also developed a system of safety measures to protect people from all manner of possible crises. Like the vegetable gardens in the Stadtrandsiedlungen, the settlement units and the regions were to form self-sufficient units that produced their own wares and agricultural products.

A subsistence economy was to give individuals security and personal independence and protect the factory workers from the effects of unbalanced economics. Hilberseimer illustrates this using the example of job insecurity in the Detroit automobile industry.[21] He suggests that two people share a job and be allotted enough land to provide for themselves in order to maintain a livelihood. His concept entails agricultural fields pervading the city, replacing a large number of buildings, as well as small factories industrializing the rural areas.

Hilberseimer and his students at the Illinois Institute of Technology in Chicago produced hundreds of studies in which cities in America, Asia, and Europe were to be transformed step by step into the idealized New City structure with a low population density. The different projects all follow the primary planning principles, but do not yield a fixed geometric structure. They conform to the topography and are drawn in such a way that while intermediate phases already mark a clear improvement according to planning principles, an ideal state is described as a final goal. This was the idea behind the "Lafayette Park" project in Detroit (1956–1963), which was planned as a small section of the New City and carried out with Mies van der Rohe as the architect and Alfred Caldwell as landscape designer. As the sole New City project that was in fact realized, this isle of parkland in a sea of conventional grid structures represents internal flexibility and process-oriented integration in a suburban environment.[22]

The plans blend urban structures with the surrounding landscape. Their rigid, schematic character is the only feature that allows the settlement units to be distinguished from real suburbanization or urban sprawl.[23] Nature and housing penetrate each other. By means of ever-finer branching structures, the contact area linking the New City to the surrounding countryside is extended infinitely, transforming it into an endless park landscape. This breaks the cities down into small units with a low population density and anticipates the thinning out, the peripherization, and the suburbanization of Western inner cities in the second half of the twentieth century.

On the one hand, the settlement areas are decentralized in order to counteract the concentration of population in the metropolises. At the level of regional and state planning, however, an equal distribution of urban structures is not the aim. Studies in the eastern United States and in the region around Warsaw show how settlement structures cluster in ribbon-like strips along the new highway systems and along natural resources. As in shrinking regions today, the already thinly settled population will become concentrated in corridors along the main traffic arteries. Far away from these transit spaces, nature and wilderness can reconquer extensive areas, while prospering suburbs will be concentrated along strategically located ribbons; for example, like along the Rhine River all the way up to southern England today.

For a short while immediately after the Second World War, emphasis was placed on radical plans for decentralization in Europe. The cities lay in ruins and had lost large parts of their populations because of the war. In Berlin, the number of inhabitants dropped to 2,807,000 in 1945;[24] in Cologne, the maximum population, which was counted as 768,000 in 1939, was reduced to 40,000 in March of 1945, but rose again to 447,000 in December of the same year.[25] The population decline in the cities was not solely due to the bombings; it was also related to a food shortage, which led to a rise in rural subsistence agriculture especially in the last year of the war and in the initial years following it.

As a student of Ludwig Hilberseimer at Bauhaus Dessau, Hubert Hoffmann had already intensively worked on in-depth studies on decentralization. He saw Germany's

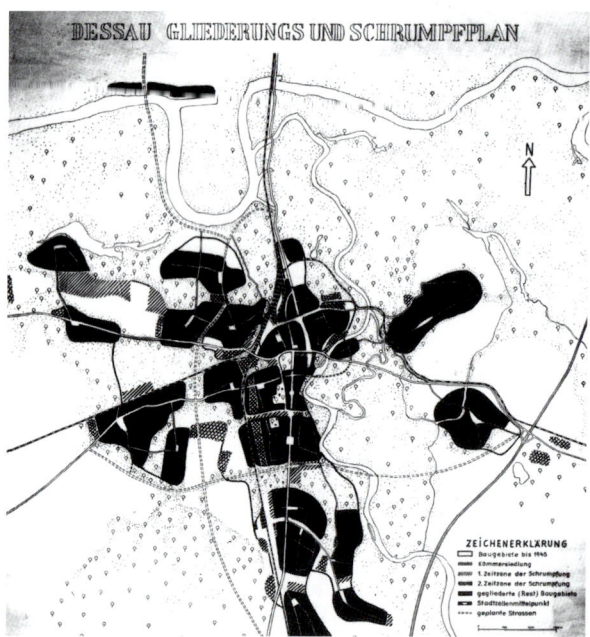

Hubert Hoffmann, a former student of Ludwig Hilberseimer, understood the war-torn cities and the deindustrialization after the war as a chance to reestablish a balance between city and countryside by reorganizing cities into less densely developed urban quarters interspersed with green areas. He put this idea to use in his 1945 "sectioning and shrinking plans" for Dessau and Magdeburg. Only those buildings that were less severely damaged were to be restored, and heavily damaged areas (hatched lines) were to be converted into green zones made available for subsistence farming.

deindustrialization as a reaction to losing the war and the destruction of the cities as a unique chance to bring the "degree of urbanization" back down to the preindustrial level seen in 1870, reestablishing what he called a "healthy" balance between cities and agricultural areas.[26] His recommendation was that huge cities with over a million inhabitants should shrink by about 50%, and cities of 200,000 inhabitants by about 10%, while the population of small cities of around 50,000 inhabitants should be increased by 50%.[27] Hoffmann created model shrinking plans for Dessau and Magdeburg in 1945 with the goal of dividing and structuring the urban fabric using parkland. While certain street blocks of Magdeburg were to remain undeveloped, the "sectioning plans" for Dessau were aimed at transforming the ruined structures into a core city with outlying satellites. Dispersed housing, counting approximately 30 to 60 apartments per hectare, was to be accomplished by building one- and two-story terraced houses using materials garnered from the rubble.

One year later, Max Taut referred to the great economic value of the underground infrastructure, which had remained largely intact, in his text *Berlin im Aufbau*.[28] He suggested the pragmatic approach of maintaining the layout of most streets and then thinning out the cities by keeping down the density of construction. The transition "from tenements to cozy living quarters"[29] was to be accomplished by building detached one- and two-family housing units with large gardens on the lots where the large tenements and their courtyards had been. As with the expressionist "Stadtkrone" (City Crown)[30] conceived by his brother Bruno Taut one year after the First World War, the evening sun was to shine over the romantic landscapes of ruins and idyllic single-family homes.

Both Hoffmann and Taut tried to strike a balance between reform ideals and pragmatic viability, thereby intentionally remaining far afield of Hilberseimer's radical approach. Plans for reconstruction developed by Hoffmann, Taut, and the Planungskollektiv centered around Hans Scharoun, which were only under discussion for a few years, are perhaps close to Hilberseimer's ideas.[31] They are, however, pragmatically oriented—and increasingly so as the end of the war lies further distant—toward the local economy and local conditions. After the Allied Forces endorsed the Marshall plan in 1947 and fundamentally changed the economic conditions for Germany's three occupied western sectors, the plans focusing on shrinking quickly became irrelevant. The reconstruction boom allowed the growth-oriented models to take precedence once again.

Translated from the German by Christina M. White

Notes
1   For example, in the cities of Berlin, Hamburg, and Cologne. See Tilman Harlander, *Siedeln in der Not: Umbruch von Wohnungspolitik und Siedlungsbau am Ende der Weimarer Republik* (Hamburg: Christians, 1988), 40.
2   See Klaus Bergmann, *Agrarromantik und Großstadtfeindschaft* (Meisenheim: Hain, 1970), 66, 79, 283; Harlander, *Siedeln in der Not,* 47–50.
3   Figures correspond to today's Berlin city limits. Source: Landesamt Berlin, *Statistisches Jahrbuch Berlin* (Berlin: Kulturbuch-Verlag, 2004).

4   Martin Wagner, "Sterbende Städte? Oder planwirtschaftlicher Städtebau?" in *Die Neue Stadt* 3 (1932/33), reprinted in *Neues Bauen, Neues Gestalten—Das Neue Frankfurt / die neue stadt—eine Zeitschrift zwischen 1926 und 1933*, ed. Heinz Hirdina (Dresden: Verlag der Kunst, 1984), 261-262.
5   Ibid., 258.
6   Alexander Schwab, "Baupolitik und Bauwirtschaft—Stadtrandsiedlungen," in *Die Form* (1931), 399-400; quoted in Harlander, *Siedeln in der Not*, 43.
7   K. von Mangoldt, "Die Städtische Kleinsiedlung," in *Die Wohnung* (1930/31), 156; quoted in Harlander, *Siedeln in der Not*, 43.
8   For example, Roger Ginsburger, Otto Haesler, Wilhelm Lotz, Adolf Rading, and Alexander Schwab in *Die Form* (1932); quoted in Harlander, *Siedeln in der Not*, 51.
9   Adolf Rading, "Erwerbslosensiedlung," in *Die Form* (1931), 101; quoted in Harlander, *Siedeln in der Not*, 52.
10 See Harlander, *Siedeln in der Not*, 47ff.
11 For example, *Soziale Bauwirtschaft*, quoted in Harlander, *Siedeln in der Not*, 44.
12 See Harlander, *Siedeln in der Not*, 68ff.
13 "Rebuilding the Cities," *Business Week* 566, July 6, 1940; quoted in Robert A. Beauregard, *Voices of Decline: The Postwar Fate of US Cities* (Oxford, UK: Basil Blackwell, 1993), 83.
14 Beauregard, *Voices of Decline*, 83.
15 Frank Lloyd Wright, *The Disappearing City* (New York: William Farquhar Payson, 1932). Another publication in the same vein is Eliel Saarinen, *The City: Its Growth, Its Decay, Its Future* (Cambridge, MA: MIT Press, 1943).
16 Ludwig Hilberseimer, *The New City: Principles of Planning* (Chicago: Paul Theobald, 1944); for more details, see Markus Kilian, "Großstadtarchitektur und New City—Eine planungsmethodische Untersuchung der Stadtplanungsmodelle Ludwig Hilberseimers" (doctoral thesis, Faculty of Architecture, University of Karlsruhe, 2002), 87ff.
17 See Ludwig Hilberseimer, *The New Regional Pattern: Industries and Gardens, Workshops and Farms* (Chicago: Paul Theobald, 1949).
18 See Hilberseimer, *The New City*, 55ff.; also see, for example, the linear-city concepts of Soria y Mata, Milyutin, and Leonidov; the garden and satellite cities by Ebenezer Howard and Raymond Unwin; as well as Wright's "Broadacre City" and Patrick Geddes's ideas on regions.
19 Hilberseimer, *The New Regional Pattern*, 72.
20 Ibid., 78.
21 Ibid., 171.
22 See Charles Waldheim, ed., *Hilberseimer / Mies van der Rohe: Lafayette Park Detroit* (Munich: Prestel, 2004).
23 See Albert Pope, *Ladders* (Houston, TX: Rice School of Architecture, 1996), 71ff.
24 Figures correspond to Berlin's present city limits. Source: Landesamt Berlin, *Statistisches Jahrbuch Berlin* (Berlin: Kulturbuch-Verlag, 2004).
25 Amt für Stadtentwicklung und Statistik, *Statistisches Jahrbuch der Stadt Köln* 32 (Cologne: Stadt Köln, 1946), 10-11.
26 Here Hoffmann's socialist-motivated ideas overlap with the Nazi rhetoric of a Bauernvolk.
27 Hubert Hoffmann, "Raumordnung und Wiederaufbau der Städte: Denkschrift der deutschen Akademie für Städtebau" [1945], manuscript, Archive of the Akademie der Künste, Berlin.
28 Max Taut, *Berlin im Aufbau* (Berlin: Aufbau-Verlag, 1946).
29 Ibid., 15.
30 Bruno Taut, *Die Stadtkrone* (Jena: Diederichs, 1919).
31 See Werner Durth, Jörn Düwel, and Niels Gutschow, eds., *Architektur und Städtebau der DDR*, vol. 1, *Ostkreuz, Personen, Pläne, Perspektiven* (Frankfurt am Main: Campus Verlag, 1998), 90ff.

THE BUFFALO IS DEAD
NEW WORK FOR SHRINKING CITIES
A conversation with philosopher Frithjof Bergmann
___
___

Frithjof Bergmann, born in Saxony and raised in Austria, was awarded a year's scholarship in Oregon in the United States at age nineteen for an essay entitled "The world in which we want to live," and he ended up staying in America. He worked as a dishwasher, prize boxer, assembly-line worker, and longshoreman, lived as a subsistence farmer in the countryside for two years, studied philosophy at the Ivy League university of Princeton, received his doctorate, and taught at Princeton, Stanford, Chicago, and Berkeley. In the 1970s he traveled in the Eastern Bloc countries, gave some attention to the issue of communism, which he found outdated, and searched for an economic model that went beyond that of a planned economy or that based on capitalist wage labor. Today he is a professor of philosophy at the University of Michigan in Ann Arbor and a guest lecturer at the University of Kassel.

In 1984 Bergmann worked together with General Motors to found the first Center for New Work in the automobile city of Flint, Michigan. Since then he has traveled around the world advising governments, companies, unions, municipalities, youths, and the homeless on questions concerning the future of work. (Ed.)

Philipp Oswalt and Tina Veihelmann: Work is the primary causal problem of shrinking cities. Cities shrink when there is no more work. The loss of workplaces also affects the cultural and public life of a shrinking city. What does the situation look like in Detroit and Flint?

Frithjof Bergmann: Detroit and Flint look like empty shells; everything that had constituted life there has died out. Detroit and Flint are automobile cities. Since the 1980s there has been a dramatic loss of jobs. Today you can drive for ten kilometers in Detroit and you get the impression of a city in ruins. Two-thirds of all stores have closed down; the windows are broken or boarded up. In the abandoned, half-burned-down houses you can still see the status that was once represented here. You can read off the facades what work brought to the city and what went down with it. The personal status represented by the villas, the activity, public life, everything.

In Detroit the whole pathology of our culture of work becomes palpable. I like to use the following comparison: what work is for us, the buffalo once was for the native Americans. The buffalo was everything. He was the bow and arrow, the teepee, the meat, the moccasins. Life was unimaginable without the buffalo. For us, work is everything. All our conceivable values are linked to work. Work is survival, status, self-esteem, fulfillment, the meaning of life. The madness of our culture is that in the same epoch in which we allowed work to accumulate this central importance, we have also let work shrink away.

Detroit and Flint are the places where you gained your first significant experiences with your debates about work ...

If you are doing research on work, you must go there where the question arises. Originally, I had a professorship at Stanford and Berkeley in California. But, as they say in America, "In California people don't even know what work is." Because I always believed that research and practice must be intertwined, I first went to Detroit and then to Flint. In Detroit I soon realized that the city was too big for things to change. With a city the size of Flint, you had a better overview. There was nothing but auto factories, and they determined every aspect of the lives of each person living there. I founded a group with a variety of people who came from the union movement, management, and companies; one was a priest, and one was the deputy mayor of the town. We predicted that 50% of the jobs would be cut—a grim prophesy that would in fact come worse in reality. After two years of preparatory work, we presented the following suggestion to the unions and the management of General Motors: instead of laying off half of the employees, the workers should work for half the year in the factory and use the other half for some kind of self-determined work. We founded the Center for New Work for this very purpose. The management accepted, and mass layoffs were prevented.

An attempt, in other words, to avoid mass layoffs through part-time work.

No. There was more at stake. As long as the premise is that a worker renounce wages and working time so that everyone can work, this kind of model is bound to fail because it depends on altruism and self-renunciation, and the worker receives nothing valuable in return. We were also primarily concerned with the quality of the new work. A big problem with work is, of course, not only that there are fewer and fewer jobs, but also that no one is really doing what he likes to do and is good at. In our discussions with the workers this was a very common complaint. The concept of new work that we decided upon in our talks with workers in Flint was: "Work that we really, really want." If the workers could work according to their inclinations, skills, and ideas, a lot of energy could be generated and possibly sensible things would develop that no one otherwise had the time or the means for under the given conditions. The Center for New Work would provide the space, time, advice, and support needed to develop one's own projects.

Were the workers compensated for their self-determined work outside the factory?

No. The management was very open to my idea as far as promoting the creativity of the workers went. They imagined that further education would be carried out at the Center for Work. They found the idea nice and charming. But as regards the question of money, they closed the door on us. Although the employees in Flint's auto industry earn so much that this part-time work was possible without further compensation, it was still not exactly what I had in mind. That was a big disadvantage.

That is, if the employees were not to be disadvantaged in an extreme way financially, then the old form of work would have to be retained—as the unions were demanding. No manager would understand why he should pay for creativity in the form of a Center for New Work.

I don't think this would work in the long run. Due to technological progress, work is being diminished more and more. You can't stop this, and you shouldn't. That would be like refusing to accept the invention of the telephone. And anyway, why shouldn't machines and computers take over dull and undignified work? My suggestion is rather simple, but radical.

Instead of defending each and every job to the last drop of blood, we should turn the strategy around 180 degrees and say: we aren't against machines taking over

OUT OF WORK, INTO REALITY!
Stuttgart and Berlin, Germany, 2004/05
bankleer (Karin Kasböck and Christoph Leitner) in cooperation with Akademie Schloss Solitude, Stuttgart Employment Office, lagalo, Salz & Wut Initiative of the Unemployed, Bündnis gegen Sozialabbau

———

In the "first-contact" zone of the Stuttgart state employment office, bankleer created a week-long installation out of office furniture that featured video screenings, flyers, banners, and a small library—the simulation of an office in the midst of everyday life in the employment center, but filled with counter-information. Together with local initiatives for the unemployed, the group organized a program during office hours with activities that changed daily, from resistance yoga and politico-hip-hop karaoke to indoor demonstrations, daily action events, and bevies of zombies.

The figure of the zombie, the living statistical corpse, is meant to make visible the excessive, nonfunctional horror that characterizes contemporary life in global capitalism and determines the automatic creation of excluded and disposable individuals. In further projects, bankleer promotes a positive expansion of the concept of work that extends beyond gainful employment: for example, "a-class"—a series of video clips and installations addressing alternative "lifestyles in full-employment science fiction" (in cooperation with workstation). (Ed.)

———

The original German title of this project is "Raus aus der Arbeit, rein mit der Realität!"

———

Zombies in the first-contact zone of the Stuttgart state employment office, now called the Agency for Employment.

human work, but we put the responsibility for this on the management. In the place of each job we demand a grant with which the worker can do meaningful work according to his own wishes.

This fundamentally contradicts the approach of the unions, which is to defend the bulwarks of classical work for an increasingly smaller clientele. This is not the way to find solutions for the increasing proportion of the population who no longer have work or never did. As long as the unions insist on their old strategy, they are condemned to fighting skirmishes on the retreat; they will lose touch with young people and offer no prospects for the future.

Your concept of creating Centers for New Work or offering grants with the aid of companies that are cutting jobs only reaches out to those people who are losing their jobs at a company. For some shrinking cities, for example in the new German states, this does not represent a solution because there are hardly any companies left.

The way the suggestion was introduced in Flint, this would be true. But the idea has been further developed since then. Precisely because of this problem. The financing for grants, the Centers for New Work, and the workshops cannot be taken over by classical companies alone because wage labor would be reduced to such an extent that it would hit a minimal level. Two sources of funding must be found in order to finance New Work. On the one hand, I'm talking about the immense sums that are currently being spent to create or retain classic jobs—investments to stimulate economic growth, and subsidies. By subsidies I don't only mean the classic subsidies for unprofitable economic branches such as coal, but also the subsidies that companies like BMW receive. And here I also mean the bribes paid to companies so they don't move jobs to countries where wages are cheap.

The second source of funding would be through a change in the tax system. All money that is related to productive work should be tax-free. On the other hand, a tax of up to 60% would be levied on money generated via financial business or speculation. If this plan were carried out, so much money would be available that we wouldn't even know what to do with it all.

Do you believe this would be easy to put into practice?

No.

If every unemployed person received a grant with which he could do whatever he wanted— is this not similar in terms of the practical consequences to a base income such as that promoted by André Gorz?

I'm not a fan of base income. To me this goes too far in the direction of social welfare. Welfare is the old way of compensating for the loss of work. Work declines, and at the same time people are maintained at a certain level, they become dependent and feel like they are taking advantage of the system. I would like not only to hold on to the principle of productive work, I would like to promote it and develop it. That's why I find it important to link a person's desired work with compensation for that work. My idea of grants is that they are linked with a particular endeavor that someone would like to carry through.

You said that old wage labor should continue to exist on a low level and a new culture of work with different forms of work should emerge: wage labor in companies, desired work in Centers for New Work ...

Imagine a model that looks like an inverted sandwich. Previously everything was held together by the hard bread, and in the middle there was a condiment, salad, and fresh tomatoes. The bread is the wage labor. In the future, salad and fresh tomatoes will predominate, and in the middle of the sandwich there will also be a layer of wage labor. The model for a system with three types of work: the rudimentary remnants of wage labor, desired work, which I have already described, and a third component that can partially secure a person's living: self-sufficiency. You produce the goods that you yourself need. This is the principle of the peasantry. For hundreds of years it worked well—if you disregard the fact of serfdom. Today we could realize self-sufficiency on a much higher level.

Are you sure that a model of peasant-like self-sufficiency is appropriate for shrinking cities? And haven't you already tried out the subsistence economy in your own life and then abandoned it?

Very much so—because I had a quite wrong understanding of something. I mistook an eco-back-to-nature dream for the project of taking my life into my own hands.

When I say "self-sufficiency," I don't mean raising sheep or struggling to barely survive on a clod of earth, but instead an additional source of income through the application of sophisticated technology in a workshop. These workshops might look a bit like photocopy shops and would be equipped with computers for production purposes. Computers that manage production, so-called fabricators, are already being researched in the automobile industry. It won't be long before they're ready for use. Just like everyone burns CDs at home today—which no one could imagine ten years ago—we will be able to make all kinds of things ourselves that are needed for daily use. Cell phones, for example, or contact lenses. It wouldn't be possible to produce absolutely all products on your own—high-tech self-sufficiency would just be an additional module in securing one's livelihood. This kind of self-sufficiency is an urban, not a rural, model and could very well be realized at a neighborhood level in shrinking cities.

How much time would one spend every day doing what kind of work?

In the future, we would still pursue wage labor for one or two days a week. We would produce high-tech items for our own use for one and one-half days a week, and for another two days a week we would work on something we really want to do.

And this "sandwich model" will generate a new culture of work?

Yes. Those who are gainfully employed in the industrial age can be compared with classical musicians who practice and play a certain piece of music. The high-tech self-sufficient people, who work one day a week in a company and otherwise carry out the work they really want to do, they're more like jazz musicians who improvise. They develop skills and creativity that make them able to lead a life in which they find fulfillment, despite an economic environment in which secure, well-paid jobs are disappearing.

You travel a lot and present your ideas to various audiences. You once said that audiences in the new German states are much more open to the idea of New Work than those in the old German states.

I call them the new states and the old-fashioned states. It is much more refreshing to talk about work in the new German states than in the old western German states. The

WORKSTATION
Berlin, since 1998
WochenKlausur and ideenwerkstatt berlin e.V.
www.workstation-berlin.org, www.wochenklausur.at, www.ideenaufruf.org

———

The project "workstation" was initiated in the spring of 1998 with a three-month intervention by the Viennese artist group WochenKlausur at the Künstlerhaus Bethanien in Berlin-Kreuzberg. As a solution to the lack of a nonbureaucratic contact opportunity for the unemployed, the group founded the association "ideenwerkstatt" with the help of Frauke Hehl. Since then, workstation has been offering space and support in various locations in Berlin for a dialogue on how to establish various forms of work and activities beyond traditional employment and the monetized economy.

The project offers individualized counseling to youths and adults on realizing their dreams and utilizing their skills, helping them with questions concerning work, securing a livelihood, financial assistance, and supporting institutions. The participants organize projects such as the "Intercultural Garden" in Friedrichshain-Kreuzberg or the recycling project "Kunst-Stoffe," which delivers materials usually not thought of as recyclable to artists and cultural workers whose main interest is to create sustainable models of work and economy via self-determined and community actions. In addition, workstation has an amateur choir and a small library focused on the issue of work, it organizes various activities for youths who sign up for a year of volunteer service, and, for example in the "a-class" project, it documents experimental lifestyles beyond classic employment. By appropriating an unused railway-service facility in Warschauer Strasse at the end of 2000, workstation started the initiative "Ideenaufruf zur partizipativen Gestaltung des Geländes" (Call for Ideas on the Participative Shaping of the Area), which is still active and serves as a walk-in service and information center for developing ideas on shaping the urban environment and the lives of people in the neighborhood. (Ed.)

WochenKlausur discovered this poster calling for a demonstration and an "Uprising of the Unemployed" while carrying out research on unemployment in the Berlin neighborhood of Kreuzberg.

inhabitants of eastern Germany's cities have already taken leave of old industrial work, a painful leave-taking. They know much better than the West Germans that the buffalo is dead. In the East a new language is already being spoken. If I talk about "self-determined work" there, they say, oh yeah, Marx talked about something like that: nonalienating work. And this is indeed what Marx said. He didn't mean exactly the same thing as I did, but this at least leads to a dialogue and ultimately to new ideas.

Don't you think you might be overburdening people by trying to redefine such a central thing in their lives as work? The old work offered first and foremost a fixed place in life, it required social conformity, subordination, and diligence. New Work, which you associate with concepts such as improvisational jazz music, requires independence, an ability to endure uncertainty, innovativeness, and improvisation.

One difficulty that we do not take lightly is what I call in my book "the poverty of desire." Before you can begin with desired work, you have to know what it is you really want. When you ask people spontaneously what they really really want, most of them look at you bewildered and shrug their shoulders. Almost all people—and not just factory workers—have learned their whole lives to do what is expected of them, but never to find out what it is they themselves want. When their ability to want something has been this wounded, it often leads to apathy, indifference, cynicism, and depression. And these are our cultural diseases. I would assert that this is the first problem that we have to deal with. This alone demands effort and innovative ideas. If there weren't so much to do still, then we wouldn't need the Centers for New Work.

Translated from the German by Christina M. White

OPERA OF THE UNEMPLOYED
Berlin, since 2001
Robert Linke and Hans-Joachim Schulze

The "Opera of the Unemployed" is an initiative by students and academics with and without jobs. They developed the concept of an opera about unemployment based on genuine correspondence with the Labor Office. The libretto documents the correspondence between the Labor Office and the unemployed artists Robert Linke and Hans-Joachim Schulze. The plot consists of a series of appeals against decisions made by the Labor Office.

The opera was supposed to be performed by unemployed people in the Labor Office itself and to be funded indirectly through unemployment benefits. However, the Labor Office refused to support the project on the grounds that unemployed people involved in producing an opera would no longer be actively seeking work or available for interviews. Unemployment benefits were denied the project's initiators, Linke and Schulze, on account of their unpaid artistic activity. (Ed.)

The original German title of this project is "Die Arbeitslosenoper."

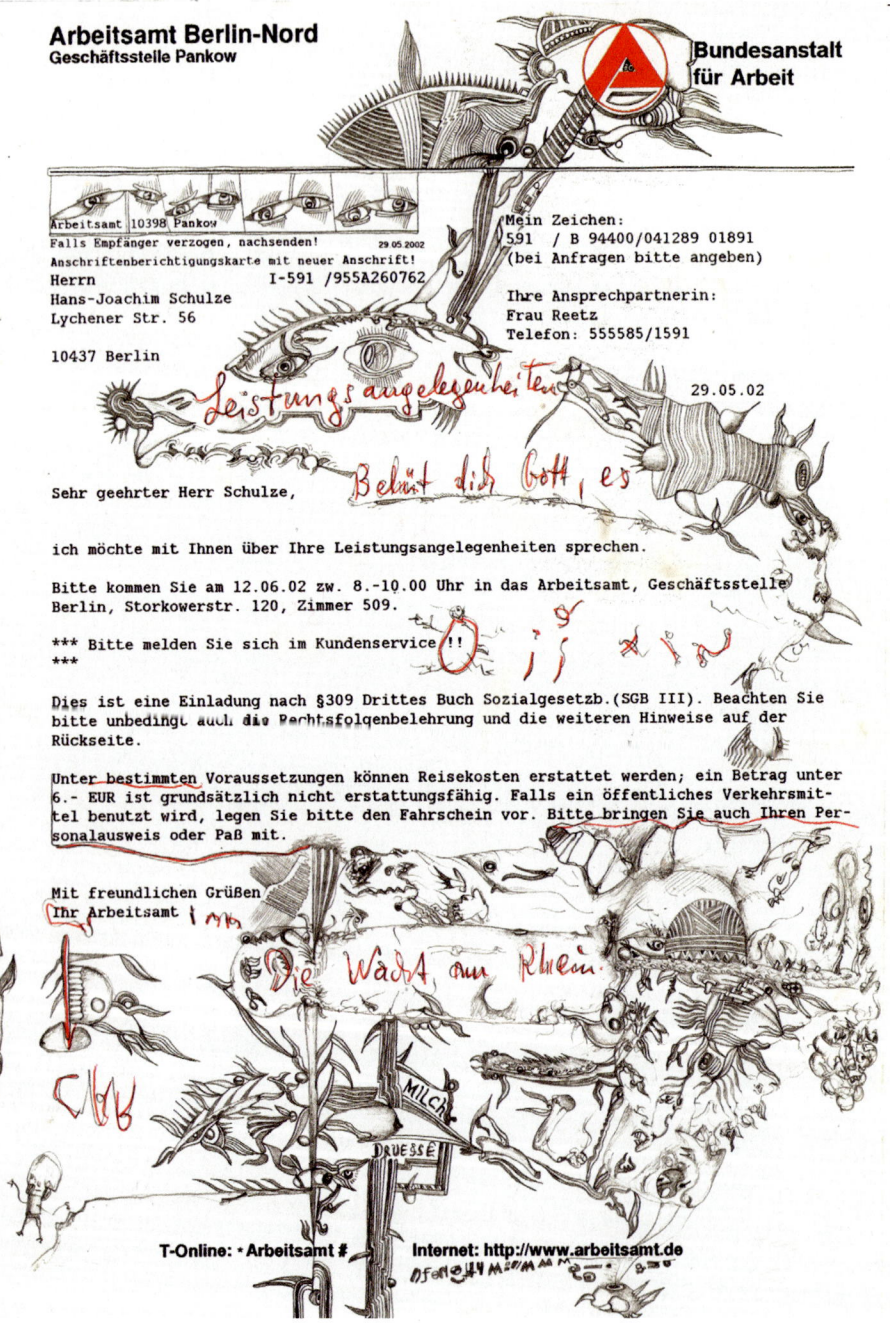

Correspondence between the North Berlin Labor Office and artists Linke and Schulze documents how absurd communication can be in the absence of a common language. Whereas unemployed people hope for assistance that takes account of their respective personal capabilities, the authorities answer in "officialese," offering only

Opera of the Unemployed_Robert Linke, Hans-Joachim Schulze

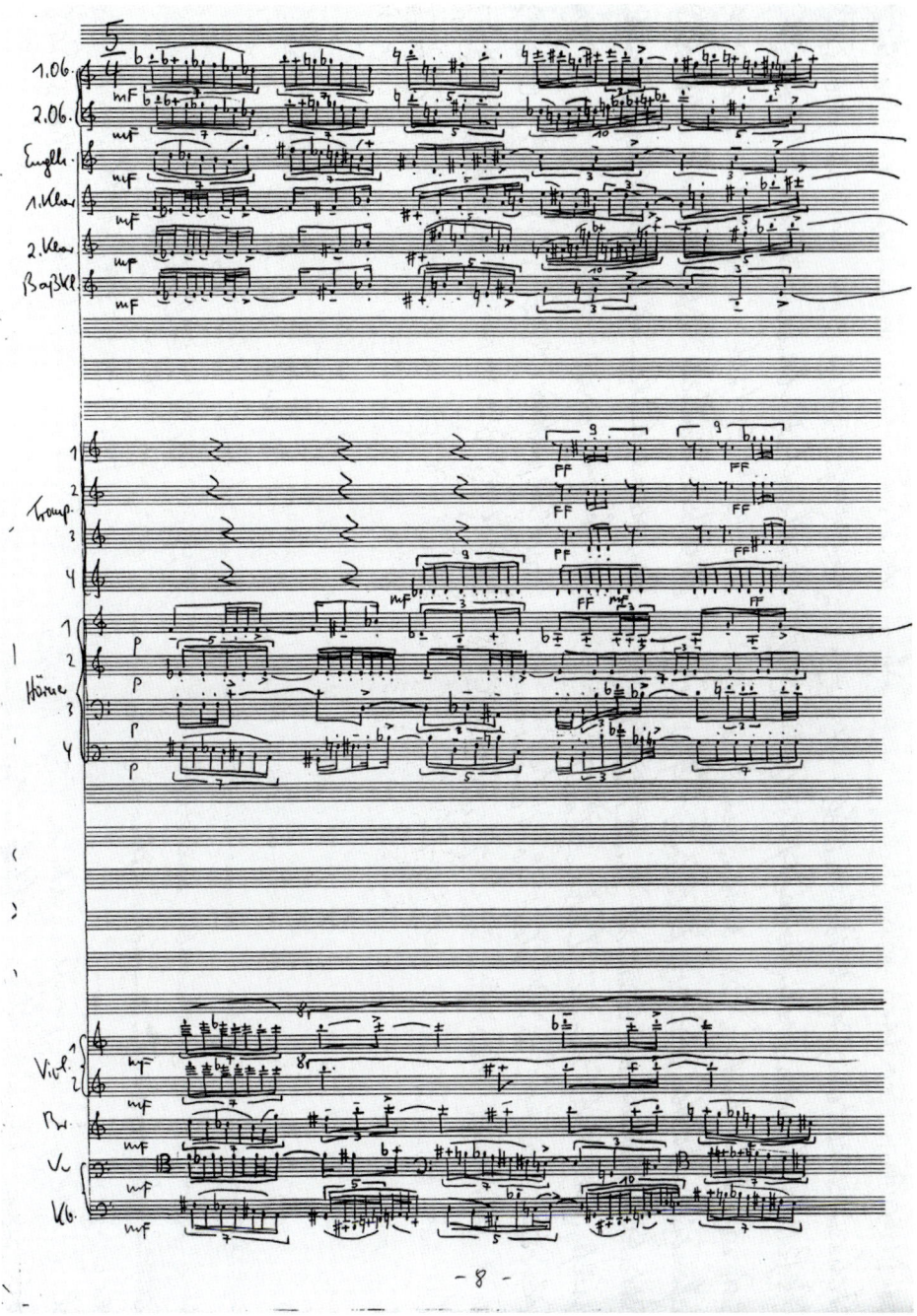

standardized schemes for training or further education. They are consequently not in a position to fulfill their actual purpose, which is to help people gain access to the labor market.

STRONG CITY

The crisis of the city can only be overcome by strengthening the city. The authority to make decisions and plan a course of action should be shifted from the state back to the municipalities, which must in turn be reorganized. The spatial expansion of the municipalities is a prerequisite for shaping urban development and balancing out regional disparities. Competencies and tasks should be renegotiated between municipalities, society, and business, yet without orienting urban development toward private economic criteria in the sense of an "entrepreneurial city."

IN TIMES OF CRISIS – BACK TO THE CITIES

A conversation between Marta Doehler-Behzadi (urban planner), Dieter Hoffmann-Axthelm (writer and urban planner), Stephan Lanz (urban studies expert), Engelbert Lütke Daldrup (construction and planning department head for the city of Leipzig), and Philipp Oswalt (architect and curator)

———
———

Philipp Oswalt: When we discuss how the shrinking of cities can be shaped, we have to turn to questions that precede the concrete act of shaping and that are thus also political questions. This is because the urban planning instruments available today don't allow us to structure change in a way that makes sense. We need new instruments and new models of action, and in my opinion these must be developed out of new ideas in urban policy.

Engelbert Lütke Daldrup: The classic body of instruments provided under today's laws were conceived of as a means for wrestling with the expansion of cities and are usually based on incentives in the form of development rights. With respect to the decreases in utilization, intensity of utilization, and development that we face today, and the distribution of losses that this implies, these laws are only of limited use. The cities have tried to identify possible plans of action by engaging with large-scale urban development concepts based on the whole area of a city. They are exploring how cities can be de-densified and thereby new qualities created over a relatively long-term period, usually over the course of up to twenty years, yet without necessarily stipulating and defining the end results in advance. In certain limited areas, the goal of "more quality through less density" is indeed possible. The objectives of funding programs have already shifted: the sole emphasis on development has been supplemented with an orientation toward sociospatial, social, and economic issues, with questions regarding the local economy and the small and medium-sized businesses in urban districts coming increasingly into focus. What is necessary here is a clustering of all subsidies from the government and the European Union so as to form "urban development budgets" that can be administered at the local level and directed toward local problems—because the problems in Wuppertal are different from those in Leipzig, where they are completely different again from the situation in Hoyerswerda.

Philipp Oswalt: The financial possibilities for German municipalities are so limited today that they are dependent on subsidies for any plans extending beyond the basic tasks at hand. For this reason, they can only act in ways that fit into the logic of the programs: only those plans that are covered by a program can be carried out. Given this situation, is it possible at all to respond to complex local problems?

Engelbert Lütke Daldrup: Each individual program only allows for funding of specific tasks according to very strict rules. The difficulty is in combining the programs—URBAN II, Stadtumbau, funding for housing development, Soziale Stadt, and so on.[1] When it is the federal government or even the EU that determine the aims of the programs and the criteria for funding, this makes it harder to find meaningful local solutions. This is why I think it's essential that the decision as to how to use the funds be shifted to the local level through this kind of "urban development budget."

But I would also caution against giving the municipalities complete responsibility for urban development issues. If there are no more national or European subsidies to complement local funds, then it will be very difficult to raise enough money at the local level. If the federal government steps back from these issues in the wake of the federalism debate and under the pressure of the states, the wealthier states will continue to fund urban development, and the poorer states, above all those in eastern Germany, will not be in a position to provide funding.

Dieter Hoffmann-Axthelm: Of course, the other question is whether urban reconstruction is politically feasible at all. The situation in Berlin today is such that in the decision-making bodies—the Senate, the various committees, and the Plenary in the House of Representatives—anything that costs money can no longer find a consensus. So structural questions are no longer up for discussion. Everything has to bring immediate returns, even if this means closing the door on future opportunities or trading off for yet more problems in the long run.

Marta Doehler-Behzadi: You can't just shift everything to the local level or even the district level in cities and then think it will all automatically get better. Many questions must be resolved from a wider perspective, including the question of the direction in which our cities should develop. If this is only dealt with at the local or district level, this leads to constellations that are by no means always productive, as the competition between city centers and surrounding areas shows. This has to be negotiated at a political level that is not just situated within a district.

Philipp Oswalt: That does not at all contradict the notion that the municipal level has to be strengthened considerably in relation to the higher level of the states, the federal government, and the EU. A second key issue comes into play here: What would the appropriate spatial unit be for the municipalities today? There is a serious misfit at the moment: urban regions constitute an important unit with respect to urban development and spheres of action, but there is no corresponding political and administrative unit, only a number of municipalities in competition with one another. This competition between the municipalities is a central factor in urban sprawl and shrinking. Only with great difficulty do municipalities get together and cooperate, for example in the greater region of Hannover, and even in such cases critical questions still go unaddressed.

In 1920 Berlin had the courage to bring together eight towns and fifty-nine communities to form one big city. Why shouldn't we be able to create a functioning metropolitan area in the Halle-Leipzig region by merging dozens of municipalities? Are we only prepared to think in terms of micro steps within the existing structures instead of taking on real change?

Dieter Hoffmann-Axthelm: Berlin, Frankfurt, Cologne, and others were rapidly growing cities in 1900, and strong growth was also predicted for them for the future. It was believed that huge spaces were needed for this. But the First World War put an end to this phase. Today the situation is reversed, and the question is how to get rid of parts of these areas again, which have meanwhile become urbanized. The idea that ever-larger containers need to be created stems from the nineteenth century, and it is also not economical because the larger such a unit is, the less profitable it is.

Stephan Lanz: The main question of how to balance out resources may well be resolved using coercion and top-down decisions. But this would by no means be effective for all other questions—especially not for the current problems in large cities: the social problems, the integration of immigrants, urban renewal, and so on. If there were political units made up of the wealthy outer-lying communities, the danger would be that the very articulate, powerful social groups of suburbia would dominate the direction of a city's entire development with their specific interests, while the problems in the city center would be neglected. Rather than such obsolete kinds of fusion, the focus must be on building networks that cooperate, and in which each different issue is approached with a different constellation.

Engelbert Lütke Daldrup: In the past few decades, a few individual tasks such as local public transit and supply and waste disposal have been regionalized. I doubt, however, that in the near future we will have functioning political and administrative structures at the regional level that are familiar with the remits of urban development. In the medium term, we will have to act regionally on questions of space utilization, traffic, and revenue-sharing. But cooperative networks are fair-weather models and will not suffice for this; competencies will have to be shifted to regional institutions. Ultimately, municipal policy will have to develop further in two different directions: on the one hand, toward the overarching regional questions and, on the other, toward issues that can best be negotiated and resolved at the local level.

Philipp Oswalt: Wouldn't this mean that the regional level would also have to be democratically legitimated? In the Rhine-Main region, for a time there was a regional association with its own directly elected parliament.

Engelbert Lütke Daldrup: A real region is only possible when it has its own budget and its own parliament. As regards the Leipzig region, this would be a particular challenge because it crosses state borders. The Leipzig-Halle agglomeration stretches through Saxony as far as Wurzen and Döbeln, and in Saxony-Anhalt all the way to Bitterfeld and Altenburg. Almost two million people live in this region. There's one big city with 500,000 inhabitants, the second largest has 200,000, and over a million live in the surrounding counties. This suggests a potential conflict, given that the majority of the population live in the outer-lying counties and not in the cities.

Philipp Oswalt: On the other hand, there's a desire to decentralize downward, to shift competencies to the local level. Mr. Hoffman-Axthelm, you recently published the book *Lokale Selbstverwaltung,* which deals with this issue. What can local self-administration offer us?

Dieter Hoffmann-Axthelm: Given the need to save money, there is no longer room for politics—you can only discuss things that don't affect the budget. So we have to ask which forms of municipal autonomy we can imagine today. Moreover, how exactly do we envisage the financing? How do we achieve cooperation between residents and a more flexible municipal administration?

Engelbert Lütke Daldrup: Shifting public responsibilities to the local citizens has two sides to it. On the one hand, there's a danger of an extreme polarization of social space, as the educational system in the United States has taught us, for example. There they have very wealthy municipalities with good schools, and very poor municipalities with bad schools. On the other hand, what is positive about this model is that many problems could be better resolved at the district level because it is closer to the issues at hand and thus more appropriate solutions might be found, as well as the fact that we could tackle the lack of funding in the municipalities. With funds from the local economy, which are directly accessible, problems at the district level can be solved without all the red tape. Local funding could be augmented with money from private investors, nonprofit organizations, or churches. The financial backers would be right there and so they would be in touch with the endeavors they are sponsoring. With the help of private financing, federal funds could also be acquired. Obtaining these funds is often conditional on the municipality's ability to raise means of its own, which isn't possible anymore today.

Stephan Lanz: This is precisely the scenario that should not be taking place. The state is no longer willing to finance certain tasks at the local level, so now they're trying to mobilize private funds under the guise of democratization. While the municipalities boast that they're giving citizens more room to shape policy, they're actually retreating from their responsibility for the urban districts.

Engelbert Lütke Daldrup: Okay, but then everything depends on how much money will continue to flow from the state's coffers. I'm a realist here. I don't believe that the state's share will be increasing.

Stephan Lanz: Today there are fewer funds than five years ago. The way these diminished funds are used, however, could be more democratic. But the question is, who controls the budget? There should be more participation here. This is what the point should be, not mobilizing private capital through alleged democratization.

Engelbert Lütke Daldrup: One problem here is that the practical implementation of the postulate of equality has led to more red tape and to some peculiarities. For example, there are exact specifications as to how large the rooms in a municipal retirement home must be. This excessive regimentation makes it impossible for the municipalities to find pragmatic solutions in these times of limited funds. Soon it will be impossible to decide anything at all at the local level.

Marta Doehler-Behzadi: When private funds are activated for local purposes, an otherwise rather loose notion of civil society becomes very concrete. Usually we associate it with a nebulous idea of volunteerism, for example through associations and church communities, which become responsible for the poor. But who shall take on this responsibility in our society? Who of us is in a position to contribute time and energy for volunteering in their district? At the same time, in all these suggestions of shifting responsibility downward, I see the danger that the poorer districts will come up with less money and the wealthy ones with more. And the poorer districts will not be able to position themselves as professionally or as robustly in economic terms as the others.

Philipp Oswalt: This is a fundamental dilemma. Individual residents are in different positions as regards their ability to become involved, so that some actors will have more influence than others and will be able to assert their interests. An unequal situation will quickly emerge. It is precisely those models that require capital that can become particularly problematic. But there are also other forms of local cooperation. For instance, at the RAW complex in Berlin,[2] the municipality acted as a guarantor for an interim project that had not been accepted by the owners of the site, and so it made an interesting project possible without spending any of its own funds. The project only had to pay the owners for the running costs of using the space. We have to think about models that would allow actors who can't contribute capital to nonetheless participate in shaping and developing cities.

Dieter Hoffmann-Axthelm: Everyone has to pay taxes. But we have a system where first everything has to be handed in to the tax office and centralized, and then it eventually flows back again via very complicated channels. This system should be turned on its head: Of the taxes that are collected, part should remain in local hands and the rest given to the municipality, which in turn hands its surplus to the state for its responsibilities. The sum of money would remain the same, but it would be distributed differently. In this kind of model, the local level would act as a public investor and could handle the money quite differently. The higher levels of government would remain in place, but they wouldn't be able to prescribe what the local level had to do, as is the case today.

Stephan Lanz: The big questions are: What happens to the equality of living conditions in this kind of model? Is this a goal that will still be pursued from the level of the nation-state? And if so, then how will the distribution of resources be determined?

Dieter Hoffmann-Axthelm: We're functionaries of equality in living conditions, which is why the municipalities no longer have a say, rather 90% of the time are on the receiving end of commands and are completely dependent financially. This is, of course, not only about justice, but also to a large extent about animosity toward the cities. The horizontal equality we strive for faces limits anyway because the horizontal plane is not really flat, but full of mountains and plains, more and less fertile soils, and so on. In other words, there are a great number of heterogeneous parameters. To the champions of the free market I would say, however, that if the goal of equality is called into question, this does not mean that the state or the municipalities should be dismantled, but that their role should be redefined.

Marta Doehler-Behzadi: Equality was the great promise of reunification. Whatever has fallen below the social average will be sponsored so that it rises up again. This apparently worked quite well in growth phases in the past, but today it is under scrutiny. In place of the principle of equality, the principle of competition has taken over. Funding is allotted according to the criteria of effectiveness and success.

Engelbert Lütke Daldrup: The equality postulate has eaten into municipal finances so much that the cities have no scope to determine their own policies anymore. The municipalities have become the helpmates of centrally dictated guidelines today. Everything is prescribed down to the last detail—the size of a room in a nursing home, the width of the streets, and so forth. If these incredibly high standards were reduced by just 10%, the municipalities would gain a lot of room to maneuver.

Stephan Lanz: But that's a false alternative. The answer can't be to hold onto the structural norms and just reduce their level. There must be a debate about the goals, the values that are implied in the norms, what should be kept and what should be updated.

Dieter Hoffmann-Axthelm: Before we discuss these political-moral questions, we should first talk about the structures within which they take place. The federal ministries with their staff of thousands have no experience with the concrete problems at hand or with the local implementation of programs. The staff receive their instructions from the upper echelons; they are completely removed from reality and spend their time presiding over norms and aligning those norms with the EU and existing law. The equality of living conditions is merely the ideology on top of it all. And then behind the system are all these normalizing institutions, and behind them the corresponding industries, associations, and lobbies—it's a huge and very powerful complex.

Engelbert Lütke Daldrup: For me, the central question is who decides. For example, who decides the size of a room in a home for the elderly? The federal ministry in Berlin, the state ministry in Dresden, or the city of Leipzig? Or are there much lower minimum standards and then it's decided at the local level how the separate areas, such as caring for the elderly and child care, and so on, should be organized?

Philipp Oswalt: Your arguments are misleading. Standards by no means always have anything to do with social equality. There are many standards in the context of neoliberal policies—just think of some of the EU regulations that impose completely economistic principles onto social areas and thereby play into the hands of the strongest actors. I agree with Stephan Lanz that the debate should not be primarily about the level of the standards, but first of all about the issue of how goals are formulated and by whom. Let's take the example of local public transportation in sparsely populated areas. The question should not be whether or not this should still be a public service, but how it should be accomplished under changed conditions with a justified level of effort. If demand has decreased, the old system can't be sustained. But it would be possible, for example, to couple the task with other functions. For instance, the local baker could transport school children. But this has so far been prohibited because of regulations to protect the taxi businesses. Precisely in the interest of keeping and raising the quality of public services, existing regulations, that is, standards, must be loosened up.

Marta Doehler-Behzadi: Today we have to ask anew what is necessary in terms of human dignity, the needs of the elderly, educational policy, etc. The regulations that have been manufactured by the bureaucratic apparatus over the decades must be held up to scrutiny. Reducing standards should be negotiated at the local level.

Stephan Lanz: I don't believe that this is about reducing standards. An unbelievable amount of social resources are being wasted with these standards. When the standards are held up for scrutiny—as bureaucratic rules and not as social values—and they are shifted over to local jurisdiction, then it must first be determined whether this will lead to a reduction in the quality that was once defined by the standards. Take Mr. Lütke Daldrup's example of the old people's home: the standards don't guarantee that the life of the elderly will be dignified, but instead lead to a situation where I may have a room of a certain size, yet I may still live in a home that does not suit my needs.

Engelbert Lütke Daldrup: The state should retract these standard guarantees to a certain extent—that is, either lower them or make them less detailed so as to enable better solutions, to allow for more freedom in the choice of means used to reach a goal, even if this means taking certain risks.

Philipp Oswalt: If an objective is formulated more generally, this implies that one must be prepared to accept a loss of control and the danger that, at the local level, some things may work worse than before. But the negative effects of a system with fixed standards outweigh these risks by far, and we should have more faith in local and informal solutions. The obsession with control has long since become the real risk. In Germany the ratio of government expenditure to gross national product is almost 50%, and we are one of the most wealthy countries in the world. So there is actually a lot of money out there. Even if this quota were to be reduced somewhat again, the question as to where and how the resources are used is still more important than debates about quantity. Thinking only in terms of reducing spending or defending assets is a dead end.

Engelbert Lütke Daldrup: At the municipal level, the share spent on social benefits such as social welfare and rent subsidies increases every year by many millions of euros. At the moment in Leipzig, we spend over 260 million in social subsidies and another 120 million in the area of child care, and the proportions are the same at the federal level. Since reunification, social spending has rapidly risen from below 30% to almost 50% of the federal budget. This trend will only be strengthened if financing for the social systems is separated from employment costs, which I think is very probable. Social spending will then form the main portion of the national budget.

Marta Doehler-Behzadi: In many areas there is still state funding, but what to do and how to do it is prescribed very precisely, without the necessary flexibility.

Stephan Lanz: What about the funding for developing commercial parks, for example, which are supposed to promote the development of local businesses? Can a community redirect this funding for the infrastructure into the budget for economic development so as to approach the goal in a different way?

Engelbert Lütke Daldrup: No, the municipalities are hardly able to support local business, although this is very much needed. Through changes in national and EU law, many of the support methods that previously were possible have fallen by the wayside now, for example selling property below the market value. All that's left is EU money from URBAN II and the European Regional Development Fund. But these budgets are minimal, not even one-hundredth of the municipal costs for social spending. We have no access to the money in the Gemeinschaftsaufgabe pot or to the EU's infrastructure funds.[3] These funds are administered at the state and federal level, which means that primarily spectacular industrial projects are funded instead of local mid-sized businesses. There are large subsidies—above all for agriculture, coal mining, or for tearing down empty housing lots—but relatively little money for future-oriented development projects.

Philipp Oswalt: Does it make sense to use public money to heavily fund capital-intensive investments that produce relatively few jobs—for example, the more than 400 million euros worth of public money that went toward opening a BMW branch in Leipzig—which is how the development programs are currently structured? Or shouldn't the municipalities at least have partial access to such funds so that they can consider different options and perhaps use them to promote local small and medium-sized businesses?

Marta Doehler-Behzadi: The call to reduce standards has different aims: building narrower streets with less traffic lights, not prescribing fixed sizes for rooms in old people's homes, and the like, in order to free up resources and then decide freely if they should be spent on education, culture, or developing the local economy. Subsidies for economic development are beyond criticism today if they prove successful.

Dieter Hoffmann-Axthelm: The crucial discussion—what do we really want?—cannot take place because it is already decided in advance how funds and spending should be distributed. In the municipalities, it is getting harder to do policy. The fundamental problem is that the mechanism for distributing funding and the mechanism for distributing responsibilities have become completely disengaged. One side is constantly setting new tasks, while the other—the municipalities—have to bear the costs for them. We can no longer afford the system we have today. Tackling this from below also means working with other methods of paying or other levels of costs. The local economy means an economy that does without standards. I am convinced that shifting administration to the local citizen's level will absorb a lot of unemployment, if we can do without the financing standards of the public coffers. If the municipalities can't put out anymore, then the residents are the remaining resource. With their intelligence and knowledge of the situation, municipal tasks can be accomplished much more affordably. Municipal tasks and bureaucracy could be reduced by two-thirds.

They have to take themselves seriously. That's the secret. In countries like Brazil or Mexico, people are much worse off than here, and yet they are able to initiate things. It's a question of self-respect; of to what extent one is internally colonized and dependent upon the state.

Translated from the German by Christina M. White

Notes
1 URBAN II: a European Union community initiative financed under the EU Structural Funds; Stadtumbau: a program for urban restructuring in both eastern and western Germany; Die Soziale Stadt (The Socially Integrative City): a joint federal and state program for urban development.—Ed.
2 A former railway repair works, part of which now houses a range of community projects and artists' initiatives.—Ed.
3 Gemeinschaftsaufgabe Aufbau Ost: Joint Mission for the Development of Eastern Germany.—Ed.

Literature
Hoffmann-Axthelm, Dieter. *Lokale Selbstverwaltung: Möglichkeiten und Grenzen direkter Demokratie*. Wiesbaden: Verlag Leske + Budrich, 2004.
Lanz, Stephan, ed. *City of COOP: Ersatzökonomien und städtische Bewegungen in Rio de Janeiro und Buenos Aires*. Berlin: b-books Verlag, 2005.
Lütke Daldrup, Engelbert, and Marta Doehler-Behzadi, eds. *Plus Minus Leipzig 2030: Transforming the City*. Wuppertal: Verlag Müller + Busmann, 2004.

WOLFEN: THE COST OF SILENCE
Tina Veihelmann

Wolfen. Start of the shift. "If you want to discover the secret of Wolfen's world fame, you have to look for it in the morning at the start of the shift," rasps a sonorous voice. The *r* in "morning" is drawn out. A flock of people with clean-cut hair hurry down the stairs at the train station. "Women and men! Your experiences, your diligence, your skillfulness!" The industrious ones smile and look young. It is 1960.[1]

When I arrive by train in Wolfen on a Monday in 2005, I go up the same steps and am the only one as far as the eye can see. In the waiting room there are no longer any service counters. Four youths are sitting on a bench drinking beer with an air of defiance. The drive to the hotel winds through housing developments for workers. Pretty little brick houses with small front yards, Easter eggs dangling in the bushes. It is quiet, like it would be elsewhere on a Sunday. When I finally find the hotel, I discover that it recently closed down. Bankruptcy. The door happens to be open, a woman is cleaning. She gives me a room anyway: it seems business has continued under the table. Besides my own room, four or five other rooms seem to be occupied, but I never meet anyone in the hallway. In the evening you can hear music somewhere until long after midnight. A party, perhaps. It seems a bit ghostly that this is the only sound that can be heard here today.

Because I can't sleep, I take a look at the film *Original Wolfen*.[2] The ORWO company and its 15,000 employees. The second-largest producer of photographic film in the world, the largest employer of women in the German Democratic Republic (GDR). Wolfen's worldwide fame. A myth. Doe-eyed ladies bustle about with the highly sensitive film, bathed in green light or completely in the dark. "Nimble hands." A grain of dust can ruin the day's work. Sabotage would be easy—but the ladies never sabotage. They talk about a peculiar intimacy that arises through their work in the dark. You have to touch someone else if you want to make contact. They know a lot about each other, bring their children to the same daycare center at the company, evenings they chat at their *Datschen*.[3] They call the factory "the film."

A white-haired man with a soft voice had researched the emulsion used for the film—the secret of ORWO. He is also a man in the dark. Because he carries a secret, he never becomes famous for his formulas. When the company closed, he received a bouquet of flowers. Garlands are hanging in the backdrop; there's a buffet with finger foods. The human resources lady hugs him and says she hopes to see him soon again. He gives her another spontaneous hug. I turn off the film. Outside the party is still going on. "What's happened to Wolfen's world fame?" I direct the question to myself, since I am sitting alone in this hotel room where no one else wants to spend the night anymore. A folder in my luggage filled with papers offers clues as to why this is so.

In 1991, the film factory presents a business plan and asks the Treuhand for DM 82 million in investments to ensure its economic survival.[4] Consulting firms think the business is viable under these conditions—if personnel cuts are made.[5] The amount requested is granted, but the money never materializes. In 1994 the company files for bankruptcy. Now DM 32.6 million are granted by the Bundesanstalt für vereinigungsbedingte Sonderaufgaben (Federal Authority for Special Tasks Related to Reunification)

Following state-funded renovation and improvement measures in Wolfen-Nord, demolition was later also subsidized in the same area.

so the company can pay off its debts, and DM 45 million are lent to a firm that takes over the business and 100 of its former employees. Total costs for the state: DM 77.6 million.

A total of DM 82 million to save a company is not a small amount, I think to myself. On the other hand: Is it cheaper to spend a comparable sum to bury a patient who has passed away? And what are the other costs that will follow after such a loss?

In order to revive the legacy of the dismantled collective combines of Bitterfeld and Wolfen, the Bundesanstalt founds a chemical park. A management company takes over all the properties that private individuals did not want to buy. Their task: clean up the area, build an infrastructure, look for investors. The first chemical park management agency for Bitterfeld and Wolfen quickly reaps public criticism because it uses the subsidies to build a disproportionately large purification plant that generates immense sewage costs. And the development of the area does not bring the desired results.[6] Hope is next invested in the Preiss-Daimler conglomerate, which receives DM 240 million to develop the infrastructure. Because the new management is in principle a construction company, it takes over several contracts itself. The company is diligent; the Bitterfeld-Wolfen chemical park is soon considered the best-constructed of its kind. Federal and state grants as well as funds from the European Union start flowing in order to attract companies to the area. Preiss-Daimler, which has meanwhile branched out in multiple directions—cleaning up contaminated sites, burning sludge, producing glass fibers, and so on—establishes several firms in the area, including its own subsidiary companies. Around 10,000 jobs are created in the chemical park.

Chemical park—a better name for it could not have been found. The morning sun shines on a broad area where a type of dune vegetation thrives. The wide streets form a checkerboard pattern. Industrial complexes are scattered about, as if someone had misplaced them here. An older man walks toward me.[7] He looks familiar. "Excuse me," I say, "I'm told that there are 10,000 jobs here." He stops and looks at me, half skeptical, half amused. "They aren't here in Wolfen," he answers. He moves the tip of his foot around in the gravel and seems to be considering whether or not he should tell me more. "You know," he says, "these companies have created something of a tax paradise here—on a small scale. The chemical park properties don't all belong to Wolfen. They belong to Wolfen, Bitterfeld, and two small towns: Greppin and Thalheim. The two villages ask for far less taxes. You see?" "And Bitterfeld?" "Some want to be in Bitterfeld because the chemical companies are all together in one place there." "And Wolfen?" He shrugs his shoulders. "A few smaller companies came here.[8] FilmoTec, for example, makes a special kind of black-and-white film and employs 25 people. You see what I mean?" The man has a gentle voice, like the researcher in the film. "All this swallowed up a huge amount of money, and it didn't do a bit of good!" I exclaim. The man raises his eyebrows. "I mean the millions of deutschmarks in funding. Who profits from it? Not the town of Wolfen, not the people of Wolfen, but just a few companies, and they're probably from Munich." The man laughs for a minute. "Are you a journalist? It shows. My name is Sandler, by the way. But you know what? Don't get too caught up in it." He makes a dismissive gesture. We leave the chemical park behind us and walk slowly down the street. I'm on the way to the city administration. My escort is apparently going the same way.

Mr. Sandler had been responsible for developing ORWO's color film. When the film company went broke, he found work again. An "ABM" job under a state-sponsored employment creation program. Disassembly. He used to associate "disassembly" with the plundering of the factory after the Second World War. Some doubted at the time whether the factory could be saved at all, he says. That's when he started working at ORWO and helped to rebuild it. They worked meticulously, found solutions. He came at night, too, if it had to be.

The next disassembly he would have to undertake himself. He remembers very well how the women sat around the table and unwound the film rolls with their nimble hands. Also ABM. "They had already started to subsidize us back then," he says. They talked little during work—though earlier they could be quite loud, there in the dark. In the dark one likes to talk loud. Now there was only this silence left. In Wolfen. You see? Wolfen is as if ... a piece of us had disappeared.

Soon Wolfen is completely dependent on ABM jobs. Up to the year 2000, over 16,000 ABM employees found work in the chemical park and 18,000 people were employed through SAM (Structural Adjustment Measures). Then the ABM positions were reduced. In 2001, children here were asked what they most wanted to have, and their answer was no longer a "a jungle gym," but "an ABM for my parents."[9]

We've arrived at the city planning office. Mr. Hermann, the director of the urban planning department, is waiting for me with coffee and cookies. He flashes a big smile and gives me a picture book titled *Gesichter (m)einer Stadt* (Faces of My Town). He would like to do something for his town, that's easy to see. My escort takes a seat at the table without being asked. The nice urban planning official pours me a cup of coffee, and I begin to understand that I am the only one who acknowledges Mr. Sandler's presence. The planning official has spread out a map of Wolfen on the table. When I ask him about new industries in Wolfen, he points to the chemical park and lifts his shoulders. I don't want to press him. "And where do you get your taxes?" is simply not a question that one asks. Not in a town that has lost its economic base and almost half of its inhabitants since 1990.[10] "Where there is a problem, there is usually a funding program," notes Mr. Sandler laconically as he steals a cookie. Apparently he is right.

At the beginning of the 1990s, for example, housing construction and renovation was still being subsidized. While residents were packing their bags, apartments were being renovated and built anew. Starting in 2001, funding was flowing in yet another form—demolition. The program was called Stadtumbau Ost (Urban Restructuring in Eastern Germany). It was primarily developed by the Bundesverband deutscher Wohnungsunternehmen, the lobby organization of the housing sector, as a means of warding off bankruptcy for housing companies that were losing their tenants. Financially, the housing companies are in the position of only being able to afford those measures for which there are subsidies. This is because, as successors to the GDR's municipal housing development associations, they must pay for old debts and are in the red. Stadtumbau Ost has one advantage for the housing companies that are deeply in debt: wherever demolition is prescribed, old debts are dissolved.

But here we are in the city planning office. According to the program, municipalities and housing companies are to work together to reconstruct the city. A challenge, and one for which there is no historical role model. Tax the shrinking city. This is an issue for Mr. Hermann. Demolition is not the only task at hand: new playgrounds, walking paths, and flowerbeds have to be created—our city will become smaller, but all the prettier.

No one should think that Wolfen will simply disappear from the map. For this reason, the community gets money to improve certain areas, while elsewhere buildings are being torn down, explains Mr. Hermann. But the municipality only gets the money if it comes up with its own funds additionally, and since it does not have its own funds, nothing happens. In the newly developed area of Wolfen-Nord, an empty lot the size of a football field—the result of demolition—cannot be transformed into a park because the properties are earmarked for development, and the municipality cannot buy them in order to use them for something else. And there where housing units have given way to bulldozers, schools and youth clubs remain standing in a flattened prairie—because they belong to the municipality and it doesn't have the money to tear them down.

"Why does the municipality have to come up with its own funds, but not the housing companies?" I ask. "To me it looks as if the program is meant to keep companies solvent and allow debts to be paid," I add, and note the thought on my escort's mind again: "You journalist, you!" Mr. Hermann does not say "You journalist" to me, but then he is the town's planning official and not Michael Moore. He pours me a coffee. "What kind of conditions do you ideally need in order to do your work better?" I ask him. "That the city has the money it needs at its disposal," he says.

Then he tells me how he himself once took the initiative to do something for Wolfen. It was his own idea, which came to him over a beer. The idea was to build an indoor water park, using only ABM jobs. There was no money, but you could get ABM jobs in large quantities. The plan worked. They had so many ABM jobs that they were able to complete 70% of the construction. He passes me more cookies. They're good, with chocolate on top. Mr. Sandler is holding his hand over his mouth, laughing to himself. "Was there no swimming pool in Wolfen?" "There where the swimming pool was, now there's a purification plant," says Mr. Hermann. The old pool had cracks in it because when the industries were dismantled, the ground water rose. I munch on another cookie and think about the unpredictable costs after a large bankruptcy.

We're ready to go. My escort wants to go home to Wolfen-Nord, where he lives. We take the bus. At the bus station he shakes my hand and says, "Here's to a new subsidy program. For fireworks, perhaps, to accompany the demolition. We could try to do something else with the money on the sly, to bring down sewage costs." Mr. Sandler wishes me luck and sets out on his way. He seems to head straight for one of the demolition lots and is suddenly gone.

All is quiet in Wolfen-Nord, and the air is good. Where the housing ends, a grassy landscape begins. Half the houses, it seems, are empty. The demolition will start here next. In front of the housing blocks are heaps of old household items that have been thrown out. People walking by make sure no one is looking and then pick out the parts that can be salvaged and reused. I meet up with the boys at the youth club, which will soon be standing quite alone in this landscape. They are happy because the stupid neighbors are finally gone, so they say. "Now we can have outdoor parties here and no one will call the police." A woman whom I ask to show me the way back to my hotel tells me her son was beaten to death with baseball bats by his own friends. On Christmas Eve. The people can't stand it here anymore, she says. The youths even less so. They can't handle the feeling that they are a nobody. "My smaller son, the one who's still alive, is told at school: You won't make it anywhere. Nowhere. It's a crime."

When I finally get back, I am almost happy to see the sign on the shiny new building that says "Travel Lodge." I look out the window at the road that looks like a village street and I hope for Mr. Sandler that his life's work will one day be appreciated, I hope for money for the brave planning official so that he can build one, two, or many water parks, and I hope that the boy from Wolfen-Nord will find an apprenticeship that he can get to on the local train.

Translated from the German by Christina M. White

Notes
1   An excerpt from the film *Orwo Film und Faser* (Wolfen: Betriebsfilmstudio ORWO, 1960).
2   *Original Wolfen,* VHS, directed by Niels Bolbrinker and Kerstin Stutterheim (Germany, 1996).
3   Many eastern Germans own a small weekend home known as a *Datsche* (from the Russian *dacha*).—Ed.
4   The Treuhand was the name of the trusteeship responsible for the privatization of former East German public property.—Ed.
5   See the interview with Mr. Gill by Andreas Sterr in Andreas Sterr et al., eds., *EF IV: Annäherung an eine Industrieruine* (Weimar: Universitätsverlag der Bauhaus-Universität, 1999), 32.
6   Holger Derlien, Tobias Faupel, and Christian Nieters, "Industriestandort mit Vorbildfunktion? Das ostdeutsche Chemiedreieck" (discussion paper FS IV 99-16, Wissenschaftszentrum Berlin, 1999).
7   This character is fictional. Any resemblance to actual living persons is purely coincidental.
8   Around two thousand jobs were created at the Wolfen chemical park site. The unemployment rate in Wolfen is 30%-35%.
9   "Blühende Landschaften—leere Städte—das Drama Ostdeutschlands," radio report by Ulrich Neumann, Südwestrundfunk, April 15, 2002.
10 In 1990, Wolfen had a population of 44,000; in 2003, there were only 26,000 inhabitants left.

THE EXPERIMENT OF RED VIENNA, 1919-1934
Rudolf Kohoutek

Taking the model of Social Democratic municipal policy implemented in "Red Vienna" between 1919 and 1934 as both exemplary and representative of other progressive municipalities of the same era, for example Red Frankfurt or the New Berlin, what can we find in it that is relevant to us today as we tackle the problems currently facing urban development policy? What does the housing and construction policy, the social and cultural policy, and the architecture of Red Vienna represent when it is isolated from its historical context?

We can certainly say that the city of Vienna following the First World War was a "shrinking city." The monarchic Reich with its population of 56 million was reduced to a republic of 6 million and, simultaneously, the number of inhabitants in Vienna dropped within a few years from 2.1 million to 1.9 million. The city's economic and political influence and its extensive markets were lost. Vienna's Social Democrats immediately recognized the new meaning of "local," even if they made attempts to create a "greater Vienna" with the goal of attaining more local autonomy in terms of the food supply while at the same time expanding local markets.

In the postwar Vienna of 1919, echoes of our contemporary problems can also be found: imbalance in economic development and clear inequalities in social development, extreme competition in the export economy, high unemployment, a lack of public funds, as well as controversial assessments as to how to tackle the crisis.

During those fifteen years or so, Red Vienna became an experiment in municipal policy in which all possible paths were explored with a high level of instrumental creativity. This was not least because the Social Democrats in Vienna—as soon as they won the 1919 election with 100 out of 165 mandates—could build on the comprehensive theoretical analyses and program formulations already carried out in advance of their victory.

Vienna's municipal policy program reflected a Social Democratic policy of a peaceful "gradual transition"—which Austria's Social Democrats ultimately laid down in the Linz Program of 1926—as well as the interests of workers and sections of the middle classes at that time. It thereby formed the basis for a stable majority.[1]

A few essential prerequisites enabled and supported the policies implemented in Red Vienna: (a) the separation of Vienna from Lower Austria and the transformation of its status as a municipality to that of a province in 1920; (b) several laws introduced during the war, such as a freeze on interest rates and the housing reclamation law; and (c) a technical infrastructure that had been extended in the Christian Socialist period in preparation for a larger Vienna. With the freeze on interest rates, begun as a wartime measure and continued consistently after the war, the proportion of a working class family's income spent on housing was reduced from 20% or 30% before the war to between 2% and 4% afterward. An integral part of these measures was also protection from job loss, which set strict limits on the possible grounds for terminating a worker's contract of employment and introduced a standard procedure for contesting and reviewing job dismissals. The measures concerning interest rates and job protection were also applicable to businesses and therefore ensured that the population was provided for and the economic base of the middle classes secured. The interest-rate freeze was essential to ensuring the survival of smaller businesses, including coffee houses, inns, and shops. With the housing reclamation law, introduced in 1917 in response to the war and maintained in force until 1925, the municipality was able to place those seeking housing into empty or underoccupied or inappropriately occupied apartments at a generally controlled, low rent. This distribution of housing according to need, which the municipality of Vienna continued even with new housing that it had constructed itself, represented a revolution in the history of housing for the lower classes. Taken together, the above measures were so popular that they could be adopted despite the opposition of those representing private property interests.

Parallel to this, the municipality of Vienna tried to revive the construction of new private housing, which had almost come to a standstill during the war due to the lack of capital and the freeze on interest rates. The first approach taken—which was also intended to curb the spread of "illicit settlements"—was cooperative housing developments. This initiative was able to draw on the settler movement in Vienna that had begun as a form of self-help.[2] Starting in 1924, the municipality began erecting its own settlements, and the autonomous settler movement lost its force in what could be called a transition from "grassroots cooperative socialism to municipal socialism."[3]

But this development of settlements was quantitatively not sufficient, and the city council thus decided in 1923 to build 5,000 apartments per year. Between 1923 and 1934, a total of 65,000 apartments were erected by the municipality, and 2,500 old apartments were fully renovated. For the construction program, the city sought properties that were cheap or temporarily devalued as a result of the interest-rate freeze and that were located within the city's closed street system and existing districts, which meant that the least possible costs would arise in developing them. This was also one of the first programs in what was to become a "city of short distances." The decision to build high-rise inner-city housing came only after vehement debates between the representatives of "low-rise" versus "high-rise" models within the city administration and among Viennese architects, also with the participation of prominent foreign proponents and critics.

Key to the housing construction plan in Red Vienna was the decision to fund it exclusively from incoming tax revenue. To this end, an earmarked housing construction tax was levied from 1923 onward. The latter was, however, only one part of an innovative municipal tax policy that was generally tailored to the social and economic circumstances after the war. This new tax policy was founded on the following principles: (a) a change from indirect taxes to as many direct taxes as possible; (b) a move away from debt accrual, and thus a dismissal of the Christian Socialists' constant demand that housing construction be financed through loans; instead, the rather extensive municipal development program was financed solely through incoming tax revenue; (c) a strongly progressive tax rate for higher incomes for the central housing construction tax and various other "luxury taxes"; thus, higher taxes for industry and commerce could be avoided, as could a tax burden on those renting small apartments; (d) the renunciation of a pure profit orientation in the municipality's monopoly services (streetcars, electricity, gas, water, etc.) and a limitation of the charge to consumers on the cost of providing the services; similarly, for rental costs in municipal housing only the costs of operation and maintenance were levied; (e) property was sold for housing construction and public works, although even in economically bad times, additional parks were created and forest and meadow zones were extended.[4]

The Karl Marx Hof, built 1927-1930 in Vienna, is a symbol of the Social Democratic urban policy of the period.

The Experiment of Red Vienna, 1919–1934_*Rudolf Kohoutek*

But it was only with the separation from Lower Austria and the granting of a new status as a province that Vienna was granted the authority to administer its taxes autonomously. Through its own taxes as well as the additional revenue from national taxes designated for Vienna as a municipality and a province, it was possible to create an innovative financing model for construction activity and for municipal policy in general.

Red Vienna can be seen in many ways as a "strong municipality" that carefully planned the extension of its competencies, but only took action where it made sense in relation to an overall strategy. Thus, for example, after the Social Democrat's victory in the 1919 election, the city initially drafted a plan to communalize property and all housing assets, but the plan was withdrawn after a few weeks on the reasoning that it would not bring in revenue but instead create high costs, for example because of the additional 40,000 caretakers who would have to be hired as city employees.

Fundamental to the municipal policy program of Viennese social democracy were clear analyses of deficits and possibilities, as well as the creation of new, specific instruments that could build on the platform developed over the preceding twenty years and on the theories of what was known as "Austrian Marxism."

The policies of Red Vienna from 1919 to 1934 constituted an integrative approach that completely reorganized municipal tasks. In addition to the regulation of housing through rent protection, housing reclamation, and municipal housing construction, other agendas for improving the quality of life were integrated into a comprehensive municipal program of tasks that included provisions for the unemployed and for health, education, social services, culture, and sports, as well as for the technical infrastructure.

This understanding of the state's tasks—that is, striking a balance between spurring on economic growth at the level of industry and small to medium-sized businesses, and securing and/or raising the standard of living for the masses, including the unemployed—included a distinct awareness of how state infrastructure should be maintained and financed. The technical infrastructure was to be owned by the municipality, optimally maintained both technologically and economically, and not oriented toward profit, but rather organized such that the running costs were passed on according to use.

The city of Vienna thus actively extended its competencies and increased its experiences, yet in a differentiated way. It also modernized the city's own construction firms and acquired additional construction material manufactories, thereby gaining exact knowledge of actual construction costs. And the use of the streetcar lines and city transport companies for delivering construction materials was also quite innovative.

Further, the complete package of municipal tasks increased consumption among the lower income classes and established effective assistance for the unemployed. By greatly lowering the cost of living and housing through vast municipal provisions, wages were kept down, which in turn improved the competitiveness of Viennese industry. For example, real wages in Berlin were 16% to 37% higher than in Vienna, in Paris they were 22% to 49% higher, and in London 92% to 117% higher.[5] "There is one component of wages that can be gotten rid of without squeezing the productivity of workers and employees, namely, compensation for housing."[6] By increasing demand, Vienna's Social Democrats were practicing a form of municipal Keynesianism, but without deficit spending.

The literature unanimously concurs that Red Vienna essentially pursued an effective industrial modernization program to which the municipal policies of the Social Democrats were much better suited than the contradictory, status-based interests of the Christian

Socialist camp with its goal of protecting property and homeowners and its lack of understanding for the intricacies of social and economic policy.[7]

Red Vienna's municipal policies were "modern" and exemplary in that they incorporated an understanding of what was then becoming an important new concept: "leisure." With the introduction of the eight-hour working day in 1918, leisure—which had been greatly reduced during the Wilhelminian era—was expanded. There was, of course, also the "leisure" of the unemployed. The city's policies were aimed at leisure in a whole new way, yet not primarily in terms of consumption. According to the notion that "the best things in life are free," a wide and yet structured spectrum of provisions for meaningful leisure time were developed and realized. This included not only administratively organized civic education, culture, and sports activities, rather a rich culture of leisure-time clubs and associations focusing on many different aspects of life emerged that had to manage without municipal funding, with the important exception of the space provided for these burgeoning groups. In Red Vienna's heyday, the Social Democratic Party itself had 650,000 members, the union 520,000 members, the consumer association 267,000 members, and the renter's association 214,000 members, and new, semi-public groupings began to emerge on the basis of specific interests in the numerous cultural clubs. This constituted the beginning of social "scenes" beyond the spheres of bourgeois high culture and petty bourgeois event culture. The Kinderfreunde (Friends of the Children) club boasted 91,000 members, the "Worker's Sports Club" 240,000, and the Naturfreunde (Friends of Nature) 75,000.[8] With its festivals and large-scale events, the municipality was able to offer many points of identification, not only in its capacity as administrator, but also as a tangible actor.

In Red Vienna's policies and concrete municipal action, socialism was generally conceived of as a philosophy of an "urban public sphere": the public sphere as a utility value, which found expression in the shape of the courtyards in residential buildings, in the construction of public baths or the stadium (1930), as well as in the whole of its municipal bill of fare. At the same time, the construction of 65,000 apartments expressed the new value of the private sphere and privacy, which were unfamiliar to the poorer population. These were subletters or "bed-goers" (people who rented daytime beds in private housing when the tenants were absent) and usually by necessity single (in 1900, 60% of the urban population was single!), or else they lived in workers' quarters where running water and toilets were shared on each floor.

Vienna was perhaps the first municipality in the world that linked together all the interconnected aspects of urban infrastructure as well as the sector of reproduction—together with housing construction and the spatial aspects of city development—to create a modern idea of municipal policy as an absolute synergy of economic and financial policy together with social, educational, and cultural policy.

What is remarkable is how this program was realized in a relatively short period of time—in the fifteen years between 1919 and 1934, which is approximately the same amount of time that has gone by since the reunification of Germany. Although there were cultural and political contradictions in—and resistance to—the programmatic appropriation of bourgeois culture and the transformation of old popular cultural traditions into a new culture of work, the programs for the construction and the shaping of urban spaces (housing construction, and the social and cultural infrastructure) represented a coherent unity. Indeed, in the subsequent phase of fascism, the highly visible municipal buildings and facilities took on a symbolic meaning that was to last.[9]

Many aspects of the innovative, radical, and at the same time pragmatic local policies of Red Vienna, given some necessary refashioning, are relevant and of interest today in countering the misconceived liberalization and privatization of public services as well as exaggerated centralism in other areas. The instruments chosen by Vienna's Social Democracy were appropriate for ensuring progress in the city's urban planning and for contextually linking the new housing developments and municipal facilities with existing city spaces, topographies, and local characteristics.

Viennese Social Democracy's historical understanding of the city was remarkable and from today's perspective "modern" in its comprehension of the meaning of public spaces, of traditional and new forms of communication in urban spaces, and of the civic institutions that constitute an urban society. Larger residential housing complexes with numerous public facilities, large open spaces, and flexibility in the design of their scale exposed a generation of architects to new tasks and new possibilities—and the city of Vienna knew to include the most important and innovative architects in its construction program. Four hundred municipal housing complexes of varying scale (including those that utilized smaller and medium-sized lots between buildings) were thus erected, providing 64,000 new apartments for over 200,000 inhabitants.

Of course, critical reference was often made to the tight discipline associated with such a strong local administration, but this discipline was seen in contrast to the chaos of living and housing conditions in the Wilhelminian era. What is still relevant today from the Red Vienna of 1919 to 1934 are the above-described efforts to conceptualize an integrated municipal program, one in which wide-ranging theoretical debates in both public and internal party discussions led to the formulation of viable approaches to the issues at hand. What is missing today is a comparable development of new instruments that is as stringent and innovative, as oriented toward the goal of sustainability, and as bolstered by expert advice as that demonstrated in the integrative municipal policies of Red Vienna. For in some respects, the problems we face today resemble those of the period between 1919 and 1934 much more than we would care to admit.

Translated from the German by Christina M. White

Notes
1. Maren Seliger, *Sozialdemokratie und Kommunalpolitik in Wien: Zu einigen Aspekten sozialdemokratischer Politik in der Vor- und Zwischenkriegszeit* (Vienna: Jugend und Volk, 1980), 142ff., 149.
2. Wolfgang Förster and Klaus Novy, *Einfach bauen: Genossenschaftliche Selbsthilfe nach der Jahrhundertwende; Zur Rekonstruktion der Wiener Siedlerbewegung* (Vienna: Picus, 1991), 28.
3. Ibid., 31.
4. Hans Hautmann and Rudolf Hautmann, *Die Gemeindebauten des Roten Wien, 1919-1934* (Vienna: Schönbrunn, 1980), 38-39.
5. Rainer Bauböck, *Wohnungspolitik im sozialdemokratischen Wien, 1919-1934* (Salzburg: Neugebauer, 1979), 64.
6. Karl Honey, *Die Wohnungspolitik der Gemeinde Wien* (Vienna: 1926), 32.
7. Seliger, *Sozialdemokratie und Kommunalpolitik*, 9; Gerhard Melinz and Gerhard Unger, *Wohlfahrt und Krise: Wiener Kommunalpolitik 1929-1938* (Vienna: Franz Deuticke, 1996), 129.
8. Alfred Georg Frei, *Austromarxismus und Arbeiterkultur: Sozialdemokratische Wohnungs- und Kommunalpolitik 1919-1934* (Berlin: DVK-Verlag, 1984), 28ff.
9. Eve Blau, *The Architecture of Red Vienna, 1919-1934* (Cambridge, MA: MIT Press, 1999), 46. For an evaluation, also see Manfredo Tafuri, ed., *Vienna Rossa: la politica residenziale nella Vienna socialista, 1919-1933* (Milan: Electa, 1980).

FROM MANAGERIALISM TO ENTREPRENEURIALISM
THE TRANSFORMATION IN URBAN GOVERNANCE IN LATE CAPITALISM
David Harvey

The concept of urban entrepreneurialism has increasingly shaped urban policy in Western countries during the past decade, and it has been implemented in both prospering and crisis-ridden cities. The revitalization policies of shrinking cities such as Baltimore, Bilbao, Birmingham, and Manchester are often cited as prime examples of the success of this concept. But as David Harvey already demonstrated in 1989, in an essay reproduced here in shortened form, in "entrepreneurial cities"—notwithstanding partial successes—the disparities between winners and losers only grow more acute. For a significant share of the urban areas and the cities' inhabitants, there have been few positive changes to the problematic trends, although dwindling state resources are being redistributed with a view to fostering economic development. Fifteen years later, Harvey's insightful analysis has lost none of its relevance. (Eds.)

In recent years, urban governance has become increasingly preoccupied with the exploration of new ways in which to foster and encourage local development and employment growth. Such an entrepreneurial stance contrasts with the managerial practices of earlier decades, which primarily focused on the local provision of services, facilities, and benefits to urban populations.

The "managerial" approach so typical of the 1960s steadily gave way to initiatory and "entrepreneurial" forms of action in the 1970s and 1980s. In recent years, in particular, there seems to be a general consensus emerging throughout the advanced capitalist world that positive benefits are to be had by cities taking an entrepreneurial stance to economic development. What is remarkable is that this consensus seems to hold across national boundaries and even across political parties and ideologies.

David Blunkett, leader of the Labour Council in Sheffield for several years, has given the seal of approval to a certain kind of urban entrepreneurialism: "From the early 1970s, as full employment moved from the top of government priorities, local councils began to take up the challenge. There was support for small firms; closer links between the public and private sectors; promotion of local areas to attract new business. They were adapting the traditional economic role of British local government which offered inducements in the forms of grants, free loans, and publicly subsidized infrastructure, and no request for reciprocal involvement with the community, in order to attract industrial and commercial concerns which were looking for suitable sites for investment and trading.... Local government today, as in the past, can offer its own brand of entrepreneurship and enterprise in facing the enormous economic and social challenge which technology and industrial restructuring bring."[1]

In the United States, where civic boosterism and entrepreneurialism had long been a major feature of urban systems,[2] the reduction in the flow of federal redistributions and local tax revenues after 1972 (the year in which President Nixon declared the urban crisis to be over, signaling that the federal government no longer had the fiscal resources to contribute to its solution) led to a revival of boosterism to the point where Robert

Goodman was prepared to characterize both state and local governments as "the last entrepreneurs."³

The shift towards entrepreneurialism has by no means been complete. Many local governments in Britain did not respond to the new pressures and possibilities, while cities like New Orleans in the United States continue to remain wards of the federal government and rely fundamentally on redistributions for survival. And the history of entrepreneurialism's outcomes is obviously checkered, pockmarked with as many failures as successes and not a little controversy as to what constitutes "success" anyway. Yet beneath all this diversity, the shift from urban managerialism to some kind of entrepreneurialism remains a persistent and recurrent theme in the period since the early 1970s. Both the reasons for and the implications of such a shift are deserving of some scrutiny.

There is general agreement, of course, that the shift has something to do with the difficulties that have beset capitalist economies since the recession of 1973. Deindustrialization, widespread and seemingly "structural" unemployment, fiscal austerity at both the national and local levels, all coupled with a rising tide of neoconservatism and a much stronger appeal (though often more in theory than in practice) to market rationality and privatization, provide a backdrop to understanding why so many urban governments, often of quite different political persuasions and armed with very different legal and political powers, have taken a broadly similar direction. The greater emphasis on local action to combat these ills also seems to have something to do with the declining powers of the nation-state to control multinational money flows, so that investment increasingly takes the form of a negotiation between international finance capital and local powers doing the best they can to maximize the attractiveness of the local site as a lure for capitalist development. By the same token, the rise of urban entrepreneurialism may have had an important role to play in a general transition in the dynamics of capitalism from a Fordist-Keynesian regime of capital accumulation to a regime of "flexible accumulation."⁴ The transformation of urban governance these last two decades has had, I shall argue, substantial macroeconomic roots and implications. And if Jane Jacobs is only half right that the city is the relevant unit for understanding how the wealth of nations is created, then the shift from urban managerialism to urban entrepreneurialism could have far-reaching implications for future growth prospects.⁵

If, for example, urban entrepreneurialism (in the broadest sense) is embedded in a framework of zero-sum interurban competition for resources, jobs, and capital, then even the most resolute and avant-garde municipal socialists will find themselves, in the end, playing the capitalist game and performing as agents of discipline for the very processes they are trying to resist. It is exactly this problem that has dogged the Labour Councils in Britain.⁶ They had, on the one hand, to develop projects that could "produce outputs which are directly related to working people's needs, in ways which build on the skills of labour rather than deskilling them,"⁷ while, on the other hand, recognizing that much of that effort would go for nought if the urban region did not secure relative competitive advantages. Given the right circumstances, however, urban entrepreneurialism and even interurban competition may open the way to a non-zero-sum pattern of development. This kind of activity has certainly played a key role in capitalist development in the past. And it is an open question as to whether or not it could lead towards progressive and socialist transitions in the future.

Conceptual Issues

It is important to specify who is being entrepreneurial and about what. I want here to insist that urban "governance" means much more than urban "government." The real power to reorganize urban life so often lies elsewhere or at least within a broader coalition of forces within which urban government and administration have only a facilitative and coordinating role to play. The power to organize space derives from a whole complex of forces mobilized by diverse social agents. It is a conflictual process, the more so in the ecological spaces of highly variegated social density. Within a metropolitan region as a whole, we have to look to the formation of coalition politics, to class alliance formation as the basis for any kind of urban entrepreneurialism at all. Civic boosterism has, of course, often been the prerogative of the local chamber of commerce, some cabal of local financiers, industrialists and merchants, or some "round table" of business leaders and real-estate and property developers. The latter frequently coalesce to form the guiding power in "growth machine" politics.[8] Educational and religious institutions, different arms of government (varying from the military to research or administrative establishments), local labor organizations (the building and construction trades in particular), as well as political parties, social movements, and the local state apparatuses (which are multiple and often quite heterogeneous), can also play the game of local boosterism, though often with quite different goals.

Coalition and alliance formation is so delicate and difficult a task that the way is open here for a person of vision, tenacity, and skill (such as a charismatic mayor, a clever city administrator, or a wealthy business leader) to put a particular stamp upon the nature and direction of urban entrepreneurialism, perhaps to shape it, even, to particular political ends. Whereas it was a public figure like Mayor Schaeffer who played the central role in Baltimore, in cities like Halifax or Gateshead it has been private entrepreneurs who have taken the lead. In other instances it has been a more intricate mix of personalities and institutions that have put a particular project together.

The new entrepreneurialism has, as its centerpiece, the notion of a "public-private partnership" in which a traditional local boosterism is integrated with the use of local governmental powers to try and attract external sources of funding, new direct investments, or new employment sources. In the United States the tradition of federally backed and locally implemented public-private partnership faded during the 1960s as urban governments struggled to regain social control of restive populations through redistributions of real income (better housing, education, health care, etc., all targeted towards the poor) in the wake of urban unrest. The role of the local state as facilitator for the strategic interests of capitalist development (as opposed to stabilizer of capitalist society) declined. The same dismissiveness towards capitalist development has been noted in Britain: "The early 1970s was a period of resistance to change: motorway protest groups, community action against slum clearance, opponents of town centre redevelopment. Strategic and entrepreneurial interests were sacrificed to local community pressures."[9]

In Baltimore the transition point can be dated exactly. A referendum narrowly passed in 1978, after a vigorous and contentious political campaign, sanctioned the use of city land for the private development that became the highly spectacular and successful Harborplace mall. Thereafter, the policy of public-private partnership had a popular mandate as well as an effective subterranean presence in almost everything that urban governance was about.[10]

The activity of that public-private partnership is entrepreneurial precisely because it is speculative in execution and design and therefore dogged by all the difficulties and dangers that attach to speculative as opposed to rationally planned and coordinated development. In many instances this has meant that the public sector assumes the risk and the private sector takes the benefits, though there are enough examples where this is not the case (think, for example, of the private risk taken in Gateshead's MetroCentre development) to make any absolute generalization dangerous. But I suspect it is this feature of risk absorption by the local (rather than the national or federal) public sector that distinguishes the present phase of urban entrepreneurialism from earlier phases of civic boosterism in which private capital seemed generally much less risk averse.

Entrepreneurialism focuses much more closely on the political economy of place rather than of territory. By the latter I mean the kinds of economic projects (housing, education, etc.) that are designed primarily to improve conditions of living or working within a particular jurisdiction. The construction of place (a new civic center, an industrial park) or the enhancement of conditions within a place (intervention, for example, in local labor markets via retraining schemes or downward pressure on local wages), on the other hand, can have impacts either smaller or greater than the specific territory within which such projects happen to be located. The upgrading of the image of cities like Baltimore, Liverpool, Glasgow, or Halifax through the construction of cultural, retail, entertainment, and office centers can cast a seemingly beneficial shadow over the whole metropolitan region. Such projects can acquire meaning at the metropolitan scale of public-private action and allow for the formation of coalitions that leap over the kinds of city-suburb rivalries that dogged metropolitan regions in the managerial phase. On the other hand, a rather similar development in New York City (South Street Seaport) constructs a new place that has only local impacts, falling far short of any metropolitan-wide influence and generating a coalition of forces that basically consists of local property developers and financiers.

The construction of such places may, of course, be viewed as a means to procure benefits for populations within a particular jurisdiction, and indeed this is a primary claim made in the public discourse developed to support them. But for the most part, their form is such as to make all benefits indirect and potentially either wider or smaller in scope than the jurisdiction within which they lie. Place-specific projects of this sort also have the habit of becoming such a focus of public and political attention that they divert concern and even resources from the broader problems that may beset the region or territory as a whole.

The new urban entrepreneurialism typically rests, then, on a public-private partnership focusing on investment and economic development with the speculative construction of place rather than amelioration of conditions within a particular territory as its immediate (though by no means exclusive) political and economic goal.

Alternative Strategies for Urban Governance

There are, I have argued elsewhere, four basic options for urban entrepreneurialism.[11] Each warrants some separate consideration, even though it is the combination of them that provides the clue to the recent rapid shifts in the uneven development of urban systems in the advanced capitalist world.

1. Competition within the international division of labor means the creation of exploitation of particular advantages for the production of goods and services. Some advantages derive from the resource base (the oil that allowed Texas to bloom in the 1970s) or location (e.g., favored access to the vigor of Pacific Rim trading in the case of Californian cities). But others are created through public and private investments in the kinds of physical and social infrastructures that strengthen the economic base of the metropolitan region as an exporter of goods and services. Direct interventions to stimulate the application of new technologies, the creation of new products, or the provision of venture capital to new enterprises (which may even be cooperatively owned and managed) may also be significant, while local costs may be reduced by subsidies (tax breaks, cheap credit, procurement of sites). Hardly any large-scale development now occurs without local government (or the broader coalition of forces constituting local governance) offering a substantial package of aids and assistance as inducements. International competitiveness also depends upon the qualities, quantities, and costs of local labor supply. Local costs can most easily be controlled when local replaces national collective bargaining and when local governments and other large institutions lead the way with reductions in real wages and benefits. Labor power of the right quality, though expensive, can be a powerful magnet for new economic development so that investment in highly trained and skilled workforces suited to new labor processes and their managerial requirements can be well rewarded.

2. The urban region can also seek to improve its competitive position with respect to the spatial division of consumption. There is more to this than trying to bring money into an urban region through tourism and retirement attractions. The consumerist style of urbanization after 1950 promoted an ever-broader basis for participation in mass consumption. Gentrification, cultural innovation, and physical upgrading of the urban environment, consumer attractions (sports stadia, convention and shopping centers, marinas, exotic eating places), and entertainment (the organization of urban spectacles on a temporary or permanent basis) have all become much more prominent facets of strategies for urban regeneration. Above all, the city has to appear as an innovative, exciting, creative, and safe place to live or to visit, to play and consume in. Baltimore, with its dismal reputation as "the armpit of the east coast" in the early 1970s, has, for example, expanded its employment in the tourist trade from under one thousand to over fifteen thousand in less than two decades of massive urban redevelopment.

3. Urban entrepreneurialism has also been strongly colored by a fierce struggle over the acquisition of key control and command functions in high finance, government, or information-gathering and -processing (including the media). Functions of this sort need particular and often expensive infrastructural provision. Efficiency and centrality within a worldwide communications net is vital in sectors where personal interactions of key decision-makers is required. This means heavy investments in transport and communications (e.g., airports and teleports) and the provision of adequate office space equipped with the necessary internal and external linkages to minimize transaction times and costs. Assembling the wide range of supportive services, particularly those that can gather and process information rapidly or allow quick consultation with "experts," calls for other kinds of investments, while the specific skills required by such activities put a premium on metropolitan regions with certain kinds of educational provision (business and law schools, high-tech production sectors, media skills, and the like).

4. Competitive edge with respect to redistribution of surpluses through central (or in the United States, state) government is still of tremendous importance since it is somewhat of a myth that central governments do not redistribute to the degree they used to. The channels have shifted so that in both Britain (take the case of Bristol) and in the United States (take the case of Long Beach, San Diego) it is military and defense contracts that provide the substance for urban prosperity, in part because of the sheer amount of money involved, but also because of the type of employment and the spin-offs it may have into so-called high-tech industries.[12]

These four strategies are not mutually exclusive, and the uneven fortunes of metropolitan regions have depended upon the nature of the coalitions that have formed, the mix and timing of entrepreneurial strategies, the particular resources (natural, human, locational) with which the metropolitan region can work, and the strength of the competition. Urban entrepreneurialism implies, however, some level of interurban competition. We here approach a force that puts clear limitations upon the power of specific projects to transform the lot of particular cities. Indeed, to the degree that interurban competition becomes more potent, it will almost certainly operate as an "external coercive power" over individual cities to bring them closer into line with the discipline and logic of capitalist development. It may even force repetitive and serial reproduction of certain patterns of development.

The reduction of spatial barriers has, in fact, made competition between localities, states, and urban regions for development capital even mote acute. Urban governance has thus become much more oriented to the provision of a "good business climate" and to the construction of all sorts of lures to bring capital into town. The search to procure investment capital confines innovation to a very narrow path built around a favorable package for capitalist development and all that it entails. The task of urban governance is, in short, to lure highly mobile and flexible production, financial, and consumption flows into its space. The speculative qualities of urban investments simply derive from the inability to predict exactly which package will succeed and which will not in a world of considerable economic instability and volatility.

It is easy to envisage, therefore, all manner of upward and downward spirals of urban growth and decline under conditions where urban entrepreneurialism and interurban competition are strong. The innovative and competitive responses of many urban ruling-class alliances have engendered more rather than less uncertainty and in the end made the urban system more rather than less vulnerable to the uncertainties of rapid change.

The Macroeconomic Implications of Interurban Competition

The absorption of risk by the public sector and, in particular, the stress on public-sector involvement in infrastructural provision have meant that the cost of locational change has diminished from the standpoint of multinational capital, making the latter more rather than less geographically mobile. If anything, the new urban entrepreneurialism adds to rather than detracts from the geographical flexibility with which multinational firms can approach their locational strategies.

The radical reconstruction of the image of Baltimore through the new waterfront and Inner Harbor development put Baltimore on the map in a new way, earned the city the title of "renaissance city," put it on the front cover of *Time* magazine, and helped it shed its image of dreariness and impoverishment. It appeared as a dynamic go-getting city, ready to accommodate outside capital and to encourage the movement in of capital and of the "right" people. No matter that the reality is one of increased impoverishment and overall urban deterioration and that the thorough study of the renaissance by Levine showed again and again how partial and limited the benefits were and how the city as a whole was accelerating rather than reversing its decline.[13]

Behind the mask of many successful projects there lie some serious social and economic problems, and in many cities these are taking geographical shape in the form of a dual city of inner-city regeneration and a surrounding sea of increasing impoverishment. Yet there is something positive also going on here that deserves close attention. The idea of the city as a collective corporation, within which democratic decision-making can operate, has a long history in the pantheon of progressive doctrines and practices (the Paris Commune being, of course, the paradigm case in socialist history). There have been some recent attempts to revive such a corporatist vision both in theory and in practice.[14] While it is possible, therefore, to characterize certain kinds of urban entrepreneurialism as purely capitalistic in method, intent, and result, it is also useful to recognize that many of the problems of collective corporatist action originate not with the fact of some kind of civic boosterism, or even by virtue of who, in particular, dominates the urban class alliances that form or what projects they devise.

A critical perspective on urban entrepreneurialism indicates not only its negative impacts but also its potentiality for transformation into a progressive urban corporatism, armed with a keen geopolitical sense of how to build alliances and linkages across space in such a way as to mitigate if not challenge the hegemonic dynamic of capitalist accumulation to dominate the historical geography of social life.

This text is an abridged version of David Harvey, "From Managerialism to Entrepreneurialism: The Transformation of Urban Governance in Late Capitalism," *Geografiska Annaler* 71 B, no. 1 (1989): 3-17. It is reprinted by kind permission of Blackwell Publishing.

The concept of the entrepreneurial city has been examined by numerous authors since Harvey's article first appeared. As no more than a representative example, see Tim Hall and Phil Hubbard, eds., *The Entrepreneurial City: Geographies of Politics, Regime and Representation* (Chichester, UK: John Wiley, 1998).—Ed.

Notes
1   David Blunkett and Keith Jackson, *Democracy in Crisis: The Town Halls Respond* (London: The Hogarth Press, 1987), 108.
2   See Stephen L. Elkin, *City and Regime in the American Republic* (Chicago: University of Chicago Press, 1987).
3   Robert Goodman, *The Last Entrepreneurs: America's Regional Wars for Jobs and Dollars* (New York: Simon and Schuster, 1979).

4   For a more detailed elaboration of and a critical reflection on this controversial concept, see, for example, David Harvey, *The Condition of Postmodernity* (Oxford, UK: Blackwell, 1989).
5   Jane Jacobs, *Cities and the Wealth of Nations* (New York: Random House, 1984).
6   See the excellent account by Gareth Rees and John Lambert, *Cities in Crisis: The Political Economy of Urban Development in Post-war Britain* (London: Edward Arnold, 1985).
7   Robin Murray, "Pension Funds and Local Authority Investments," *Capital and Class* 20 (Summer 1983), 102.
8   Harvey Molotch, "The City as a Growth Machine: Towards a Political Economy of Place," *American Journal of Sociology* 82 (1976): 309-332.
9   H. W. E. Davies, "The Relevance of Development Control," *Town Planning Review* 51 (1980), 23; quoted in Michael Ball, *Housing Policy and Economic Power: The Political Economy of Owner Occupation* (London: Methuen, 1983), 270-271.
10 See, for example, M. Levine, "Downtown Redevelopment as an Urban Growth Strategy: A Critical Appraisal of the Baltimore Renaissance," *Journal of Urban Affairs* 9, no. 2 (1987): 103-123.
11 David Harvey, *The Urban Experience* (Baltimore, MD: Johns Hopkins University Press, 1989), chap. 1.
12 Ann Markusen, "Defense Spending: A Successful Industrial Policy," *International Journal of Urban and Regional Research* 10 (1986): 105-122.
13 Levine, "Downtown Redevelopment."
14 For the former, see Gerald Frug, "The City as a Legal Concept," *Harvard Law Review* 93, no. 6 (1980): 1059-1153; for the latter, Blunkett and Jackson, *Democracy in Crisis*.

THE URBAN TASK FORCE AND ITS URBAN RENAISSANCE
Anna Minton

"New" has been the essential prefix to Britain's Labour Party government—elected on a landslide in 1997 after eighteen years of Conservative Party rule—and no matter what many skeptics may feel today, the early heady days of the new government were indeed characterized by a feeling of immense change.

In the immediate aftermath of the New Labour victory, an unprecedented raft of "task forces," "units," and "czars" was appointed to oversee the radical policies promised by the new government. In the sphere of regeneration, the Urban Task Force was chief among these and symbolized the image that the new design-conscious government was keen to be associated with, from continental-style urban café life to hip, iconic architecture.

Appointed to lead the thirteen-strong group of prominent luminaries, Richard Rogers (the eminent architect and Labour Party Lord who designed the Pompidou Center—together with Renzo Piano—and the Millenium Dome), was the embodiment of a fully paid-up member of the new establishment that had so comprehensively swept to power. When, a year later in 1999, the task force produced its report, *Towards an Urban Renaissance,* in "urban renaissance" it coined a term that has become one of the defining buzzwords of this government.[1]

Yet, while his influence on the political rhetoric of New Labour is undeniable, seven years on Lord Rogers is working for Blair's erstwhile opponent, London Mayor Ken Livingstone, and has repeatedly spoken of his disappointment that so few of his report's recommendations have been taken up by the government.

The task force was set up, according to its mission statement, to "identify causes of urban decline in England and recommend practical solutions to bring people back into our cities, towns and neighbourhoods." The clear aim was to attract people back into the United Kingdom's shrinking cities and to promote continental-style, high-density urban living, in contrast to the English suburban ideal. The context was the 3.8 million additional households expected to form in the United Kingdom in the period to 2021, a demographic time bomb seen by the task force as an opportunity to revitalize declining towns and cities.

The substantial document included more than one hundred recommendations in five sections and specified measures to deal with declining inner cities. The first section, "The Sustainable City," argued for high-quality, compact, and mixed-use urban developments under a national urban design framework that would inform all planning policy and public expenditure. Part two dealt with the importance of stronger local government to drive forward the defining theme of "urban renaissance"—a concept examined in the third section. The fourth part, "Making the Investment," made the case for regional investment companies, while the final section, "Sustaining the Renaissance," called for an ambitious 25-year program to oversee the renaissance at national, regional, and local levels.

Since the launch of the task force in 1998, what is undeniable is that a transformation has occurred in the way that many British cities, particularly city centers, are perceived, especially in the traditionally depopulating North of the country. Up and down the United Kingdom, from London's Docklands to Leith in Edinburgh and the Albert Dock in Liverpool, the waterfront areas surrounding the country's empty dockyards have seen the metamorphosis of former industrial warehouses into spruced-up apartments, art galleries, bars, and restaurants, providing a vibrant evening economy and playground for the young professionals who are flocking back to city-center living.

But while it is clear that this transformation has coincided with a sea change in political rhetoric and a genuine shift in city-center living, it is less certain to what extent the task force had been riding the crest of the wave of postindustrial change and to what extent it actually influenced the direction of that change.

It is also worth examining what is actually meant by the term "urban renaissance," which, in common with a great many current policy buzzwords, is very loosely defined. Although there is no doubt that the driving force behind the "renaissance" is the desire to revitalize city living, the form this should take is less clear. The foreword to the task force report is written by the former Mayor of Barcelona, Pasqual Maragall, and the thrust of the rhetoric surrounding the launch was the need to introduce a more continental-style café culture in tune with the open public spaces and squares of the continent. But a closer look at Rogers's own work in this respect reveals the championing of privately owned and privately managed city spaces, such as Potsdamer Platz in Berlin, which have a more complex relationship with public access.

Critics of the "renaissance" concept argue then that it champions, in particular, what is becoming known as "private-public" space, typified by the new mixed-use developments of yuppie penthouses, restaurants, and bars in the trendy converted warehouses that have sprung up on the old industrial sites of the city. The problem with this is that these developments, often with a visible private-security presence, are not seen as inclusive for the population of the city as a whole and are derided as consumption-and-leisure playgrounds open only to the high earners of the postindustrial knowledge economy.

As to Rogers's own disappointment with the way government viewed the work of the task force, that is down to the fact that while the rhetoric of "urban renaissance" is never far from government ministers' lips, very few of his report's 105 recommendations have actually made it into policy, in terms of both the broad thrust of the report and the more specific recommendations.

The key plank required to underpin the urban renaissance was clearly identified in the report as the need to strengthen local government to ensure it was the leading local actor behind city change, and it is this, above all, that has not been taken on board. The report stated: "There is a need to re-think the role, the responsibility and structures of local government in our urban areas. Our towns and cities need strong leadership and democratic structures which are meaningful and accessible to citizens. Local authorities must be empowered to lead the urban renaissance."[2] It recommended that the government push aside any ideological opposition to involving local authorities left over from their Conservative predecessors and increase their powers and funding, enabling them to undertake a pivotal role as "urban managers."

However, regeneration policy remains highly centrally driven, concentrating on the creation of four new growth areas in the South alongside the "market renewal" of declining areas in the North. The possible exception to this local-government weakness is London, where Mayor Ken Livingstone is serving his second term as elected mayor. It is surely no coincidence that Lord Rogers is now heading up the mayor's Architecture and Urbanism Unit, alongside a number of other members of the task force who have also taken on prominent roles with the Greater London Authority.

Alongside the dramatic changes witnessed in a great many postindustrial city centers, the other big shift in the social and economic climate since the publication of the report has been the dramatic rise in house prices, leading to a housing affordability crisis across the country, particularly in London and the Southeast. Consequently, first-time buyers and public-sector workers such as nurses and teachers can rarely afford to buy their own homes, while the decline in the "social rented" public-housing sector means that subsidized renting is not an option either. The result has been a "key workers crisis," with nurses, firefighters, and teachers unable to afford either to buy or to rent and in many cases forced to abandon their careers.

There is no doubt that this has been a key factor behind the government decision to promote the growth areas in the Southeast, an aim that clearly runs counter to the concept of "urban renaissance," with the task force having stated in its interim report that "the current concentration of economic opportunity and wealth in London and the southeast is bad for the country and not even sustainable in London."[3]

Instead, policy towards the growth areas is more reminiscent of the centralized new towns' expansion programs of the postwar years. Similarly, the large-scale demolition and rebuilding proposed by the "Pathfinder" market-renewal strategy in the North also brings to mind the centralized "slum clearance" of the 1950s and 1960s, not least in terms of the widespread local opposition to the policy.

Behind this, and behind the failure of the Rogers report to find its way into policy, has been a schism in approaches between government departments. On the one hand, the most dominant department, the Treasury, has consistently backed a market-led approach to tackling regeneration through economic renewal and the building of more new homes. This is in contrast to the department officially tasked with regeneration, the Office of the Deputy Prime Minister (ODPM), which has been more sympathetic to the task force recommendations and their emphasis on converting what is already there. The recent appointment of former Treasury minister Yvette Cooper to the ODPM signals that it is, unsurprisingly, the Treasury agenda that remains in the ascendant.

With the publication of the "Urban White Paper" in 2000, a year after the task force report, it immediately became clear that most of the recommendations in the Rogers report had been ignored.[4] In particular, the two most important ones, which contained fiscal measures, were dismissed by the Treasury. These were the creation of urban priority areas with special powers and incentives to aid urban renewal, and the removal of value-added tax (charged at 17.5%) on conversions (it is not charged on newly built homes). Clearly, it is anomalous that while repair and refurbishment is often the most sustainable option, particularly for city-center living, the tax system favors new construction. With the Urban White Paper, a relatively weak document strong on the rhetoric of the "urban renaissance" but utterly lacking in the policy teeth to implement it, the consequence has been that the increasingly criticized Communities Plan is the template for today's urban policy.[5]

The other area heavily emphasized by the task force was the importance of design-led regeneration, with a key recommendation being the need for a national urban-design framework. Here, too, Rogers has been particularly vocal in his concerns about the quality of new housing currently being built. Once again the feeling is that ever-more house building, often on greenfield sites, is seen as the only answer to the housing crisis. And despite the government's emphasis on the need to build sustainable communities that will stand the test of time, the fear among a growing body of experts is that precisely the opposite is under way.

Now, the task force is apparently preparing to re-form, either temporarily or as a more permanent body able to play a high-profile yet critical role with regard to current policy. However, with a number of members currently running key government agencies, it is unlikely that their criticisms will be too trenchant. As for Rogers himself, although he has continuously expressed his disappointment, he has largely managed to stay within policy-making circles, while he shared a platform with Deputy Prime Minister John Prescott to launch the Urban White Paper.

The likelihood is that when and if the task force does come together again, its main role will be to press for stronger local government to drive through regeneration, probably through elected mayors with real powers and able to serve a number of terms, according to the model in London, Barcelona, and New York. But whether or not the Treasury is genuinely prepared to relinquish power to local government would seem, on the basis of the evidence so far, more than a little unlikely.

Notes
1. United Kingdom Department of the Environment, Transport and the Regions, *Towards an Urban Renaissance: Final Report of the Urban Task Force Chaired by Lord Rogers of Riverside* (London: E & FN Spon, 1999).
2. Ibid.
3. United Kingdom Department of the Environment, Transport and the Regions, *Urban Renaissance—Sharing the Vision: Interim Report of the Urban Task Force* (Wetherby: Free Literature, 1999).
4. United Kingdom Office of the Deputy Prime Minister, "Our Towns and Cities: The Future—Delivering an Urban Renaissance (Urban White Paper 2000)," www.odpm.gov.uk/stellent/groups/odpm_control/documents/contentservertemplate/odpm_index.hcst?n=2866&l=2.
5. United Kingdom Office of the Deputy Prime Minister, "Sustainable Communities: Building for the Future (2003)," http://www.odpm.gov.uk/index.asp?id=1139868.

RETHINKING LOCAL SPECIFICITY AND COMMUNITY
Ash Amin

We have got accustomed to thinking of cities and regions as territorial entities: local economic systems, political regimes, home. The local continues to be seen as the space of the intimate, the familiar, the near, the embodied; a space deemed constitutively separate from the global, a space seen as the afar, the abstract, the virtual, the encroaching. It is odd that this interpretation continues to grip the imaginary, given the rise of forces that are transforming cities and regions as sites immersed in global networks of organization and therefore routinely implicated in distant connections and influences. These are forces we have come to associate with globalization, which includes the everyday transnational flow of ideas, information, knowledge, money, people, and cultural influences; the growth of translocal networks of organization and influence, such as transnational corporations, global financial institutions, international governance regimes, and transnational cultural networks; and the ripples of distant developments such as stock-market swings, environmental disasters, global trade agreements, and policy decisions in powerful nations.

In this emerging order, spatial configurations and spatial boundaries can no longer be seen as territorial or scalar, since the social, economic, political, and cultural inside and outside are constituted through the topologies of actor networks that are becoming increasingly dynamic and varied in spatial constitution.[1] These spatialities are decisive in the constitution of the local, but they continue to be written out of the hegemonic territorial imaginary of the world. They require a relational reading of place that works with the new ontology of flow and connectivity, so that cities and regions can be imagined through their plural spatial connections, with no automatic promise of territorial or systemic integrity, since they are made through the spatialities of flow, juxtaposition, porosity, and relational connectivity.

It matters politically in quite profound ways whether we see cities and regions as territorial or relational entities, because very different sensibilities of the political spring out of each reading of place. Each one offers a different understanding of local community and sense of place, with profound implications as to what to do about the problem of shrinking cities and declining regions.

Territorial Politics
Twenty years ago, few policy-makers in the advanced economies would have expected localities facing sustained economic hardship to sort out their own problems, especially through the route of rebuilding local community. There was still a sense that urban and regional fortunes were intertwined and influenced by embedded power asymmetries within and between places, such that an effective local economic development strategy would have to regulate interregional competition and mobilize state action through active urban, regional, and welfare policies to redirect investment, jobs, and income to the less favored areas.

Community, when invoked, as during the famous community development projects of the 1970s, was invoked as a differentiated category (attentive to divisions of class, gender, and race) and as a means of socially empowering hard-hit localities. It came with no major economic regeneration expectations other than the sense that well-being was good for labor-market participation or that community could spawn small-scale activity in the alternative economy.

Then along came neoliberalism—backed up by a vengeful New Right and a relieved international business community—to sweep away this mode of thinking and acting, arguing that the society of connections and commitments interfered with the efficient market allocation of resources and growth potential, created a culture of dependency and expectancy in the assisted areas and their inhabitants, was a drain on public resources and perpetuated unnecessary state intervention in the economy, conceded too much to the weak and their organizations, and, to boot, failed to stimulate entrepreneurship and growth in declining or lagging cities and regions. In the United Kingdom, the cradle of New Right thinking, a policy revolution was unleashed in the 1980s involving cuts in regional aid, giving business free rein, reorienting state support to underpin growth in the prosperous regions, introducing measures to promote entrepreneurship and innovation in the less favored regions, replacing democratically elected institutions by unelected quangos and business-led organizations as key players in local regeneration, and refashioning welfare as workfare and welfare dependency as moral and social degeneracy. In the meantime, urban and regional inequality intensified across a wide range of indicators—including health and morbidity, education, economic prosperity, housing, social breakdown and alienation, and fear and insecurity—without stimulating self-sustaining growth in the less favored areas.

Most recently, along has come the Third Way—driven by new Social Democrats vengeful of both the Old Left and the New Right—to harness the idea of the society of connections and commitments to the principles of market freedom and unhampered growth in the core regions. Here, too, the United Kingdom government under New Labour, balancing on the shoulders of the likes of Hayek, Giddens, Etzioni, and Putnam, has led the way in experimenting with a new trickery that simultaneously works in sociospatial inequality and equality.[2] Third Way thinking is not confined to the United Kingdom, but is also inscribed in the policies of the European Union in the form of active measures to promote social cohesion and equally active measures to promote competitiveness through market liberalization and deregulation, as it is increasingly conjured up by left-of-center governments hampered by rising social and regional budgets. The Third Way, sharing New Right concerns over redistributionist regional policies, has chosen to accompany market-led policies working for the more prosperous regions with a series of measures to boost the competitive potential of the more disadvantaged and the less prosperous regions. Regional competition, thus, is forecast to work for both the core and the periphery through processes of regional specialization and the mobilization of latent potential. The Third Way has spawned a new localism underpinned by policies to build regional capacity through the promotion of locally referenced activity such as industrial clusters, technopoles, and local knowledge transfer, harnessed to various institutions of regional promotion such as regional development agencies, business-led regional assemblies, and devolution in general.

This new regionalism is based on the assumption that territorial autonomy will: (a) restore local control and democracy; (b) increase economic returns; and (c) strengthen the sense of place attachment and social capabilities. All three expectations spring from a strongly territorial imaginary of place and place politics, and one that is increasingly problematic.

Limitations of the Politics of Territorial Management

At one level, it is hard to fault the politics of localism. Has it not long been argued that the regional problem is the product of the centralization of capital and control? Does it not follow therefore that devolution and localization are a necessary first step in reducing regional inequality? Is local capacity-building not a way of helping less favored cities and regions to shed a culture of dependency on central state solutions? Indeed so, but only if nonlocal influences on cities and regions can be held in check. Contemporary experiments in devolution, with their endless concern with clusters, regional assemblies, development agencies, and the like, seem largely blind to the evidence that shows that in the majority of contemporary corporate and industrial contexts, supply chains, linkage arrangements, and knowledge networks are not locationally restricted, but highly dispersed spatially.[3] Such evidence casts serious doubt on the potential of cluster initiatives and promised local returns. In turn, the new localism is unable to control the forces—material, virtual, and immanent—that are implicated in new spaces of transterritorial organization. These are forces that, in the form of share prices and interest rates, shifts in standards and rules, corporate and banking investment decisions, financial transfers, flows of information, people and knowledge, and decisions in faraway places, routinely get around, distort, or annul brave efforts to organize for local benefit. Only too often devolution and local institution-building—despite the rhetoric of wresting control away from the central state—comes without any serious attack on the might of defining others.

My argument is not against building regional voice and representation. Instead, it is against the assumption that there is a defined geographical territory out there over which local actors can have effective control and can manage as a social and political space. In a relationally constituted modern world in which it has become normal to conduct business—economic, cultural, political—through everyday transterritorial organization and flow,[4] local advocacy, it seems to me, increasingly must be about exercising nodal power and aligning networks at large in your own interest, rather than about exercising territorial power (unless you have access to the core sources such as control over the means of coercion and enrollment as do some in some powerful regions and states). There is no definable regional territory to rule over.

The Localization of the Social

But, the territorial imaginary remains unshaken. In many ways, it suits the state to think of the national social and economic map as subdivided into distinct regions. Devolution and its successes and failures can then become the responsibility of the regions, who can then also be asked to put their own social houses in order for regeneration purposes, thus breaking the idea of a single national community that the state has equal responsibility towards. I take up this argument next, with reference to the emblematic policies of the Blair government.

The repackaging of the economy and polity as a series of self-reliant territorial entities evident in current regional-policy thinking has been accompanied by a similar repackaging of the social as the special feature of hard-pressed areas affected by high levels of unemployment and social stress or breakdown. The rediscovery of the social by the Third

Way as a policy instrument for local renewal has been most actively pursued by the Blair government. This localization of traditionally national policy domains differentiated on social rather than territorial grounds is in part the product of a reconceptualization of the problem of social exclusion *as a problem of local origin* and the challenge of local regeneration as a challenge for local actors.

The core assumption is that the society of commitments is one that is spatially circumscribed. Local authorities, local communities, local organizations of various sorts, and local branches of national bodies are expected to interact in the local public sphere and work as a local political community, often in designated spaces such as regional assemblies, to attend to local problems directly or by pressing for more resources from the center. The local is viewed as a political community that, through mechanisms of deliberation, partnership, and shared interest, knows what is best for the locality and can deliver solutions that work for the common good. Local regeneration is premised around the assumption of a multiheaded, but consensual, political community with localized concerns. At face value none of this seems problematic. Indeed, set against the legacy of state-driven or market-based cultures of local intervention in the hands of remote and context-blind actors, the new thinking can be praised for recognizing at long last the power and potential of an enlarged democracy that draws on the creative impulses of an active civil society and a devolved polity. Such a shift has long been advocated by the democratic Left concerned with spatial equality.

So, why is it problematic? It is problematic because it suffers from a romance of local community, one that will be assailed from all directions and will be modest in its economic and political returns, especially in the areas in which it is most expected to deliver. While deprived or declining areas are thrown the expectations of local community, paradoxically a plural, less functionalist and geographically promiscuous understanding of the social is retained for other spaces such as the nation or prosperous cities and regions. In imagining a future for the less favored and more hard-pressed areas, the rich tapestry of the social conceded to other spaces is conjured away, as is the obligation to explain why the social thus defined should provide for economic and democratic vitality. Lack of community is blamed for local degeneration without any critical appraisal of other contributing factors[5]— local and translocal—or of alternative forms of social connectivity that do not fit the stereotype.[6] In turn, the restoration of community is seen to be the mainstay of local economic and political regeneration, once again without critical assessment of what community really means and without serious analysis of the drivers of change and renewal beyond community.[7] The problem of "failed" places becomes a problem of eliminating bad community and replacing it with good community, under the unwritten assumption that if and when the policy efforts fail, the communities will have only themselves to blame.

The consequence is less talk about the less favored regions in terms of lack of job opportunities, state obligations, equipping people for social and spatial mobility, rights and entitlements, the consequences of uneven development, productive ways of external linkage, sustained investment in the local infrastructure, enabling citizenship, and other drivers of well-being. Instead, there is plenty of talk of ensuring participation in local and national associations, elections, organized leisure pursuits, circles beyond the immediate family or interest group, work and leisure communities, and so on, with the results, when negative, thrown back to the hard-pressed communities as evidence of lack and degeneracy.

These observations are not intended to devalue the significance of strategies of social empowerment and bottom-up development. My objection, instead, lies with the idea of government by community itself—with its narrow and parochial understanding of the society of commitment and connections, as well as with the unrealistic and excessively high regeneration expectations laid at the doorstep of local community. The relationship between social empowerment and economic enhancement is not at all straightforward. First, an empowered citizenry that lacks the means to control its destiny as well as wrest power from or enroll others who routinely shape the world and its ways—others who are never that easy to identify or access, inscribed as they are in instituted practices and habits, diffuse networks, hidden immanence, and distant places—does not possess the autonomy to make and distribute resources. Second, an empowered citizenry never comes with a common set of interests, which is precisely why so many programs on the ground are assailed by a politics of uneven voice, social manipulation, conflicting interest, and power imbalance; a politics that regularly compromises the needs of the socially excluded and marginalized. Third—*pace* the communitarians and social capitalists—there is no direct link between social empowerment and economic regeneration or development, because this relationship is intermediated by structures of market relationships, regulations, institutional arrangement, power configuration, and values and norms. Thus, social intervention in one place may lead to economic enhancement somewhere else or require other interventions both there and afar in order to ensure local economic returns.

My argument is that effective local economic regeneration requires a multipolar polity in which the regions can run discrete areas of national life (rather than just a limited set of their own affairs) as well as count on action by the state to redirect opportunities towards them, bolster their bottom-up strategies, and regulate interregional competition. This is not an argument for a 'handout' approach to local regeneration, but recognition of the principle of spatial mutuality and connectivity. Without attention to the wider institutional and market circumstances that shape local fortunes, community-led strategies will never amount to more than a fob to the hard-pressed cities and regions, possibly even a cold towel, as state welfare support and other redistributive measures are subtly rolled back in the name of support for a community empowerment approach, while the lion's share of policy attention and institutional arrangements for national economic development remain biased towards the most prosperous cities and regions. It is simply perverse that the "social" should be privileged as a tool for economic regeneration for those areas in which it is thought that the "social" is somehow deficient, while other avenues for regeneration and other constraints on regeneration—national and regional—in these areas are left unexamined.

The regeneration areas—yes, they too—are spaces of plural publics, contested claims, and irreconcilable understandings of the good life, in possession of a vitality that is only too frequently crushed or manipulated by the dominant sectional interests. In these circumstances, social empowerment is a must so that vested interests and old hierarchies can be challenged through opposition and dissent. Community-building can end up as an act of disempowerment, as yet another consensual fix for regeneration is put into place, now in the name of active citizenship. Social empowerment programs should be stripped of the language of community cohesion and social capital formation, and justified on their own terms as acts of enhancing the capabilities, voice, rights, and presence of the excluded and the marginalized, so that these social actors can become legitimate claimants upon the social turf, even when the claims are not consensual.

It is important to retain a more promiscuous sense of the political and a more cosmopolitan sense of social and spatial connectivity and commitment in imagining regeneration strategies. Regeneration cannot be a localist affair or a matter of local responsibility alone, but part of a wider political economy of decentered power and redistributive justice. Local society—at least in areas facing social and economic hardship—cannot be caricatured in the way that the Third Way has tended to, but deserves to be understood as part of a cosmopolitan society, not blamed for its symptoms, but empowered without expectations. There is a democracy to be preserved and a right to difference to be respected in such areas, including the right to engage freely, the right not to agree, the right not to play community, the right not to resolve your own affairs. This is not asking for a return to the old days of dependency on the state and others, only the suggestion that community empowerment alone will not remake economy and society in the hard-pressed areas, and also the question why such places only deserve local community while others are allowed to enjoy cosmopolitan society.

A Relational Politics of Place

In this final section, I wish to explore an alternative regional approach, a politics of place that is consistent with a spatial ontology of cities and regions seen as sites of heterogeneity juxtaposed within close spatial proximity, and as sites of multiple geographies of affiliation, linkage, and flow.[8] We could summarize the political challenges of these two spatial registers of place respectively as the *politics of propinquity* and the *politics of connectivity* (or transitivity). What follows is a hesitant sketch of place politics in relational terms.

A politics of connectivity

The plural public sphere that is involved in the making of a region is a spatially diffuse and geographically mobile sphere. It follows that a politics of place, whether we like it or not, has to work with the varied geographies of relational connectivity and transitivity that make up public life and the local political realm in general in a city or region. What is deemed "local space" and what is deemed to be a local priority cannot be determined territorially; rather, it has to be determined in other ways. A start would be to define regional priorities programmatically, contested through relationally constituted communities of attachment and resistance. The result is a regional "inside" constructed through public debate over a particular political program or vision of the good life. Indeed, this should happen in ways open to both local and distant actors to sign up to a given program, thereby—at the very least—freeing proximate strangers who inhabit different worlds from the tyranny of belonging to a "local community" with shared interests.

There are significant changes in the conduct of regional politics that follow from this emphasis on a politics of program conducted through spaces of relational connectivity.[9] Two examples—one related to regional economic priorities and the other related to regional cultural priorities—might help to illustrate the difference. First, in a relational politics of place, decisions concerning what is good or bad for the local economy would not be decoupled from scalar or territorial assumptions, which in the new regionalism routinely hold that "local" autonomy is empowering, while "external" control is disabling;

that local agglomeration increases local returns, while global commodity chains seep profits away; that homegrown institutions are locally oriented, while distant institutions are predatory or indifferent. Instead, judgement over economic worth would be based on public scrutiny of alternative models of economic prosperity and well-being (e.g., neoliberal versus social democratic) and competing visions of the economic good life, which would be approved of or not by residents on the basis of how well a vision fits with their interests that may well be locked into spatial connectivities beyond the region.

The debate on local economic priorities—within the development corporations, in regional assemblies, in the public arena—would become that of discussing what kind of regional economy is desired, instead of relying on the make-belief that economic localism in its own right promises regional competitiveness and rewards for all. Whatever fictions there may be regarding the inevitability of neoliberal economics or the inevitability of "container" policies, even the most cursory glance at experience in different parts of the world reveals the work of plural models of economic prosperity and organization.

Similarly, in the area of cultural priorities, attention in a frame of a politics of connectivity would fall on the actual, material dynamics of cultural formation, since no ontology of origin or indigeneity would be assumed. The imperative is to arrange for active debate over different models of cultural connectivity, over the kind of cultural connections that people in a region wish to defend, over the value of relational interactions beyond the region.

For example, we can compare two very different versions of cultural connectivity circulating in current debates on multiculturalism. One is a "consumer" cosmopolitanism, typified by the European Union program on European Cities of Culture, which celebrates cities and regions as cultural gateways and plays on the virtues of world music, minority ethnic food and festivals, regeneration based on multicultures and multiethnic public spaces, and the exoticism of the stranger. A raft of contemporary urban and regional regeneration strategies play on this aspect of belonging in the world in order to reboot the local economy through new consumption, as well as to demonstrate an openness to multiculturalism and multiethnicity. Another version of cultural connectivity is a cosmopolitan ethos of solidarity and rights that has been growing in different parts of the world as a form of local response to global poverty, ethnic intolerance, and Empire. It frequently involves local groups developing voice and impact through worldwide solidarity networks and social movements in order to shape and influence cultural politics both "at home" and in other regions. While cultural connectivity in both examples rejects an idea of the region as a place of reminiscence and cultural preservation, neither share the same sense of place in the world.

The point is that the politics of connectivity is not about the balance between localism and globalism. It is a matter of making explicit and of choosing between different senses of place and place attachment on the basis of agonistic engagement between different coalitions of cultural and geographical attachment. Thus conceived, a region should be able to be claimed by distant others and, in turn, be able to link up with developments elsewhere on the basis of genuine normative complementarity.

A politics of propinquity

The politics of a local society made up of bit arrangements and plural cultures that never quite cohere or fit together can no longer be cast as a politics of intimacy or shared regional cultures. What, then, are the alternatives? If there is something distinctive about the politics of place as a *spatial* phenomenon, it is that different microworlds find themselves on the same turf, and that the pull on turf in different directions and towards different interests needs to be actively managed and negotiated, because there is no other turf. In other words, spatial propinquity produces a local politics shaped by the issues thrown up by living with diversity and sharing a common territorial space.

The politics of propinquity can be read as a politics of negotiating the immanent effects of geographical juxtaposition between physical spaces, overlapping communities, and contrasting cultural practices. As such, the politics of propinquity is neither automatically benign nor malign. It has no pregiven remit, institutional composition, and conduct, and it comes with no territorial restriction of its spatial architecture and alignments. Instead, all it can be sure of is to take spatial juxtaposition seriously as a field of agonistic engagement. This means seeing the local political arena as a field of claims and counterclaims, agreements, and coalitions that are always temporary and fragile, always the product of negotiation and changing intersectional dynamics, always spreading out to wherever a claim on turf or on proximate strangers is made or to where novelty is generated by juxtaposition.

One implication of this interpretation is that the politics of propinquity must be as much about what is struggled over as it is about the conduct of local politics in allowing agonistic engagement (contra the politics of governmentality), and also about who or what counts as political through its recognition of the acts of expression and organization across local society (contra the powers of designated institutions).

We now have a politics of place that looks very different from the politics of regional management or regional destiny that have become the hallmark of territorial regionalism. It accepts that a regional agenda has to be fashioned out of the disparate interests and the different worlds of connectivity that overlap in a given place through active public discussion of different visions of what kind of local turf is desired and in whose interest (from the vested classes and majority communities to minorities, outsiders, and distant strangers). "Region-building" becomes altogether different in a politics of place that works with and through the fragments. It becomes an act of the free play of an active and plural regional body politic and a plural public sphere; an act of making the invisible part of the register of political life. It becomes an act of acceptance that the shared commons that we choose to call a regional way of life is only ever relationally and discursively constituted.

In this very brief consideration of thinking regions relationally, my aim has been to begin to articulate a regionalism freed from the constraints of territorial jurisdiction. Cities and regions express, perhaps more than other sociospatial formations (nations, households, organizations, virtual and imagined communities), the most intense manifestations of propinquity and multiple spatial connectivity. They are distinctive "nodal" formations and, as such, they illuminate a particular kind of spatial politics. They could be seen as the forcing ground for challenges that are thrown up when difference is so visibly gathered in one place and when a globality of myriad flows and connections is temporarily halted in one place. There might be something to be gained from thinking about cities and regions as generators of a kind of democratic energy as they continually act to remind citizens what the stakes are in living with difference and everyday global connectivity.

This paper is a synthesis of two more detailed publications by Ash Amin ("Regions Unbound: Towards a New Politics and Place," *Geografiska Annaler B* 86, no. 1 (2004): 31–42; and "Local Community on Trial," *Economy and Society* 34 (2005): 612–633). Reprint with the kind permission of Blackwell Publishing and the Taylor & Francis Group (http://www.tandf.co.uk/journals).

Notes
1   See Ash Amin, "Spatialities of Globalisation," *Environment and Planning A* 34, no. 3 (2002): 385–399.
2   See Stuart Hall, "New Labour's Double-Shuffle," *Soundings* 24 (July 2003): 10–24.
3   See Ash Amin, Doreen Massey, and Nigel Thrift, *Decentering the Nation: A Radical Approach to Regional Inequality* (London: Catalyst, 2003).
4   See John Urry, "Connections," *Environment and Planning D: Society and Space* 22 (2004): 27–37.
5   See, for example, Putnam's negative observations on amoral familism in southern Italy and the excess of bonding social capital in Black U.S. urban areas.
6   For example, diaspora-based social capital and citizenship, variety in types of social capital in different types of association, or friendship-based forms of trust and solidarities in new forms of family arrangement.
7   Defined and measured in highly selective ways, such as individual and social groups with particular "social capital" endowments, mixed neighborhoods, citizens' juries, engagement in shared spaces.
8   See Doreen Massey, *For Space* (London: Sage, 2005).
9   See Amin, Massey, and Thrift, *Decentering the Nation*.

COMMODIFIED CITY

In capitalism, the city is a commodity. Economic commodification of urban spaces shapes the city; the logic of market growth determines the rules. Contrary to the assumptions underpinning the ideal model of the economy, the individual drive toward economic efficiency sometimes works against the goal of achieving overall prosperity. Communal forms of granting loans and utilizing property can open up new possibilities and promise greater prosperity for both the individual and society as a whole, particularly during times of crisis.

COMMUNALIZATION OF PROPERTY?
Holger Lauinger

In dealing with shrinking cities, planning discourses have been increasingly focusing on the question of society's understanding of property rights. The municipalities currently have no practical instruments for gaining—or coercing—the cooperation of property owners who possess fallow real-estate lots. For this reason, renaturation proceeds in many places less according to city planning criteria than to the given local ownership relations.

German legal tradition generally bases its understanding of property on the concept of "dominium" in Roman law:[1] The owner of a property has the sole right to administer his/her land, and impingement upon this right or restrictions on an owner's use of his/her land on the basis of public considerations is limited. But because of increasingly pressing problems, more and more prominent voices are demanding that municipalities should have greater power and more options available to them for administering fallow real-estate lots. Albert Speer, an urban planner from Frankfurt, complained in an interview with the *Frankfurter Allgemeine Zeitung* about the lack of legal authority for municipalities to expropriate property in the public interest.[2] And Michael Krautzberger, departmental director in Germany's Ministry of Transport, Construction, and Urban Development, has referred to the expropriation practices in England in the early 1970s—"a square meter for a British pound"—and noted that "other European countries with comparable value systems have recognized that the problems cannot be solved without significant intervention as regards property."[3]

Municipalities have the de jure right to expropriate property for reasons pertaining to urban planning under paragraphs 85ff. of the Federal Building Code *(Baugesetzbuch)*. But the owner has to be compensated at a rate comparable to the property's market value, which is usually exaggerated. Given the scarcity of municipal funds, this obligation makes expropriation an unrealistic option. The situation has led Benjamin Davy, professor for land management at the University of Dortmund, to appeal to lawmakers to reinstate feasible means for municipal action on behalf of urban planning exigencies. "The Federal Building Code should stipulate that property owners who do not participate in creating sustainable urban planning structures may be dispossessed at a rate below market value."[4]

Alternatively, the idea of raising property taxes for unutilized real estate is being discussed as a measure to encourage the transfer of privately owned fallow lots to municipal hands. This strategy would serve to further depreciate unutilized real estate by raising taxes on it, thereby increasing the pressure on property owners to either find a use for the land or find another sponsor. This would mean that municipalities would gain more control over city properties, which would, for example, allow them to lease the land to other occupants using the alternative property concept of hereditary leasehold. The idea of raising the property tax for unused land is also promoted by other actors in order to stimulate the property market and to keep real estate in dynamic economic circulation. For example, since 1992 a special tax has been levied on empty lots in Japan, a country with very scarce development property resources. And in the United Kingdom, the Urban Task Force suggested raising property taxes in 2000 in order to give developers better access to fallow land.

These examples show that the suggestions for reforming land-property rights from the various actors have been tied to very specific interests and objectives. The planners are looking for solutions that are in the interest of urban development and that will also accommodate the interests of the different actors. Private development agencies concentrate on plots that are appropriate for reutilization; they seek easier access as well as maximum financial and logistical support from public institutions. The municipalities, on the other hand, are trying to find ways to further their role in shaping urban development despite their minimal financial resources. The primary interest of the housing sector is to obtain state subsidies for dismantling unutilized real-estate lots in an effort to create a "balanced market." In contrast, community housing and employment projects are trying to improve the possibilities for socially engaged actors who usually lack capital. Given these diverging interests, in recent years specific instruments have been formulated for dealing with various cases of unutilized properties in shrinking cities.

Urban Planning Concepts
Exemplary for the perspective of planners, who are oriented toward serving the common good, are instruments that use price incentives to stem an increase in new settlement areas and thereby hinder the spread of suburbanization. Instruments such as land management, land-utilization management, land-value tax, soil-sealing duty, and transferable development rights can mobilize fallow inner-city lots by making development permits either hard to come by or expensive, thereby leading to the recycling or redensification of lots, depending on the concept at hand, or to an effective scaling back and change in the designated utilization.[5]

For example, transferable development rights: Analogously to the environmental policy of emissions trading practiced in some countries, the concept of transferable development rights means that the right to develop land can be traded. This method constitutes a reformulation of the link between land ownership and development rights. Practiced in the United States since 1968 and also employed in other countries, in recent years Germany and Switzerland have also been considering the application of this method.[6]

In 2004, the Nachhaltigkeitsbeirat Baden-Württemberg (Baden-Württemberg Board for Sustainable Development) proposed the introduction of a system of transferable development rights as a means of quantitatively and qualitatively administering land use. Under this system, after a goal has been set at the regional level, the municipalities are allotted a quota for new land development. An exchange market for land development allows them to buy or sell quotas. Because the municipalities will try to avoid having to buy, they have an incentive to use existing fallow lots and gaps between buildings. This strategy gives shrinking cities with fallow inner-city lots the possibility to avoid the suburban sprawl effect. Other models of transferable development rights would allow the owner of a lot marked for renaturation to auction his development rights to another property owner. In this way, an existing right to develop a piece of land set for renaturation could be voided without the municipality having to pay expropriation costs.[7]

State Concepts
At the federal and state level, broader and more concerted redevelopment strategies can be pursued. In addition to implementing and financing policy programs, the federal states

REALITY PROPERTIES: FAKE ESTATES
New York, 1973
Gordon Matta-Clark

In the summer of 1973, Gordon Matta-Clark discovered that the city of New York was auctioning off very small and inaccessible plots of land. The idea of inaccessibility fascinated Matta-Clark and moved him to buy fourteen lots, thirteen of them in Queens and one in Staten Island, each for between $25 and $75. Later he described his purchases as a way of getting at the absurdity of existing property boundaries, for the lots were the result of arbitrary decisions in city planning and mistakes on the part of land surveyors.

The intention of the artist was to create an awareness for these "leftover spaces"—public sidewalks, driveways, or unusable lots between buildings. Usually they were sold to the owners of adjacent property and remained vacant, or they were used for speculation. Matta-Clark took the opportunity to make these abandoned urban spaces accessible again. After he bought them he created collages using photographs of the lots, corresponding excerpts from the land register, and urban planning designs. The work, entitled *Fake Estates*, was meant to question the economic implications of private property.

Twenty-six years after Matta-Clark's death, the art and culture magazine *Cabinet* devoted its issue on "property" to this project and during its research discovered that of the lots in Queens, ten had since become the property of the city because the annual property taxes on them had not been paid. The magazine secured the leasing and title rights to the properties, initiated the project "Odd Lots," photographed the lots in Queens again, and commissioned contemporary artists Jimbo Blachly, Matthew Northridge, and Clara Williams to develop a series of imaginative projects for these spaces. (Ed.)

Literature
Kastner, Jeffrey, Sina Najafi, and Frances Richard, eds. *Odd Lots: Revisiting Gordon Matta-Clark's Fake Estates*. New York: William Stout, 2005.

Communalization of Property?_Holger Lauinger 573

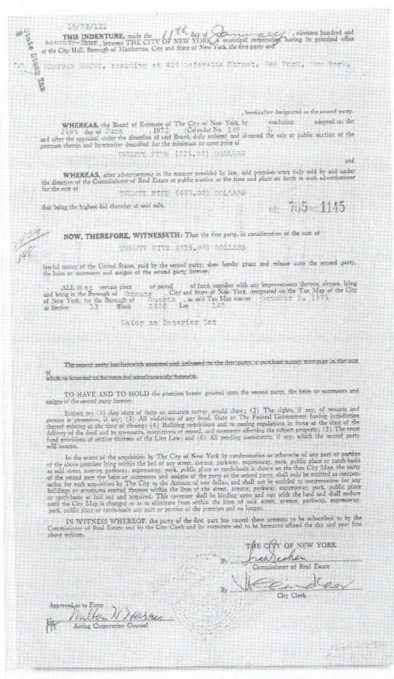

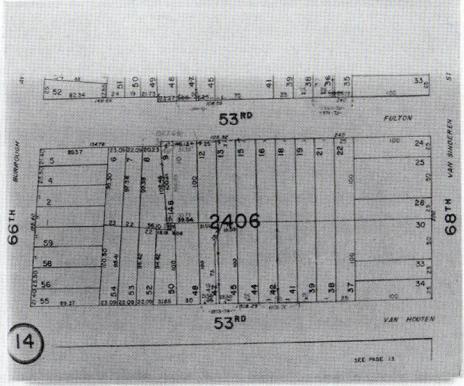

A surplus lot bought by Matta-Clark in 1973 for $25 at an auction in New York City for the project "Reality Properties: Fake Estates."

can also develop and apply concrete instruments for administering individual properties that are no longer profitable, with a view toward sustainable development. Collaboration with private actors is increasingly sought, along the lines of a policy seeing the state in an activating role.

For example, property funds: For the past 25 years, the Landesentwicklungsgesellschaft (LEG) Nordrhein-Westfalen (North Rhine-Westphalia State Development Association) has been using a property fund as a key instrument for recycling fallow lots.[8] The municipalities commission the LEG to buy privately owned properties that are no longer profitable. Through a development policy agreed at the regional level, the aim is to reactivate land for long-term utilization by cleaning up old industrial waste sites, newly parceling the land, and improving the infrastructure. Thanks to this fund, since 1980 investments totaling €1.7 million have gone into redeveloping about 61% of the acquired lots (1,626 hectares out of a total of 2,650 hectares) and it was possible to put 83 out of 188 acquired sites on the market again. Industry and commercial enterprises settled on 624 hectares of the land, and other sites were made into public green zones. A total of €440 million were invested in the purchase of properties, and an additional €1 million were spent to develop the sites and projects. The financial deficits in the property fund are balanced out with sales proceeds, funding from the state budget, grants from state support programs (regional economic and urban development funds), federal aid (structural funds), and grants from the European Union. Prominent projects engendered by the fund include the Landschaftspark (landscape park) in Duisburg-Nord, the Zeche Zollverein XII (industrial monument) in Essen, and the Jahrhunderthalle (concert hall) in Bochum.

The North Rhine-Westphalia land fund is an exemplary, if cost-intensive, model for property funds. With respect to today's shrinking regions, we must explore how such development models could function if they received only interim financing and much smaller grants. To this end, learning from the experiences of municipalities in the United Kingdom could be helpful.[9]

For example, land assemblies: In the United Kingdom, the Town & Country Planning Act of 1990 offers municipalities the legal means to expropriate land when necessary and to create "land assemblies" (property pools) in order to clean up and prepare lots for future development. Studies have shown that in most cases, the obstacle to the development of fallow urban lots are problems with property owners. The Urban Task Force's report thus recommends that the instrument of Compulsory Purchase Orders should be further improved and points to good experiences with this in the cities of Leicester, Bristol, and Medway.[10] The basis of the British model is a business-oriented municipal policy in which the cities buy—when necessary through expropriation—depreciated fallow lots that have good potential, apply purposive development measures to refurbish their value, and then sell the land again. The sales profit should be enough to cover the costs of the improvement measures, and the municipality therefore only receives interim financing.

Municipal Concepts
The municipalities in Germany are also important actors in the process of redevelopment, although at present they do not have enough options at their disposal. Instruments such as funding, planning rights, and urban development agreements are predicated on the

cooperation of property owners. If they are not willing to cooperate, the municipalities are almost powerless to act. In addition, the pervasive practice of neoliberal privatization that has also extended to state and government real-estate properties has robbed the municipalities of further options. But when the municipalities have a larger stock of property—for example, as is the practice in Amsterdam or Hong Kong—they have more room to maneuver, and the long-term effect is advantageous for both municipal economics as well as for the economy at large.

In practice, however, the prominent instruments at the moment are those with which the municipalities, who hold sovereign power with respect to planning, show goodwill toward the interests of property owners, who in turn reciprocate with cooperation, for example by allowing interim utilization. Another prevalent scenario today is that municipalities act as mediators or guarantors for various actors and support those groups that are less established but that act in the general interest. The municipalities make use of their institutional and sovereign power for the above measures, yet without having to spend substantial funds. They therefore at times function as enablers.

For example, neighborhood associations: The urban development and construction department of the city of Leipzig and the housing association pro Leipzig e.G. introduced the neighborhood association model. By bringing together various individual properties in an association, the overarching urban development policy goal is to override private property owners' blockades of efforts to scale back development (the "pick-up-sticks" effect: whoever makes a move loses). The former owners receive shares in the association in proportion to the amount of real estate they contributed, yet all association members equally share the responsibility for utilization and the burden of costs. Those interested in using the real estate can also become association members if they acquire shares on the basis of capital and self-help. In Leipzig, a district association is being founded for which specific utilization concepts have been developed for fifteen houses in the Anger-Crottendorf district. As a starting project, these properties are to be fully renovated with the participation of association members and the utilization of available sources of funding.[11]

For example, permit agreements: The city of Leipzig makes use of permit agreements for the temporary utilization of fallow lots in private hands. This form of legal agreement between the city and owners is primarily used to create green zones in urban spaces. As an incentive for owners to give over their property at no charge for a limited period of time, the municipality organizes subsidies to remove unwanted building structures on the property. In certain cases it also waives the property taxes due during a period of interim utilization that must last at least eight to ten years. The existing right to build on the lot is not affected. More than one hundred private parcels in Leipzig amounting to a total area of 14 hectares were redeveloped on the basis of permit agreements. A prominent example is the Dunkler Wald park in Wurzner Straße—a part of the Rietzschkeband green strip on the east side of Leipzig.[12]

Housing Association Concepts

Because of the enormous economic burdens caused by vacant housing, the housing industry has become the main actor in the process of urban redevelopment. In Germany, for example, the vhw-Bundesverband für Wohneigentum und Stadtentwicklung (German

ACQUISITION OF THE PROPERTY AT THE CORNER OF TIBUSSTRASSE/ BREUL, MÜNSTER AREA, FIELD SECTOR 5, NO. 672
Münster, Germany, 1997
Maria Eichhorn

As a contribution to the exhibition "Skulptur.Projekte in Münster" (1997), Maria Eichhorn together with the Westfälisches Landesmuseum (Westphalia State Museum) bought a piece of property from the city and then, as agreed, sold it back again after a few months. The proceeds from the sale were signed over to the Verein zur Erhaltung preiswerten Wohnraums e.V. (Association for the Preservation of Affordable Living Space) for the purpose of renovating buildings. The artists accompanied and documented the process and, among other things, put together a brochure on the question of property, which considered topics such as: "Who does the city belong to?" "How does a city come into being?" and "Acquiring property." In the brochure text, Maria Eichhorn outlined the socialist property theories of Pierre Joseph Proudhon and Gustav Landauer, the legal history of the land register, the property practices in the shrinking city of New York in the 1970s, the progressive thematization of property/real estate in several artistic and social projects, and the relativity of public and private property. This material was supplemented with local studies, for example on squatting and the housing battles in Münster in the late 1980s, the expropriation of Jewish property in Münster during the Nazi period, and the city planning of the 1990s. With this project Maria Eichhorn highlighted and called into question the constitutive role of society's understanding of property in the development of cities and society.

The concept of artwork as it is reformulated here includes processes such as buying and selling property with all the legal steps this entails; resurveying, researching, and documentation; and the material parts of the artwork that thereby emerge or are collected. The refusal to allow the work an object character means that it is not reduced to a single location, rather encompasses many locations and institutions in addition to the property itself, for example the land register, the land office, the Westfälisches Landesmuseum, the Landschaftsverband Westfalen-Lippe (Landscape Association of Westphalia-Lippe), and the Verein zur Erhaltung preiswerten Wohnraums e.V. (Ed.)

The original German title of this project is "Erwerb des Grundstücks Ecke Tibusstraße/Breul, Gemarkung Münster, Flur 5, Nr. 672."

Communalization of Property?_Holger Lauinger

▲ The property on Tibusstraße/Breul in Münster. ▼ The artist at the signing of the sales agreement.

Association for Housing Property and Urban Development), with its 1,400 members from the municipal, real estate, and credit sectors, is strongly engaged in debates about property problems in times of shrinking cities, as described in the organization's publications. In order to take the diverging interests of the housing industry into account and avoid future blockades in the process of scaling back development, various models of balancing out the burdens on companies are being discussed.[13]

Community Project Concepts
Socially engaged community projects could stand to benefit the most from the dramatically changed conditions in the real-estate market. With the increasing focus on civil-society solutions, more and more room is being created for projects oriented toward social appropriation and experimental communalization of real-estate property. Some of the first examples of this are the models developed by Projekt GmbH, which promotes the social redistribution of funds, as well as foundations and loans. The question arises as to the extent to which public projects can be shaped through a modification of these strategies.

For example, syndicalist housing projects: Many aspiring alternative housing and living projects in the new German states are currently seeking support through the Mietshäusersyndikat, a rental property syndicate operating out of Freiburg. The goal of the syndicate is to pull real estate from the rental market and use it to create new spaces for socially and politically emancipatory projects. The projects are organized in a solidarity-oriented business association of homeowner limited liability companies and financed with transfers from old to new projects, direct private loans, and bank credits from the GLS Gemeinschaftsbank (an ethically and ecologically oriented German bank). The property title does not immediately belong to the individual housing associations, but instead to an association with limited liability. This limited liability company has two bodies: the housing association, and the Mietshäusersyndikat as a control organization. In certain situations—such as the selling of a house, the conversion of apartments into condominiums, or similar undertakings with real-estate properties—the syndicate has a right of veto. Internal decisions affecting the housing project lie with the housing association. Thus far, sixteen projects and twenty-two project initiatives in western Germany are participating. In 2002, the VEB Wohnfabrik in Halberstadt was integrated as the first project in eastern Germany. Interest in the syndicate idea has grown rapidly in eastern Germany due to the low real-estate prices there.[14]

For example, foundations and loans: Like the syndicate above, the Projektwerkstatt initiative acquires real estate for collaborative and self-organized living, housing, and work-related projects. But the purchases or investments are carried out by a nonprofit foundation. The real estate is loaned to the groups for utilization purposes, thereby instituting a separation between property and utilization. The binding reciprocal conditions are laid down in a lease agreement (covering, for example, maintenance, management costs, asset depreciation, and insurance for the buildings). The groups utilizing the properties participate with equal rights in the superordinate activities of the Projektwerkstatt: they are members and have the right to vote, and they are involved in decisions about funding further projects. They take on responsibility for the foundation's properties, yet without becoming owners of the living, housing, and work-related projects. The Projektwerkstatt sees itself as a financing instrument based on solidarity and neutrality as regards property that can be used by project initiatives to realize their goals through active participation. It is based in Berlin and supports projects in the Brandenburg area.[15]

A New Understanding of Property?

The phenomenon of shrinking cities and the related loss in monetary value of real-estate properties has unleashed a quest among all involved players to develop new conceptions of property. The different interests of the various social actors are reflected in the wide spectrum of models introduced above. Many of the approaches point in the direction of a communalization of real-estate property. Might this mean that a social process has been set in motion in the shrinking cities that will lead to a new understanding of "property"?

Translated from the German by Christina M. White

Notes
1 See Philipp Oswalt and Wolfgang Kantzow, "Property: Whose City?" in *Shrinking Cities, Vol. 1, International Research,* ed. Philipp Oswalt (Ostfildern-Ruit, Germany: Hatje Cantz, 2005), 693–699.
2 Albert Speer, "Wir altern im wachsenden Schatten von Riesen," *Frankfurter Allgemeine Zeitung,* no. 45, February 23, 2005.
3 Michael Krautzberger, "Strategien und neue Leitbilder auf Bundesebene," in *Schrumpfende Städte fordern neue Strategien für die Stadtentwicklung,* ed. Deutsche Akademie für Städtebau und Landesplanung (Wuppertal: Verlag Müller + Busmann, 2002).
4 Benjamin Davy, "Grundstückswerte, Stadtumbau und Bodenpolitik," *vhw Forum Wohneigentum* 2 (2005): 67–72.
5 See Bundesamt für Bauwesen und Raumordnung, ed., *Steuerung der Flächennutzung, (Informationen zur Raumentwicklung),* no. 8 (1999), 492–576.
6 See Markus Gmünder and Andreas Süess, "Weniger Zersiedlung durch handelbare Flächennutzungszertifikate?" *DISP* 160 (2005): 58–66; Nachhaltigkeitsbeirat der Landesregierung Baden-Württemberg, *Neue Wege zu einem nachhaltigen Flächenmanagement in Baden-Württemberg* (Stuttgart: NBBW, 2004); and Hartmut Dieterich, Dirk Löhr, and Stephan Tomerius, eds., *Jahrbuch für Bodenpolitik 2004* (Berlin: VWF, 2004).
7 See expert opinions at http://www.nachhaltigkeitsbeirat-bw.de.
8 LEG Stadtentwicklung GmbH, ed., *25 Jahre Grundstücksfonds: Zwischenbilanz* (Düsseldorf: LEG Stadtentwicklung GmbH, 2005).
9 See http://www.leg-nrw.de.
10 See United Kingdom Department of the Environment, Transport and the Regions, *Towards an Urban Renaissance: Final Report of the Urban Task Force Chaired by Lord Rogers of Riverside* (London: E & FN Spon, 1999), 223ff.
11 See http://www.leipziger-osten.de.
12 See a draft of the agreement at http://www.ratgeber-bauen-wohnen-finanzieren.de.
13 See Jürgen Goldschmidt and Markus Terboven, "Lastenausgleich im Stadtumbau," *vhw Forum Wohneigentum* 2 (2005): 86ff.
14 See http://www.syndikat.org.
15 See http://www.gegenseitig.de.

OPENING EMPTY LOTS TO THE PUBLIC
Amsterdam, Brussels, Alcorcón, 2000–2002
Lara Almárcegui

In opening up empty lots to the public I wanted not only to question the use of public spaces and private property, but also to reclaim territory for the citizens.

The city authorities in Amsterdam did not allow me to open an empty lot to the public on the grounds that such an action would put the population's health at risk. In Brussels, I was able to open an empty lot for one day, and whoever wanted to could walk into this space that was normally closed off under lock and key. In Alcorcón, I was able to open an empty lot for a week. It was a piece of private property that was normally off-limits to the public. I did not add or remove anything from the place, and during the week it was open we talked spontaneously about its past and future.

CLAIMING LAND
Liverpool, UK, 2004/05
Stefanie Bremer, Dirk E. Haas, Päivi Kataikko, Henrik Sander, Andreas Schulze Bäing, and Boris Sieverts

---

In the classic theories of the real-estate market, there is a positive correlation between urban planning and land prices. When a municipality earmarks previously undeveloped land for future development, open fields become "land awaiting development." The municipality's announcement of the intention to allow development is enough to make the land value rise. If local authorities then produce an official entitlement to build on a particular property, this then becomes the even more valuable "greenfield development site." The next step in the spiraling staircase of land-value appreciation, as described by Willy Bonczek in the 1960s, is that of a "ready-to-build site," which results when the municipality has carried through the measures necessary for development to begin, that is, built roads and other infrastructure. Thus, planning leads to land-price appreciation. This rise in land value—which is not the work of property owners, yet is reaped by them—was heavily criticized in planning debates well into the 1970s, and various models for the fiscal absorption of these planning gains were discussed.[1] But then the Bonczek staircase model was forgotten again.

The question of land-price appreciation disappeared from public debate as concepts for prudent urban renewal emerged in the 1970s and 1980s. Then a new phenomenon appeared: land prices were no longer climbing, despite the completion of urban reconstruction measures, but were remaining stable. At first this was seen as a success. The problem of rising land prices seemed to have vanished. But the apparent solution to the problem turned out to be the harbinger of an even bigger problem. If the value of a property does not increase following a planning measure, this is a sign that the market is no longer functioning properly.

In shrinking cities, what are known as "hardcore sites" appear. This is the term used by a recently published study for the English Partnerships regeneration agency to define spaces or plots that can no longer be permanently mobilized for the real-estate market—despite the availability of infrastructure, full-scale renovation, or careful urban repair.[2] No further appreciation can be gained, and the value of the property drops.

The causes of this value depreciation are manifold. Sometimes it is because a site is located along a main traffic artery, which makes it unattractive for long-term development projects. Or the size of the property no longer meets today's demands. Or the lots are in areas that have a cumulative trend toward depreciation. The behavior of property owners leads to further depreciation when they become caught up in the narrow logic of property laws, and instead of reacting to negative developments in the area with countermeasures, they decide to wait it out and hope for a better utilization in the future. There are also "passive property owners" who have no interest in an active real-estate utilization of their land. This might be due to the particular tasks they are responsible for or to their specialized competencies, for example because they represent public interests. Other "passive" owners may have special planning tasks, such as administering and stockpiling land for highway or waterway use. This produces

The project "Claiming Land" suggests working against the depreciation of unused lots in Liverpool by symbolically staking claims on the land.

▼ The staking of claims was enacted by a group of urban planners and architects and documented by photographer Bas Princen.

individuals for a piece of land in Europe could be the first harbinger of a movement that could lead to new forms of property markets and property relations in the modern urban environment.

Translated from the German by Christina M. White

This project was developed for the *archplus* competition "Shrinking Cities: Reinventing Urbanism."

Notes
1 Peter Conradi, Hartmut Dieterich, and Volker Hauff, *Für ein soziales Bodenrecht: Notwendigkeiten und Möglichkeiten* (Frankfurt am Main: Europäische Verlagsanstsalt, 1972).
2 See http://www.englishpartnerships.co.uk/images/D8B222B7AC3A43299A6A0D072F0674D8.pdf (September 2003).

LOANS FOR SHRINKING REGIONS
Rolf Novy-Huy

Eastern Germany, the new German states: immediately after the fall of the Wall in 1989 and in the years following, the territory was considered gold-rush country, and there was a feeling that one had to get there quickly in order to stake a claim. The banks recruited personnel and quickly put up trailers so they wouldn't arrive too late. Loans were given out freely. After all, the region had to be reconstructed and introduced to the blessings of the free-market economy.

But everyone soon sobered up. The personnel wasn't properly trained, the expectations for returns were too high, the rate of market growth was overestimated. The consequence was that all too frequently large loans were not repaid. Then came a complete about-face in lending policy. The high losses in these initial years led to restrictions on those applying for credit.

Parallel to this particular problem, banks were increasingly adhering to the American ideal of "shareholder value," in other words, returns for shareholders, as has recently and most spectacularly been demonstrated by the chairman of the board at the Deutsche Bank, Josef Ackermann, who sought a 25% return on capital for his financial institute.

What does this mean in practice? A large northern German bank that until a few years ago had financed young alternative cooperatives in Berlin suddenly told its old clients that it was now only interested in financing at a minimum level of €5 million. Companies constituted under civil law, which is the legal form of choice for group endeavors, are no longer being financed by some banks. The reason lies in the notorious Section 18 of the German Banking Act, according to which borrowers must disclose their economic situation to the banks. If there are several people involved, this creates a lot of work for the banks. Small loans are uninteresting from a business perspective, for what banks are concerned about are the costs per transaction. Charging for the costs of this work is simply not enough; today, every transaction must bring a profit. Mixed calculations or long-term perspectives—such as gaining contacts to future clients—are not important anymore, or at least no longer seem to be.

The banks' behavior is understandable in terms of business management, but it is disastrous for the economy. The bank system's responsibility for the development of the nation's economy, so often evoked in the past, has crumbled under the dictates of high returns. Today, start-up entrepreneurs who need small loans (of less than €100,000) have no one to whom they can turn. The risk is too high, and the work involved is too great. The reconstruction programs run by the Kreditanstalt für Wiederaufbau (KfW, German Development Bank) are only of limited help here. Bank employees are under such pressure to work hard and produce returns that it would take an above-average amount of commitment to carefully and vigorously pursue such cases beyond the usual workload. When banks are drawing up extensive plans for processing development financing in "loan factories," just imagine what it would mean on the other hand to apply meticulous workmanship to a start-up business.

To a limited extent, it is the *Sparkassen* (saving banks, mostly operating at a local level) and *Volksbanken* (cooperative banks)—although these, too, are also often criticized—that are open to a more flexible policy because of their local presence, the responsibility felt by the local sponsor, or the traditional sense of cooperative duty to be of help to the banks' members.

Basel II

One cannot write about banks today without mentioning Basel II. On the surface, the goals of the World Trade Organization commission referred to as Basel II are the stabilization and risk management of national banking systems, as well as ensuring that the banks have sufficient equity capital. Two points are up for debate in this context: price policy, which is subject to a capitalist, not to mention a Darwinist, logic, and requirements pertaining to the quality of the accounting records and the business management of the borrowers.

Nothing can be said against the latter. It is surely in the interest of all economic players that borrowers maintain a well-educated management that documents and regularly updates its revenue and returns. A more critical view should be taken of a price policy that operates according to the logic that the good customers should not have to pay for the bad ones. At first this idea might seem acceptable. But in practice it means that companies that have lower returns or have gotten into trouble and therefore have a worse credit standing will have to pay very high interest rates, while good borrowers only pay a minimum interest. How then could a company ever recover if it must pay even more interest when it is already in a difficult situation?

Does this paint a dark picture of the banking industry? Only in part. In addition to the critical aspects mentioned here, there are, of course, also bankers and institutions that feel a responsibility toward their region and their activities and that often come to the aid of others.

Negative statements coming from the borrowers can often be traced to the poor quality of their projects. In these cases, the bankers can at most be accused of not being honest enough about their reasons for denying credit. Who wants to look an applicant in the eyes and say "I don't believe you have the necessary business skills to be successful"?

Real Estate as Security

The developments in recent years have, of course, made the use of real-estate securities very difficult. Here, also, exaggeration in the early years has meant that after the initial euphoria, the pendulum has now swung in the opposite direction. The new buildings on the city outskirts erected only for speculative purposes, the trend toward homeownership, and migration have all led to a dramatic increase in vacant lots in many areas. It is in part difficult to deny the impression that among western German banks, real-estate properties in all eastern German states, regardless of the local situation, are automatically rated as unmarketable. The fact that real estate in reasonable and even poor locations is still being sold is completely buried due to the mostly negative media coverage.

This leads to an irremediable and self-perpetuating cycle. Lacking loans mean a lack of investments, which leads to a further drop in economic activity. Only those cities with a special location or particular quality can escape this downward spiral. But not every town has a Goethe or is a UNESCO World Heritage site or has such a favorable location that people migrate there en masse.

To escape this vicious circle of the capitalist loan industry, various instruments have been developed that allow actors in economic crisis regions who are weak on capital to take out loans for projects that are badly needed by the local community.

Which Tools Are Available?

In the past few years, new approaches have been developed in the area of microloans for small-scale commercial financing. The founder of the Grameen Bank in Bangladesh, Professor Muhammad Yunus, introduced this financing model as a development instrument in 1976. Actors lacking sufficient capital are granted small loans without having to put up securities or pay risk interest. In the past thirty years, the bank has given out 4.5 million small loans on this basis, thereby creating a model for the successful promotion of self-help that is now recognized worldwide.

Now industrial countries are learning from developing countries as they try to adapt this model. The Deutsche Mikrofinanzinstitut e.V. (www.microlending-news.de) should be mentioned in this context. The KfW is still dragging its feet, but seems to be moving closer to adopting this model. In Germany, anything in the range of €5,000 to approximately €15,000 is considered a microloan. An essential aspect is guidance. The new entrepreneurs are offered guidance on everything from business plans to marketing, which they receive at so-called start-up centers, for example in Germany at the Enterprise Verbund (www.enterprise-netz.de), Enigma Gründungszentrum, Hamburg (www.enigmagruendungszentrum.de), Exzet Existenzgründerzentrum, Stuttgart (www.exzet.de), and KIZ Existenzgründung (www.kiz.de).

The KMU Genossenschaft zur Mittelstandsförderung e.G. (a cooperative for the promotion of small and medium-sized businesses, www.kmueg.de) is taking a somewhat different approach in Halle an der Saale. An inadequate equity position is a typical reason for the failure of start-ups. The KMU raises capital via cooperative shares and then makes it available to young businesses as equity capital. The cooperative also offers intensive guidance during the starting-up phase and in crisis situations, to the point of taking on management responsibility if necessary. A bookkeeping service also ensures that account records are in order and provides advice. Today, the businesses associated with KMU constitute a small network of companies that help one another out.

A classic deficit in every start-up, yet also in growing businesses, is the lack of ability to offer securities for loans. A few years ago the Bürgschaftsbank für Sozialwirtschaft GmbH (Security Bank for the Social Sector, www.bbfs.de) was founded in Cologne to aid the social sector in this regard. If a business is financially viable, the bank provides the securities necessary to implement the project by taking over an indemnity bond. If state credit guarantees were allowed, as has long been called for, such an institute would be in a much better position to meet the demand for funding.

For the commercial sector there are security banks that are owned by the individual states, but they do not deal in small loans because the hedges do not pay off in comparison to the workload invested.

Where Are We Headed and What Happens Next?

As becomes clear when considering projects such as the Daksbau eG Dessau, addressed by Birgit Schmidt elsewhere in this volume, it is necessary that we recall old virtues. This becomes quite apparent with cooperatives that are fundamentally based on the idea of "members mutually helping one another." Solidarity and the willingness to take on responsibility beyond one's own personal needs are evident in this case, for example in the form of small guarantees: equity capital has been able to close the gaps in those situations where banks did not provide loans.

In May 1998, a housing cooperative that had been founded only a few months previously acquired the former Koch hardware store in Dessau. The cooperative paid €30,000 at the foreclosure sale. How would the financing work? There was no other bidder at the auction besides the group itself. From the perspective of a bank, this meant that if the building were auctioned again, it would not sell. Thus the building could not be ascribed any value, strictly speaking.

But the project group not only put forth a convincing plan for renovation and later use as housing and commercial real estate, it also showed the GLS Gemeinschaftsbank eG Bochum that it was prepared to become personally involved in the project and assume responsibility for it. In addition to raising equity capital in the form of cooperative shares and personal loans, a group of people joined together as a borrowing community, thus enabling the Alternativbank in Bochum to grant further loans. Each individual backs a maximum amount of €3,000, and the group makes sure that the installments are paid on time. In addition, active parties and supporters from the area took out small guarantees also of a maximum sum of €3,000. This setup was convincing enough to the GLS Gemeinschaftsbank that it granted the necessary loans, now sufficiently secured by the real estate. These means were complemented with the above-mentioned guarantee loans and commercially attractive "renovation funds" from the KfW. Today, the building is a beautiful site, situated next to the new Federal Environmental Office in Dessau. All its rooms are rented out. Further small-scale extensions are already being carried out.

The Markus-Gemeinschaft Hauteroda in Thuringia, a living community made up of families and individuals with various kinds of handicaps, has created very interesting self-help and network structures for its social and craft-oriented projects. It was sponsored by European Union funds from the Equal and LeaderPlus programs, but also via regional financing structures.

In public debates it is readily admitted that it is the small and medium-sized businesses that create jobs and open up new fields of economic activity. Experience has shown that it is a long time before tax laws, funding programs, and associations are activated and support this process. Given this situation, it is not very productive to chime in to the general lament about a lack of economic development. It would make sense instead to find examples of success, analyze them to find out why they were successful, and propagate them. This is the only way to create new impulses.

Those who start up new businesses, whether as individuals or with a group project, need to be very tough in order to accomplish their aims. In addition to tapping into conventional state programs and the banking sector, they also need to build personal networks.

Taking a look at the funding policy of public coffers, it is clear that one must get away from the mammoth structures of an institution like the KfW in order to promote instead the opportunities offered by an initiative such as the KMU. If the decision on a loan becomes an abstraction in the large cogs of a bank that functions like a public authority, it is necessary to choose local, flexible actors who are closer to the endeavors at hand. Turning to regional statutory foundations is an additional possibility. A syndication in Brandenburg/Havel in which the chambers of commerce, banks, foundations, project advisors, and free individuals all worked together is a good example of what kinds of structures are necessary today. Why is it that this initiative had to fail due to a lack of financing from the state?

Germany Needs New Financing Structures
When bank staff cannot adequately support start-up businesses or structural financing from a business perspective and do not have the time or the know-how for the kind of thorough guidance that is necessary, it is better to put tax revenue money into start-up centers and other alternative financing structures rather than to squelch economic regeneration. The point here is not to chastise the banks, but to recognize that such undertakings require a certain amount of energy and knowledge, which the banks are no longer able to supply. We need new structures, which means that the state and, for example, the Bundesamt für die Finanzierungsaufsicht (Federal Financial Supervisory) must create new opportunities for these structures to develop. These would include foundations, regional networks, or equity capital funds. Existing structures, for example the Bürgschaftsbank für Sozialwirtschaft GmbH, must be strengthened. But we also need people who are prepared to support young pioneers and take on responsibility for development in their own region.

Translated from the German by Christina M. White

FICTITIOUS VALUES, IMAGINARY MARKETS: THE HOUSING MARKET IN EASTERN GERMANY
Matthias Bernt

If the widespread notion that markets are an effective instrument for distributing goods is true, then we shouldn't be witnessing a problem with overabundant vacant buildings in eastern Germany. According to the predominant neoclassical view, when supply and demand meet, they produce an "equilibrium" that allows the supplier and the buyer to conduct business without the accumulation of a surplus of products that cannot be marketed or a demand that cannot be met. If prices wobble, the supply is automatically reduced or the price adjusted such that the market regains its equilibrium.

Looking at the housing market in eastern Germany, one begins to doubt whether the idea of self-regulating markets makes any sense. The game played by property owners, banks, and urban planners seems to have little to do with whether or not there is a demand for the apartments being offered. The relations between these players instead resemble an occult science in which fictitious debts, tax gains, and inscrutable accounting serve as the rather unnatural laws. The following examples attempt to explain how this strange science functions, how one can make a big profit in a market economy even without a market, and why housing that no one needs is not simply torn down.

Before and After Tax

Intense doubt about the validity of the market-economy view could be felt in eastern Germany as early as the mid-1990s, when almost 800,000 new apartments were built despite the fact that the population was declining. In other words, available housing was expanding while the population was shrinking. In a "normal" market, no businessman in his right mind would invest in such an enterprise.

But the situation was not normal in this case. Under German tax law, homeowners can finance a significant portion of the costs for a full renovation of their real-estate properties through "tax deductibles." This means that they are able to reduce their taxable income by writing off part of their losses from the renting and leasing of their properties, thereby lowering their total taxable income. The allowances for these kinds of write-offs were particularly generous in the 1990s. Up until 1996, the rate was 50%, and then through 1998/1999, a hefty 40% of renovation costs could be deducted in the year following the investments. For example, if a real-estate company took in DM 1 million in 1995 (for which they would normally owe DM 500,000 in taxes), and yet showed losses of DM 2 million, they could write off 50% of these losses—that is, DM 1 million—thereby owing nothing. They would get to keep the DM 500,000 that would otherwise have gone to the state treasury. These high indirect subsidies made development investments—especially in view of the low rents and high costs for construction—very lucrative for investors with high taxable incomes, given that the investment "costs" could be transformed into tax savings for the shareholders.

The housing deals that this precipitated took a similar course everywhere. First a businessman bought a dilapidated piece of real estate in the East. In order to renovate it, he set up a real-estate fund for investors. When they paid into the fund, the investors became shareholders, meaning that they would share in the gains and losses of the business according to the amount they paid in. Because real-estate investments are so expensive, in the first years following completion of the construction primarily losses would be recorded. This usually hinders most investors from becoming involved in real-estate ventures. But in eastern Germany, losses were a good thing because they could be deducted from the investor's taxable income as "exceptional write-offs." It was in particular those who pay very high taxes who stood to benefit from the write-offs. As a result, lawyers from Munich and dentists from Hamburg flooded the real-estate funds, reduced their taxes to nothing, and let the German state pay for the expansion of their assets. Through such investments in rental properties alone, it is estimated that DM 3.5 billion in tax revenues were lost.

Prices, locations, and future market prospects were almost negligible considerations in these tax-saving schemes, and investors could afford to build even in places where the demand did not justify the costs. Investments thus proceeded largely independent of demand, anticipated rental returns, and even the location of a property. The result can be seen today in many eastern German cities and towns: a huge housing surplus everywhere.

Even the fact that houses with top-quality renovations are unable to find renters has not been a problem. Because the deductible investments were made just a few years ago, interest and redemption payments are still due that result in "losses from renting and leasing," which can be written off yet again. Only when these benefits have been completely soaked up and the debts overtake the amounts being saved will alternatives be sought. Until then, investors can wait it out and reap the profits. Lesson One of the housing market in eastern Germany could thus be formulated as follows: investing is worth it even with declining demand because the state will cover part of the bill.

Old Debts and Real Liabilities

But this maxim is not true for everyone. At the same time that Munich's lawyers and Hamburg's dentists were reaping profits, eastern Germany's housing companies were being asked to cough up. Here, too, the circumstances are skewed and seem to fly in the face of basic common sense.

To explain why, we must look back in history. In the German Democratic Republic (GDR), new housing was financed through long-term loans from the GDR Staatsbank (State Bank). However, redemption and interest were not paid by the housing company but by the municipalities and/or out of the national budget. Although this arrangement was considered a simple matter of accounting, a mountain of debt piled up. This became a huge problem with the changeover to a market economy in 1990. On average, every newly constructed apartment building in eastern Germany carried a debt of DM 15,000, and thus the eastern German housing companies were all but broke when they entered the market economy. In order to avoid the collapse of the housing sector, in 1993 Germany passed the *Altschuldenhilfegesetz* (Old Debts Assistance Act), which stipulated a cap of DM 150 per square meter for outstanding debts and allowed any additional debt to be taken over by the state *Erblastentilgungsfonds* (Redemption Fund for Inherited Liabilities). Because the *Altschuldenhilfegesetz* repeatedly led to difficulties, it was revised several times—the last time in 2001 when Section 6a was added, which allowed old debts to be canceled for housing that had been torn down.

If we sum up this operation, we again find a situation that has little to do with a market economy. In the first step, the "people's" businesses took out loans with the "workers and farmers state." Because the GDR was a planned economy, these loans could hardly be denied, nor other banks sought out as partners. The state posted the loans at the Staatsbank, and the allocations became real debts. After the state had been dissolved, the Staatsbank was privatized and the "debts" ended up with private business banks. These banks were not the ones who had lent the money originally, but they now had lending agreements on the basis of which they could demand payment for interest and redemption of the "old debts." Although the housing company and the bank did not have a previous business relationship, this arrangement granted the one the right to collect interest and redemption payments, while the other had to pay. But here, too, the state jumped in again after a while and took over part of the bill. The rest of the old debts—between around €0.50 and €1.00 per square meter per month—remained with the housing company, who in turn passed the costs on to the renters. As vacancies increased, however, this system didn't work anymore either. So the state jumped in again and took over the "old debts" for vacant housing—on condition that it had been torn down. As a result, the demolition of housing suddenly became lucrative, and in contrast to all other property owners, former GDR housing companies started tearing down buildings left and right.

If we sum up this arrangement, Lesson Two can be formulated in three parts: (a) Not everyone is free to make his/her own decisions in a free economy; (b) even when the state creates debts and pays off a great deal of them itself, this is still a market economy; and, finally, (c) the reduction of a surplus must also be subsidized in order to be lucrative.

Accounts and Balances

What has influenced the course of events on the housing markets in eastern Germany, however, is not only the "market distortion" due to state funding, but also the appraisal practices of real-estate companies, through which a house made of stone and mortar—via several intermediate steps—enters into a relationship with international financial markets.

Here, too, the forces at work are not immediately apparent. A textbook mortgage transaction works as follows: A builder takes out a loan from a bank in order to finance a real-estate property and secures this loan with a mortgage on the property in case he becomes unable to pay off the loan. If the borrower is unable to make the required payments, the lender can redeem his right to cash in on the mortgage, for example through a public auction of the property. In addition to its estimation of the general credit standing of the borrower, the mortgage is the most important security the bank has for protecting itself in the event that payments are not made. The mortgage appraisal therefore becomes the tricky hoop through which fresh capital enters the real-estate market.

But the question of how secure this form of security is will depend upon developments on the market. If there is a surplus on the market, the prices that could be expected if the mortgaged real-estate property were to be auctioned will fall, and the security will then be worth less. Real-estate property thus loses its traditional status as one of the most stable securities.

In order to protect themselves against this risk in a situation where prices are plummeting, the banks would really have to demand additional securities. Take, for example, a homeowner who borrowed at a rate of €400 per square meter for a property of

1,000 square meters. If the market value of his property were to fall to €200, he would have to come up with €200,000 worth of additional securities. If he can't, the bank could demand full payment for the loan and thereby drive the owner into ruin.

Property owners want to avoid this, of course, and so they have an acute interest in keeping the recorded value of their properties high. In order to continue to have access to credit, they will do anything to appear in the eyes of the bank as productive, efficient, profitable, and solvent. So even for a piece of real estate that no longer shows real returns, it may make more sense to continue to record a high value and keep the property on the books than to remove it from the accounting records. In times of weak markets, many businesses will carry a never-ending string of properties that have no real value but that allow them to look solvent. Here, too, real business practices look different from those in the textbooks. Whereas those trading in housing really should respond to a fall in demand by lowering prices or reducing volume in order to stay on the market and sell their properties, these owners try to keep the value of their assets high and thus maintain their credit standing.

But this means that they simply pass the problem on to the banks, because on the international financial markets it is not the real-estate moguls who are being assessed, rather the banks that lend to them. Because the banks acquire a large portion of their capital on the international financial markets, just like their own clients they must submit to an analysis of their credit standing. If, for example, a Bavarian mortgage bank tries to lend money on the London stock exchange, it must subject itself to the watchful eye of, let's say, an American finance specialist who evaluates its present and future revenues and expenses. If this analyst determines that the bank has too many "bad" credits that have a poor chance of being paid back, he will set a high price for the borrower and slap him with a deduction for risk. If a bank has many accounts receivable in a region with a high rate of housing vacancy, for example in Niederlausitz, this creates a bad impression on the London exchange, where they will have little knowledge about the situation on the ground. This becomes a problem for the bank because it will either have to offer additional securities or accept higher borrowing costs.

Thus, the sorry state of the real-estate market in eastern Germany becomes a liability for the banks that agree to do business there. They will end up paying for their involvement in a difficult region by paying higher borrowing costs on the capital they acquire on international markets. Overall, this sector expects a "valley of tears," as the director of an eastern German banking association described the situation during a conference. They are already sifting through their investments with a fine-toothed comb to sort out the risks that are looming, and they are more stringent than previously in assessing the risk on a given loan. In many cases this means a complete exit from the eastern German real-estate market. In order to make a better impression on the international money markets, some banks are even selling off existing loan contracts—at a markdown. What is decisive here are not the real circumstances, for example the actual demand for low-cost housing projects or affordable unrenovated apartments in a particular district, but instead the impression that is made on the financial markets.

The end result of these interactions between borrowers and lenders is again a paradox. While the former will do everything to create a favorable impression on the market, including keeping problematic real estate in their portfolios, the latter are willing to get rid of even those real-estate properties that are marketable, likewise in an effort to make a good impression on the markets. Lesson Three of the incredible eastern German shrinking real-estate market could read as follows: bluffing is half the game, and/or save your own bacon if you can.

Voodoo Economics, Not Market Economies

If we sum up the absurdities of the real-estate market in eastern Germany, it becomes clear that the idea espoused by many urban planners as to how real-estate property owners must cooperatively take part in the consolidation of the market in order to avoid depreciation is grounded on thin ice. Instead of being a collective attempt to create a balanced market, the practices more closely resemble a combination of bluffing and blaming in which everyone tries to make a good impression and pass the buck. Revenue from "losses," depreciation as a business deal, souped-up credit criteria, and perceived values are the result. This has nothing to do with the conventional notion of self-regulating markets that has been handed down in neoclassical economics. Much of what is going on in the real-estate market in eastern Germany brings to mind not so much Adam Smith's "invisible hand" as the theater of the absurd. A voodoo production is on the bill, a play addressing "the revitalization of markets through the conjuring of their existence." How long this show can go on remains to be seen.

Translated from the German by Christina M. White

COLLATERAL IN HAND, TREUHAND, AND THE INVISIBLE HAND THEATRUM MUNDI OECONOMICUS/STAGES OF A MARKET MECHANISM
Leipzig, Germany, 2005
Andreas Siekmann

One consequence of the economic restructuring and privatization following reunification are the shrinking cities in eastern Germany. The Treuhand was the central coordination office for the privatization of businesses and real estate. Their transformation into corporate entities, their commodification, was understood as a form of collateral in hand that would allow for economic consolidation—a prerequisite for the ability of the "invisible hand" of the private economy, as described by the economist Adam Smith, to ultimately provide a second economic miracle: the revitalization of eastern Germany. But the Treuhand and its successor, the Bundesanstalt für vereinigungsbedingte Sonderaufgaben (Federal Authority for Special Tasks Related to Reunification), instead created an official state debt of €136 billion.

In order to represent this mechanism, which continues today, this project takes up the model of the mechanical theater. Up until the end of the nineteenth century, the regions of Saxony and Thuringia had a particular folk-art tradition practiced by disabled or retired miners. They built mechanized marionette theaters called theatra mundi. In these theaters they reconstructed natural catastrophes, world events, and scenes from their own former workplace. The marionettes were mounted on conveyor belts and moved around in stage-like cabinets. These theatra mundi were shown at fairs.

"Theatrum Mundi Oeconomicus" illustrates the measures outlined above. The privatization of all economic structures in eastern Germany was often also represented as an automatism. The mechanical theater explicates this historiography and at the same time satirizes it.

This project was developed in the context of "Shrinking Cities" with a grant from the Museum of Contemporary Art Leipzig. The original German title is "Faustpfand, Treuhand und die unsichtbare Hand. Theatrum Mundi Oeconomicus/Stationen eines Marktmechanismus."

Commodified City

The Theatrum Mundi Oeconomicus tells the story of privatization as carried out by the Treuhand, Treuhand personnel, bankers, consulting firms, and investors. These agents of privatization move along on a conveyer belt past the various backdrops presented by important political and economic institutions: for example,

the European School of Management and Technology (ESMT) in the former East German State Council building in Berlin, the capital-city offices of Bertelsmann AG in the restored Prussian army commandant's headquarters, and the head office of the Treuhand Agency in the former Reich Ministry of Aviation.

HOANG'S BISTRO
Leipzig, Germany, 2005
Christoph Schäfer, with Deborah Schamoni

In the middle of Leipzig, unnoticed by most of its inhabitants and overlooked by officials and politicians, a covert Asian world has emerged. Three short videos entice us into this unknown part of Leipzig: three places where the city proves itself to be a city because it is open to the outside, incorporating compacted differences and the presence of the Other.

Dong Xuan Center
A huge Asian market has sprung up, spread over six large industrial warehouses: an endlessly branching labyrinth of markets and wares; worlds of Afghan, Vietnamese, and Chinese clothing and food; card players; Vietnamese children on their tricycles.

Casino Petersbogen
The hunger for a city: Times Square, New York. In the top floor of the Piranesi-like, half-finished shopping center, the casino owners have installed a real-time video projection. With the film's dry, long takes, the casino proprietors are attempting to project an urban situation onto their establishment, to have the metropolis present in the casino.

Hoang's Bistro
A busy restaurant in the central train station with a large mural of the Chinese Wall. In this last film sequence, what has so far been a documentary turns into a tremendous dance scene. The artist, disguised as a rabbit, performs a ritual fertility dance to entice foreigners into the city. Dance scenes in front of, in, and over "Hoang's Bistro": a growing city! Prosperity, a baby carriage ballet, growing more and more.

This project was developed in the context of "Shrinking Cities" with a grant from the Museum of Contemporary Art Leipzig.

Dong Xuan Center, Leipzig.

Hoang's Bistro_*Christoph Schäfer*

A sketch from the storyboard for the film *Hoang's Bistro*.

Hoang's Bistro_*Christoph Schäfer*

Hoang's Bistro, Leipzig Central Train Station.

URBAN TRANSFORMATION AS UNINTENDED SIDE EFFECT
PLANNING AND ITS LIMITS IN THE RESTRUCTURING OF THE AMERICAN METROPOLIS
Robert Fishman

—

—

The transformation of the American metropolis in the course of the last hundred years has been a complex interaction of deep structural forces and national policies. What we call the "unintended results" of these policies are usually instances of a national policy reinforcing structural trends—leading to an unexpectedly far-reaching transformation of the urban environment. For the years 1930-1990, these transformations were almost invariably in the direction of radical decentralization and the shrinking of the central cities—what Rem Koolhaas has called "dysurbanism."[1] But since 1990 another set of trends and policies has come to prominence, leading to what I call the "reurbanism" of at least some urban cores.

During the age of dysurbanism, the most important "deep structure" was automobile-based decentralization, and the most important government policy in the United States was the creation, starting in 1956, of the 41,000-mile interstate highway system, "the largest public works program in the history of the world." The new highway system worked in tandem with the long-term decentralization of industrial production to produce an unexpectedly radical redistribution of jobs within individual regions from the central city to its suburbs; at the national level, the shift was from the Northeast and Midwest to the South and the West, the emerging "Sunbelt." Similarly, government policies promoting low-cost mortgages for new suburban homes unexpectedly intensified the long-term trend toward the exodus of population from the core to the suburban periphery.[2]

Although regional form is invariably "unintended" because the scale of a metropolitan region always exceeds what planners can control or imagine, the decentralized region represents a particularly intense break between conscious plans and results on the ground. This is because dysurbanism is always a process of the fragmentation of the urban. Unlike dense cities, where some degree of control and coordination is both possible and necessary, the low-density sprawl environment is both uncontrollable and radically flexible. This fragmentary regionalism can accommodate unanticipated development precisely because the fragments need not relate to each other. Thus we are familiar with the perceived chaos along any highway, where the random succession of discordant housing, retail, and commercial fragments produces an impression of extreme discontinuity. But such fragments need not cohere into any traditional urban form. They constitute an unexpected and unintended form of "strip highway urbanism," a linear city that has come to define the new American region as much as pedestrian streets define the traditional downtown.

The best examples of this "linear city" are the "beltways" that were built around every major American city as part of the interstate highway system. These beltways were conceived by the highway engineers of the 1940s and 1950s as ways for long-distance automobile and truck traffic to bypass a congested city on their way to other destinations. But property developers soon realized that rural locations close to a beltway (especially where the beltway intersected a radial road heading toward the urban core) offered very convenient access from locations in the central city and throughout the region. Soon that cheap rural land along the beltway was filled with massive industrial parks, shopping centers, office parks, and housing. The whole region was unexpectedly pulled out toward the beltway "linear city," thus shrinking the central city and swelling its suburbs.[3]

This is one example of the interaction of government initiatives and unexpected entrepreneurial responses that resulted in a radical restructuring of the American metropolitan region that neither group could have envisaged or accomplished on its own. In this case, the real-estate speculators who transformed the beltways into linear cities were at least as radical in their conception of the region as were Le Corbusier and the other visionaries of the Congrès Internationaux d'Architecture Moderne. Or, perhaps more accurately, these speculators had no fixed conception or goal for the region: they exploited immediate opportunities with little concern that they were revolutionizing established principles of planning and regional form.

Insofar as there was an overall vision and strategy for the American "age of dysurbanism" in the years 1930-1990, it came out of the New Deal—the reform administration of President Franklin D. Roosevelt—during the years of the Great Depression. Many reformers and economists believed that the root cause of the depression was that the U.S. economy was too centered on the great cities of the East and the Midwest, where potential for growth was limited. The key to reviving the American economy was thus to move growth from the central cities to their suburbs, and from the East and Midwest to the then underdeveloped South and West. Some key elements in this 1930s regional development strategy were the Tennessee Valley Authority in the South and the massive Hoover and Columbia dams, which brought cheap electric power and irrigation to the South and the West, and the Federal Housing Administration with its new long-term, low-interest, low-down-payment home mortgages. These well-known programs were joined by an equally influential group of smaller federal programs to fund regional sewer and water systems as well as highways, and by "invisible subsidies" that used tax policy to promote new investment.[4]

But these New Deal dysurbanist policies aimed only at a modest correction of what they saw as excessive centralization in cities of the East and the Midwest. If these policies took on a wholly unexpected and unintended force after 1945, it was because Roosevelt and his planners never understood the weight of corporate and populist power that would unite behind the banner of regional restructuring. Nor could they understand the radical power of dysurbanism itself, the ways in which the special flexibility of the low-density, automobile-based environment could uniquely accommodate rapid and highly profitable speculative development. Dysurbanism first showed its strength during the Second World War, when new defense plants were disproportionately built in suburban locations or in the South or the West, outside the traditional urban centers. But it was only in the post-1945 period that the full impact of decentralization was seen. The policies that were intended to drag a sluggish economy out of the Great Depression now took on an unintended "supercharged" power in the explosive postwar economy.

Where the Federal Housing Administration mortgage policy of the depression had aimed at a modest revival of home-building, this same mortgage policy in the postwar boom led to the production of more than a million new housing units per year, almost all of them single-family suburban houses.[5] Moreover, whereas the depression-era tax

Emerging City

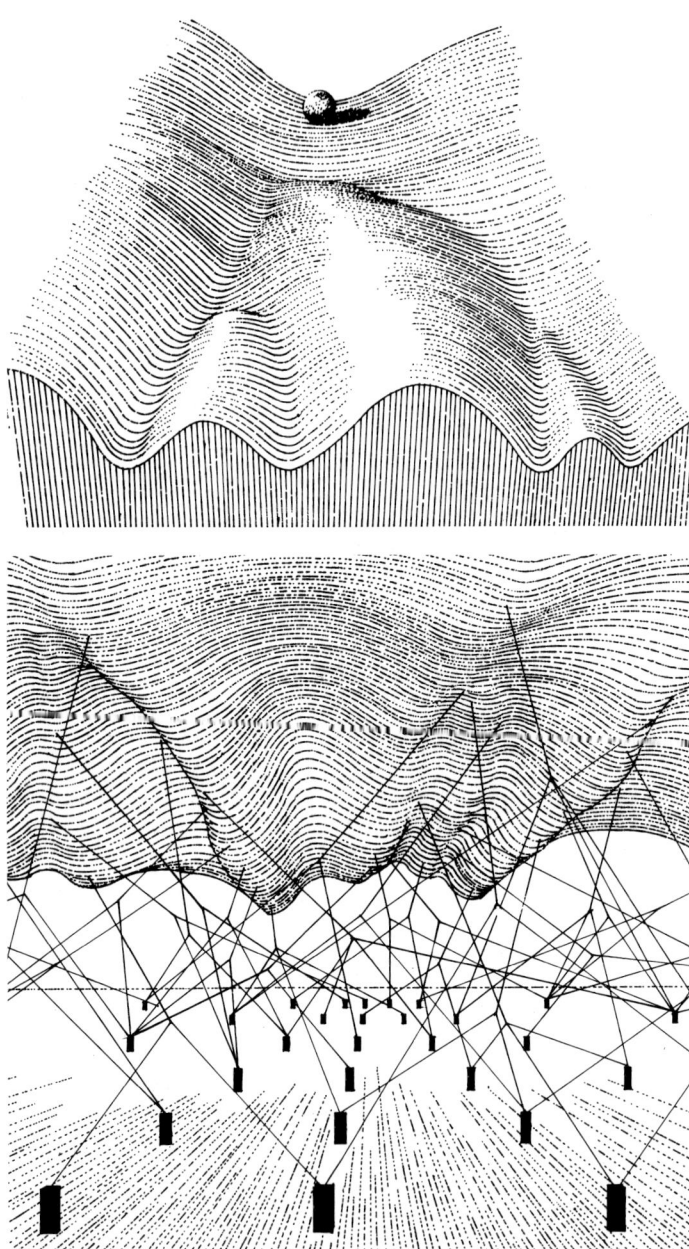

The epigenetic landscape after Conrad Waddington (top) shows the nonlinear effect of genes on the development of living beings. The complex interplay of many genes (bottom) creates a landscape of possibilities, the concrete effects of which will only be decided over the course of time (the rolling of the ball, top). Analogously, many different factors have an effect on today's urban development, which is why the form, structure, and development of cities cannot be immediately shaped.

incentives for new industrial plants and other facilities had operated within very modest bounds, these incentives during the postwar era helped fuel a massive rebuilding of the nation's industrial plants, as tax policies greatly favored building new factories in the suburbs or the Sunbelt over renovating old ones in the core rust-belt cities. These older plants and their workers were exploited as "cash cows," as facilities that could be "milked": they were run down and eventually abandoned, while new investment was directed elsewhere in the region and the nation.[6]

This relocation of industrial jobs during the years 1950–1985, surely the most important factor in the shrinkage of the great American cities, anticipated on the national scale our contemporary globalization of production. American corporations learned to exploit the differentials between the high-wage cities of the East and the Midwest and the relatively low-wage South and West. Perhaps equally important, the conservatism of the Sunbelt meant that trade unions were weak there, a very important factor for American managers who had never reconciled themselves to sharing power with unions.[7]

These initial industrial relocations would not have been possible without the massive investment by the U.S. federal government that created superhighways, massive electrical power grids, and other vital infrastructure in parts of the United States that had lacked them. These infrastructure initiatives had an equally important impact on retail location. A. Alfred Taubman, the shopping-center magnate who has endowed the School of Architecture and Planning at the University of Michigan, where I teach, has often emphasized to our students and faculty the key importance of the interstate highway system and its beltways in the transformation of his business. As early as the 1950s, he realized that the new highways would at least quadruple the number of suburban households that would be within an easy ten- to fifteen-minute drive of a well-located shopping center. This massive enlargement of the customer base meant that crucial economies of scale were reached. For the first time, a suburban shopping center at the edge of the region could offer enough selection to compete effectively with downtown. A new generation of American shopping centers, many designed by the Viennese-born architect Victor Gruen, were, like the nearby suburban industrial parks, a major unintended consequence of the interstate system of highways.[8]

This redistribution of production and retailing, moreover, has been reinforced by another set of unintended consequences. The American practice of funding crucial services like schools from local property taxes has given a wholly new meaning to local government boundaries, especially those between a central city and its suburbs. As these suburbs gained not only population but also industrial parks, office parks, shopping malls, and other lucrative tax sources, the local boundary lines that once served to demarcate quiet agricultural villages have now become critical social and economic barriers that separate the haves and have-nots within a metropolitan region.[9]

This localism or "home rule," which includes not only local services but land-use policy (zoning) as well, had further consequences that lie somewhere between the intended and the unintended. "Home rule" divided regional land-use policy among a multitude of suburban jurisdictions and thus made a coherent regional land-use policy impossible.[10] Developers like Taubman became expert in playing one suburban town against another, almost always succeeding in winning support in small, semirural peripheral towns where farmers and speculators were eager for the profits that development generated. Because the major infrastructure investments were already in place thanks to the federal government, the incentives to approve virtually any project at the rural fringes were overwhelming—even if one obvious result was the shrinkage of the central city.

What seems surprising in retrospect was that this profound shrinkage of the American central city was allowed to continue unchecked even after the destructive "unintended consequences" were evident. Indeed, the worst period of the urban crisis in terms of depopulation, deindustrialization, and the near bankruptcy of the central cities came in 1967–1977, that is, in the decade after the riots that tore so many American cities apart. The explanation requires some understanding of the American political economy of the period. First, the federal government, the overwhelming force behind decentralization, remained disproportionately dominated by the interests of the South and the West. The pro-urban policies of the "Great Society" of President Lyndon Johnson (1963–1968) were always subordinate to the continuation of federal subsidies to roads, suburban houses, and decentralization in general.[11]

Within older metropolitan regions, the local elites were often deeply split. Every large city had its "downtown coalition" headed by local bankers and industrialists who promoted downtown offices and cultural centers. But these were often the same men who were directing the decentralization of the factories that they controlled out of the central city and the region. Moreover, the stark racial divide between "chocolate cities, vanilla suburbs" made it easier to isolate the central cities politically. For both the corporate elite and the new majority of white suburban voters, the shrinking American cities of the 1970s and 1980s were like the unprofitable divisions of a large corporation. As management doctrine taught, one cuts back on the unprofitable divisions, and invests in the profitable ones: hence the period's seemingly unstoppable trend toward the abandonment of the central cities and the frantic growth of their suburbs and the Sunbelt.[12]

If this trend has slowed and even reversed in some American metropolitan regions since 1990, the reason lies, I would argue, in another set of unintended consequences stemming from globalization. The deeper international trend has been the reorientation of the global economy around the cores of certain favored cities that centralize finance, information, culture, and tourism. In the United States, this deeper trend has been most importantly reinforced by the unintended consequence of the Immigration Act of 1965. Enacted to redress some inequities from the highly restrictive and indeed racist immigration policies going back to the 1920s, the 1965 act opened the door to more than eighteen million legal immigrants (and millions more "undocumented" ones), who flocked directly to those "immigrant gateways" (e.g., Los Angeles, San Francisco, Chicago, New York) that also were becoming the most important American nodes of the global urban system.[13]

The unexpected consequences of the interaction between the heights of the global financial system and the millions of new immigrants have been, in my view, the principal story of the American metropolitan region over the last twenty years. Initially the immigrants provided the cheap labor for the luxury services that made core cities attractive to the global elite. Although millions of immigrants remain stuck in this low-wage sector, others have succeeded in creating a small-scale immigrant economy that now produces goods and services for a wider range of the American population. This immigrant surge has reversed the depopulation that cities like New York and Chicago suffered from 1950 to 1990, and has made the central cities far more attractive to an American middle class that once sought to escape them.[14]

The interaction of these widely disparate sets of unintended consequences—those that shrank the cities and those that now are growing them—has resulted in an unusually wide variation in regional form within the United States. The American regions most favored by globalization—New York, Los Angeles, Chicago, Boston, Seattle, and the San Francisco Bay Area—enjoy feverish growth which even the "tech bust" of 2000 has not stopped. In these regions one finds a lively pedestrian-oriented downtown surrounded by rapidly revitalizing neighborhoods that have reversed the seemingly inevitable pattern of depopulation and job loss at the core.[15] The main problem for such regions is intolerable congestion and the lack of affordable housing, not only for the poor but even for much of the middle class.

Some of this feverish growth is now spilling over into once shrinking cities like Portland, Oregon; Santa Fe, New Mexico; Burlington, Vermont; and Portland, Maine. These cities combine natural beauty with beautiful older neighborhoods. They have attracted affluent older residents who are freer to move and who find that, for the price of a cramped, uncomfortable house in a booming region, they can afford good housing in a pleasant, uncongested environment.

These growth trends work off the global economy, and for that reason require little assistance from a federal government that is, in any case, increasingly paralyzed by structural deficits, an antigovernment philosophy, and an unending "war on terror." Unfortunately, these global trends will do little for industrial centers like Camden, New Jersey, which once grew prosperous through their domination of a national market. Some of the largest centers—Detroit, Cleveland, Saint Louis—still retain enough multinational corporations, major cultural institutions, and traditional urban amenities that their eventual recovery is at least possible. Perhaps the worst off are those small-to-medium-sized "gritty cities" like Camden; Gary, Indiana; Syracuse, New York; and Flint, Michigan (made famous by Michael Moore's film *Roger and Me*): here toxic waste dumps outnumber scenic or cultural amenities. Although these cities have largely lost their industrial base, they retain a tradition of strong unions and high wages sufficient to discourage potential employers like Mercedes-Benz, Honda, Toyota, and Hyundai—all of whom recently located large automobile plants in rural, low-tax, anti-union Alabama.[16] At the same time, older cities like Flint have little to attract immigrants, tourists, global capital, or Richard Florida's "creative class."[17]

Planner Mike Wallace has recently proposed a "new" New Deal: a national growth policy that would counteract the lingering long-term effects of New Deal dysurbanist policies through transportation subsidies, tax policies, job-location policies, and other incentives to direct growth back to the "shrinking cities" of the Northeast and the Midwest.[18] But with the federal government dominated by followers of Herbert Hoover rather than Franklin Roosevelt, no deal (new or otherwise) seems possible. Instead, I predict a continuing divergence of regional experiences. The dynamic regions and cities will be those global centers that continue to attract a diverse mix of immigrants and well-educated young people. Meanwhile, the shrinking cities and regions will attempt to exploit their very limited advantages—affordable housing, less automobile congestion, a slower pace of life—in order to cushion their decline.

Notes

1. Rem Koolhaas, "Atlanta," in *S, M, L, XL* (New York: Monacelli Press, 1995), 836.
2. Dolores Hayden, *Building Suburbia: Green Fields and Urban Growth, 1820–2000* (New York: Pantheon, 2003).
3. Robert Lang, *Edgeless Cities: Exploring the Elusive Metropolis* (Washington, D.C.: Brookings Institution Press, 2003).
4. Alan Brinkley, *The End of Reform: New Deal Liberalism in Recession and War* (New York: Knopf, 1995).
5. Kenneth T. Jackson, *Crabgrass Frontier: The Suburbanization of America* (New York: Oxford University Press, 1985).
6. Jefferson Cowie, *Capital Moves: RCA's 70-Year Quest for Cheap Labor* (Ithaca, NY: Cornell University Press, 1999), introduction and chap. 7.
7. Ibid., chaps. 1–6.
8. M. Jeffrey Hardwick, *Mall Maker: Victor Gruen, Architect of an American Dream* (Philadelphia: University of Pennsylvania Press, 2004).
9. Jon Teaford, *City and Suburb: The Political Fragmentation of Metropolitan America, 1850–1970* (Baltimore: Johns Hopkins University Press, 1979).
10. Gerald Frug, *City Making: Building Communities Without Building Walls* (Princeton, NJ: Princeton University Press, 1999).
11. Jon Teaford, *The Rough Road to Renaissance: Urban Revitalization in America, 1940–1985* (Baltimore: Johns Hopkins University Press, 1990).
12. John R. Logan and Harvey L. Molotch, *Urban Fortunes: The Political Economy of Place* (Berkeley: University of California Press, 1987).
13. Audrey Singer, *The Rise of New Immigrant Gateways* (Washington, D.C.: Brookings Institution Press, 2004).
14. See especially the important research in Bruce Katz and Robert Lang, eds., *Redefining Urban and Suburban America: Evidence from the 2000 Census* (Washington, D.C.: Brookings Institution Press, 2003).
15. James W. Hughes and Joseph J. Seneca provide strong evidence for the New York metropolitan area, perhaps the only U.S. region where population and job growth at the core equal or even exceed that at the edge. See their *The Beginning of the End of Sprawl?* Rutgers Regional Report No. 21 (New Brunswick, NJ: Bloustein School of Planning and Public Policy, 2004).
16. Susan Carney, "Alabama Strong with Autos," *Detroit News*, April 3, 2003, p. B1.
17. Attracting this "creative class" has become as much a panacea among American urban planners as attracting "high-tech jobs" was a decade ago. As I have suggested, immigrants are at least as important to "reurbanism" as these young, skilled, middle-class professionals. See Richard L. Florida, *The Rise of the Creative Class* (New York: Basic Books, 2002).
18. Mike Wallace, *A New Deal for New York* (New York: Bell & Weiland, 2002).

SHRINKAGE AND IMMIGRATION
Franz-Josef Kemper and Olaf Schnur

Demographic change manifests itself not only in the pension system or the economic output of a nation, but also in its "space." In addition to regional variations in age structure and fertility rates, population shifts due to immigration and internal migration play an important role. The result is a very complex mosaic of patterns of growth and shrinkage that seem to point in opposite directions. If the idea is that increased immigration will greatly alleviate the problem of shrinkage and its effects on the social system at the national level, from a geographic perspective it must be cautioned that such simple conclusions are inadequate. Immigration certainly is desirable, but it could bring new problems by aggravating spatial disparities and the unresolved problem of integration in the receiving areas. Today we may safely assume that future immigrants would move to one of the few remaining growth regions in the south and the west of Germany. In other words, "Large parts of the Federal Republic will be ... unaffected by immigration—in both the good and the bad sense."[1]

Migration and the City System

In highly industrialized countries, immigration from abroad is primarily directed toward cities because it is expected that the chances of finding work are higher in an urban setting. But there are very significant differences between the cities as regards the proportion of immigrants. The bigger and more important a city is, the more immigrants it will attract. There are also regional differences: a South-North divide within the old German states, and a West-East divide. The spatial and temporal development of the influx of so-called guest workers *(Gastarbeiter)* in the 1960s and 1970s is reflected in the South-North divide, which brought a movement from the south to the north within West Germany, in particular into the regional centers and industrial agglomerations. The West-East divide reflects the different migration policies of the two former German states. The "new migrations" since 1989 (refugees and asylum seekers, as well as "resettlers" *[Aussiedler]* of German heritage from countries to the east), which were channeled to various locations by state allocation, have in part led to a balancing out of these spatial differences. But to a certain extent the previous disparities have intensified because migrants motivated by the prospect of finding work move to economically prospering cities and regions, above all in southern Germany (e.g., skilled migrants or qualified information technology workers granted special "green cards").

The proportion of foreigners living in southern Germany's large cities is therefore particularly high. The regional metropolises of Munich and Stuttgart both have shares of foreigners that make up 24% of the total population (2002); Frankfurt am Main has 22%; whereas Hamburg with 15% and Berlin with 13% show much lower proportions. The highest rates are found in some of the industrial cities of the south, for example in Offenbach (26%) and Ludwigshafen (22%)—cities that drew in many immigrants during the guest-worker phase. Although foreign migrants were hard hit by deindustrialization and have since shown an above-average rate of unemployment, these industrial cities and regions in the old German states are still experiencing immigration, primarily due to families bringing over their relatives. Social networks can keep driving migration movements even when the original factors that attracted people (e.g., industrial jobs) are no longer present. This explains why the migration of Turks to Germany in the 1990s, contrary to the prognoses of economics-based migration theories, was for the most part to those German states and regions that show a high rate of unemployment (such as North Rhine-Westphalia and Berlin).[2]

In the new German states, the relevance of deindustrialization as a factor in shrinkage and migration is quite a different story. Monostructured industrial cities have very low proportions of foreigners compared to the overall figures in eastern Germany, which are quite low in general. Hoyerswerda, for example, which saw a population decline of 24% between 1995 and 2002, is one of the cities most affected by shrinkage, and it shows a quota of foreigners of just 1.5% (2002). In contrast, the large regional centers in the new German states show significantly higher figures: Dresden and Chemnitz are at 4% and Leipzig is at 6%. The general decline of the population in these cities has recently been softened by an overall increase in the foreign population. A similar influx of migrants can be seen in slightly growing cities such as Jena and Weimar.

The figures representing the percentage of foreigners mentioned here do not, however, include the entirety of people with a migrant background. There are, in addition, naturalized foreigners and "resettlers" of German heritage, who in the past few years have still been arriving primarily only from the former Soviet states, above all Russia and Kazakhstan. The total number of immigrants arriving in Germany between 1991 and 2002 was 3.84 million; of them, 1.55 million were of German nationality, mostly resettlers. The distribution of resettlers across Germany is determined by the official quotas for residency allocations, which are intended to ensure equal distribution, including between the old and the new states as well as cities and rural areas. Thus, even shrinking cities and regions in eastern Germany show an influx of resettlers. Asylum seekers and refugees are likewise distributed across the country according to regional quotas, including in the new states. But the allocation of foreigners to areas outside the main locations for settlement, for example former military sites, has proven unfortunate for the objective of local integration—insofar as integration has been a goal at all.[3]

When people come to Germany from abroad, often their move is not intended to be permanent or even long-term; they plan on a stay of limited duration. Many highly qualified foreigners in the large key cities are among those who intend to stay for a limited time, as are many migrants from eastern Central Europe. Depending on current developments on the German job market, bilateral agreements are drawn up annually with Central European countries which stipulate quotas for the temporary migration of workers. Most important in this respect is the program for seasonal workers, which primarily pertains to the agricultural and hotel and catering sectors. The numbers of these workers have increased steadily since 1994 and accounted for a total of almost three hundred thousand contracts in 2002. Another segment of immigrants who are drawn particularly to the cities are temporary workers, primarily from Poland and largely employed in domestic services. Even the shrinking cities in eastern Germany have a share of this "transnational" migration, which, however, is not associated with lasting demographic effects.

Demographic Selectivity and Its Effects

The process of migration is selective. Young adults are highly mobile, whereas older people show little tendency to migrate. Hopes are placed on young people and families with children when migration is lauded as a remedy against population decline and aging.

Foreigners living in Germany are on the whole much younger than the rest of the population. But there are big differences between the various categories of settlers. In the core cities that have a high percentage of foreigners, after the group aged 15–25 it is the children under 15 that have an above-average representation. A good third of the inhabitants of Offenbach, Stuttgart, Frankfurt, and Ludwigshafen who are under age 25 do not have a German passport. On the other hand, in rural areas the group of foreigners aged 20–50 is overrepresented.[4] One characteristic of the cities is thus a high percentage of children with foreign heritage; this situation calls for specific efforts in education and support for children.

In the new states, however, not only is the percentage of foreigners much lower than in western Germany, but the relative overrepresentation of children is also much less prominent. Apparently migration is a relatively new phenomenon in eastern Germany, and the families and relatives of migrants are not yet following in tow. Significant in this context are temporary migrants who come to Germany without their families, a group largely represented by men. Excluding Berlin, in the eastern states women make up only 37%–38% of the population (2001); in the western states the figure is 47.4%. Migrants do not necessarily have more children than the native population. The fertility rate of all foreigners together—the number of children per woman—is below the level needed to sustain the current population. If there is nonetheless a surplus of births, this is only due to the age structure. Only certain groups, such as the Turks, have a higher fertility rate. And even in this case the United Nations population prognoses predict that by 2015 the fertility rate in their home country of Turkey will also drop to the minimum necessary to sustain the population.

But the shrinking and aging of the population in Germany can still be mitigated through immigration, as various prognoses and models demonstrate. In this context, the population prognosis of the German Federal Office for Building and Regional Planning is worth mentioning because of its regional differentiation. According to the prognosis of this office, immigration from abroad will have an effect on three different levels.[5] Primary effects constitute the direct demographic effects as regards total population, age structure, and spatial distribution. Secondary effects will be brought about indirectly by births and deaths and possibly surplus births among migrants. Immigrants are also involved in internal migration, which will create a tertiary effect through geographic redistribution across Germany. A comparison of model projections with and without immigration from abroad (according to status quo estimates) demonstrates the demographic effect of internal migration. Without immigration, the number of primary and secondary-school students (ages 6–16) would decline by one-third from the year 2000 to 2020; with immigration the figure would be one-fourth. This effect due to internal migration would be most tangible in western Germany in the large core cities and the densely populated suburban areas, whereas in eastern Germany it would only be felt in the core cities and even there to a lesser extent. Similar results would be seen for other age groups. The total demographic effect of migration would vary regionally. Within the new German states, Berlin and the Leipzig/Dresden/Chemnitz region would profit most; other parts of eastern Germany's "shrinking landscape" would not be helped by migration.

The Urban Housing Market and Migration

Urban housing markets are very complex because "housing" as a commodity is highly sensitive. Housing is an essential human need, but it is also quite expensive and difficult to produce: the product itself varies greatly, and it is very dependent on location. Those looking for housing would like to maximize the quality of what they are getting while keeping the costs (e.g., rent, transportation) at a minimum; the neighborhood must also be the "right" one. This sociospatial sensitivity means that the market is highly segmented, that is, there are partial urban markets with different consumers who remain within a given segment either voluntarily or because they are forced to (due to their level of income, ethnic discrimination, etc.).

These particular market characteristics steer migration currents in the context of shrinkage, as the following trends show:

1. Because the number of shrinking cities will increase in the future, while some cities will continue to grow (with varying degrees of new construction), there will be some (urban) regions with relaxed markets and some with tight markets. The former may at first seem attractive to those searching for housing, but not to those offering housing. The situation in growing cities will be the exact opposite. These differentiations in the market will in turn influence investment decisions in the housing industry, which will only exacerbate the disparities.

2. Irrespective of this development, different situations ranging from a scarcity to a surplus of housing will result in the different market segments for various target groups (e.g., migrants). Market access for migrants will become more complex than in previous times, in parallel with the increasing regional dynamics of demographic change.

3. As households become increasingly smaller while the housing space desired per person grows larger, the prognosis is that housing needs will initially still climb and then later taper off.

The conditions of shrinkage thus represent a complex spatial mosaic of simultaneous concentration and dispersion, and thereby constitute a multilayered, inter- and intra-regionally differentiated housing market. For migrants, however, the job market is generally more important than the housing market. They go where the jobs are, that is, to the few remaining regions where the economy is still strong (the exception here is socially motivated migration to deindustrialized regions). Areas with a strong economy will always have a greater pull and thus will gain most from immigration. At the very least, they will show an increase in the number of residents and thus be designated as growth regions. And it can be expected that future immigrants will behave as others have in the past: they will pay attention to costs and flexibility, request rental property according to a specific set of criteria, and move to the core cities of large, centrally located urban regions rather than to the suburbs. In the future, certain neighborhoods in the city centers will continue to be chosen more or less voluntarily depending on the market segment and the migrant group in question, in particular as a result of chain migration. But cumulative growth will bring its own set of problems. The mostly inner-city housing market segments for migrant households will remain relatively expensive; the segregation tendencies apparent today will persist in many places; and integration problems will only grow as the migrant population becomes increasingly concentrated (given that the majority society will also probably shrink overall in the growth regions).

Shrinking cities with structural economic problems will hardly profit from the flow of migration. But there are nonetheless potential pull factors—in particular for internal migration. Due to the typically relaxed housing market, affordable housing with above-average space is easier to find, meaning that the quality and standard of living will be higher in such areas. Shrinking cities could, for example, become a retirement destination for people with a migrant background who have an independent economic base (e.g., a pension). Among resettlers, in particular, it was observed that one main reason for moving is to obtain a higher level of comfort—regardless of the job-market situation—given that government subsidies for resettlers, like pensions, are sufficient enough to serve as an economic base for a more or less modest standard of living. In addition, job-market niches potentially exist in shrinking cities, waiting to be filled by migrants. But the relaxed housing market in cities with declining populations also harbors a potential danger. It can be expected that greater housing choices and low rent and/or property prices will quickly contribute to social and ethnic homogenization. Increased segregation could become a problem in Germany's shrinking cities—as it has become in large cities in the United States, where there is a pervasive segregation of blacks, whites, and Hispanics.

Urban Job Markets and Migration
Shrinking cities will thus not become preferred destinations for migrants seeking work—regardless of whether they are highly skilled or unskilled.[6] Generally, competition for human capital will in fact further strengthen the already prospering cities. Just as immigration will decline in a given area when it hits an economic slump, during a phase of intense demographic change immigration will be concentrated in the few urban job-market hot spots. Further, in the large, old, industrialized cities, many migrant groups—regardless of their generation—are among the most affected by the decline in jobs in the industrial sector and are thus likely to move away in search of a better future.

For "ethnic" migrants with a low level of qualification, access to the urban job market is in general difficult—and has even become significantly more difficult in the past twenty years. The lack of qualifications and language skills among many migrant groups serves as a potential basis for employers to exclude them, and individual forms of discrimination and structural disadvantages resulting from red tape are the norm for migrants in urban job markets. Opportunities exist primarily in the area of personal and domestic services: migrants will be able to find work in "assisted living" arrangements or caring for ill and/or elderly persons, in particular because shrinking cities will have an above-average proportion of elderly persons due to demographic aging. For less-qualified migrant groups, there are also perspectives in the area of "ethnic businesses." The experience in German municipalities has been that migrants are generally eager to start up their own businesses—whether in order to serve their own ethnic group and thus to occupy an economic niche, or in order to ensure the survival of a certain branch of business. In shrinking cities where the infrastructure is slowly thinning out, there is a certain stabilizing potential in this respect. Ethnic entrepreneurs can satisfy some of the local needs in the sense of a "supplemental economy" (e.g., the retail sector, skilled crafts, everyday services, the catering trade) and settle permanently with jobs in shrinking areas. This can, in turn, lead to new impulses (i.e., the generation of jobs) or create chains of internal migration. In order to strengthen these effects and create incentives for migrants in shrinking cities, the existing restrictive prerequisites for ethnic businesses in Germany must be eased (e.g., the rules on practicing handicrafts and trades).

Migration in a New Europe
The eastward expansion of the European Union (EU) has proved to be a political sticking point in this context. When the Central and Eastern European accession candidates joined the EU on May 1, 2004, the labor mobility stipulated by the EU charter did not yet become a reality. Germany, as well as other countries of the old EU, feared that labor mobility would lead to a quick rise in labor migration, thereby resulting in wage dumping and growing unemployment among native populations. So a transition phase of a maximum of seven years was established in which labor mobility for dependent employment is prohibited. The basis for this decision was a series of reviews by economic research institutes on the prognoses for immigration from the accession countries if the previous restrictions were suddenly lifted. The relevant econometric models, based on empirical migration figures in the United States and for so-called guest workers, estimated an annual net migration from the accession countries to the old EU of three hundred thousand to six hundred thousand people, which would taper off over time and lead to a total of three to five million migrants settling in western Europe.[7] Given that Germany was expected to receive two-thirds of this net migration if the distribution seen in the year 2000 remained constant, this implied a future net immigration of 2.0 to 3.4 million people for the country. In the long term, however, the rapid drop in births since 1989 and the more or less prominent shrinkage in Central Europe means that the potential number of migrants from these countries could be expected to decline. Starting in the year 2010, the most mobile group, that of 20- to 30-year-olds, will be significantly affected by the drop in births. For cities in the new German states, this means that immigration from Eastern and Central Europe will affect the region's shrinkage only minimally in the long run. EU expansion will thus not result in a job-market horror scenario nor an anti-shrinkage scenario for the new German states. Nonetheless, particularly in eastern Germany, certain professions, ethnic businesses, and locations will present opportunities for migrants to settle and thereby possibly help shrinking cities consolidate their future development.

Conclusion
The overall trend that can be expected is a dynamic polarization of growing regions and shrinking regions due to economic and migration effects. In order to prevent drastic disparities, shrinking cities should offer both direct incentives to immigrate as well as measures that encourage internal migration, for example through targeted job-market policies or regional incentives for migrants to start their own businesses. To avoid endangering social cohesion during times of demographic transformation, efforts toward the social integration of migrants need to be significantly strengthened.

Translated from the German by Christina M. White

Notes

1. Hansjörg Bucher, Martina Kocks, and Claus Schlömer, "Künftige internationale Wanderungen und die räumliche Inzidenz von Integrationsaufgaben," *Informationen zur Raumentwicklung* 8 (2002): 415–430, here p. 429.
2. See Franz-Josef Kemper, "Außenwanderungen in Deutschland – Wandel der regionalen Muster in den 80er und 90er Jahren," *Petermanns Geographische Mitteilungen* 144, no. 1 (2000): 38–49.
3. See Jörg Becker, *Die nichtdeutsche Bevölkerung in Ostdeutschland: Eine Studie zur räumlichen Segregation und Wohnsituation,* Potsdamer Geographische Forschungen 15 (Potsdam, Germany: Institut für Geographie und Geoökologie, Universität Potsdam, 1998).
4. See Ferdinand Böltken, Hans-Peter Gatzweiler, and Katrin Meyer, "Räumliche Integration von Ausländern und Zuwanderern," *Informationen zur Raumentwicklung* 8 (2002): 397–414.
5. Bucher et al., "Künftige internationale Wanderungen," 424.
6. See Hansjörg Bucher and Claus Schlömer, "Der demographische Wandel und seine Wohnungsmarktrelevanz," *Forum Wohneigentum* 3 (2003): 121–126, here p. 121.
7. Heinz Fassmann and Rainer Münz, "Auswirkungen der EU-Erweiterung auf die Ost-West-Wanderung," *WSI-Mitteilungen* 17 (2003): 25–32.

TO PLAY WITH SHRINKING – AND SHRINK PLAYFULLY?
Friedrich von Borries

A man in a strange yellow costume with thick padding runs through the city, his cell phone in his hand. He runs around street corners, turns around, and is followed all the while by other people, likewise oddly dressed, who in the end jump on him. These people are not crazy: they are playing Pac-Manhattan,[1] the translation of a video game into reality. Pac-Man was one of the most successful video games in the 1980s. In Pac-Manhattan, a grid map of Manhattan takes the place of a virtual labyrinth. A player dressed as a Pac-Man runs through the city collecting virtual points, just like in the video game, while the other four players try to catch him. All the players are in communication with a control room via cell phone, by which their positions are transmitted via specially developed software. In Pac-Manhattan, not only has the old Pac-Man game been reinterpreted, transformed, and adapted for a new playing space, but also the city has been transformed. A functional space, the urban infrastructure, has become a playing field. The perception of what the city is has been transformed. Can this transformation of meaning, this playful distancing from reality that creates a new perspective on the city, also be implemented in urban planning? Can we gain new approaches to the problem of shrinking cities? Or: Can we play with shrinking in order to shrink playfully?

Three Shrinkage Games: P2-Ripdown, BürgerMeister, Halle an Salle
Where population is declining, buildings are supposed to disappear. But how does this happen? What are the alternatives to the usual course of demolition? In P2-Ripdown, a game developed by urbikon,[2] an architect group located in Berlin and Leipzig, any layman can become an architect and playfully try his hand at experimenting with concrete slabs. In a flash animation accessible via the Internet, the player can remove parts of a P2-type precast concrete building piece by piece per mouse click, thereby creating a new building through the act of demolition. The results can be seen on the Web site: there are realistic designs, such as the diminution of blocks, as well as experimental, futuristic skyscrapers. Static problems don't play a role—it's only a game, after all. Though P2-Ripdown is more than just a game, in fact, because it symbolically explores hidden possibilities and gives the player—who may be someone from the affected region—a new role and new competencies: he becomes a planner.

The reality of planning in shrinking cities is that it is not the inhabitants who decide which buildings are renovated or restored, but the owners and city planners. The inhabitants also are not the ones who make decisions about funding and planning for the future; this is left to political committees. So why not imagine oneself in the role of mayor in a game? This is the idea behind the game BürgerMeister, a strategic board game developed by the Berlin agency raumtaktik.[3] At the beginning of the game, up to four players make a sketch of the most important sites in their city on the empty board. The city is constructed from the basic building blocks of single-unit houses, city streets, and concrete slabs. Small colored stones are placed on the most attractive buildings, and, finally, people are placed in the houses. Now the game begins. If a player lands on an "E," he picks an event card (e.g., floods, European Union funding programs). With a strategy card, a move is made to shape the city, for example by bringing in a waste incinerator or selling a school and leasing it again. In exchange, the player can bring in or remove inhabitants or the colored stones—he develops the future. This political maneuvering is counteracted by an "X," which stands for shrinkage. If, for example, you roll the dice and get a four, you can remove four residents from a building with one colored stone, or one resident in a house that has four colored stones. According to which criterion does shrinking take place—mass or class? The game is over when a player has no inhabitants left. The winner is the one who has the fewest number of victims of the shrinkage process.

BürgerMeister is a board game. The children's city called Halle an Salle, on the other hand, explores the task of the city's administration by way of a model city. Initiated by Thalia Theater,[4] a small city was constructed in 2001/02, after one year of preparation, in empty exhibition halls. The city was modeled, built, and administered by children—adults were forbidden entry. "Children decide what belongs in their city, how it should look, and how it can function; they help build their city. This process set into motion very exciting developments: the children's wishes were spontaneous and full of fantasy."[5]

During the five weeks that the children's city was open, the community quickly grew. Over seventy institutions were established: a bank and a detective agency as well as a swimming pool, fire station, restaurant, and theater. The city had its own currency and binding laws and rules, developed by the children themselves, which they ratified during the daily citizens' meetings and then implemented in the everyday life of their young city.

Games As Interactive Planning Instruments
The three games related to the theme of shrinking cities demonstrate the need to define planning in a new way and to integrate the subjects of planning into the planning process. They are thus part of a long tradition of participatory efforts. But are there any relevant results from the application of such playful instruments?

Often instruments that try to simulate reality are called "games." Particularly in the military, such role-playing and strategy games have a long tradition; there are, for example, complex strategy games in which the possible course and outcome of battles are planned and tested.[6] In addition, the military uses games for training as well as for recruiting[7] and for the simulation of political decision-making.[8]

To what extent are games used in actual city planning? In the United States, the classic city-planning computer game Sim City is used in planning bureaus to simulate possible courses for a city's development. But this track is doomed to failure because a simulation tool based on given parameters produces predictable results, that is, it cannot imagine anything beyond the setting of its familiar parameters. And the media-based participatory process developed by the Bundesamt für Bauwesen und Raumordnung (Federal Office for Building and Regional Planning) and tested in 2000/01 with the title "Planspiel Innenstadt" (Inner-City Planning Game) is not really a game.[9] When citizens present their ideas at workshops, when virtual-city models are developed, and when those who will be affected are allowed a vote via the Internet, this may be a step in the right direction of Net-based participation—but a single mouse click alone does not constitute a game.

The real potential inherent in games is communication. For example, in the context of Copenhagen X, an international planning exhibition in which the future of Copenhagen up

Emerging City

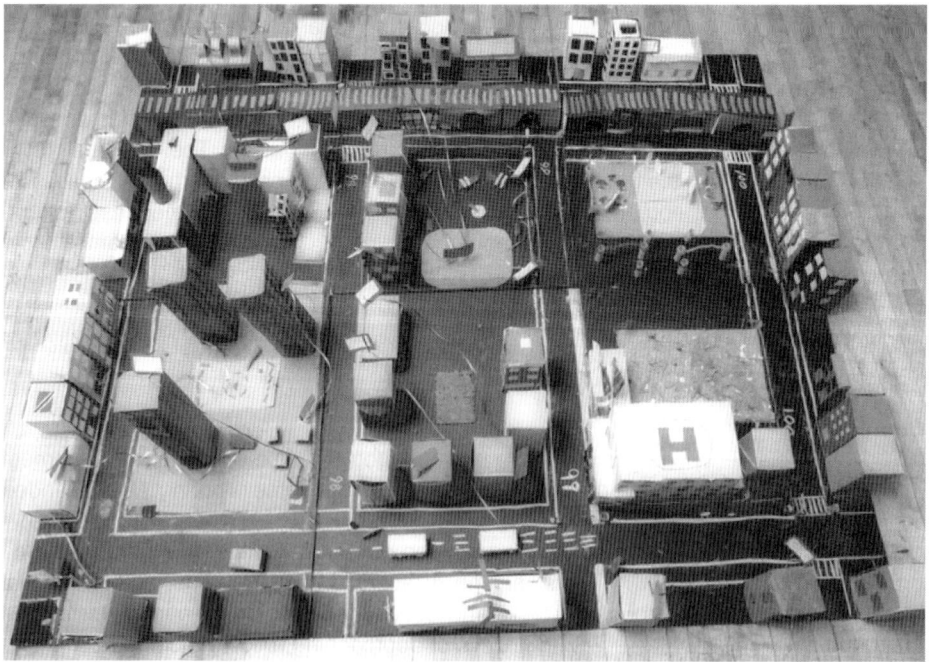

In 2002 students at Heritage High School developed and built a model that allows them to study the development dynamics of East Harlem (Center for Urban Pedagogy, New York).

Being absorbed in the game rather than in the real world implies, however, that one maintains a distance from the object of the game. In order to be played, games must necessarily create a distance to the events played out. So, for example, the board game Monopoly, originally developed as "The Landlords' Game" by Elizabeth Magie, lost its original aim as social critique long ago.

But it is also the distance created by games that constitutes their potential. Participants gain distance to their own routines and open themselves to new ways of thinking. Games do not produce solutions, but their generation of surprises prepares players to imagine new possibilities, leave behind fixed positions, and dive into a new role. On a small scale they encourage people to join in and to have their say. And the ironic distance to reality that they produce enables people to leave behind their habitual thought patterns and to try out new possibilities—in other words, to "play."

This letting go of convention is precisely what is needed in shrinking cities, where decisions are difficult, controversial, and painful. It is perhaps the most important prerequisite for a meaningful urban planning concept and for effective planning action. Only when disciplinary routines are broken down can there be room for new solutions.

Translated from the German by Christina White

Notes
1   See http://www.pacmanhattan.com.
2   See http://www.urbikon.com/_new/seiten/products/p2ripdown.htm#.
3   See http://www.raumtaktik.de.
4   See http://www.kinderstadt-halle.de.
5   Cora Hegewald, project coordinator, in the documentation brochure for Thalia Theater, 2002.
6   A precursor to the type of strategy games that are popular today above all as computer games is the table game developed in 1811 by Georg Leopold Reisswitz for the Prussian General Staff, in which a battlefield is constructed out of combinable landscape elements and battles are played out.
7   The most famous example is the online game America's Army.
8   The German army uses the game Polis for educational purposes. In it, world politics are simulated in the form of role-playing, and thus possible action and reaction models are practiced as they relate to the given economic and political parameters.
9   See http://www.virtuelle-stadtplanung.de/start.htm.
10 See http://www.copenhagenx.dk.
11 See http://www.chora.org/urban.html.
12 See http://www.anothercupdevelopment.org/.

EXCEPTIONAL CITY

Territorial islands allow for experimentation with special rules or measures to balance out local weaknesses, for example by granting unique privileges. Since the Middle Ages, cities have been granted special rights upon their founding or during periods of decline, making them attractive for immigrants and enabling them to revitalize the economy. The special economic zones of today are limited exclusively to offering economic incentives. Emancipatory projects and social-libertarian experiments, by contrast, are very rare.

Exterritories – Practice Challenges Theory

Paula Bialaziewicz

In contrast to political practice, which has largely accepted the existence of Exterritorial Communities (ECs), political science is still struggling to digest the idea of externally ruled enclaves within foreign states. Living examples such as CT HALLE (the Chinese Special Economic Zone in Eastern Germany) or Detroit's ADA (a gated inner-city community administered by South Africa) go against the very fundamentals of political thinking - e.g., self-determination of nations, integrity of territories - and they do not have any historical precedent. However, their appearance follows a logic which this article will attempt to trace.

When external rule is mentioned, comparisons to colonialism are invariably invoked. Colonialism was based on the overwhelming economic and military power of states imposing their organization upon territories which were – at the time – too weak to resist. In its mature form, the physical logic of colonialism was geographic expansion and the creation of coherent areas, not enclavic rule. But the older patterns of trading posts and coastal strongholds (capitanias in the case of Portugal) did have isolated character and many, such as Singapore, Hong Kong and Macao, lasted well into the 20th century. Others, like Gibraltar and Ceuta/Melilla only recently merged into their surrounding states. The Russian-governed enclave of Kaliningrad still exists. It is a heritage not of colonialism, but of earlier forms of colonization. However, all of the cited cases are coastal strongholds, none of them fully enclosed. And - another contrast to today's ECs - external rule there arose by imposition, not by invitation.

Other examples of political enclaves were products of ethnic conflicts: the "Homelands" created by apartheid South Africa or the infamous Palestinian "Autonomous" Territories installed by Israel in the late 20th century. They were based on the idea of segregation of ethnic groups

---

PAULA BIALAZIEWICZ is a political scientist with CRNS in Paris. She lectures at the European University in Gdansk.

within one territory, with a dominant minority imposing the terms of limited self-governance upon the majority. Both examples have fortunately been swept away by the currents of history and they do not offer any model of explanation for today's developments.

So, then, what is the genealogy of exterritorial communities? How did developed societies come to invite external rule within their borders? According to polls, a majority of the British electorate is likely next March to vote in favor of establishing the Indian Territory of "New Liverpool." How can this be explained?

One must recall the character and the dynamics of the globalization process around the millennium, which obviously prepared the ground. With social and economic settings converging after the collapse of the Communist alternative, investment capital became extremely mobile and volatile, allocating and withdrawing resources at short notice, according to the assessment of profits and risks, without following long-term-strategies. Such behavior was supported by the attitudes of shareholders, who would themselves shift their engagements rapidly and allocate their assets wherever profits beckoned. In this process, the criteria for geographic allocation shifted dramatically. Neither the availability of natural resources – the issue in early industrialization - nor the existence of local markets were sufficient criteria for investment allocation. In the end it was the regulative framework – the entire system of labor legislation, taxation, licensing and governance - which shifted the balance toward one location and away from another.

When considering regulation as the key to capital allocation, one must take a glace back at the post-World War II era. Out of the war economies, Europe and Japan, the Communist Block and the United States had developed the highly successful Fordist system: stable, state-guaranteed frameworks for industrial investment. An array of securities and subsidies was available and infrastructure was provided by the state. Gauging the relatively high costs of industrial production in such a regulated economy against lower production costs in low-wage countries with weak regulation, the benefits of the former always prevailed. But excessive regulatory demand by trade unions and consumer groups (prompted by repeated neo-liberal currents) during the 1980s led to a widespread erosion of regulation capacities in these countries towards the end of the 20th century. Even as local governments pledged to guarantee standards, globalization had simply deprived them of the sovereignty and the means to do so.

On the other hand, with globalization on the rise, the political risk of

Paula Bialaziewicz

investment in countries like Mexico, India and finally, China, diminished. During this process, a variety of rather informal exterritorial practices came into being. Privately run labor-intensive production units, so-called maquilladoras, sprang up in Central America. They were based upon special terms negotiated between external investors and local governments. The core element in such deals was limited labor regulation for higher pay. Maquilladoras always had a rather questionable reputation, but they made economic sense to all parties involved. Politicians like Mexico's then-president Vicente Fox was known for addressing national values before elections, and selling national sovereignty against foreign investment when they were over. This kind of opportunism did pay off in political and economic terms. As the Mexican political scientist VALLADARES laid out in his analysis of the Tijuana Region[1], people did not care what miracle was behind the investment boom, as long as local conditions and individual revenues improved. Real benefits from state institutions and social security systems had never really been witnessed, so their disappearance went largely unnoticed. Another form of creeping exterritorial rule was the one linked to the energy sector in large parts of Russia and other former Soviet republics. Companies like Turkey's Turen conglomerate ran, and still run, oil exploration and a wide array of key services in countries like Azerbaijan, Abkhazia and Turkmenistan under special arrangements with local authorities. These arrangements provide not only economic privileges, but also substantial influence in governmental issues. With practically all of the energy and water supply in the hands of Turen, these countries are so entirely dependent on external management that any action by the local governments must respect this reality.

One reason why populations - both in the Caucasus as well as in Central America - came to accept the reality of external rule can be seen in the fact that it did not create any distinct physical image. No foreign armies patrolling, no representative buildings, just a few dusty compounds – fenced, of course, like any other structure of value in these countries. Nor do the foreigners appear on official occasions. The people at center stage are one's own compatriots, the usual corrupt characters known through generations of feudal or totalitarian rule. Academically speaking, external rule is implicit and informal.

The phenomenon of "private government" constitutes another genetic line of today's exterritories. First appearing during the 1990s, privately

---

[1] VALLADARES, Eugénio, Regulación Exterritorial en America Central, Merida 2005

Exterritories – Practice Challenges Theory

managed territories with parastatal behaviour now abound globally. Whether theme parks, golf estates or suburban residential areas - they may encompass the area of entire counties or districts, sometimes housing more than 500.000 people, and they are owned and managed by companies or homeowner associations. These organizations not only regulate access, the social composition of the populace and the use of the property, but they also draw up and enforce rules, and impose fines and evictions. Some areas in the United States, Brazil or South Africa are now so fragmented by all sorts of gated estates that it would probably go unnoticed if one of them were an EC- governed by just another unknown organization. This was the case with Detroit's ADA (African Detroit Area). Its installation did not stir up a lot of emotions among the white middle-class. For this group, Downtown Detroit had been off limits for a long time already. Today, some people would even point at the positive effects of the enterprise. ADA is not only access-controlled (as are the other gated communities), but it is also exit-controlled, a fact which is highly appreciated by the local middle class.

However, in the wake of the anti-state currents during the "innocent" years of globalization, no real exterritorial community would have come about. It was the destruction of the New York World Trade Center by Islamic terrorists in 2001 that initiated a reevaluation of the principle of the "State", starting with its most archaic function, the provider of security. Although the "State" has never regained the all-encompassing meaning it had during most of the 20th century, it did, however, resurface as a regulating instance. This was accompanied by the emergence of some effective elements of global regulation, not the least driven by the traumatic experience of the Bush administration in the US until 2005. The emergence of exterritories must be attributed to the renewed belief in the benefits of state organization, among other factors.

Back to the economy: with a basic system of global taxation and jurisprudence becoming available during the Zeroes, there was little reason for global capital to remain in the old "developed" societies, where the legacy of high social and ecological standards lingered on, without however providing investors with the amount of security and political embedding enjoyed during past Fordist days. The result was a drain of investment towards the reforming societies of Eastern Europe, India and East Asia, most prominently towards China. For some time, these movements followed the traditional center-periphery logic. The "old" societies gained substantial profits from exporting know-how and technology, as well as capital. But the inherited advantages began to wear out as the receiving

Paula Bialaziewicz

societies outgrew the suppliers. One must remember that growth rates in 2005 were 11.5% in China and 9,2% in India, compared to a mere 2.8% in the US and 1.3% in the Euro Zone. Even African states like Mozambique or Ghana boasted 3.2% and 4.3% respectively[2].

The effect on the "old" societies was disastrous. It was a final blow to the industrial districts which had survived earlier waves of de-industrialization. In these years, much of Germany appeared as a stretch of poverty on the way to the prospering landscapes of Poland. Economists agree that it was the backlog of structural reform in countries like Germany and France which caused this severe setback. It became obvious that the former Communist countries, due to the complete re-boot of their economies, were better prepared for global competition than were the former welfare-states with their the timid approach. These latter disintegrated socially into tow groups: pre-globalization privilege holders on the one hand; and the rest of the population, bearing the double burden of reduced competitiveness and continuing high public levies, on the other.

It has been mentioned above that exterritorial schemes were practiced even before the advent of CT HALLE or ADA. What remains to be explored is the reason why these projects were granted the formal status of state rule. One compelling explanation has been given by GONZAGA[3]: In a cultural analysis, she comes to the conclusion that Protestantism plays a central role - not as a religion, but rather as a public attitude. Protestant societies are particularly concerned with order – formal order, to be precise. A Protestant society tends to "pour its sinful behaviour into laws," in contrast to Catholic one, which would practice sin without regulation. GONZAGA cites the Nazi Rassengesetze or South Africa's apartheid legislation as extreme examples of the Protestant's need for formalization. External rule on one's own territory might not exactly qualify as a sin, but it is certainly regarded as disorder – although a necessary one. So, the Protestant logic goes, if something has to be done, it should be done in an orderly way. This would explain why, so far, the only formally declared exterritories are located in countries of Protestant orientation, with another one about to be created in England. Other societies have their exterritories, too, but they are not eager to formalize them. Their cultural background allows them to practice disorder without laws that make it look like order.

But apart from such philosophical aspects, formalization of exterritorial

---

[2] THE WORLD BANK: World Development Indicators 2005
[3] GONZAGA, Tullia, Themes of Post-Liberal Urbanization, MIT Press 2008

Exterritories – Practice Challenges Theory

rule also has more tangible effects. On the basis of the 2006 Treaty between the German Republic and the Republic of China (endorsed by the European Parliament on the 12th of January 2007), the German Federal State collected some EUR 3,2 billion in royalties (Hoheitsentgelt) by the end of 2010, and some EUR 25 billion in taxes per year, 80% of this amount being channeled to the Land of Obersachsen. Further direct revenues come from the lease of infrastructure (such as Leipzig airport), from concessions in public transport and from emission licenses. From the perspective of the Land, the Chinese deal is highly profitable. Before the installation of CT HALLE, the tax-base of the area concerned was estimated at merely EUR 14,2 billion/year, whereas costs related to public services were calculated at EUR 23,5 billion[4].

Certainly, such fruits can only be reaped when there is a sound contractual basis and when implementation is backed by accountable institutions on both sides. With informal exterritorial rule - as in the case of the Central Asian republics mentioned before - direct profits are shared between the few actors in the deal – the higher ranks of government, influential clans and the foreign investor - but relatively little of this trickles down to the population as such. Nevertheless, such informal schemes do create employment, stimulate local markets and improve infrastructure.

Summing up, one can identify two conditions which seem to guarantee exterritorial success: a.) that external rule is invited and not imposed; and b.) that clear terms are set. What seems obvious in retrospect analysis is difficult to achieve in political practice. To Germans, the idea of inviting the Chinese to run a part of one's own country was certainly not easy to sell, nor would it be to anyone else. This is not a subject that would grow over time to become a public demand, an issue that one or the other political group would be eager to adopt. No examples, no references were available. Had the concept not been articulated by Peter Hartz, the notorious innovator at Volkswagen and long-time adviser to then chancellor Gerhard Schröder, no one would even have listened. First, he was cited as to encourage competition between Volkswagen production sites world wide. Those sites which offered the best conditions would be awarded contracts for new models. In order to beat this kind of competition, German plants would have had to reduce labor costs by 30%.[5] Then, a few months later, on the occasion of the inauguration of another Volkswagen plant in Guangzhou

---

[4] ALTHAUSER, WEINFURT: Die Ökonomie der sächsischen Regionen, Studienblätter des Instituts für Wirtschaftsgeographie, Jena 2005
[5] „VW heizt Wettbewerb der Fabriken an" Handelsblatt, August 26th, 2004

Paula Bialaziewicz

in May 2005, Hartz said: "If a place wants to compete with China, it must become like China."[6]

Peter Hartz may have been a visionary, but he was certainly not a dreamer. Talks between the German Federal Government and the Republic of China were already under way - and Mr. Hartz's statement was meant to prepare the ground for the news that would soon begin to leak. After all, the logic was striking: to prevent German production units from going to China, China would have to come to Germany. Once this was understood, it appeared more feasible to accept the complete set of Chinese standards in a limited area inside the country than to try to introduce Chinese standards for the country as a whole. From the Chinese point of view, the scheme was just another Special Economic Zone, a familiar practice since the early 1990ies.

However, CT HALLE would not have materialized if there had not been a number of "soft" factors easing the entire process. One was a widespread nostalgia among members of the East German population who had grown up under Communist rule and regarded China with sympathy, as a regulated market economy based on Socialist ideals. The post-communist PDS Party exploited such sentiments and played a pivotal role in creating public acceptance. But conservatives also let their admiration for Chinese (Prussian!) discipline override religious or ethnic concerns. Even the far right expressed hopes that the creation of a confined territory would contribute to reducing the presence of foreigners in the rest of the country.

But in the end, the entire concept had to be poured into a legal mold. The core idea called for Germany to waive its legislation and standards in a part of its territory, so ways had to be found to accommodate this objective within the constitutional framework. The German constitution being based on the equal application of law regardless of place and person (Gleichheitsgrundsatz), the only way to achieve exemption was the ceding of the territory in question to an other state – for a limited period. It was up to the Chinese to accept the continuation of certain elements of German regulation within the Territory – not as German law, but on contractual terms, to be laid down in the treaty. In principle, each item was subject to negotiation, but the core issues – such as property rights and the ban of capital punishment – were never actually questioned.

For political science, the emergence of ECs opens an entire range of new

---

[6] „Volkswagen prefers China to Germany", Financial Times, May 25th, 2005

Exterritories – Practice Challenges Theory

fields to be explored. What is the role of the global regulative framework in the process? Does it encourage the venture by offering implicit guarantees and a reliable arbitration forum? To what extent has the principle of "State" changed during the globalization process? Could it be that the "State" is losing its national connotation –becoming just another legal format for global economic activities? Will "State" organization one day become a commodity, like a franchising system? Those interested in engaging in studying this phenomenon should do so quickly – in order to keep up with reality unfolding.

RECRUITMENT OF SETTLERS IN THE HISTORY OF PRUSSIA
Carsten Benke

Historically, the revitalization of cities and rural regions that had declined economically and demographically following natural catastrophes, wars, or other crises often required—in addition to local initiatives—active public aid and settlement measures. If the local structures had been irreparably damaged, reconstruction was almost impossible without outside help. In such cases, the intentional recruitment of new settlers was an indispensable part of revitalization measures. In times of limited population growth, recruitment of external populations necessitated the guarantee of special rights in order to compete with other territories for qualified immigrants.

Already in the Medieval period, when thousands of new cities and towns were being established in central Europe during the twelfth to fourteenth centuries, measures to recruit settlers and strategies to create successful local communities could be found. In parts of the Ostsiedlung (the German settlement area in Central and Eastern European territories) and in areas of internal colonization in the old Reich, towns and villages were planned and settled in order to develop regions that were considered underdeveloped. While the older, "unplanned" towns had fought with the local lords to wrestle out a set of special rights, newly founded and laid-out towns were often granted a rights ordinance from the start that provided extensive privileges and served to secure an economic base and attract settlers. The special privileges were aimed at both the individual citizen—"Stadtluft macht frei" ("city air makes you free")—and the town community as a whole. In its ideal form the medieval town was largely self-administered and had the right to engage in commerce, markets, and trade, as well as having its own court. Even nonfree foreigners who arrived later were eligible for the town's special privileges after a certain period of time. The special status of the town was symbolically represented by the wall around it that separated it from the surrounding feudal lands.

The growing strength of several German territorial states in the Early Modern period gradually reduced the importance of the towns' special privileges after 1500. Economic and political crises also contributed to the further decline of the role played by the free cities. The Thirty Years' War (1618–1648), in particular, had a lasting crippling effect on the city system. The regions that were particularly affected lost between a third and a half of their previous populations. Some areas were slow to regenerate after the war, many towns had deserted lots, and some agricultural fields even became overgrown. These areas were in need of planning, long-term revitalization measures, and external impulses. Though it cannot be said that there was a modern development policy with a clear agenda in place, the state did greatly contribute to the revitalization of settlement structures and the economy.

The example of Prussia illustrates typical measures to regenerate ravaged provinces and towns. From the perspective of the immigrants who were so central to revitalization, most areas of the rather poor region of Brandenburg-Prussia were not initially attractive in comparison to other territories. But the religious intolerance found during the Counter-Reformation in the seventeenth century led to large waves of migration all over Europe, and those who were on the move could be enticed to Prussia with targeted recruitment measures. Potential settlers in other countries learned about the privileges and attractions of the newly developed territories through announcements in foreign newspapers and from traveling solicitors for the new settlements. The harsh realities in the new, rather backward territories did not precisely reflect the advertisements, but for those in need they did represent a new prospect.

Incoming settlers were not usually recruited as individuals, but rather as whole colonies. These communities, organized by religious confession, were granted the right to self-administration in religious and legal questions. The initial motivation that spurred the new settlers—Bohemians, Jews, Huguenots, refugees from the Netherlands, and Protestants from Salzburg—was the promise of religious freedom in the new colonies. Other important privileges were exemption from taxation and military service for several years, personal and economic liberty, and financial support for building a home and setting up a business. Often immigrants were given tools for work, construction materials, and farming land at no charge.

Depending upon where the settlers came from, the rights they were granted differed. While some groups were required to enter into long-term contracts for a certain location in order to receive benefits, other colonists were largely allowed to choose for themselves where they would like to settle. The degree of the tolerance shown depended upon the group in question, which was placed within the following hierarchy of sorts: Lutherans, Calvinists, Evangelical sects, and Catholics. Persecuted Jews were given a limited right of stay, while highly qualified Huguenot tradesmen were granted much greater concessions.

Taking in refugees was not a goal in and of itself; it served to stabilize absolutist rule and the mercantilist economic system. Yet solidarity toward fellow members of one's own confession was also an important motive. It was necessary, however, to ensure that investments to attract foreigners, paid for from the king's treasury, proved good investments, meaning that immigration was not to be a form of temporary asylum but rather was meant to lead to permanent settlement. According to state theory of the time, a growing population was considered "the country's treasure chest" that promised long-term political and military might. More important than the demographic effects in the long run were the economic and cultural impulses that skilled immigrants brought with them.

Since the 1660s, Brandenburg-Prussia had been pursuing a systematic "active settlement policy for large areas" that was to last until the death of Frederick II in 1786.[1] In the years 1661–1683, as many as seven decrees on immigration were issued. During the same period, a system of public support aimed specifically at science and commerce arose, as well as the systematic development of regional infrastructure through the construction of channels and roads.

Most remembered today is the settlement of French Huguenots, who were forced to leave France after the Edict of Nantes was abolished in 1685, thereby stripping them of their protection. Prince-elector Frederick William of Brandenburg offered the Huguenots refuge and a new home in his territory under the Edict of Potsdam, guaranteeing them tolerance and support. Those who were willing to migrate were then put to the test by the bureaucracy of Brandenburg-Prussia, which did not desire to take in the poor and unskilled. But the Prussian state had limited possibilities because most Huguenots—and particularly those who showed economic potential—preferred to emigrate to England or Holland, that is, to countries that were economically further developed.

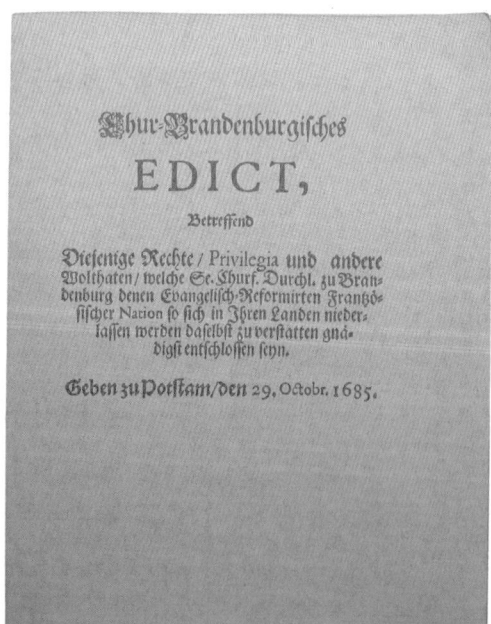

The Edict of Potsdam of 1685 allowed French immigrants to settle freely in Prussia. ▲ "The Great Prince-Elector welcomes the refugees to his territory." ▼ The title page of the historical edict.

The Edict allowed the French immigrants to settle wherever they thought it would "be most comfortable for their profession and lifestyle."[2] But at the same time, certain settlement areas were suggested to them. Up to the year 1699, 52 Huguenot colonies were developed in Prussia. The Uckermark, which was then, as it is now, an economically and infrastructurally underdeveloped region afflicted with population decline, became a center for agricultural settlements. A large proportion of immigrants settled in the cities and towns, however. As many as 3,008 Huguenot refugees found a new home in Magdeburg, which brought the town new impulses for regeneration after the devastating destruction of the Thirty Years' War.

Deserted lots and empty homes in the towns and cities were taken over by the immigrants, and in part new suburbs were constructed. In Berlin, the Huguenots settled largely in Dorotheenstadt and Friedrichstadt. Later, Bohemian religious refugees also settled in these areas. In order to ensure a continual influx of skilled tradesmen, they were subject only to a mild assimilation policy.

One of the largest settlement measures during this period was the reconstruction of East Prussia following the plague epidemic of 1709-1711. More than a third of the population died of the disease, which compounded the devastating population decline that had been ongoing since the mid-seventeenth century. It was a "blessing" for Prussia under King Frederick William I when approximately 16,000 Protestants expelled from Salzburg settled in the vacant towns and villages of this province in 1731-1732. To aid reconstruction and improve regional infrastructure, new *Retablissementsstädte* (revitalization towns) were founded: for example, Gumbinnen, Darkehmen, and Pillkallen. These new towns were granted certain privileges, though by and large there was no place for self-administered citizenship in the old Prussian concept of state.

The new devastation brought by the Seven Years' War (1756-1763) made it necessary to continue with the settlement measures. In this context, under Frederick II around 300,000 new settlers arrived, often settling on new land created by water drainage, for example in Oderbruch. By 1786, every fifth Prussian was from a family of colonists.

But the Prussian peopling policies do not represent an unqualified success story, and they were not as targeted as the Borussian myth would lead us to believe. Many settlement projects went nowhere, and some immigrants left again. The privileged acceptance of religious refugees often caused envy and resentment among the local people, and even the settlement of Calvinist protestants in Lutheran Prussia was not without its conflicts. Integration was eventually successful, however, though it occurred more rapidly in the larger towns than in rural areas. Many towns were able to escape stagnation and decline due to the influx of settlers and state infrastructure measures. This made the settlement policies successful overall and accelerated reconstruction and development. The economic impact of any given immigrant group should not be overestimated, but the settlers did contribute significantly to the revitalization of many towns and the establishment of new trades, for example wallpaper and, in particular, textile manufacturing. They thus played a role in creating new and lasting economic structures.

Another good example of the special communities established specifically for immigrants in the smaller German territories were the privileged towns for exiles founded by the princes. Friedrichstadt, Glückstadt, Freudenstadt, and Erlangen were established solely as places of refuge for those exiled for religious reasons, yet they also served as an impulse for regional development. The immigrant communities were granted extensive rights, although they were still subject to the supervision of the state. Many of these exile towns did not develop beyond a modest start, founded as the economic project of an often inexperienced and overburdened prince. Many settlers moved on after such a bad start, or once again became the victims of wars in their new homes. In other cases, taking in religious refugees led to unexpected positive effects, for example in the mining towns of the Erz Mountains in Saxony, where Bohemian refugees arrived with knowledge of the textile industry and the manufacture of musical instruments. These special trades often became an essential economic base for the region after the mining industry declined.

The immigrants of this era were not necessarily all paupers; they were able to assert themselves in relation to those who were handing out the benefits. The free imperial city of Frankfurt initially showed tolerance toward the Reformists from the Netherlands, to whom they granted asylum. But the settlers' rights were limited by the Lutheran majority in 1593 and 1596. When the Prince of Hanau then signaled his interest in giving them further refuge, these economically powerful Calvinist reformers were in a better bargaining position than the ruler of an insignificant small territory. They were thus able to strike an advantageous compromise to settle in the new town of Neu Hanau in 1597 with expanded rights.

The majority of these recruitment and development measures of the Early Modern period—particularly in Prussia—were carried out by the state, while most towns did not have much of an opportunity to independently manage their own development because they lacked the necessary legal autonomy. Fundamental change came to Prussia with the new Städteordnung, the municipal reform that granted local self-government for towns from 1808 onward, following the decisive defeat against Napoleon in 1806. Reformers associated with the most influential minister, Baron von Stein, wanted to use the changes to transform stagnant communities into independent towns with active citizens, thereby revitalizing the war-ridden regions. The new self-administration for towns also spread to other German territories and allowed the towns to respond more self-sufficiently to the challenges of the nineteenth century. The towns' new right to self-administration, however, led to a loss of the old privileges for the Huguenot communities within them, who had long since been integrated.

Targeted settlement policies were no longer necessary in the nineteenth century due to the enormous growth of the overall population; in fact, for a long time overpopulation was feared. Only at the end of the century, when birthrates were dropping and populations declined in some regions, was there another change of paradigm. State-initiated population and settlement policies became relevant again, but this time in the form of a racialist drive to propagate one's own people. In order to counter the shrinking numbers of German-speaking residents in some eastern provinces of Prussia, the settlement law of 1886 was passed as part of the Germanization policy, hereby promoting the settlement of Germans with special privileges on Polish land. The plan was not very successful in the way envisioned by its initiators; what it did accomplish, however, was an enduring poisoning of relations between the different peoples.

Although Germany became less and less open to immigration, many commercial sectors remained dependent upon foreign workers. Before the First World War, approximately one million foreigners were working in Germany as seasonal laborers with very precarious rights. After the period of seasonal labor was over, most of them were expelled again in order to prevent their permanent settlement. The citizenship law of 1913 further buttressed this policy of expulsion by introducing the principle of *ius sanguinis* (i.e., citizenship according to one's ancestry and ethnicity and not according to the place of birth) to the relatively young German nation-state, which had been united in 1871. This law, which fixed the status of immigrants and generations of their descendants as "foreigners," would not be fundamentally changed until around ninety years later.

Historically, supporting immigration by privileging rather than disadvantaging it proved to be very successful, bringing decisive demographic and economic impulses. Today we cannot afford to do without external impulses, social support in combination with local self-organization, and the importation of people and ideas. Historical experiences with immigration where special rights were granted for certain locations and immigration was actively supported can contribute a wealth of knowledge to contemporary debates about economically disadvantaged and shrinking regions.

Translated from the German by Christina M. White

Notes
1   Gerd Heinrich, "Toleranz als Staatsraison: Ursachen und Wirkungen des Potsdamer Edikts (1685)," in *Geschichte als Aufgabe: Festschrift für Otto Büsch,* ed. Wilhelm Treue (Berlin: Colloquium Verlag, 1988), 29-54, here p. 35.
2   Quoted in Eckart Birnstiel and Andreas Reinke, "Hugenotten in Berlin," in *Von Zuwanderern zu Einheimischen: Hugenotten, Juden, Böhmen, Polen in Berlin,* ed. Barbara John and Stefi Jersch-Wenzel (Berlin: Nicolaische, 1990), 13-152, here p. 53.

Literature
Engel, Evamaria. *Die deutsche Stadt des Mittelalters.* Munich: Beck, 1993.
Hipp, Hermann. "Friedrich III: Die Stadt und die Fremden," *Stadtbauwelt* 24 (1993).
John, Barbara, and Stefi Jersch-Wenzel, eds., *Von Zuwanderern zu Einheimischen: Hugenotten, Juden, Böhmen, Polen in Berlin.* Berlin: Nicolaische, 1990.
Kathe, Heinz. *Preußen zwischen Mars und Musen: Eine Kulturgeschichte von 1100 bis 1920.* Munich: Koehler & Amelang, 1993.
Neugebauer, Wolfgang. *Zentralprovinz im Absolutismus: Brandenburg im 17. und 18. Jahrhundert.* Bibliothek der brandenburgischen und preußischen Geschichte 5, Brandenburgische Geschichte in Einzeldarstellungen 4. Berlin: Verlag Arno Spitz, 2001.
Planitz, Hans. *Die deutsche Stadt im Mittelalter,* 5th ed. of 1954 original. Wiesbaden: VMA-Verlag, 1996.
Schoeps, Hans-Joachim. *Preußen: Geschichte eines Staates,* new edition. Berlin: Ullstein, 1995.
Stoob, Heinz. "Über frühneuzeitliche Städtetypen," in *Forschungen zum Städtewesen in Europa,* vol. I, *Räume, Formen und Schichten der mitteleuropäischen Städte: Eine Annäherung,* ed. Heinz Stoob. Cologne: Böhlau, 1970.
Wehler, Hans-Ulrich. *Deutsche Gesellschaftsgeschichte,* vol. I, *Vom Feudalismus des Alten Reiches bis zur defensiven Modernisierung der Reformära 1700-1815.* Munich: Beck, 1987.

NON-PLAN

Great Britain, 1969/1977
Reyner Banham, Paul Barker, Peter Hall, and Cedric Price

"Non-plan: An Experiment in Freedom" is the title of a lead article from the March 20, 1969, issue of the left-liberal magazine *New Society*. The four authors—architecture critic Reyner Banham, architect Cedric Price, geographer Peter Hall, and the magazine's publisher, Paul Barker—make a call for a radical experiment in urban planning: "Town-and-country planning has today become an unquestioned shibboleth. Yet few of its procedures or value judgments have any solid basis, except delay. Why not have the courage, where practical, to let people shape their own environment?"[1]

The authors maintain that conventional planning is determined by the assessments of conservative, middle-class elites and seldom leads to the desired results. They see bureaucratic planning restrictions and preservation lobbyists as being responsible for the present stagnation in growth. If construction and development in cities and regions were allowed to proceed without regulation, the existing pressure to develop could progress unfettered. "What would happen if there were no plan? What would people prefer to do if their choice were untrammeled?... This is what we're now proposing: a precise and carefully observed experiment in non-planning."[2]

For three clearly defined zones, exemplary English urban regions, the authors sketch various scenarios that might develop if all forms of spatial planning regulation were stopped. Increasing individual mobility, highways, and airports are the most important factors in development. They make another kind of urbanism possible, one that takes pressure off the core cities: low-rise buildings spread out over the countryside. What emerge are leisure-time landscapes of single family units, highways, and gas stations, local recreation areas, and shopping centers.

According to the authors, free rein in planning and shaping development would allow the true taste of the people to show through in urban spaces: "At the least, one would find out what the people really want; at the most, one might discover the hidden style of mid-20th century Britain."[3] The American "strip"—a business district which is ideal for cars and is lit up with advertising billboards—is thought here to represent the aesthetic impact of pop culture on urbanism, an influence the authors say should be allowed to assert itself.

The authors' passionate suggestions manifest an uninhibited belief in growth, progress, and mass prosperity. The first signs of crisis are countered with the deregulation of planning. There is no fear of urban sprawl, rather an acknowledgment of new (sub)urban forms of development. Above all, however, this is about a true experiment in laissez faire—one that could go wrong—and/or about garnering information from a spatially limited experiment under changed conditions.

"It would be a good zone in which to tack on to the basic Non-Plan scheme a number of other possible try-outs: freedom for local authorities to raise money in ways they see fit (a sales tax, a sail tax, a poll tax, a pony tax); 'pot' shops instead of all those declining tobacconists (and see how different the population seems, or how similar, after five or ten years) ..."[4]

NEWsociety

20 March 1969 No 338 1s 6d weekly

Robert Holman	WRONG POVERTY PROGRAMME
John Berger	MAGRITTE RECONSIDERED
David Marquand	EDUCATION BACKLASH
Rayner Banham Paul Barker Peter Hall Cedric Price	NON-PLAN: AN EXPERIMENT IN FREEDOM

"Write it in neon: NON-PLAN IS GOOD FOR YOU." The authors of the article "Non-plan: An Experiment in Freedom" explain, "We seem to be so afraid of freedom."

That the libertarian-anarchical impulses motivating both this attack on conservative planning culture and the critique of the overregulated welfare state have much in common with a neoconservative and economically liberal position becomes clear in the further development of the non-plan idea in later contexts.

The Freeport Solution

In a lecture at the annual conference of the Royal Town Planning Institute in 1977, Peter Hall expands on the non-plan concept, bringing it into the economic context. The urban and economic situation is now clearly affected by the crisis of deindustrialization, and Hall's suggestions refer to the phenomenon of shrinking in British inner cities. For the very difficult cases, he describes a special visionary solution:

> If we really want to help inner cities, and cities generally, we may have to use highly unorthodox methods.... It would result in a final possible recipe, which I would call the Freeport solution. This is essentially an essay in non-plan. Small, selected areas of inner cities would be simply thrown open to all kinds of initiative, with minimal control. In other words, we would aim to recreate the Hong Kong of the 1950s and 1960s inside inner Liverpool or inner Glasgow.
> The first element would encourage entrepreneurs and capital. The area would be outside United Kingdom exchange controls. Businessmen from the Third World would be welcome to come in and set up their factories. Since the area would be outside UK customs limits, all goods would be imported and sold free of duties and indirect taxes, including VAT. Such an area would thus be a Shannon Airport, or Canary Islands, right in the heart of one of our cities.
> Secondly, this area would be based on fairly shameless free enterprise. It would be free of United Kingdom taxes, social services, industrial and other regulations. Bureaucracy would be kept to an absolute minimum. So would personal and corporate taxation. Trades' unions would be allowed, as in Hong Kong, but there would be no closed shops. Wages would find their own level.
> Thirdly, residence in the area would be based on choice. Since the special taxation and customs arrangements would render the area ineligible for Common Market membership, it would be mostly appropriately administered as a British Crown Colony or protectorate: the Isle of Man provides one model. Existing residents—and there would not be many—would be free to stay or leave, since they would hold UK passports. However, if they stayed they would have to do so on new terms, under the laws and regulations of the Crown Colony. Their tax levels would be much reduced, but so would their benefits. And, if they then tried to enter the United Kingdom, they might not be allowed to do so until their social security payments were made up....
> Such an area would not conform at all to modern British notions of the welfare state. But it could be economically vigorous on the Hong Kong model. Since it would represent an extremely drastic last-ditch solution

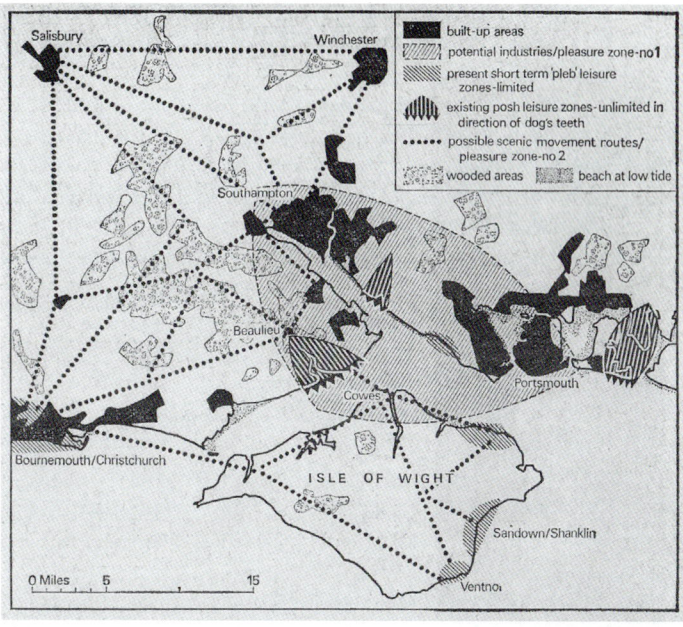

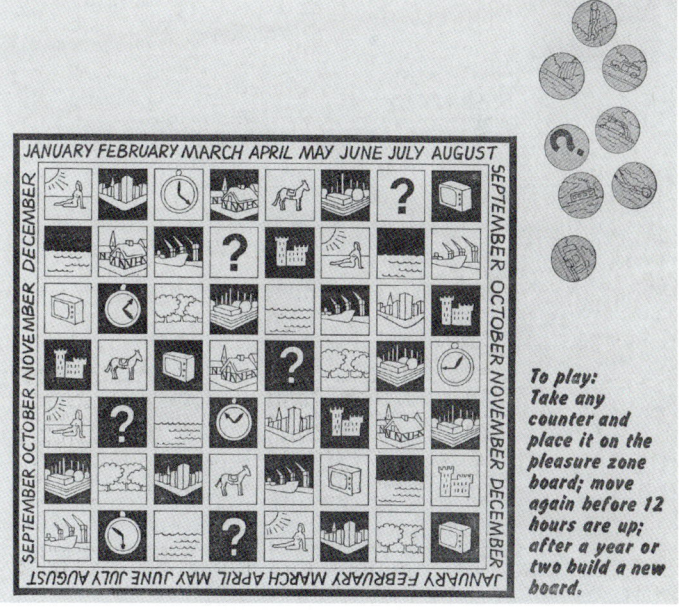

▲ Cedric Price drafted a development scenario with industrial, residential, and new-age leisure and recreation areas for one of the "Non-plan" test regions—the agglomeration Southampton-Portsmouth and the Isle of Wight.

▼ "Non-plan" celebrates liberation from regulations and permanent instability. With this game plan, Cedric Price challenges players to change location every twelve hours and to construct a new playing board every one or two years.

to urban problems, it could be tried only on a very small scale. It is most appropriate to those inner city areas which are largely abandoned, and denuded of people; or [alternatively] areas with very grave social and economic problems. I envisage it as an appropriate solution for a decaying seaport such as Liverpool. Here, it could help build the basis of a vigorous tourist trade, since it should encourage a huge movement of buyers both from the United Kingdom and mainland Europe. Again, the vast tourist boom in recent years in Hong Kong and Singapore, based very largely on the rock-bottom competitive prices in their shops, provides a foretaste of what could happen.[5]

Hall's vision was taken up and further expanded just one year later by the (conservative) Tory politician Sir Geoffrey Howe. In a speech before the Bow Group, a renowned planning and development agency, Howe called for the designation of deregulated and debureaucratized inner-city development areas, which was later realized in the form of "enterprise zones" following the inauguration of the Thatcher government. The critical-emancipatory moment that underlay the original non-plan concept was no longer to be found. (Ed.)

Translated from the German by Christina M. White

Notes
1   See Reyner Banham, Paul Barker, Peter Hall, and Cedric Price, "Non-plan: An Experiment in Freedom," *New Society* 338 (March 1969): 434–443. Republished in *Non-plan: Essays on Freedom, Participation and Change in Modern Architecture and Urbanism*, ed. Jonathan Hughes and Simon Sadler (Oxford, UK: Architectural Press, 2000).
2   Ibid.
3   Ibid.
4   Ibid.
5   This text is an excerpt from Peter Hall, "Green Fields and Grey Areas," in *Proceedings: Royal Town Planning Institute; Annual Conference* (London, 1977), 1–12.

ENTERPRISE ZONES IN THE UNITED KINGDOM
Klaus Zehner

The problem of shrinking cities and regions has been recognized in the United Kingdom since the 1920s. In those years, for the first time in the country's history, entire city regions were sinking into a spiral of recession, deindustrialization, and unemployment—above all the old industrial regions in the North: Greater Manchester, Merseyside (Liverpool), Tyneside (Newcastle), Teesside (Middlesborough), Clydeside (Glasgow), and South Wales (Cardiff, Newport). Precipitated by worldwide competition and flagging sales in the traditional and heavily export-dependent key industries, in particular mining, textiles, and shipbuilding, the old industrial regions slowly lost their economic base. The result was a decline in population due to people moving to other regions, for example to prospering southeast England.

Great Britain thus developed concepts for supporting economically disadvantaged regions as early as the years between the wars (starting in 1934), when Germany had yet to develop its own regional development plans. First, regional "special areas" in need of aid were identified. In order to stimulate the local economy in these regions, the government granted businesses willing to settle there direct subsidies and low-interest loans. In addition, several new "trading estates" and "industrial estates" were designated that were to attract businesses with their solid infrastructure.

Over the next four decades, British economic aid policy alternately extended the special areas receiving support to include larger areas under the Labour government and then cut them down again under the Conservatives.[1] In the late 1970s it became clear, however, that, regardless of the size of the subsidized regions, the general "watering can" method had not worked. In the spring of 1979, on the eve of the Thatcher government's inauguration, the United Kingdom presented the image of a socially torn and politically split country, in which not enough had been invested in industry over too long a time and where the economy had been paralyzed by strikes.

The Main Features of Urban Development and Economic Subsidies under Margaret Thatcher

The Conservative government made waves shortly after it entered office with a radical paradigm shift in business development and urban development policies. The "New Right philosophy" emphasized the advantages of the market economy, the importance of the private economic sector, and the dangers that lurked for businesses if government or nongovernment organizations (for example, unions and associations) had too heavy a hand in the economy. This basically meant a farewell to the welfare principle. Margaret Thatcher even went a step further by dissolving the social contract drawn up between the social classes during the Second World War. In the place of government regulation and welfare, a laissez-faire understanding of socioeconomics and regional development and an emphasis on deregulation took over.

Thatcher explained her position in unambiguous terms at the Conservative government's first convention following her election as prime minister: "Let me give you my vision: A man's right to work as he will, to spend what he earns, to own property, to have

Exceptional City

Population decline in cities with > 100,000 inhabitants
- \> 50%
- 25%–49%
- 10%–24%

- ■ Enterprise Zone 1st generation
- ◆ Enterprise Zone 2nd generation
- ▲ Enterprise Zone 3rd generation

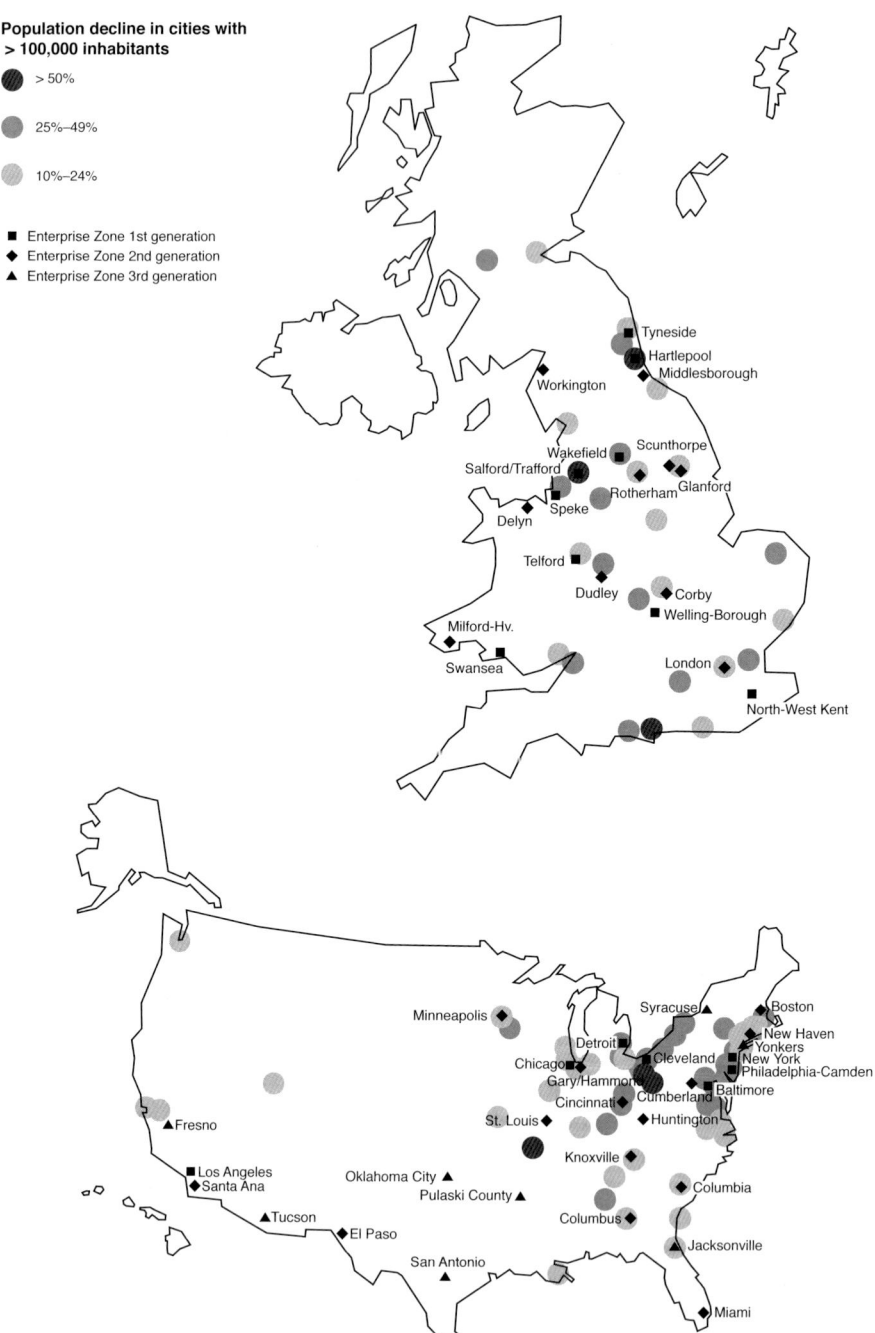

▲ In 1981 the British government under Thatcher introduced special economic zones with the aim of reviving designated inner cities through comprehensive deregulation.
▼ The United States later adopted the concept and developed it further.

the state as servant and not as master. These are the British inheritance. They are the essence of a free country, and on that freedom all of our other freedoms depend."[2]

The neoliberal strategy for business development and urban development policy was that the private business sector, rather than the government and municipalities, should play the leading role in urban renewal. What was new, above all, was that subsidies and funding instruments were not to be divided among whole regions, but rather concentrated in limited urban areas. Those areas to profit most from this plan were inner-city industrial districts and working-class neighborhoods, where abandoned docks and train depots as well as industrial wastelands had long since become visible signs of economic decline.

The Concept of Enterprise Zones

A main instrument for realizing this strictly market-based planning approach were the "enterprise zones," which were small economic zones (of 50 to 454 hectares), usually in brownfield areas, that were granted special status. Between June 1981 and April 1982, the government designated ten enterprise zones in Great Britain and one in Northern Ireland. With only one exception (the steelworks town of Corby in eastern England), the enterprise zones were in large cities with severe economic development problems. Also considered for special status was London (the London Docklands), which was faced with a steep drop in industrial jobs in the 1970s. In the years 1983 to 1984, fourteen other enterprise zones were established. These were, however, in smaller, more remote cities and towns. Since 1984, fourteen more enterprise zones have been established. The measures will expire in 2006.

The special advantages granted the enterprise zones were as follows:
- exemption for businesses from commercial taxes for a period of ten years,
- easier write-offs for investors,
- exemption from land development taxes (taxes on the value appreciation of property),
- exemption from education taxes,
- exemption from the obligation to supply the government with statistical information,
- relief from customs duties,
- exemption from industrial development certifications (a measure to reduce the concentration of industrial works, introduced in 1960),
- easier access to permits,
- a timely processing of construction proposals (within a maximum of two weeks).

In declaring the enterprise zones, the Conservative government adopted a concept developed in the late 1960s by Sir Peter Hall, Professor of Urban Planning at the University of Reading and former director of the Fabian Society, which promotes democratic socialism in the United Kingdom. The concept went down in international planning history as the "Non-plan." Hall's idea was to create the prerequisites necessary for the development of highly skilled jobs in the subsidized region, for example in research and development. These jobs, Hall postulated, were decisive for the future of the city's economy: "We should encourage science-based industry in the cities, especially in their inner areas. The value of such industry is first, that it is the only kind of manufacturing that still shows real growth in an advanced industrial economy."[3] In addition, attractive milieus for businesses in the finance, media, and cultural sectors were to be established: "That means encouraging activities like banking, finance and insurance; the mass media, including publishing of books and magazines and newspapers, television and radio, all kinds of new audio-visual technologies, advertising and PR, plus entertainment; consultancy activities ... and higher education and culture."[4] In order to achieve this goal, disadvantaged districts in the "inner cities"—which in Great Britain refers not to the city centers but to the industrial and working-class districts bordering them that emerged in the Victorian period—were granted a special legal and fiscal status: "If we really want to help inner cities, and cities generally, we may have to use highly unorthodox methods.... It would result in a final possible recipe, which I would call the Freeport solution.... Small, selected areas of inner cities would be simply thrown open to all kinds of initiative, with minimal control. In other words, we would aim to recreate the Hong Kong of the 1950s and 1960s inside inner Liverpool or inner Glasgow."[5]

Under the direction of public-private partnerships, less used or abandoned urban spaces were to turn into flourishing and attractive locations for the post-Fordist service industries. It was precisely this aspect of Hall's approach that the Conservatives took up and transformed into the enterprise zones. It is worth noting that Sir Geoffrey Howe, finance minister at the time, declared the enterprise zones an "experiment" and not a political concept—presumably because he would thus be better able to defend the plan if it should fail. Experiments may fail; business development concepts, on the other hand, must bring results.

The Wider Effects of the Enterprise Zones

The designation of the enterprise zones had its most immediate effect, of course, in transforming fallow lots into new, and often spectacular, economic zones within a short period of time. The Canary Wharf at the London Docklands and the Salford Quays in Manchester are perhaps the best examples of this. But of greater interest was the question of whether the enterprise zones would contribute to a stimulation of the regional economy and thus have a wider effect. The experiment could only be considered successful if it could be shown that there were meaningful external effects.

A small-scale analysis of changes in the unemployment rate between 1984 and 1990 clearly shows, however, that the first generation of enterprise zones, primarily in large industrial cities, was only able to minimally stimulate the city's economy. The second generation, on the other hand, proved more successful. The zones brought tangible relief not only at the municipal level, but in some cases also in the regional labor markets.[6] The map on page 650 shows that in the labor market regions of Telford (West Midlands), Scunthorpe, and Glanford (East Midlands), as well as Middlesborough and Hartlepool (Northeast), the jobless figures were lowered at a significantly faster rate than the national average.

Overall, however, the enterprise zones were only a modest success, with the few above-mentioned exceptions. In other words, their contribution to the regional economy was mostly only minimal. One of the main reasons for the failure of the approach is that too few growth industries were involved. Instead of bringing in sustainable businesses, a high number of businesses were established in the zones that were bound to have a weak effect on the regional economy. Examples include retail and wholesale. In the enterprise zones of Dudley (West Midlands) and Newcastle, for example, regional shopping centers were built that could not be expected to integrate adequately with the local economy and that, in addition, were a threat to businesses in both city centers. In Wellingborough (East

Midlands), the central location and easy access to the national highway system attracted logistics enterprises, which also had a weak effect on the regional economy. In addition, important retail businesses set up their central delivery warehouses here. In Swansea, the enterprise zone brought in large retailers, car dealers, and even a hotel. These developments were perhaps understandable given the complete deregulation as regards which types of businesses were allowed to settle in the zones, yet with the single exception of the London Docklands, they did not accomplish the goals set out by Hall.

The concept of enterprise zones was nonetheless internationally renowned and even copied in some countries. In the United States, enterprise zones became an important policy element of the Reagan era, but ultimately the program did not pass in the U.S. Congress and was thus never enacted. As a result, the 400–500 enterprise zones designated in the United States beginning in 1981 never developed beyond the status of small-scale models. Critics often spoke of the program as a "toothless tiger."

This changed when Bill Clinton entered office in 1993. Clinton set up a funding program that went by the name "Empowerment Zones/Enterprise Community Initiatives" and was enacted in the same year. The empowerment zones were a central element in Clinton's "new contract" with the cities. Overall, eighty cities profited from the measure, which Clinton used primarily to revitalize social and economic life and urban development in the inner cities. The program specifically mandated that, in addition to economic goals, the social and ecological effects of the proposed measures must be taken into account. And one of the main prerequisites for the designation as an empowerment zone was that activities be linked and coordinated by various formal and informal local actors, that is, people and organizations from the affected districts and neighborhoods. It was presumably this overly ambitious array of goals that ultimately led to the minimal impact of the empowerment zones.

More recently, enterprise zones have been used in threshold countries and new European Union member states as business development instruments. Examples are the "special economic zones" in Poland, Slovakia, and the Czech Republic.

Summary

Despite isolated successes, the experiment of enterprise zones must ultimately be declared a failure. The decisive reason for this can be found in the false interpretations of Hall's original idea. His goal was to attract sustainable growth industries and key industries. The spatial concentration of these businesses, on the other hand, played a lesser role in his theoretical considerations. In practice, however, the complete deregulation of businesses entering the zones opened the door to too many that did not qualify as key or growth industries as designated by Hall. The desired external or spillover effect thus necessarily remained rather minimal.

If such an experiment is to be carried out again—for example in the eastern German states—this aspect must be taken into account. This means that every industrial sector under consideration must be evaluated and ranked with respect to its potential feedback effect and potential value for the region. In granting access to space in the enterprise zones, attention must be paid to these rankings. In addition, in choosing the location for such zones, the quality of the individual locations must be closely considered. The potential of a given location must serve as a crucial factor. If the potential is not high enough, for example due to inadequate linkage with supraregional highway systems, then it may be assumed that after the subsidy measures expire, businesses will leave again.

Translated from the German by Christina M. White

Notes

1. Heinz Heineberg, *Großbritannien: Raumstrukturen, Entwicklungsprozesse, Raumplanung* (Gotha: Klett-Perthes, 1997), 151ff.
2. Andrew Thornley, ed., *Urban Planning under Thatcherism: The Challenge of the Market* (London: Routledge, 1991), 86.
3. Peter Hall, "Green Fields and Grey Areas," in *Proceedings: Royal Town Planning Institute; Annual Conference* (London, 1977), 1–12, here p. 3.
4. Ibid., 4.
5. Ibid., 5.
6. See Klaus Zehner, "'Enterprise Zones' in Großbritannien: Eine geographische Untersuchung zu Raumstruktur und Raumwirksamkeit eines innovativen Instruments der Wirtschaftsförderungs- und Stadtentwicklungspolitik in der Thatcher-Ära," *Erdkundliches Wissen* 128 (Stuttgart, 1999).

SPECIAL ECONOMIC ZONES IN POLAND
Uwe Rada

—
—

When a commission headed by former Hamburg mayor Klaus von Dohnanyi declared in April, 2004, that the Aufbau Ost (Eastern Recovery) program had been a failure, it not only called for a concentration of subsidies on so-called core growth centers or flagship developments, but also for the establishment of "special economic zones" in the eastern German regions along the Polish and Czech borders: "We have to look very carefully at what can be deregulated there and what is feasible in terms of taxation," said Dohnanyi. The reason for this, he stated, is that precisely these eastern German regions bordering Poland and the Czech Republic are currently facing very stiff regional competition as a result of the enlargement of the European Union.

The call for special economic zones in eastern Germany is not new. In the autumn of 1990, the then Federal Minister of Economics, Helmut Haussmann (of the FDP party), proposed establishing a low-tax region in the East, where most taxes would be reduced by a quarter in comparison to those in the West. The proposal was supported by the foreign minister at the time, Hans-Dietrich Genscher (FDP), as well as former SPD economics minister Karl Schiller.

Poland's experiences with special economic zones were what led the Dohnanyi Commission to reach once again—fourteen years later—for the "evergreen of economic policymakers" *(Berliner Zeitung)*. The shining example here was the opening of a brand-new Opel factory in the special economic zone Gliwice/Gleiwitz.

As early as 1994, the government in Warsaw had approved the establishment of fourteen special economic zones *(strefa specjalna ekonomiczna)*. The decision was prompted by the reality of the growing regional polarization in booming post-Communist Poland. Economist Łukasz Burkiewicz observed back then: "Because of their geographic location, certain regions on the periphery of the country have no economic relations with the larger cities, and these regions are confronted with major problems, many of which cannot be overcome without government assistance."[1] According to Burkiewicz, the government agreed to create special economic zones, that is, regionally circumscribed areas that would attract companies—largely through a radical reduction in corporate and income taxes—because it lacked the financial resources to actively promote trade.

In contrast to the German debate in 2004, however, Warsaw did not concentrate its special economic zones on the German border, but scattered them across the country. Special economic zones were formed in Mielec, Katowice, Suwałki, Legnica, Łódź, Wałbrzych, Kamienna Góra, Słupsk, Starachowice, Tarnobrzeg, Sopot, and Olsztyn, and in the form of a technology park in Krakow. In Łódź, for example, high-tech companies and research institutes were to compensate for jobs lost as a result of the decline in the textile industry. Spinning off small textile shops could not halt the decline, however, and by the end of the 1990s all that remained of the former textile center of Poland was a gigantic bazaar—located in Tuszyn on the freeway heading toward Katowice, and housed in former hangars imported from the Ukraine.

The only special economic zone set up on the German border was the Kostrzynsko-Słubicka Strefa Specjalna Ekonomiczna in Kostrzyn and Słubice (KSSSE). When the latter

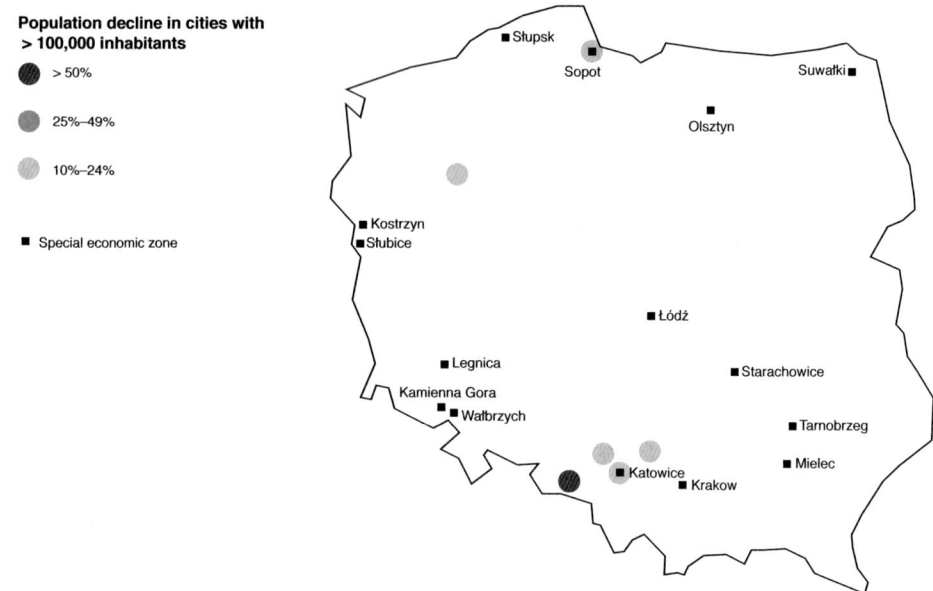

Special economic zones were introduced in Poland in 1994 as an instrument for regional economic development.

was founded in 1997, the misgivings were loud on the German side; they feared that the Polish side of the border region would overtake the eastern German side in economic dynamism. These concerns often came in the guise of benevolent advice. In particular, the *maquiladora* industry, which offers low-wage production in world-market factories on the United States–Mexico border, was held up as the ultimate example of horror. In Kostrzyn and Słubice, however, such fears were shrugged off. Their focus was not so much on cheap labor production as on quality, like Opel in Gleiwitz.

In the end the Polish side proved to be right. No cheap labor production has emerged on the German-Polish border. Stefan Krätke, an economic geographer at the Europa Viadrina University in Frankfurt/Oder, summed up the situation in 2003 as follows: "The so-called job-processing industry, that is, companies that invest only because of the low wages, has already left Poland and the Czech Republic. These companies are now in Romania. Poland, on the other hand, is only interesting as a business location for qualified investments requiring a lot of know-how."[2]

This especially affected the special economic zones located near Polish cities with their large pools of highly qualified labor. But the KSSSE in the German border region has stagnated. By 2002 only one German company had settled there—the Bremen sausage manufacturer Könecke, which has its salami packed in Słubice. Like the KSSSE's model company—the Croatian soup manufacturer Podravka—Könecke was less interested in profiting from low wages when it chose its location than in developing the Polish market from the new base in Słubice or Kostrzyn. The attempt to establish a special economic zone so as to help revive the structurally weak region in the dukedom of Lubuskie appeared to have failed. Competition regulations issued from Brussels in the run-up to

Poland's accession to the European Union (EU) only complicated the matter. A ten-year exemption from corporate tax as well as a further reduction of 50% for another ten years could not be reconciled with EU competition laws.

Pressure from the competition watchdogs in Brussels led to a reduction in tax concessions. Since 2000, only 50%–65% of investment sums can be written off in taxes. Nevertheless, the Polish special economic zones have not been a failure. Not in Kostrzyn, nor in Słubice. On the contrary, the KSSSE has experienced a new boom since EU enlargement. German companies, in particular, are now showing interest in investing in Poland, says KSSSE spokesman Dariusz Lesicki. In comparison to 2002, investments have now doubled to €220 million. And a total of 1,800 new jobs have been created in the same period. What makes the KSSSE interesting for German investors is its proximity to the border. Since the customs frontiers have been done away with, traffic congestion at the border crossings has also vanished.

But the recent upswing cannot conceal the reality that tertiarization is also in full swing in Poland. Special economic zones represent a good deal for international companies specializing in industrial manufacturing; they play no role in the service sector, however. One could say that the more the service industry comes to the fore, the more the different levels of prosperity will be evened out—not in the special economic zones on the Polish side, but on the German side.

The bogey today are not the special economic zones in Poland, but the rock-bottom wages paid in Germany to Polish service providers. The current debates about the implementation of a services directive *(Dienstleistungsrichtlinie)* and a law for foreign subcontractors *(Entsendegesetz)* bear testimony to this. Special economic zones exist not only in Poland, but on every German construction site and in every German household.

Translated from the German by Nancy Joyce

Notes

1 Łukasz Burkiewicz, *Die Sonderwirtschaftszonen im internationalen Vergleich: Die Sonderwirtschaftszone Kostrzyn-Slubice und ihre Auswirkung auf die deutsch-polnische Grenzregion* (master's thesis, Europa-Universität Viadrina, Frankfurt/Oder, 1998).
2 Stefan Krätke, "Polen ist in vielem schon weiter," *die tageszeitung,* October 19, 2002.

SPECIAL TAX ZONES AS A FATAL STRATEGY
Corell Wex

———

———

"Are you (still) paying trade tax? Save your money!" Because: "We have abolished the trade tax! Enjoy a 0% tax rate right now!" This is how Freudenberg AG advertises itself on its Internet home page in order to attract companies willing to locate there. It could be thought to be satire if the German Constitutional Court had not become involved in the case when Baiersdorf-Freudenberg, a small town 40 kilometers northeast of Berlin, used this strategy to promote itself. Whereas the town collected only €13,600 in trade tax eight years before abolishing it, it now takes in €150,000 a year in rent and incidental costs. Jobs have been created for 32 people, four of whom actually come from the town itself. Yet, although a community may have some success with this strategy, it is collectively fatal for all communities: "It damages our reputation and destroys the solidarity principle," says Karl-Ludwig Böttcher of the Städte- und Gemeindetag Brandenburg (an association of municipal authorities in Brandenburg). "All German town councils are moaning about their poor funding. Nobody can afford to dispense with a source of revenue."

Accordingly, the federal government put a stop to such actions in 2004. The tax may not be set at zero, rather must be at least 200%. The Constitutional Court has confirmed this rule as well. Since such tax havens mostly attract letter-box companies, and companies do not choose their locations solely based on trade tax, this measure has little use as a regional development strategy.

Tax Exemption and Tax Justice
This can be demonstrated with yet another example, one that Freudenberg explicitly cites: Norderfriedrichskoog in Schleswig-Holstein. Owing to special circumstances, no municipal tax is levied in this village of 45 persons, and at the end of the 1990s the number of companies "relocating" here—though only on paper—skyrocketed. Rooms were rented from farmers, but nobody could really say the companies had settled there.[1] The damage to the treasury, however, was considerable: The Federal Republic lost one billion euros a year in taxes alone because of this "tax haven behind the dike." A particular example of perfidy is the Deutsche Bank. First it moved its tax residence by relocating its computer center in Eschborn, so that Frankfurt am Main lost trade tax revenue; then it moved to Norderfriedrichskoog as a letter-box company, and Eschborn suffered the same fate as Frankfurt. In the end such ruinous tax competition hurts everyone.

For this very reason, tax havens—whether national or international—are an assault on tax justice. Most tax havens are located overseas, but there are certain conditions that turn parts of or entire European countries into tax havens. There are, for example, the Belgian Coordination Centers (CC), which are made available to corporations with profits exceeding €500,000. Having a CC enables them to outsource their asset management and be rewarded with a corporate tax rate of only 2%. According to conservative estimates by the Tax Justice Network (based on figures from the Bank for International Settlements), at least 255 billion tax dollars a year are lost to tax havens worldwide, money that is then not available for developing countries, nor for eastern Germany.[3] The classical tax havens do not per se create jobs, nor do they generate any self-supporting economic growth.[4] There has been talk recently about so-called special economic zones, of which the best-

A German magazine addresses "The Advent of the Special Economic Zone East?"

known examples are in China and Mexico. Insufficient taxation makes a national regional policy impossible; most foreign companies are not tied to the region and spend their profits where their likewise tax-exempt head office is located. Furthermore, such special economic zones, when they do function, hurt other countries by luring away companies and thus reducing their tax revenues—until yet another new region opens up with even better conditions for capital. All in all, European and international "tax competition" harms everyone: countries, because they can no longer raise the taxes needed for economic development; employees, because their jobs are outsourced and eliminated; and the companies themselves, because this zero-sum game generates no new domestic demand.

Germany's corporate tax reform of 2000 is further evidence that the fundamental argument does not hold up empirically. Tax cuts do not create more jobs, only more profits.[5]

Special Economic Zone East or Mezzogiorno: A Belated Debate

This "corporate community" strategy is based on the growth pole theory: The growth of a few poles is supposed to catalyze the growth of other areas—a theory that does not work in practice. The goal of achieving "equal living conditions on German territory" has long been discarded,[6] as has—since the publication of the Dohnanyi report (declaring the

Eastern Recovery program a failure) and the subsequent debate—that of raising living conditions in the eastern part of the country to western German standards.[7]

What remains is a German Mezzogiorno. This is what they call the South of Italy, which has received transfers from the North for sixty years without anything substantial to show for it.[8] What strategy could counteract this? The trade associations would like to turn all of eastern Germany into a tax-privileged zone, that is, one big Freudenberg. Aside from the resulting legal issues with the European Union,[9] this is actually a belated debate about the annexation of the East, for the reunification agreement and the 1:1 exchange rate destroyed the industrial cores and left nothing to subsidize.

The real alternative to these ineffectual efforts would be a radical tax reform, such as that proposed by Attac and the trade unions in the form of a *solidarische Einfachssteuer*— a fair and simple flat-tax system.[10] This reform would generate more tax revenue by eliminating loopholes. If inheritance and property taxes were similarly streamlined, and tax evasion and sales tax fraud combated, along with other measures, a new tax volume of at least 100–150 billion euros a year could be mobilized. Then all discussions about the allegedly empty coffers would be settled as fast as those about "tax-free communities." And that would really be something to cheer about.

Translated from the German by Nancy Joyce

Notes
1. See Hans Schmiederer and Ernst Weiss, *Asoziale Marktwirtschaft: Insider aus Politik und Wirtschaft enthüllen, wie die Konzerne den Staat ausplündern* (Cologne: Kiepenheuer & Witsch, 2004), 47ff.
2. See Sven Giegold, *Steueroasen trockenlegen! Die verborgenen Billionen für Entwicklung und soziale Gerechtigkeit heranziehen*, AttacBasisTexte 4 (Hamburg: VSA-Verlag, 2003).
3. See Tax Justice Network, "The Price of Offshore," March 2005, http://www.taxjustice.net/cms/upload/pdf/Price_of_Offshore.pdf (accessed April 2006).
4. See Giegold, *Steueroasen trockenlegen*, 40.
5. See Albrecht Müller, *Die Reformlüge: 40 Denkfehler, Mythen und Legenden, mit denen Politik und Wirtschaft Deutschland ruinieren* (Munich: Droemer, 2004).
6. See Neil Brenner, "Die Restrukturierung staatlichen Raums: Stadt- und Regionalplanung in der BRD 1960-1990," *Prokla: Zeitschrift für kritische Sozialwissenschaft* 109 (December 1997).
7. See Ulrich Busch, "Ostdeutschland: Wirtschaftspolitische Optionen für 2005 bis 2019," *Utopie kreativ* (February 2005): 133–145.
8. See Joachim Tesch, ed., *Ostdeutschland: alternative Entwicklungsmöglichkeiten oder deutsches Mezzogiorno? Beiträge eines Workshops in Leipzig, November 2004* (Leipzig: Rosa-Luxemburg-Stiftung Sachsen, 2005).
9. See RWI Essen, "RWI Essen fosters scepticism towards 'special economic zone Ruhr'" (press release, April 25, 2005), http://www.rwi-essen.de (accessed April 2006).
10. See Attac, "Konzept einer solidarischen Einfachsteuer," May 2004, www.attac.de/aktuell/steuer.pdf (accessed April 2006).

SPECIAL SOCIAL WELFARE ZONE FORST
Forst, Germany, 2004/05
Jesko Fezer, Stephan Lanz, and Uwe Rada

> *What would it be like if there were no plan? What would people do if they had a free choice? Would things get better or worse or just stay the same?*
>   Reyner Banham, Paul Barker, Peter Hall, and Cedric Price, *Non-plan*, 1969

> *The idea of a guaranteed basic income as a human right serves as a foundation for the human being in this world, acknowledges him unquestionably, and is satisfied in establishing his claim ad hominem: You are born in this world—live in it free of superfluous anxieties.*
>   Wolfgang Engler, *Bürger, ohne Arbeit*, 2005

> *If this goes on, then eventually the day will come when we will have to consider closing down the town.*
>   Jürgen Goldschmidt, head of the Forst building department, 2004

I. Starting Points
1. Forst

Before the war, Forst in the Lausitz region was the "German Manchester," the second-largest center of the textile industry. Every fifth man's suit came from Forst, they said; later every fifth man's uniform. After the war, Forst became a divided town. Eighty-eight percent of the buildings had been destroyed, including most of the factories. The Soviet city commandant considered declaring Forst a "dead town." But then refugees started flowing in from the East, and Forst revived. In the German Democratic Republic, textile production picked up again, yet the town still shrank. Unlike other industrial towns on the Polish border, like Schwedt, Eisenhüttenstadt, and Guben, Forst's population fell from 40,000 to 29,000.

After 1989 the textile industry collapsed for good, and the population dropped to 23,000. Nowadays even the old people are moving away—following their children to western Germany. In the town center the population has decreased by 30% since 1990, and the vacancy rate is just as high. Forst is no longer a shrinking city, it is a dying one.

And as the town shrinks, the state is pulling out of Forst. Although funds are available from the Stadtumbau Ost (Urban Restructuring in Eastern Germany) program, urban development planners are debating whether to change Forst's designation as a secondary regional center. This would mean that even less public funding for business development, infrastructure, and culture would be available than before. South Brandenburg is also in danger of losing its Target 1 status with the European Union structural funds as a result of a "statistical effect." Forst is thus increasingly being abandoned to its own fate.

2. Special zone

Eastern Germany already has concrete experience with special zones. Not just historically, as in the colonist villages of the eighteenth century, but today as well. Western German collective bargaining law, for example, is in force in very few companies between eastern Germany's Baltic coast and the Erz Mountains. As a low-wage region, eastern Germany has already become a German Mezzogiorno.

And now, after the failure of the economic revival in eastern Germany, politicians are deliberating on whether to focus subsidies on a few "growth cores" or "flagships." In Brandenburg this is now the declared policy of the grand coalition between the Social Democrats and the Christian Democrats. Thus, the establishment of parity in living conditions, which is anchored in the German constitution, has been de facto set aside.

Since then talk has repeatedly turned to finding special solutions for the regions from which the state is pulling out. Mayors of towns on the Polish border, for instance, are calling for opening up the job market to workers from the EU's new member states. Economic vitality for their towns is otherwise no longer feasible. If need be, each federal state must be allowed to decide for itself whether to introduce the free movement of labor or not. In the eastern states, economics ministers across party lines are advocating radical deregulation for development projects and other investments.

In reality, the border regions play a pioneering role in loosening up the rules and creating special regulations. In the German town of Herzogenrath, Dutch companies from Kerkrade were given permission to build cheap, Dutch-style houses, even though German buildings laws actually prohibit this type of construction. The towns of Herzogenrath and Kerkrade joined forces in a municipal joint body called "Eurode" and began clamoring for a "minimization of the obstructive effect of national statutory provisions." And further: They are also striving "to arouse interest in a certain degree of anarchy in circumventing statutory provisions or taking on a pioneer role to change them." Towns on the German-Polish border are aware of these actions and want to develop them further.

Special regulations now exist not only on the German side but also on the Polish side of the border. In 1996 the government in Warsaw established fourteen special economic zones where investors are exempt from corporate taxes for ten years. After initial start-up difficulties, these special economic zones are now considered a success. A few years ago this inspired even the reform-communist PDS party to call for a cross-border special economic zone agreement between Germany, Poland, and the Czech Republic for the Lausitz region.

EU structural funding also constitutes a special regulation. This funding is granted to those European regions whose GDP is less than 75% of the EU average. Up until now, all of Brandenburg has benefited from "Target 1 funding." Whether this will remain so with the accession of the ten new EU countries is doubtful. The "statistical effect" has lowered the EU average, and the eastern German states are now considered "rich."

But with less money coming from Brussels and funding, the regions that are not "flagships" are increasingly being left to fend for themselves. Their path thus automatically becomes a special path.

3. Social welfare zone

Special zones, however, do not automatically culminate in special economic zones. They have always been experimental grounds and laboratories for new forms of social coexistence.

In the middle of Copenhagen in Denmark, the "local free state" Christiania was founded on a vacated and then squatted military compound, and the Danish state has more or less kept its nose out of its affairs. A local community has evolved there with structures built on a grassroots democracy with strict restrictions on who can move in.

In the past few years numerous new rural communes and projects have been set up in Brandenburg. So-called space pioneers have moved here and established their own rules and regulations. Unlike many of the former residents, they perceive the "emptiness" not just as a loss, but also as a "luxury."

4. Special social welfare zone

Let us assume that the conditions of shrinking worsen until a town like Forst can no longer guarantee an adequate urban infrastructure nor equal living conditions with the conventional resources available to it from the federal and local government. Let us assume that despite substantial government grants, local living conditions continue to worsen, the local economy totally collapses, and ongoing emigration steadily increases the amount of money needed to maintain a minimal urban standard. Would it not then be necessary to fundamentally rethink the social and economic conditions of such a community? Would it be possible to permit a far-reaching experiment in an area in which the usual attempts to "normalize" the situation have failed and the state is no longer willing or no longer able to act? Could it possibly get worse?

The model of the special social welfare zone is one possibility for a radical rethinking. It connects the deregulation of the special economic zones with the social security measures provided by welfare projects on the basis of municipal self-administration and direct democracy. The special social welfare zone is a response to the end of the labor society and to the radical shrinking on the shadow side of the affluent society. It is a contribution to the discussion on civil society and political self-administration in those regions where citizens are no longer able to define themselves through classical wage labor.

The main features of the special social welfare zone are indebted to this synthesis—local self-administration, a guaranteed basic income, municipalization to the furthest extent possible, and deregulation of labor, building, commercial, and social law. Using these measures as a foundation, residents can reorganize their social living conditions, economic activities, local culture, and how they use the city. The special social welfare zone is not a model or planning concept for phasing out or revitalizing a dying city, but an open experiment aimed at changing the foundations of the urban economy. The goal is to enable the development of a self-organized community based on grassroots democracy and to create space for local initiatives.

The "dying city" of Forst—once a central location of the textile industry—was already shrinking in the days of the German Democratic Republic, then lost another 30% of its population after 1989.

II. Principles of a Special Social Welfare Zone
1. The special social welfare zone is a place of local self-administration and direct democracy.
Supported by the EU and a given German state, the federal government establishes the special social welfare zone by means of a unique law. The federal government and the municipality enter into a social welfare zone agreement that defines its rules. Within the scope of this experiment, the municipality is no longer an administrative level which is politically subordinate to the federal government, but becomes a largely autonomous local political system not subject to any general legal supervision from higher levels. The special social welfare zone is the product of a constitution that has been negotiated through grassroots democracy and is based on local self-administration and direct democracy. There are local civil rights. The German public services law and budget law are not in force in the special social welfare zone. Existing forms of administration and their regulations will be replaced; and the categories of departments and public officials dissolved. A solution for existing claims that run counter to these principles is included in the special social welfare zone agreement.

2. The special social welfare zone guarantees an unconditional basic income that secures the livelihood of all its residents.
The main feature of the special social welfare zone is the guaranteed basic income. The municipality is obliged to guarantee its residents a comfortable subsistence as an

unconditional basic financial security. This basic income should cover the essential costs of a simple standard of living, thus enabling each member to participate in society without the compulsion to engage in gainful employment. Each resident is entitled to it—much like the monthly child benefits offered by the German government—in addition to all other income and earnings. The local self-administration determines the specific amount. There are no means tests, no compulsory measures, and no compulsion to work. In this it differs from a negative income tax, which creates a base income only in the form of a negative tax available to eligible unemployed persons and which is thus still based on the privileged status of gainful employment.

The administrative effort involved in providing a guaranteed basic income is commensurate to that of a bank standing order. The state reimburses to the special social welfare zone the costs it saves in administering recipients of unemployment or welfare benefits. Unlike Hartz IV, it is not linked to wage labor, and it prevents poverty. Community work in education, social services, and healthcare is paid and is valued in the same way as gainful employment or work in the private sector. At the same time, however, community work represents the transition between gainful employment, social engagement, and forms of domestic labor. The local self-administration decides in each individual case where and how to draw the lines between paid employment and unpaid engagement.

Specific concepts on basic income, which not least of all prove their financial feasibility, have been around for a long time.[1] A regional basic income, for example, can be linked to the empirical results of the negative income-tax experiments of the 1970s and 1980s in the United States. The primary objection against a comfortable basic income—that its recipients will become lazy and do nothing if the compulsion to work is removed—was not confirmed here. On the contrary, participation in the job market increased, since the extra income could be pocketed. Moreover, economic and psychological research on happiness also confirms that people want an opportunity to use their skills.

The current organization of labor and income reduces the idea of the usefulness of work to what is useful for the economy. To facilitate the transition from a gainful employment society to an active society, the special social welfare zone builds up a strong infrastructure with DIY agencies and centers, advisers, and public places for people to engage in the labor they want to do. With this kind of reinforcement, the basic income can notably expand the spectrum of useful work and its social recognition—in the field of social reproduction as well as in relation to new products and services.

3. The special social welfare zone is based on a radical municipalization and deregulation of labor, construction, commercial, and social law.

Apart from self-administration and a basic income, the third fundamental principle of the special social welfare zone is extensive municipalization and deregulation of labor, construction, commercial, and social law, as far as this is possible on a local level. The German building code, for instance, will be completely suspended. Certain public services, hitherto subject to the authority of higher governmental levels, will be entrusted to the municipality. This applies to schools and the entire urban development industry on the territory of the special social welfare zone. Social insurance can be partially municipalized, provided that it is embedded legally and economically in larger contexts such as mechanisms to balance risk distribution. The basic income will replace unemployment insurance. Existing pensions or rights to a pension should be treated separately in the transition phase. Regulations that make little sense to municipalize, such as criminal and civil law, environmental protection, and the like, will remain unaffected. The municipality merely has the contractual obligation to use the public funds it receives to provide its residents with vital community services as well as a basic income. But it itself decides on the standards.

This stipulation rests on the thesis that the existing density of regulations and supralocal competence in many areas of everyday life blocks citizen initiative. At the same time existing regulations, in building or commercial law for instance, define standards whose level and financial investment bear little relation to the shrinking and dying of entire cities. These arguments are common. Yet, the wrong conclusions are usually drawn. Current deregulation redistributes the resources of a society in favor of the private sector, leave the privileges of powerful groups untouched, and take back social rights fought for tooth and nail over the course of many years. The special social welfare zone reverses this process: the social right to a basic income makes it possible to deregulate labor law, for instance, thus generating a new dynamic between economic and nonprofit activities. At the same time, this alone renders an entire bureaucracy superfluous, namely the one responsible for administering social transfers.

4. The special social welfare zone continues to receive the same amount of public funds, but as a lump sum and no longer earmarked for a specific purpose.

The special social welfare zone does not relieve the state of its responsibility. It requires the same amount of financial assistance. The special social welfare zone assumes that the amount of public funds received up to now is sufficient to guarantee a public infrastructure at a local level provided that these funds are used and distributed in a different way than is now the case. Therefore the amount of public funds, whether from financial aid programs, investment funds, or social transfers, EU, federal government, or state funds, will be transferred in the future as a lump sum to the municipality, which decides itself how to use it. Consequently, funding allocation is no longer determined by state stipulations, but by a participative civic budget. The special social welfare zone is thus cost-neutral for the public authorities.

These funds are guaranteed for a specific period. Later the underlying calculation can be updated.

5. A radically participative civic budget determines the use of funds in the special social welfare zone.

A civic budget administers the lump payments from the government as well as any money generated by the municipality. This goes far beyond any current concepts, which usually limit themselves to improved transparency, public consultation, and budget accountability. Instead civic budget in the special social welfare zone means local self-administration in a direct democracy, and thus the direct participation of the residents in the making of the budget: the decision making, the realization, and control over the budget.

The example of the Orçamento Participativo in the Brazilian city Porto Alegre shows that this is by no means an unrealistic utopia. In a multiphase process spanning several months, around 30,000 residents participate in citizen and delegate conventions to plan and draw up a budget together with the town council. The town councilors normally pass this budget without modifications. The experience shows not only remarkable civic engagement, but also a more just distribution of municipal resources and funds. Similar forms of self-administration can also be used in other areas of municipal action. Previous "citizen participation" is hereby transformed into a genuine self-administration, in which experts in the town council only take on advisory, moderating, and technical roles.

6. The special social welfare zone promotes municipal management of wasteland in the interest of the users.

High vacancy rates and wasteland are the main characteristics of shrinking cities. Owners of unprofitable real estate, who are faced with running expenses for an unforeseeable period, can turn them over to the town. One possibility here would be *Erbpacht* (long-term leaseholds), which leave open the possibility of a later return to the owner. The special social welfare zone can set up a "real estate fund" in the form of a foundation or a cooperative association, that is, as neutralized capital, which also manages all public properties and real estate. All residents have the right to use vacant real estate in return for a minimal fee. The suspension of the building laws, with the exception of certain standards for security, environmental protection, and historical monument conservation, and all land use and development plans makes it possible to realize uncomplicated, cheap, and temporary land use such as agriculture, living space expansion, livestock breeding, leisure, collective activities, cultural use, small businesses, restaurant and catering trade, commerce, and car repair.

7. Citizens in the special social welfare zone decide on the taxation of income and assets.

The municipal self-administration also decides on the levying of taxes and the appropriation of tax money. The result is not per se a tax haven. On the contrary, higher taxes for residents and companies here as compared to elsewhere in the country are justifiable and can be expected, because they have the basic income at their disposal in addition to other income and property. The special social welfare zone, however, is a model created on structures other than economic growth and participation on the primary job market. If access to participation in society is no longer primarily regulated through a dependence on wage labor, other social groups come back into play. Basic financial security can lead to self-determined, experimental, and smaller forms of producing and providing services and thus overcome the duality between wage labor and unemployment.

8. The special social welfare zone is open to new residents.

The special social welfare zone is an open system. Admission is not restricted. Regardless of their residence permit status in Germany, all residents have an unlimited right to settle, work, and start up a business, as well as to enjoy the social rights entitled to those living in the special social welfare zone. For each person in Germany who moves into the special social welfare zone, the state calculates the social transfers that person would otherwise receive in comparison to the taxes they would pay. If transfer payments predominate, these go to the special social welfare zone, but if taxes predominate, the special social welfare zone must pay the appropriate amount to the state. Thus the influx of employed taxpayers reduces the total budget of the special social welfare zone, and the influx of transfer recipients increases it.

It must also be possible for residents to leave at any time. The special social welfare zone agreement should provide a way for residents to return to national insurance schemes.

9. The residents themselves will introduce the special social welfare zone incrementally and will modify it to suit their local needs.

The special social welfare zone will be introduced step by step. Changes can be made at any time. The testing of each step will be followed by modification and the formulation of the next step. This introduction, however, will most likely raise more problems, for instance the issue of windfall effects, the potential of overtaxing the residents with the burdens of self-administration, the regulation of influx and migration, the relation between local and national structures of social security, the questions of whether the well-off are also willing to participate in the experiment, whether the special social welfare zone can only function as an isolated solution or as an exemplary model, and so forth.

The authors do not assume that a special social welfare zone will automatically halt shrinkage, nor will it necessarily produce a happier community and economic prosperity. The assumption, however, is that dependency on transfers and the helplessness it breeds can be overcome and that existing opportunities and ideas can make another kind of city possible, one that cannot be worse than the status quo. The special social welfare zone is no master plan, but rather an open experiment that shapes its own modalities through intensive local self-administration and that takes advantage of the absence of a local, functioning capitalist market.

Translated from the German by Nancy Joyce

This project was commissioned by the Bauhaus Dessau Foundation in the context of "Shrinking Cities." The original German title is "Sonderwohlfahrtszone Forst."

Note
1   See http://www.archiv-grundeinkommen.de.

TEMPORARY AUTONOMOUS ZONE
New York, 1991
Hakim Bey

In 1991 the American author, journalist, and "ontological" anarchist Hakim Bey published the book The Temporary Autonomous Zone, Ontological Anarchy, Poetic Terrorism, *in which he outlined the concept of enclaves, limited in time and space, in which an existence free of power differentials can be realized. The book had a significant influence on the discourses of network theory and communication guerillas in the early 1990s. (Ed.)*

To say that "I will not be free till all humans (or all sentient creatures) are free" is simply to cave in to a kind of nirvana-stupor, to abdicate our humanity, to define ourselves as losers. I believe that by extrapolating from past and future stories about "islands in the net" we may collect evidence to suggest that a certain kind of "free enclave" is not only possible in our time but also existent. ...

The concept of the Temporary Autonomous Zone (TAZ) arises first out of a critique of Revolution, and an appreciation of the Insurrection. The former labels the latter a failure; but for us *uprising* represents a far more interesting possibility, from the standard of a psychology of liberation, than all the "successful" revolutions of bourgeoisie, communists, fascists, etc.

The second generating force behind the TAZ springs from the historical development I call "the closure of the map." The last bit of Earth unclaimed by any nation-state was eaten up in 1899. Ours is the first century without *terra incognita*, without a frontier. Nationality is the highest principle of world governance—not one speck of rock in the South Seas can be left *open,* not one remote valley, not even the Moon and planets. This is the apotheosis of "territorial gangsterism." Not one square inch of Earth goes unpoliced or untaxed—in theory. ...

... We are looking for "spaces" (geographic, social, cultural, imaginal) with potential to flower as autonomous zones—and we are looking for times in which these spaces are relatively open, either through neglect on the part of the State or because they have somehow escaped notice by the mapmakers, or for whatever reason. ...

... The TAZ is like an uprising which does not engage directly with the State, a guerilla operation which liberates an area (of land, of time, of imagination) and then dissolves itself to re-form elsewhere/elsewhen, *before* the State can crush it. Because the State is concerned primarily with Simulation rather than substance, the TAZ can "occupy" these areas clandestinely and carry on its festal purposes for quite a while in relative peace. Perhaps certain small TAZs have lasted whole lifetimes because they went unnoticed, like hillbilly enclaves—because they never intersected with the Spectacle, never appeared outside that real life which is invisible to the agents of Simulation.

Quoted from: Hakim Bey, *T.A.Z. The Temporary Autonomous Zone, Ontological Anarchy, Poetic Terrorism,* http://www.hermetic.com/bey/taz_cont.html.

DRESDEN'S COLORFUL REPUBLIC OF NEUSTADT
Dresden-Neustadt, Germany, 1990–2005
Residents and other stakeholders
www.brn-dresden.de

On June 20, 1990, the residents of Dresden declared the city's Neustadt district the "First Colorful Republic of Germany," which boasted a "monarch without a portfolio" and a government of which each resident should become a member. A white line was drawn to separate this self-defined territory from the city of Dresden, and the "Neustadt mark" was introduced as the district's new form of currency.

The background for this symbolic act of resistance was the decline of the district, 20% of which was vacant and set for demolition already back in the days of the German Democratic Republic. Even before 1989, a creative niche society had emerged here around squatters and cultural and political activists. The interest group Outer Neustadt also participated in this inspired protest by articulating concrete political demands such as a stop on demolition, renovation measures, and the reconstruction of a swimming pool. The protest prompted the city to earmark the district for urban renewal under the designation "Outer Neustadt." The "Colorful Republic" has since become a neighborhood festival with less of a political edge since the resignation of the provisional government in 1994, but which continues today, albeit as an increasingly commercialized event.

Riots at the event in 2001 and 2002 have meant that there is now a large police presence. Since 2002 the festival has been run without a central organizer and has developed into an open, multicultural street festival. (Ed.)

This newspaper of the provisional government of the "Colorful Republic of Neustadt" ("Bunte Republik Neustadt") from 1991 proclaims: "Scandal: The Mob Rules in Neustadt." The provisional government's decisions and schedules are published here.

COMMUNICATING CITY

Cities are places of communication and exchange. Yet this basic condition of urban life is critically undermined by the effects of shrinkage—migration, population decline, fragmentation, and introversion. Artistic interventions foster communication and new relationships between individuals, a city and its residents, the people who moved away, and those left behind. At the same time, novel forms of representation and changes in perception lead to reflection about oneself and a reappraisal of one's environment. The very diversity of conflicting opinion lends a new quality to public space.
—

ON THE CRISIS OF URBAN PUBLIC LIFE
Jörg Dürrschmidt

The American urban sociologist Sharon Zukin coined the saying that public spaces are the window to a city's soul.[1] This is even more patently the case when a city is in upheaval, when the self-evident integration of urban space and urban everyday life no longer seems to function and urban identity is consequently put to the test. This constellation of factors applies in particular to shrinking cities on the periphery of East Brandenburg. Deindustrialization, migration, and general decline have led to a situation that is not, to say the least, conducive to urban public life. The city of Guben in East Brandenburg shall serve as a case in point, for the discrepancy between the ambitions and the reality of urban development in Guben cannot be overlooked. Whereas the town—along with its Polish counterpart, Gubin—has on the one hand been officially promoted as a "European model town," it is perceived in the everyday experience of its residents as "a dying town."[2]

Should a visitor to Guben make his way on a sunny spring day from the railway station to the center, its reputation as a dying town seems at first unfounded. A neat station forecourt that ends in a small park greets the visitor. The way to the town center leads past the premises of an apparently prosperous small company and a row of more or less well-kept houses, of the sort one might find anywhere in Germany. The closer one comes to the center, however, the more obvious it becomes to the visitor that this town really has suffered substantial losses in the last fifteen years. One passes the abandoned premises of the Guben Wool Works, where broken windows permit a glimpse into the prestigious past of a former East German town that developed around a state-owned combine. Then, on the right, a typical snack shop serves its typical customers: people with a daylong thirst for beer, people whose desire for discussion extends to the stoops and the street. In the three-story tenement blocks that flank the road, curtains are few and far between, and some windows are boarded up with pressboard. Here and there, occasional villas—now empty and run-down—bear witness both to the textile industry's rapid growth in the town around 1900 and to the legal battles for restitution of property that have continued since 1989. Then a short curve and one enters Frankfurter Street, a newly renovated promenade with a travel agency, a bookshop, an ice-cream parlor, and the restored stucco facades of chic apartment buildings. Yet something here gives one pause for thought: there are no people around to bring the promenade to life. The seats in front of the cafés and the ice-cream parlor remain largely unoccupied.

The people of Guben confirm that these impressions are not exclusive to outsiders. In interviews they repeatedly mention the strange feeling of loneliness evoked by staring into empty, curtainless windows, by pavements that are dead by five o'clock in the evening, and by the gradual closure, one after the other, of the town center's bars. And they long for their town to come back to life, for it to be like "back then" again, when even people from the larger nearby towns would come to Guben. Here we find articulated not only discontent with the disappearance of public spaces but also a clear correlation between urban public life and social behavior. Public life requires not only the physical spaces of bars, cafés, and squares. It must also be supported by forms of interaction that are open to noncommittal chance encounters with other people and by ready contact to the new; that must, in the end, be embedded in civic values such as curiosity about the rest of the world and pride in one's own.

Considered from this perspective, shrinkage and the decline of public life are causally related to one another. Those people whose biographies were drawn into the maelstrom of simultaneous postindustrial and postsocialist transformation often lack, understandably, the composure necessary for enjoying public interchange, and often lack as well the requisite confidence in their own biography to commit themselves to a predestined role in public life. Instead, there ensues the retreat into one's own four walls or the idyll of one's allotment. The evidence of shrinking cities makes clear, furthermore, that the problem of the erosion of urban life concerns not only shrinking in social terms—migration (for the most mobile) or retreat into one's own four walls (for the discouraged)—but also the increasingly problematic issue of the remaining residents' potential identification with their city's built environment. Both demolition and rebuilding projects give rise to questions about the compatibility of the (dis)continuity of the built environment and the (dis)continuity of people's biographies. In what follows, some aspects of the relationship between shrinkage and the erosion of public life will be discussed further.

Urban Public Life without a Civic Milieu?

In considering the causes of the decline of public life in a town like Guben, it is illuminating to first of all lend an ear to everyday discourses on the subject. These voices hold the migration of the restless and the young to be directly responsible for the decline of public life. This phenomenon appears to be part of a general pattern, described by M. Rainer Lepsius in his study of the culture of resignation in southern Italy as the "negative selection of the people left behind regarding activity and the spirit of enterprise."[3] And yet this explanation appears to be only partly satisfactory, for the people of Guben who have been left behind are actively involved in the community. The impressive list of local associations and clubs proves this beyond any doubt.[4] It is, however, a kind of activity that has more to do with riding one's own hobby horse (albeit in a group) than with urban public life. The link between the various niches established by associations—be these concerned with angling, allotments, or pensioners—and any true civic consciousness, with all the conflicting interests and chance encounters that this entails, has yet to be forged. The people involved spoke to us about their tendency to remain "too wrapped up in their own interests and concerns."

This description of what one might be tempted to call aimless activism points to the core of the problem. If we bear in mind that public life always exists in part to generate and coordinate "social capital" (to quote Robert D. Putnam), then a differentiation introduced into the debate on shrinking by Christine Hannemann becomes important indeed.[5] In particular with regard to small towns, one must differentiate between "community" and "civic" engagement. The former functions within consensual norms of solidarity in a close-knit community, whereas the competence of the latter lies precisely in the links that it forges between its own interests and a wider public arena. From this perspective, what is missing in shrinking cities is not so much the will to community involvement, but rather a functioning civic milieu that can bundle the various niche activities at the municipal level and connect them with wider issues and reference points for (further) action. The urban sociologist Hans-Paul Bahrdt has described in this respect the existence of an urban citizenry that repeatedly attempts "to break out of an 'insular' local orientation" as a basic requirement of urban public life.[6] On the same tack, in the aforementioned study Lepsius argues that the failure of an urban milieu to generate such communication is a significant indicator of a "shrunken society." No longer challenged by impulses from outside the locality, a shrunken society is characterized by "people's over-integration into the remaining social fabric," even if—as in Guben's busy clubs and associations—they appear to be outgoing and actively involved.

For towns like Guben, which formerly were dominated by a single state industry, this structural question has an additional edge. Did a civic milieu actually ever exist before migration began in 1989? It is a question that one would first certainly have to answer empirically. Yet two analytical objections give pause for thought. First, the case for a "socio-structural desiccation" of the civic milieu,[7] as described by Wolfgang Engler in the context of former East Germany's "workers' society," cannot be dismissed out of hand. Second, such a manufacturing town is a child of industrial society. The social structures of towns created in this period were defined primarily by their respective major industrial plant (a synthetic fibers combine, in the case of Guben), and a tendency to devalue local public life vis-à-vis "public life in the workplace" could be noted. All in all, then, it was a development that produced towns whose inhabitants "are townspeople but not civic-minded."[8]

Impulses from Beyond: *Le Week-End*

For communities in crisis, the frequently observed retreat of residents into their own four walls is not the only typical reaction. A complementary development can be observed with respect to the symbolism of public life, namely, the retreat to the safe anchorage offered by local history, which is often actively promoted by local authorities facing structural constraints. What certain individuals experience as a shameful retreat, necessitated by a sense of personal failure, is echoed on a municipal level by the "political taboo made of shrinkage."[9] In Guben this development is made manifest by the revival of its tradition as an "Apple Town." At the start of the twentieth century, Guben's vineyards and apple orchards were a popular destination for the region's day-trippers. Most especially when the apple trees were in bloom, special trains were organized to bring Berliners to the more than one hundred open-air restaurants surrounding the town. Since 1995 Guben has celebrated its Apple Festival annually, along with all the usual rituals of folk festivals, such as electing an Apple Queen as a symbolic representative of the town. Yet the "Apple Town" image conjured by these few days of festivities contrasts sharply with the reality of people's daily experience of shrinkage and increasing insignificance. The festival is by no means an effective catalyst for civic consciousness, for the latter would require that a critical review of the town's current situation lead to links with other localities and to viable options for the future. It is more about navel-gazing than networking. So, at least, the critical opinions that can be garnered on the edge of the festivities: "Well, to have an Apple Festival every day wouldn't be bearable. Once a year is all right."

Amidst the circumstances of structural shrinkage—retreat into the private sphere, the lack of or inadequacy of a civic-minded citizenry, local authorities' treatment of shrinkage as a political-symbolic taboo—what courses of action for the creation of civic consciousness are even imaginable?

One possible strategy is to open up to impulses from "beyond." The social history of the "outsider" has long since shown that the stranger who is here today and gone tomorrow can play an important role in the communities that he passes through. He has a critical eye for the inner machinations of an established group and is able to express this precisely because he does not really belong, because he is not "too wrapped up in it all." Furthermore, the fact that he will soon move on means that, although not totally insensitive to social exclusion, he is not existentially threatened by it. The outsider is consequently the perfect person when it comes to firing up dormant civic consciousness.

Such was the case of Gregor Mirwa, a doctor from Berlin who practiced for some years in Guben. This self-confessed "outsider" really did succeed in pulling Guben's townspeople out of their insular hustle and bustle for a short while and—over the course of occasional weekends, hence the title *Le Week-End*—trying out new forms of public life with some of them.[10] He revamped an old toyshop as an exhibition space for contributors from London, New York, Paris, Poland, and Germany, and organized film screenings, workshops, and a soccer tournament between teams from Berlin and Guben. The third *Le Week-End* posed the greatest challenge to Guben's urban consciousness. In cooperation mainly with younger residents of both Guben and Gubin, he publicly took issue with the partition of the town and with the shared challenge of mass migration. Under the slogan "To Come—To Go—To Stay," the group erected six four-by-four-meter billboards showing portraits of townspeople and short statements by them at various important public locations. The residents' reactions ranged from interest and curiosity to daubed graffiti.

This "pioneer of public life," who astutely exploited his position of having one foot in and one foot outside local life, actually did create new structures of public life in at least three ways. He turned empty premises—the toyshop—into a venue for artistic communication; he involved local protagonists—the towns' youth clubs—in wider, international networks; and he won the financial and moral support of various state institutions such as the Heinrich Böll Foundation and the Federal Ministry for Family Affairs. He thus succeeded in achieving that which the self-confessed navel-gazing Guben associations and clubs do not—namely, he brought outsiders in and helped open Guben up a little to the wider world. He thus in a very real sense generated a critical public consciousness that exceeded the bounds of a close-knit community.

A sympathetic observer might regard such experimental practices of extending public life as "acupuncture for public space" or as a "minimalist intervention" in the sense of a homeopathic remedy.[11] Sociological analyses of shrinking communities have, however, shown that a rather different tendency takes holds for them; namely, the extended horizons and the subsequent increase in normative claims disappear "as soon as an exterior impulse ceases to have an effect."[12] *Le Week-End* in Guben rather confirms this pessimistic prognosis.

Spatial Imagery and (Concrete) Utopias

Identification with the built environment of a town is a catalyst for urban public life. Civic pride feeds in part on residents' identification with significant public edifices. Conversely, representative buildings may function as the architectural expression of a collective commitment to urban development. To the extent that individual biographies are closely

6 Hans-Paul Bahrdt, *Die Moderne Großstadt: Soziologische Überlegungen zum Städtebau* (Hamburg: Rowohlt, 1971), 14.
7 Hartmut Häußermann, "Von der Stadt im Sozialismus zur Stadt im Kapitalismus," in *Stadtentwicklung in Ostdeutschland: Soziale und räumliche Tendenzen,* ed. Hartmut Häußermann and Rainer Neef (Opladen, Germany: Westdeutscher Verlag, 1996), 10, 23.
8 Bahrdt, *Moderne Großstadt,* 116–117.
9 See Philipp Oswalt, "Akupunktur des öffentlichen Raums—Künstlerische und architektonische Strategien minimaler Intervention," in *Der öffentliche Raum in Zeiten der Schrumpfung,* ed. Heinz Nagler, Riklef Rambow, and Ulrike Sturm (Berlin: Leue Verlag, 2004).
10 This and the following details refer to the manuscript by Gregor Mirwa, *4 x 4 Sachen machen* (2003), and his workshop lecture on January 18, 2003, in the context of the Shrinking Cities project.
11 Cf. Oswalt, "Akupunktur des öffentlichen Raums."
12 Cf. Lepsius, "Immobilismus."
13 Maurice Halbwachs, *Das kollektive Gedächtnis* (Frankfurt am Main: 1991), 127ff.
14 Hartmut Häußermann and Walter Siebel, "Die Politik der Festivalisierung und die Festivalisierung der Politik: Große Ereignisse in der Stadtpolitik," in *Festivalisierung der Stadtpolitik: Stadtentwicklung durch große Projekte,* ed. Hartmut Häußermann and Walter Siebel (Opladen, Germany: Westdeutscher Verlag, 1993), 12–13.
15 See http://www.guben-gubin-stadt2030.de.
16 See *Lausitzer Rundschau,* April 16, 2005, p. 13.

LE WEEK-END
Guben/Gubin, Germany/Poland, since 1998
D. Gregor Mirwa and others

In 1998, "because he and Guben were lacking something," D. Gregor Mirwa, a doctor and author who had moved to Guben from Berlin, initiated the art festival *Le Week-End,* the first theme of which was encounters between periphery and center. An exhibition by young photographers from Guben and artists from Berlin, held in a former toyshop, was complemented by a program of readings and screenings. The following year, *Le Week-End* responded to the death of Farid Guendoul, an Algerian who had been driven to his death by neo-Nazis in Guben. Under the motto "I Will Survive," a group show by artists from London, New York, Poland, Paris, and Germany, along with schoolchildren from Guben/Gubin, attempted to close the gap between pop culture and politics.

Le Week-End 3 in 2001 strove for new forms of public outreach with two projects on the theme "Kommen – Gehen – Bleiben" (To Come—To Go—To Stay). Twelve billboards at prominent locations in Guben/Gubin showed four-by-four-meter portraits of inhabitants of the German and Polish areas of the town who had moved there, intended to stay, or were planning to move away, along with excerpts from interviews with them. During the same period, German and Polish teenagers produced the newspaper *Portal.*

Lastly, *Le Week-End 4* set out to apprehend reading as an active and collective process. Under the title "Guben/Gubin reads *The Heart of Darkness* by Joseph Conrad," Gregor Mirwa and Saskia Draxler arranged for a bookshop close to the border to distribute fifteen hundred free copies of the novella by Conrad—who was born in Poland—along with notebooks. By assuring that hundreds of people in a small town knew that they and others were simultaneously reading the same book, they intervened in the town's public discourse. They then invited people to a series of Long Nights with discussions, readings, and screenings and, most important, the presentation in a temporary library of the readers' personal notebooks. A further edition of the festival is planned for 2006. (Ed.)

Poster from the project *Le Week-End 3,* "Kommen – Gehen – Bleiben" (To Come—To Go—To Stay), depicts Michael F. and his family. A locksmith, he married a woman from Guben in 2000 and moved there from Eisenhüttenstadt.

Ramadan D., a hairdresser from Kosovo (here with his German girlfriend), came to Guben in 2001 as a refugee. He would like to leave: "I can't stay here. It's shit! It's boring here. Working isn't permitted."

A MONUMENT FOR THE WOMEN'S CENTER
Wolfen, Germany, 2004/05
Isa Rosenberger with Elke Allmer, Christel Baer, Brigitte Heinicke, Diana Hiller, Sonja John, Rotraut Niess, Elvira Radek, and Birgit Wessel

In discussions about shrinking cities in eastern Germany, women are often described as the losers—and quite rightly, considering the financial and professional discrimination that they face. Yet the passive connotations of this label reflect neither the complexity of women's situations nor their diverse ways of dealing with it. What alternative strategies do women invent when paid labor, an essential component of their identities, becomes an increasingly scarce commodity? And, as the social scientist Petra Drauschke has asked, what role might women's centers play as "places where alternatives can be considered, visions be made manifest, and political demands be formulated?"

Prompted by these questions, the artist Isa Rosenberger invited the manager of the Wolfen Women's Center in Wolfen-Nord, Birgit Wessel, to cooperate on a project. The project team numbered eight women, aged between 30 and 67 and with very diverse professional backgrounds. All are active in the women's center and each is a quasi expert on her own situation.

In the course of several workshops the project team discussed how perceptions of women as the losers might be challenged by other (self-) images, and how artistic intervention might communicate the activities and significance of the center to a wider audience.

After drafting numerous ideas (e.g., a documentary soap about the center or a newspaper supplement), the team agreed on *Monument for the Women's Center*. This idea tied in with the local tradition of erecting monuments to women. Until recently, the statue *Die Chemiearbeiterin (The Chemical Worker)*, erected in 1965 in front of the ORWO administrative offices in Wolfen, had commemorated the eight thousand women employed in the film factory: more female workers than in any other factory in former East Germany.

But how should a monument to women look today? A concept by Rotraut Nieß anticipated a field of flags along the street-side facade of the low, inconspicuous women's center building, rendering it highly visible. Today, a collectively written poem, printed on six flags, communicates to the outside world both the center's work and the personal vision and opinions of women involved in it: "STAY – AND GO – DARING TO TRY – IS OUR STRENGTH – COLORFUL NOT GRAY – A PERSONAL REVOLUTION." Even the antagonistic reactions this was expected to generate would draw attention to the center's work and encourage public debate about the situation of women in Wolfen and about forms of self-organization.

An essential part of the project was the decision to visit local policy-makers, show them a model of the monument, and try to win their financial and moral support (e.g., through funding and speeches at the opening ceremony). These preliminary steps provided a pretext for discussions about the situation of women in Wolfen with public personalities and people in power, for example with Wolfen's mayor, Ms. Wust.

A former employee at ORWO, Magdalena Brandl was the model in 1964 for the recently dismantled *Chemical Worker* monument. Today she is active in the Wolfen Women's Center. Video-stills from the film *The Making Of // A Monument for the Women's Center*.

Mayor Wust: Following the reunification of Germany, it became clear that women, in particular, are badly hit. It was said we should create opportunities for women: create places for them to meet as well as offer training and further education. The Women's Communication Center in Wolfen has developed into an effective organization, and has received very positive feedback, which is entirely due to the commitment of the women involved in it, who do everything they possibly can. And if we are to put up a monument to women, then that is certainly the place for it.

Sonja John: We thought about it for ages: A monument or a memorial? I personally thought from the start that it is first and foremost a work of art. During a discussion with Mr. Ruprecht [manager of the Ernouerungsgesellschaft Wolfen-Nord mbH, a company responsible for local regeneration], it was considered that the project might be misunderstood as a revival of former East Germany's use of flags. For me, flags connote hope. That's how I feel about them. I think it will look wonderful when the flags wave in the wind, their color bright against a background of endless gray. And because of the statements on them, they also convey an "inner message": they are not "just" flags.

Mayor Wust: What is the task of art? To represent something, obviously: the artist wants to express something. Yet what other task should art fulfill? It should stimulate whoever sees it to discuss the artwork. And if that happens, then the artist has achieved all that he intended. And that is precisely what I will be able to achieve here with the flag project. It's like an arrow pointing at the Women's Communication Center. I like the idea very much.

Translated from the German by Jill Denton

This project was developed in the context of "Shrinking Cities" with a grant from the Museum of Contemporary Art Leipzig. The original German title of the artwork is *Ein Denkmal für das Frauenzentrum*.

CONFLICT AS PRODUCTIVE POTENTIAL
COMMUNITIES AND PUBLIC SPACES
Nina Möntmann

—

—

Communities and Public Spaces
In shrinking cities, public spaces as social locations often find themselves in crisis. Urban space constitutes the most visible of all public spaces, and it is here that the crises, conflicts, and reorganization of democracy become most apparent. Shifts in the discussion about the composition and value of publics are particularly relevant when considering shrinking cities. The public is today, at last, acknowledged to be a problematic issue and not a solution to be conjured at will. Reflections on the form (or formation) of public space have subsequently shifted: from Habermas's unrealized ideal of a harmonious and homogeneous whole to a space structured by diversity, in which parallel different interests coincide in conflictual relationships. Democratic theories, as expounded by Claude Lefort or Chantal Mouffe and Ernesto Laclau, are fundamental to the latter interpretation. Mouffe, for instance, describes this space as an "agonistic public sphere."[1] Given the current trend in public spaces toward more privatization, supervision, rivalry, and exclusionary practice, a homogeneous democratic space in which extremely diverse interests might be manifested concurrently and harmoniously is unthinkable. In its stead, the "agonistic model" describes a plurality of different public spaces. Acknowledging the dissonance generated by such plurality to be the productive potential of public spaces poses a new challenge to urban planners, politicians, the media, public institutions, and indeed anyone who uses public spaces. The challenge, namely, is to deal with this diversity and to channel conflict productively. Nancy Fraser posits that participation is an essential factor in this process: "Together, these two ideas—the validity of public opinion and citizens empowerment vis-à-vis the state—are essential to the concept of the public sphere in democratic theory. Without them, the concept loses its critical force and its political point."[2]

Such concepts of space correspond with newer or recently revived notions of community which represent a critique both of the 1980s communitarian consensual politics of shared values and of Marxist ideas of community as a group united in class struggle. In *The Inoperative Community,* Jean-Luc Nancy demands that the radical diversity and multiple voices within a community be acknowledged.[3] Nancy speaks of community as a relational social organization constituted not by the fact of belonging but by the coexistence of singularity and shared experience. This view is shared by Giorgio Agamben, who in his turn completely dismantles the dichotomy of identity and difference.[4] Both Nancy and Agamben proclaim the community to be a political project. Nancy perceives the community's permanent struggle against immanent power as a central quality, whereas Agamben adheres to a somewhat idealistic concept of a "coming community" arising from collective resistance to an external power and hence to some degree approximates Michael Hardt and Antonio Negri's concept of "multitude." The community that best accords with Mouffe's concept of an agonistic public space would thus correspond to Nancy's conception of the permanent inner conflict of a community.

The issues of public space and community are also closely linked in contemporary art. When citizens' empowerment is formulated as an artistic goal, it is commonly attained by means of participatory practice. This phenomenon has led increasingly since the early

1990s to collaboration with various communities. "Community-based art" encourages active participation in public space by challenging certain social groups or the art public to take action and communicate in a cooperative process. This approach poses the fundamental question of how such communities are respectively defined in the context of art projects.

Community-Based Art

The early 1990s witnessed an increased interest in the politically serviceable value of artistic work.[5] Because the ensuing benefits were intended to accrue to socially disadvantaged groups, the term "community-based art" was coined in the debates on the topic in the United States. Such projects are characterized by cooperation between artists and a select group of people who have certain circumstances in common, for which reason it is treated as a "community." In the mid-1990s, Suzanne Lacy used the term "New Genre Public Art" to present this new orientation of art in public space: "It actually is a genre of public art work, not in the traditional sense, referring to a monument placed in a central area of the city, but because it deals with the public in an interactive way."[6] Art thus defined does not take place in public space, nor is it placed there: it is by its very nature public. With "Culture in Action" in Chicago in 1992/93, Mary Jane Jacob curated the first comprehensive and groundbreaking exhibition of participatory art projects in public space which aimed to work with local communities. For this exhibition, Iñigo Manglano-Ovalle—in cooperation with the group Street-Level Video—organized the video workshop "Tele Vecindario" for members of youth gangs in Chicago's West Town, which ended with a one-day block party. This resulted in a kind of video dialogue. Participants reacted on video to the videos of their neighbors. In this way video was employed as a communication tool: to promote contact between the members of various gangs and other urban residents, on the one hand, and to integrate the project in the life of the community, on the other.[7] In another project, the HaHa group set up a garden that was tended by local artists and HIV-positive volunteers. In cooperation with a local chapter of the Bakery, Confectionery, and Tobacco Workers' International Union, artists Christopher Sperandio and Simon Grennan initiated the production of a "We Got It" chocolate bar, which was created by workers in a local candy factory. In such New Genre Public Art projects, community is conceived in essentialist terms and the participants' identities reduced to characteristics that they have not personally chosen, such as social exclusion, poverty, HIV infection, criminality, or use of drugs. Use of the term community in this context proves problematic when it is applied by external sources as a potentially coercive label, when participants are defined as a group on the basis of a single characteristic that they have not personally chosen, and when, furthermore, independent action by participants is not encouraged. This understanding of community is characterized by exclusion and marginalization. Accordingly, the notion persists of public space as a hegemonic construct in which it is possible to create niches or "counterspaces."[8] Christian Kravagna correctly maintains that in many of the projects defined as New Genre Public Art, "the lack of political analysis" is replaced by "a pastoral mix of public welfare and education" that has "pseudo-religious traits."[9] Against this background and in accordance with Mouffe's concept of agonistic public spaces, a suggestion by Gerald Raunig appears particularly convincing: community projects should preferably establish the reality of a situation, taking into account the differences between respective groups rather than ignoring these. They should "insist on structural transformation, the accessibility of marginal areas, and the constant collision of differences," most effectively by means of interventionist practice.[10]

Experimental Communities

To prevent art's attempted mission from being misguided, it is of fundamental importance to recognize the temporary nature of communities.[11] "Provisional communities" are in fact constituted at certain locations or for limited periods, frequently in order to deal with a particular problem. Such constraints allow solely for an intervention in existing structures and a creation for a limited period of an exemplary situation which might challenge the existing structures. In their article about communities' involvement in recent contemporary art projects, Carlos Basualdo and Reinaldo Laddaga pose one of the central questions about the necessity of both respecting and challenging diversity in public space: "How can very diverse intentions be brought together on behalf of unified actions that acknowledge their diversity as well as their shared value?"[12] They answer the question with the term "experimental communities," which acknowledges both the temporary and the exemplary nature of communities in participatory art forms. The involvement in collaborative processes of individuals with diverse knowledge and experience appears in this respect to be an essential resource and one that differentiates these projects from the aforementioned, in which community membership is defined by a categorical, essentialist characteristic. Projects with hybrid experimental communities can be found, for example, in the work of Jeanne van Heeswijk or in the "Park Fiction" project in Hamburg, which involves residents of the St. Pauli district as creative coproducers of "personal wishes" pertaining to long-term use of the district, and not because they typified a single social characteristic.[13] In 2002, for the "Face Your World" project that took place in Amsterdam and Columbus, Ohio, Jeanne van Heeswijk installed computers in a bus that traveled a route, among others, between three urban "Children of the Future" centers. Children riding the bus were able to use an interactive program to manipulate, redesign, or reinvent their immediate environment, and their urban visions were displayed at bus stops in interactive kiosks.[14] The project united the everyday use of public transport with innovative computer technology and creative thinking. For van Heeswijk, the electronic medium is neither an end in itself nor a unifying characteristic of the community addressed. Rather, it is employed as a tool that demonstrates children's ideas productively and thus allows them to be acknowledged as creative coproducers of an imaginary urban space.

Virtual Communities

In contrast, the term "virtual communities" describes communities that define themselves according to their use of a common medium, such as the Internet, television, or cell phones. These, too, initially promised liberation from fixed identities. Above all, the Internet offers new forms of participation in public democracy in that it facilitates activity bound neither by ethnicity nor by gender in public space that is not organized by the state. Individuals from far-flung geographical locations and diverse cultural and ethnic backgrounds are thus able to contact one another directly, without regard for the social barriers encountered in local public spaces. At first there were online forums such as "The Thing," founded in 1991 in New York and still used today by a community recruited more or less from the arts field, or the now defunct New York mailbox "Echo," which was set up in 1990 and used by intellectuals from all disciplines. In contrast to Howard Rheingold, who offers a somewhat esoteric and idealized conception of a harmonious and homogeneous media community,[15] approximating Habermas's concept of the public, Echo's founder, Stacy Horn, reports in her book *Cyberville* that power relations are reproduced on the Net in exactly the same way as in local physical communities. She thereby dispels any notion of the Internet's democratic leveling effect in and on public space.[16] In the meantime, the virtual bubble has burst and interest in the dashed hopes of "another world" has long since dwindled. The tendency has instead been toward the constitution of media publics that comprise both physical and virtual space and that synergistically exploit the communication potential of both. The Indymedia network, set up initially as a "Web site for alternative countercultures," is particularly interesting in this regard. As well as hosting wikis and e-mail lists, it provides live coverage of political protests, functioning at such moments as a Web site with a real physical base, as "a sort of alternative Internet café in the immediate vicinity of a political action, with computer access and the possibility of uploading audiovisual and written documents."[17] This amalgamation of virtual and physical public space gives rise to a community that no longer distinguishes between real and virtual.

Whereas in Net communities interactivity is a priori one of the medium's key qualities, the passive viewer of the centrally organized medium of television continues to personify the late-capitalist consumer. The possibility of "interaction" is here limited to TV-shopping and dialing telephone sex numbers, which merely reinforces the prescribed role of consumer. The other possibility of actively broadcasting oneself is to be typecast for participation in a "reality show" and then display oneself before a public of millions. Quiz shows, too, in which one can appear and perhaps show one's ignorance, merely confirm the prescribed and completely de-individualized possibilities of participation, the only aim of which is to trade one's dignity for a rating in the voyeuristic entertainment sector. Several participatory TV channels and programs that counter such passivity and pseudo-participation have emerged from the arts field, for instance, "Superchannel," Internet TV produced since 1998 by the Danish group Superflex in cooperation with Sean Treadway, and "tv-tv," a broadcasting slot on a local public access channel in Copenhagen which is used by a group of artists and art theorists associated with the Copenhagen Free University.[18] Superchannel devises various methods of participation. Temporary studios are occasionally created as a contribution to exhibitions in institutions, such as in the Kunsthalle in Vienna. The Kunsthalle put together a program on the theme "Europe?" whereby use of the medium in this case did not diverge from the traditional one-way transmission of a discussion in an art institution. Another, more long-term project was established in a housing estate in Liverpool. For "Tenantspin," the medium was used to draw attention to problems arising locally in high-rise housing, to promote social exchange among residents by means of collaborative work on the project, and to communicate with other groups via the Internet. Because the respective channels were unable to take up independent, direct contact with one another but instead had to run all contributions through the Superchannel common server, the potential radicalism of the Internet's communication structure, namely, the decentralization of news-reading, publishing, filmmaking, and broadcasting, was capped at the systemic level. The tv-tv project, in contrast, uses a centralized TV-broadcasting structure, while decentralizing this by drawing on a broad network of local production groups. In this way public media are defined not only by the common use of a particular medium but to a much larger extent by the fact that the groups are constituted in a decentralized structure on account of the independent program material that they produce. For Mark Poster, the Internet's technological potential for decentralization is its decisive achievement, for it marks the end of the era of public space as face-to-face communication and hence calls for a new interpretation of the concept of democracy with respect to the potential of electronic communication, even beyond the virtual communities of mailing lists, chat rooms, and commercial or institutionalized networks.[19] Such democratization primarily affects the constitution of the subject, which on the Internet can be chosen at will.

Imaginary Communities

In the aforementioned art projects, definitions of communities and of public spaces accord with one another to the extent that they abrogate models that depend on concurrent identities—such as were reproduced in early community-based art projects and which hence affirm communitarian ideals—and instead explore in various ways models of public participation which are informed by the diversity and creativity of virtual and experimental communities. The attractiveness of the currently popular concept of the "imaginary"[20] leads one to suspect that, with hindsight on modernity, the conflict-ridden discussions on the status of imaginary communities in a fragmented public space might be raised to a narrative, symbolic-political, or possibly even utopian level, from which real effects might yet still be stimulated: "These imaginary communities are 'nowhere' ... precisely to the degree that they make somewhere possible, offering a mechanism by which people will invent anew the communities as well as the places they inhabit."[21]

Translated from the German by Jill Denton

Notes

1 Chantal Mouffe, *The Democratic Paradox* (London: Verso, 2000); see also Claude Lefort, "The Question of Democracy," in *Democracy and Political Theory*, trans. David Macey (Minneapolis: University of Minnesota Press, 1988).
2 Nancy Fraser, "Transnationalizing the Public Sphere," Republic Art Web site, http://www.republicart.net/disc/publicum/fraser01_en.htm (published on the site in March 2005).
3 Jean-Luc Nancy, *The Inoperative Community*, trans. and ed. Peter Connor (Minneapolis: University of Minnesota Press, 1991).
4 Giorgio Agamben, *The Coming Community*, trans. Michael Hardt (Minneapolis: University of Minnesota Press, 1993).
5 See also Stella Rollig's contribution in this volume.
6 Suzanne Lacy, "Cultural Pilgrimages and Metaphoric Journeys," in *Mapping the Terrain: New Genre Public Art* (Seattle: Bay Press, 1995), 19–47.
7 "Video itself emerged as the artist's tool for engaging the neighborhood, enlisting students, meeting other people, and learning the terrain" (Mary Jane Jacob, *Culture in Action: A Public Art Program of Sculpture Chicago* [exhibition catalog; Seattle: Bay Press, 1995], 76–87).
8 Henri Lefèbvre defines the production of "counterspace" as a subversive strategy: "forces that run counter to a given strategy and occasionally succeed in establishing a 'counterspace' within a particular space." See his *The Production of Space* (Cambridge, MA: Blackwell, 1995), 367.
9 Christian Kravagna, "Modelle partizipatorischer Praxis," in *Die Kunst des Öffentlichen*, ed. Marius Babias and Achim Könnecke (Dresden: Verlag der Kunst, 1998), 28–47, here pp. 34–35.
10 Gerald Raunig, "Spacing the Lines: Konflikte statt Harmonie, Differenz statt Identität, Struktur statt Hilfe," in *Dürfen die das?*, ed. Stella Rollig and Eva Sturm (Vienna: Verlag Turia + Kant, 2002), 118–127, here p. 125.

11 See Beatrice von Bismarck on the concept of temporary communities: "Verhandlungssachen: Rollen und Praktiken in der Projektarbeit," in *Kunst des Ausstellens,* ed. Hans Dieter Huber, Hubert Locher, and Karin Schulte (Ostfildern-Ruit, Germany: Hatje Cantz, 2002), 229-236, here p. 235.
12 Carlos Basualdo and Reinaldo Laddaga, "Rules of Engagement," *Artforum* 43, no. 7 (March 2004): 166-169, here p. 169.
13 Park Fiction, realized since 1995 in the Antoni Park in the St. Pauli district of Hamburg, is a cooperative project realized by the artists Margit Czenki, Christoph Schäfer, and Cathy Skene; residents of the St. Pauli district; other activists; and a landscape architect. See also the contribution to this volume by Stephan Lanz.
14 The interactive program was created in collaboration with the media collective V2_lab in Rotterdam and Maaike Engelen. Atelier van Lieshout designed the interactive bus-stop kiosks.
15 Howard Rheingold, *The Virtual Community: Homesteading on the Electronic Frontier* (Reading, MA: Addison-Wesley, 1993).
16 Stacy Horn, *Cyberville: Clicks, Culture, and the Creation of an Online Town* (New York: Warner, 1998).
17 Marion Hamm, "Indymedia—Zur Verkettung von physikalischen und virtuellen Öffentlichkeiten," in *Publicum: Theorien der Öffentlichkeit,* ed. Gerald Raunig and Ulf Wuggenig (Vienna: Turia + Kant, 2005), 176-186.
18 The project "tv-tv" was founded by Kristina Ask, Stine Eriksen, Joachim Hamou, Kent Hansen, Henriette Heise, Christian Hillesøe, Ulla Hvejsel, Jakob Jakobsen, Marie Reynolds, Katya Sander, and Simon Sheikh.
19 Mark Poster, "CyberDemocracy: Internet and the Public Sphere," University of California, Irvine, School of Humanities Web site, http://www.humanities.uci.edu/mposter/writings/democ.html.
20 See, for example, Anselm Franke and Hila Peleg, eds., *The Imaginary Number* (exhibition catalog; Berlin: 2005). In the exhibition and an accompanying essay, Franke examines "the artistic imagination in relation to the imaginary work in a society at large."
21 Cf. Phillip E. Wegner, *Imaginary Communities: Utopia, the Nation, and the Spatial Histories of Modernity* (Berkeley: University of California Press, 2002), xvi-xvii.

[MURMUR]

Toronto, Vancouver, and Montreal, Canada, since 2003
Gabe Sawhney, James Roussel, and Shawn Micallef
http://murmurtoronto.ca, http://murmurvancouver.ca, and http://murmure.ca

"This is [murmur], what's the code?" asks a voice, when one dials the number on one of the audio stations that can be found in public spaces in Toronto, Vancouver, and Montreal. Dialing a further code allows one to listen to site-specific stories and histories of the district's inhabitants.

The project "[murmur]" was initiated in 2003 in the Canadian city of Toronto in Kensington Market, a district reputed to be boring and unspectacular. On the premise that even ordinary parts of a city are full of experiences, the developers of [murmur] collected inhabitants' anecdotes about different locations. This resulted in an audio archive of diverse urban histories from past and present, along with futuristic interpretations of what particular locations might become.

The stories introduce new perspectives on the city to listeners. Perception and interpretation become more complex, and an unusual body of knowledge emerges about otherwise ordinary, everyday places. (Ed.)

Map of audio stations in the Kensington Market district of Toronto.

IMMAGINARE CORVIALE
Rome, 2003–2005
Osservatorio Nomade/Stalker and Laboratorio Territoriale West Rome
www.corvialenetwork.net

Corviale, a building almost one kilometer in length and with 6,500 inhabitants, was designed by the architect Mario Fiorentino and built on the southeastern periphery of Rome in the late 1970s. Despite facilities such as a senior citizen's center, a library, education centers, and district committees, Corviale conforms to the stereotype of an alienated and forlorn estate on the city margins. In 2004 its demolition and replacement by a neomedieval village hung in the balance.

The development of new forms of urban democracy was seen as an alternative strategy. The main concern of the residents was the need to create a new identity for the district, based on tangible redevelopment of the area. This concern prompted the architects' group Osservatorio Nomade/Stalker and the Laboratorio Territoriale West Rome, commissioned and largely financed by the city administration of Rome, to embark on a search for solutions. This evolved into a one-year project, curated and cofinanced by the Adriano Olivetti Foundation, which aimed at artistic production and the encouragement of residents to get involved. The project took an experimental approach to researching how the spaces and immediate vicinity of Corviale are experienced, imagined, and transformed. The city implemented a redevelopment scheme for the building during the same period.

The result was an atlas of micro-transformations and an appropriation of space which demonstrates residents' liberal interpretations of the models of accommodation and social life put forth by planners. A "Manual for the Use of the Building" was intended to raise awareness of how one might live in an architectural prototype for a community utopia. A local "street-TV" station was set up for one and one-half months to counter media coverage condemning the district. "Corviale Network" was produced in cooperation with Corviale's residents and broadcast by cable to the entire building. The channels Sky and Roma Uno broadcast weekly fifteen-minute excerpts from programs such as *La prova dell'ascensore* (casting residents in the elevators) and *Casa Fraterno* (featuring conversations between architects, planners, and a long-time resident during dinner in the latter's apartment), as well as from opinions polls about Corviale conducted with residents of other districts and the comments of Corviale residents about the workshops offered by the Corviale UniverCity established by the Osservatorio Nomade. (Ed.)

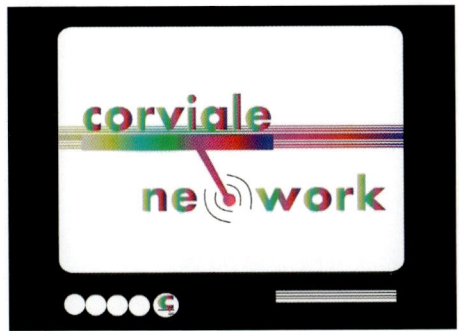

"Corviale Network" street-TV.

TENANTSPIN (SUPERCHANNEL)
Liverpool, UK, since 2001
Superflex with Sean Treadway, FACT (Foundation for Art & Creative Technology)
www.tenantspin.org and www.superflex.net

"Superchannel" is a communication tool for social self-empowerment. It enables individuals to set up their own TV channel and broadcast their own program on the Internet. What initially transpired in a small gallery in Copenhagen as an experiment by the group Superflex has in the meantime grown into a network of 26 small TV studios. Broadcast via the Internet permits viewers to use chat rooms to contact the producers and other viewers during live transmissions. The studios, which are located at diverse, primarily European locations, thus function as discussion forums, a means of presenting programs, and a meeting point for local communities.

The first studio to emerge outside an artistic context was set up in 2001 in Coronation Court, a tenement block in a district of Liverpool. Some years ago, when plans to relocate tenants were made in response to imminent urban redevelopment, fears arose that contact between neighbors would be adversely affected. This led the Housing Action Trust, which owned the building, to cooperate with the state-funded cultural center FACT (Foundation for Art & Creative Technology) in developing new media projects with the residents. In the course of the project the population of Coronation Court, mainly elderly people, learned various stages of Internet film production, from research through to presentation. They produced features about their lives and their neighborhood that were broadcast once a week. Although the Coronation Court channel was shut down following demolition of the building in spring 2002, FACT and the Arena Housing Association have continued the concept with the "Tenantspin" channel, for which residents of various high-rise blocks in Liverpool create their own program collectively.

Another Liverpool project set up to facilitate access to broadcasting media is "Toxteth TV" (TTV). It operates somewhat differently, however. In contrast to Superchannel, TTV is not a TV station but a nonprofit production company that uses profits accruing from the subletting of TV studios to finance an education center for young people and young entrepreneurs: a place where the residents of a deprived district are taught how to use communication media.

The construction of a production studio for TTV in Windsor Street in Liverpool corresponded with project participants' wishes for sustainable redevelopment of the district. The complex of buildings has functioned as a catalyst, leading to job creation and the economic revival of a neglected area. (Ed.)

"Superchannel" as a TV station for residents of the Coronation Court tenement block in Liverpool.

Programs produced by residents were broadcast once a week on the "Tenantspin" channel.

KARLSKRONA2 (SUPERCITY)
Karlskrona, Sweden/virtual, 1999–2002
Superflex with Rune Nielsen
www.karlskrona2.org and www.superflex.net/tools/supercity/karlskrona2

The southern Swedish town Karlskrona—which until the fall of the iron curtain occupied a relatively peripheral situation on the Baltic Coast and declined economically due to crises of the steel and shipbuilding industries—has aspired since 1990 to a new role as a regional economic center founded primarily on the development of service industries and IT-related or knowledge-based centers. Simultaneously, the city has made an enormous effort to improve and market its public profile as an attractive place to live and work. It was during this period of economic upswing that the city of Karlskrona commissioned the artists' group Superflex to develop a public art project that would offer a democratic platform for public communication.

Superflex created the "Supercity" *Karlskrona2* (K2), a virtual replica of Karlskrona city center. This was to serve as a field of experimentation in which residents of Karlskrona could create a digital character or virtual alter ego and interact online. In this way, the Internet is used as a local medium of exchange. Residents of Karlskrona have exclusive rights to interact on the site, whereas people from elsewhere must log into K2 as tourists. The virtual Karlskrona and the real city are thus at least partially "inhabited" by the same people, who communicate with one another in chat rooms. K2 began as an exact replica of the real town and was changed over time. In the "open space" of K2 users or, rather, their alter egos could take part in designing the city at both the urban-planning and the social levels. Subsequently, new objects were designed or existing buildings assigned a new function, social hierarchies were disrupted, and existing laws were amended.

For financial reasons, the original concept—which had anticipated presenting users' suggestions and discussions by screening the alternative virtual world of K2 in the real city of Karlskrona—was not realized. (Ed.)

Communicating City

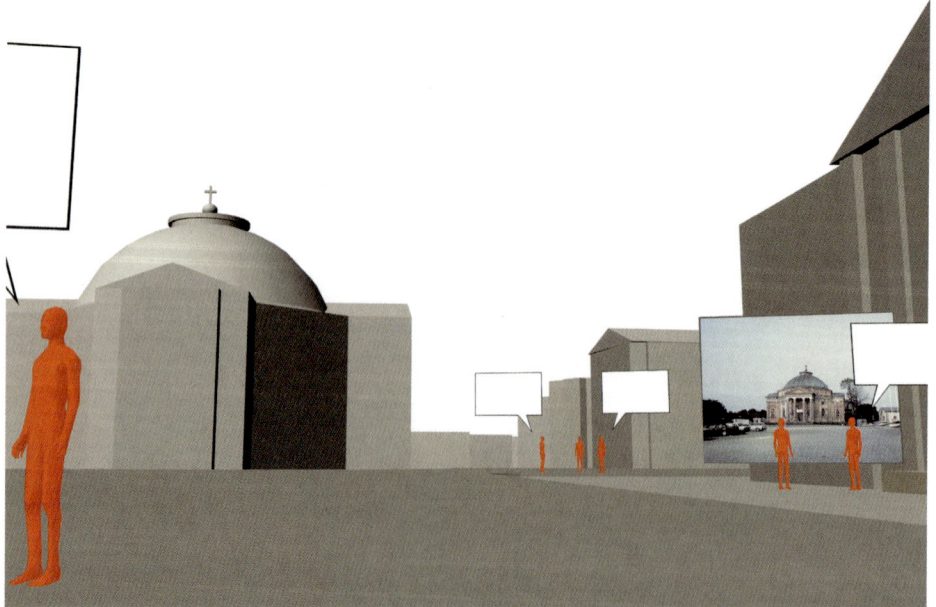

Public screenings of its virtual replica, *Karlskrona2,* were planned for the city of Karlskrona. Its residents can manipulate and develop the interactive virtual world of *Karlskrona2* online.

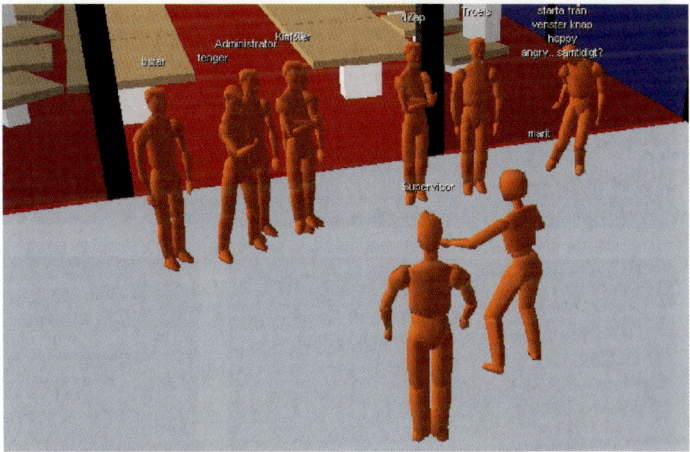
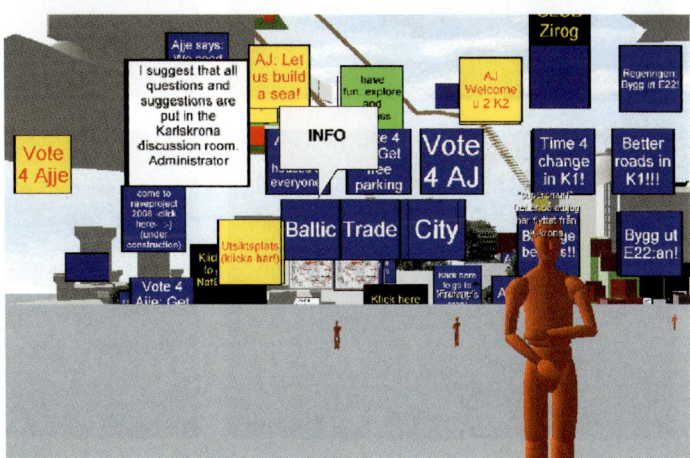

WALK THE CITY, FLEX YOUR MIND
WALKING AS AN ARTISTIC AND EVERYDAY PRACTICE
Gregor Harbusch

When, in 1957, Guy Debord created his now renowned collaged maps of Paris *(The Naked City* and *Guide Psychogéographique de Paris)* and thereby depicted various significant city-center districts as free-floating islands that were related to one another merely by a plethora of arrows, an almost incidental side-effect was the premonition of the structural characteristics of suburban space, such as were to establish themselves in the following decades. Debord's poetic representation of a fragmented city, inspired by the impassioned practice of walking through distinctive Parisian districts and researching their particular position and atmosphere, comes to mind in a more prosaic variation today when conversation turns to sprawling, unassigned spaces on the city margins. Whether these are expanding or shrinking is irrelevant to the general picture: suburban space is a city's stepchild, not only neglected by town planners but most of the time simply ignored. Quite aside from the fact that the proliferation of suburban structures is a problem faced by numerous shrinking cities, it is the ignorance of public consciousness regarding certain urban areas' very existence that allows parallels to be drawn with how marginal spaces, an increasingly permanent feature of shrinking cities, are dealt with. This ignorance in everyday perception is, however, being countered by several projects that follow, so to speak, in the footsteps of Debord and his colleagues in the Situationist International, whose favored method of perceiving the city was to consciously walk or drift through it.

The Situationists had developed their theory of *dérive* (drifting) in reference to Dadaist and Surrealist practices and in the context of a decidedly antibourgeois, utopian-revolutionary attitude and orientation. Accordingly, to drift about the city presented them not only with playful but also with excessive moments. They attempted to describe the relationships between space, time, and passions by conducting an affective survey of the city and by abandoning themselves to the stimuli offered by the spaces explored. The resulting psycho-geographic maps facilitated a completely novel regard for the atmospheric qualities of spaces which had hitherto been neglected.

In order to clarify both the range of the Situationist theory of "drifting" and walking as a conscious act, it is helpful to consider Michel de Certeau's constitutive thoughts on walking as a spatial practice. For de Certeau, the relationship between the act of walking and space is analogous to the relationship between the act of speaking and linguistic elements. Just as the speaker is able to delve into a trove of viable linguistic elements in order to appropriate these—in his personal style—and by uttering them actually make language manifest, so the walker draws on spatial elements, appropriates these in his individual manner of strolling, and thus comprehends space as an organic structure of meanings. By availing himself of forms in the sense intended by a system or, equally, by subverting this sense, the subject constructs personal meaning. In this respect, the act of walking and the immediate experience of space—as an everyday or artistic activity—are potential means of experiencing supposedly unviable spaces in a new way and of making them one's own. Regarding the fragmentation of urban structures—also and in particular in shrinking cities—the tropes of synecdoche and asyndeton on which de Certeau focuses are relevant here. The synecdoche is the rhetorical figure of the part instead of the whole. It replaces totalities with fragments and thus delivers a less instead of a more. The asyndeton, in contrast, describes the omission of connections, a destruction of continuity, and a challenge to the latter's likelihood: "space is transformed into enlarged singularities and isolated islands."

It is precisely the extreme forms of such isolated islands—characterized most frequently by disused land or derelict buildings—that are perceived as problematic in shrinking cities, for they conflict with traditional ideas of urban density. Lucius Burckhardt—the "father of the science of walking," who coined the term "strollology"—said of rural wasteland something that applies equally to its urban counterpart. Although as an individual phenomenon it might occasionally be of aesthetic interest, wasteland nevertheless interrupts the totality of the spatial construct that a person taking a walk habitually expects to find, and thus requires some explanation. In Burckhardt's terms, wasteland refers to any arrangement of spatial elements that appears illogical, and thus connotes any rupture with established expectations regarding space per se. Burckhardt's criticism of romanticized concepts of landscape (which expound the picturesque qualities of agrarian regions and ignore their exploitative economic aspects) leads him to plea for a renewed perception of contemporary forms of landscape—namely, by taking a stroll in a manner that raises awareness of the constructed nature of established images of landscape.

Artistic works that employ the practice of walking in public spaces are informed by this briefly sketched and purely subjective selection of theoretical positions. They are focused expressly on sensitizing the subject in a particular space to its qualities, and interweave space, recipient, and movement with narrative elements or emphasize performative moments.

Following the Lucius Burckhardt tradition, Boris Sieverts's Bureau for City Trips (Büro für Städtereisen) organizes extensive guided walks, primarily around Cologne, that convey both the aesthetic potential of cities' marginal areas and individuals' private and personal relationship to them. The areas covered by Sieverts's guided walks evince characteristics of suburban spaces that can be found in shrinking cities as well, and for this reason his approach is of interest in regard to the latter. The guided walks focus on walking and on participants' experience of successive spaces; they are precisely composed and, in order to convey the spaces' essential qualities on more than a merely visual level, are enhanced by diverse activities such as picnicking or swimming, making a fire, or chatting with local residents. Sieverts describes his activity as a way of simultaneously compressing and poeticizing experience (and plays thereby on the German words *dichten,* meaning to write poetry, and *Verdichtung,* meaning compression). The course of a tour is organized in a way that allows an area's richness to become apparent and its aesthetic qualities—he speaks of the aesthetic sustainability and complexity of space that only appears to be lacking in signifiers—to be experienced.

Sieverts writes that he is not interested in establishing a dichotomy of actual and in-between spaces: he is not walking through gaps in space but through space itself. A new form of perception and aesthetic appreciation is asserted here, and its applicability to the shrinking context must be examined. To present arguments solely from an aesthetic perspective is dangerous, as this would imply the total complex of problems associated with the modern visual primate (distance, clarity, and so forth). In contrast, Sieverts's study of a wild settlement, to which he attributes an exemplary exposition of the conditions of

LOVE AT LEISURE. HELP ME STRANGER. ROUNDABOUT.
North Adams and Williamstown, Massachusetts, USA, spring 2004
e-Xplo: Rene Gabri, Heimo Lattner, and Erin McGonigle
www.e-Xplo.org

North Adams was once the largest city in the United States of America and yet today it has only fifteen thousand inhabitants. Following the closure of the last major company in 1986, efforts to revitalize the city failed until the Massachusetts Museum of Contemporary Art (MassMoCA) opened in 1998. An upturn has since begun: tourists come, along with the wave of residents who moved to rural areas in the wake of 9/11.

Using interviews with stockbrokers, politicians, and residents, the e-Xplo group has turned the area's history, its current situation, and its hopes for the future into an audio play that was broadcast as part of a bus tour. The tour went from North Adams to nearby Williamstown and back again. On the outward trip one could listen to excerpts from interviews and unedited audio material, whereas in the second part local residents told their own stories as characters in a play. The bus tour ran for two months, departing from MassMoca every two hours. (Ed.)

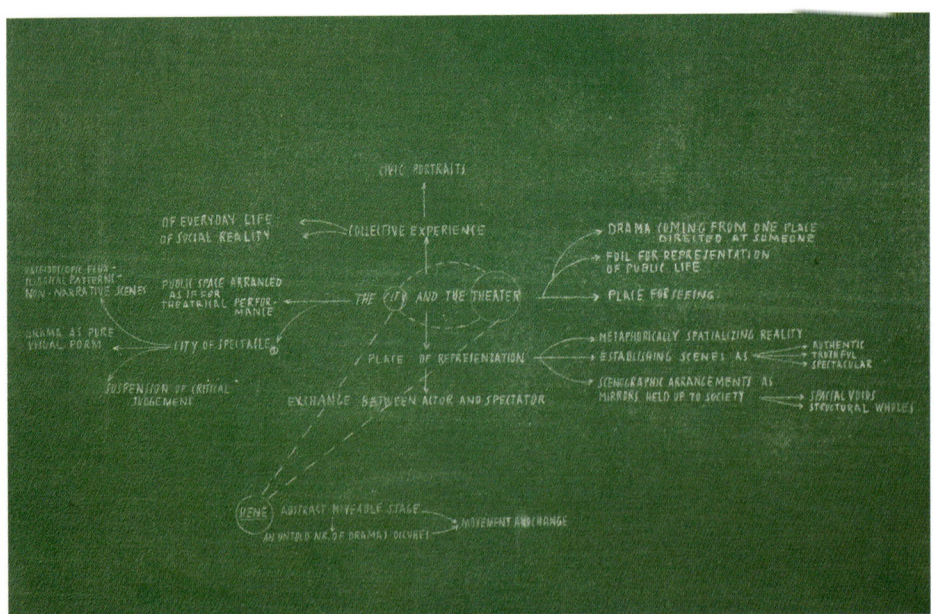

Diagram of the structure and dramaturgy of the bus tour.

suburban forms of life, seems instructive. Sieverts investigated the historical origins, property relations, and social structure of an illegal settlement in the Wiedenpesch district of Cologne. He concludes that the settlement does indeed represent a free space within society and that the "patchwork" structuring principle characterizes both its architecture and the lifestyles of its residents. The settlement therefore epitomizes a space for self-determined lifestyles and shows that the indeterminate, transitory, and wildly seeded aspects of such areas not only are articulated on an aesthetic level but also—due to free spaces or niches in society, as well as to administrative neglect—possess a subversive potential, whereby one might without further ado assert that here, in societal terms, an in-between space has indeed emerged, for it is indisputable that illegal settlements constitute a socially marginal phenomenon. To go for a walk under this premise can indeed broaden one's cognitive facilities with regard to perceptions of the city.

The so-called audio walks, created by Canadian artists Janet Cardiff and George Bures Miller, work with multifarious combinations of space, recipient, movement, and narration and point in quite another direction. The audio walks are a kind of deeply atmospheric "air-waves theater": complex narratives listened to via Discman while following a certain route on foot. Cardiff and Miller use a binary-aural recording technique that immerses the recipient in the simulation of an extremely differentiated and realistic sonic space (e.g., the tonal complexity of a busy street). This sonic space is overlaid by visual impressions, which are lent a cinematic quality through this sound. Complex narrative fragments, observations on the spaces walked through, and a permanent play with the various levels of perception and reality conjured by the work are superimposed on these sonic spaces.

The audio walks have not yet taken place in suburban areas; their settings have been in the palimpsest of a city center, inscribed by countless historical and individual moments that are mirrored in the nonlinear narratives. Certain themes appear in these repeatedly: disappearance and loss, a vaguely constituted narrative "I", and a diffuse longing. The superimposition of these sufficiently familiar psychological motives on the spaces walked through opens up a field of interpretation that links the urban space to indefinite forms of loss and a blurring of contours which are perceived either with melancholy or with a tinge of excitement. The work of Cardiff and Miller has an audio-immersive power that is difficult to describe and that nevertheless really does succeed in raising the experience of being-in-space to a level at which the narrative establishes a connection between the person walking and space, making the latter's constructed nature and historicity tangible.

A reference to cinematic techniques is equally appropriate when describing the bus tours created by the art group e-Xplo (comprising Rene Gabri, Heimo Lattner, and Erin McGonigle), which invite one to ride rather than walk. In particular, e-Xplo organizes nocturnal bus tours that offer a combination of narratives, theoretical and literary texts, music, and field recordings related to the area traveled through. The bus tour becomes a vehicle of a distanced perception of the city, yet it simultaneously employs various mechanisms to break down this distance, cite forms of cinematic reception, and link various urban areas, thereby creating a new consciousness of a city's contexts and hidden qualities. The group e-Xplo also always makes efforts to convey the complex political and social contexts that determine the formation and self-perception of urban spaces.

Communicating City

Someone standing directly behind you whispers in your ear; horse-drawn carriages sweep by so close it makes you jump, perhaps you even witness a secret romance.... This is the kind of experience that participants in Janet Cardiff's audio walks in Münster can expect, listening via Discman to voices and sounds, such as street noise or birdsong, mixed with people's narratives and personal reflections on places along the route. These conjure extremely varied atmospheres and associations, fuse real and fictitious space, and invite the listener to take a new look at the city around him.

Walk the City, Flex Your Mind_Gregor Harbusch

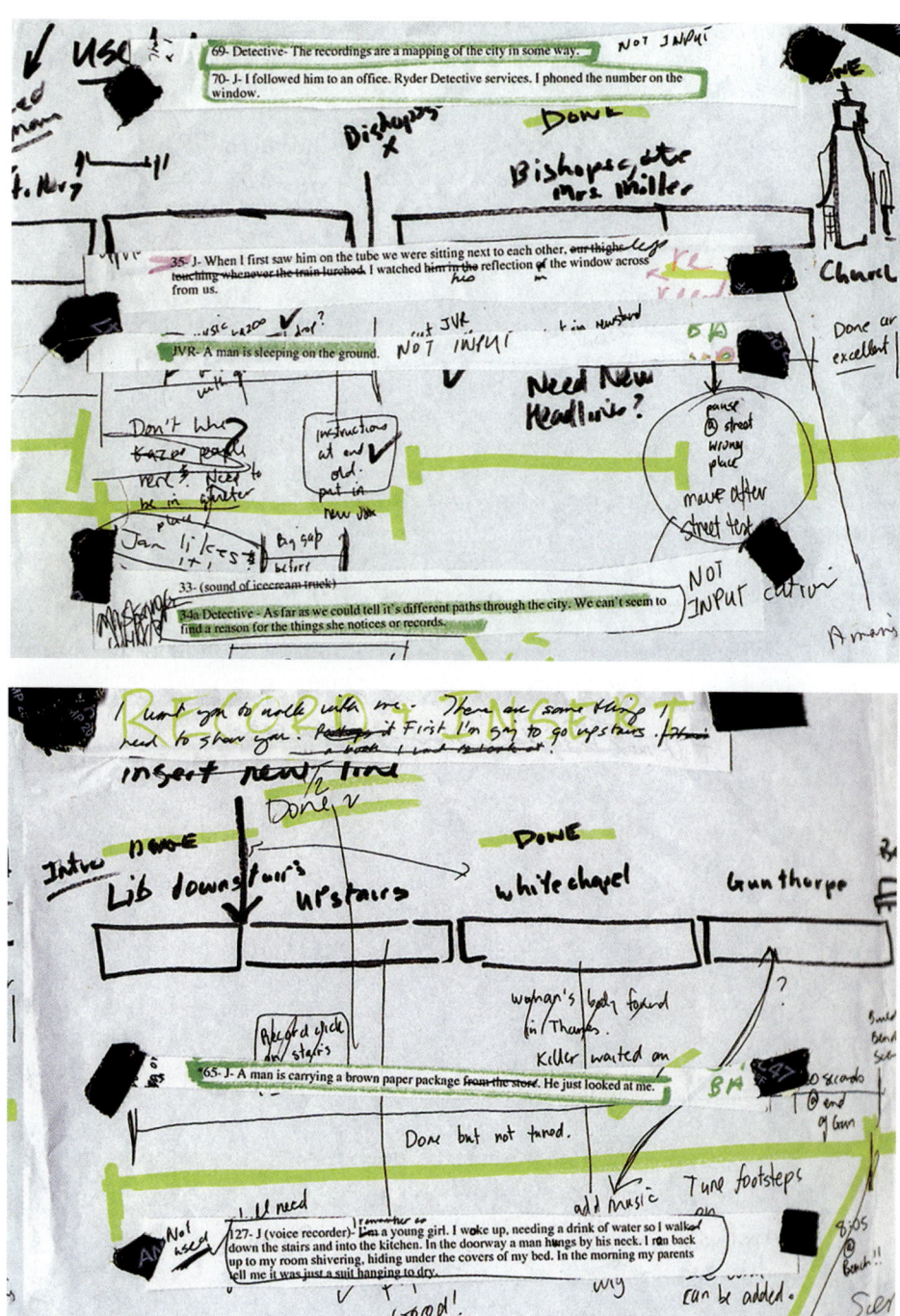

Score for the interplay of real space and narratives. The audio walk *The Missing Voice (Case Study B)* by Janet Cardiff for the Whitechapel Gallery, London, 1999.

Its bus tour *Love at Leisure. Help Me Stranger. Roundabout.* was conducted in spring 2004 in an area of Massachusetts faced with the effects of shrinkage. Interviews about the precarious issues of property and local politics were carried out with the residents of two very different towns, Williamstown and North Adams. The ensuing audio material was listened to during one half of the bus tour, the drive from North Adams to Williamstown. By way of contrast, the drive back to North Adams had a more cinematic and fictional character. The tour not only created a spatial connection but, by permitting a glimpse of the biographies of local residents, turned the experience into a portrait of an area characterized by shrinking. The classic bus tour through apparently unremarkable districts thus became a means of propagating unprejudiced perception: the local residents' personal narratives countered the distancing effect that a bus tour habitually creates.

Perhaps the core of conscious walking—motion as a means of connecting physical and mental spaces—can be rendered equally fertile by far simpler strategies. San Keller's action *The Long Way Home—San Keller Accompanies You Home* succeeds in combining walking and social contacts by employing very simple performative elements. It also inspires one to consider transposing this artistic strategy from its original location—New York in winter—to the context of shrinking cities. The basic idea of *The Long Way Home* is delightfully simple. Flyers were used to invite potential participants to meet the artist at ten o'clock on a certain evening in New York's Grand Central Station, from where the impromptu group would set about accompanying each other home. It was decided first of all which route would be most practical and, hence, in which order the participants would reach their respective homes. Once a participant arrived at home, he took leave of the group or perhaps invited the remaining participants to briefly warm up inside before continuing on their way. As most of the participants met for the first time through this shared activity, it and their common route through the city were an obvious topic of conversation. They talked about the city, as perceived through the lives of people living there.

The shift of emphasis from perception per se to a more social experience, as exemplified by Keller's action, might perhaps lend a new quality to walking in shrinking cities: one that combines the act of walking with a heightened awareness of the problematic and ongoing decline of public life there; that encourages a readiness to experience coincidental and playful moments (such as were encouraged by the Situationists' practice of "drifting"); and that, simply due to the physical exertion of walking for several hours, simultaneously creates an earnest and actual physical connection to the spaces walked through. Keller acknowledges that his function consists in serving the group: he does nothing more than set a framework and rules for the action, within which the route and communication can then develop freely. It is neither a case of exploring a precisely composed, linear route and experiencing its suggestive power, nor a case of endowing the spaces explored with a preconceived store of stories and memories and subsequent legibility. Instead, quite simply, social factors come into play, spaces are walked through for the most absurd reasons, and the private poles of existence in the frayed fabric of public life are consciously addressed.

Nocturnal wanderings in wintry New York perhaps lie closer to the pessimistic self-perception of some shrinking cities than one might initially want to believe—and perhaps, in the shared experience of space lies the key to a new perception of it. Under this premise, one might once again glean from the late work of Lucius Burckhardt how he imagined a successful and potent postmodern landscape. Beyond the established formulas such as "wasteland plus talkativeness" (in reference, for example, to semantically overloaded buildings in a green meadow) or "total predetermination of form and roles" (as in shopping malls and Disneyland, for example, or in historical cities that have been renovated to death), he posited this: a postmodern landscape as a mixture of human activity and leisure and chance.

Translated from the German by Jill Denton

Literature
Burckhardt, Lucius. *Warum ist Landschaft schön?—Die Spaziergangswissenschaft*. Edited by Markus Ritter and Martin Schmitz. Berlin: Martin Schmitz Verlag, 2006.
Careri, Francesco. *Walkscapes: Walking as an Aesthetic Practice*. Barcelona: Gustavo Gil, 2002.
Certeau, Michel de. *The Practice of Everyday Life*. Berkeley: University of California Press, 2002.
Höger, Hans, ed. *Lucius Burckhardt: Design = unsichtbar*. Ostfildern-Ruit, Germany: Hatje Cantz, 1995.
Sadler, Simon. *The Situationist City*. Cambridge, MA: MIT Press, 1998.

RAINWATER RETENTION TANKS ON LAND AWAITING DEVELOPMENT – A CITY WALK
Leipzig, Germany, 2004
Boris Sieverts with Karin Geiger and Stefan Hostlettler
www.neueraeume.de

Since 1998 Boris Sieverts has been offering tourists and local people guided walks through German suburbs. Walks to these seemingly indistinct urban spaces are intended to highlight their respective aesthetic qualities and the specific realities experienced there. As part of the seminar "Learning from Leipzig," held by Professor Joachim Brohm for advanced students of photography at Leipzig's Academy for Visual Arts, Boris Sieverts led walks through areas of Leipzig with which students and academic staff had hitherto been unfamiliar. The goal of "land reclamation"—enlarging one's own local field of activity—was to focus on those diffuse urban structures to the north and the east of Leipzig that do not generally figure in local residents' image of the city. The route, which was partially covered by bike, starts at a shopping mall, cuts across land awaiting development, passes by pre-1939 and prefab housing estates, through a ditch (where one's feet get a good soaking) and the overgrown margins of housing estates, before ending in a large meadow with a view of the motorway. Breakfast in an association's canteen, or chance conversations, for example in front of a family's detached house, assure some contact to the local population. Photographs taken during the walks and further research activities were exhibited and later published as a book.

Boris Sieverts brings his specific style of observation to bear on planning processes, too. His contribution to plans for village development in Ödenwaldstetten in the Schwäbische Alb was to read the village as a "labyrinth" and "prairie," elaborating and mapping out its specific spatial qualities. He thus interpreted informal spaces such as a vacant lot or a yard entrance as an actual village square, where villagers might play boules or watch TV together—activities that local participants in "guided village walks" have sometimes taken up. (Ed.)

The original German title of this project is "Regenrückhaltebecken im Bauerwartungsland – Ein Stadtspaziergang."

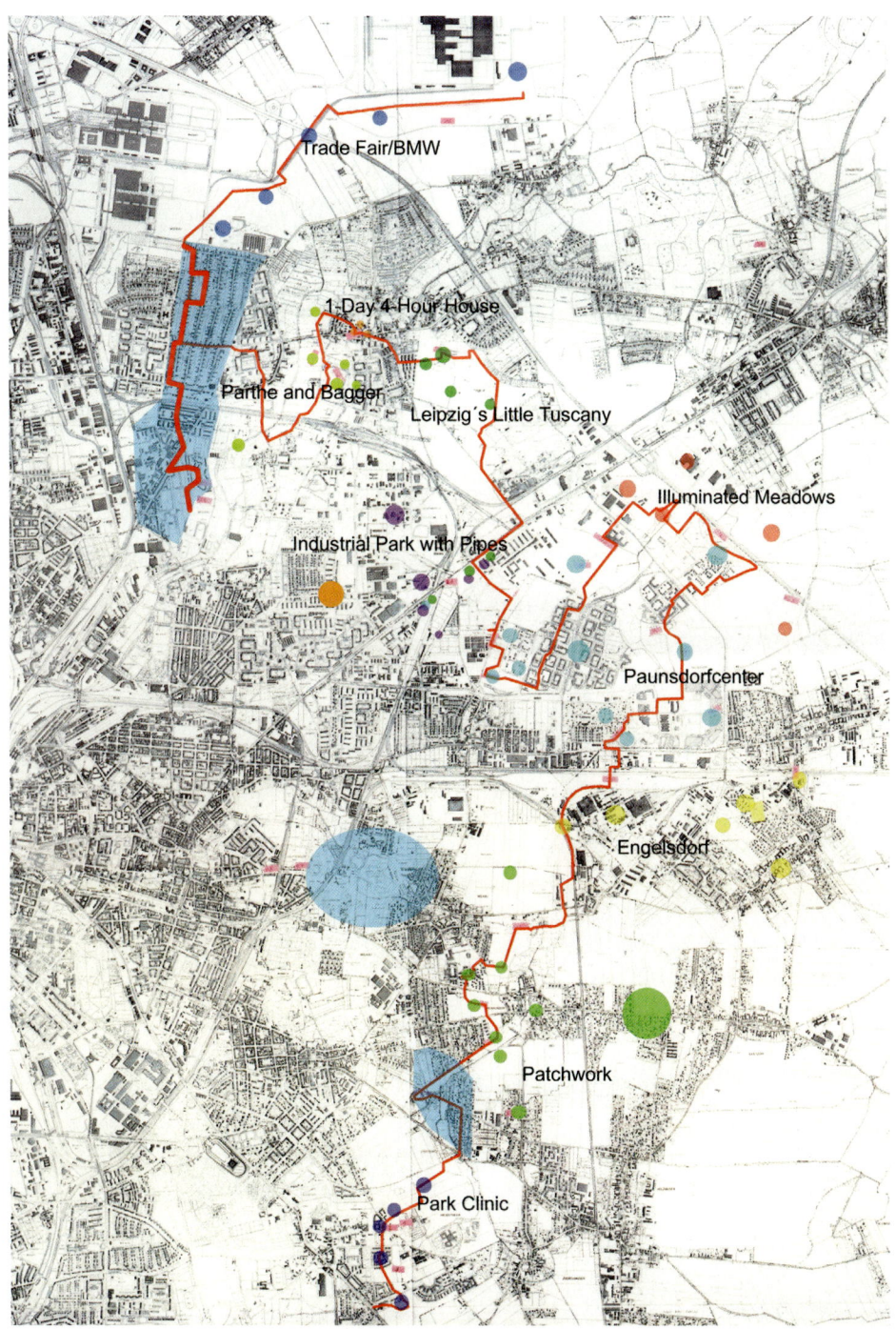

Map of the guided walk through eastern Leipzig, 2004.

The walk in the eastern periphery of Leipzig led through in-between spaces that are otherwise overlooked.

COMMUNICATION WITH THE ONES WHO LEFT
THE SIGNIFICANCE OF THE INTERNET FOR TRANSNATIONAL SOCIAL NETWORKS
Mirjam Struppek

In Berlin districts with a large immigrant population, one frequently comes across small shops offering Internet access and cheap calls abroad. The need to remain in touch with one's homeland is manifest here, a need that can be fulfilled increasingly by the new media.

Since the mid-1990s, theoretical approaches in the field of migration research have sought models that take better account of the social causes and attendant circumstances of migration. One focus of this revived interest is the proliferation of social networks, the social capital that ensues, and the way in which these accelerate the course of migration patterns. It can be observed that such networks lead to a stronger development of transnationalism: the emergence of new types of migration in complex migratory networks.[1] The prognosis is that the numbers of people commuting between their homeland and their new place of residence will increase. People, information, and goods are in circulation, which leads to a close relationship between the society of origin and the target society. A transmigrant's social field of reference is no longer bound to one particular location, but extends over various geographical areas. In view of these developments, in 1997 the sociologist Ludger Pries introduced the concept of "transnational social spaces," in which migrants' cultural, economic, and social activities unfold.[2]

Studying the forms of communication and exchange used by migrants who maintain an active relationship with their native country can be instructive when considering the problem of economic and social continuity in communities in shrinking cities. What communication and information needs ensue from the lifestyle of commuter migrants? What role do the new media play in maintaining transnational social spaces, and how do they contribute to their stability?

Mobile telephones have made it possible to communicate with acquaintances in a way that is simpler and cheaper than ever before, wherever one might be. Satellite transmissions and digitalization facilitate the reception of specifically tailored programs from geographically distant regional TV and radio broadcast stations. Contact with one's native country can thus be maintained over great distances. In the following discussion, however, I intend to concentrate primarily on the Internet. Because of its great potential for presenting information to a broad public or to specific communities and, equally, for communicating directly with individuals, the Internet is a particularly interactive means of communication with multipurpose applications. Its technical requirements are relatively minor. The same is true of the knowledge required for active production of content. The participatory generation, dissemination, and storage of information that ensue from the Internet's various interactive elements (e.g., wikis, blogs, chat rooms, newsgroups, forums, and guest books) make it an unusually accessible space for communication. In the same way as older mass media, however, it too disseminates images and narratives that affect its mostly passive users and thus puts its stamp on their perception of reality and feeling of belonging.[3]

In their essay "Networked Diasporas,"[4] the ethnologists Joanna Breidenbach and Ina Zukrigl posit four theses on the effects of the Internet, which are discussed in detail below.

1. The Internet strengthens the "diaspora family." An inexpensive medium, it stimulates contact with family and acquaintances in the country of origin, as well as with the "family of like-minded persons" elsewhere. A broad spectrum of means of expression is available, which can be extended by the integration of texts written by others, by the dispatch of visual material and electronic postcards, or simply by forwarding news. In Internet cafés and community centers in Belize, one frequently sees middle-aged women scanning family snapshots and sending them to their relatives in Los Angeles or on the Cayman Islands. The Web site *www.karaganda.de,* for example, is a small, independently created platform that illustrates what kind of information natives of the shrinking town of Karaganda in Kazakhstan require after migrating to Germany. The site's primary feature—in a sense serving as its catalyst—is a photo album of the hometown, which is open for further contributions. Various exchange mechanisms, such as a guest book, forum, and online chat room, point to the deep need for very diverse forms of active exchange. The notice board "Finding Friends" is helpful for resuming contact with acquaintances, and another link informs users about the latest cheap precodes for telephone calls to Kazakhstan. On the German-Turkish ethnic platform *www.vaybee.de,* special "rewards" beckon to anyone who helps build up the community. Anyone who distinguishes himself by regularly submitting good contributions or by showing reliability or fairness can become "Member of the Week" or be endowed by the Vaybee team with special privileges that permit active intervention in communication within the community.[5] Nor should the members' meetings organized by Vaybee be underestimated: these enable face-to-face contact and are subsequently documented on the site. The archival aspect of the Internet can be helpful in establishing a community's collective memory.

2. The Internet intensifies the relationship between a state and the diaspora. States make a conscious effort to establish close relationships with "their emigrants" and thus to strengthen loyalty to the native country. They speculate primarily on financial support for the relatives who have remained at home and investment or support for social projects. On the site *www.armenlanddiaspora.com,* for example, the Armenian government endeavors to provide its emigrant citizens with information about business networks and current events and thus involve them in native developments in economic and political fields. In former war-torn regions such as Bosnia and Eritrea, the emphasis lies decidedly on transnational participation in national reconstruction.[6] Additionally, the Internet allows migrants to articulate their concerns and interests regarding both their native and their adopted country and to formulate demands for power and participation. In online solidarity networks—and their attendant mailing lists, blogs, discussion groups, and platforms—activists and communities in exile attempt to exploit the power of the new media in order to draw wider public attention to various grievances and problems. The Net is thus particularly attractive for groups such as women and adolescents, who lack a strong public voice. The Internet's new, unfiltered possibilities of organization and self-expression promote greater self-confidence, not least because users are able to choose their own themes and emphases when submitting reports or commentaries.[7]

3. The new media offer diaspora communities a space in which their distinctive cultural characteristics can be nurtured. Various ethnographic research projects have described how the Net is used in the adopted country as a stage for the presentation of cultural

characteristics and how it clearly strengthens collective identities. Web sites such as *www.australians-abroad.com, www.farsinet.com,* and *www.indiansabroad.net*—which respectively address Australians, Iranians, and Indians living abroad—are full of culturally specific offers. Trinidadian migrants watch festivals in Trinidad live via webcam, for example, and the importance of characteristic figures of speech for their communication in chat rooms is conspicuous. The Internet offers migrants a space in which those parts of their identity that are oppressed in everyday life in a new country can be expressed. It thus contributes considerably to the process of establishing an identity "between two worlds."[8]

4. The new media are instrumental in the cultural regeneration of diaspora communities. Some portals have been developed—*www.niniveh.com* for example, the Assyrian Nineveh Online—to serve as the guardians and keepers of a specific marginalized cultural legacy. These refer primarily to the value of retaining or maintaining their specific cultural characteristics. In a shrinking process in which a whole town is threatened with extinction, as in the case of Hoyerswerda, such portals can acquire a commemorative function and document and archive local characteristics.

A fifth thesis should be added here as a final aspect. The Internet is a source of information that offers practical support in difficult situations. The sheltered space of discussion forums and chat rooms can help people living "between two worlds" to process the emotional upheaval of their particular circumstances or to solve specific problems. The Net offers a third space, so to speak, a virtual home: a "healthy distance" from the conflicts and problems that arise both in the new home and in the "native" environment of the place left behind. Steven Vertovec further emphasizes the importance of social networks when it comes to finding jobs, accommodation, services, and new or used goods.[9] In this regard, Internet platforms that target particular groups or needs can be an invaluable resource, for the "amateur" knowledge of people who have gone through similar experiences can easily be mobilized.

But how might these insights into such forms of communication as they pertain to international migration patterns be applied to small-scale migration in the context of shrinking? Nils Zurawski emphasizes the self-management potential of the Internet, supported by "ethnicity as a resource of self-management."[10] Defining the sense of belonging to a particular region or even to a city as ethnicity is a trend consistent with current moves in urban marketing to reinforce regional identities and promote particular locational advantages: both important factors in an era of globalization. The following four examples present online projects that deal specifically with a shrinking region or town and their "transregional" migrants.

The Web site *www.hoelle-saale.de* is an unusual information platform that confirms many of the aforementioned theses. It has become a permanent "hobby project" of the Vröhliche Vagabunde (Merry Vagabonds) in Halle. Creative provocation is used here to attract attention, promote community understanding, and, hence, strengthen the "diaspora family." The site also encourages a sense of community by instigating lotteries, fan clubs, and a "Photo of the Month." A humorous look at daily life in the shrinking city of Halle prompts widespread discussion and reflection on the negative image and menacing decline of the (home)town. A countdown ticks toward the day of its demise, for example, and former residents of Halle can immortalize themselves in the "Joldenen Buch"

(Golden Book) or explain why they may eventually return. A guest book and a chat room (in which one can also chat with local politicians) offer a channel for everyday problems and criticism, through which demands for participation in policy-making regarding the hometown's development are articulated. A dictionary encourages people to learn the regional dialect, and traditional products from the region are presented in an attempt to promote and preserve local specialties. The ever-growing photo archive of the changing city helps establish the collective memory of its current and former residents. Finally, somewhat sardonic tips on the practical aspects of moving home are offered to Halle's "People Still Here."

The site *www.hoywoy-online.de* emerged from the Agentur Borchert's sample homepage and shows how information platforms can be put together with relatively minor effort. It offers comprehensive information about Hoyerswerda, where the Borchert Agency is based. By bundling links to various information sources for cultural events, online sites of local newspapers, and information about other practical matters such as the weather forecast, city maps, local transport, and local history, the site at first resembles typical official municipal sites, which doubtless cover the needs even of former residents regarding what is going on "back home." This agency site, however, also offers a small ads supplement that is free of charge to anyone wishing to buy or sell, rent or let, borrow or lend. Theoretically, this practical tool offers support for the creation of a flexible transregional lifestyle.

The agency mv4you *(www.mv4you.de)* illustrates how the Internet is employed also by state agencies to nurture an intensive relationship between the region of origin and those people who already left. Initiated by three active citizens—the proprietor of the Internet Commerce GmbH, the managing director of the Evangelischer Jugend (Evangelical Youth) in Schwerin, and an employee of Mecklenburg's ministry of labor—the site is now funded by Mecklenburg-Vorpommern's Ministerium für Arbeit und Bau (Ministry for Labor and Construction). A communication network supported by the Internet is intended to create an "electronic bridge" for individuals to their hometown and thus to make their eventual return easier. As the slogan says, "Wander and Return." Any judgment of the decision to leave is consciously suspended. Leaving is instead treated as a temporary necessity. It is hoped that communication through the Internet will help establish a personal and consistent communication flow that can accommodate the constantly fluctuating demands of employers and employees. Another aim is to promote mutually enlightening discussions about labor market policy among all those concerned. Interested participants can enter their personal profile and wishes and be accordingly informed by e-mail about current local economic developments, business enterprise funding, job offers, and potential contacts.

A similar group is targeted by the Internet portal *www.sachsekommzurueck.de* of Oberland e.V., an association set up by nine businesses in the rural district of Löbau-Zittau and Dresden's Chamber of Industry and Commerce to promote further education and training opportunities. Its aim is to guarantee adequate provision of trained personnel to local businesses and diverse job opportunities to unemployed people. The aforementioned projects clearly attempt to serve the information needs of migrants and to cater to people's desire to stay in touch with their hometown or country. Drawing in particular on her experience of the project "mv4you" as well as her experience of southern European transnational migrants' networks, the social scientist Christiane Dienel—in her final report on the research project "Future Chances for Young Women and Families in Saxony-Anhalt"[11]—strongly recommends the founding of contact agencies at the municipal level, supported by Internet portals, as a means of "allowing a personal connection between a federal state and its people in order to grow and remain stable." The various elements of the Internet offer a complementary locus of exchange with new operative possibilities and thus can help balance the loss of a stable home and work environment. This space becomes a unifying element in the construction of the transnational or transregional lifestyles of people "between two worlds." It nurtures the ability to react with spontaneity and flexibility to changes in real, geographically distant spaces.

Voluntary involvement and participation play a very significant role in this. Many ethnic portals were developed on the initiative of young people within the communities concerned. The vibrancy of networks depends considerably on the courage to accept diversity and address conflict.[12] Dealing with conflicts in shrinking cities can—as the site *www.hoelle-saale.de* clearly shows—by all means be seen as a positive motor of exchange.

Translated from the German by Jill Denton

Notes
1 Sonja Haug and Edith Pichler, "Soziale Netzwerke und Transnationalität: Neue Ansätze für die historische Migrationsforschung," in *50 Jahre Bundesrepublik—50 Jahre Einwanderung,* ed. Jan Motte, Rainer Ohliger, and Anne von Oswald (Frankfurt am Main: Campus, 1999), 260.
2 Ludger Pries, "Neue Migration im transnationalen Raum," in *Transnationale Migration* (Soziale Welt, special volume 12), ed. Ludger Pries (Baden-Baden, Germany: Nomos, 1997), 15-44.
3 Urmila Goel, "Die virtuelle zweite Generation" (a research project, updated 2005), http://www.urmila.de/UDG/Forschung/forschungsstand.html (accessed April 1, 2005).
4 Joana Breidenbach and Ina Zukrigl, "Vernetzte Diaspora," politik-digital.de Web site, http://www.politik-digital.de/archiv/globalisierung/diaspora.shtml (published February 21, 2002; accessed April 1, 2005).
5 Seref Ates, "Internet in der Türkei," in *Zwischen kultureller Zersplitterung und virtueller Identität: Türkische Medienkultur in Deutschland III* (Loccumer Protokolle 17), ed. Jörg Becker and Reinhard Behnisch (Loccum, Germany: 2003), 156-157.
6 Steven Vertovec, "Transnational Social Formations: Toward Conceptual Cross-Fertilization," Working Paper 01-06n (Center for Migration and Development, Princeton University, NJ: 2001); see http://www.transcomm.ox.ac.uk/working%20papers/Vertovec2.pdf (accessed April 1, 2005).
7 Breidenbach and Zukrigl, "Vernetzte Diaspora."
8 Daniel Miller and Don Slater, *The Internet: An Ethnographic Approach* (Oxford: Berg, 2000), 95.
9 Vertovec, "Transnational Social Formations."
10 Nils Zurawski, "Internet und Virtuelle Ethnizität: Macht, Repräsentation und transnationale Identität," in *Zwischen kultureller Zersplitterung,* ed. Becker and Behnisch, 102.
11 Christiane Dienel, Antje Gerloff, and Loreen Leske, "Abschlussbericht—Zukunftschancen junger Frauen," in *Zukunftschancen junger Familien in Sachsen-Anhalt,* ed. Federal Government of Saxony-Anhalt (Magdeburg: Federal Government of Saxony-Anhalt, 2004), 458, 497. Also see http://www.sgw.hs-magdeburg.de/menschen/index.html (accessed April 1, 2005).
12 Geert Lovink, "The Principle of Notworking: Concepts in Critical Internet Culture" (Amsterdam: HvA Publicaties, 2005); also available at the HvA Publicaties Web site, http://www.hva.nl/lectoraten/ol09-050224-lovink.pdf (April 1, 2005).

MARKETING CITY

Cities thrive on an influx of residents, tourists, and investors. After losing economic sectors once vital to their identity, cities seek to create a new profile and promote their locational advantages by means of marketing campaigns, major events, and prestigious architectural projects. Urban marketing targets a public beyond the city as well as local residents and thus must attempt to satisfy contradictory demands.

CITY MARKETING: ORIGIN AND CRITIQUE
Stephen V. Ward

Few things are more challenging for civic leaders than the loss of the core economic functions that sustained their city for generations. Not only is there a material loss—of jobs, income, and population—but also a loss, at least partially, of cultural identity. Alongside problems of unemployment and poverty, there arises the question of what places that formerly derived their identities from coal, steel, shipbuilding, heavy engineering, or seaport activity have now become. In a world where there are few barriers to international shifts of capital or economic activity and where market forces reign supreme, it has become almost inevitable that the stricken cities will themselves, sooner or later, attempt to address these various problems by engaging in marketing.

Creating a more entrepreneurial marketing approach within the government of a shrinking city is no easy task. There are, for example, at least three broad and fairly discrete target groups that have to be addressed by marketing efforts. This task is complicated because each is far from being a homogeneous group but instead contains many diverse interests. The first group is potential *investors* in the city, who have to be persuaded to lay the basis for new wealth creation. They are likely to be relatively few in number and especially difficult to generalize, and therefore are likely to require quite precise, often individualized, targeting. Second are the potential *consumers* of the city, who need to be convinced to come to the city and spend (more) money there. Tourists, shoppers, cultural visitors, and others (e.g., students) constitute potentially large target groups that need therefore to be reached through mass communication media. Finally, and most problematically, there are the *residents* of the city. These include members of the two other groups but, as actual residents, they have their own, very special concerns that require (but do not always receive) great sensitivity from marketers. Thus, they need to be encouraged to take pride in their city despite its (and perhaps their own) economic travails and anxieties. They also need assurance that the new postindustrial identity for their city, and themselves, is worthwhile, both as an object for civic expenditure and in a much deeper, emotional sense.

Initially, residents and city leaders might well want to rage against the closure of their industries. At this stage marketing techniques are sometimes used in efforts to persuade (or shame) higher governments into giving them assistance. In 1983, for example, the deprived London borough of Hackney launched an advertising and public relations campaign that proclaimed it to be "Britain's Poorest Borough." Yet if its leaders thought they could by this approach convince Mrs. Thatcher's hard-faced government to grant Hackney special assistance, they were sadly mistaken. It was to be another, trend-setting city-marketing campaign of the same year, one with quite a different message, "Glasgow's Miles Better," which won the admiration of "the iron lady." Though Glasgow was a city that was, on many indicators, poorer even than Hackney, the jaunty double optimism of the slogan (miles better/smiles better) combined with the Mr. Happy cartoon character were definitely about looking on the bright side of life. The tremendous success of the campaign over the next few years can be seen as opening the present era of European city marketing as a strategy to address the various dilemmas faced by postindustrial places.

The idea for Glasgow's campaign had come directly from New York State's "I ♥ NY" campaign, launched in 1977. Though not strictly a city-marketing campaign, this famous slogan had played a key (if unforeseen) part in boosting tourism in the city of New York. In doing so, it also helped to draw city government back from the brink of bankruptcy. By deliberately adopting this same approach, Glasgow's left-wing leaders were recognizing that government intervention, especially at the level of the individual city, could never change the realities of increasingly globalized market forces. They saw that cities should instead work with these market forces to position, refine, and promote their "product" within the global market for places to invest and consume.

At much the same time, other cities began to find their own ways to these same conclusions. The cities of the United States, where perpetual mobility of capital and population was a traditional theme in the narrative of national development, came earlier to this recognition than did their European counterparts. New York and other older industrial or port cities such as Detroit, Cleveland, Saint Louis, Boston, and Baltimore were already peering into an economic abyss in the 1970s. The reductions in federal programs and regulatory powers under President Reagan in the 1980s brought these and many other cities much closer to the reality of economic freefall. City marketing accordingly became a key part of their attempts to avoid this fate and reposition themselves for a post-industrial afterlife.

Yet the leaders of these beleaguered American cities soon realized that advertising alone was not enough. The experience of industrial decline is never one that leaves a city in a fit state to be immediately packaged and "sold." The nature of market capitalism is such that new investors do not spontaneously rush to put money into places that other investors are quitting. A new narrative of "success" must first be created or at least convincingly promised. Nor are the newly broken places of decline suitable attractors for all but the most idiosyncratic of tourists and consumers of culture. And residents looking at the silent workplaces where they were once employed are understandably quite unable to believe that their city can possibly be "miles better."

To get the target audiences of city marketing to think differently, tangible signs of a new postindustrial city need to emerge in order to lend some concrete reality to the marketing slogans and images. During the late 1970s, many of these cities launched controversial new projects based on services and tourism that were intended to be real down payments on the notion of reborn cities. Of these it was the trend-setting regeneration of Baltimore's Inner Harbor from 1978 that really set the tone for what soon became the new orthodoxy on both sides of the Atlantic. Here was the basis for a new city economy based on tourism and cultural consumption.

That British cities largely took the lead in introducing these American city-marketing practices into Europe reflected a long-familiar pattern of transatlantic policy diffusion. In the specific circumstances of the 1980s, it was also a local symptom of the emergence of a larger Anglo-American model of political economy associated with the Reagan and Thatcher regimes. Yet a few other cities in other parts of Europe were also gaining their own direct understandings of American experiences. Foremost among these was Barcelona, a deindustrializing port city freshly emerged from the sterile authoritarianism of the Franco years. Its mayor from 1982 to 1997, the socialist Pasqual Maragall, drew from his direct, personal knowledge of Baltimore's efforts to reposition and project itself as a city of postindustrial consumption. Even more than Glasgow, Barcelona's dramatic

In 1983 Glasgow began a successful image campaign with the appealing mascot Mr. Happy.

successes over the next few years soon made it another potent model of the new city-marketing approaches.

Like the leaders of the pioneering American cities, their European equivalents soon realized that city marketing must go beyond mere advertising. In Glasgow, the evidence to support the proposition of being "miles better" was achieved only through a sustained program of investment in cultural development and spectacle throughout the 1980s. By means of specific steps, public and private investments were used to create a new cultural infrastructure and build a momentum for change. These early successes were crowned when the city was designated European Capital of Culture for 1990. This tumultuous year unlocked still more opportunities which Glasgow, its marketing capacity now further reinforced by Saatchi & Saatchi, did not fail to capitalize upon. Subsequent initiatives, though less ambitious, have been sufficient to continue the momentum and embed Glasgow as a destination for cultural tourism.

The marketers of Barcelona, from the mayor downwards, were even more successful in imagining and realizing a new city built on art, design, culture, and spectacle. Modest but highly visible transformations in the urban cultural fabric in the early 1980s were taken to new heights when the city won the bid for the 1992 Olympic Games. This accomplishment remains the greatest marketing coup ever staged by any shrinking city (albeit one less demoralized than most because its long-suppressed desires for democracy and regional identity had so recently been freed). Even greater amounts of public and private investment than those in Glasgow followed. The event itself showed an apparently transformed and stylish city to the world and triggered a major growth in tourism throughout the 1990s. The 2004 Forum of the Cultures represented another, albeit less convincing, attempt to work the same magic.

In their different ways these trend-setting efforts by Baltimore, Glasgow, and Barcelona had a major influence on many other cities. Yet the new ascendancy of the marketing ethos within city governments has not gone uncriticized. At the simplest level, it (at least in its more superficial aspects) seemed to many to be an unseemly display of mindless cheerfulness during what should be a period of mourning. The Glasgow's Miles Better campaign faced criticisms of just this type. In this view, the campaign was insultingly patronizing to the many working-class Glaswegians whose life prospects remained dismal after the jobs that had traditionally maintained their lives were gone. Yet in this case, at least, the criticism did not stick, ultimately perhaps because its wordplay and humor struck a chord (even if it had an ironic edge) with most people.

Many other image campaigns have worked less well, usually because they were simply too vacuous to hold anyone's interest for more than a moment. Yet a few engendered real irritation, revealing much about the dangers of mixing marketing and place identity. In the late 1980s, another shrinking city, Newcastle-upon-Tyne, tried to emulate Glasgow's approach. In place of Mr. Happy, its campaign proposed using the much-loved comic-strip character Andy Capp, an incorrigibly idle flat-capped Geordie (Tynesider), whose life revolved around the pub, gambling, and cigarettes. Here was a classic figure drawn from a landscape of shrinking industrial employment, for whom unemployment on state benefits was no hardship. His hardworking and long-suffering wife Flo was expected to subsidize and service his every need without complaining, and without the slightest assistance from him. One might reasonably have thought, as did the city's advertising consultant, J. Walter Thompson, that giving him a makeover, so that he shed his flat cap

PROMOTING DETROIT
William J. V. Neill

Promoting present-day Detroit is a challenge. The image of gangsta rap amidst the overgrown remains of a city, as portrayed in the recent movie *8 Mile,* adds to the Hollywood depiction of Detroit as a place of the imagination that is associated with societal breakdown and failure. Although the struggle to find meaning in music among the ruins below 8 Mile Road, Detroit's northern boundary, is an image improvement over the nihilistic militarization and commercialization of law enforcement in the 1980s film *RoboCop,* the overall effect is still the presentation of Detroit as a place to be feared. Nevertheless, against the background of the void of meaning at the center of the consumer culture satirized in *American Beauty,* Detroit and other landscapes of urban dereliction also conjure up a different imagination. Alluded to, for example, in the film *Fight Club,* this visceral sensibility seeks—alongside the frisson of danger and the allure of possibility—what is "real" in the abandoned streets of the shrinking city. The city of Detroit thus both repels and attracts through a bundle of place meanings, which city marketing must approach with some caution. The result, as elsewhere, is often a retreat to blandness.

Since Detroit went into image freefall, especially after the riots in 1967, various attempts have been made to use urban planning and major development projects to promote an image revival. In this contribution I review such efforts and also consider the tensions between the promotional rhetoric on place identity and the feelings of African American Detroiters, many of whom live not just in a city of the imagination, but in an urban nightmare in which grassroots identity struggles for a voice. The uphill task of promoting Detroit over the last 35 years has ultimately proved nearly impossible, with the city in 2005 on the brink of receivership and the *New York Times* declaring in a headline, "Shrinking: Detroit Faces Fiscal Nightmare."[1] Despite the current financial difficulties of the automobile industry in Michigan, Detroit is situated in what is still a wealthy metropolitan region. However, cutthroat civic entrepreneurialism in a de facto racially segregated metropolis without strategic regional planning creates a situation in which, in the words of a recent director of planning and development in the city, "Detroit is forced to run the 100 meters race wearing combat boots."[2] In the birthplace of Edge City,[3] the exurban metropolitan fringe sprawls further outwards at the rate of 10,000 acres per year,[4] propelled in part by the desire for racial separation. Old Detroit shrinks, but since the 1970s no one outside Detroit has really cared. With the focus of state concern in 2005 on the competitiveness of the Michigan economy as a whole, this is unlikely to change.

The Failed Promise of the Flagship Renaissance Center
The 1970s were the last best hope for turning around the image and the reality of what one Detroit journalist called at the end of that decade the phenomenon of "the incredible shrinking city."[5] A central element of re-imaging Detroit under its first African American mayor, Coleman Young, was a prestige development strategy harking back to the 1950s and concentrating in particular on the rebuilding of downtown. Shamed by the pace of economic disinvestment from what was becoming an African American city and alarmed at the rage animating the 1967 "disturbances," Henry Ford II flexed his corporate muscles, bringing the private side of Detroit's public-private partnership to life in a way that has

Coleman Young, Detroit's first African American mayor, was faced with the paradoxical task of creating an image for the city that appealed both to its African American majority population and to the white-dominated world of investment.

Marketing City

Feature films and news reports create a predominately negative image of Detroit. The project "De-TRO-it" by Ursula Faix, Anders Melsom, and Kathrine Nyhus (bad-architects.network) contrasts differing and yet concurrently created media representations of the city which appeared in the national weekly *Time*, the local paper *Detroit Almanac*, feature films, and TV series.

This project was developed for the *archplus* competition "Shrinking Cities: Reinventing Urbanism."

THE POTT'S BOILING
The Ruhr District and nationwide, Germany, 1998–2001
Springer & Jacoby

Following the major advertising campaign "The Ruhr District – A Strong Part of Germany," which ran from 1985 to 1995, the Ruhr District Municipal Federation began a further campaign to spruce up the region's image, which was to coincide with the completion of the ten-year project "Emscher Park IBA." The main slogan of this campaign, "The Pott's Boiling" ("Der Pott kocht," which plays on the area's nickname, "Ruhrpott"), proved controversial. The municipal federation's confrontational use of the term "Pott" was meant to evoke positive associations, but critics feared it was strongly reminiscent of the region's former "grubby image."

On the one hand, Springer & Jacoby's advertising campaign cleverly drew on traditional clichés of the working class, suggesting down-to-earth attitudes and solidarity, for example; at the same time, they contrasted these images with examples of postindustrial developments intended to signalize skillful innovation and structural change. Polls conducted in and beyond the Ruhr District to assess the campaign's reception revealed that its concept and imagery were mainly judged positively, whereas its lack of clarity and of pertinent information gave cause for frequent criticism.

The campaign has been running in the Ruhr District on a relatively slim budget since 1998 and was launched nationally in 1999. Approximately DM 3.8 million was invested in the first year and a further DM 5 million in subsequent years. (Ed.)

Literature
Kisters, Sebastian. "Ruhrpott, Ruhrpott! Wie die Europapokaltriumphe von Schalke 04 und Borussia Dortmund Image und Identität des Ruhrgebiets veränderten." *Materialien zur Raumordnung* 56 (2000).
Kommunalverband Ruhrgebiet, ed. *Ein starkes Stück Selbstbewusstsein: Der Pott kocht.* Essen: Verlag Peter Pomp, 2000.
Prossek, Achim. "Mittelmaß – Sehnsucht – Metropolenentwürfe: Image und Selbstverständnis im Ruhrgebiet." Opening lecture at the congress "OUT 4 – Popkultur, Ruhrgebiet, Internet," Oberhausen, Germany, November 1999.

A billboard from the Ruhr District's campaign for a new image plays on the conversion of industrial locations to cultural locations: "His grandpa worked in the coal mine. His father worked in the coal mine. Now he works there."

Marketing City

▲ "If God won't give us mountains, we'll make our own."
▼ "Until recently the foreman set the pace here. Today it's the conductor."

▲ "Everyone can find his personal dream factory in the Ruhr District."
▼ "Performances, visual worlds, and art installations. Visiting a brewery is back on the program."

LEIPZIG FREEDOM
Germany and international, since 2002
Orange Cross
www.leipziger-freiheit.de

Marketing Leipzig GmbH was founded in July 2001. Commissioned by the city council's "Leipzig Initiative" and chaired by Mayor Wolfgang Tiefensee, it is to act as the city's official marketing agency and coordinate the national and international campaign "Leipziger Freiheit" (Leipzig Freedom), which it developed in cooperation with the advertising agency Orange Cross.

The theme of freedom was chosen for the campaign in order to highlight a long-standing tradition in the city—Leipzig was one of the first free trade centers, for example, and also was home to the world's first daily newspaper. The slogan also builds on current unique selling points: the "freedom" of a good climate for investment and an attractive range of housing and cultural events.

The campaign refers quite explicitly to the low rent levels that have ensued from a temporary decline in population and a subsequent housing surplus. Among the first ad concepts one could find, for example, "3 rooms, city center, 120 sq. meters, stucco, balcony, bright, 600" and "Why live in cramped, overpriced apartments? Why study at overcrowded universities? ... Why not come to Leipzig instead?" In this way, the phenomena arising from urban shrinkage, which generally are perceived negatively, are employed creatively and put in a positive light. (Ed.)

An ad in the nationwide campaign for a new image, "Leipzig Freedom," asks, "Dear students in Tübingen, Munich, Hamburg, or wherever. Why do you live in cramped, overpriced apartments, study at crowded universities, and put up with early closing times?"

THE GUGGENHEIM EFFECT
Lorenzo Vicario and Pedro Manuel Martínez Monje

Today, after two decades of swift and devastating deindustrialization that eventually made Bilbao a prime example of an old industrial city in decline, the city has enjoyed a spectacular turnaround and is now in the midst of an extraordinary urban renaissance, which has its basis in a number of initiatives undertaken in the 1990s to restructure and re-image the city. As a result of such strategies, Bilbao—with the Guggenheim Museum as its hallmark—appears to have become a standard reference for urban studies, or even *the model* of urban regeneration for other cities affected by decline.

However, although the urban regeneration strategies deployed in Bilbao are touted as unique, innovative, and exemplary, in fact they are a rather recent continuation of a model first devised years ago by numerous cities in the United States and the United Kingdom. Indeed, the intervention model followed in Bilbao was explicitly inspired by strategies developed earlier in cities such as Pittsburgh, Birmingham, and Glasgow. Bilbao is, therefore, a significant example of the well-known approach dating from the 1980s in which flagship, property-led redevelopment projects are central ingredients of urban regeneration. The city visions and trajectories adopted by Bilbao clearly reflect the themes and discourses of the "new urban economies" and the practices of what is known as "urban entrepreneurialism."

Urban Regeneration Strategies in Bilbao

In the late 1980s the Bilbao and Bizkaia councils became convinced of the need to devise and implement planning strategies designed to combat the steady decline begun at the end of the 1970s, to revitalize the economy, and to reposition the city within the new context of a global economy. This thinking gave rise to the Strategic Plan for the Revitalization of Metropolitan Bilbao (initiated in 1989 by the Basque government and the provincial council of Bizkaia), the Master Plan for Bilbao (initiated by the Bilbao City Council in 1985), and the Metropolitan Bilbao Zoning Plan (initiated in 1992 by the Basque government and the provincial council of Bizkaia).

Generally speaking, the revitalization strategies adopted in these plans were based on six key elements. First, planners embraced a new vision for the city, a "postindustrial vision," whose prime objective was to secure Bilbao's place among "world-class" metropolitan centers, to turn Bilbao into a "global city."

Second, if urban regeneration was to take place, it would first be necessary to alter the city's image in order to "put Bilbao on the map." That is, the negative picture associated with deindustrialization and decline would have to be done away with, and a new image associated with art, culture, and advanced services created in its stead—an image of Bilbao as a better-looking, competitive, attractive city.

Third, this change in image would be achieved through transformation of the city's physical environment and the use of aggressive place-marketing campaigns. This strategy opened the door to large emblematic projects and riverfront redevelopment undertakings (Abandoibarra and the Isozaki "Gateway" project), the creation of new cultural facilities (the Guggenheim Museum and the Euskalduna Conference Centre and Concert Hall), the construction of new trade-fair and conference infrastructures (the Bilbao International Exhibition Centre), and public transport infrastructures (a striking new metro system). To ensure that these additions would stand out as symbols of modernity and "renaissance," and that they could be featured in place-marketing campaigns, the authorities resorted to big-name architects for their design: Frank Gehry, Sir Norman Foster, Cesar Pelli, Arata Isozaki, Zaha Hadid, and so on.

Fourth, there was a downtown bias to the urban regeneration strategies adopted. As happened in other old industrial cities, deindustrialization created profitable opportunities for reinvestment in the urban core. The existence of derelict industrial sites and obsolete waterfront areas near the central business district and in the heart of the affluent residential area provided the city council with its "opportunity areas": strategically located sites with high potential for commercial property development where flagship schemes could be undertaken. Thus, from the very beginning, the transformation of the downtown area through the production of new urban landscapes was considered crucial to the attempt to restructure the image and the economy of the city as a whole.

A fifth feature of urban regeneration is the increasing importance of urban leisure economies. Judging by the results obtained to date, the ambitious original objective of turning Bilbao into a world-class advanced services metropolis appears to have faded into the background. The so-called Guggenheim effect seems to have been more successful at attracting visitors and possibly developing a cultural tourist industry than at attracting international capital investment and strategic functions. Thus, the local authorities have had to rely increasingly on economic revitalization strategies based on culture, tourism, and entertainment.

A final feature is the emergence of a new urban governance system in which an increasingly important role is being played by novel agencies such as Bilbao Ría 2000, an urban development corporation engaged in revitalizing degraded areas or industrial zones in decline for new property investment, and Bilbao Metrópoli-30, a public-private partnership set up to implement the Strategic Plan and operating in fact as a lobbying institution. The presence of these new agencies in which market logic predominates, together with the top-down approach to urban regeneration preferred by the local authorities, raises critical questions about issues of local democracy and public involvement.

Flagship Redevelopment Projects and the Remaking of the Central Urban Landscape

Once in place, the regeneration strategies devised for Bilbao have been subject to a great deal of criticism. However, two main issues are of special interest because of the sociospatial consequences that they entail: the predominance of market logic in devising the redevelopment projects and the downtown bias inherent in this regeneration model.

Regarding the first issue, it is clear that the strategists who devised the redevelopment projects see the city basically as a commodity with exchange value, where "opportunity sites" are said to exist wherever there is room for profitable reinvestment, and where the principle of self-financing adhered to by Bilbao Ría 2000 and the overwhelming emphasis on efficiency and financial feasibility have left the projects the captive of a short-term-return maximization logic that subordinates the strategic component to the requirements of speculative redevelopment. To be sure, much criticism has been directed

The construction of luxury apartments in the immediate vicinity of the Guggenheim Museum in Bilbao is part of the Abandoibarra investment project extending over 35 hectares.

at redevelopment operations that give precedence to market laws and to a pragmatism whereby only the economically profitable is seen as desirable for the city; operations in which projects are adapted to suit the objectives and interests of the private enterprises eager to invest in them; operations that the public authorities use to provoke a rise in residential property prices in order to finance their planned projects.

The second issue, the downtown bias, is easy to understand in light of the above. As a result of deindustrialization and decline, the heart of the city was dotted with "opportunity sites." Thus, from the outset, urban regeneration strategies concentrated on the physical restructuring of the downtown area, relegating to a lower priority other districts which, though deteriorated and in need of investments, did not offer the same "opportunities." This, then, gave rise to a new central urban landscape and waterfront, featuring high-priced, high-rise housing and office blocks, luxury hotels, new shopping and entertainment facilities, museums, convention centers, riverside promenades, and so forth. Although the powerful presence of the Guggenheim Museum Bilbao seems to give the downtown a touch of "originality," it is actually the same urban landscape that can be found in cities all around the world from Baltimore to Barcelona and Sydney to Shanghai.

These issues are well illustrated in downtown Bilbao by two large-scale redevelopment projects, both located near the site of the imposing Guggenheim Museum Bilbao, which today is considered both the symbol and the driver of the city's regeneration. The two new projects are known locally as Abandoibarra and the Isozaki Gateway project.

Abandoibarra, a 35-hectare site previously devoted to port facilities and a shipyard, is considered the most emblematic project of those undertaken by Bilbao Ría 2000. The area skirts the river between the Guggenheim Museum and the Maritime Museum. Its redevelopment, which began in 1997 and is not yet finished, has had to be refocused since first conceived. The initial project, designed by Cesar Pelli, called for the development of a new directional center that would attract international investments and strategic functions, thereby driving the economic revitalization of the city. However, the lack of companies interested in locating their activities there, plus saturation of the offices market and the relatively better investment prospects of the luxury housing market, forced a change in the original plan: greater emphasis was given to residential and commercial uses, to the detriment of office space. Today, therefore, the project's main elements include seven blocks of luxury flats (around one thousand new dwellings), a Sheraton hotel, a shopping and entertainment center, the Euskalduna Conference Centre and Concert Hall, and office space that has been reduced to one emblematic high-rise designed by Pelli and set to be occupied partly by Iberdrola—a private electric utility whose old headquarters on prime land in the city center will be reclassified to allow luxury housing to be built in its stead. In short, the redevelopment concept for Abandoibarra has been transformed from a directional center to a new and exclusive residential area, from a production-oriented development to a consumption-based renovated space catering to the demands of the urban elite.

The Isozaki Gateway, begun in late 2002 and still under construction, is a project designed to transform Uribitarte, a quayside area just up river from the Guggenheim Museum, where the city's old customs depot was located. The architect's striking design calls for the construction of a small "citadel" containing five new buildings set off by twin glass towers rising 83 meters high. The project envisages a building area of 80,000 square meters with 317 luxury flats, parking garages, and commercial space. Unlike Abandoibarra,

"More than a museum." The Guggenheim Museum became such an icon of marketing and branding that it was even used to promote other products (here BMW).

the Isozaki Gateway is a project undertaken by private initiatives on privately owned land. Nevertheless, the local authorities not only have paved the way for its development (e.g., amending the zoning laws to allow a change in land use from commercial to residential, approving an increase in allowed building height), but also have included the Isozaki venture in their place-marketing campaigns as if it were one more emblematic project produced by public initiative. The Isozaki Gateway, which has been the object of a great deal of criticism, affords a clear example of the pragmatism and the commercial philosophy behind most of the recent property-led redevelopment projects.

The "perverse effects" of this regeneration model—the sociospatial consequences of these projects—seem obvious. Within the wider context of steeply climbing housing prices all over the country, the high expectations of economic revitalization generated by the new projects (the so-called Guggenheim effect) have sent prices soaring in adjacent neighborhoods as well, eventually affecting the entire city. According to a recent report from a real-estate appraisal company, Abando—the city's central district where Abandoibarra is located—was by early 2005 one of the three most expensive residential areas in Spain, with purchase prices of over €7,000 per square meter in Abandoibarra proper and adjacent streets. Between the years 1997 and 2004, the average cost of housing in the open market rose nominally by 150% in metropolitan Bilbao. Consequently, by early 2005 Bilbao had become one of the most expensive cities in Spain.

Second, the regeneration model has exacerbated social and territorial disparities in the city. The downtown residential areas, always inhabited by the city's more affluent citizens, have had their socially exclusive nature reinforced to the detriment of the less-favored sectors of the population and the more peripheral neighborhoods, which did not offer the same "opportunities." Clearly, then, the new emblematic projects, with their combination of luxury housing, commercial and leisure spaces, new associated city image, and consequent evolution of the real-estate market, are all enabling the city's central district—an already privileged area—to become ever more exclusive and "privatized." Thus, as has happened in other European cities, Bilbao is becoming another example of how large-scale urban development projects can actually accentuate social exclusion and polarization in the city.

The "Guggenheim Effect" and the "New" Bilbao: Lights and Shadows of a Changing Metropolis

This final section offers a preliminary and tentative evaluation of the urban regeneration strategies in Bilbao by summarizing their economic, social, political, and cultural impacts on the city and its population. It is a tentative assessment for two reasons. First, very little time has passed since most of the regeneration strategies were launched (a mere seven years since the opening of the Guggenheim Museum, for example), and the major flagship projects are either still under construction (e.g., Abandoibarra and the Isozaki Gateway) or have not yet begun (e.g., the recent Zorrozaurre project designed by Zaha Hadid). Second, what happens to a city's economy is determined not only by local political factors but also by larger forces and processes on different regional, national, or global spatial levels. So, when explaining the city's recent development, the problem is to disentangle the effect of urban regeneration policies from what would have happened anyway.

How to evaluate the Guggenheim effect, therefore? As noted earlier, it does not appear to have worked when called upon to attract international capital and advanced services, although it did prove effective in creating a new city image associated with art and culture, thereby making it possible to pursue an economic revitalization strategy based on the "new leisure economies." In many respects, the success of the Guggenheim Museum appears undeniable. As a symbol, for example, its success could not have been more complete. The museum building is now the icon of the new Bilbao, an emblem of urban renaissance, and has contributed to the re-imaging and marketing of the city: it has put Bilbao on the world map. With regard to its economic impact, the results appear highly satisfactory as well. Since its grand opening in October 1997, the Guggenheim Museum has attracted some seven million visitors, 60% of whom were foreigners. It has contributed to the maintenance of approximately 4,500 jobs, principally in transport, hotels, restaurants, bars and coffee shops, and retail establishments, and has generated added value amounting to nearly €1.2 billion, which has produced an increase in local fiscal capacity and tax revenues of close to €200 million. Finally, the Guggenheim effect has also made itself felt in the realm of the psychological. It has helped to recover civic pride and heighten citizens' self-esteem.[1]

However, there are doubts about the museum's capacity to adequately spearhead the rise of a dynamic, flourishing culture and tourist industry. Some claim that it is simply a transnational corporation's "franchise"—a museum financed and owned by the Basque administration but "remote controlled" from New York by the Guggenheim Foundation. A museum that, in any case, is a mere cultural showcase, contributing nothing to cultural production per se. A museum that was created at enormous public expense, drawing funds away from other cultural activities.

Be that as it may, although the Guggenheim project is clearly the most emblematic urban renewal project to have been undertaken in Bilbao, it is not the only one. Accordingly, the specific effect of the museum on the city is not the only factor to be taken into account when evaluating urban regeneration strategies in the city. So far, what we have seen is basically the highlights, the bright side of the Guggenheim effect on the new Bilbao. Now it is time to look at the other side of the coin. As some of the criticism drawn by the model has already been outlined above, we shall now simply summarize the main issues in this regard.[2]

Because the city's approach to "regeneration" was quite narrow—equated basically with physical regeneration—the Bilbao model tended to focus primarily on physical renewal through flagship projects on selected sites, without at the same time developing coordinated strategies for economic and social revitalization. The city government has promoted physical change in the belief that property development equals economic regeneration, and with the expectation that a better-looking city is also a better city.

As for economic impact, the type of investment encouraged by Bilbao's regeneration projects is inherently unstable (this is the case for the tourism market and the retail sector, for example) and highly speculative (like the real-estate sector). Moreover, the patterns of employment created in urban redevelopment projects tend to be highly polarized. They are characterized by a relatively small number of highly paid managerial jobs and a far larger number of low-paid, unskilled jobs in sectors such as construction, retail, catering, hotels, and restaurants.

With regard to social issues, recent figures on the rise of inequality and poverty in the city make it impossible to consider the Bilbao model a success. For example, severe poverty has increased in Bilbao since 2000 by 33% and today affects 11.5% of Bilbao groups. You repeat this process many times and pull everything together until the moment comes when you think, "Well, there's now enough stuff on the drawing board." Then we try to make sense of what we've heard and to sum it all up.

After that we present what I call a "sacrificial scheme." By this I mean not that we say what has to be done, but rather that we present our understanding of what has been said—that this is roughly what it looks like. We produced a sixteen-minute film to show our results to residents, some of whom appear in the film. We showed it to an audience of five hundred people, and they were very enthusiastic. This is the visioning phase. At that point there's a need for something else. Which is where branding comes into play.

Beyond the dreams of local residents?

A lot of people say, "Good old Barnsley. Not much changes in Barnsley. Barnsley is Barnsley," and it seems quite nice. When you first go there, it looks ugly. Then you notice, the more people you get to know the more comfortable you feel. You can't find fault with the place. But in reality, perhaps you can. So we came up with the slogan "Barnsley—a Tuscan hill town." Barnsley does lie on a hillside, surrounded by farmland in a quite beautiful landscape. It's situated halfway between two major economic centers, Sheffield and Leeds. Therefore Barnsley isn't an economic center, nor will it ever be. But it could be a pleasant place to live.

So the input by local people is not used as a classic participatory consultation, as literal proposals, but rather it fires your imagination, stimulates ideas, and gives you a better feeling for the place?

That's right. I don't give up my role as an architect. I can adopt an idea, take a look at it: it feeds my imagination. This is exactly the same method I use when I paint completely abstract images of architectural projects. The way the paint behaves suggests possible structures for the building. And in that respect people are very much like the paint.

On the one hand you want to create a vision that will encourage people to identify with this place, and on the other hand there's the desire to attract new investment. These might be two different tasks. When you speak of rebranding, does this differ in any way from classic commercial strategies?

This is a difficult field. If you go back forty years and look at towns in England—not at all of them, but at Barnsley, Northampton, Coventry, and so forth—many of them were in chaos. Traditionally they had all had work to offer: Sheffield was steel, Manchester textiles. But all that's over now. So what identity is left? This is why rebranding is important. "Barnsley—a Tuscan hill town": that's what can help the place evolve. The slogan will somehow always sound a little odd, yet it also helps wake people up. When you hear about it in the media—and our project did get a lot of national coverage—it sounds like a joke; but the joke is gradually taken seriously. "Barnsley? A Tuscan hill town? I must go and have a look." That did begin to work. But that is only the first step. After the visioning phase we entered a more conventional phase. We investigated where opportunities lay, examined all the site boundaries and densities, came up with a master plan, and identified potential investors: all of which related to the vision and helped make it a reality. About £150 million is being put into Barnsley, a mixture of private and public investment.

There seems to be a strong need in shrinking cities for iconic architecture that gives them a new image; and architects who tend toward eccentric designs, such as Frank Gehry, Daniel Libeskind, and yourself, therefore receive commissions from these cities. Your project "The Fourth Grace," in Liverpool, and the library in the deprived London district of Peckham exemplify this very well.

I think it is more complicated than just saying "iconic architecture." I'm very happy if you find that Peckham Library, a quite modest building, has become iconic. Yet in the beginning we just developed something that was right and appropriate for the location and its architecture. The local authority had the intelligence to recognize that one or two civic buildings at the heart of the area would have a spin-off effect on the regeneration of the district. We initially worked with the residents of Peckham and asked them the simple question, "What does a library mean to you?" There were all sorts of answers, such as "I'd like to get married in a library." They talked about the relationship between plays in printed form and actual performing. We talked about the sort of buildings people have to visit to deal with social problems. We tried to pull together a lot of factors and to respond to that actual location, to its current urban conditions. The only problem the library has today is that there are too many visitors, which to me is not a problem. It has become a symbol of regeneration.

The Fourth Grace in Liverpool is a different matter, for it was developed for a competition. There wasn't a tender as such, nor was there really a brief. The brief was the location. The site lies next to three existing iconic buildings: the Royal Liver Building, the Cunard Building, and the Port Authority. And as far as we were concerned, if three iconic buildings are standing in a row, then there should be a fourth. We won the competition and our scheme generated a lot of media coverage. This was exactly what the city was after, as it was bidding for selection as the European Capital of Culture.

Initially the people of Liverpool didn't like our design at all. Nor did they want it to be built. The problem was that this was a traditional competition, where you are not allowed to consult in advance the very people you ought to talk to. So it was impossible to initiate the kind of participation here that we had achieved in Barnsley and elsewhere. After Liverpool was selected as the European Capital of Culture for 2008, the scheme was dropped.

In your exhibition project "Supercity," you describe the north of England as a single gigantic city called "Coast to Coast."

It has long since become reality. People travel from one place to another just for the pleasure of it. There's shopping in Leeds, a good club scene in Manchester, a good market in Doncaster. In everyday terms this whole area has long since merged into a single city. Northerners are in that sense much more mobile than we are in London, in the Southeast.

You already mentioned the need to differentiate between various locations that are in competition with one another. You've identified three "Supercities" in England. The one in the North extends from coast to coast; the second cuts a diagonal across the country and includes, among other places, London; and the third, on the southern coast, is shaped like a wave. Each has different characteristics and a very distinct identity.

One would hope so. It's a model of compaction. There are exceptions at many points, and places like Norwich and York will remain completely isolated. Parts of the remaining farmland will be left to run wild, to renaturalize. This is how differentiation looks on a large scale. Equally, however, when one zooms in for a closer look, one finds places with very different qualities within individual regions. Our proposal for Bradford is practically the exact opposite of the one for Barnsley. We anticipate compaction for Barnsley, whereas the idea for Bradford is to open it up, to display its locational qualities: its architectural heritage, its proximity to other towns, and so forth.

So on the one hand there's your idea of Barnsley as a compact city. It is surprising that you, an avant-garde architect, formulate the most conservative idea of a city in the face of processes of shrinkage, whereas, in response to processes of shrinkage in Berlin in the 1970s, Oswald Matthias Ungers, a conservative architect, proposed a very avant-garde concept of urban development, namely, "the urban archipelago." Was your proposal for a compact city influenced by the guidelines of the Urban Task Force, which helped shape British urban development policy in recent years? The Urban Task Force propagated a very pragmatic and ultimately uninspiring form of urban compaction.

My concept is probably not influenced by those guidelines. The task force's work was very good. The most important messages were that we should build on brownfield sites wherever possible and not squander the land we have, that we should reduce distances between places of work and residence and build a sense of community, and so forth. On the other hand, the task force is very old-fashioned. And the North today is different. I like that. They have a sense of community, yet at the same time they feel like part of a greater entity.

Not everyone wants to or can afford to live in places like London or Manchester. And it's therefore impossible to simply say, "Cars are bad." You can't disenfranchise people who have already bought a house in the suburbs. They exist, they are real people, they made a choice. How do you deal with that? Many planners simply use existing twentieth-century models and don't ask themselves any fundamental questions. I call them the carpet-layers. They just roll out their same old carpets. The landscape in between towns is absolutely vital, however. From the center of Leeds, it takes less than half an hour to reach the splendid isolation of the Pennine Mountains. For me, there's a very special poetry to this. I shouldn't like to destroy it. So how might one approach this question differently?

Landscape is playing an increasingly important role in contemporary urban development, and you have been fascinated by it for quite some time already. So I was almost astonished that the concept of an urban agrarian economy was not explored in your "Coast to Coast" project. On other occasions you've proposed bringing sheep into Manchester's city center.

What interests me is the introduction of technology into agriculture. The second agricultural revolution has only just begun. If we shop for food in supermarkets, we can have strawberries at any time of year, yet these come from southern Spain, Israel, or wherever. However, it's possible today to cultivate strawberries throughout the whole year here, in this country, and to market them directly. That changes the supermarket's and the farmer's roles, as well as the way we shop for food and so on. It can also result in a new type of building.

All your schemes promise growth and stabilization, to attract new residents, generate new investments, and so forth. Could you also imagine a strategy of retreat, of letting a place shrink, accepting that it's becoming smaller, and working with that? Might this be thinkable, or even appealing?

Very appealing. Liverpool has a smaller population today than it had in the past. Vienna, for example, had 2.6 million inhabitants in 1910 and now has 1.7 million. In the UK and Germany, the total population figures have remained more or less constant. What we're talking about, therefore, is reorganization and relocation in exchange for certain benefits: quality of life, being able to choose a pleasant place to live, and reorientation.

... at the regional level?

It's an issue for the whole of Europe. You could build a town one mile wide along the Mediterranean coast and house all of Europe in it, or even more. People would live in a warmer climate, consume less fuel, and harvest a greater diversity of crops. The whole of northern Europe would return to a state of wilderness. Would that be a bad thing? There are lots of Germans and British people doing it already, by building houses in Spain or Turkey: admittedly, in a horrible form. That's where we should start an architectural debate.

An interesting aspect of your scheme for Bradford was the step-by-step development of the design—that you proposed test steps, such as blocking a street for a day or a month to see what effect this would have. Have you already implemented a design based on this approach?

Nothing so radical, as yet. My former teacher Cedric Price fostered the idea that all of our endeavors actually represent a sort of test. You don't have to be definitive, because you can have ideas and try them out on a temporary basis: see how something works and learn from the situation. We perhaps have great visions but we never really know what effects they will have. Many transport engineers first try out their ideas for traffic control by erecting wooden barriers and seeing what happens. We could follow their example.

In Northampton, for example, there are calls for a new art gallery; and rightly so, I must say. All the town with its 200,000 residents has at the moment is one theater. We responded with a project: a cultural mall. We converted the top floor of one of the downtown multistory car parks into a gallery for one weekend. Lots of people came and it was a great success. The local press then reported that Northampton needs a gallery. And then people said, "Look where this was done. No one ever parks there." With some simple bars around the edge and a little heating, you have a gallery with pretty views, right in the middle of the town. We don't need to do anything else.

And did this happen?

No. We wanted the gallery as a symbol, as an iconic building. That particular project has now entered the round of, "OK, they want the gallery, but how to fund it?" We're presently working on a very complex financial package—that's a part of the architect's job too. It's always about a vision, a master plan, about the role played by architecture and also by money, a very important factor.

I would like to raise the issue here of deregulation and neoliberalism, with particular reference to the 1960s project "Non-plan" by Banham, Barker, Hall, and Price. On the one hand, Non-plan was a leftist idea of emancipation. Yet it ultimately came to underpin Margaret Thatcher's neoliberal politics.

In talking about liberalizing the rules for architecture or design and proposing—as you did for Manchester—to open up the city, to make it a place where anything is possible, where people are invited from all over the world to test ideas and so on, how would you differentiate that from classic commercial enterprise strategies?

Having no rules is a very important thing. I think that it's about openness, and about all things being possible. When we talk about Non-plan, I take it to have a more particular meaning than Cedric did. I add something else, and I am sure that Cedric was thinking about it as well when he talked about delight and joy: beauty, points of high energy, places where people simply feel very comfortable. There are many different types of space for that. Some are known; some could be reinvented or tried out.

If we look at existing free enterprise zones such as the London Docklands, or those in Detroit or Poland, in the end they yield only extremely banal business activities that have nothing whatever to do with experimentation, innovation, or inspiration. They are money machines. In speculating on experimental zones in the way you just did, there is certainly a need for other conditions if they are to be more challenging and productive in a cultural sense.

Let me attempt an analogy. Let's say you're giving an architecture course at a university. To me that whole course is about creating an environment in which students will come and try things out. When I teach, I don't invent the program. I prefer to say, "Let's have a discussion. Let's try it out a bit and see where it goes." The same could be true of our towns and cities. To me it's much more interesting to say, "Come and share your dreams with us and let's see if we can make some of it, or all of it, a reality."

We can be far more relaxed. Not everything is forever, and that's the point. We must be prepared to take risks instead of always trying to hedge our bets.

Adapted by Jill Denton and Anna Minton

TWENTY-FIRST-CENTURY HOMESTEADING: NEW ATTEMPTS TO RESETTLE THE AMERICAN FRONTIER
Kate Stohr

In 1862 the United States Congress enacted the Homestead Act. Considered by some the most important piece of legislation in the country's history, the act allowed settlers to claim up to 160 acres (about 647,000 square meters) of land, provided they could demonstrate that they improved the property, built a house, and had lived there for five years.[1] By 1900 some 600,000 farmers had received clear title under the act to lands covering some 80 million acres, an area equal to approximately 10% of the country's landmass, according to the National Park Service. Ultimately, more than 1.5 million homestead applications would be fulfilled. During the same period, America experienced its first great surge of immigration. As industry took root in American cities, the companies suffering labor shortages encouraged, even solicited, immigration. Some 25 million immigrants arrived on America's shores in three great waves from 1820 to 1860.[2]

Together, this open-door immigration policy and the Homestead Act would forever change the landscape of America. Ethnic neighborhoods shaped by shared cultural ties would shape the country's inner cities, while pioneers would turn the seemingly limitless expanse of grassland in the country's Great Plains into freestanding family farms.

Today, however, many of the towns and cities formed by these two major population shifts are suffering from population loss, decay, and blight. According to Census Bureau figures, whereas cities such as Las Vegas have nearly doubled in population in the last ten years, their counterparts in the Midwest, cities such as Cincinnati, Minneapolis, and Saint Louis, have lost between 25 and 60% of their populations between 1990 and 2000.[3]

The population loss in rural areas has been no less dramatic. According to census figures, rural areas of the twelve-state Great Plains region have lost more than a quarter of their populations since 1950—a gradual exodus of more than a half million people.[4] Today hundreds of rural counties in the center of the country—covering roughly a million square miles—have six or fewer inhabitants per square mile, the nineteenth-century definition of frontier land.[5]

The concept of homesteading has deep roots in the American psyche, and not just in rural areas. When once stable neighborhoods were on the brink of collapse in New York City in the 1970s, city activists developed an "urban homesteading" program to enable residents to take ownership of abandoned buildings.[6] Today's city planners, desperate to resuscitate their emptying cities and towns, are inventing new variations on the same theme. Where once cities looked to big business to salvage their ailing economies, today's planners are attempting to revive communities one resident at a time by luring modern-day pioneers with promises of everything from high-speed Internet to tax breaks to free land.

Indeed, the concept of "homesteading" has come full circle. For instance, in Ellsworth County, Kansas, there are 23 lots available for free to individuals provided they are prequalified to build a house that is at least 1,000 square feet and they agree to build the house on the land within two years' time.[7] Families with children are eligible to receive an additional credit of between $1,500 and $3,000 towards a down payment when they buy in the area. Many of the lots, which are located in town centers, have been donated by private owners who receive a tax deduction for the value of the property. According to Anita Hoffhines, director of Ellsworth County Economic Development, eleven families have relocated to the county since the program began in 2004.

Kimberly and Paul Bayless moved there from Las Vegas after learning about the program through a newspaper article. A former software engineer, Paul now drives long-haul truck; Kimberly is a substitute teacher. Although the family has had to make some adjustments—"I sometimes forget that I can't just run out and buy anything I want any hour of the day," Kimberly Bayless has said—they enjoy the town's slower pace of life.[8]

Ellsworth is just one of a dozen communities throughout the Great Plains which is hoping to reverse decades of population decline by offering free land and other incentives to qualified newcomers. Most are jolted into action by the threat of school closings, the last bastion of small-town life. "The thing about the school is it's the very backbone of the town," said Steve Piper, who launched a similar land giveaway program in Marquette, Kansas, when the town's elementary school was on the verge of being shut down. "People aren't going to move to a town if there's no school there."

Free land is not the only incentive that town planners are offering. Many communities offer tax breaks aimed at recruiting—and keeping—younger residents. In Iowa, legislators concerned about the state's aging population are offering a $600 tax credit to residents under the age of thirty. The program is part of an effort to stem the state's "brain drain." The state's legislature is also considering a bill to abolish the state income tax for people under thirty years of age.[9] In Nebraska, boosters hope to lure former residents back to their hometown with job placement programs, tax breaks, and business incentives. Using slogans like "Do you remember when the night sky looked like this? It still does," the program, called Business Beyond the Farm,[10] aims to lure mid-career professionals who moved away in their twenties back to the area with promises of a better quality of life. Postcards and other recruiting materials are sent to former high school graduates.

Conversely, some communities are specifically recruiting seniors. Mississippi budgets $350,000 a year to recruit "active adults" between the ages of 50 and 65. In its marketing campaign the state "certifies" cities that meet the needs of retirees and profiles them in marketing materials sent to prospective residents. According to Diana O'Toole, the program's manager, each relocated retiree household is the economic equivalent of 3.7 factory jobs to the community. She says the initiative, called Hometown Mississippi Retirement, has snagged 3,500 retirement-age households since its inception in 1994.

The population crisis has become so acute in rural areas that Congress is considering whether to enact the New Homestead Act, which would allocate $30 billion to incentives for people to relocate to counties that have lost at least 10% of their populations in the past twenty years. The bill, sponsored by Senator Byron Dorgan of North Dakota, offers up to $10,000 in student-loan forgiveness to recent university graduates who live in a depopulated area for at least five years. People buying homes would receive $5,000 in tax credits. Another $3 billion would be allocated for new business loans.[11]

Urban areas in the so-called rust belt of the Midwest and Northeast are also actively recruiting newcomers. The industrial city Schenectady, New York, which once had about 90,000 residents, has lost nearly 30,000 jobs since the 1960s because its main employer, General Electric, gradually moved branches of production and in the end its company

Twenty-First-Century Homesteading_Kate Stohr

headquarters out of the city. By the late 1990s many of the tree-lined streets had succumbed to blight and abandonment. However, former mayor Al Jurczynski noted that a small but close-knit Guyanese community had taken root in the city. The mayor began to actively recruit prospective Guyanese homebuyers—even going so far as to give busloads of Guyanese personal tours of his city.

The unconventional campaign worked. Today as many as five thousand Guyanese have settled in this former company town. Many have taken jobs at nearby health facilities that had long suffered labor shortages, and property values have risen as the new recruits have renovated homes and rejuvenated the city's streetscape. Most were attracted by lower housing costs. "If you were to compare the house we are living in right now for $100,000, the same property would have sold in New York City for $500,000," said Kamla Sahabir, a real estate agent who moved from New York City to Schenectady two years ago.

Schenectady may seem like an unlikely destination for Guyanese immigration, but newcomers say they feel welcome and plan to stay. "At first, I was thinking it was maybe not such a good idea to come up here after all. I was accustomed to having many things to do. Here it's a bit different. You have to plan your life," said Ravi Shivnath, an engineer who recently moved to Schenectady after getting a job nearby. "After a few months I made some friends and began to see the place ... I got more involved in sports ... It didn't hurt that I had Guyanese and Hindu friends who were here and propagating the Guyanese tradition and culture."

However, Shivnath thinks that Schenectady's success could be difficult to replicate. Most of the immigrants who have come to the city are highly educated, and many were living in nearby New York and had already assimilated to American life. In addition, he added, because of their existing network, many were able to remodel their new homes on the cheap with help from friends and family members. Finally, because Schenectady is located between two large centers for Guyanese immigration, New York and Toronto, it makes for an ideal halfway point. "There are some things that are very peculiar about this situation in Schenectady," he said. "If someone tried this model with another group, I wouldn't say it would work the same way. There could be some growing pains and personality conflicts."

Indeed, a similar strategy met with mixed success in parts of rural Spain. The village of Aguaviva lies in the desolate hills of Teruel, one of Spain's poorest provinces. After generations of decline, Luis Bricio, the village's mayor, initiated a campaign two years ago to recruit immigrants from abroad. Initially the village turned to South America, posting advertisements in newspapers in Argentina which offered free flights and a job for families with school-age children which were willing to relocate to Aguaviva for a minimum of five years. More than five thousand families applied, and, as a result of the campaign, enrollment at the town's school, which once had only twelve pupils, doubled.[12]

But retaining the village's new recruits proved difficult. The village had targeted immigrants from Argentina, hoping that a shared language and culture would make integration easier. Yet many of the immigrants came from big cities and were unable to adapt to village life.[13] Of the first seven families recruited to the town, five left within the first two years. "We made a big mistake because successful integration doesn't depend on the language, nor is it guaranteed by a shared Hispanic heritage," Bricio explained to the BBC.[14] "What really matters is the work ethic and that the skills that they come with match

The village Eustis in Nebraska's "Frontier Country" has about five hundred inhabitants. It hopes to attract new residents with its clean air and the slogan "Sausage Capital of Nebraska ... You'll Love Our Wurst!"

Twenty-First-Century Homesteading_*Kate Stohr*

the sort of jobs we can offer here." The town has since adapted its campaign to recruit immigrants from rural communities, many from eastern Europe. "In many ways, the East Europeans have adapted better than the South Americans," said Bricio.

Despite these success stories, some policy-makers and others have begun to question the effectiveness—and fairness—of what they consider government-subsidized settlement. How do cities choose which ethnic or age groups to recruit? And are they discriminating against other groups? Columnist Derrick Jackson of the *Boston Globe* has pointed out that many of these incentives find their way to predominantly white communities, unfairly rewarding less diverse communities. "The white heartland of America could eventually get tax credits, college loan repayments, and guarantees against losses. It is affirmative action and reparations all rolled into one," he complained to a *New York Sun* editorialist. "When black folks want it, we're beggars. When white folks want it, they're hard workers." Others have called the proposed incentives "pork-barrel giveaways to empty spaces" that command political weight "far out of proportion to their actual population and economic productivity."[15]

More to the point, few of these programs address the root cause of population loss: lack of employment. At a time when most families depend on two incomes, small towns find it increasingly difficult to offer a wide-enough range of jobs to attract both partners in a working family. At the same time, while new business incentives encourage start-ups, small towns and shrinking cities often lack the support industries needed to buoy growing businesses.

For example, when Shawn and Esther Oehlke moved from Albuquerque, New Mexico (population 1,819,046), to Crosby, North Dakota (population 1,200), to start a small high-tech business making precision laser parts, they found it was easier to meet with the governor than to hire a plumber. "There were drawbacks that we hadn't anticipated and one of them was the kind of support services you take for granted in a city," said Esther Oehlke, who had moved to take advantage of incentives offered through the state's Prairie Opportunity program.[16]

Moreover, studies have shown that grassroots efforts to encourage entrepreneurialism have done little to change the region's fortunes. In their census research on rural population loss, David A. McGranahan and Calvin L. Beale of the Economics Research Service of the United States Department of Agriculture found that over half of America's frontier counties had falling population figures between 1990 and 2000. However, of the 56 frontier counties that gained in population during the same period, their study found that in most cases this growth had come from outside forces. According to their research, the employment created in these counties tended to be low-skill jobs in meatpacking or feedlot facilities, casinos, and prisons. "In no case did small business entrepreneurship alone appear to be the critical factor," wrote McGranahan and Beale.[17]

The region's continued decline has caused some to question whether the populations of communities on the verge of extinction should be bolstered at all. In 1987 Deborah and Frank Popper, both urban planners at Rutgers University at the time, wrote a landmark article that suggested a radically different approach to land use in the Great Plains region.[18] They argued that the 1862 Homestead Act had wrongly encouraged settlement in America's frontier areas: everything from the blizzards, locust plagues, and droughts of the late 1800s to the dust bowl of the 1930s had led to cycles of economic and environmental ruin that had forced newcomers off the land. The population of the area had in fact been declining, they pointed out, even before the act was abolished in 1936. What is more, farming was stretching the region's environmental resources to the limit. Water shortages loomed, and soil erosion was once again approaching dust-bowl rates, they warned.

Calling the Homestead Act the "longest-running agricultural and environmental miscalculation in American history," the article called for an end to government subsidies for rural growth. In addition, the Poppers proposed that the government buy back large parcels of land, repopulate it with natural plant and wildlife, and encourage sustainable land uses such as ecotourism and bison ranching. Dubbed the "Buffalo Commons," the concept sparked a maelstrom of controversy when it was first introduced. However, less than twenty years later, the Poppers' vision for the Great Plains has come to pass in many areas—sometimes through the intervention of conservationists and others, but often by default.

It is too early to tell whether or not new attempts to resettle the Great Plains will work, said Popper of the latest homesteading initiatives. But, he said, "One thing you can say for sure is that these things have been tried before and haven't worked." Still, the concept of homesteading lingers on in the American psyche. Few could have imagined the profound effect that the Homestead Act would have on the landscape a century ago. "The red grass was disappearing, and the whole face of the country was changing," wrote the early-twentieth-century American novelist Willa Cather of the vanishing Nebraska prairie in 1918. One can only wonder what the American frontier will look like a century from now.

Notes

1. National Park Service, http://nps.gov/home/homestead_act.html.
2. The James Madison Center, http://www.jmu.edu/madison/center/main_pages/teacher/curriculum/chap9.htm.
3. Demographia/Wendell Cox Consultancy, http://www.demographia.com/db-intlcityloss.htm.
4. Blake Nicholson, "Buffalo Commons Professors Find Theory Gaining Acceptance," Associated Press, April 11, 2002.
5. Errol Luis, "Slicing the Bread," *New York Sun,* August 8, 2003.
6. Homesteading Assistance Board, http://www.uhab.org/about/history.htm.
7. See http://kansasfreeland.com.
8. Sarah Max, "Free Land in the Heartland," CNN, December 23, 2004.
9. Les Christie, "Stopping the Great Plains Brain Drain," CNNMoney.com, February 9, 2005.
10. See http://www.businessbeyondthefarm.com.
11. "New Homestead Act Highlights," *The Wichita Eagle,* March 17, 2003; http://www.kansas.com/mld/eagle/business/5410105.htm.
12. "Returnadores: A New Life in the Old World," *Guardian,* February 21, 2003.
13. "No es lo que esperábamos," *La Nacion,* June 17, 2001.
14. Michael Voss, "Rural Spain Welcomes Immigrants," BBC News, June 19, 2003; http://news.bbc.co.uk/2/hi/europe/3002928.stm.
15. Luis, "Slicing the Bread."
16. See http://prairieopportunity.com.
17. David A. McGranahan and Calvin L. Beale, "Understanding Rural Population Loss," *Rural America* 17, no. 4 (Winter 2002).
18. Deborah Epstein Popper and Frank J. Popper, "The Great Plains: From Dust to Dust," *Planning* 53 (December 1987); http://www.planning.org/25anniversary/planning/1987dec.htm.

FLAGSHIP DEVELOPMENTS
1988–2005
Various architects

Name: Guggenheim Museum
Location: Bilbao, Spain
Function: Art museum
Surface area: 26,500 sq. meters
Construction costs: 77 million euros
Built: 1991–1997
Population of Bilbao 2003: 352,317
Population decline 1981–2000: 78,700 / 18.18%

Name: Selfridges
Location: Birmingham, UK
Function: Department store
Surface area: 23,225 sq. meters
Construction costs: 53.6 million euros
Built: 1999–2003
Population of Birmingham 2003: 992,100
Population decline 1960–2000: 98,070 / 28.77%

Name: Aronoff Center for Design and Art
Location: Cincinnati, USA
Function: Faculty building
Surface area: 25,400 sq. meters
Construction costs: 26.95 million euros
Built: 1988–1996
Population of Cincinnati 2000: 331,285
Population decline 1950–2000: 172,710 / 34.27%

Name: Rosenthal Center
Location: Cincinnati, USA
Function: Art museum
Surface area: 8,500 sq. meters
Construction costs: 28.05 million euros
Built: 1998–2003
Population of Cincinnati 2000: 331,285
Population decline 1950–2000: 172,710 / 34.27%

Name: Universum Science Center
Location: Bremen, Germany
Function: Museum
Surface area: 4,000 sq. meters
Construction costs: 34.77 million euros
Built: 1999–2000
Population of Bremen 2004: 546,000
Population decline 1970–2000: 53,130 / 8.93%

Name: BTU University Library
Location: Cottbus, Germany
Function: Library
Surface area: 12,667 sq. meters
Construction costs: 30 million euros
Built: 1998–2005
Population of Cottbus 2004: 106,731
Population decline 1987–2003: 19,043 / 15.04%

Name: Volkswagen Transparent Factory
Location: Dresden, Germany
Function: Manufacture and commerce
Surface area: 83,000 sq. meters
Construction costs: 186.6 million euros
Built: 1999–2002
Population of Dresden 2005: 480,801
Population decline 1987–2003: 36,187 / 6.1%

Name: Science Park
Location: Gelsenkirchen, Germany
Function: Landscape park and commerce
Surface area: 2,850 sq. m. (buildings), 30 hectares (park)
Construction costs: 38.35 million euros (buildings),
12.78 million euros (park)
Built: 1989–1995
Population of Gelsenkirchen 2004: 270,107
Population decline 1990–2004: 23,607 / 12.44%

Name: Aquarium
Location: Genoa, Italy
Function: Aquarium
Surface area: 10,000 sq. meters
Construction costs: 62 million euros
Built: 1988–1992
Population of Genoa 2001: 604,000
Population decline 1970–1998: 200,680 / 23.83%

Name: MARTa
Location: Herford, Germany
Function: Art museum
Surface area: 6,000 sq. meters
Construction costs: 28.8 million euros
Built: 2001–2005
Population of Herford 2004: 65,097
Population decline 1962–2004: 1,207 / 1.82%

Name: Imperial War Museum
Location: Manchester, UK
Function: Museum
Surface area: 6,500 sq. meters
Construction costs: 41.3 million euros
Built: 2000–2001
Population of Manchester 2003: 422,302
Population decline 1951–1991: 298,220 / 42.43%

Name: Hôtel du Département des Bouches-du-Rhône
Location: Marseille, France
Function: Regional administration
Surface area: 44,000 sq. meters
Construction costs: 143.8 million euros
Built: 1991–1994
Population of Marseille 1999: 798,430
Population decline 1968–1999: 90,600 / 10.19%

Flagship Developments_Various Architects

Name: Liverpool Cloud
Location: Liverpool, UK
Function: Hotel, offices, commerce
Surface area: Not specified
Construction costs: 217–318 million euros (estimate)
Built: 2002–2007
Population of Liverpool 2003: 441,477
Population decline 1951–1991: 336,210 / 42.63%

Name: Peckham Library
Location: London, UK
Function: Library, job center
Surface area: 2,300 sq. meters
Construction costs: 7.2 million euros
Built: 1998–2000
Population of London 2001: 7,172,036
Population decline 1951–1991: 1,668,324 / 19.98%

Name: National Centre for Popular Music
Location: Sheffield, UK
Function: Museum, education center
Surface area: 4,000 sq. meters
Construction costs: 21.73 million euros
Built: 1995–1999
Population of Sheffield 2001: 439,866
Population decline 1981–2001: 30,819 / 6.55%

Name: Therme
Location: Vals, Switzerland
Function: Thermal spa
Surface area: Not specified
Construction costs: 16.6 million euros
Built: 1992–1996
Population of Vals 2000: 885
Population decline 1970–2000: 152 / 14.66%

PROFILED CITY

Cities acquire a profile by building on their singular local strengths. This gives the urban transformation of shrinkage—at first a disintegration imposed by external forces—direction and contour. Conflict, crises, and difference can be catalysts for the development of new identities and local character. Urban profiling is imperative in order that cities with uneven spatial development can assert themselves as competitive locations.

THE URBAN SELF
Anke Haarmann

The city is a film set. City subjects move as if scripted through urban space. But which role do we assign to these subjects? Do they have a part to play or are they merely extras? Is urban space an effect crafted by a brilliant director, or does the urban self introduce its own directorial cues? What is this film anyway? Which images structure the cities? And with whom shall we reckon in the other roles?

Image and the City
A trade-fair city in the German Democratic Republic (GDR) and now the regional capital of eastern Germany, Leipzig quotes Goethe as a way of characterizing itself. Leipzig is Little Paris. Leipzig is, however, also "L.E." (pronounced "L.A." in German), and thus abbreviated flirts with the image of the American media metropolis. Already during the era of the GDR, Leipzig jokingly and disrespectfully nicknamed its east the Bronx, thereby claiming to be related to that famous scenario of urban wilderness. Paris, Los Angeles, and the Bronx: all these comparisons are visually potent, for they draw on existing images of cities. Paris, Los Angeles, and the Bronx are topoi in cultural space. They signalize parameters of meaning within which certain urban conditions are posited: the metropolitan character of Los Angeles, Parisian culture, or the reprobate Bronx. Urban imagery is differentiated and global, widely comprehensible and as ready at hand as language. Yet in this case it is a visual language—a symbolic arrangement of moving scenarios.

The City and Power
That Leipzig stages itself as Little Paris, L.E., or the Bronx, thereby appropriating for itself the character of a European city or an American metropolis, demonstrates that the relationship between role model and reality is not constituted in a vacuum. Whether a place might be considered a topos depends on a cultural-historical legacy within which certain cities occupy a central position of power. Paris and Los Angeles are or were, economically and culturally, hegemonic centers of power, and this is precisely what makes them attractive cities and such covetable role models. In their function as a cultural and economic center of power, the metropolises have structured the images that are associated with them. And in this tradition, to conjure these images simultaneously affirms existing (or former) dominant power relations. Affirming the dominant arrangement of images is, however, as unavoidable as an escape from language is impossible. This cultural-historical legacy so irrevocably interweaves any idea of the city per se with the social position of particular cities that any refusal to define oneself in relation to the latter would not connote an autonomous definition of a city but rather amount to a nondefinition. Perceptions and definitions of the city function in the context of existing symbolic arrangements that are structured by established norms and dominant power relations.

Imagery and Power
The symbolic arrangement of cities is rehearsed and perpetuated by public imagery circulating on the global market of cultural industries. Cinema, television, newspapers, and advertising all communicate images of the city that are not merely superficial and

Film poster for Anke Haarmann's project *The Secret of L.E.*

visual but also convey contextual knowledge of urban norms. The "urbanness" of a city is in play when cinematic car chases lead us through chaotic traffic, across bridges that give a view of the skyline, and then end in derelict areas where industrial wasteland, graffiti, and homeless people set the scene for the final shoot-out between urban subjects. Urbanness, says the message, is action and speed, crowds and cars, inhabited or empty buildings, and subculture. Urbanness is the tension between ambitious infrastructure and grim trash, between social isolation and technical prowess. But that is only one version of the film. Cosmopolitan urbanness acquires quite another face when the camera pans along the facades of bourgeois apartment buildings on nocturnal boulevards, catches some eccentric characters in a lively alley, and pauses momentarily before a brightly lit café, restaurant, theater, or cabaret, in front of which a taxi draws to a halt and an urban subject steps out onto the streets: a flaneur in search of distraction. The message of this urban setting is that the city offers cultural excess, the pleasures of night owls, unconventional individuals, bourgeois capital, the opulence of grand boulevards, consumerism, and endlessly available wares. These images define norms and people's expectations: they structure the habitual and the imaginable. What counts as "urban" appears here as a stage set, standardizing the urbanness of cities.

The City as a Metaphor of the Social

Perception of the city is structured by images of the city, but urban space is also exquisitely suited to be a draft for the production of scenic imagery. The close interaction between urban space and the collective imagery of space is related to a particular dimension of urbanness. The city is architectonically multidimensional and is in this regard a multifaceted metaphor for society. Down to the microcosm of gutters and aerial cables, the formation of urban space mirrors forms of human cooperation. Above and below the neutral "zero level" of street life, the catacombs and roofs of the city comprise further dimensions of engineered construction, in which the dirty depths and the airy heights of city life are manifest. The view from the twentieth floor is the paradigmatic survey of society's "bigger picture." Rearguard action in the canalization and cellars that serve as housing epitomizes places of resistance and misfits' lifestyles. The cultural elite, the left wing, the bourgeois individual, petty criminal, or big capitalist: each has a particular, carefully staged place in this urban architecture—and each takes his or her place within it in accordance with these images.

Power and the Self

At this point, however, it becomes evident that urban spaces are not characterized by a single image, nor do dominant images correspond to a single view of a city. They are run through with the threads of many different urban perspectives. These do not have a monocausal effect, but rather combine to create specific urban networks. Within such an ensemble of views of the city, individual urban subjects are embedded differently and regulated in their conduct differently. Typecast characters are hence conformist and yet simultaneously diverse. They are a template and a change of clothes in one. This variability is a prerequisite of the urban self as a transformer.

Precisely at that point where cities are not exemplary and not inhabited by standard subjects, the production of the urban self stands out against a predetermined range of images. Torn between all the possible varieties of urban self, the urban production of self is only ever partially successful vis-à-vis the symbolic standard. Possible consequences of this lapse are willful behavior and unexpected productions of self. Gaps emerge between the urban ideals, symbolic topoi, and well-known films, creating space for deviant production both of the self and of urban imagery. Individual urban subjects will possibly intervene at this juncture in existing ideas of the city and change its reality. They create new urban dramaturgies in transformational transit between established ideas of the city and standardized self-images. The urban subject's potential scope consists in either conforming incompletely or using this unsuccessful affirmation of the ideal as a springboard for transformation. It is about nothing more than emphasizing this dual approach of the urban self to its relationship with the city. The philosophical question that emerges is, to what extent the urban self and the city might be perceived as specific junctures of media references—and to what extent the urban subject as a protagonist in the interplay of such references is able to "pull the strings." The multidimensionality of urban imagery and the complexity of the production of self prove to be a prerequisite of any possible proactive behavior. It is thus necessary to consider how much emancipatory potential urban subjects have to create themselves in their own image, and to place this in a critical relationship to dominant, influential urban imagery. The productive aspect of the interaction between city, image, and self must be emphasized. It is important not only to interpret urban reality as an effect of power relations but also to positively subvert this reality.

The Unexpected Dimension of Ambiguous Cities and Subjects

Leipzig is Little Paris and an ironic L.E. It is a shrinking city in eastern Germany and a capitalist shoppers' paradise. It stages itself as a second Berlin and is unhappy with its role as a first-class backwater. All stage sets are locally available, and the appropriate images for any of these ideas of the city could be blended in at will. However, Leipzig is neither Paris, nor Berlin, nor a provincial town. It is not at all exemplary. It is as ambiguous as it is ambitious in striving to correspond to norms that it fails miserably to meet. This failure can, however, be read as an unexpected dimension of an ambiguous city, just as the in-between position of the urban subject can be turned into something liberating. The affirmative surplus, with which Paris, New York, Tokyo, or even the Bronx or Detroit reproduce themselves as types, draws a blank in unspectacular and ambiguous places. These indistinct cities are neither free of role models nor beyond symbolic ranking, yet they always function unsatisfactorily. Let us then play a role in this film and assume that at the heart of the imperfection is obstinacy of the subject, and in all that is dissatisfactory is the disquiet of a city!

Translated from the German by Jill Denton

THE SECRET OF L.E.: THE SELF/IMAGES PROJECT "CITY"
Leipzig, Germany, 2004/05
[AHA] Anke Haarmann with Irene Bude

Developed over the course of a year in cooperation with residents of Leipzig, the film *The Secret of L.E.* employs various genres such as feature film, sci-fi, and animation. It focuses on a variety of urban settings with which the project participants are confronted in their daily lives: examples of former East Germany's architecture, such as the Brühl prefab housing district and the Winter Garden high-rise block in central Leipzig; the alternative subcultures and squatters' scene in redundant industrial sites in Südvorstadt and Plagwitz; allotments on disused land in the east of the city; and municipal gentrification of the *fin de siècle* Waldstrasse district as an example of Leipzig's history as a "citizens' city." Project participants illustrate their relationship to the shrinking and growing city through actions that include occupancy, conversion, design, or intervention in existing processes. In their film "roles," they demonstrate various strategies with respect to the city. The result is a playful and provocative reflection on urban space.

This project was developed in the context of "Shrinking Cities" with a grant from the Museum of Contemporary Art Leipzig. The original German title of the film is *Das Geheimnis von LE*.

The following residents of Leipzig participated in the project: Brita and Fritz Will, Klaus Schuknecht, Eberhard Friedrich, Karo, Clarotte, Thomas Pracht, Nora Gitter, Paavo Patz, Roland Löbel, Alexander Lebe, Mamat, Leyla, Yilez, Nuri, Zeki, and Anke-Maria Kops-Horn.

The film demonstrates various forms of urban action from the respective viewpoints of project participants.

THE NATIONAL MUSEUM OF STATISTICS
Halle/Leipzig region, Germany, 2004/05
Eva Grubbauer, Martin Luce, Joost Meuwissen and Johannes Weisser

---

In terms of statistical inquiry, the phenomenon of shrinkage is the observation of greater or lesser levels of density. Once these levels have been assessed in the light of fundamentally diverse data, however—an arbitrarily determined surface area in which density, in the majority of cases, is not regularly but, rather, randomly distributed—density is a relative factor.[1] While Leipzig is shrinking the world is growing: whereby shrinkage can signify aggregation at other locations or the growth of other objects in the area under investigation. If every category to be measured, be it the farmer's or the civil servant's, spreads itself discretely over the same area, it is axiomatic that this chosen area is not equally advantageous for the various categories being measured. In this regard, density is relative in a double sense: in the first place, the disposition of the surface in and of itself and, second, the suitability of this surface for the categories to be measured. One or the other of these statistics is consequently false. In the light of such disequilibrium, any statement about density necessarily infers an institutional, political, or moral preference. According to Karl Marx, "capital" as a complex and all-encompassing set of social relations must be differentiated from money as such. In the same way, densities and processes of shrinkage have an inherent social aspect and should not be viewed purely as a quantification, by means of which they are frequently represented in the economic, urban planning, and architectural fields as an empirical calculus that accords with reality. In the latter two fields, therefore, it is during the stocktaking stage of a survey, and not just at the drafting board, that the question of representation becomes pertinent.

It is admissible today to demand some form of transparency not only of political administrations but also of architectural and urban planning processes. Because stock (or an inventory thereof) plays an essential role in the context of shrinking, our approach addresses the acceptance of existing factors. In the framework of qualitative evaluation, populations, buildings, and infrastructures are also instances of economic and biological (physical) exchange and hence cannot be understood merely as artifacts in space. Such analyses posit the extensity of natural space over the extensity of the objects under inquiry. Conversely, it would be possible—and in the case of processes of shrinkage even desirable—to examine the potential optimal size of each object (which is to say, its own size) once a correct statistic has been determined. In this way statistics would cease to be factual absolutes that subject towns to the strict and mostly indecent regime of expectations; they would instead encourage, in the tradition of ancient philosophy, a perception of growth and shrinkage as attributes rather than as extrinsic constraints.

When searching for appropriate statistics it is imperative to promote the inclusion of the informal economy, elderly people, and the preservation of monuments. Our procedural approach in this regard is neither to mix the various densities that occur in a certain area nor to make an issue of their potential conflicting interests, but rather to illustrate them by means of representative institutions that are provided directly by the people concerned.

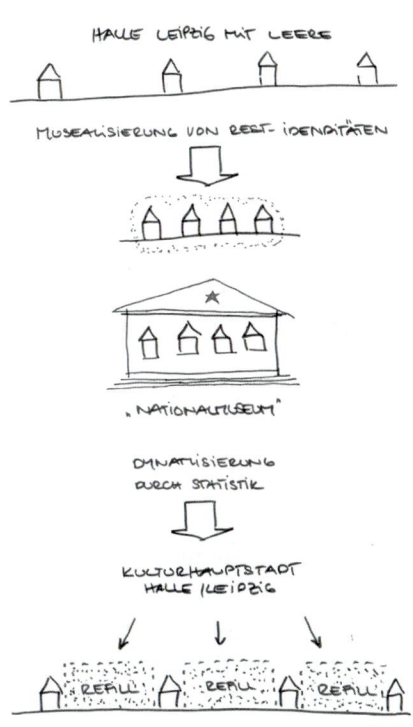
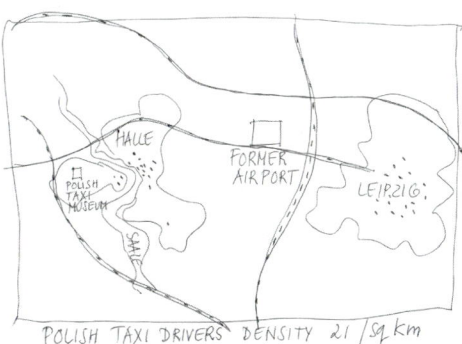
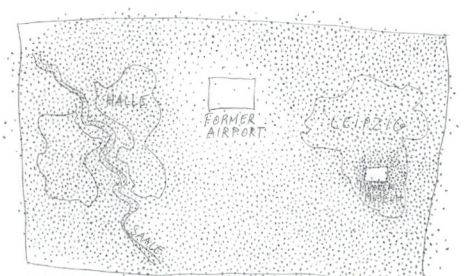
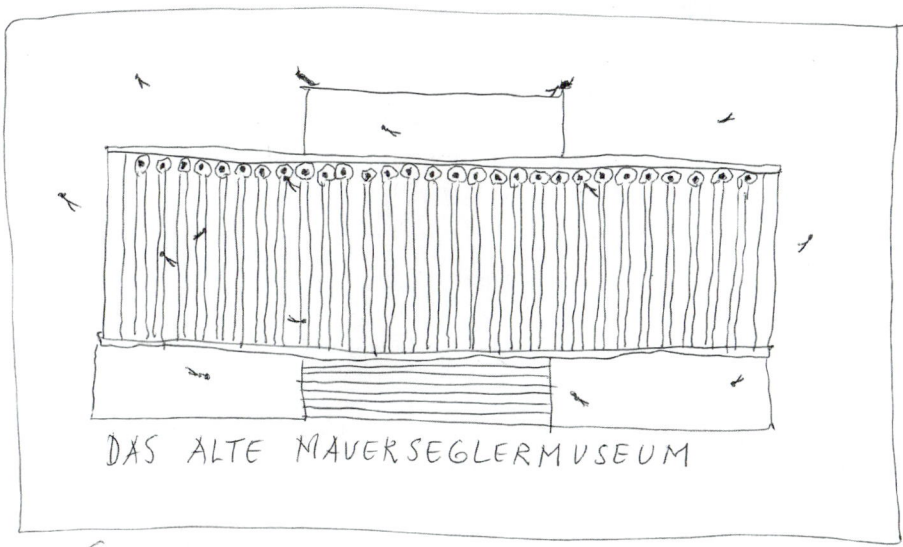

Sketches for the museums' display of residual identities.

Profiled City

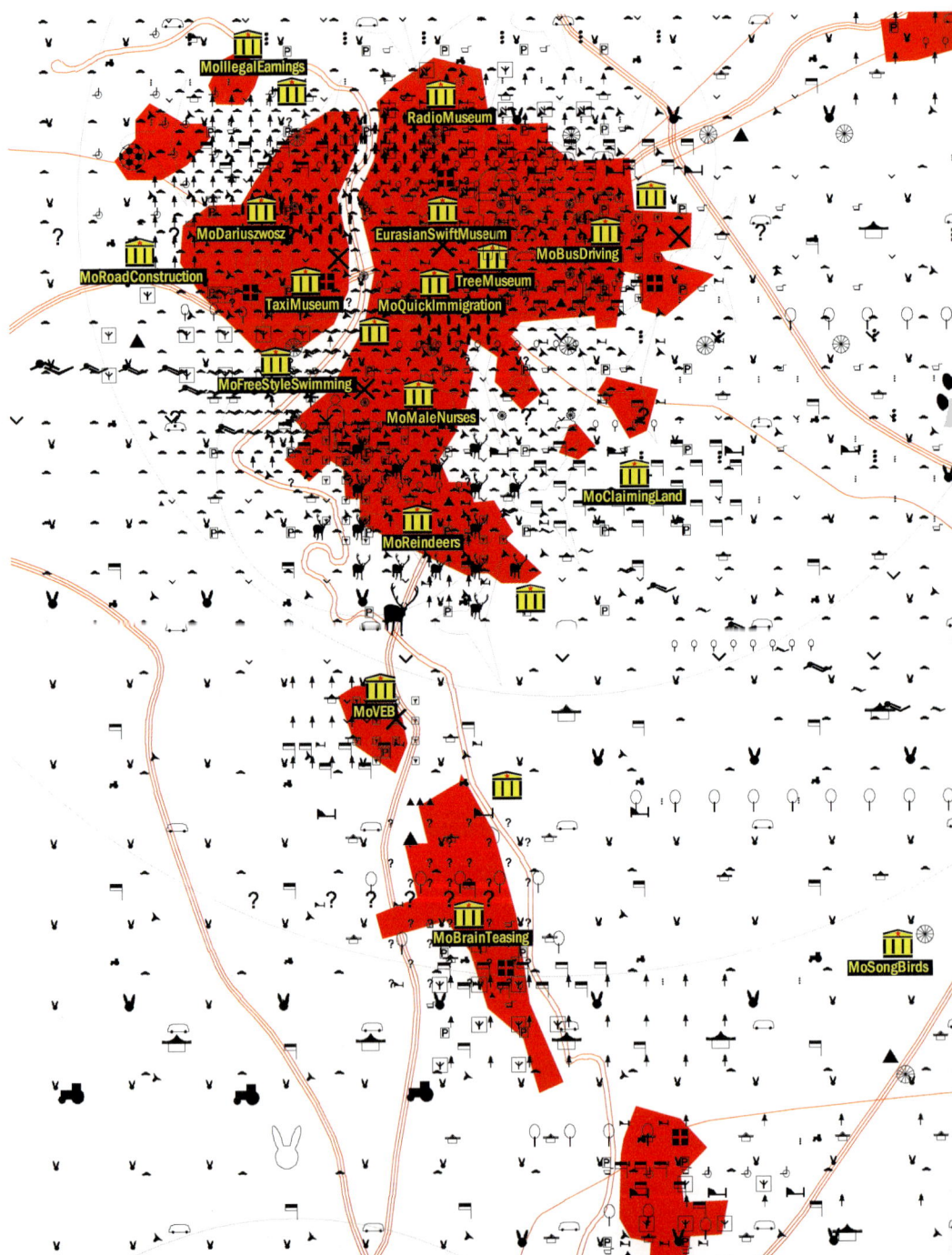

Map of the Museums of Residual Identities.

The National Museum of Statistics_Eva Grubbauer, Martin Luce, Joost Meuwissen, Johannes Weisser

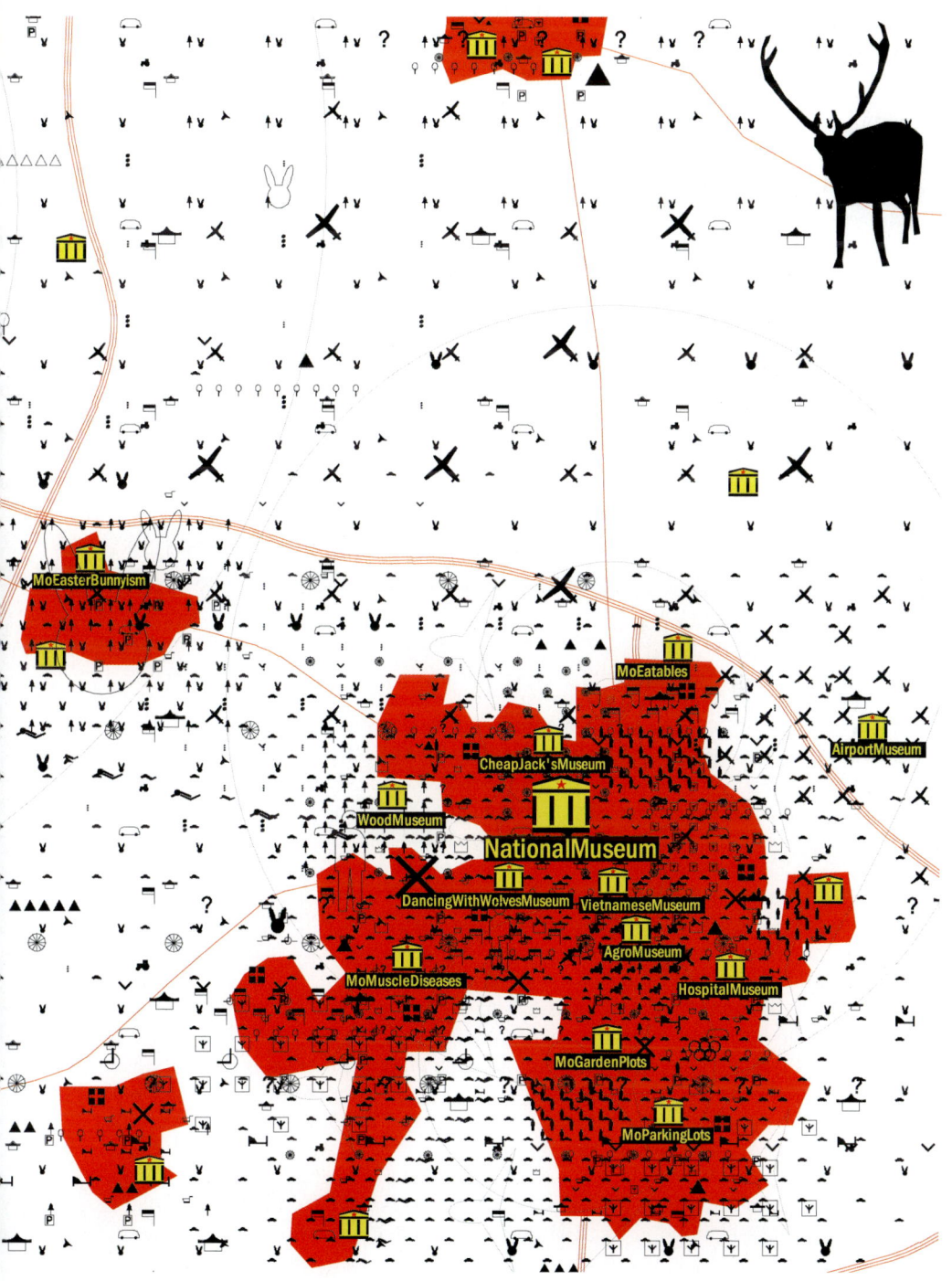

That a certain tension between citizens' initiatives and representational democracy has always existed was discussed extensively as early as the 1970s, both in reference to that era's "advocacy planning"[2] and in view of the so-called contradiction between the flexibility and the legal security of planning. Our project surmounts the problematic aspects of this area of conflict by focusing exclusively on the representative value of citizens' initiatives. We call these representations "museums." They do not have any collections but they collect relevant facts on the basis of which correct decisions—on which everyone agrees—can be made. It would, in our opinion, be an important step if urban planning facilitated people's self-organization in this way and, consequently, by representing the citizens involved, such organizations communicated to a greater extent with representative democracy—which is to say, through associations or through the "social middle ground," as it is known in the Netherlands.

Individual Phenomena

Our proposal for Halle and Leipzig therefore anticipates the following four logical steps. The first step is to acknowledge what is there. Such acknowledgment requires a classification of what there is to perceive, irrespective of whether this is relevant or pointless: cab drivers, mosquitoes, wolves, elderly women with dyed hair and those without, Vietnamese people, or members of the Association of Friends of Nesting Boxes for the Common Swift. Such classification is as indispensable for analysis as it is in principle impolite. The data of shrinkage are to be collated, not the everyday difficulties that ensue from it.

One next has to establish which categories might gradually and incidentally obtain their correct statistics. Although general statistics, such as the level of unemployment, the number of sick or old people, or economic growth rates do not register the activities of the persons listed, we also know that there are few people more active than unemployed or elderly persons, whose considerable contribution in economic statistics is, however, not registered, due to the very impossibility of formally determining its extent. Third, contemporary art and cultural projects that have arisen in the context of the debate on shrinking cities are for the most part independent artworks and partial: their catalytic effect is marginal, and the very concept of shrinkage will vanish from these cultural agents' field of activity at some point. Not we, the authors and artists contributing to a temporally and financially limited "Shrinking Cities" project, but only the people or groups concerned are able to adequately elucidate the specific and correct statistics.

Our task might then consist in a fourth step, namely, in formalizing a compatibility or comparability between the various informal or formal statistics. Let us call it "public processing." Because democracy demands manageable representation, the museum can function as a representative instance for those initiatives that cannot be formally or permanently represented by the electoral process. This extended concept of its function apprehends the museum as a cipher for a societal nexus of representation or of collection.[3] Instead of art, however, aspects of citizens' initiatives relevant to everyday life are collected and thus formalized. In order to become representative and to gain a voice within urban and cultural planning procedures, every initiative should create its own museum and visualize relevant data.

A National Museum

The formation of communities necessitated by identity investment resembles conventional citizens' initiatives in that micro-practices of visualization are rendered constant. The self-monitoring practiced by citizens potentially leads to changes in their own behavior: they may attempt to manipulate statistics positively by raising their personally generated density rates. The statistics' own momentum thus leads to an unexpected distribution of densities and activities in space, the repetition of which leads to previously overlooked readings of density and to new geographies of regional identity. Furthermore, there is a drastic increase in the density of museums due to the hyperplastic foundation of countless museums in the Halle and Leipzig areas. It is a museum-oriented concept of geography and increased density that can counter the continuing depletion of real physical spaces.

The main concept for this dispersed urban level is, therefore, not a dispersal or urban sprawl of increasingly lower densities within the natural unity of a continuous landscape, but dispersed identities in and of themselves without reference to their environment. Our contribution is the realization of a National Museum of Statistics, which shall be founded amidst the ruins of Germany's political future. The museum is, however, merely a container for potential real activity, for every citizen can open a museum. Whether the creation of museums will have a positive effect on citizens' self-esteem is something we cannot know, either now or later.

Translated from the German by Jill Denton

This project was developed for the *archplus* competition "Shrinking Cities: Reinventing Urbanism." The original German title is "Nationalmuseum für Statistik."

Notes
1 "By almost any measure, Halle is the worst place in Germany, a symbol of what's wrong with the nation." Charles P. Wallace, "A Brand New Start?" *Time Magazine*, July 18, 2004; http://www.time.com/time/europe/html/040726/economy.html.
2 See David Eversley, *Planning without Growth*, Fabian Research Series, no. 321 (London: Fabian Society, 1975).
3 See Boris Groys, "Sammeln und gesammelt werden," in *Logik der Sammlung* (Munich: Hanser, 1997).

INTERNATIONAL BUILDING EXHIBITION "URBAN REDEVELOPMENT SAXONY-ANHALT 2010"

Saxony-Anhalt, Germany, 2002–2010
www.iba-stadtumbau.de

> *Every city follows its own course of development. Identify each city's particular qualities and integrate these in the regional urban network.*
> - *Every town determines its prospective development in the light of its historical configuration, which defines its position in the regional network of Saxony-Anhalt and beyond. Opportunities for consolidation and development arise both from its endogenous potential and its regional significance.*
> - *Disparities in infrastructure and rates of development in urban space offer opportunities for diverse lifestyles: characteristic regional differences should not be effaced; rather, their dynamics should be augmented in a productive way.*
> - *The formulation of city typologies aims to create clear contours and attractive urban configurations in the region's cities. It is intended as a guideline for municipal authorities' drafts of overall concepts and their development of modernization strategies.*
>
>   IBA Guidelines, point 5

The International Building Exhibition (Internationale Bauausstellung – IBA) "Urban Redevelopment Saxony-Anhalt 2010" has been closely linked since its inception with the formulation of integral approaches to urban redevelopment at the municipal level. The IBA's basic requirement of all towns participating in the exhibition is nothing more and nothing less than a concept of its future role—in as concrete terms as possible—based on its respective local and/or regional strengths, resources, and potential.

The quality of urban life and economic productivity are dependent not on an increase in population or land use but on the qualitative growth of sustainable sectors and projects. Only in this way can processes of shrinkage be slowed down. Each town participating in the IBA addresses an issue that is fundamental to urban redevelopment and that has overall significance for the development of a sustainable profile.

In Saxony-Anhalt eighteen towns are currently participating in the IBA with a total of seventeen issues. In the course of formulating and concretizing these IBA issues, four closely interwoven strategic approaches have emerged. It is evident that the creation of a profile is not just the initial step in each town's IBA process: it also features in the course of further developments, partly as the background to spatial interventions, and partly at the core of project work.

The majority of towns deal with the issue of urban redevelopment ostensibly at the *spatial, architectural, and planning levels.* Yet the issue of urban identity is inherent in any discourse about public space, as is exemplified by Halle, where work on new bridges across the river Saale and the development of concepts for a cultural center in

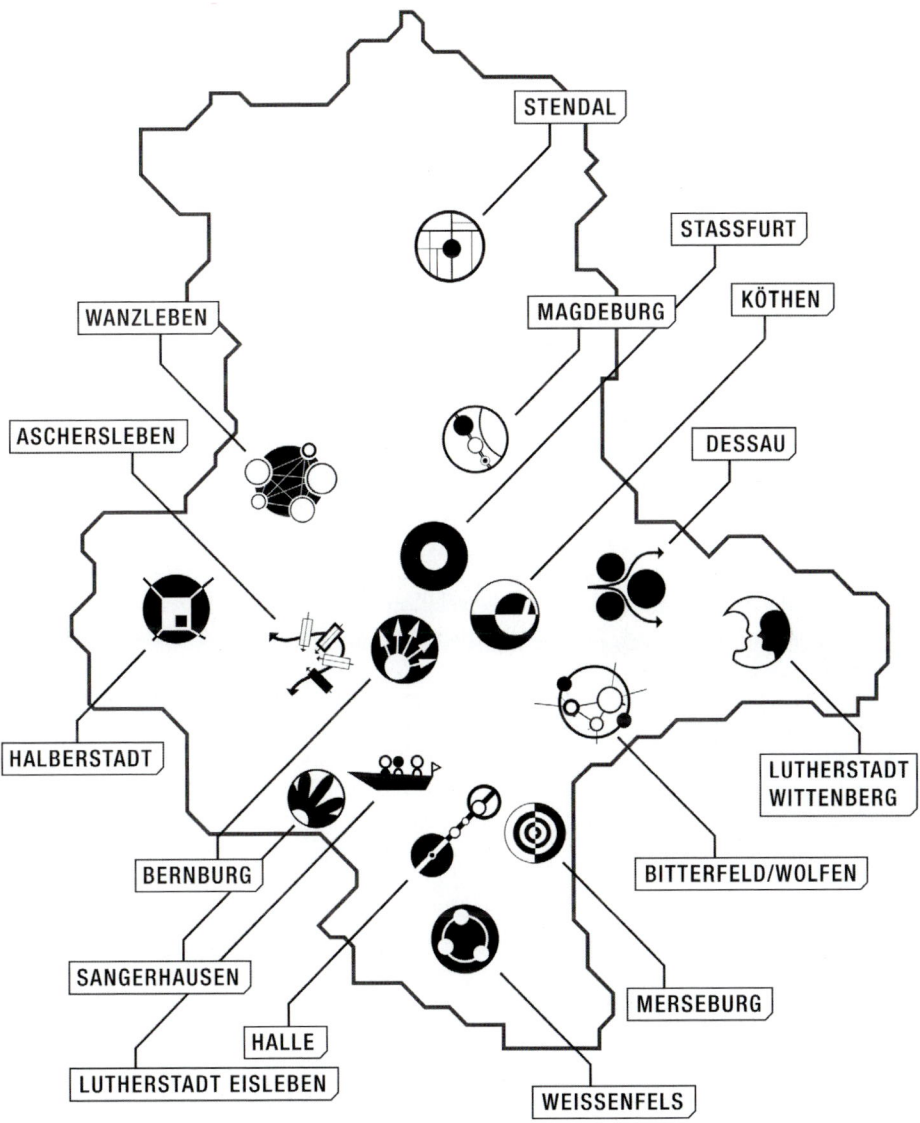

Each IBA town pursues an individual profile that is symbolized by a logo.

the Halle-Neustadt railway station serve to stabilize the city's double identity: as the historic city of Halle and the socialist prototype Halle-Neustadt.

The second group of towns focuses on *society, social structures, and culture*. Köthen is an unadulterated instance of extensive profile management. The work of Samuel Hahnemann—the founder of homeopathy who worked for some years in Köthen—has become the primary motif of the town's identity in ways that far exceed the usual parameters of urban image policy: the thematic level has been complemented by the design process for the built environment. In addition to decisions to invest in homeopathic institutions in the town, the question of whether homeopathic principles and methods might be applied to issues of urban development is also under discussion.

The third group pursues issues of *infrastructure and networking tools*. Stendal is the main municipal agency in a scheme that encompasses the entire, extremely depleted region of Altmark. The issues here are how a region so badly hit by shrinkage might retain any urban qualities and identity at all, and what forms of modern infrastructure must be created in order for it to do so.

The fourth group's approach centers on *the economy and knowledge*. The local foodstuffs industry in Weissenfels is one of the agencies in the IBA process. It combines a quite traditional interest in creating a positive image with unusual interventions in and emphases on urban redevelopment.

The active inclusion of local citizens in processes of urban redevelopment is extremely important. Broad-based support for vital urban identities cannot be generated from above: it can be generated only through civic engagement and the use of all possible means to guarantee transparent and accessible policy-making procedures.

Text by Martin Krems

Translated from the German by Jill Denton

URBAN IDENTITIES
Ulf Matthiesen

An insidious rumor circulating in the regional and urban marketing trade suggests that it is only when economic development leaves a lot to be desired that cities and regions begin to consider whether their image and identity strategies are on the right track. If this were true, strategic efforts to create a city's identity could be understood first of all as symptoms of crisis—whereby crisis can always also be the cradle of new beginnings. The explanation offered by "New Regionalism"—that urban and regional identities are consciously promoted simply in response to the intensification of the worldwide and European "regional battle" for essential markets—is hardly more sympathetic.[1] A third interpretation tends to emphasize the growing significance of soft locational factors as well as the increasing impact of processes of cultural codification of space in a post-traditional knowledge society.[2] Last but not least, urban and regional identity policies are also intended to have an internal effect, namely, by offering incentives for proactive developments and encouraging the urban populace to undertake new ventures.

These four readings of current forms of urban identity development are evidence of the extreme diversity and complexity of the interests, discourses, standardizing mechanisms, and subterfuges that affect the new hybrid compositions of strategic urban imagery and substantive identity models. A number of renowned urban and regional researchers therefore remain consistently dismissive of any attempts to apply the term identity—which in the first instance refers essentially to persons—to more highly aggregated "things, spaces, or systems."[3]

On the other hand, even before the "cultural turn" in the spatial sciences, there was little doubt that generic themes and supra-individual identities can be brilliantly exploited for political ends. Proving that culturally coded transpersonal forms of identity or collective identities yield real, objective structural effects is therefore not difficult—particularly in the case of cities and regions. In addition, the four above-mentioned readings demonstrate how and when the effects of transpersonal identity structures and policies on the dynamics of urban development increase, which is the case in particular when competition is acute. Furthermore, highly aggregate forms of identity sometimes become so deeply entrenched that they can hold their ground quite easily against the pertinacity of the hard locational factors of infrastructure.

Nevertheless, a certain caution is required with the use of "holistic" terms and generic themes. Metaphorical and model-oriented governance and planning attempts to develop space or identities can quickly become nebulous, with the result that the gap between the fact and the fiction of urban identities grows too wide. It is therefore worthwhile to take a brief look at the highly differentiated theories of identity as they pertain to individuals.[4]

1. First of all, "genetic" identity theories since Erik Erikson have proven that identity is a dynamic *process,* as opposed to a static condition. Personal identity is thus bound up with educational and developmental processes. We can stimulate and foster identity. We can also, however, fall short of it or lose it.

2. Developmental *phase models* have further shown that individuals do not move to and fro along a "developmental track" at will; rather, their (eventual) development unfolds

in *developmental phases* that occur sequentially in a structured order.[5] This process takes place in line with their specific personal development rate. In this sense, respective urban societies may indeed strategically construct complex identity concepts, developed in accordance with their overall image, and thus "stimulate" development. However, they cannot determine or impose forms of identity by simply providing "recipes" from an "identity cookbook."

3. A central role in the developmental phases of an individual's identity is played by *crises of maturation and development* and the ways in which these are dealt with. One can fruitfully differentiate here between

- social crises associated with certain periods in a person's life (e.g., adolescent crises, "empty nest" syndrome, retirement);
- individual crises (e.g., an accident, illness, unemployment); and
- individual crises of meaning (e.g., coming-out, religious conversion).

In all three respects, there are close correspondences to urban identity processes.

4. Since George Herbert Mead's and Erving Goffman's epochal studies, the social sciences differentiate between a *personal* and a *social* construct of identity. *Personal identity* is understood as the subject's individual response to his environment. This also encompasses reflexive forms of a person's description of himself, and thus the self-image that is developed by the subject in personal interaction with respectively identical others (mother-child dyad, etc.). *Social identity,* in contrast, denotes a subject's cognitive expectations of typical relationships in typical social situations with concrete and "generalized others" (G. H. Mead). Social identity has, furthermore, an emotional subdimension, namely, the identification of a subject with a collective, a role, or a certain group or, alternatively, with a native community, a district, a city, or a region.[6]

5. Periods of social uncertainty, such as followed 1989 in eastern (and western) Germany, are characterized by the proliferation of new forms of social identity. It is a process that can be particularly well observed in the conflict-ridden actions undertaken by collective subjects. Under pressure of conflict or crisis, collective subjects' identity changes. Admittedly, it does so within a framework of options and windows of opportunity that are again organized by identity structures or identity types. Such *crisis-ridden identity development* manifests itself in specific demands and forms of action and their associated argumentation cultures and descriptions of self, as well as in the characterization of the respective "opponent" and dominant power relations. The appearance of new social actors and constellations of actors on the historical stage generally leads to a transformation of those characteristics of social identity that hitherto had been the constitutive base of "structural" trust.

6. The "relative" stabilization of new social identities rooted in trust, confidence, and reliable forms of interaction shows us that a social learning process has been concluded successfully: one has effectively come to terms with a phase of critical uncertainty. This is generally synonymous with the attainment of a new, though not necessarily higher, phase of development.

The above six concepts pertaining to personal development and identity formation appear to be particularly informative and instructive for current discussions about the intermediate levels of urban-regional forms of identity. In addition, they facilitate an ongoing review of the frequently somewhat confused discourse on identity conducted by cities and regions themselves. The following seven points briefly define these aspects:

- The construction of identity is primarily and essentially a process: a self-organized process, to be exact. In contrast, urban-regional drafts for a self-image or identity are often produced ad hoc, deliberately, schematically, and to a deadline, and are constrained by the pressures of time and limited resources. A genetic-historical perspective on the process of creating urban identity, with sufficient options and capacity to accommodate the development of a particular place's strengths when these are under pressure, is still extremely rare. In general, the seemingly more marketable normativity of a glossy urban image campaign sets the dominant tone: branding is hip (though often unsuccessful).

- The construction of identity is a vectored step-by-step process, in the course of which innovative spurts frequently are precipitated by periods of developmental crisis. Yet, absurdly, crisis as the cradle of new developments, and hence also of new forms of identity, usually tends to be played down or even systematically excluded from concepts of urban or regional identity. Local authorities engaged in creating a sleek self-image that rests on political symbolism seem to perceive crises as unsightly blemishes, instead of grasping and exploiting their potential for creativity and innovation (which lies in their heterogeneity). This is precisely why so many "urban creativity" image campaigns have a uniform look characterized by design-obsessed superficiality.

- The construction of identity can be stimulated but not directly taught. Consequently, the process cannot be planned as a whole. Identity policies should thus be confined to the initiation of learning processes that take account of the risks inherent in the logic of internal development, in available competencies, and in limited planning effects. Media image campaigns may stimulate, but they cannot replace this process of creating an identity. Image campaigns geared only to one particular end therefore contribute significantly to the frequent failure of instrumental identity planning.

- The construction of identity is a genuinely social process in which personal and social forms of identity are constituted simultaneously. Consequently, the capacities of cities to describe themselves ("How do we see ourselves?") and their external image ("How do others perceive us?") are more closely and systematically connected than the usual image-construction processes drafted by the planning committees and tourism and marketing departments of city administrations would like to have it. Of particular interest here is the relationship between "personal" and "social" identity, or between internal and external identities. This points beyond the usual antinomy of strategic images versus intrinsic identities; it leads us toward hybrid forms that, to quote Rolf Lindner, really do mold "a town's habitus."

- Many "structures of identity" that were successfully reconstructed in the field of individual personal development are in danger of becoming metaphorical or even misplaced should one apply them naively and arbitrarily to more highly aggregated, "holistic" developmental processes. If used with the necessary caution and in the appropriate context, however, they point us toward promising structural dimensions that urban identity policies must consider if they want to be committed, successful, and innovative. "Real" urban identity structures are constituted largely through civic negotiation processes—although strategic images play an increasingly significant role within such deliberations, for example as an incubator for the *invention of tradition* in posttraditional configurations of urban society.

- Information and knowledge media, governance procedures, and reflexive mechanisms are increasingly crucial at the structural level of collective identities, even more so than at the psychological level. The media and reflexive mechanisms are differentiated in this respect: on the one hand by technological innovations and the demand for these; on the other by new institutions, local elites, or regional agencies that are in touch with local needs. Together they can help reinforce a civic society's capacity for self-governance, which is of growing importance to "a city's identity." Admittedly, media overkill can lead to socially divided constructs of identity and trigger social disintegration. The question of the right dose and the appropriate style must be answered for each town individually, in light of its own civic knowledge and media culture. It cannot be generalized or answered abstractly.

- The rise and eventual fall of collective identities ultimately follows a quite different pattern of development than is the case for individual fates and aging processes. The latter, as is well known, succumb to our physiological dowry and necessarily end in the death of the specimen concerned. In the peripheral towns and regions of eastern Germany, for example, one finds a whole string of localities that are labeled "dying towns" by *younger* inhabitants who are considering leaving them. Yet this kind of death is neither natural nor necessary for a town. The crisis-ridden implosion of a community can be avoided and steered in another direction, for example by means of identity policies that put the maxim "crisis is opportunity" to concrete use, hence orienting the people concerned to perceive the strengths of specific locations in a new light.

To sum up: within urban-regional contexts, identity always has to integrate and manage at least four things:

- first, the internal view that a city and its citizens have of themselves: local self-confidence and the idiosyncrasies—frequently coupled with pride—of its inhabitants. Even this internal view is necessarily "differentiated" and "socially divided."
- Second, the concept of identity includes the external face that a city shows the wider world, one that is conveyed primarily by the media rather than by direct experience. This aspect pertains to a city's reputation on a local, regional, or even international level—for example in the recently expanded European Union, with its harsh competitive dynamics.
- The third aspect is the image that a city strategically creates and conveys via the media to both external and internal (!) target audiences. This is becoming increasingly significant. The term "image" is normally reserved for this marketing process.
- Fourth, these three sociocultural constructs—self-image, reputation in the wider world, and the image that a city markets—now merge or overlap within new urban identity typologies. They are hence subject to changes that vary extremely from case to case.[7] Indeed, it is only in their hybrid form that urban identities actually become proactive. Many variations are possible here. Wolfgang Kaschuba, for example, addresses the urban profiling strategy of "styling and scaring": nowadays, not only attractive but also ugly aspects are exploited for the purposes of identity strategies. Even "unlovely" artifacts are integrated into current heterogeneous urban image-policies. In general, it suffices to say that cities under pressure from increasing competition tend to culturally codify both their external reputation and their self-image much more intensively than ever before. In

this respect, Europe's cultural capitals and knowledge-economy centers constitute only the tip of the iceberg of branding campaigns. Identity is anything but a fixed state, therefore. At the municipal level, in particular, it proves on the contrary to be an ongoing, developmental learning process that is frequently accelerated by crises.

In posttraditional knowledge societies like that found in Germany—and in particular in eastern German urban society—there seems to be no way of escaping the compulsive megatrend of inventing traditions. This is true especially when new functions and, subsequently, new identities have to be developed for areas facing continual depletion. The employment of traditions as tactile, tangible remains of historical cultures—for alternative purposes, for example—plays an increasingly important role, not least in that it serves as a temporary docking station for the creation of identities that can be regularly updated to stay abreast of new developments. This development has to do with the ever-shorter time span of the validity of knowledge in posttraditional knowledge societies—a fact (among others) that accelerates the decline of traditions considerably. Certainly we never begin at the beginning when we reinvent them. This is as true of efforts to regenerate eastern German shrinking inner cities as it is of the reinvention of the "European city." A new elite of identity designers does not hesitate to incorporate the (re)invention of urban cultural traditions into its image campaigns and develop them at will. Hence, "buzz," the busy sound of vibrant urban interaction and negotiation, becomes the goal of urban development and the measure of its identity: there is barely a town left that has not been branded with "urban heterogeneity"[8]—and, of course, a touch of Mediterranean flair too.

Whenever one taps into local everyday culture by means of "new or reinvented traditions," one must remain aware of how strongly constructionist this process is and, equally, of the degree of liberty which it entails. Indeed, the degree of liberty inherent in social constructs of urban identity must be exploited more forcefully, so that cultural differences and collective identities might no longer be treated as opposites but rather as complementary patterns in a city's shared history. This approach now seems to be the only way to make the qualities of local forms of "staying rooted" more adaptive. It is precisely in this regard that local idiosyncrasy and the specific "habitus of a city" (Rolf Lindner) can contribute considerably to the complex learning process of urban identity formation.

It is a fact, above all in those smaller eastern German cities and cultural landscapes threatened by marginalization, that a city's identity and its wider reputation are being pushed further away from the images promised by professional identity-designers, be these external marketing or tourism agencies or local planning offices. For quite some time such promises have been directed not only at external but increasingly also at internal targets—namely, at the self-image and the capacity for self-description of each respective city. How this complex network of strategic forces might really affect identity remains nonetheless difficult to forecast, for the urban process of identity construction continues in its essence to be tied up closely with civic processes of self-organization. Marketing and identity-planning processes that lose touch with this fact generally ricochet off the actual town profile in no time at all and without further consequences. Although newly created landmarks and synthetic points of reference for urban and urban regional identity—signposted "city image"—frequently attempt to disassociate themselves from the respective posttraditional traditions of their area, history catches up with them on this same track. All this proves that the civic social milieu and its various forms of self-organization continue to constitute a decisive sounding board for successful and compatible constructs of identity as well as for the profiling of hybrid forms of identity at a concrete location.

Translated from the German by Jill Denton

Notes
1 Martina Koll-Schretzenmayr, "Die Welt ist ein Dorf – Und die Stadt wird zur Stadtregion," *DISP* 152 (2002), 2.
2 See Ulf Matthiesen, "Zur Kultur gewachsener Kulturlandschaften," in *Kulturlandschaften als Herausforderung für die Raumplanung,* ed. Rainer Danielzyk et al. (Hanover: forthcoming).
3 See Wolfgang Aschauer, "Regionale Identität als empirischer Untersuchungsgegenstand," *Geographische Revue* 1 (2000): 55-60; Detlev Ipsen, "Was trägt der Raum zur Entwicklung der Identität bei? Und wie wirkt sich diese auf die Entwicklung des Raumes aus?" in *Räume der Identität – Identität der Räume,* ed. Sabine Thabe (Dortmund: Institut für Raumplanung, Universität Dortmund, 1999), 150-159, here p. 150.
4 For a summarized survey of their reception, see Rainer Döbert, "Identitätsformationen und Gesellschaftsstruktur im Schatten von Globalisierungsprozessen: An der Schwelle zur multikulturellen Identität?" in *Konstruktivistische Sozialisationsforschung,* ed. Matthias Grundmann (Frankfurt am Main: Suhrkamp, 2001), 290-323, here pp. 290ff.; Hartmut Esser, *Sinn und Kultur,* vol. 6, *Soziologie: Spezielle Grundlagen* (Frankfurt am Main: Campus, 2000), 335ff.; Thomas Luckmann, "Persönliche Identität als evolutionäres und historisches Problem," *Lebenswelt und Gesellschaft* (Paderborn, Germany: Schöningh/UTB, 1980), 123-160.
5 On developmental phase models, see Lawrence Kohlberg, *The Psychology of Moral Development* (San Francisco: Harper & Row, 1984), and Jane Loevinger, *Technical Foundations for Measuring Ego Development* (Mahwah, NJ: Erlbaum, 1998).
6 See, for example, Esser, *Sinn und Kultur,* 341-342.
7 On the complex of the personal and the alien in postsocialist processes of the constitution of hybrids, see Ulf Matthiesen, "Fremdes und Eigenes am Metropolen-Rand: Postsozialistische Hybridbildungen in den Verflechtungsmilieus von Berlin mit Brandenburg," in *An den Rändern der deutschen Hauptstadt,* ed. Ulf Matthiesen (Opladen, Germany: Leske + Budrich Verlag, 2002), 327-350.
8 For the advancement of concepts of the posttraditional constitution of tradition in the context of urban and identity politics, I am indebted to the work of Maurice Halbwachs, Edward Shils, Eric Hobsbawm, S. N. Eisenstadt, Jürgen Habermas, Klaus Eder, Peter Wagner, and Anthony Giddens.

Literature
Kaschuba, Wolfgang. "Urbane Identität: Einheit der Widersprüche?" In *Urbanität und Identität zeitgenössischer europäischer Städte,* edited by Wüstenrot Stiftung, 8-28. Ludwigsburg, Germany: Wüstenrot Stiftung, 2005.
Krappmann, Lothar. *Soziologische Dimensionen der Identität.* Stuttgart: Klett-Cotta, 1971.
Matthiesen, Ulf. "Deutungsmuster und Lebensstile im 'problematischen' Konstitutionsprozeß regionaler Identität." In *Lebensstile und Raumerleben: Zur Analyse und Empirie von Strukturveränderungen in der sozialen Raumerfahrung* (REGIO – Beiträge des IRS, no. 8), edited by Institut für Regionalentwicklung und Strukturplanung, 31-44. Berlin: IRS, 1995.

THE CITY MUST BE INVENTED
Regina Bittner

—

—

At some inchoate corner of Dessau, between a gas station turned hotdog stand, prefab apartment blocks, a hypermarket, and a mainstream UCI cinema, there stands a billboard. Its text, "We get up earlier," is at first glance perfectly obscure. It's not an ad for a sports team, for a service company, or even for the federal railways. It's about a whole federal state: Saxony-Anhalt. The small print alongside the photograph of an idyllic sunrise sheds some light: "We are always ahead of our time. Years, sometimes; decades, even; and a few minutes, every day. The people of Saxony-Anhalt." The slogan "We get up earlier" is based on a representative survey conducted by the forsa institute for market, opinion, and social research, which showed that the people of Saxony-Anhalt get up nine minutes earlier every day than the average German.

Saxony-Anhalt numbers among those federal states of eastern Germany that arguably have been hardest hit by the post-1990 wave of deindustrialization. Aside from a few token gestures, Aufschwung Ost (the state program for economic regeneration of the new federal states) barely made a dent. Inhabitants of the region used to be early risers, without a doubt, for the rhythm of chemical production and lignite mining had their body clocks tight in its grasp. What is interesting about the billboard is that it seeks to create a connection between Saxony-Anhalt's early risers—whose rhythm remained unchanged even in 2005, despite the waning of their working days—and an image of local innovation that is, so to speak, backlit by the glow of the region's history. A sunrise denotes a new start, albeit a new start with tradition. The billboard is intended to arouse inhabitants' pride in their region and its traditions and idiosyncrasies. Naming names—be it Fürst Franz, Junkers, Weill, or Gropius—is consciously avoided. The message is aimed at a community that appears to stretch back in time. The industrial era's early riser bears the same yoke as local reformers, men of letters, and inventors from centuries past, the rather populist intention being to strengthen inhabitants' identification with their region.

A Bauhaus Town in the Garden Realm (Gartenreich)

The billboard campaign is one of many diverse political attempts to promote a sense of identity in the shrinking region of Saxony-Anhalt. In an attempt to retain some visibility between Berlin and Halle/Leipzig, Dessau—like many other places—falls back on the displaced artifacts of its history. In this process various historical elements become associated with extremely varied projections of future development.

In the early 1990s, Dessau hit the headlines with a series of architectural competitions for the new center between the railway station and the city hall, preparatory studies for areas due for redevelopment, and extensive plans for local transport. Posters for local elections showed the mayoral candidate against a dense background of cranes: the promise of Dessau's rapid economic and social revival as a service town. The town's public relations brochures also spoke of the rise of a "large modern city that, with its historical buildings and parks, will be one of Saxony-Anhalt's centers." The gigantic construction site between the tower blocks to the north and the south, which hitherto sheltered an extensive covered market, is a case study of private inner-city development. The project management firm ECE and the Karstadt retail chain together built the Rathaus

Center, a town within a town that has been a magnet since the mid-1990s for Saturday shoppers from the entire rural hinterland. The same era's second major project, the Fürst-Leopold-Karree, intended to offer a four-star hotel, high-end apartments, and countless commercial units. Now almost all of the apartments and offices are vacant. The Rathaus Center has completely absorbed the region's buying power. The smaller businesses at the museum crossroads have closed down and been replaced by discount stores and secondhand shops.

What card should Dessau play if the service-town scheme fails to work? The rhetoric about the city's comeback was spun from historical threads stretching from the aviation engineer Hugo Junkers to the Bauhaus: an attempt to draw on the city's tradition of engineering élan and innovation. From 1994, the new mayor consciously steered policy toward the preservation of industrial core areas. Himself the child of a family of engineers that had worked for Junkers, he tried to encourage unity among the majority population that still had close bonds with industrial culture. Despite the failure of attempts to rescue the little that was left—such as, in 1995, wagon construction, Dessau's one remaining industrial complex—his policy was very popular, for it exploited the resentment of the frustrated, disappointed, and largely unemployed population. A second strategy reactivated and even invented traditions that pointed to Dessau as a "Sporting Town" and consciously attempted to latch on to the history of "a workers' town," including the period of the former German Democratic Republic (GDR). Dessau had made a name for itself as a sporting town before 1989. Every major factory had its own sports association, and soccer was particularly popular. After all, Dessau's wagon builders made history in 1949 as the soccer team SG Waggonbau—the first cup-final winners in the GDR. In an industrial town like Dessau, it was mainly sporting associations that offered a healthy balance to heavy work.

Many sports venues were renovated or newly built after 1990 in order to further the city's reputation as a location for international competitions. New fitness studios were set up alongside the remaining older associations founded within GDR combines. Enthusiasm for physical achievement and competition is a long-standing popular tradition. Historically, it was working-class culture that drew attention to the relationship between alienated work and the desire for physical experience in sport, the circus, or other popular pursuits during leisure time. Even though the world of work—which needed to be balanced—has now dwindled, its social networks created a framework for mutual acknowledgment and a sense of identity that are as important today as they ever were. Even newly founded sporting associations—whose membership is drawn almost exclusively from the recently self-employed—follow the often rigid rules and rituals of the former combine sport groups. Nowadays sport is for many people a means of balancing the stress of facing the imponderability and the menacing bankruptcy of small businesses in eastern Germany.

It is therefore no wonder that the image of Dessau as a "Sporting Town"—created by elite urban management—comes closer to the townspeople's principles of self-organization than does the image favored by the tourism and marketing board, namely, of the "Bauhaus Town in the Garden Realm." For years the board has stubbornly pushed these two flagship projects—which are on UNESCO's World Cultural Heritage list—in the belief that they alone might make Dessau internationally identifiable. The public relations brochures thus concentrate on these two unique selling points: the Bauhaus and its buildings, and the Garden Realm at Dessau-Wörlitz with its castles and parks. Whereas at the start of the 1990s there was talk of the rise of a modern city, the town's portrayal in the course of the decade was reduced to a few cultural highlights: "... the city, characterized at many points by prefab housing, retains in the area around the city hall something of the charm of the former royal residence."

Consonant with a conscious "visibility policy," Dessau is developing a positive image intended to guarantee it the attention of international investors, potential residents, and, above all, tourists.[1] As in Dresden, history and identity are here considered to be "localized" and "manifest." Yet whereas Dresden's Baroque city center is becoming increasingly alien to its own population and giving rise to competing identities, Dessau's "visibility policy" remains ambiguous outside the pages of the image brochures. The mayor prefers to speak of Dessau as "... [having] room for ideas."

Celebrations

The reinvention of tradition must be compatible with local everyday culture. Festivals and events can be instrumental in creating such bonds. The boom in urban festivals and events emerged in the context of a new urban economy of symbols. Festivals and events help cities to assert themselves in the national and global competition for the favor of investors, tourists, and subsidizing bodies. That festivals are celebrated in towns is nothing new; what is new is the sociopolitical context in which these are now embedded. The event and festival circuit is calculated not only on the financial level: its populist political intent is to strengthen citizens' identification with their city. Dessau, too, particularly in the summer months, celebrates its festivals, which draw on the history of its two flagship features. What relationship do the events planned from above have to the grassroots culture of a city like Dessau? Are they perhaps cultural red herrings that bear no relation to social reality? Or do such festivals function as "in-between spaces" that offer possibilities of transgression?[2] To what extent do such events invent when they "reinvent tradition"?

It is true that the first Leopold Festival in July 2004 courted the descendants of Anhalt's aristocracy in the city hall and provided various spectacles on the square before it, including local manufacturers and their produce. On the whole, however, it remained faceless. Events organized by the Dessau-Wörlitz Foundation are less ambiguous. Oranienbaum's "Small Festival in a Large Park" was aimed at the new middle class in and around the region, for whom a truly royal evening held promise of cultural distinction. The announced reintroduction of foxhunting is aimed at a comparable group. In particular for the region's emergent middle class, which is slowly polishing up its differentiated profile, such events provide a repertoire of symbols and codes with which the social group can identify on a cultural level. Such events have added importance as a means of establishing social contacts and local small business networks. In contrast, the annual eastern German men's cycling tour through the Garden Realm on Ascension Day is a collective ritual. It ties in with a specific tradition, namely, that of male workers in the GDR who used to make a holiday of Ascension Day (which is also Father's Day) in order to "spit in the eye" of state regulations on public holidays, which did not include this particular day. On Ascension Day, countless exclusively male and mostly quite drunken groups line the Fürst-Franz-Weg, the route to Wörlitz. The baronial educational program that accompanies the route has little in common with this pagan East German tradition of rambunctious men. Or perhaps the enlightened perception of nature as freedom, as epitomized by the Garden Realm, really is a motor for such excesses? These increasingly popular activities support the inversion of such groups, for what is evident here are rituals whose content is repeated or even radicalized every year by the same participants. Yet what they offer—which is perhaps precisely why they are so popular—is a collective community experience in a changing society increasingly characterized by individualization and privatization.

The Bauhaus, too, has developed a festival circuit over the last five years. The annual Festival of Color at the Bauhaus—organized cooperatively by the city council, the theater, and the Bauhaus Dessau Foundation—takes place concurrently with a free open-air concert. The rediscovery of the Bauhaus festivals was bound to happen. Yet whereas the festivals in the 1920s served the self-assurance of creative bohemians, the Festival of Color is now a major event in the city. Allusions to a carnival parade—fireworks and dressing in the festival colors—work well in a town that also celebrates an ever-growing carnival on Mardi Gras of each year, even though it is neither a religious nor a local tradition here. Carnival functioned in the GDR as a protest against a situation of deadlock. A topsy-turvy world that turned hierarchy on its head and encouraged profanity, carnival was a way of expressing discontent with the state's unreasonable demands.[3] Carnival clubs lived a shadowy existence in the GDR and experienced a veritable renaissance after 1989. The revival of a carnival spirit at the Bauhaus festival can build on this local significance.

None of this leads to any architectural improvements in Dessau, but the annual Festival of Color has managed to turn the "Laboratorium" behind the railway station into a public space. The Bauhaus has a different meaning for each visitor, according to the respective music, colors, and atmosphere on hand. In this respect, the Festival of Color perhaps exemplifies the fact that processes of identification are not a one-way street but the cultural practice of manufacturing heterogeneous meanings.

Does Dessau invent these cultural strategies anew, both externally and internally? People live here because they work here, have their families here, and like the landscape and the people; but to move house, they say, is always possible. This at least was how young people expressed their feelings toward their native town in a survey conducted by the local youth radio station Sputnik. Unlike the early risers and the avant-garde who lay personal populist claims to Saxony-Anhalt, they see nothing special about the place. The city does not get a mention in the interviewees' statements. The few displaced artifacts of urban culture—cafés, bars, and salsa clubs—are scattered randomly throughout the city and would attract their respective publics even if they were situated in a mall at the A9 freeway exit. The city as an encompassing space has no tradition in this postindustrial region. And perhaps for this very reason should not be reinvented.

Translated from the German by Jill Denton

Notes

1   Susanne Hauser, "Stadtentwürfe," in *Die Stadt als Event,* ed. Regina Bittner (Frankfurt am Main: Campus, 2002), 194.
2   In this regard, see the concept of "liminal spaces" in Victor Turner, "Variations on a Theme of Liminality," in *Blazing the Trail: Way Marks in the Exploration of Symbols,* ed. Edith Turner (Tucson: University of Arizona Press, 1992), 50.
3   Mikhail Bakhtin, *Literatur und Karneval: Zur Romantheorie und Lachkultur* (Munich: Hanser, 1985), 49.

URBAN BLINDNESS
Ruedi Baur

The brain processes selectively what our eyes see: only new, exceptional, or unexpected impressions are registered consciously, whereas the rest is filtered out. We only see that which merits our interest, preoccupies us particularly, or attracts us naturally. After a while we cease to hear repetitive sounds, background music, the hum of daily life, the freeway, or even the noisy passage of a train. The mind can become alarmingly somnolent in the face of repetitive similitude. Yet, in the midst of indifference, one look can awaken sudden interest of the sort inspired by a most spectacular monument. A certain light in early spring and, suddenly, what was invisible becomes a magnificent tableau that moves us—to say nothing of the effect of a melody or the revolutionary awakening of a people too long oppressed. These phenomena of disappearance and sudden reappearance remain difficult to explain, just as certain objects, by reason of their aesthetic, or the interest, singularity, or memory that they evoke, succeed in drawing our constant attention, despite their familiarity. A first-class architect, exceptional designer, or talented artist succeeds in creating signs, objects, or spaces that emerge more easily from the unseen than does the rest of our environment. Conversely, everything that seems to us common and banal, neither lovely nor ugly—in a word, all that might become dead weight on our personal cerebral databank—is systematically and automatically eliminated from our conscious field of vision.

What is more, we all know that to walk regularly through a familiar area reduces our level of awareness considerably. Many a day we realize that we have walked quite some way without noticing the slightest thing: not the least detail held us up; the territory left us completely unmoved. Conversely, as a tourist or new arrival, we see things that we don't register in everyday life. Nevertheless, even in this context we don't see everything: far from it. We need only to go for a walk and focus on a particular object, such as gray junction boxes, to realize how very selectively we see, how very little of our daily environment we register. Beyond sensitivity, receptivity, and an open mind, our capacity to see, to observe, is directly determined by our knowledge and comprehension. An electrician will perceive within our invisible junction boxes all the workings of an electricity supply system. He will be unable to prevent himself from noticing each one's singularity. A person with knowledge of architecture or art history will cross a town with an eye for details that remain hidden for the uninitiated. A lawyer, in turn, will read a city in terms of the "visual consequences of legislation." An economist will extract other details relevant to his interests. But most of us will see in the city only the display of new goods in a store window, posters, and similar objects that contribute to the ongoing visual transformation of everyday urban space. In short, we will see those things designed to appeal to us.

A greater cause for alarm is the growing uniformity of urban landscapes in the planetary megalopolis. The uniform city threatens to sink little by little into the nondiscernible, the nonperceived, and, hence, the nonexistent. Soulless and endlessly boring suburbs already demonstrate the widespread risk of obliteration by undifferentiated urban policies. The same threat hangs over the considerable number of hyper-rationalized cities unable to maintain or create a singular profile. These are seriously at risk of disappearing into unattractiveness or even invisibility if functional, economic, security-minded, and industrial logic and, equally, the logic of unifying signs imposed by the global market cannot be overcome.

On the brighter side, it is certain that certain places, places that are identifiable without resort to artificial, costly, and superfluous ad campaigns, will quickly gain in attractiveness and significance in the global context. It is not utopian to imagine that the planetary megalopolis, with its simplifying dialectic, will at some point only differentiate between what is normal and what is extraordinary. Normal will mean everything that ensues from the logic of rationalism, the economy, and maximum security: everything that excludes aesthetics or extraordinariness. This leads automatically to uniformity, already a planetary phenomenon. The majority of urban spaces fails to escape such engineered normality and will become increasingly unworthy of attention. Tourism already demonstrates how catastrophic selective obliteration can be. Whereas places with an impressive cultural legacy or outstanding geological attractions can sit back, placidly holding their trump cards, the others—faced with irrevocable cultural standardization and the rapid disappearance of most customs and traditions—will soon be hard put to build on local strengths. Dialects, local construction or production methods, rituals, and customs can unfortunately only be kept alive by artificial means; and for how much longer? The very act of preserving them robs them of their authenticity. In the future, a place's identity will derive less from a traditional and local cultural logic than from a conscious will, a design, a plan. Striving for that specific something no longer will be synonymous with withdrawal from the wider world, which is in any case impossible, but will, on the contrary, be a conscious striving for the qualitative difference that will suffice to attract a foreign public. Any singular place will be open to the world, whereas any place that limits itself to appearing global will sink into the anonymity of being everywhere and, therefore, nowhere. However, it is not a matter of creating originality for originality's sake. To be credible and, above all, to escape being reproduced elsewhere, such originality must be justified and inscribed in the logic of its location.

Competing to see who can build the highest tower or the largest museum is not an option for everyone. It is also a rather risky undertaking in the medium term, precisely because it can be copied: a fact that makes its fascination soon wane. Yet even in this arena of competition to be the highest, the biggest, the strongest, it nonetheless makes sense to analyze the iconic power of a truly original object such as the Eiffel Tower in Paris: to compare the fascination that the latter continues to exert with all the countless buildings in the world that have the highest of towers and yet become uninteresting practically from the moment they are built. An architectural icon and a prime example of a useless monument, the Eiffel Tower is directly related to the technological aspirations of a certain epoch and to a concrete event, namely, the "World Exhibition" of 1889. Its form is an expression both of supreme technological functionality and of the uselessness of a celebratory monument that was not designed for eternity. A reproduction of the Eiffel Tower at any other location would be absolute nonsense. This is what makes it unique and internationally identifiable as an icon and a symbol of its place. Unfortunately, apart perhaps from China and certain rapidly growing major corporations, no territory today would have the ability or temerity to erect such a completely useless, although ultimately highly profitable, monument. Must we be reminded, to our consolation, that the Eiffel Company was at the time obliged to invest personally in order that the project might be realized?

Urban Blindness_Ruedi Baur

During my stay in eastern Germany in the years following the fall of the Wall, I had the opportunity to be directly involved in a scarcely less modest endeavor. It concerned the gigantic "conveyer bridge" in the Südraum district of Leipzig, a metal giant on tracks, of dimensions that more or less corresponded to an Eiffel Tower lain on its side. Our proposal was to remove this metal monstrosity from its original site at the bottom of a strip mine and to show it to advantage and endow it with new symbolic significance by erecting it in an open pit that was to be transformed into an artificial lake. As a kind of archeological park or tourist attraction, the object was meant to symbolize the brief period of heavy industry's megalomania. However, the local and, even more so, the national political and economic leadership was so intent on eradicating the past, on not undertaking anything that was not immediately functional and profitable, and so worried about equaling former West Germany by establishing a general normality as quickly as possible, that they thoroughly underestimated the potential fascination of such an object. With its location at the gates of Leipzig, so to speak, and visible as it was from the freeway that runs through all of eastern Germany, its symbolic effectiveness was practically guaranteed. And although that era may still seem banal at the moment, there is little doubt that the Herculean efforts of the industrial age will fascinate future generations. But no: to save a few million, which were, incidentally, spent instead on a stupid advertising campaign and the artificial attempt to host the Olympic Games in this very city, this irreplaceable icon was destroyed in 2002 and replaced by nothingness. Normality, uniformity, even banality had again gained the upper hand: the hand that also poses the threat of obliteration.

More generally speaking, these eastern German regions had a unique opportunity in that, within the course of only a few years, considerable sums of money for reconstruction came their way. They completely failed to use these resources to create something different, special, or even exceptional that would have drawn attention to them in a positive way. Instead, every new measure succeeded only in obliterating yet another of the territory's unique characteristics. I am not speaking here of monuments but of the possibility of benefiting from a process of transformation by introducing that little extra something that would make it worthy of interest, and also of coordinating these possibilities so that, in the sum of its parts, the whole would appear fascinating. Woe betide those politicians who were not prepared to take a risk, preferring to work in secret and spending money without creating any visibility. They can perhaps be excused by the speed of developments, which bereft them of the planning phase that would have facilitated a visual coordination of the various measures. Other explanations are the lack of sensitivity to this visual dimension; without a doubt the national leadership's declared intention of eradicating all that differed from the rest of the country; and, finally, a deeper reason related to the history of the place: a lack of self-confidence that inhibits one from being different. Creating an identity always requires that one assert oneself and stand up for whatever it is that makes one different. The hyper-positivistic approach of marketing generally builds an identity based only on positive attributes and is prepared to camouflage anything that could harm that image. For my part, I plea loudly for what is natural, which means taking on what exists and modifying it progressively in order to make it interesting again. The most important thing, it seems to me, is the parallel construction of a reality based on the contextual specificities that one accepts, and of the mirror that serves to communicate this construction to third parties. Reconstruction is now over, and the mistakes made are a thing of the past, or almost so; nonetheless, the problem is not yet solved. What can be done to make this part of Germany fascinating? The issue of its cities' shrinking populations can be seen as a new catastrophe that is to be kept hidden at all costs. But one can, on the contrary, accept the situation by trying to investigate its positive potential in the light of this question of differentiation.

The thermal spa at Vals—which was built between 1992 and 1996 by the architect Peter Zumthor at one of the most inaccessible spots in Switzerland and which is visited nonetheless by people from all over the world—demonstrates rather well that it is not always necessary to build a Herculean-size monument in order to make a place fascinating. Gigantism is only one of the ways in which singularity can be accentuated. Moreover, a territory's identity cannot be conjured from thin air. To be credible it must necessarily be rooted in concrete historical or contemporary realities. The work of creating a regional identity must comprise the parallel tasks of enhancing local singularities in situ and developing a visual language that can reflect those singularities in other places. This mirror of communication can be effective only when based on something real that has the genuine potential to fascinate. The latter cannot under any circumstances emanate from normality. The act of dealing with existing differences—which need to be enhanced, strengthened, communicated, and, indeed, reinterpreted—constitutes the core of the creative process that enables a territory to step out of indifference.

A critical situation such as this presents a perfect opportunity, if one faces up to it, to work on this positive typology. One must, however, have the courage to abandon the standard recipes of marketing and political correctness, and perhaps also those of the capitalist mechanism of supply and demand, in order to seek the really special solutions that allow a territory's problems to be linked to more general problems: to build communities, temporarily make space for living and working available, invite confrontation with the situation, grant liberties that are not guaranteed elsewhere, visualize these actions, and work on the law and the facts of the exception. In brief, to find a way of dealing with one's own territorial difference and of being open to the world and to modernity at the same time. It must be said, however, that such a situation more than any other demands a sensitivity to the question of the visual, which lies, it seems to me, at the core of any question of credibility and fascination. How to get out of the rut that creates negative obsessions if not by working on one's appearance, to reiterate, not in an artificial manner but by creating and communicating one's own mirror in a professional manner? The serious work of visual identity allows one to anticipate and coordinate potential transformations in a way that creates the necessary synergy between a specific reality and its transmission through the media. The instigation of a highly qualitative system of visual territorial identity is in this respect nothing other than an analysis of the potential in situ and its transformation into a sort of visual vocabulary that permits a location and its mirroring to the media to proceed toward a place worthy of being seen, and even a "remarkable" place.

Translated from the French by Jill Denton

THE RAILWAY UNDERPASS AT TOURCOING
Tourcoing, France, 1995–1999
Intégral Ruedi Baur et associés

The underpass renovation project in the French town of Tourcoing was initiated in order to improve connections between districts that are divided by a former railway line. Hundreds of eye-witness reports on the localities were collected through research in the town archives and conversations with the districts' residents. Excerpts from these were mounted on glass bricks and inserted into the underpass walls, to accompany pedestrians on their way through. In contrast, the underside of the railway bridges illustrates translocal connections. Place-names represent the countries of origin of Tourcoing's immigrant population and point out a range of possible destinations. Reference is made also to the train from Loos, which gained notoriety as the vehicle that carried children deported from the region across these very bridges on the way to German concentration camps. These textual elements were complemented by a new lighting concept and a choice of colors for the underpass's exterior which visually detract from the impression of being a barrier. (Ed.)

A REGIONAL IMAGE FOR SÜDRAUM LEIPZIG
Leipzig region, Germany, 1999–2001
Unverzagt und Albrecht, Visuelle Kommunikation, with Ruedi Baur, Peter Bilak, and Paul Schellschmidt

The Südraum Leipzig Forum, a municipal federation comprising the administrative district Leipziger Land, the City of Leipzig, and a further seventeen local authorities, commissioned the development of a regional marketing concept and a new image. The region's specific aesthetic is characterized by the last traces of vanishing industry, the flooding of former strip-mining areas, and the impression that everything is one huge construction site. Taking account of changes occurring in the region, the branding designers developed a process-oriented corporate identity composed of a catalog of graphic elements symbolizing the transition from an industrial to a postindustrial area. Users—namely, the region's key institutions and any other entities that feel they belong to the Südraum area—can draw on elements in the catalog in order to assemble a customized and alterable corporate identity that nevertheless states their regional affiliation. (Ed.)

Absence of the smallest common denominator

Bundling

Dominant individual identity, similar regional identity

Similar regional identity

Parallel regional identity

Uniform regional identity, no individual identity

The region's logo can be customized to meet the needs of each local enterprise or institution.

1999 2050

Not least due to the flooding of former strip-mining areas, the landscape of Südraum Leipzig will change dramatically in the coming decades, as will its image.

Black/White

Monochrome

Two-tone

Density: high

Density: low

Symbol size: large

Symbol size: variable

Symbol size: small

Text: at the (very) top

Text: at the top

Text: uniform

Computer software enables numerous variations of the logo to be generated online.

IMAGINARY CITY

Imagination generates different pictures of the past and the future. Practices of remembrance mold our understanding of history and in this way influence how we see the present. Desire designs another future, opens up space for new possibilities, and thus sparks off change in the present. Urban action is born of the power of our imagination.

TO THE SISTERS OF CARL MÖGLIN
Wismar, Germany, 2004/05
Wiebke Loeper

———

Carl Möglin, the youngest of four children and poverty-stricken, left Wismar in 1854. Recently confirmed, he set out as a poor ship-boy and landed five years later in Australia. There he bought land, struck gold, and grew rich. His unmarried sisters followed him from Wismar to Australia. Carl Möglin died at the age of 34. Throughout their lives, his sisters sent paintings they had commissioned and other exotic objects to Wismar—from a Chinese vase to a stuffed kangaroo—to keep their native town informed. The kangaroo served for a time as a visual aid in natural history lessons. The Möglin Collection is now housed in Wismar's Museum of City History.

> **Lad** [low German dialect]: a trunk on wheels containing the most important household objects [documents, valuables, memorabilia, crockery, linen, and so forth] of people put to flight [by fire, floods, or war].[1]

In 2005, young high-school graduates were facing the decision of whether to leave home. Wiebke Loeper told them about the "Lad" (memory box) that she had packed when change swept through her life and her parents' house was demolished.

The question was, What might people who had recently come of age pack in a Lad to protect, conserve, or take along in case of a sudden departure, in order to be able to tell other people about it or to ensure themselves a continuing sense of their native town? Students from the Geschwister-Scholl Grammar School in Wismar took photographs of their town: of the things, places, and people that mean something to them. The photos and boxes of memorabilia were exhibited in "RAUM—Philosophie und Zeitgenössische Kunst" (SPACE—Philosophy and Contemporary Art) in Wismar town center, in cooperation with Jan Apitz.

———

This project was developed in the context of "Shrinking Cities" with a grant from the Museum of Contemporary Art Leipzig. The original German title is "An die Schwestern des Carl Möglin."

———

Project participants: Johanna Benz, Marlen Bernier, Sara Bock, Hiun Dangtran, Franziska Deffke, Hanna Drabon, Hella Fassauer, Sabrina Hankel, Susanne Heise, Marie Keimel, Friederike Koch, Tanja Reese, Ann-Christin Ringel, Anne Suderow, Sabine Töpper, Monique Troche, Antje Vagt, and Marius Wolter.

Note
1 See Goldrausch Künstlerinnenprojekt, ed., *Wiebke Loeper: Lad* (Berlin: 2001), 4.

Hanna Drabon, Wismar, 2004.

Imaginary City

The contents of schoolgirl Hanna Drabon's "memory box."

Hanna Drabon's "memory box."

MAKING MUSEUMS OF INDUSTRIAL HERITAGE SITES: PRACTICES OF REMEMBRANCE
Susanne Hauser

Between 1970 and 1990, industrial museums were founded in all of Europe's primary industrialized nations and in many former industrial regions. In Germany, for example, the Museum für Technik und Arbeit (Museum of Technology and Labor) opened in Mannheim, the Centrum Industriekultur (Center for Industrial Culture) opened in Nuremberg, and in North Rhine-Westphalia the industrial museums of the Landschaftsverbände (Landscape Associations) have been extended. Campaigns for the preservation of industrial monuments have grown louder, and the preservation of entire industrial sites is being considered, as are demands to preserve working-class settlements.

Up to that point, the preservation of industrial heritage sites had been—at least outside England—a largely exotic concept, albeit one that in the course of turbulent discussions in the 1970s increasingly appeared to be the next logical step in a long-standing process. Calls to preserve old machinery date back to the zenith of industrial prowess around 1900, and designs for an open-air museum of technology and industry were drawn up as early as the 1930s. Bochum's Bergbaumuseum (Museum of Mining)—the industry's own public-relations undertaking—also dates from the1930s, and parts of the famous Falun Mines in Sweden have been used as a museum since the1940s.

Yet by around 1970, the interest of isolated specialists and enthusiasts in preserving redundant industrial sites had come to be shared by a broad public. One reason for this increased interest was that, by the end of the 1960s, it became impossible to overlook the transformation or relocation of traditional industries. The belief that new production sites would ever fill the void created by widespread industrial closure was dwindling. These signs of fundamental structural change coincided, moreover, with the emergence throughout the Western democracies of a strong political movement that went far beyond the student revolts of 1968. Demands for more democracy applied to the present and, equally, to the past. From this perspective, not only the nobility and the middle class have a history worth documenting: so, too, do working-class men and women. Subsequently, the objects of their daily lives and their general living and working conditions acquired a commemorative value. It is in this context that moves to preserve industrial heritage gained acceptance and popularity. This development constituted one among several possible answers to questions that are central in former industrial regions to this day, namely: how the emotional consequences of economic collapse might be dealt with; how the latter effect local, regional, and national notions of identity; and how planning processes might deal with the remnants of traditional modes of production.

Urban Planning and Industrial Heritage

Discussions about industrial heritage began somewhat earlier in England than in other former industrialized nations. Aesthetic appreciation of redundant industrial sites increased around 1955, along with the desire to preserve them. A significant trigger for this development was the impending demolition of a prominent industrial monument, the Neoclassicist Euston Arch, a portico in Doric style and over twenty meters high, which stood at the entrance to the pompously decorated Victorian railway station of the same name and was its most visible landmark. Many citizens joined the campaign for its preservation, which was organized primarily by the Victorian Society, founded a short time previously and still influential today.

The railway station was rebuilt in 1962 nevertheless, and its old landmark vanished. Yet by then public debate had established arguments for the preservation of industrial monuments. Characteristic for ensuing developments has been the fact that the debate on the preservation of industrial remains is conducted as a debate on national identity. The idea of presenting England as the cradle of the so-called industrial revolution and of preserving "the evidence" has gained in popularity and readily won the attention of public-funding bodies. Research projects have been initiated, although, admittedly, concrete preservation schemes for industrial buildings have not been immediately forthcoming.

The complex museum project in the Iron Bridge Gorge, developed gradually since the 1960s, set a new benchmark of quality. Here, for the first time, the new and prolifically publishing industrial archaeologists met with local urban planners to carry out a common project. Urban development of the New Town of Telford and the development of the adjacent Iron Bridge Gorge, industrialized some four hundred years earlier, were conceived as a single comprehensive project. The result was the first industrial museum landscape, one of the world's largest, even today.

A pattern crystallized in the Iron Bridge Gorge project that was to be decisive for all future museum developments at former industrial sites: the integrated planning of the urban region incorporated the preservation of several hundred buildings in various industrial villages as well as the construction of eight major heritage sites. Today these draw on a wide range of presentation styles: the classic display of commentated collections, products, and machines; visits to fully reconstructed residences and workplaces from various eras of industrial labor; tours of furnaces almost four hundred years old; "working museums" that employ old production methods; reenactments of historical events; and a new, interactive Design and Technology Museum. The Iron Bridge—the world's first—lends its own quite singular flair to this varied program.

The Iron Bridge Gorge was staged from the start as "the cradle of industry," as the first step in British industry's triumphal march—an interpretation that was much criticized and ridiculed by serious historians. Yet this interpretation helped to focus preservation initiatives on one particular location and to acquire public funding for it in the form of a foundation. The inhabitants who remained after industrial collapse and over whose heads the heritage bandwagon rolled found themselves being styled in the 1990s as the heroes and heroines of an economic dry spell: a characterization that was by no means unanimously welcome. The servicing of day-trippers does indeed sustain the settlements within the heritage sites, and there is business enough to provide for more than just the local population: the old houses, most of them perfectly restored, bear witness to new prosperity. The Iron Bridge Gorge was, incidentally, the first industrial monument to be included in the UNESCO World Cultural Heritage list.

Regional Development and Industrial Culture

The industrial-ecological museums, or *Écomusées,* in France, Belgium, Sweden, and Canada have a comparable size and agenda. The first was founded in Le Creusot in France in 1971. Here, too, the question of identity was central from the start, albeit in this case local and regional identity, rather than national identity, was at the forefront. The

The overburden conveyor bridge F60 in Lichterfeld is now used for exhibitions and art actions. The steelworks in Brandenburg is used as a museum, and even hosts concerts by the Brandenburg Symphony Orchestra.

program of the first French Écomusée was (and still is) to turn whole landscapes into heritage sites that function on behalf of local inhabitants and to develop tourism as a new economic base for former industrial areas. The intention was not to turn a region into a moribund museum but to open up new perspectives. The positive transformation of postindustrial conditions and tangible economic improvement were on the agenda from the start.

Because it is meant to constitute the collective memory of an entire area rather than of one particular line of production, an Écomusée combines the creation of industrial heritage sites with the development of a cultural landscape that is simultaneously old and new. It aims to help the whole population take a proud look at its past. This is an important component, for Écomusées attempt to counter the depression that ensues from economic collapse. There is no reason to devalue the past even further, once it proves to be economically unviable. Its fruits and the experience born of it should be perceived as riches and, above all, as a resource for new developments that point to the future.

The collection illustrating vanishing cultures and forms of labor attempts to be as comprehensive as possible. So-called mobile goods are preserved as historical and ethnographic evidence, as are "immobile goods"—castles, factories, fields, and forests, preferably with their traditional husbandry intact. Typical plants and domestic animals, the "fungible goods," are recultivated or rebred, and sometimes old strains are revived. "Immaterial goods"—practices, skills, all kinds of techniques, and dances and songs, for example—are recorded and archived.

A centrally located permanent exhibition of the region's natural and cultural history is typical of the Écomusées, which otherwise operate throughout the region by means of "antennas": natural and cultural sites of particular interest. Those industrial regions that now have, or are, an Écomusée are mostly accessible by hiking trails, and they carry out intensive advertising campaigns. The result has been described as a vibrant "museum burst open."

The Concept of Heritage Preservation

Since the 1970s, numerous industrial sites and regions have to a greater or lesser degree mutated into museums or Écomusées with extremely different styles. Of the developments that have emerged in connection with a sizable area rather than a single site, the reconstruction of Lowell, a former textiles city, must be cited as an outstanding North American example. A National Historical Park illustrating the transition of Massachusetts from an agrarian to a textile state—which for a time was the center of the textile industry—has been developed since the 1970s. Its founders present arguments similar to those of their French colleagues: Lowell should represent history that people can identify with. The park today comprises functional factories such as a cotton mill, nineteenth-century merchants' houses, workers' dwellings, and almost ten kilometers of canals. Particular aspects treated are the history of women's work—farmers' daughters were the first to be employed—and the question of how immigration affected developments in the textile industry.

The two large-scale interventions described above demonstrate the limits and possibilities of heritage preservation strategies with respect to development in former industrial regions—strategies that cannot, however, be repeated indefinitely. The circle of enthusiastic fans and expert historians is by no means large enough to support all of the now

Imaginary City

The former "Hannover Colliery" in Bochum is today part of the Westphalian Industrial Museum and is called "Zeche Knirps" (Coal Mine for Tots). Children can learn here how a coal mine works.

numerous industrial heritage sites. Likewise, potential income from tourists, albeit considerable, cannot be increased indefinitely. The competition with other sights and forms of entertainment for tourists' money and time is acute, particularly in the case of industrial heritage sites that are not embedded in a wider local entertainment network. The preservation and running costs of industrial and working museums consequently depend to a large degree on public funding.

Other limits apply with respect to expectations about how museums might preserve sites and about the identities that these sites project. The creation of a heritage site necessarily implies a certain distance from the original practices and production processes which are subsequently made available as consumable memorabilia. The setting and role of workers' songs have been irrevocably transformed, along with all the other paraphernalia of yesteryear, in the heritage site stores. The same holds true of locations and buildings in the museum context: tourists dine among the turbines of an engine room, then follow hiking trails through landscapes offering the bonus of special attractions ... which often have been especially constructed as such.

Museums turn available "live elements" into collected and commentated wares, which thereby acquire new meanings. The process begins the instant a material or immaterial object—a tool, a building, an ensemble, a district, a song, or a dance—is extricated from its original context and field of reference. It is isolated. It is placed in the context of a museum's collection and thereby subjected to new parameters of classification. These then determine how and to what extent the object will be restored, and the finished product may well bear little resemblance to the original object. The various practices and media effects employed to display exhibition material are a further distancing mechanism. The very act of preserving and displaying historical artifacts assigns them their future meaning, thereby defining their historical and cultural relevance in the light of heritage preservation. This process does not efface these artifacts, yet their current manifestation is alien to the people for whom they once played a role in everyday life.

Effects

To answer the question of how regions have been altered by their transformation into heritage sites—above and beyond the alienation described above—it is worth taking a look at the respective contexts. Lowell's unique former industrial sites were perceived as an attractive location by a software company that was, initially, extremely prosperous. Although the software boom has ended, the potential of such symbolic capital is not yet exhausted and can be exploited further. Without the Écomusée in Belgium's Central Region, the Walloon coalfields probably would attract fewer transit tourists than they do now, as the area faces the problems typical of most other relatively sparsely populated former industrial areas, namely, bad infrastructure, marginalization, and limited prospects. The museum or heritage site is a tourist attraction.

The contributions that a museum might make to the "identity" of an area or region are likewise extremely variable. Some industrial heritage sites emerged in the 1970s from the idea of tapping into the living memory of recently discontinued production processes. These museums were thus perceived as a kind of substantive collective regional memory that would constantly nourish and renew remembrance. The nexus cannot be so easily maintained, however, once the generation with a vital connection to slate quarries and textile mills or to mines and steelworks has died. In addition, new conditions assert

themselves when the focus of industrial production in these areas completely shifts: conditions that gradually push former industries into the background and, in the long term, render these as alien to the local population as any further-flung foreign cultures. Museums must respond to such developments.

Moreover, museums were often created long after industrial closures had bereft a region of its competitive profile. When Belgium's Central Region Écomusée was conceived in the early 1990s, scarcely a resident was left who had a personal connection to the former mine of Bois-du-Luc. The intention here from the start, therefore, was to embed this site in the larger picture of the Central Region, thus ensuring the preservation of valuable monuments and highlighting a supralocal and regional social history. To take another example, the Iron Bridge Gorge had been economically unviable for more than one hundred years when its resurrection was initiated. Along with the bridges and old furnaces, it is possibly this very circumstance that facilitated the establishment at this location of a nationally conceived and locally confirmed narrative of the origins of industry.

It makes little sense, in any case, to consider heritage sites as simply the results of "postindustrial cultural policy," at least if relegating them to "retrospective space" is to be the last word on the subject. The alienation inherent in museums—alienation even from familiar processes or objects—is precisely what offers great potential for discoveries, both to local people and to passing tourists. Museums traditionally are, after all, places in which new kinds of perception can be formed and new concepts can be articulated. They can be an archive and a theater, bearing witness to expeditions into the unknown, into supposedly familiar or vanishing worlds. They invite exploration by permitting a playful confrontation with alien objects, circumstances, and processes. In this light, it is not surprising that many designs for former industrial arenas lay claim to the vision of industrial museums and of the use of former industrial sites as living heritage laboratories. At best one can trust that, in and due to such laboratories, important visions for the future will develop and that, with intelligent regard for old material, new identities can unfold.

Translated from the German by Jill Denton

Literature
Hauser, Susanne. "Denkmalpflege und industrielles Erbe: Zur Begründung der Industriekultur im 20. Jahrhundert." *Industriedenkmalpflege und Geschichtskultur* 1 (2005): 20–24.
———. *Metamorphosen des Abfalls: Konzepte für alte Industrieareale.* Frankfurt am Main: Campus, 2001.

THE POWER OF DESIRE
Stephan Lanz

"Wishes will leave the house, take to the streets ... and put an end to the reign of boredom and bureaucratically managed misery," declares *Park Fiction,* a film by Margit Czenki about an art project of the same name which had real-life repercussions and became known through its inclusion at the Documenta 11 exhibition. "Operating from a subordinate position, local residents—organized as the Harbor's Edge Association (for Self-Determined Lives and Housing in St. Pauli, Hamburg)—prevented the construction of a multimillion-euro project that was planned for the slopes of the Elbe in the St. Pauli district, then overturned Plan B, and succeeded in creating in its stead a park with a view of the Elbe which is run by the residents themselves."[1] Like Henri Lefebvre, *Park Fiction* argues that urban revolution will begin at home. Living accommodations can be viewed as the subconscious level of a city's existence, for this is where objects encapsulate people's desires and their relationship to what is possible and imaginary. Czenki's film suggests that personal wishes lead an undervalued existence among favorite belongings, dismissed fragments of novels, dusty holiday souvenirs, and sad stamp collections.

After working for years in its own planning office-trailer, making house visits with its mobile "action kit," putting on "infotainment" events, setting up a telephone hotline in the park (for people who wanted to pass on their brain waves at night) and an archive of wishes, the art project "Park Fiction" managed to get encapsulated wishes onto the streets and translate them into a self-organized planning process. Activists had blithely squatted the wasteland they had set their sights on, replaced the rubbish with plants, visibly announced their appropriation of it with construction signs, and then defended it against covetous claims and local authority obstacles. It took ten years until, in 2005, a major part of the park with its Flying Carpet, the Tulip-Patterned Tartan Field, Poodle-Hedges, Palm Island, the Neighborhood Gardens, and the Bamboo Grove of the Modest Politicians could finally be realized. Park Fiction, to use Lefebvre's terms, therefore stands for that aesthetic spatial practice which is able to extend the scope available to dominated spaces of the imaginary.

Lefebvre understands urban space as a configuration in which a society's spatial practices, the vision of space as construed by scientists and technocrats, and space as it is lived and experienced are superimposed upon one another. Accordingly, a city comprises material space as well as imaginary space, everyday spatial practice as well as conceptional ideology. Spatial practice is the lived space of everyday production and reproduction of life, and thus is material space. Construed space—construed by plans, concepts, and regulations—corresponds to the social modes of production and signifies the political and technical domination of space. Spatial disciplines such as architecture and urban planning formulate the dominant representation of space for their respective institutions. Such conceptions denote power because, in the exclusionary procedures of their development and manifestation, they define which types of use and form are desirable or undesirable, permitted or forbidden. In contrast, space that is lived or experienced through images and symbols is the dominated space of the imaginary and of resistant thinking. The power of its users' imaginations attempts "to variegate it and to appropriate it for itself."[2] In everyday city life, confrontations about issues of urban space aim "at the

▲ BOX HEDGES TRIMMED IN POODLE SHAPES.
▼ The Park Fiction project came up with a variety of tools to encourage local residents to develop and articulate their wishes for a park in the St. Pauli harbor district of Hamburg. These tools included a "planning container," a "model-making office," an "action kit," a "photo studio," "interview equipment," and a "garden library."

borders between dominant and dominated spaces and, by shifting these borders, attempt to extend the scope both for renegotiating conditions for action and for articulating interests. One possible means of widening this scope is an aesthetic spatial practice in which imaginative power can transgress these borders and approximate a utopian existence free of dominance, and visualize that which is repressed within the parameters of dominant ideology."[3]

Art Is Not Innocent
Park Fiction's slogan, "Art Is Not Innocent," points to the key role played by (sub)cultural production in the "city image game" of current urban development, which, according to Lefebvre, is diametrically opposed to its explosive resistant potential. In the global battle for economic standing, cities that have been bled by the migration of both industry and the middle classes use the new leading economies of consumerism and tourism as arenas of entertainment. Urban development is increasingly enacted as a spectacle: municipal image-policy markets major projects as cultural events and (sub)cultural spaces as tourist attractions. At the same time, "Government by Fun"—the "festivals for all" circuit—attempts to integrate the urban milieu's splintered realities at the symbolic level. Local economic policy begins to focus on urban culture because event managers need images and themes for their productions. "Be Creative!" is also the categorical imperative of the new urban service sector. Hence, nonconformist artists—the latest social "role models"—personify the chain of conceptual resourcefulness, creativity, and self-marketing that postindustrial urban culture now expects of everybody. The structures of desire and models of practice of formerly subcultural counterworlds now appear to be major players in urban economies. Cities' subordination to the imperatives of a cutthroat global economy also produces hotbeds of conflict in which their losers gather. The local authorities govern in this setting by means of community concepts that rely on help through self-help or charitable donations rather than on a redistribution of public funding. From an urban manager's viewpoint, artistic interventions and participatory cultural projects have an increasingly important role to play in this respect as well: namely, to produce social adhesion, polish up a district's image, and jolt marginalized residents out of their lethargy.

Lefebvre's work poses the question of whether the current urban significance of art and culture extends the scope of the imaginary. If art serves location competition as a creative promoter at all, then almost certainly it does so in ways that benefit the dominant representation of space. Art that works on a participatory level with local residents is more ambiguous. If it succeeds in liberating trampled desire, it extends the imaginary's scope for resistance. If, however, it merely produces images and events that paper over the cracks in social structures, it participates in the dominant mode of producing and using urban space.

How Did Art Arrive at the City?
Referring to Berlin, Diedrich Diederichsen described how a preoccupation with the city became the refuge of various cultural scenes at a time when these were splintering into marginal "mini-publics" and losing their common cultural, political, and moral orientation.[4] The city as an issue and as immediate experience seemed to promise a way out of seemingly illegible social complexity. It created the feeling of being able to participate in social negotiations and conflict. Local intervention became the primary motif of an art

THE SQUARE OF PERMANENT REORGANIZATION
Arnhem, The Netherlands, 1993
Andreas Siekmann

As part of the exhibition "Sonsbeek 93" in Arnheim, Andreas Siekmann discussed with local residents their ideas and wishes for the design of a central square in the city, the Gelerijders Plein, and translated these ideas and wishes into seven scenarios: Self-activation Square, Gardeners' Square, Teenage Square, Winter Square, Wastage Square, Planning Agency Square, and Central Perspective Square. Siekmann illustrated these with a series of drawings which were exhibited for the duration of the project behind construction fencing on the Gelerijders Plein—the drawings could be viewed through peepholes. For Teenage Square—a meeting place for young people with a fountain, a bar, and walls for graffiti—Siekmann took issue in his drawings not just with the square but also with questions about planning procedures and financing (e.g., the collection drive "Running for Money") which had come up in discussions with teenagers.

In the course of the exhibition, the construction fencing was smeared with graffiti and some of the drawings in display cases were replaced by critical commentaries. Yet what the public decried as vandalism, the artist understood as feedback, and he used it as a starting point for further communication with local residents. (Ed.)

The Power of Desire _Stephan Lanz

The scenarios for "Teenage Square" show the desires, fears, and potential conflicts of its users and local residents.

The group Freies Fach in protest against the demolition of former East Germany's Ministry of Foreign Affairs, Berlin, 1995.

The Power of Desire_Stephan Lanz